S0-BLN-762

BEHAVIORAL HEALTH CARE

Assessment, Service Planning, and Total Clinical Outcomes Management

Edited by
John S. Lyons, Ph.D.
&
Dana A. Weiner, Ph.D.

CRI
Civic Research Institute
4478 U.S. Route 27 • P.O. Box 585 • Kingston, NJ 08528

Copyright © 2009

By Civic Research Institute, Inc.
Kingston, New Jersey 08528

The information in this book is not intended to replace the services of professionals trained in psychiatry, psychology, or any other discipline discussed in this book.
Civic Research Institute, Inc. provides this information without advocating the use of
or endorsing the issues, theories, precedent, guidance, resources, or practical materials discussed herein. Any application of the issues, theories, precedent, guidance,
resources, or practical materials set forth in this book is at the reader's sole discretion
and risk. The authors, editors, and Civic Research Institute, Inc. specifically disclaim
any liability, loss or risk, personal or otherwise, which is incurred as a consequence,
directly or indirectly, of the use and application of any of the contents of this book.

All rights reserved. This book may not be reproduced in part or in whole by any
process without written permission from the publisher.

This book is printed on acid free paper.

Printed in the United States of America

Library of Congress Cataloging in Publication Data
Behavioral Health Care: Assessment, Service Planning,
and Total Clinical Outcomes Management

ISBN 1-887554-69-6

Library of Congress Control Number: 2008943208

Dedicated to Kenneth I. Howard

Our view is from his shoulders.
—John S. Lyons and Dana A. Weiner

About the Editors and Contributors

John S. Lyons, Ph.D.

In 2008, John S. Lyons became the first Endowed Chair of Child and Youth Mental Health on the psychology faculty at the University of Ottawa and the Children's Hospital of Eastern Ontario. Prior to that, he was a professor of psychiatry and medicine at Northwestern University's Feinberg School of Medicine and the founding director of the Mental Health Services and Policy Program. He has published nearly 200 peer-reviewed articles and five books, including *Redressing the Emperor: Improving Our Children's Public Mental Health Service System*. Dr. Lyons has developed and implemented outcomes management tools, such as the Child and Adolescent Needs and Strengths (CANS) and Adult Needs and Strengths (ANSA), which are widely used in systems of care in the United States and are also used in Canada, Europe, and Asia. He actively works at the interface between behavioral healthcare, child welfare, juvenile justice, and education. He received his doctorate in clinical psychology and methods and measurement from the University of Illinois at Chicago in 1982 and then completed a two-year postdoctoral fellowship with Donald Fiske, Ph.D., at the University of Chicago.

Dana A. Weiner, Ph.D.

Dana A. Weiner has worked for the past seven years on evaluating the progress and outcomes of programs that deliver mental health services to children and youth in child welfare. Her work includes developing strategies for applying technology to build awareness of services and understand the gaps between regional needs and resources. In her current position in the Director's Office at the Illinois Department of Children and Family Services, she uses continuous clinical assessment data to inform child welfare policy, and to this end she has linked clinical child assessment data with service recommendations that can be incorporated into provider search and geomapping tools. The Statewide Provider Database search tool, launched in March 2008 to caseworkers and administrators across Illinois, allows caseworkers to search for providers close to children based on individual child need, and allows system planners to assess the local capacity to meet the needs of the local population. In her role as assistant professor in the Mental Health Services and Policy Program at Northwestern University, Dr. Weiner teaches courses in statistics and mental health services research. She has overseen many program evaluation projects for the State of Illinois, including an evaluation of a pilot implementation of evidence-based treatment for trauma, an ongoing outcomes monitoring system for a foster-care stabilization program, and a residential performance-monitoring unit. She is the author of numerous publications stemming from this work. Dr. Weiner received her doctorate in clinical psychology from Northwestern University in 1999 and her bachelor of science degree in human development from Cornell University in 1992.

Rachel L. Anderson, Ph.D.

Rachel Anderson is an associate professor with the Department of Health Management and Policy in the College of Public Health at the University of Iowa. She completed her graduate training in social policy at Northwestern University and a two-year National Institutes of Mental Health-funded postdoctoral fellowship in mental health services research at Rutgers University, as well as a two-year NIMH mentoring and education program in mental health services research. Dr. Anderson is director of the Mental Health Services and Policy Collaborative and associate director of the National Health Law and Policy Resource Center in the College of Law, and she holds secondary appointments in the colleges of nursing and law. Her research interests are in mental health services and policy research. She is engaged in a variety of research efforts that contribute to policy debates and the development of legislation, as well as advising policy agencies and other research organizations. Her research examines strategies for connecting service systems in an effort to maximize the effectiveness of usual care practice and to identify prevention and early intervention strategies for persons with mental health challenges and their families.

Lise M. Bisnaire, Ph.D.

Lise Bisnaire received her doctorate in clinical psychology in 1988 from the University of Ottawa, Canada. She has been at the Children's Hospital of Eastern Ontario since 1996 and is currently the director of the Autism Intervention Program at CHEO, where she is involved in the development and implementation of the Total Clinical Outcomes Management approach to services for children, youth, and their families. At the time this chapter was drafted, she was the clinical director of the Inpatient Psychiatry Program and a professional practice leader in psychology at CHEO.

Margaret E. Blaustein, Ph.D.

Margaret Blaustein is a practicing clinical psychologist who specializes in the assessment and treatment of complex childhood trauma. Dr. Blaustein is the director of training and education at the Trauma Center at the Justice Resource Institute in Brookline, Massachusetts, and co-developer of the Attachment, Self-Regulation, and Competency (ARC) treatment framework. She has provided extensive didactic and interactive training to clinicians, educators, professionals, and consumers regarding the impact of and intervention for childhood-onset trauma. She received her doctorate in clinical psychology, with a specialization in children and families, from the University of Miami, and completed her internship at Boston Children's Hospital/Harvard Medical School.

Jason Brennen, B.A.

Jason Brennen has a background in health policy research. He was the project coordinator for the Mental Health Juvenile Justice (MHJJ) evaluation for three years under the supervision of Dr. John S. Lyons at Northwestern University, and in 2005 he served as an appointee to the State of Illinois Juvenile Justice Task Force Committee. His other research efforts have included Chicago's System-of-Care and the Department of Human Services of Illinois Sex Offenders project. Prior to his experience at Northwestern, he was employed at the Rhode Island Division of Mental Health as a program development associate. After a year teaching English as a second language in China, Mr. Brennen has returned to the United States where he is currently an associate director of Events Management for Hyatt International. He received his bachelor's degree in psychology from Brown University in 1999.

Inger Burnett-Ziegler, M.A.

Inger Burnett-Ziegler is a student in the clinical psychology doctoral program at Northwestern University and is currently teaching psychology courses at Chicago State University. She has worked in myriad clinical settings, including a Veterans Administration Medical Center, private hospital, and outpatient mental health center, conducting individual and group psychotherapy as well as psychological assessments. She has also worked for the Inspector General's office for the Illinois Department of Children and Family Services and as a consultant for the State of Illinois Department of Mental Health. Ms. Burnett-Ziegler plans to continue her work as a clinician to those with chronic and severe mental illness and to work for improvements in policy related to the provision and receipt of mental health services in the community. She received her bachelor's degree in psychology from Cornell University.

Julita Caliwan, M.S.W.

Julita Caliwan has nearly twenty-five years of experience in human services. She is currently with New Jersey's Division of Developmental Disabilities, coordinating efforts to address the cross-system challenges in serving children and adults with developmental disabilities and co-occurring behavioral health disorders. She previously served as an assistant division director of Policy, Planning and Quality Improvement at New Jersey's Division of Child Behavioral Health Services (DCBHS). Her experience with the DCBHS includes directing and overseeing the development of annual plans; coordinating federal, state, and foundation grant activity; developing policies and procedures, including regulations and Medicaid State Plan amendments; developing training activities; and developing and managing a continuous quality improvement (CQI) unit to infuse all DCBHS operations with a CQI culture of accountability and excellence. She was also on the faculty of the 2005 SAMHSA National Technical Assistance Center Policy Academy. Ms. Caliwan received her master's degree in social work from the Graduate School of Social Work at Rutgers University in 1983.

Stacey Cornett, M.S.W., L.C.S.W.

Stacey Cornett is the director of Intensive Youth Services at the Community Mental Health Center in Lawrenceburg, Indiana. In this position, Ms. Cornett is responsible for the development and administration of intensive home- and community-based services and a systems of care initiative for youth from infancy to age twenty-two. She has served as a consultant to the State of Indiana in the development of the Indiana Comprehensive Child and Adolescent Needs and Strengths Assessment, birth to five version. In addition, she has worked with Allegheny County, Pennsylvania's early childhood system of care initiative to develop an early childhood version of the ANSA. Ms. Cornett serves as the co-chair of the Indiana Association of Infant and Toddler Mental Health and is endorsed as a distinguished mentor in infant mental health. She serves as a consultant to various early childhood programs and trains mental health and early intervention providers throughout the country. She received her master's degree in social work from Saint Louis University in 1988.

Keith Cruise, Ph.D., M.L.S.

Keith Cruise is an assistant professor of psychology at Fordham University, where he teaches both graduate and undergraduate courses and contributes to clinical research and supervision as part of the clinical-forensic training specialization. Before joining the Fordham faculty in 2006, Dr. Cruise was an assistant clinical professor of public health at Louisiana State University Health Sciences Center in New Orleans, with a primary appointment to the LSUHSC Juvenile Justice Program. He earned his doctorate in clinical psychology in 2000 from the University of North Texas and his master's degree in legal studies from the University of Nebraska in 1995.

Norin Dollard, Ph.D.

Norin Dollard is a research assistant professor in the Department of Child and Family Studies, Louis de la Parte Florida Mental Health Institute, University of South Florida. She has over fifteen years of services research and evaluation experience in the behavioral health needs of children and families in child welfare, juvenile justice, and education systems. Prior to her work in Florida, Dr. Dollard was a research scientist with the New York State Office of Mental Health. She received her doctorate in curriculum and instruction with a specialization in child and family policy from the University of South Florida in 2003.

Elizabeth M. Durkin, Ph.D.

Elizabeth Durkin received her doctorate from Northwestern University and is currently on the university's faculty in the Department of Psychiatry and Behavioral Sciences. She conducts research in the areas of mental health services, health care organizations, and health policy. She has collaborated on two evaluations of federally funded programs for homeless individuals with co-occurring substance use and mental health disorders. Dr. Durkin is also a lecturer in Northwestern University's master's degree program in public health.

Murielle Elfman, M.S.S., L.S.W.

Murielle S. Elfman currently manages the CANS Unit for the Philadelphia Department of Human Services' Behavioral Health and Wellness Support Center, where she oversees all aspects of the CANS process in Philadelphia, including training, quality assurance, utilization of CANS data in strategic planning, and development and management of the CANS database. She also acts as a consultant to child welfare and mental health organizations as well as to state agencies on the implementation and use of the CANS and has co-presented with Dr. John Lyons on the use of the CANS in child serving systems. Prior to her work at the Philadelphia DHS, Ms. Elfman spent twenty-five years at several private child welfare agencies in the field of adoption and adoption search. She holds a master's degree in social work from Bryn Mawr Graduate School of Social Work and Social Research.

Heidi Ellis, Ph.D.

Heidi Ellis is a licensed clinical psychologist and instructor of psychiatry at Children's Hospital Boston/Harvard Medical School. Dr. Ellis's primary focus is the development and dissemination of interventions for traumatized children and their families, particularly refugees. She has also conducted research with the Somali community on issues of stigma, mental health, and service utilization. Before joining Children's Hospital in 2007, she was on the faculty of Boston University School of Medicine. She completed her doctorate in clinical psychology at the University of Oregon in 2000.

Philip Endress, L.C.S.W., A.C.S.W., M.B.A.

Philip Endress is the Commissioner, Erie Department of Mental Health in Buffalo, New York. He previously held the same position in Oneida County for eighteen years. His primary interest is developing systems of care for children and adults that are responsive to the evolving needs of individuals. Mr. Endress received his master's degree in social work from the State University of New York in Buffalo in 1977 and a second master's degree in business administration, also from SUNY Buffalo, in 1984.

Marcia Fazio, M.S.

Marcia Fazio is the director of the Hudson River Field Office of the New York State Office of Mental Health. At the time of the writing of this chapter, she was the assistant director of New York's Office of Mental Health, Division of Children and Families, and was involved in overseeing the transformation of children's services. Ms. Fazio has twenty-five years' experience working in the public mental health system in New York State. She received her degree in rehabilitation counseling at the State University of New York at Albany in 1977.

Jason Fogler, Ph.D.

Jason Fogler is a clinical associate at the Brookline Mental Health Center in Brookline, Massachusetts. At the time of the writing of this chapter, he was a National Institutes of Mental Health (NIMH) postdoctoral clinical research fellow at the National Center for Posttraumatic Stress Disorder and Boston University Medical Center, where he specialized in the study and treatment of posttraumatic stress in children, adolescents, and combat veterans. From 2003 to 2006, he was part of the research development team and a project coordinator for the initial studies of Saxe, Ellis, and Kaplow's Trauma Systems Therapy (TST); which informs many of the ideas in Chapter 17. Dr. Fogler earned his doctorate in clinical psychology from Boston University in 2005.

Susan Furrer, Psy.D.

Susan Furrer is the executive director of the Behavioral Research and Training Institute and the Violence Institute of New Jersey at University Behavioral Health Care, University of Medicine and Dentistry of New Jersey. Dr. Furrer administers a number of statewide training and technical assistance efforts (funded by the New Jersey Department of Human Services) and directs a variety of research and program evaluation projects focused on violence prevention. She administered the statewide training and technical assistance program for the New Jersey System of Care from its inception in 2001 until 2005. Dr. Furrer earned her doctorate in clinical psychology in 1990 from the Graduate School of Applied and Professional Psychology at Rutgers University.

Stephanie L. Greenham, Ph.D.

Stephanie L. Greenham is a clinical psychologist and research coordinator with the inpatient psychiatry program at the Children's Hospital of Eastern Ontario in Ottawa, Ontario, Canada, where she has been involved since 2000 in the development and implementation of an outcomes management approach to inpatient mental health services. Dr. Greenham earned her doctorate in clinical psychology in 1999 from the University of Ottawa.

Grant R. Grissom, Ph.D.

Grant R. Grissom is the president and CEO of Polaris Health Directions. Dr. Grissom is a leader in the field of outcomes management. He holds advanced degrees in mathematics, computer science, and counseling. He served as social science research director of Philadelphia's University City Science Center and as vice president for research and development for Compass Information Services and Integra. Dr. Grissom has been the principal investigator for more than twenty-five grants by the National Institutes on Drug Abuse (NIDA), Mental Health (NIMH), Alcoholism and Alcohol Abuse (NIAAA), and the federal Departments of Education, Justice, and Defense.

Bruce Hillman, M.S.

Bruce Hillman is the chief executive officer of Campagna Academy in Schererville, Indiana. Campagna Academy is a multi-service agency that serves the child welfare, juvenile justice, and education systems in northwest Indiana through its residential treatment, foster care, and charter school programs. Before coming to Campagna Academy in 2005, Mr. Hillman was the Lake County Director for the Department of Child Services. Mr. Hillman served as department director for ten years and supported the initial use of the CANS in Lake County before it was adopted for use throughout the State of Indiana. Mr. Hillman is a doctoral candidate at Walden University in the area of nonprofit management and leadership. Walden is headquartered in the Mills District in Minneapolis.

Stacey Hirsch, M.S.W.

Stacey Hirsch is the Director of the PMHCC Best Practices Institute (BPI) (PMHCC was formerly the Philadelphia Mental Health Care Corporation.). Her expertise is in resource development, capacity building, and program and organizational development for nonprofit and public agencies serving children and families. Ms. Hirsch manages twenty staff members who provide technical assistance and consulting support to two major departments within the City of Philadelphia Social Services Division: the Department of Human Services and the Department of Behavioral Health/Mental Retardation Services. Prior to joining BPI, Ms. Hirsch spent four years working for the Child Welfare League of America in the National Center for Field Consultation, providing consultation services to public child welfare agencies. In addition, she was the director of the Philadelphia Interdisciplinary Youth Fatality Review Team; she also spent several years as a kindergarten teacher and child care worker. She received her master's degree in social policy and program planning from Temple University and her bachelor's degree in human services from the University of Delaware.

John A. Hunter, Ph.D.

John Hunter is a research associate professor of psychology at the University of Virginia. He is well-known for his clinical study of the etiology, assessment, and treatment of juvenile sexual aggression. He has published over forty articles and book chapters on the subject of juvenile sexual offending and sexual trauma, and has been the recipient of seven federal research grants. Most recently, Dr. Hunter received a Career Development Award for the National Institutes of Mental Health to further his study of subtypes of sexually aggressive youth and their differential developmental trajectories. He has directed both community-based and residential treatment programs for juvenile sexual offenders and is a former member of the board of directors for the Association for the Treatment of Sexual Abusers. He currently serves on the Kempe Center National Task Force on Juvenile Sexual Offending, the University of Oklahoma Center on Sexual Behavior National Advisory Committee, and the Center for Sex Offender Management National Resource Group.

Frits J Huyse, M.D., Ph.D.

Frits J. Huyse is a professor of psychiatry and medicine at Groningen University Medical School in Groningen, the Netherlands. He was recently awarded the Thomas Hackett award for career contributions to Consultation-Liaison Psychiatry for his work on the INTERMED.

Crystal Jackson, M.A.

Crystal Jackson is a doctoral student of sociology at Loyola University of Chicago. Ms. Jackson has worked on many program evaluation projects for the Mental Health Services and Policy Program at Northwestern University, where she has been primarily responsible for the local evaluation site for a national program aiming to improve service utilization through school-based linkages. She is also a certified CANS trainer. Her current research interests focus on social policy as a vehicle for addressing social and economic inequality. She received her bachelor's degree from the University of Louisville and her master's degree in clinical psychology from the University of Detroit—Mercy.

Peter de Jonge, Ph.D.

Peter de Jonge is an assistant professor in the Department of Internal Medicine and Psychiatry at the University of Groningen, the Netherlands.

Cassandra Kisiel, Ph.D.

Cassandra Kisiel is a research assistant professor at Northwestern University Feinberg School of Medicine and a trauma consultant and project director for the Illinois Department of Children and Family Services, where she is responsible for developing and implementing trauma-focused training plans and materials related to best practices for child trauma assessment and treatment, both within the Illinois child welfare system and with mental health providers across the state. In this capacity, she conducts evaluations and research related to complex trauma adaptation and protective factors for child trauma. Before joining Northwestern in 2006, Dr. Kisiel was the training director for the SAMHSA-funded National Child Traumatic Stress Network through the University of California, Los Angeles. Dr. Kisiel earned her doctoral degree in clinical psychology at Northwestern University Feinberg School of Medicine and completed her internship at Cambridge Hospital, Harvard Medical School, and postdoctoral fellowships at the Cambridge Hospital and the National Violence Against Women Prevention Research Center at the Stone Center of Wellesley College.

Corine H. M. Latour, C.N.S., R.N.

Corine H. M. Latour is a consultation-liaison psychiatric nurse in the Psychiatric Consultation and Liaison Service, Vrije University Medical Center in Amsterdam, the Netherlands.

Renanah K. Lehner, Ph.D.

Renanah Lehner is a psychologist at Trilogy, Inc., a psycho-social rehabilitation agency for individuals with severe mental illness. She received her doctorate from the Northwestern University Feinberg School of Medicine clinical psychology program, with a concentration in mental health and policy research. She also completed a post-doctoral fellowship at the Northwestern University Institute for Healthcare Studies focusing on mental health services.

Scott C. Leon, Ph.D.

Scott Leon is an assistant professor of clinical psychology at Loyola University in Chicago, where he teaches and mentors in the undergraduate and graduate psychology programs. Dr. Leon received his doctorate in clinical psychology from Northwestern University Medical School in June 2002. During his graduate studies, he developed research interests in mental health services evaluation. He has conducted research in community mental health centers, schools, and child welfare agencies, with the primary goal of improving the appropriateness and effectiveness of mental health services delivered to youth. Dr. Leon also practices psychotherapy as an associate in a private group practice.

Zoran Martinovich, Ph.D.

Zoran Martinovich is a research assistant professor at the Northwestern University Feinberg School of Medicine. He received his doctorate in psychology from Northwestern University in Evanston, Illinois in 1998, and has provided teaching and statistical support services within Northwestern's Mental Health Services and Policy Program since that time. His research has primarily concerned statistical methods and products with real-world applications for outcomes management in mental health care.

Mitch Mason, M.S.W.

Mitch Mason is the Chief of Governmental Relations for the Los Angeles County Department of Children and Family Services. He is responsible for providing leadership on the department's legislative agenda, coordinating efforts with the County Welfare Directors Association and other stakeholders. He also oversees the department's Policy, Training, Education and Licensure, and Accountability and Outcomes sections. Mr. Mason participated in the development of the department's Title IV E Waiver Demonstration Project; in 2003 he served as the Structured Decision-Making

(SDM) Project Manager. He has been involved in the field of child welfare for over twenty-seven years. He started as a field social worker in South Central Los Angeles in 1980. From 1990 to 1996, he was employed by the Los Angeles County Inter-Agency Council on Child Abuse and Neglect to coordinate the county's child death review team. He has worked in the department's Training Section, coordinating and presenting training to nearly 5,000 social work and support staff, and has held a number of executive support positions. Mr. Mason received his master's degree in clinical and counseling psychology from California State University at Los Angeles, and his master's of social work degree from California State University at Long Beach.

Joan Mechlin, M.A., M.S.N., A.P.R.N.B.C.

Joan Mechlin is a consultant to various child serving systems in Philadelphia, Pennsylvania, having recently retired from her position as director of the Mobile Response Services for New Jersey's Child Behavioral Health Division.

Angelica Oberleithner, M.S.

Angelica Oberleithner is the program director of the Orange County Partnership for Young Children in Chapel Hill, North Carolina, a local Smart Start agency. Angelica oversees and manages program evaluation, program monitoring, and program development for the agency and its twenty funded providers in the areas of early childhood education, early intervention, and family support. Before relocating to North Carolina, Angelica was the director of the PMHCC Best Practices Institute (BPI) in Philadelphia, Pennsylvania, where her work focused on treatment foster care reform, a key initiative in the Department of Human Services' permanency reform agenda. Before joining BPI, Angelica served as division director for health promotion and wellness at one of Philadelphia's largest social service providers, overseeing and managing a multitude of programs in the areas of domestic violence, HIV prevention and intervention, child welfare, and maternal health. Angelica holds a master's degree in sociology from the University of Vienna, Austria and is fluent in German, English, and Spanish.

Thomas W. Pavkov, Ph.D.

Thomas Pavkov is an associate professor of psychology at Purdue University, Calumet, and the director of the Institute for Social and Policy Research located on the same campus. Dr. Pavkov has served as the principal evaluator for the Residential Treatment Center Evaluation Project along with the Circle Around Families Child Mental Health Initiative Evaluation. Dr. Pavkov's work as an evaluator has spanned numerous initiatives, including Head Start, juvenile justice, and child welfare. Prior to working at Purdue, Dr. Pavkov was a research associate at Chapin Hall for Children at the University of Chicago. Dr. Pavkov earned his doctorate in human development and social policy from Northwestern University.

Irene Podrobinok, B.A.

Irene Podrobinok received her bachelor's degree in psychology in 2004 from Knox College in Galesburg, Illinois, and shortly thereafter began working for the Mental Health Services and Policy Program at Northwestern University. Ms. Prodrobinok worked as a project assistant for the System of Care evaluation, helping to measure agency effects on child outcomes. She also worked on the development and pilot of the CANS 0-5 items. She is currently a graduate student and will receive her master's degree in child development from the Erickson School of Psychology in Chicago in 2009.

Michael Rauso, Psy.D., M.F.T.

Michael Rauso is the director of Wraparound Services for the Los Angeles County Department of Children and Family Services (DCFS). He oversees the DCFS's Family to Family Initiative, Family Group Decision-Making, and its crossover prevention program. He is also the chair of the California Welfare Directors Association's Wraparound subcommittee. Dr. Rauso started as a therapist in a group home and then came to the DCFS in 2003 as director of Wraparound, where he grew the program from an initial 175 enrolled children to a current census of 1,157. He holds a doctorate in clinical psychology and also is a licensed marriage and family therapist.

Mary Beth Rautkis, Ph.D.

Mary Beth Rauktis received her doctorate from the University of Pittsburgh School of Social Work in 1993. She is an assistant professor of research in the Child Welfare Research and Training Program at the university. Prior to this appointment, she was the director of research and evaluation at Pressley Ridge, an international nonprofit provider of services to children and families. She was also an adjunct at the University of Pittsburgh School of Social Work and Robert Morris University Business School in nonprofit management, and a visiting professor at the University of Minho, Institute of Child and Family Studies in Portugal.

Purva Rawal, Ph.D.

Purva Rawal currently does health and social policy work in the United States Senate, where she drafts legislation and provides briefings on a range of health and social policy issues. Prior to her current position, she was a Congressional Fellow through the Society for Research on Child Development and the American Association for the Advancement of Science. She received her doctorate in clinical psychology from Northwestern University in 2005, and completed her predoctoral internship at Johns Hopkins University.

Laura L. Rogers, L.C.S.W.

Laura Rogers is currently an executive director at the Stockon site of the Victor Community Support Services in northern California. Prior to this, she was the director of Children and Family Services at Oneida County Mental Health in Oneida, New York, where she was charged with establishing and implementing a seamless process called Single Point of Access (SPOA) for children's systems in the areas of mental health, child welfare, juvenile justice, and education.

Glenn N. Saxe, M.D.

Glenn Saxe is associate chief of psychiatry at Harvard Medical School and Children's Hospital in Boston, where he is also the director of the Center for Behavioral Science. His main area of expertise is traumatic stress in children. His research concerns bio-behavioral processes and intervention development related to children who have experienced trauma. Dr. Saxe is the lead developer of Trauma Systems Therapy (TST), an integrated treatment model for traumatized children and families who live in the most challenging of environments. He also directs the Center for Refugee Trauma, a treatment adaptation center within the National Child Traumatic Stress Network. He received his medical degree from McMaster University Medical School in Hamilton, Ontario and completed his residency in adult psychiatry at Harvard Medical School/ Massachusetts Mental Health Center.

Joris P. J. Slaets, M.D., Ph.D.

Joris P. J. Slaets is a professor of geriatrics and Chairman of the Internal Medicine Department at the Gronigen University Medical School in Groningen, the Netherlands. He is well known for his work in geriatrics, particularly with the frail elderly.

David Sliefert, M.A.

David Sliefert is Director of Quality Assurance and the Fetal Alcohol Disorder Community Team Coordinator at the Sitka Developmental Center in Sitka, Alaska. He received his M.A. from the University of Alaska.

Wolfgang Söllner, M.D.

Wolfgang Söllner is an associate professor of psychosomatics and psychotherapy at the Department of Psychosomatics and Psychotherapy, General Hospital, Nurenberg, Germany.

Jena H. Stallings, M.A.

Jena Stallings is a clinical psychology doctoral candidate at Northwestern University Feinberg School of Medicine. She has six years' experience in the area of outcome assessment and program evaluation as a research assistant in the Mental Health Services and Policy Program. She has worked on several different projects, including structuring a database for a sex offender treatment center, evaluating community based mental health and substance abuse services for homeless individuals in Chicago, and examining differences in outcomes across residential facilities for children in Illinois. Her research interests include children's mental health services and more specifically outcome evaluations of residential mental health services for children.

Friedrich C. Stiefel, M.D., Ph.D.

Fredrich C. Stiefel is a professor of psychiatry, Service de Psychiatrie d Liaision, Centre Hospitalier Universitaire Vaudois, in Lausanne, Switzerland.

Linda L. Toche-Manley, Ph.D.

Linda Toche-Manley is principal investigator at Polaris Health Directions, where she is the primary scientific developer of Polaris's public sector products for youth, for the severely and persistently mentally ill, and for domestic violence and child welfare. Dr. Toche-Manley received her doctorate in applied psychology from Claremont Graduate University in Claremont, California. She has extensive experience based on her consultant and evaluator work on national and state systems of care and public sector agencies.

Nynke van der Wal, A.N.P.

Nynke van der Wal is a consultation-liaison psychiatric nurse, Consultant on Integrated Care, Department of General Internal Medicine, University Medical Center, Groningen, the Netherlands.

Keren S. Vergon, Ph.D.

Keren Vergon is a research assistant professor in the Department of Child and Family Studies, Louis de la Parte Florida Mental Health Institute, University of South Florida. Dr. Vergon has twelve years of behavioral services research experience in the areas of older adults' and children's mental health. She received her doctorate in aging studies from the University of South Florida in 2006.

Notes on the
Organization of This Book

The overall goal of this book is to bring to life a variety of applications of communimetric tools with the long-term objectives of fully implementing the principles of Total Clinical Outcomes Management (TCOM). Part 1, Setting the Stage (Chapters 1 and 2), is a general introduction to TCOM and the Child and Adolescent Needs and Strengths (CANS) tool. The remaining chapters in the book provide a variety of case studies of various aspects of the TCOM approach and the development and use of communimetric tools. These case studies are organized based on the level of the implementation.

Part 2, Cross-Program Applications Within Systems, includes six chapters describing experiences with system level implementations. Chapters 3 and 4 narrate the story of statewide CANS implementation in New York. In Chapter 3, Fazio describes the state level use of CANS, first in a need-based planning study and then in support of the implementation of systemwide efforts at transformation. In Chapter 4, Rogers and Endress provide a parallel description of New York's transformation process at a county level rather than from the state perspective. The New York State Office of Mental Health (OMH) works to facilitate adoption of innovation at the county level because so much system control occurs at the county level. By requiring that a Single Points of Accountability (SPOA) system adopt some standard measure, and by recommending the CANS as this measure, the OMH both encourages adoption and respects local control.

In Chapter 5, Caliwan and Furrer describe one of the most comprehensive applications of this approach in New Jersey. New Jersey's vision, the most ambitious effort nationally, is to implement TCOM across the state's entire child-serving system through the use of a common assessment strategy. In Chapter 6, Hirsch, Elfman, and Oberleithner describe an interesting implementation in Philadelphia's child welfare system. This chapter describes the oldest and most successful implementation of an eligibility approach to decision model implementation. The success of the treatment foster care eligibility model has spawned expansion into thresholds for group homes and institutions and applications within the juvenile justice system.

Pavkov and Hillman in Chapter 7, and Rauso and Mason in Chapter 8, describe county-based applications in Indiana and California, respectively. Lake County, Indiana, in the northwest corner of the state, is a complex and diverse county. The Lake Country implementation has led to a statewide approach in Indiana. Los Angeles County's population would make it the fifth largest state; implementation is well underway.

Part 3, Managing Single Programs Across Systems, describes TCOM implementations that focus on single programs in statewide systems. In Chapter 9, Leon describes one of the one of the most mature applications of TCOM in the mobile crisis services in Illinois. Recently, the method described by Leon has been expanded as the mobile crisis program has grown to include all Medicaid-eligible youth. In Chapter 10, Furrer and Mechlin describe how New Jersey used its Information Management and Decision Support tool (IMDS) to support the implementation of its mobile response component to its expanded children's system of care. To conclude Part 3, Burnett-Ziegler, Brennen, and Jackson present in Chapter 11 the Mental Health Juvenile Justice Initiative's approach to TCOM. Data on the impact of this program was successfully used to secure its expansion to all county detention centers and it has become a model for Illinois's Department of Juvenile Justice.

Part 4, Program-Level TCOM, presents three chapters that describe TCOM approaches at the program level in areas where systemwide implementation has not been undertaken. In Chapter 12, Bisnaire and Greenham describe the first program-level effort at TCOM at the Children's Hospital of Eastern Ontario. This program is seen as an innovation at the provincial level, with funding from Ontario's Center for Excellence, representing the first externally funded TCOM implementation. In Chapter 13, Lehner and Durkin present the development and implementation of TCOM within a program for adults with serious substance use and housing problems. Implementation occurs here in the context of an under-funded environment that uses staff with less training and experience than many service delivery settings. In Chapter 14, Anderson describes a process to improve mental health services in an adult prison. The challenge of needs-based planning and service system transformation in an environment that is historically unfriendly to mental health is an interesting application of the person-centered approach advocated in TCOM.

Part 5, Treatment Management for Special Populations, offers four chapters that cover the design and implementation of communimetric tools for special populations. In Chapter 15, Huyse and his colleagues describe the development of the INTERMED, which is used in medical/surgical populations. This tool has been successfully used to support biopsychosocial assessment and intervention in a wide variety of complex medical and surgical settings, both inpatient and outpatient. In Chapter 16, Hunter and Cruise present research on the version of the CANS developed for use with sexually aggressive youth. The authors compare the communimetric CANS tool with other tools that come from psychometric theory. Kisiel, Blaustein, and colleagues describe in Chapter 17 the collaboration within sites of the National Child Traumatic Stress Network to develop a special version of the CANS-Trauma Experiences and Adjustment version. This development was the foundation for the CANS version that is now used statewide in child welfare in Illinois. To round out Part 5, Cornett and Podrobinok in Chapter 18 describe the early development version of the CANS used for children five years old and younger. Currently, early development interventions are an important area of interest and program expansion. Few comprehensive, strength-based assessment approaches exist for this age group.

Part 6, TCOM Methods, presents methods applications for TCOM. Rawal and Lyons in Chapter 19 describe the methods for needs-based planning, which can be used as the foundation of developing TCOM in complex systems (e.g., New York State, Philadelphia, Illinois State, and Los Angeles County). In Chapter 20, Dollard, Rautkis, and colleagues present the development of a file review method to match assessment information to service planning and treatment impact documentation. Effective use of information technology is an important aspect of successful TCOM implementation, and this technique, Service Process Adherence to Needs and Strengths (SPANS), is an excellent method of quality improvement consistent with the TCOM philosophy.

In Chapter 21, Toche-Manley and Grissom present a computer-based management system that supports TCOM implementation at a program level. Weiner in Chapter 22 discusses the development of a method for building matches between assessment data and provider information, an important contribution for anyone interested in managing complex systems. Chapter 23 presents an innovative statistical approach to using communimetric data for outcomes. Martinovich and Stallings use hierarchical linear models to build trajectories of recovery for children and youth in residential treatment settings. In Chapter 24, Lyons describes the philosophy and methods for developing decision models, and in Chapter 25, Lyons and Weiner discuss the future of TCOM and offer their reflections on what it needs to succeed in the long run.

In sum, the design of the book is to provide a series of case studies that describe aspects of the TCOM approach, using communimetric measures, from a variety of levels and perspectives. As yet, no implementation represents a full implementation of TCOM. However, together these stories provide a useful way to understand the philosophy and approach.

Table of Contents

PART 2: CROSS-PROGRAM APPLICATIONS WITHIN SYSTEMS

Chapter 3: Implications of Needs-Based Planning in New York for the Children's Public Mental Health Services System
Marcia Fazio, M.S.

Chapter 6: Managing Treatment Foster Care With Decision Support and Outcomes
Stacey Hirsch, M.S.W., Murielle Elfman, M.S.S., L.S.W. and
Angelica Oberleithner, M.S.

Chapter 7: Introducing Outcome Management Measures Where None Exist: The Lake County, Indiana, CANS Implementation Experience
Thomas W. Pavkov, Ph.D. and Bruce Hillman, M.S.

Chapter 8: History of Placement Control and Utilization Management in Los Angeles County
Michael Rauso, Psy.D., M.F.T. and Mitch Mason, M.S.W.

PART 3: MANAGING SINGLE PROGRAMS ACROSS SYSTEMS

Chapter 9: Understanding Psychiatric Hospital Admissions and Outcomes
Scott C. Leon, Ph.D.

Chapter 10: Building a Mobile Response and Stabilization System
Susan Furrer, Psy.D. and Joan Mechlin, M.A., M.S.N., A.P.R.N.B.C.

Chapter 11: Illinois's Mental Health Juvenile Justice Initiative: Use of Standardized Assessments for Eligibility and Outcomes
Inger Burnett-Ziegler, M.A., Jason Brennen, B.A. and Crystal Jackson, M.A.

PART 4: PROGRAM LEVEL TCOM

Chapter 12: Implementation of Total Clinical Outcomes Management in an Acute Care Pediatric Inpatient Setting
Lise M. Bisnaire, Ph.D. and Stephanie L. Greenham, Ph.D.

PART 5: TREATMENT MANAGEMENT FOR SPECIAL POPULATIONS

Chapter 15: Integrated Care for the Complex Medically Ill With the INTERMED Method

Frits J. Huyse, M.D., Ph.D., Friedrich C. Stiefel, M.D., Ph.D.,
Wolfgang Söllner, M.D., Joris P. J. Slaets, M.D., Ph.D.,
John S. Lyons, Ph.D., Corine H. M. Latour, C.N.S.,
R.N., Nynke van der Wal, A.N.P. and Peter de Jonge, Ph.D.

**Chapter 16: Use of the CANS-SD in the Treatment and
Management of Juvenile Sexual Offenders**
John A. Hunter, Ph.D. and Keith Cruise, M.L.S., Ph.D.

**Chapter 17: Treating Children With Traumatic Experiences:
Understanding and Assessing Needs and Strengths**
*Cassandra Kisiel, Ph.D., Margaret E. Blaustein, Ph.D., Jason Fogler, Ph.D.,
Heidi Ellis, Ph.D., and Glenn N. Saxe, M.D.*

Chapter 18: Use of the CANS—Early Childhood in Effecting Change in the Lives of Young Children and Their Families
Stacey Cornett, M.S.W., L.C.S.W. and Irene Podrobinok, B.A.

PART 6: TCOM METHODS

Chapter 19: Needs-Based Planning Using the CANS
Purva Rawal, Ph.D. and John S. Lyons, Ph.D.

Chapter 20: Service Process Adherence to Needs and Strengths: A Quality Improvement Tool
Norin Dollard, Ph.D., Mary Beth Rautkis, Ph.D., Keren S. Vergon, Ph.D. and David Sliefert, M.A.

Chapter 21: Recovery Outcomes Management System: Combining the Adult Needs and Strengths Assessment With Consumer and Support Informant Self-Report

Linda L. Toche-Manley, Ph.D. and Grant R. Grissom, Ph.D.

Chapter 24: Creating Decision Support and Eligibility Models Using Clinical Assessments
John S. Lyons, Ph.D.

Chapter 25: Reflections and Future Directions
John S. Lyons, Ph.D. and Dana A. Weiner, Ph.D.

Part 1
Setting the Stage

Chapter 1

An Introduction and Overview of Total Clinical Outcomes Management and Communimetrics

by John S. Lyons, Ph.D. and Dana A. Weiner, Ph.D.

INTRODUCTION

Initial Efforts at Outcomes Management

Beginning in the 1980s, based on the work of Ken Howard, Michael Lambert and others, interest developed in using the outcomes of behavioral health services to help understand how these services were performing (Howard et al., 1986; Lambert, 1989, 1983). Work on understanding outcomes was a natural evolution from Glass, McGaw & Smith's (1981) seminal meta-analysis on the impact of behavioral health services, which identified a large average effect size. Lipsey & Wilson (1993) later demonstrated that this effect size was larger than many effects of commonly accepted medical treatments. Initially, measuring outcomes was seen as an effort to extend science into field settings. With the advent of managed behavioral health care, however, it did not take long for people to see the potential for actually using data on outcomes to assist in the management of a behavioral health service system. With this interest, the field of outcomes management was born.

Unfortunately, despite considerable interest and a large number of conferences and meetings, initial efforts at outcomes management failed to deliver on its early promise. There are a number of possible reasons for this shortcoming:

- There was a general attempt to implement traditional, basic science approaches in field settings without respect for the differences between research methodology and approaches that are feasible within service delivery settings.

- Choice of outcomes measures did not always mirror the goals and objectives of the services being monitored. For example, psychiatric hospitals collected measurements on functional status when the hospital intervention was no longer attempting to improve functioning, but instead was focusing on stabilization and risk management.

- Measuring outcomes was an unfunded mandate. Few states or insurers paid for the additional costs of collecting outcomes data. Few resources were invested in the infrastructure of analyzing and interpreting findings within reasonable time frames.

- Existing technologies did not support efficient data management. The Internet was brand new and its potential far from realized. Most behavioral health service settings had limited computer access/capacity.

- No guidelines existed with regard to how to use outcomes. So even when findings were available it was not clear how best to use them to evolve service systems.

For these and other reasons, few settings successfully implemented routine measurement of outcomes in a manner that was available in a time frame relevant to program or system management. As the light of the outcomes management movement began to dim, many leaders in the field shifted to an emphasis on evidence-based practices. The logic was persuasive. Rather than trying to see whether services were actually working in the field, why not simply identify treatments that are known to be effective in clinical trials?

Evidence-Based Practices

Over the past decade our ability to distinguish categories of best practices, promising practices, and evidence-based best practices has lead to major advances in how we understand the science of clinical efficacy. A number of treatments have been identified in each category. Now controversy has developed over whether treatment providers must implement an evidence-based practice in its totality, or may identify key active components and implement these active aspects without using the entire practice. A second controversy in the evidence-based practice literature concerns the growing realization that efficacy (i.e., the treatment works in clinical trials) and effectiveness (i.e., the treatment works in service delivery settings) are very different constructs. This disparity may in part be related to the failure to maintain the fidelity of the evidence-based practice in its field implementation; however, it is possible that this difference is much more complex than that.

The flickering embers of the outcomes movement have recently been revitalized. Ironically, the obvious limitations of the movement to implement evidence-based practices appears to be the reason for this. Disparate findings such as an 80 percent efficacy rate for Prozac in clinical trials and a 20 percent to 40 percent rate of the drug's effectiveness in clinical practice (Shasha et al., 1997) made clear to anyone paying attention that implementing evidence-based practices is by no means straightforward. Further, most evidence-based practices have limited indications. Therefore, the full and effective implementation of evidence-based practices requires both an assessment process to ensure that the right practices are provided to the right recipients *and* an indication that the treatments are as effective in the field as in clinical trials. The only viable strategy to achieve these goals is to fully implement an outcomes management approach.

TOTAL CLINICAL OUTCOMES MANAGEMENT

A Practice/System Management Approach

In *Redressing the Emperor*, Lyons (2004) proposed an expansion of traditional outcomes management approaches to a full practice/system management strategy. He termed this approach Total Clinical Outcomes Management (TCOM), a title designed to imply the following:

Total—The use of assessment in all aspects of the service delivery process, from work with an individual recipient and/or family, to supervision, program management, and system management. All aspects of management should be directed toward the needs of the people the system is intended to serve.

Clinical—The focus on recipients should be a focus on their needs and strengths. Traditional quality improvement efforts have focused on the functioning of services (e.g., how soon an appointment is made following hospital discharge, how quickly a phone call is answered, how long the wait time prior to an appointment). While such quality indicators may be meaningful for service management, a clinical focus means shifting these measurement processes away from the services and toward the people we are attempting to serve.

Outcomes—The clinical focus described above must be further refined to maintain the focus on those aspects that represent the goals of the treatment, service, or intervention. There are few universal outcomes in a complex behavioral health system. Hospitals aim to manage risk and mobilize resources. Outpatient treatment often has the goal of improving subjective well-being and reducing symptoms. Rehabilitation services target functional improvements. An outcomes focus means that program management targets the goals and objectives of that program. The outcomes question is really central to managing services from a TCOM perspective. However, outcomes expectations may not be that everybody "gets better" over time. Rather, the outcomes question requires that we first define the rationale for the service/program/intervention and then understand its place within a larger service system. Outcomes then refers to monitoring the clinical rationality of the service/program/intervention.

Management—This term implies that the information collected is used to make decisions in real time about how services and programs are staffed and managed. The information that system and program managers collect should be used to inform all of their decisions. From decision-making with an individual recipient to supervision to program management, the focus should remain on the needs and strengths of the person being served. Management of the service is about maintaining the focus on that shared vision. Use of collected data for management decision-making represents a fundamental change in business strategy for many behavioral health care providers. However, a focus on outcomes is a fairly standard approach in most other industries and sectors of the business community.

TCOM and Organizational Theory

Over the past several decades a number of conceptual frameworks have been proposed as strategies to improve health care generally and behavioral health care services specifically. Concepts such as total quality management and continuous quality improvement have been promoted as strategies for improving efficiency and effectiveness. The main difference between TCOM and such other approaches lies in the difference between the construct of quality versus the construct of outcomes.

The behavioral health field's focus on quality assurance and quality improvement efforts can be understood within organizational theory. In his seminal work on organizational theory, Max Weber (1947) distinguished a bureaucracy (i.e., a rational-legal authority) from two other forms of authority—traditional (leadership by tradition) and charismatic (leadership by charm). In a rational-legal authority, people in leadership follow a legally established order and must act within established rules or face legal jeopardy. Weber described the bureaucracy as the most evolved form of rational-legal authority. According to Weber, an ideal bureaucracy has these key characteristics:

- Fixed areas under the jurisdiction of the authority exist, and the boundaries of responsibility are clear.

- Within a fixed area, required duties are assigned to individuals whose training or expertise is consistent with their responsibilities.

- A clear division of labor exists among individuals.

- No individual has the power to give a command that does not coincide with the rules of the organization.

- A hierarchical system is created where higher officials govern lower officials, and communication is standardized and regulated along these established chains of command (i.e., a standard corporate structure).

- Rules and regulations are documented and readily available to anyone in the bureaucracy.

According to Weber, bureaucracies emerge as a reaction to market economies where centralization becomes valued. Centralized bureaucracies are particularly important in markets in capitalist economies, as such markets emphasize rationality and coordination to maximize profitability. As markets grow in size, the bureaucracies should become more complex and differentiated and, therefore, interdependent with other bureaucracies.

More recently, Perrow (1967, 1993) has argued that Weber's model of bureaucracy is idealized and, thus, not suited for real world applications, for three primary reasons:

- While bureaucracies attempt to eliminate the effect of individuals, only in an ideal world would all members of the bureaucracy always act in the best interest of the organization. In reality, people in organizations have their own agendas.

- Bureaucracies, by creating rules and regulations that must be followed, grow into organizations that struggle with rapid change. In fact, the bureaucratic structure actually discourages change. Change is a threat to the routine. The inertia of the routine maintains the system.

- Bureaucracies are designed to handle routine and stable processes and tasks. In the absence of either foresight or planning, it is impossible to establish effective rules and regulations for new processes.

Evolving from the original theory of bureaucracy, contingency theory posited that organizations with different products or processes develop differently (Galbraith, 1973). In other words, the purpose of the organization will influence exactly how it becomes organized. Further, different technologies require different types of organizations (Hage & Aiken, 1969). Routine technology (e.g., building cars) requires formal and centralized structures. Craft technology (e.g., art) requires a decentralized, less hierarchical structure with flexible decision-making. Engineering technology (e.g., software development) requires a flexible centralized authority (e.g., it is helpful for different software products to be compatible with each other). And non-routine technology requires more of a matrix structure with multiple points of centralization.

Behavioral Health Care a Non-Routine Technology

Behavioral health care is best conceptualized as a non-routine technology. The recent focus on individualized, culturally sensitive treatment is just one clear indication that behavioral health care is non-routine. One can make an argument that a medical procedure such as coronary bypass is a routine technology. We know who needs it, when not to do it, exactly how to do it, and in what sequence. While many therapies have become "manualized," a great deal of flexibility is built into even evidence-based practice approaches. Therefore, at this stage of our knowledge, it is reasonable to conceptualize behavioral health care as non-routine technology.

A key component of contingency theory is that the technology to be managed must be easy to model. Essentially, management under contingency theory flows from the assumption that everyone should be doing what he is supposed to be doing at the time he is supposed to do it. To accomplish this goal, you have to clearly know the when and where of all processes. This contingency-based approach leads to management efforts to measure processes and ensure that the processes are carried out. However, this approach is primarily useful only for routine technology. Monitoring the quality of processes on the assembly-line is very helpful for maintaining the output of the line.

Quality assurance and quality improvement models derive from the application of contingency theory to behavioral health care. The basic assumption is that we know what we should be doing (e.g., answering the phone within three rings, scheduling an outpatient appointment within seven days of hospital discharge), and all that has to be done is measure and manage these quality indicators. Unfortunately, behavioral health care is much more complicated than that—it is a non-routine technology. You cannot treat everyone the same because, in fact, they vary on important individual difference characteristics. Quality models may enhance the routinization of treatment, but there is no reason to believe that improving management of protocols will by definition improve outcomes associated with the treatments. Only when the routine is *very* closely tied to the outcome can we make this leap. Although we have some break-throughs in identifying evidence-based practices, we do not believe we are anywhere near establishing behavioral health care as a routine technology.

As a non-routine technology, then, a different type of organization is required, and management should not simply target processes. It is not until processes have become routine (and they should become so) that they can be monitored and managed. Rather, flexibility in process is required. Therefore, accountability cannot be applied to quality but rather to the impact of the efforts. The focus on the product rather than the process is how TCOM differs from quality assurance and quality improvement efforts.

MEASUREMENT AS COMMUNICATION—COMMUNIMETRICS

A key challenge in the implementation of TCOM is the choice of measurement strategies. In fact, the assessment strategy chosen is the foundation of the TCOM approach. Unfortunately, one reason outcomes management floundered in its earliest implementation was a lack of fit between how measurement was conceptualized and operationalized and how it was applied in the field. To resolve the tension between measurement theory and TCOM, we propose an alternative theory of measurement designed specifically for implementation in service delivery environments. We refer to this measurement theory as communimetrics because the primary reason for measurement in the TCOM approach is communication.

Since the early 1900s, when Sir Francis Galton created statistical methods of psychological measurement, measurement in behavioral health care has been predominantly the enterprise of the field of psychology. While measurement exists in all science, calibration of laboratory tests and physical assessments require limited theory. It is only when measurement strays from the directly observable that theories of measurement become desirable in the design of assessment strategies. When human judgment moderates the direct application of a measure apparatus, special attention must be placed into the design of that approach.

Psychometric Theories

The initial measurement theories have been named psychometric theories after the field that developed them. There are several classic texts on psychometric theory. The focus is the precise measurement of an individual on a construct that cannot be directly observed. While precision as assessed through reliability and validity are the paramount values of psychometric theories (Nunnally, 1976), all of these texts discuss the goal of communication among scientists. This goal is to facilitate replication, which is a foundation of scientific progress. However, among psychometric theorists communication can be thought of as a less important goal relative to reliability and validity.

Although a number of measures developed from traditional psychometric theories are commonly used in behavioral health care, it is reasonable to say that the routine application of these types of tools has not been widely observed. Psychometric tools have proven quite useful for specialized assessment processes. In general, however, measures derived from psychometric theory have failed as universal assessment strategies in service delivery settings. There are a variety of reasons for this failure, but the two primary ones include the length of these types of measures (i.e., reliability is created by combining less reliable single items into scales) and the need to score the measure prior to interpretation.

Clinimetric Measures

In the mid-1950s, Virginia Apgar introduced the Apgar score, which was to become known as the first clinimetric measure. As elaborated by Feinstein (1999), a clinimetric measure observes the following principles:

- Selection of items is based on clinical rather than statistical criteria.
- No weighting factors are needed—scoring is simple and readily interpretable.
- Variables are selected to be heterogeneous, not homogeneous.
- The measure is easy for clinicians to use.
- Face validity is required.
- Subjective states are not measured, as they are severely limited in terms of sources of observation.

Thus, clinimetric measures involve single or a small set of items rated in a fashion that the physician knows immediately what the implications of a particular score might be. There is no deception in the presentation of the items. There is a complete trust that the person making the rating is making a good faith effort to be as accurate as possible. This is very different than some psychometric tools that involve self-report and build in validity scales to detect deception.

Communimetric Theory

Over the past decade, we have evolved the principles of clinimetrics into a theory of measurement that emphasizes the communication value of the measure—i.e., communimetrics. The theory of communimetrics takes the clinimetric approach farther, observing the following additional principles:

- Levels of items directly translate into action levels.

- Measures are reliable at the item level, and ongoing inter-reliability is critical to all applications.

- Measures should be malleable to organizational process in order to fit into service delivery operations with minimal friction.

- A "just enough information philosophy" drives measure design. An item is only included in an application if it might influence what happens in the service delivery setting.

- All partners involved in the communication process should be involved in the design of the measure.

- The measure must be meaningful to the service delivery process.

- The value of the measure is determined by its communication utility.

This characteristic of communimetrics involves the design of individual items. Specifically, anchored definitions are created that are intended to immediately translate into action levels. Several types of action level ratings have been used. For needs, the most common strategy is a four-level (0, 1, 2, 3) rating system with the following action definitions:

0 *No evidence.* No need for action.

1 *Watchful waiting/prevention.* This need should be monitored, or efforts to prevent it from returning or getting worse should be initiated.

2 *Action.* An intervention of some type is required because the need is interfering in some notable way with the individual's, family's, or community's functioning.

3 *Immediate/intensive action.* This need is either dangerous or disabling.

For strengths (or assets), these four action levels are commonly used:

0 *Centerpiece strength.* This is a strength that is so powerful and important to the person that it can be used as the focal point for a strength-based planning process.

1 *Useful strength.* While by no means as powerful as a centerpiece strength, this level indicates a strength that still could be useful for strength-based planning. It is real and ready to be included in the plan.

2 *Identified strength.* This is a strength identified as having the potential to develop but is not useful at the present time. Examples are interest in music or a hobby that is not being developed, or a vocational preference that is not being pursued. Strength-building activities would be indicated.

3 *No strength identified.* This level indicates that there is no known strength on the item. Strength identification and building are indicated.

Critical Elements of Communimetric Measures

A communimetric measure is designed to work so that once an item is identified, anchor definitions are then created that translate into the four action levels above (or whatever action levels are being used for any specific measure). People who use the measures are trained to consider the anchored definitions within the context of the action levels and, if indicated, use the action levels instead.

Partner Involvement. This characteristic is relatively novel in the field of measurement. Most psychometric measures are created by measurement experts. While this approach has the advantage of statistically sophisticated and psychometrically valid measurement, it has the disadvantage of removing the measurement process away somewhat from the applications. Clinimetric measures have generally been created by practicing physicians. This characteristic has enhanced the meaningfulness of the measure to clinicians. Communimetric measures must be fully reviewed by all partners in the communication process. Thus, if patients and families are an intended target of communication, representatives of this perspective should participate in the development of the measure to ensure that the communication goals are met. Communication involves both the communicator's ability to articulate and the receptor's ability to interpret. No communication occurs without both parties' success (i.e., a tree falling in the forest makes a sound but it is not heard unless someone is present to hear it).

Malleable to Organization. Different service delivery settings operate in different ways. The more complex settings have separate people serving in the different roles, which are all intended to be coordinated to create efficient and effective care. No two organizations are precisely alike, and the variability in how health care services are organized across settings can be remarkable. Therefore, any standard approach to measurement must be flexible so that it can be readily inserted into any service delivery operation at the most opportune time for that operation. For example, in some settings a physician must complete any assessments. In others, nurse practitioners first see the patient and complete certain assessments. In teaching hospitals, residents may have a role in the assessment process. Sometimes the patient is available to participate in the assessment, sometimes only the family. In complex medical environments, a uniform measurement strategy must be flexible enough to allow for assessment, regardless of who is party to the process.

Just Enough Information Philosophy. One of the most common complaints physicians and medical staff have about the health care field is the amount of paperwork required. Documentation requirements vary by settings, but it is clear that health care practitioners' primary interest is in providing health care, not in documenting provision of that care. Given this, it is incumbent upon anyone designing a uniform measurement strategy to respect this fact and not require documentation that is not relevant to the work at hand. Communimetrics allow for the addition and/or deletion of individual items from a measure to fit the information needs of the setting. Since the measures are reliable at the item level, they can be modular so that items can be removed or changed without affecting the tool's reliability or validity.

Meaningfulness to Decision Process. Actual use of the results of a measurement tool in the decision-making that occurs in the service delivery setting is the single most important characteristic to ensure ongoing reliability and validity. If a measure is strictly a documentation requirement, there is risk that reliability will decay over time, particularly where the documentation is not used for ongoing quality improvement activities. The ideal circumstance is for the measure to provide an information structure that can guide the decision-making process within the service delivery setting. For example, we use crisis assessment tools that support decisions to admit children to the psychiatric hospital or provide community stabilization services (Lyons et al., 1998; Leon et al., 1999). These tools provide crisis workers with a framework to understand the key pieces of information important to this decision. As such, the field reliability is high (Lyons et al., 2002).

Reliability at Item Level. There is folklore in the measurement field that you cannot have item-level reliability. That is simply not true. Achieving item-level reliability requires the careful design of items; however, we have demonstrated that it is possible to achieve item-level reliability even with relatively long, sophisticated assessment strategies (Anderson et al., 2003). The many existing clinimetric measures, most of which are single items, also demonstrate the possibility of obtaining item-level reliability. Inter-rater reliability at the item level is a key requirement of communimetric measures.

Utility of Measure Based on Its Communication Value. Given the different priorities of communimetrics, we must redefine validity to be consistent with the goals of this measurement approach. Inter-rater reliability has already been mentioned as a key measurement characteristic. A second key element is the ability of all parties using the measure to understand it. A third is the relationship of variation in the measure to variation in decision-making; that is, there should be a clear statistical relationship between scores on the tools and decisions made in the service delivery setting. This characteristic would be referred to as "predictive validity" in the psychometric literature. A fourth element in evaluating a communimetric measure is how implementation of the measure affects the service delivery process.

Use of these tools for decision support and outcomes management should have value for improving the efficiency and effectiveness of service delivery systems. Without evidence of improvement, there is little reason to continue to use such a measurement approach. The various ways that the impact of a communimetric measure can be evaluated are beyond the scope of this chapter.

In sum, measurement strategies developed with an emphasis on their communication functions will be different from measures developed with an emphasis on other priorities. To further understand the potential value of this conceptual shift in how measures are developed, it is useful to explore in detail specific applications of these types of measures.

IMPLEMENTING TCOM

This book provides a wide variety of examples of how the basic principles of TCOM can be implemented. The process of implementation is an incremental one, and it faces many barriers. Understanding the process and recognizing and overcoming the barriers is critical to success. The basic implementation process has the following eight general steps.

Step 1: Determine Responsible Organization's Needs and Capacity

As we have noted, the challenge of behavioral health care is that different organizations have different needs within the larger, interdependent behavioral health care system. The first step of any implementation process is to identify the organization that is responsible for the implementation and then define that organization's specific needs. If other organizations are involved, a new layer of complexity is introduced, as all participating organizations must have their needs at least identified if not addressed.

For example, if a state is implementing a TCOM process within a service system, the state's goals may be somewhat different than those of the agencies that provide services. One of the strengths of the TCOM approach, however, is that by focusing on individual-level outcomes, differences in perspective can be managed. For example, states want to spend less money while provider agencies want them to spend more money, but both the states and the agencies agree that they would like to see recipients experience fewer symptoms, reduced risk behaviors, and improved functioning. By focusing on the intended benefits of the service to the recipients, different organizations within complex systems can find points of agreement even if they disagree on process (e.g., quality) indicators.

Step 2: Determine What Will Be Measured

Measurement decisions refer to the outcomes question. The first question must be, what is the expectation of the treatment or service and how does it fit into a larger system of care? Multiple types of data can be important in implementing TCOM, including:

- *Clinical status data.* These data include assessments of symptoms, risks, functioning, strengths, and other information on how the individual served is doing in his or her life.

- *Utilization data, including disposition.* Utilization data are common information sources for utilization management (UM) processes. The focus of most UM activity is to ensure that patterns of utilization are predictable and fit within the business model. TCOM uses data on service use with a slightly different perspective. For example, information on disposition from the hospital or residential treatment is an important outcome. In substance abuse treatment, duration of treatment is an excellent indicator of treatment outcome (i.e., people who stay in treatment remain abstinent longer).

- *Treatment facility data.* Treatment facility data reflect what is happening within the episode of treatment. Monitoring the degree to which evidence-based practices are actually followed in the field is an important TCOM challenge. While the focus of TCOM is on outcomes, monitoring processes provide the information necessary to inform practice changes.

Step 3: Work the Organization

Any significant change in how an organization works will be met with enthusiasm in some parts of the organization (*It's about time!*) and with resistance in other parts (*What do these people think they're doing now*?). In general, it is useful to attempt to harness the enthusiasm of those who readily embrace change. Technology innovation research suggests that about 10 percent to 15 percent of the workforce can be expected to be such "eager adopters" (Weil & Rosen, 1997). Those in the middle, the bulk of the workforce, will comply with a new approach if they see the benefit in it for their work. They require some proof of value before fully embracing change. The "resistors" will struggle with any change and likely will react with active hostility or passive aggression. These individuals will require changes in job descriptions and the threat of sanctions before they embrace a change in practice. Implementing TCOM in an organization will follow similar patterns. It may initially be easy, will require evidence of benefit to expand, and finally will require the rewriting of policy and procedures and the intervention of supervisors with recalcitrant staff to reach full implementation.

Effective organizational change requires at least a two-part intervention. First, it is critical that leadership support the introduction of TCOM. Many times, an organization's leaders will not view outcomes management and quality improvement as a part of the organization's core mission. Instead, they may see them as activities that funders require them to perform to ensure continued funding but that do not directly benefit the organization. Managing based on this belief is a major strategic mistake on the part of organization leadership. In fact, an effective organization should make its management decisions based on information about what is effective and what is not. When organizational leadership embraces data-based decision-making and management, a climate is established that supports an effective TCOM implementation.

However, leadership support is insufficient for full implementation. There must be a grass-roots strategy to engage, involve, and evolve the direct service staff who will be collecting and using the strategies with individual recipients. The best course is to make sure that the assessment approach supports the work of direct service staff and that data collection strategies have minimal operational friction with the way services are transacted. Approaches that are both clinically meaningful and easy to use are the best ways to manage the grass-roots transformation process.

Two other strategies also help ensure full implementation by direct service staff. First, it is advisable to involve staff representatives on implementation decisions—understanding the staff's perspective has inherent value, and the "illusion of inclusion" provides socio-political benefits within the organization. Second, it is important to receive feedback, initially on compliance and then on findings. The fact that everyone knows the information is actually used is critical to its being valued when it is collected.

Step 4: Pretest the Instrument and Procedures

Flexibility and willingness to change "on the fly" is a good approach to any implementation process. One way to manage expectations in this regard is to initiate new processes with a pre-testing, or piloting, stage. A well-designed pre-test can become the start of an implementation process. However, where mistakes are made in the original approach, a pre-test allows changes without demoralizing staff. In fact, these adjustments can be made in a way that staff will experience changes based on a pre-test or pilot as responsive to their input.

Step 5: Train and Initiate

The foundation of the TCOM approach is the use of assessment information to fully represent service recipients at all levels of the system. For this goal to be achieved, the assessment information must be as accurate as possible. Thus, training that establishes the reliable use of any assessment tools is required. Following training, certification that the trainee is able to reliably complete the assessment is recommended. We have routinely used a criterion of an intraclass correlation coefficient of 0.70 or higher. Some jurisdictions use a higher reliability standard.

One-time training is insufficient, however, unless the assessor turnover rate is very high. For example, crisis services employees often stay less than one year. In these circumstances, a single training experience at the start of employment is sufficient. To maintain reliability, we recommend a set of steps including:

- *Recertification.* Recertification should be performed at least annually, and more often when eligibility decision models are used (e.g., see Chapter 6).

- *Audits.* This strategy involves reviewing parallel information (usually in text form) from the same time frame as the assessment and then calculating reliability. Anderson et al. (2003) have demonstrated item-level reliability of the Child and Adolescent Needs and Strengths (CANS) measure at audit.

- *Meaningful use.* The most important strategy to maintain field reliability is to ensure that assessment information is used at the individual case level, in supervision, and in program and system management. When people completing assessments know that others are actually using those assessments, they take them far more seriously. If they think the assessment is just a form that goes into a file or database never to be seen again, it is hard for them to take seriously accurate completion of the form.

Training is also necessary in procedures and in the TCOM philosophy. Full implementation of TCOM is a very different way of working for many individuals, particularly for those who have been in the field for some time. Redirecting all decisions back to the best interests of the service recipients may sound simple, but applying this principle in practice can be challenging. In addition, many workers in human service systems are not particularly comfortable with numbers and statistics. Creating accessible reports that aggregate individual recipients' experiences is an important goal. Training these employees on how to use data is necessary.

Step 6: Maintain and Manage

TCOM processes require a sufficient investment in infrastructure to allow the timely and effective use of information to provide management structures. Technological innovations of the past several decades reduce the human capital costs of maintenance and management of the TCOM process but do not eliminate the need for people to ensure that full implementation occurs. Some administrators see an investment in TCOM as an unfunded mandate. The change in thinking that has to occur before this approach can be widespread is a realization that the TCOM approach is actually the optimal way to manage the business of behavioral health care. In other words, it is not a required aspect of running a behavioral health interest. It *is* running a behavioral health interest.

Even with strong leadership, the implementation of TCOM approaches can be challenging. Not everyone "gets with the program" immediately; as we noted there are people who resist any new policy or procedure. Therefore, compliance reports are an important management tool. A compliance report provides staff level data on who is completing the assessments at the mandated time in the service delivery process. Complete collection of assessment data is critical to fully representing all recipients in the TCOM process.

Ongoing reliability checks are recommended particularly in environments in which assessments are used to make level of care decisions that have financial implications. We generally recommend annual recertification on the CANS and the Adult Needs and Strengths Assessment (ANSA) tools unless the staff turnover is so high that the average tenure is less than one year. In settings in which level of care decisions are made, semi-annual or even quarterly recertification is recommended.

Step 7: Analyze and Provide Feedback

Most of the chapters in this book will provide examples of analysis and feedback processes. There is enormous potential variety in analytic approaches; therefore, it is difficult to provide a full discussion of these options in this chapter. There are essentially three types of analyses:

- *Prevalence reports.* What are the needs and strengths of recipients in different parts of the system?

- *Decision analysis reports.* What happens to recipients at key decision points relative to their clinical presentations?

- *Outcomes reports.* What is the effect of specific programs, treatments, or services and who is more or less likely to benefit?

Analyses often require some statistical expertise. Clinical managers and staff may think they should defer to the statistician with regard to what analyses are performed, but any such deferral is a major tactical error. Most statisticians do not know which clinical or administrative questions will provide meaningful analyses. Therefore, the clinical manager must help guide specific questions addressed, with the statistician supporting the selection of methodological and statistical options for that question.

Step 8: Re-Engineer

There are two levels of re-engineering relevant to the TCOM process. First, findings can be used to adjust how and which services/treatments/interventions are provided. The core output of the TCOM process is support for these types of management decisions. In general, data from TCOM processes only point to the areas where improvements are needed. The decision on which changes to make requires you to establish a process to interpret findings and develop implications for change. Such a process is best managed within the organization's clinical and administrative leadership. Many organizations have quality improvement committees. These types of committees might be a foundation for re-engineering within the TCOM system; however, the following skill sets are required within the committee membership:

- *Ability to understand findings.* Some level of methodological and statistical sophistication is required.

- *Knowledge of evidence-based practices and other innovations.* There should be an available knowledge base to apply when outcomes are not optimal.

- *Clinical sophistication with the target populations.* Any transformations must respect the needs and potential complexities of specific clinical populations.

- *Willingness to make changes.* Sometimes leadership may be risk averse, which limits opportunities for change.

The second level of re-engineering is of the TCOM process itself. Since the goal of TCOM is to help manage services and systems for optimal effectiveness and efficiency, it would be hypocritical not to hold the TCOM process to the same standard. Thus, building in continuous adjustments to the TCOM process is an important part of the process itself.

References

Anderson, R. L., Lyons, J. S., Giles, D. M., Price, J. A. & Estle, G. (2003). Reliability of the child and adolescent needs and strengths—mental health (CANS-MH) scale. *Journal of Child and Family Studies, 12*, 279–289.

Feinstein, A. R. (1999). Multi-item "instruments" vs. Virginia Apgar's principles of clinimetrics. *Archives of Internal Medicine, 159*, 125–128.

Galbraith, J. R. (1973). *Designing complex organizations.* Reading, MA: Addison Wesley.

Glass, G. V., McGaw, B. & Smith, M. L. (1981). *Meta-analysis in social research.* Beverly Hills, CA: Sage.

Hage, J. & Aiken, M. (1969). Routine technology, social structure, and organization goals. *Administrative Science Quarterly, 14*, 366–376.

Howard, K. I., Kopta, S. M., Krause, M. S. & Orlinsky, D. E. (1986). The dose-effect relationship in psychotherapy. *American Psychologist, 41*, 159–164.

Lambert, M. J. (1989). The individual therapist's contribution to psychotherapy process and outcome. *Clinical Psychology Review, 9*, 469–485.

Lambert, M. J. (1983). Introduction to assessment of psychotherapy outcome: Historical perspective and current issues. In M. J. Lambert, E. R. Christensen & S. S. DeJulio (Eds.), *The assessment of psychotherapy outcome.* New York: Wiley.

Leon, S. C., Uziel-Miller, N. D., Lyons, J. S. & Tracy, P. (1999). Psychiatric hospital service utilization of children and adolescents in state custody. *Journal of the American Academy of Child and Adolescent Psychiatry, 38*, 305–310.

Lipsey, M. W. & Wilson, D. B. (1993). The efficacy of psychological, educational, and behavioral treatment. *American Psychologist, 48*, 1181–1209.

Lyons, J. S. (2004). *Redressing the emperor: Improving our children's public mental health service system.* Westport, CT: Praeger.

Lyons, J. S., Mintzer, L. L., Kisiel, C. L. & Shallcross, H. (1998). Understanding the mental health needs of children and adolescents in residential treatment. *Professional Psychology: Research and Practice, 29*, 582–587.

Lyons, J. S., Rawal, P., Yeh, I., Leon, S. & Tracy, P. (2002). Use of measurement audit in outcomes management. *Journal of Behavioral Health Services & Research, 29,* 75–80.

Nunnally, J. (1976). *Psychometric theory.* New York: John Wiley & Son.

Perrow, C. (1967). A framework for the comparative analysis of organizations. *American Sociological Review, 32,* 194–208.

Perrow, C. (1993). *Complex organizations: A critical essay* (3d ed.). New York: McGraw-Hill.

Shasha, M., Lyons, J. S., O'Mahoney, M. T., Miller, S. I., Howard, K. I. & Rosenberg, A. (1997). Serotonin reuptake inhibitors and the adequacy of antidepressant treatment. *International Journal of Psychiatry in Medicine, 27,* 83–92.

Weber, M. (1947). *The theory of social and economic organization* (A. H. T. P. Henderson, tr.). Glencoe, IL: Free Press.

Weil, M. M. & Rosen, L. D. (1997). *TechnoStress: Coping with technology @ work @ home @ play.* New York: Wiley.

Chapter 2

CANS and
ANSA Instruments:
History and Applications

by John S. Lyons, Ph.D.

INTRODUCTION

Chapter 1 provides the theoretical framework of the development of the communimetric tools that are designed to support the Total Clinical Outcomes Management (TCOM) system of behavioral health care management. The majority of this book describes applications that use two specific measures developed within this theory—the Child and Adolescent Needs and Strengths (CANS) measures and the Adult Needs and Strengths Assessment (ANSA). This chapter details the history, development, and applications of these tools.

The beginning history of these tools involves a personal story of my career development. After finishing a postdoctoral fellowship in mental health services research at the University of Chicago, I joined the faculty at Northwestern University's Feinberg School of Medicine. My primary activity was research in consultation/liaison (C/L) psychiatry. This was the early 1980s, and the big issue in health care was the prediction of hospital length of stay because it was one of the biggest factors in health care costs. We engaged in research demonstrating that psychiatric comorbidities were associated with increased length of stay (Fulop et al., 1987) and that timely and effective behavioral health interventions reduced these associated costs (Lyons et al., 1985; Strain et al., 1991). I then became interested in studying psychiatric hospitalization due to the failure of psychiatric diagnosis-related groups to successfully predict length of stay for this service. Like most health services researchers at the time, the primary method I used involved the application of sophisticated statistical analyses to large convenience databases (e.g., claims data) to model utilization of services. In the very first study of psychiatric hospitalization, I found that the only reliable predictor of psychiatric length of stay was the psychiatrist (Lyons & Larson, 1989). Twelve percent of psychiatric length of stay was accounted for by the identity of the attending psychiatrist. The next best predictors were insurance coverage and diagnosis, both at about 4 percent. Just like with surgery, the highest volume psychiatrists were the most efficient—having the shorter average lengths of stay compared to their colleagues who admitted few patients. This finding intrigued me until I had a conversation with a colleague in the Department of Medicine, Joe Feinglass. He reported that he found exactly the same practice pattern variation in medical admissions. The difference was that about 40 percent of the variation in medical length of stay was predicted by diagnosis.

I immediately was struck by a completely different interpretation of our earlier study. Rather than having an enormous practice variation in psychiatry, the real problem was that we had no clinical information that was relevant to predicting how services were used. Mental health services research was locked in a model that applied health services methods where they did not actually apply. People were not hospitalized because of a psychiatric diagnosis. The most common diagnosis among psychiatric hospital admissions is depression. The vast majority of people with depression never require psychiatric hospitalization. Only those who become suicidal or whose self-care becomes so impaired as to put their well being in jeopardy would be considered for hospital admission. (This definition of medical necessity was new thinking at the time, as traditionally the clinical thresholds for voluntary psychiatric hospitalizations were sometimes quite low. Cost containment efforts including managed care shifted the criterion for psychiatric hospitalization more towards the civil criteria for involuntary hospitalization.) So the necessary innovation was to create large convenience databases that contained clinical information that was actually relevant to the decision-making about the use of psychiatric hospital services. This was the thinking that led to the development of the Severity of Psychiatric Illness (SPI) rating scale (Lyons et al., 1995).

GENESIS OF CANS AND ANSA

In the early 1990s, I was impressed with the work on severity of illness and disease staging going on in health services. In particularly, Susan Horn's severity of illness utilization review tool (Horn et al., 1986) demonstrated a useful relationship to service use within diagnostic categories. The original SPI scale was designed to be a behavioral health adaptation of this approach, hence its name. The very first version of the SPI had seven items—danger to self, danger to others, severity of symptoms, self-care impairment, vocational functioning, interpersonal functioning, and residential stability. The first three items demonstrated a strong relationship to psychiatric hospitalization admissions and hospital outcomes (Lyons et al., 1997).

Northwestern Managed Behavioral Healthcare adopted the SPI for utilization management, and its success with respect to decision-making attracted the attention of Harry Shallcross, Ph.D., a managed care consultant. In consultations with the Illinois Department of Children and Family Services (IDCFS), he suggested that the department use the same approach with children in its design of a management system for residential treatment services. I had been working with Mina Dulcan, M.D., and John Lavigne, Ph.D., on the development of a child version of the SPI. Because a number of people were involved in discussions about which characteristics of children should drive decision-making in the use of these services, this work naturally transformed into the design of a decision support tool for residential treatment in child welfare (Lyons et al., 1998). Out of these focus groups and consultations, the Childhood Severity of Psychiatric Illness tool (CSPI) (Lyons, 1998) was developed.

The success of the IDCFS's transformation of its use of residential treatment services garnered some national attention (Lyons, 2004), and a second project was instituted in Florida. By this time, I had become aware of the "strengths" movement that was taking hold, particularly in children's services. During a planning study for a proposed Medicaid bundled rate in Florida, we added a brief assessment of strengths (child and adolescent strengths assessment). We found that strengths and behavioral health symptoms have significant but independent relationships with level of functioning and the probability of high-risk behaviors (Lyons et al., 2000). Thus the optimal approach to the treatment of children requires simultaneous attention to both needs and strengths. Based on this experience, the original version of the CANS was created through the auspices of the Buddin Praed Foundation. At the University of Iowa, Rachel Anderson, Ph.D., expanded the SPI for use with community populations (Anderson & Lyons, 2001), and then took the strengths items and integrated them back into the SPI to create the first version of the ANSA.

CANS APPLICATIONS

Decision Support

The first widely used version of the CANS was one designed for youth with mental health challenges (CANS-MH). Table 2.1 presents the item structure of the CANS-MH. This version was used in planning studies in New York, Nebraska, Arizona, and Iowa. Table 2.2 shows rating samples for two items, "psychotic symptoms" and "danger to self."

Table 2.3 presents the three-level decision model adopted by the Alaskan Youth Initiative to use for eligibility into wraparound services (see discussion of Alaska pilot study in Chapter 20). Providers would complete a CANS assessment, and the statewide program coordinator would apply the decision model to assist in decisions about eligibility for the program. This model has served as the basis for several similar models used by Single Points of Accountability (SPOA) in New York State. SPOAs are decision-making or "gatekeeping" bodies that include multiple stakeholders in coordinating and managing mental health care.

Review of the decision model in Table 2.3 indicates that the default referral is outpatient only. Intensive outpatient (more than weekly intervention, such as day treatment) would be indicated by a combination of behavioral health needs and a complication of a recent (actionable) risk behavior. Intensive community services (ICS) were reserved for complicated cases with behavioral health problems, risk behaviors, and caregiver capacity concerns (which is why you would go into the home to provide services).

Outcome Measure

The CANS is also used as an outcome measure. There are two basic approaches to this application. First, the percent of actionable needs (score of 2 or 3) or useable strengths (score of 0 or 1) at the initiation and end of a service episode can be used to identify met needs or built strengths. Second, dimension scores can be calculated by averaging the items within each dimension (e.g., risk behaviors) and multiplying by ten. This creates a thirty-point scale that can be used like a psychometric tool to study change over time.

Table 2.1
Item Structure of the CANS-Mental Health

Problem Presentation	Care Intensity/Organization
Psychosis	Monitoring
Attention deficit/Impulse control	Treatment
Depression/Anxiety	Transportation
Oppositional behavior	Service permanence
Antisocial behavior	**Caregiver Needs & Strengths**
Substance abuse	Physical/Medical/Behavioral
Adjustment to trauma	Supervision
Attachment	Involvement
Situational consistency	Knowledge
Temporal consistency	Organization
Risk Behaviors	Resources
Suicide risk	Residential stability
Danger to others	Safety
Elopement	**Youth Strengths**
Sexually abusive behavior	Family
Social behavior	Interpersonal
Crime/Delinquency	Relationship permanence
Functioning	Educational
Intellectual	Vocational
Physical/Medical	Optimism
Family	Talents/Interests
Sexual development	Spiritual/Religious
School attendance	Community inclusion
School achievement	
School behavior	

The use of the CANS has expanded to many jurisdictions. Child welfare applications currently exist in Alabama, California (Los Angeles County), Florida, Illinois, Massachusetts, Pennsylvania (Philadelphia), Tennessee, and West Virginia. New Jersey developed a cross-systems application and Indiana is in the process of implementing a cross-systems approach.

ANSA APPLICATIONS

At the moment, the ANSA is less widely used than the CANS. There are a variety of reasons for this disparity, the most significant being that their use is based on referrals from others already using the tools, as neither tool is "marketed" in the traditional sense. The more widely an approach spreads in this model, the more people consider

Table 2.2
Two Sample Items from the CANS-Mental Health

PSYCHOTIC SYMPTOMS

This rating is used to describe symptoms of psychiatric disorders with a known neurological base. DSM-IV disorders included on this dimension are schizophrenia and psychotic disorders (unipolar, bipolar, NOS). The common symptoms of these disorders include hallucinations, delusions, unusual thought processes, strange speech, and bizarre/idiosyncratic behavior.

0   This rating indicates a child with no evidence of thought disturbances. Both thought processes and content are within normal range.

1   This rating indicates a child with evidence of mild disruption in thought processes or content. The child may be somewhat tangential in speech or evidence somewhat illogical thinking (age inappropriate). This also includes children with a history of hallucinations but none currently. The category would be used for children who are below the threshold for one of the DSM-IV [*Diagnostic and Statistical Manual*, 4th ed.] diagnoses listed above.

2   This rating indicates a child with evidence of moderate disturbance in thought process or content. The child may be somewhat delusional or have brief intermittent hallucinations. The child's speech may be at times quite tangential or illogical. This level would be used for children who meet the diagnostic criteria for one of the disorders listed above.

3   This rating indicates a child with a severe psychotic disorder. Symptoms are dangerous to the child or others.

DANGER TO SELF

This rating describes both suicidal and significant self-injurious behavior. A rating of 2 or 3 would indicate the need for a safety plan.

0   Child has no evidence or history of suicidal or self-injurious behaviors.

1   History of suicidal or self-injurious behaviors but no self-injurious behavior during the past 30 days.

2   Recent (last 30 days) but not acute (today) suicidal ideation or gesture. Self-injurious in the past 30 days (including today) without suicidal ideation or intent.

3   Current suicidal ideation and intent in the past 24 hours.

---

adopting it based on talking to current users. To date, the majority of ANSA applications have resulted from successful CANS implementations. The most widespread use of the ANSA is in Illinois, Iowa, Indiana, New York, and Pennsylvania. Nearly all ANSA applications are in public mental health settings, often with individuals with coexisting substance-related disorders.

Table 2.4 provides a list of the items in the standard version of the ANSA. It is noteworthy that the dimensions are similar to that of the CANS. The caregiver section is smaller, as many adults with serious mental illness have no involved caregiver. However, many of the same concepts are embedded as characteristics of the assessed individual rather than his or her caregiver (e.g., motivation for care, residential stability).

Table 2.3
Decision Algorithm for Alaskan Youth Initiative

Criterion 1. Behavioral Health Needs
At least one Problem Presentation (through Attachment) with a rating of 3
OR
Two or more Problem Presentations (through Attachment) with a rating of 2

Criterion 2. Persistence of Symptoms
Temporal Consistency of 1 or greater

Criterion 3. Risk Behaviors A
At least one Risk Behavior with a rating of 3
OR
Two or more Risk Behaviors with a rating of 2

Criterion 4. Caregiver Capacity
At least one Caregiver item with a rating of 3
OR
Two or more Caregiver items with a rating of 2

Criterion 5. Risk Behaviors B
Any Risk Behavior with a rating of 2

RECOMMENDATION:

LEVEL 3:   Intensive Community Treatment
Meets Criteria 1, 2, 3 and 4

LEVEL 2:   Intensive Outpatient
Meets Criteria 1 and 5

LEVEL 1:   Outpatient Services
All other youth

As with the CANS, multiple versions of the ANSA are being developed for different applications. For example, a transitional version has been developed for use with young adults. Versions for substance abuse treatment and geriatric services are in the design stage.

Several jurisdictions are in the process of developing decision models for the ANSA. A version of the three-level model from the CANS is currently used in some places. Oneida county in New York is working to create a model that crosses three levels of case management with four levels of housing support to provide a comprehensive guide for case management for persons with serious mental illness living in the community.

Related tools have been developed and are now in use, all using the communimetric theory. The INTERMED is a tool for use with medical/surgical populations (Huyse

Table 2.4
Item Structure of the Adult Needs and Strengths Assessment

PROBLEM PRESENTATION	CARE INTENSITY
1. Psychosis	25. Monitoring
2. Impulse Control	26. Treatment
3. Depression/Anxiety	27. Transportation
4. Antisocial	29. Service Permanence
5. Substance Abuse	29. Self-Care
6. Stage of Recovery	30. Medication Compliance
7. Adjustment to Trauma	
8. Personality Disorder	
9. Situational Consistency	CAREGIVER CAPACITY
10. Temporal Consistency	31. Physical/Behavioral Health
11. Motivation for Care	32. Involvement
	33. Knowledge
RISK BEHAVIORS	34. Resources
12. Danger to Self	35. Organization
13. Danger to Others	36. Safety
14. Sexually Abusive Behavior	
15. Social Behavior	
16. Crime	STRENGTHS
17. Victimization	37. Family
	38. Interpersonal
FUNCTIONING	39. Relationship Permanence
18. Intellectual	40. Vocational/Educational
19. Knowledge	41. Well-Being
20. Physical/Medical	42. Spiritual/Religious
21. Family	43. Talents/Interests
22. Employment/Education	44. Inclusion
23. Living Skills	
24. Residential Stability	

et al., 2001; see also Chapter 15). Gregg Lichtenstein and Tom Lyons (2001) applied the communimetric model to an assessment for their work with entrepreneur development. The Entrepreneur League System Skill Assessment has been used successfully in this area (Lichtenstein & Lyons, 2001).

References

Anderson, R. L. & Lyons, J. S. (2001). Needs-based planning for persons with serious mental illness: The severity of psychiatric illness of persons residing in intermediate care facilities. *Journal of Behavioral Health Services & Research, 28,* 104–110.

Diagnostic and statistical manual of mental disorders (4th ed.) (1994). Washington, DC: American Psychiatric Association.

Horn, S. D., Horn, R. A., Sharkey, P. D. & Chambers, A. F. (1986). Severity of illness within DRGs. Homogeneity study. *Medical Care, 24*, 225–235.

Huyse, F. J., Lyons, J. S., Stiefel, F. C., Slaets, J. P. J., De Jonge, P. & Latour, C. (2001). Editorial, Operationalizing the biopsychosocial model. The INTERMED. *Psychosomatics, 42*, 5–13.

Lichtenstein, G. A. & Lyons, T. S. (2001). The entrepreneurial development system: transforming business talent and community economies. *Economic Development Quarterly, 15*, 3–20.

Fulop, G., Strain, J. J., Vita, J., Lyons, J. S. & Hammer, J. S. (1987). Impact of psychiatric comorbidity on length of hospital stay for medical/surgical patients: A preliminary report. *American Journal of Psychiatry, 144*, 878–882.

Lyons, J. S. (1998). *Severity of psychiatric illness scale—Child and adolescent version.* San Antonio, TX: Psychological Corporation.

Lyons, J. S. & Larson, D. B. (1989). A proposed value matrix for the evaluation of psychiatric consultations in the general hospital. *General Hospital Psychiatry, 11*, 345–351.

Lyons, J. S., Hammer, J. S., Wise, T. N. & Strain, J. J. (1985). Consultation-liaison psychiatry and cost-effectiveness research. A review of methods. *General Hospital Psychiatry, 7*, 302–308.

Lyons, J. S. (2004). *Redressing the emperor: Improving our children's public mental health service system.* Westport, CT: Praeger.

Lyons, J. S., Colletta, J., Devens, M. & Finkel, S. I. (1995). Validity of the severity of psychiatric illness in a sample of inpatients on a psychogeriatric unit. *International Psychogeriatrics, 7*, 407–416.

Lyons, J. S., Mintzer, L. L., Kisiel, C. L. & Shallcross, H. (1998). Understanding the mental health needs of children and adolescents in residential treatment. *Professional Psychology: Research and Practice, 29*, 582–587.

Lyons, J. S., Stutesman, J., Neme, J., Vessey, J. T., O'Mahoney, M. T. & Camper, H. J. (1997). Predicting psychiatric emergency admissions and hospital outcomes. *Medical Care, 35*, 792–800.

Lyons, J. S., Uziel-Miller, N. D., Reyes, F. & Sokol, P. T. (2000). Strengths of children and adolescents in residential settings: Prevalence and associations with psychopathology and discharge placement. *Journal of the Academy of Child and Adolescent Psychiatry, 39*, 176–181.

Lyons, T. S. & Lyons, J. S. (2002). *Assessing entrepreneurship skills: The key to effective enterprise development planning?* Presented at the 44th annual conference of the Association of Collegiate Schools of Planning, Baltimore, MD.

Strain, J. J., Lyons, J. S., Hammer, J. S., Fahs, M., Lebovits, A., Paddison, P. L., Snyder, S., Strauss, E., Burton, R., Nuber, G., Abernathy, T., Sacks, H., Nordlie, J. & Sacks, C. (1991). Cost offset from a psychiatric consultation-liaison intervention with elderly hip fracture patients. *American Journal of Psychiatry, 148*, 1044–1049.

Part 2
Cross-Program Applications Within Systems

Chapter 3

Implications of Needs-Based Planning in New York for the Children's Public Mental Health Services System

by Marcia Fazio, M.S.

The best way to predict the future is to invent it.
—Alan Kay

INTRODUCTION

The New York State Office of Mental Health (OMH) serves approximately 140,000 children and their families annually. Although New York spends over $300 million per year and has one of the largest and most comprehensive service delivery systems for children and families with mental health needs in the country, the state still faces significant challenges with timely access to appropriate services. Addressing those challenges has been the work of New York's policy planners over the course of the past thirty-five years. The following time line summarizes the key events that have shaped the history of children's mental health services in New York over the past three decades.

1969-1972—Six children's psychiatric centers opened in New York State, providing separate inpatient mental health services for children for the first time. Up to that point, children were served in the state's adult psychiatric centers.

1982—Jane Knitzer's publication, *Unclaimed Children*, outlined the failure of public responsibility to children and adolescents in need of mental health services and underscored for New York's child serving agencies the need to work collaboratively (Knitzer, 1982).

1984—The National Institutes of Mental Health (NIMH) released the Child and Adolescent Service System Principles (CASSP) to highlight that children with serious emotional disturbance and their families need a comprehensive, community-based system of care. The federal government provided states with the opportunity to apply for innovative service grants to test out new approaches to delivering services to children and families in a coordinated system of care approach. New York applied for system of care grants and began a statewide effort to build its community-based services (CASSP, 1984).

1988—The Children and Youth Needs Methodology was developed to define the target population and services available, and to assess the unmet need for additional children's mental health services (OMH, 1988).

1989—The first national advocacy group for families, the Federation of Families for Children's Mental Health, was formed in Washington, D.C. by parents of children with emotional, behavioral, and mental disorders. This group set the stage for the development of state chapters, and New York's Families Together subchapter was formed. New York's families became partners in system planning and a driving force behind system change.

1992— New York Child and Adolescent Mental Health Services released *At the Crossroads*, a comprehensive strategic plan, on the heels of a major change in leadership in the governor's office and below. The plan was the culmination of four years of assessment and planning activities by service recipients, advocates, state agency partners, and children's mental health professionals. The plan, which called for significant increases in service capacity, was never formally implemented (Armstrong et al., 1992).

1993—The New York legislature signed into law the Community Mental Health Reinvestment Act (Chapter 723, Laws of 1993). This legislation fundamentally restructured the way local governments in New York receive state aid. The act amended the mental hygiene law to allow for the "reinvestment" into community-based services of funds available from the reduction of state-operated inpatient care for adults. The act provides help to local communities and state workers affected by anticipated inpatient service reductions. By the end of the period covered by the original legislation, a total of $212 million was provided to localities to support reinvestment. Twenty-four percent of the funds were allocated to support children's programs. This important shift in resources permitted a fundamental restructuring of the mental health system in New York from a primarily inpatient-based system to a primarily community-based system.

1999—U.S. Surgeon General David Satcher, M.D., released the first report by a surgeon general on mental health. With a full chapter on children's mental health, this document provided a comprehensive compendium of the latest and most effective treatments for children with serious emotional disturbance. This document provided a comprehensive, research-based source for program planning (Satcher, 1999).

2000—John Lyons and Harry Shallcross completed the first study of the children's mental health system in New York, outlining the characteristics of children using services and the pathways into and out of those services. With an historic influx of $42 million into the mental health system in 2000, made possible with a special governor's office initiative, the study provided the foundation for directing those resources (Lyons & Shallcross, 2000).

2001—The New York State OMH released its strategic plan for children, outlining its system priorities and thirteen action areas to accomplish them, based on state-of-the-art research findings and stakeholder input (Lyons & Shallcross, 2001).

2001—President Bush convened the New Freedom Commission on Mental Health, which identifies six goals to transform the national mental health system to promote access and excellence. Highlights that began to shape our thinking about the future direction of children's mental health services include:

- Americans should understand that mental health is essential to overall health.
- Mental health care should be consumer- and family-driven.
- Disparities in mental health should be eliminated.
- Early mental health screening, assessment, and referral to services should be common practice.
- Excellent mental health should be delivered.
- Research should be accelerated.

2001–2004—The OMH significantly expanded service capacity in New York's most effective services, as follows:

- The home- and community-based services waiver was increased from 178 to 610 slots.
- Family-based treatment increased by 125 slots.
- Family support services increased by $2 million.
- Community residence beds increased by eighty-eight.
- Home-based crisis intervention increased by four teams.
- Case management increased by 2,500 slots.
- Mental health services to children in juvenile detention facilities was increased by five new teams.
- $7.1 million was provided to support single points of access.
- $3.1 million was designated to support discharge planning for children in residential treatment.
- $1.7 million was allocated to support school-based mental health services.
- Seven new positions were added throughout the state to support parent education programs to assist parents in dealing with difficult children at home.

2003—NIMH released the findings of its National Co-Morbidity Survey Replication Study to answer questions about the levels of disability and severity associated with mental disorders, the economic and health impact, the delay between onset and diagnosis, and the progress achieved in providing evidence-based treatments to those who require care. Findings from this study sparked an interest in shifting the policy agenda to prevention, public awareness, and recovery. The findings focused on increasing awareness that mental health is treatable, empowering children and families to seek higher quality mental health treatments, and spreading the knowledge that children do get better. Some findings were (NCS-R, 2001-2003):

- Over a twelve-month month period, 60 percent of those with a disorder classified as serious or moderate received no treatment.
- For those with impulse control and substance abuse disorders, nearly one-half of all lifetime cases were never treated.
- Among those who did receive treatment, only 32.7 percent reported that they received services that met minimal standards.
- Those with mental or substance disorders were more likely to receive treatment from a general medical professional (primary care physician or nurse) or from a complementary alternative source such as an Internet support group.
- Respondents were as likely to receive services from a spiritual advisor as they were from a psychiatrist.

2005—The OMH provided qualifying clinic providers with rate enhancements to promote the development of continuous quality improvement initiatives, the expansion of evening and weekend hours, and more flexibility for school-based mental health services.

The evolution of the OMH's children's mental health system has been supported by an understanding of the needs and strengths of the children and families we serve, changes in the funding formula to support the development of community-based services, and progression in the methodology used to plan services and the emergence of new research.

STUDY TO DETERMINE SERVICE NEEDS IN NEW YORK

Need for Capacity

In 1988, New York launched the first of its kind needs assessment study for children and youth requiring mental health services. The overall goal of the Youth Assessment Study (OMH, 1988) was to determine the number and characteristics of people age eighteen or younger who were in need of mental health services and to determine what services they needed. A comprehensive survey of client characteristics was conducted, a needs methodology was developed, and an extensive planning process occurred that included family members, researchers, practitioners, state and local providers, and local planners. The study projected increases in capacity (see Table 3.1) and was incorporated into a comprehensive planning document entitled *At the Crossroads*, which created a framework for resource planning throughout the early 1990s.

Services evolved from state-operated inpatient facilities to the community, and they expanded over time to meet and exceed the need projected in the 1988-1992 planning document, as shown in Table 3.2.

Needs and Strengths of the People Served

Despite the consistent growth in the system, problems with lack of access persisted. System planners began to question the utility of completing a needs assessment,

Table 3.1
Projected Capacity Need, N.Y. Child and Adolescent Mental Health Services

	Projected Capacity (2000)	Current Capacity (1992)
Total number (Clients seen per week)	38,000	19,716
Ambulatory emergency crisis	One in each geographic area (5)	Undetermined
Acute inpatient/Crisis residence	900	512
Home-based crisis intervention	500	64
Intermediate inpatient	500	600
Residential treatment facility	1,577	448
Community residence/Family-based treatment/Teaching Family homes		250
Day treatment/Clinical support services	13,000	3,123
Intensive case management	3000	950
Ambulatory/Supportive services	22,000	15,700

Table 3.2
Evolution of Services From State-Operated to Community-Based Facilities

Program	Percentage Growth/Decrease Since 1992
Family-based treatment	+ 277%
Crisis residence	+ 200%
Community residence	+ 318%
Teaching family homes	New program
Residential treatment facility	+ 8%
Local inpatient	+ 54%
State inpatient	−17%
Home-based crisis Intervention	New program
Home and community-based waiver	+ 327%
ICM/SCM blended case management	New program
Clinic	+ 30%
Day treatment	+ 3%

since the need for additional service capacity seemed infinite. Convenient for requesting funds from the budget division, the approach left us without sufficient information about which services were effective and which should be expanded.

To explore this issue further, the OMH initiated a second planning study in 1999. The purpose of the second study was to move beyond the prior needs methodology to develop an understanding of how the system actually worked. The study provided the opportunity to:

- Describe services offered statewide and understand innovative single site demonstrations;

- Create a portrait of the strengths and needs of children and their families in these service types;

- Describe outcomes in the current system;

- Locate aspects of the current system that need improvement; and

- Provide recommendations for new investment of resources based on services with positive outcomes.

The intent was to uncover new information about services that had positive outcomes for the children and families served so we could expand the services that actually worked. Study results were used to develop long- and short-term strategies for financing, organizing, and delivering services to bring about better outcomes for families and children with serious emotional disturbance.

Study Design

A stratified (by region and program type), random sample was used to study ten program types across the state. Reviewers used the Child and Adolescent Needs and Strengths Survey for Mental Health (CANS-MH) to describe the children as they entered these programs. The CANS was reliable (ICC=0.86) [intraclass correlation coefficient] across participating reviewers, which included representatives from the statewide advocacy group Families Together. A total of 1,594 cases were reviewed across all program types: residential treatment, state-operated hospitals, community hospitals, day treatment programs, outpatient clinics, intensive case management, community residences, home- and community-based waiver, home-based crisis intervention, and family-based treatment.

Key Findings

Study results indicated the following:

- New York State has a comprehensive system that relies heavily on state hospitals and residential treatment facilities to serve children and adolescents with the highest needs and risk behaviors. However, there appears to be a linkage problem in the service system between these high intensity treatment settings and outpatient clinics. More than one-half of the youth admitted to residential treatment facilities (RTFs) had no documented history of outpatient treatment, although the vast majority had been hospitalized at least once.

- Psychiatric hospitalizations in the community, which appear to be a key stop in the pathway into state hospital and residential treatment services, appear to be preventable in many cases, and home-based crisis intervention programs appear to be effective alternatives even for high-risk children.

- Community residences represent effective alternatives to larger residential treatment settings by providing residential services that are more natural environments and closer to the child's home community. Community residences generally provide housing for eight children in a home located in a neighborhood or community. These programs provide twenty-four hour staff and some programming in the residence, but they link to community-based services for the majority of programs.

- Mental health clinics, which constitute the largest part of the state's outpatient system, are not structured to serve the high-need population and their families as effectively as possible. Two-thirds of outpatient cases simply stop coming to services.

- Use of psychotropic medication as a component of treatment is commonplace, particularly in high intensity settings. Antipsychotic medications are often used off-label for reasons other than treating symptoms of psychosis (e.g., behavioral control). Despite a lack of psychosis, children were found to be on multiple medications.

APPLICATION OF FINDINGS TO SYSTEM PLANNING

The study findings provided valuable information to system planners about how and why various services were being used and which ones were most effective. The study became a road map for restructuring the system. The following sections describe the journey.

Meetings With Involved Parties

Governor's Office. In state fiscal year 1999-2000, New York's public mental health system received an infusion of over $100 million as the result of the convergence of two events. A highly publicized serious incident, in which a seriously mentally ill individual killed a young woman by pushing her to her death in a subway station, highlighted the financial shortfall and fragmentation of services in the mental health system. There was also an influx of funds from the tobacco industry's legal settlements, which the governor directed to strengthening the mental health delivery system and correcting the problems identified by the tragic incident. For the first time in history, a significant percentage of the funds, $42 million, was specifically set aside for the children's mental health service delivery system.

The study findings were complete and were used to support spending in areas found to be most effective. Study results were discussed with the governor's office. The OMH was directed by the governor's office to use the resources to expand existing services that worked and to use the emerging research base to develop new services.

Stakeholders and Agency Partners. A series of nine regional forums were held around the state to stimulate discussion about the findings and to gather public input for planning purposes. Family representatives, advocates, representatives from all licensed and nonlicensed programs, and staff from other state agencies listened to the study findings and reacted. A facilitator recorded the feedback.

Study findings were shared with key agency partners: The New York State Education Department (SED), the Office of Children and Family Services (OCFS), the Administration of Children's Services (ACS), the Council on Children and Families (CCF), the Department of Probation and Correctional Alternatives (DPCA), the Office of Alcoholism and Substance Abuse Services (OASAS), the Conference of Local Mental Hygiene Directors (CLMHD), Families Together, and the Coalition of Children's Mental Health Services. System partners discussed possible ways to collaborate to improve the system of services across agencies.

Development of a Multiyear Strategic Plan

Setting Goals. Feedback from the planning forums, the study results, the 1999 surgeon general's report findings, and the newly published "Effective Treatment for Mental Disorders in Children and Adolescents" (Burns et al., 1999) provided the basis for the creation of a multiyear strategic plan, which was released in 2001. The plan contained strategic directions with a set of action steps. The following summarizes the strategic directions the OMH implemented over the next several years.

1. Expand and restructure outpatient and community services to provide flexible, intensive, mobile, community-based services that are responsive to children and adolescents with the highest needs and risks and their families.

2. Improve clinical services, drawing on state-of-the-art research in evidence-based practices.

3. Enhance accountability for serving high-needs youngsters in the community and for improving clinical outcomes, including a county-by-county reporting on the new initiatives and statewide rollout of the data warehouse.

4. Improve and expand crisis management services.

5. Expand alternatives to inpatient services.

6. Expand alternatives to residential treatment facilities and enhance linkages between institutional and community-based services, including linkages between state and local mental health providers.

7. Establish single points of access to identify youth with the highest risk of placement out of the home, to develop adequate plans to serve them in their home communities when possible, and to manage access to residential services when necessary.

8. Improve transitions from child mental health services to independent living to enhance opportunities for recovery for young adults, especially in the area of work and employment retention skills.

9. Develop local systems of care, integrating mental health with other child-serving systems with particular emphases on the child welfare system, the expansion of school-based clinics, and collaboration with the courts.

10. Enhance responsiveness to, and support for, families and community caretakers as partners in care of youth with serious emotional disturbance.

11. Address human resource issues, including recruitment and retention of professional and paraprofessional staff, training for work in new service models, and assurance of cultural competence.

12. Address the trauma needs of children who have been victims of disaster and abuse.

Systematically Restructured Delivery System. After analyzing all the study results, feedback from stakeholders and the existing research, it was clear to the system planners that to achieve true system change, it would be necessary to systematically restructure the delivery system. The following steps were required:

1. *Diversion to community services.* Step 1 was to divert the pathway from local hospital emergency rooms and inpatient units to community-based outpatient alternatives. To accomplish this, children and families needed improved coordination and access to services in the community. If they did not know who to contact for help in their communities and were not helped in a timely manner, their tendency to rely on local emergency rooms for treatment would not change.

2. *Improved quality of service.* Step 2 was to improve the quality of services at all levels. We needed to more fully understand the medication prescribing practices in all licensed programs and to align those practices with state-of-the-art science to find out why two-thirds of the people who get to clinics drop out, and why some do not even show up for appointments in the first place. Finally, we needed to move children through the system more quickly and reduce the length of stay in existing programs.

3. *Infrastructure to maintain quality.* Step 3 was to set up an infrastructure to maintain quality over time. We implemented a web-based information system called the Child and Adolescent Information Reporting System (CAIRS) as well as evidence-based practices education and training and set up an infrastructure for ongoing training and dissemination.

4. *Financial incentive.* Step 4 was twofold—to set up a financial incentive for clinics to operate expanded hours evenings and weekends and in school settings, and to use the data to monitor performance for systematic improvement.

IMPROVING COORDINATION: THE SINGLE POINT OF ACCESS

Our intent was to stop the direct pathway into high intensity services through local hospital emergency rooms. Children and families sought treatment at local hospitals in crisis mode. Most of the time, they completely bypassed the local clinic and mental health system. The typical pattern was that after several admissions to the local hospital, children would be transferred to a state facility for intermediate care and from there be discharged to one of nineteen residential treatment facilities in the state. Most of these service recipients had bypassed local clinics and mental health services completely. Many that did try to use clinics were dissatisfied. They either did not get an appointment or dropped out after the first appointment. Thus, there was no incentive for recipients to use community-based clinic services. By improving coordination and access at the local level, our goal was that recipients would have needs met with community-based services and their reliance on high intensity services would decrease.

To accomplish this, the OMH initiated the idea of a single point of access (SPOA) as a way to improve coordination of the service delivery at the local level. With SPOA, high-risk, high-need children could be identified and assessed in their communities and a service plan specifically tailored to their needs and strengths could be developed at that level.

Each of the sixty-two county mental health departments in the state was required to set up a SPOA process. Funds were provided to each county based on population size to support the effort. Some counties received as little as $22,000. To date, fifty-eight counties in the state have SPOA. With the impact of September 11, 2001, New York City SPOA development was delayed several years. The Bronx developed a SPOA in 2002, and the remaining four boroughs that comprise New York City fully implemented in 2005.

The SPOA remains a central part of how children's services are managed. The majority of SPOAs in the state use the CANS to guide objective assignment of service level based on individual needs and strengths. The CANS is also used to measure outcome of service involvement. CANS assessments are implemented over time as individuals progress from one level of service to the next. Approximately 50,000 children and families in New York have had service plans coordinated through SPOAs since the initiative began in 2001.

IMPROVING QUALITY OF CARE

After considering the study findings and relevant research and listening to our constituents, we saw clearly that numerous opportunities existed for improved quality in the delivery system. We established priorities in the following order: the need to address the widespread use of off-label medications, the need to improve the quality of clinic services so that children and families would start using them, and the need to improve the clinical content of treatment services to promote the concept of recovery and accelerate movement in the delivery system. Our expectation was that a combination of carefully selected initiatives would provide an alternative to inpatient hospital services.

Guidelines for Use of Antipsychotics

The use of antipsychotic medication was first noted during the 1999-2000 planning study conducted by John Lyons. Very few of the children studied who were receiving antipsychotic medications were actually diagnosed with a psychotic disorder. This meant that most of the medications were being used for off-label purposes. There are few studies showing that antipsychotic medications are effective in reducing aggressive behavior.

The Columbia University Center for the Advancement of Children's Mental Health, in collaboration with a consensus panel of national experts in child psychiatry, developed a set of treatment guidelines for using antipsychotic medications called the Treatment Recommendations for Use of Antipsychotics with Aggressive Youth (TRAAY) (Pappadopulos et al., 2003; Schur et al., 2003). The guidelines include a monograph and tool kit to train all psychiatrists in the OMH inpatient system. The tool kit provides tables and selected rating scales to promote best approaches to tracking target symptoms, assessing and managing side effects, and possible drug interactions. The long-range plan is for all OMH physicians to be trained in the TRAAY protocol, followed by physicians in RTFs, community-based inpatient hospitals, and outpatient settings.

Quality and Content of Clinic Services

The findings called for a concentrated effort to improve clinic services. The first step was to gather more information about why wait lists at clinics are so high and why so many people drop out of clinic programs. We initiated a series of studies in the five regions throughout the state to find out. After examining the available research base, we implemented several evidence-based practices specifically to improve engagement and retention in clinic settings.

Functional Family Therapy. Functional family therapy (FFT), an evidence-based therapeutic approach, was introduced to nineteen clinic providers in 2002. FFT has shown itself to be highly effective with young people who have disruptive behavior and/or who have been involved in the juvenile justice system. Presently, there are twenty teams in the state. FFT is a short-term model, averaging twelve sessions, administered by a trained therapist working exclusively in the family setting. Training and certification to practice FFT occurs in a team environment, with team sizes ranging between three and eight therapists. FFT has had a significant impact on improving retention rates for children and families attending clinic programs; 64 percent of the families that begin treatment in FFT remain in treatment. This is a significant improvement over data that previous studies have demonstrated.

Telephone Engagement. In 2004, the OMH initiated the New York City Learning Collaborative. This initiative involved fifteen children's outpatient clinic providers who are working with the OMH, the New York City Department of Mental Health, the Citizen's Committee for Children, and Mount Sinai Hospital to examine current clinic engagement practices and retention rates and to identify, implement, and evaluate evidence-based practices designed to improve these practice areas. The methodology consists of using an evidence-based telephone engagement strategy providing training for reception, intake, and treatment staff and generating agency-specific solutions. The interventions have resulted in overall improvement rates for the participating clinics in relation to improved attendance at first appointment and improved attendance subsequent to the intake appointment. The OMH has plans to expand this initiative statewide.

Bringing More Effective Clinic Services to Children Where They Are

The OMH has operated school-based clinic and mental health programs since the early 1990s. In 2001, these services were strengthened with the addition of evidence-based assessments and treatments. School support projects in New York City received resources and training in evidence-based practices. All projects use the Children's Global Assessment Scale (CGAS) (Schaffer et al., 1983) and the Strengths and Difficulties Questionnaire (SDQ) (Goodman, 1997, 1999), including the parent, teacher, and youth versions. Additionally, all treatment staff received training in cognitive behavioral therapy (CBT) and interpersonal therapy for adolescents (IPT-A). Preliminary data demonstrate that teachers rated 41 percent of the students in school support projects in the abnormal range for hyperactivity on the SDQ at the point of entry into the program. Approximately 60 percent of students with severe hyperactivity had improved by the end of the program as rated by the same teachers.

Improving the Quality of Residential Treatment

In 2003, New York received federal funds, pursuant to passage of the Olmstead Act, which were used from 2003 to 2005 to support a project to reduce the length of stay in New York's RTFs. Each RTF was asked to choose three areas of focus for developing plans to improve operations in trauma sensitive treatment, family partnerships, moving from a controlled environment to one of collaboration, and using evidence-based interventions. An evaluation is presently underway to track the outcomes of the RTFs' plans on their overall operation. The OMH is looking for improved outcomes in these areas:

- Child and family skills learned
- Increased awareness of family and child strengths
- Improved and sustained connections to community
- Improved family and child satisfaction with services
- Earlier and more successful reintegration into the community

DEVELOPING INFRASTRUCTURE TO MAINTAIN QUALITY

Better Reporting of Data

All OMH licensed providers of children's mental health services are required to use CAIRS, the web-based data system described earlier. Programs receive comparative data from CAIRS showing them how long children are staying, the percentage of children meeting treatment goals upon discharge, the percentage of planned versus unplanned discharges, the number and types of serious incidents, and the percentage of children discharged to lower levels of care. Management indicator reports have been developed for provider use in measuring program effectiveness. Providers can see how they rate on various indicators compared to their colleagues.

Evidence-Based Practice Dissemination

The OMH's Evidence-Based Practice Center has been developed to expand the use of evidence-based practices through sustained clinical training. Practitioners throughout the state have the opportunity to participate in the center, which surveys local mental health needs using national and state research resources to identify evidence-based programs that can meet emerging needs.

MONEY TALKS

In 2005, the OMH successfully negotiated with the state's budget division for a fee increase for clinic providers. Rate increases are available to clinics that increase their hours to accommodate evening and weekend visits, more flexible school-based services, and continuous quality improvement initiatives geared to help them use data to monitor their own performance. If clinics fail to implement the qualifying changes, rate increases will be eliminated.

OVERCOMING OBSTACLES AND CHALLENGES

Achieving Buy-In

When initiating a new initiative, or in this case a series of initiatives, buy-in at all levels is important. The most effective strategy we implemented was to bring the study findings to our constituents, listen to their concerns, and brainstorm solutions with them. The plan we came up with reflected their concerns head-on and contained action steps they helped us develop.

Using Scientists and Their Research to Move an Agenda

It is easy to dispute government bureaucrats; it is less easy to argue with scientists who can present evidence from the latest research. In proposing our ideas and solutions, we repeatedly hosted forums with providers and researchers to educate them about current scientific findings. Providers and practitioners are hungry to learn about new techniques that work but are hesitant to participate in training opportunities that take them away from billable hours. Finding ways to fund their participation in training so that they could increase skills while staying financially intact was important to them. This was made possible through grant funding and was critical to their continued involvement. Our FFT training initiative was federally funded through the Office of Juvenile Justice and Delinquency Prevention (OJJDP) and our training of school support project sites was state funded with SED funds.

Engaging Families

New York is serious about its partnership with families. The state employs nine staff members who are senior policy advisors and advocates for families with children with serious mental illness. This staff ensures that policy reflects the needs of families and includes families as partners. New York spends over $13 million annually in family support services to assist families to get the services they need to sustain themselves in the community, and its families are true partners in policy and program development.

Dealing With a Changing Political Landscape

The key to successfully sticking to a reform agenda during inevitable leadership changes is to continuously educate staff at all levels about the philosophy, values, and mission of the reform efforts. Every new administration has a tendency to want to reinvent the wheel. By keeping all staff informed, progress continues despite changes in political leadership and the chaos a change sometimes creates. The message we focused on and that is at the heart of program planning and development is steadfastly maintained at home, in school, and in the community.

Overcoming Inertia

Borrowing a concept from the Institute of Healthcare Management, the OMH incorporated the concept of the learning collaborative as an opportunity for providers to get together, learn new techniques, measure progress, and most important, learn from each other. Collaboratives of clinic, RTF, and community residence providers were convened to allow providers to meet and help each other understand common strengths, challenges, and what needed to be changed. The OMH's role was to support the effort by convening it, providing the coffee, informing about the research, and disseminating the results.

LOOKING TO THE FUTURE

Empowerment theory moves away from the idea of a professional as the sole expert, and suggests instead that change results from collaboration between professionals and community members. The concept implies that people who may have felt little power to affect change will recognize their potential to do so. Studies of programs designed to enhance empowerment in their participants have found an increased sense of personal control on the participants' part, an increased participation in community organizations, and positive adjustment within the program (Burns & Hoagwood, 2002).

In New York, we're imagining a mental health world of the future where family members and youth recipients provide feedback to providers and that feedback shapes service delivery. Both groups will know what the signs and symptoms of mental illness are, what treatments are most effective, and how they may gain access to those services. Youth will understand how to cope with symptoms and how to successfully function in life. Family members will have the skills they need to deal with difficult behavior and the support they need to deal with challenges at home.

The planning study was critical because it helped us to understand how our delivery system works. Taking knowledge about our system and combining it with information from the research about techniques that really work set the direction of our planning efforts and program development. The next steps are:

- To continue to raise the clinical bar to improve the quality of the care we provide by bringing evidence-based treatments to clinical settings;

- To empower providers to hold themselves accountable by using data to monitor performance and outcomes;

- To increase public awareness about the signs and symptoms of mental illness and the treatments that work;

- To empower families and children to access the care they need and to provide feedback about the services that work;

- To deliver the message that there is hope and that with treatment, recovery is possible; and

- To provide financial incentives for providers to take down or convert residential and inpatient beds and to discharge children more quickly to less restrictive settings.

References

Armstrong, M., Grosser, R. & Palma, P. B. (1992). *At the crossroads*: *Expanding community-based care for children and families*. Albany, NY: New York State Office of Mental Health.

Burns, B. J. & Hoagwood, K. (2002). *Community treatment for youth*: *Evidence-based interventions for severe emotional and behavioral disorders*. New York: Oxford University Press.

Burns, B. J., Hoagwood, K. & Mrazek, P. J. (1999). Effective treatment for mental disorders in children and adolescents. *Clinical Child and Family Psychology Review, 4*, 199–244.

Child and adolescent service system program (CASSP) (1984). Washington, DC: National Institutes of Mental Health, U.S. Department of Health and Human Services (currently under the auspices of the Center for Mental Health Services, Substance Abuse and Mental Health Services Administration).

Goodman, R. (1997). The strengths and difficulties questionnaire: A research note. *Journal of Child Psychology, Psychiatry, and Allied Disciplines, 38*, 581–586.

Goodman, R. (1999). The extended version of the strengths and difficulties questionnaire as a guide to child psychiatric caseness and consequent burden. *Journal of Child Psychology, Psychiatry, and Allied Disciplines, 40*, 791–799.

Knitzer, J. (1982). *Unclaimed children*: *The failure of public responsibility to children and adolescents in need of mental health services*. Washington, DC: Children's Defense Fund.

Lyons, J. & Shallcross, H. (2000). *Matching the needs of children and families to mental health services*. New York State Office of Mental Health, Children Services Planning (unpub.).

Lyons, J. S. & Shallcross, H. (2001). *The needs and strengths of children and adolescents served by the public mental health system in New York State*. A report to the New York State Office of Mental Health.

Lyons, J., Lee, M., Carpinello, S., Rosenberg, L., Zuber, M., Fazio, M. & MacIntyre, J. (2001). *Assessing the needs and strengths of children and adolescents in a state public mental health service system*. New York State Office of Mental Health, Bureau of Children and Family Services, Children's Plan for Action (unpub.).

National co-morbidity survey replication study (NCS-R) (2001–2003). Washington, DC: National Institutes of Mental Health, U.S. Department of Health and Human Services. The study was funded by NIMH, the National Institute of Drug Abuse, the Substance Abuse and Mental Health Services Administration, and the Robert Wood Johnson Foundation.

Office of Mental Health (1988). *Youth assessment survey*. Albany, NY: New York Office of Mental Health.

Office of Mental Health (2001). *Strategic plan for children's behavioral health in New York State*. Albany, NY: New York Office of Mental Health.

Pappadopulos, E., MacIntyre, J. C. II, Crismon, M. L., Findling, R. L., Malone, R. P., Derivan, A., Schooler, N., Sikich, L., Greenhill, L., Schur, S., Kranzler, H., Carpinello, S., Felton, C., Sverd, J., Finnerty, M., Ketner, S. & Jensen, P. (2003). Treatment recommendations for the use of antipsychotics for aggressive youth (TRAAY), Part II. *Journal of the American Academy of Child and Adolescent Psychiatry*, *42*, 145–161.

Satcher, D. (1999). *Mental health: A report of the Surgeon General*. Washington, DC: U.S. Department of Health and Human Services, Office of the Surgeon General, Substance Abuse and Mental Health Services Administration.

Schaffer D., Gould, M. S., Brasic, J., Ambrosini P., Fisher, P., Bird, H. & Aluwahlia, S. (1983). A children's global assessment scale (CGAS). *Archives of General Psychiatry*, *40*, 1228–1231.

Schur, S., Sikich, L., Findling, R., Malone, R., Crismon, M., Derivan, A., MacIntyre, J., Pappadopulos, E., Greenhill, L., Schooler, N., Van Orden, K. & Jensen, P. (2003). Treatment recommendations for the use of antipsychotics for aggressive youth (TRAAY) Part I: A review. *Journal of the American Academy of Child and Adolescent Psychiatry*, *42*, 132–144.

Stroul, B. A. & Friedman, R. M. (1986). *A system of care for severely emotionally disturbed children and youth*. Washington, DC: National Technical Assistance Center for Children's Mental Health, Child and Adolescent Service System Program, Georgetown University Center for Child and Human Development.

Chapter 4

Establishing a Foundation for Collaboration Among Child-Serving Systems

**by Laura L. Rogers, L.C.S.W. and
Philip R. Endress, L.C.S.W., A.C.S.W., M.B.A.**

OVERVIEW

This chapter outlines a process designed and put into operation in Oneida County, New York to enhance inter-system collaboration and improve outcomes for families with children and youth diagnosed as having a serious emotional disturbance or behavioral disorder. As the newer systems of care demonstrate, outcomes can be improved where service provided by a child-serving system is well coordinated, culturally responsive, family centered, child focused, and supported by best-practices research. Oneida County has made its services more responsive to the unique needs and risks facing youths. Using the Single Point of Access and Accountability (SPOA/A) system and the Children and Adolescents Needs and Strengths (CANS) measure, together with Total Clinical Outcomes Management (TCOM) methodology, researchers and providers have discovered more successful protective practices and have improved coordination of services. This chapter also highlights some of the changes in structure and financing mechanisms the county has implemented to fully operationalize these individualized approaches.

BACKGROUND

Oneida County, located in upstate New York, is classified as a small city suburban area with significant rural areas. The county has a proximal population of 235,000 people, and as of 2001, there were 24,000 youths between ages ten and eighteen. Oneida County prides itself on its caring nature, especially toward new immigrants and individuals suffering from a mental illness or developmental disability. In recent years, Oneida County has become the new home for refugees from Southeast Asia, Bosnia, Croatia, Romania, and sub-Saharan Africa. At their peak in the early 1960s, with three large institutions and a population over 30,000, the City of Utica and Oneida County were home to large numbers of individuals suffering from mental disabilities. Historically, Utica was home to the second institution built for the mentally ill in the United States; this facility was the first to offer specialized treatment for alcohol and drug addiction. All that now remains of these institutions is one inpatient facility with less than 120 beds.

Once a center for industry, Oneida County is currently facing a declining industrial and tax base, an aging population, and an increasing Medicaid-eligible population. The closure of the Griffiths Air Force Base and the departure of several large manufacturing plants in the late 1990s compounded these problems. In an attempt to reinvent itself and recapture its economic prominence, the government of Oneida County was open to new ideas for addressing these and other pressing issues.

Beginning in the early 1990s, the Oneida County Department of Mental Health, in association with the Department of Social Services and several community-based providers, initiated a series of community efforts to reduce the county's dependence on foster and residential care for children and adolescents. The Robert Wood Johnson Foundation, through its replication grant program, rewarded Oneida County for its efforts with a $75,000, one-year grant to formally launch a coordinated care system for mentally ill children and their families. With vision, commitment, and strong political leadership, Kid's Oneida, a program serving high-needs youth and families with limited resources, became a reality. Kids Oneida has been in operation for nearly eight years and has emerged as a successful multi-system effort that blends child welfare, Medicaid, and mental health funds into a single system of care for children and youth with serious emotional and/or behavioral disorders.

On the preventative end, the services in Oneida County include Families Foremost (an agency that provides a multi-systemic therapy, or MST, model to the juvenile population), supportive case management, a school partnership for youth program, a family nurturing center, case planning, and mental health and substance abuse outpatient counseling. At-risk services include residential treatment facilities and centers, Kid's Oneida, intensive case management, and day treatment. To this end, whichever system a child enters, the child and family will be provided services across child-serving systems.

CROSS-SYSTEM BARRIERS

Children and their families often enter public systems during a period of crisis. This crisis may be exacerbated as they face a fragmented and at times overlapping and conflicting array of services. Families, legal guardians, probation officers, judges, principals, guidance counselors, child welfare caseworkers, mental health professionals, and other parties find these systems complex and difficult to navigate. For example, those entering the juvenile justice system can expect to be involved with as many as six different and independent systems designed to provide treatment and support services consistent with a multiplicity of regulations. This complexity might be overlooked if the systems were well coordinated—but often they are not.

As each system focuses on a particular aspect of a child's actions, it fails to address the family's needs in an integrated and comprehensive manner. To add to this complexity, each system may include multiple programs with separate and discrete providers replete with a comprehensive set of regulations governing such issues as record keeping and confidentiality. As agencies seek to provide a variety of services to address the needs of the child and family, these services may be governed by different systems, and the agency may be required to maintain separate and independent records for each child and/or family member. Too often, a child is removed from the home and community and started down path toward failure and recidivism. The following are some typical and salient cross-system barriers:

- *Service system*—Services are provided only in the system the child/family enters, despite the family's having multiple issues.

- *Finger pointing*—Systems state that their particular system is not responsible and that another system should be taking over the care of the child. In other words, "Because this child has a MH diagnosis, the MH system should handle him."

- *Uncoordinated care*—Care is not coordinated for the multiple needs of the child and family.

- *Monitoring*—Services are not uniformly monitored for quality assurance.

- *Reactive versus proactive approach*—Many children end up in higher need, more expensive services; there is little detection of these children at the preventative end.

- *Monitoring*—There is no mechanism in place that identifies and monitors children that end up in high-end services.

- *Move from high-end to community-based setting*—There is no mechanism in place that periodically observes children in high-end services such as residential placement and can help move them into community-based programs.

- *Instant replay*—There is a high recidivism rate of children who were placed in a residential treatment center.

- *Servicing guidelines*—Services are not efficiently used, as there is no mechanism in place that works as a guideline in identifying which service would best meet the needs of the child and family.

REFORM INITIATIVES—THE SPOA/A

Oneida County's SPOA/A process was established to address the above barriers. In January 2001, the New York State Office of Mental Health (OMH) announced its New Initiatives (OMH, 2001), which include guidelines for developing a SPOA/A for children and adults. The OMH recognized that the target population of high-risk children and youth entered the public systems via multiple routes. One of the tasks it charged each county with was to develop or adopt a risk assessment tool that would ensure this population's access to appropriate services through an integrated, virtual SPOA/A. In Oneida County, the major systems/points of entry that were identified as primary system of care partners included the departments of mental health, juvenile justice, social service, and education, and they are all currently the county's SPOA/A partners.

The public mental health system in New York delivers an extensive array of quality services. The OMH wants to promote improvement-oriented action within its current system. Improvement means a broadly available and flexible system that addresses families' stated needs and that is focused on strengths, individually customized, evidenced based, and responsive to each individual's need. In essence, SPOA/A oversees the provision of a broader array of services, organizes and manage services, and ensures that the care provided is based on core values, individualized service planning, family and professional partnership, and culturally competent services. The overall goal is to get children and families the services they need, when they need them, without waiting lists or eligibility barriers.

The first year of the SPOA/A initiative was dedicated to pulling systems processes together and fostering collaboration among the systems for the best interest of the child. The county chose the CANS assessment tool and then rolled out its use. Getting stakeholders to buy into and accept the use of this tool was a primary and sometimes difficult goal. The process was piloted at the entry point into SPOA/A on the MH side. Any child and family referred for the process had a CANS completed, and the information from the CANS was the basis for a service plan to be implemented and adhered to by responsible parties across systems.

The second year involved training various system partners and the line staff responsible for administering the tool. This took much time and energy, as some resisted changing to a new format. The resistance had mostly to do with paperwork and confusion about how to use the information learned from the CANS assessment. Also, four system levels needed to be trained. Eventually, whole divisions were trained on the CANS to teach new staff. The SPOA/A committees were also beginning to take formation in the second year, and CANS assessments were being received and housed in a database. The SPOA/A management information system was also being built.

In addition to the CANS, the Oneida County SPOA/A draws on the philosophies and methodologies of a number of reform programs. One is the Child and Adolescent Service Systems Program (CASSP), which sets forth values and principles for a system of care (Stroul & Friedman, 1993). CASSP principles apply to social services, probation, education, and mental health, and all of these interact with SPOA/A. Another related program is Communities that Care (CtC), which enlists the help of community leaders and professionals as well as local citizens to support positive youth development (Hawkins & Catalano, 2007). In addition, the county has established its own database, called C-Info, to manage information from the various service providers and agencies. The SPOA/A, however, is the overarching process within the county's system of care. It coordinates the delivery of services offered by the various systems components into an integrated plan of care and support for children and families. Each of the major child care serving systems has its own process for accessing services. The SPOA/A brings together the various systems into an integrated system of care.

SPOA/A System of Care

The purpose of the Oneida County's SPOA/A for children and families is twofold. First, this process occurs on the preventative end; that is, the SPOA/A can identify early the children and families needing a referral to an appropriate system or treatment. Second, the SPOA/A can identify children with the highest risk of placement in out-of-home settings, which helps in developing appropriate strategies to manage those children in their home communities. Through early identification and definition of a child's and family's needs, targeted evidence or promising practice services can be developed. The SPOA/A partners assist in developing a creative and individualized plan using services across systems. The quantification of need and service outcomes is valuable and necessary for the individual child and family as well as for informing the systems on emerging needs of children and families.

The SPOA/A system is designed to be child-centered and family focused, with the needs of the child and family dictating the types and mix of services provided. In other words, issues the families are facing are brought to the forefront by case managers, clinicians, and physicians. The family decides which issue(s) to address, and the system will provide access to the service.

Services are community based; the locus of services as well as the management and decision-making responsibility is at the local level. Oneida County representatives who sit on or chair service committees have the authority and responsibility to approve the decisions made through this family process.

The SPOA/A continuum strives to be culturally competent, with agencies, programs, and services responsive to the cultural, racial, ethnic, and linguistic differences of the children and families served. In addition, based on the outcomes from the CANS data, SPOA/A will ensure the implementation of evidenced-based and best practices strategies within the provider community. The needs of the family are first identified through a CANS assessment, which identifies not only the needs and strengths of the family, its risk and protective factors, but the service gaps and service needs within the community. This information can be fed back, for example, to the CtC to address the concern and meet the needs of the community it serves.

SPOA/A Guiding Principles

The guiding principles of SPOA/A include the following:

- Children with social welfare, emotional disturbance and/or juvenile justice needs will have access to a comprehensive array of community-based, culturally competent services that serve the child's physical, emotional, social, and educational needs.

- Children with social welfare, emotional disturbance, and/or juvenile justice needs will receive individualized services.

- Children with social welfare, emotional disturbance, and/or juvenile justice needs will receive services within the least restrictive, most normative environment that is socially and clinically appropriate.

- Children with social welfare, emotional disturbance, and/or juvenile justice needs will be provided case management or similar mechanisms to ensure that multiple services are delivered in a coordinated and therapeutic manner.

- SPOA/A will promote early identification and intervention for children with social welfare, emotional disturbance, and/or juvenile justice needs to enhance the likelihood of positive outcomes.

- Families of children with social welfare, emotional disturbance, and/or juvenile justice needs will be participants in the aspects of planning and delivery of services.

- Children with social welfare, emotional disturbance and/or juvenile justice needs will receive integrated services with linkages between the various systems for planning, developing, and coordinating services.

- The rights of children with social welfare, emotional disturbance, and/or juvenile justice needs will be protected, and effective advocacy efforts for children and youth with emotional disturbances will be encouraged.

- SPOA/A will follow the rules and guidelines of the Health Insurance Portability and Accountability Act (HIPPA) and provide access to parent and family advocates.

- Children with social welfare, emotional disturbance, and/or juvenile justice needs will receive services without discrimination.

- Children with social welfare, emotional disturbance, and/or juvenile justice needs will be ensured smooth transition to the adult SPOA as the child reaches maturity.

These principles empower SPOA/A participants to collaborate. The excitement and promise of collaboration, instead of the traditional, fragmented, single system treatment, helps the system support itself. Collaboration is essential to achieve the promise held by integrating services in flexible, high-leverage models, because most of our children and their families are involved in multiple agencies and systems. This network approach partners with the participating SPOA/A systems as well as with other public and private providers for children and adolescent services in an efficacious and accountable fashion.

USE OF THE CANS

The decision to implement a single, comprehensive screening tool was critical in bringing these multiple systems together. Following an exhaustive review of various psychometric tools and assessments available, Oneida County system partners chose to use the CANS methodology because of its ability to transcend cross-system barriers. Characteristics of the CANS assessment include:

- A focus on service delivery needs versus simply identifying a pathology;

- Identifying both current status and historical context for clinical needs;

- Various versions, to give caretakers a common language while respecting each system's focus, including the CANS-MH, CANS-CW (child welfare), CANS-DD (developmental disabilities), and CANS-JJ (juvenile justice);

- Highly flexible structure;

- Treatment plans that can be developed at the table with the child and family;

- Service providers using the outcomes of the assessment;

- Monitoring of the child's progress over time; and

- Encouragement of cross-system collaboration.

The CANS is administered to evaluate not only the child and family, but the systems and providers who interact with the family unit. The child is screened at the point of current access for risk, clinical need, and family strengths. Uniform screening ensures consistent criteria for the development of an accurate and effective care plan. A family care plan is developed based on the outcome of the CANS assessment. This information becomes a working document to be used by the SPOA/A committee. The committee will implement the program/services needed to establish uncomplicated care and to get services authorized and delivered effectively and efficiently. The CANS, then, works for multiple purposes, enhancing communication, collaboration, accountability, and coordination across systems, as follows:

- *Communication.* Through the use of the CANS and Oneida County's C-Info data base, SPOA/A partners and their affiliates are able to access information and communicate with other providers *and* systems about the child and family they are servicing. Use of the CANS has created a standard language to describe the challenges the child and family face and a standardization of the types of services being offered.

- *Collaboration.* The use of the CANS identifies service needs and service gaps. This information can be communicated to providers and funders alike. Where the CANS identifies a need for services that must be provided through multiple or divergent systems, the work of the SPOA/A committees will commence. As noted, the primary function of the SPOA/A is to bring together systems, services, and families for the exclusive purpose of developing a plan that addresses the multiple and complex needs of the family in a coordinated way. At SPOA/A meetings, a facilitator reviews the CANS assessment, particularly the 2s and 3s identified in the needs and strengths. These 2s and 3s make for an individualized service plan with the child and family. (This numbered rating system is described in more detail in Chapter 2, which provides a sample table with the ratings.)

- *Accountability.* The CANS is also used as a quality assurance/utilization review mechanism. It justifies that the service a child is currently receiving is appropriate and/or that the service provision is necessary. Periodic use of the CANS to reassess a child's and family's needs ensures that services are achieving the desired outcomes for the child and family. This reassessment has the added benefit of allowing children and families to move through the systems in an expeditious manner consistent with changes in their situations.

- *Coordination.* To reiterate, a primary use of the CANS is to aid in the coordination of services for children and families that present as having needs that can best be addressed through a multi-system strategy. A service provider will be deemed the lead manager in coordinating and implementing an individualized service plan (ISP) for the child and family. The ISP will specify the following: needs/concerns and strengths, action plan, and responsible party to ensure implementation and follow-through for the child and family. The CANS will be used to track the progress, or lack thereof, of the ISP and revisions will occur as needed.

In Oneida County, any agency that receives county dollars is required to administer a CANS assessment on families the agency is servicing. That is, children entering any county-funded program or receiving a service provided by mental health, juvenile justice, social services, or education will receive a CANS assessment. Children and families identified as being high-risk will receive a follow-up CANS assessment. Children who are not deemed at-risk will have the CANS completed only once. Where a child is not deemed at-risk but begins to decompensate, the provider, using sound clinical judgment, will readminister the CANS to assess the child's and family's current needs. These readministrations follow the uniform case record (UCR) time line of the child welfare system.

Based on the CANS, C-Info, in compliance with the HIPAA standards, will aid in coordinating the various system services with its capacity to share information about mutual clients. This process creates a multi-systemic effort to help children and families with social welfare, emotional disturbance, and/or juvenile justice needs.

OTHER RELATED PROGRAMS

Child and Adolescent Services System Program

As noted above, Oneida County's SPOA/A is also based on the federal CASSP principles and guidelines. The premise of these guidelines is to provide nontraditional community services, especially in the home or other natural environments, drawing on the strengths of the child, family, and community. Like the SPOA/A, these guidelines identify the need for the development of "systems of care" built on strong collaboration among all child-serving systems. The core CASSP values hold that the locus of services, management, and decision-making belong at the community level, with the child and family directing which types of services they should be provided.

The C-Info System

Oneida County recognized that its SPOA/A needed a coordinated management information system to help the various agencies collaborate their efforts. To meet this need, the Oneida County Department of Mental Health in 2001 embarked on the development of its own comprehensive, cross-system MIS—the C-Info system—to store and manage clinical evaluation information that can be used to support treatment efforts from all levels of systems, governments, providers, and the community. This system allows for the development of an individualized service plan anchored by a strong service coordination approach and based on a comprehensive assessment of each individual's need(s). As services are provided, C-Info tracks the individuals and families across the various systems (child welfare, mental health, vocational, probation agencies, etc.). It also collects information from the various sources identified on the New York State Quarterly Form, including a breakdown of cases referred from hospitals, emergency rooms, mobile crisis units, community mental health centers, juvenile justice, and schools, among other sources.

The local implementation of the CANS on the C-Info system allowed Oneida County to gather and analyze data as a first step toward developing a family-oriented "report card" on services and providers. Access to timely, locally generated data is essential in improving the quality of services for children and families. Allowing families to have access to this information is also critical in the overall restructuring of services and, eventually, in the funding of these services. With the detailed level of monitoring C-Info provides, the county, department, and provider agencies will be able to develop a local system of best practices.

BUILDING AN INTEGRATED SYSTEM

A Child-Centered, Family-Friendly System

Oneida County uses a sound clinical and family advocate team approach to assess for needs, strengths, and risk and protective factors as well as recommended services. Based on the CANS assessment, a family can advocate for the services that they think will best support them as they work through the current challenge. From a systemic perspective, the CANS can be used to determine whether a case is appropriate for preventative or at-risk services.

The elements of collaborative services include:

- *Implementation of the following key elements into a coordinated care package*:
  - Individualized service plan
  - Family-centered perspective
  - Strengths-based planning
  - Commitment to unconditional care
  - Community-based perspective
  - Culturally competent planning

- *Family support network*. The support team develops and monitors a family support network (FSN) that connects families to other parents and support services to ensure that the individualized service plan is child and family centered. The FSNs are family-run organizations that provide direct parent support and assistance to family members of children with emotional and behavioral disturbances. The FSNs track parent assessment of care (PAC) and youth assessment of care (YAC) surveys (as requested by the state in its New Initiatives) and base services and supports on the feedback from these surveys.

- *Clinician network*. The support team establishes, monitors, and supervises a clinician network. This network should consist of master's level mental health professionals and caseworkers who will work with a parent advocate from the FSN. The clinician/caseworker responsible for collecting CANS information adds his own data as well as information gained from the parent advocate. Typically, the service provider collects information from life domain functioning, acculturation, child strengths, child behavioral/emotional, trauma, child risk, educational, substance abuse, juvenile justice, and sexual behavior modules, while the parent advocate collects the caregivers needs and strengths module. The clinician will provide a list of recommendations based on this overall assessment.

- *Child/family team meeting*. The clinician and parent advocate will act as a team in conducting the child/family team meeting. This occurs before the child and family meet with the team of providers. The clinician and parent advocate will do the following preliminary steps:
  - Assess strengths. Strengths are assets or talents that can be mobilized to ameliorate or counteract the impact of problems or adverse circumstances. Examples of strengths that can be used as the focus of a strengths-based treatment plan are spirituality, well-being, or talents and interests. These are rated using the CANS,

with a score of 0 indicating significant strengths around which a treatment plan can be designed;

— Identify the members of the team;

— Clarify the roles of worker, advocate, and family;

— Sign the interagency release, which gives family members permission to sit at the table to make a plan for the child and family;

— Arrange a meeting date and location; and

— Invite team members, the individuals identified to provide support to the child and family (e.g., representative from social services).

- *SPOA/A team meeting.* When the SPOA/A team convenes, they will conduct the following steps in the team meeting:

— Introduce themselves and their professional capacities;

— Clarify the purpose of the meeting;

— Present family strengths;

— Present ground rules for brainstorming;

— Normalize, which means that given the circumstances and situations the child and family have experienced, others may have well reacted the same way;

— Identify needs;

— Prioritize, or identify the needs ands strengths with higher importance (of all those identified) that the child and family would like to address;

— Plan.

The SPOA/A Team

The SPOA/A team reviews and evaluates the initial level of care decision with the family and child. Depending on their unique needs, this decision could possibly include various levels of mental health treatment, case coordinator services, residential or living arrangements (i.e., home with parents, kinship, family foster care, therapeutic foster care, residential programs, inpatient treatment) and the use of other nontraditional support services such as mentoring, in-home family supports, or community supervision.

The SPOA/A director is designated as the responsible individual for monitoring progress and evaluating outcomes. SPOA/A establishes, implements, and monitors a universal intake process that includes all single points of access and residential treatment facility (RTF) referrals. The elements of this process comprise a data set, a CANS assessment with needs, concerns, and strengths identified, an action plan or SPOA/A committee disposition, and the party responsible for ensuring implementation. To ensure coordinate care across these four system partners, CANS assessment units for the various systems include:

- *Mental health*—Any mental health provider. If none, the Tier I clinician/parent advocate team will administer the CANS.

- *Child welfare*—Any program or service supported by the Department of Social Services (DSS). This could be the county caseworker or private provider staff.

- *Juvenile justice*—Probation officers or juvenile justice liaisons.

- *Educational system*—District liaison or CANS district evaluator. These are typically psychologists, school social workers, guidance counselors, nurses.

These units ensure that the universal assessment tool (data set & CANS assessment) will be administered at intake and at the sixty-, ninety-, and 180-day intervals until discharge, and at discharge to monitor for progress. The C-Info database assists in this aspect of the process. The SPOA/A process also has a utilization review system for families to evaluate outcomes and present findings to the SPOA/A oversight committee.

SPOA Oversight Committee

A SPOA/A oversight committee includes the following members: commissioners of mental health and social services, the Board of Cooperative Educational Services (BOCES), district superintendents, the senior family court judge, a family advocate, the probation director, a representative from the New York State OMH, the RTF administrator, and the SPOA/A director. It is the SPOA/A team's job to resolve any issues presented, implement services, and manage any follow-up. If the team is unable to resolve issues at the table or has exhausted all services/resources, or if its recommendation was to make an RTF referral, the oversight committee steps into the process.

The SPOA/A team, using the universal referral form discussed below, will establish an action plan to address any 2s or 3s indicated. For any such indications, the specific needs or concerns will be explained, along with the action that will remedy the 2 or 3 rating and the persons or agencies responsible for implementing the action.

Universal Referral Form

A child who enters any of the systems under the SPOA/A receives a screening assessment called the Universal Referral Form. This assessment consists of a data set and the CANS evaluation. The data set included demographics, background information, clinical information, history of substance use, history of high intensity services use, safety scores, rater/rating information, and sources of information. The last page of this data set includes a "tracking form," which identifies the service provider that will implement the supports for the child and family.

In some systems, Oneida County developed new versions of the CANS to meet needs of specific systems. For example, in the juvenile justice system we added a "compliance" item, and in the educational system we added items specific to academics and attendance components. One provider combined the CANS-DD and CANS-CW versions. Adding or deleting items does not change the validity or reliability of this instrument, however.

Oneida County's SPOA/A has moved to using a single version of the CANS with two assessment formats, the bubble sheet and interview format, to facilitate use of a common language. As mentioned earlier, the CANS assessment is put into the action (i.e.,treatment) plan format as well.

Anyone who is introduced to the CANS uses the bubble sheet format. It consists of the manual with the score card or "bubble sheet" to highlight the scores for the particular youth. This format is used with *all* children coming into the system. More specifically, any child who enters the mental health system through a public or private provider is required to have a CANS completed using this format. If a child is a new referral to a unit within social services, the caseworker (or referrant, if trained) is required to complete a CANS. All CANS are submitted to the SPOA/A director for data entry into a database.

The interview format is used for youths who present with multiple needs or who have involvement in multiple systems. The interview format is the format used to present the case-specific information to the SPOA/A committee for the system into which the child has entered. In this format, the CANS is used as a psychosocial/psychometric tool. From the case-specific information, the SPOA/A committee establishes a family care plan (action/treatment plan) from the 2s and 3s identified.

These formats are considered the Universal Referral Form for the child and family. In this method, the family does not have to repeat the paperwork process again and again with the various services and the providers get information from the assessment for program specific information. This uniform screening of completing the CANS for all programs ensures consistent criteria for an accurate and effective treatment plan.

CANS Readministrations/Follow-Up

CANS assessments are readministered only on those children identified as high risk and high need. If a child who was originally deemed low risk demonstrates decompensation, the CANS will be readministered. Readministrations occur sixty, 120, and 180 days after initial assessment until discharge, and at discharge. This is an SPOA/A process of monitoring progress and evaluating care effectiveness. More specifically, the SPOA/A will:

- Maintain continuous utilization review of cases for program efficacy (readministrations of the CANS);

- Complete quarterly reports on capacity expansions (reporting to the state);

- Use a performance management system via readministrations of the CANS;

- Monitor inpatient utilization and hospitalization slots, and manage RTF slotted beds;

- Collaborate with the OMH on screening and level of care determination tools and receive technical assistance in piloting the single point of access;

- Use outcomes evaluation and management;

- Access web-based clinical and administrative decision support via the C-Info database;

- Actively use evidenced-based practices; and

- Oversee satisfaction surveys administered to the child and family.

A Philosophy of Resilience and Change

SPOA/A and the use of the CANS is a philosophy of and about change. These programs bring a message of hope and resilience that is all too often buried and overlooked in each of us. In participating in this initiative, Oneida County wanted to reopen everyone's eyes to the potential of those whom many consider the most difficult to reach and most lost among society. When we pretend the problems do not exist, we continue to ignore them. SPOA/A and CANS bring a fundamental change that helps ensure the acceptance of this philosophy by all partners and providers involved with this project. By making use of research and data, we need to make everyone understand the true long-term costs, in dollars and lost human potential, of every child placed in an institutional setting. One juvenile at a time, we need to change common perceptions held by communities about our youth.

Aside from the ideological or theoretical changes, Oneida County expects to demonstrate that the data-driven, services-based practices research can produce individual changes only when supported by the actions of every other system.

Transitional Care

Learning from the Kid's Oneida experience, we expect that the new systems will develop an array of integrated community living options for individuals returning from a residential treatment center or correctional facility. Very few of those returning to the community make a successful adjustment without supports and reminders of what they learned in the institution. The systems need to begin to accept and understand that many young people discharged from an institutional setting need a transitional environment before returning home. As Oneida County seeks to develop new and more responsive living arrangements, we expect to demonstrate that the length of time spent away can be reduced and in some cases eliminated altogether. New alternatives to residential care must be incorporated into the mainstream of the community.

The focus is to keep youth integrated and involved in the community instead of being sent away only to return without the necessary services to keep them home. For example, youths ages sixteen to eighteen and possibly as young as fourteen can receive residential services or other levels of care while attending a public school setting. This allows a youth to remain in or be reintegrated into his or her community while receiving the necessary education, treatment, and residential structure required to begin a new future. Part of the SPOA/A plan aims to phase out this type of transitional service, so that an individual can remain in a residential program while working to reduce the number of days each week spent there. Transitional resources are scarce, sometimes involving "bed-sharing." Remaining flexible—for example, changing the current service delivery rules where necessary—is needed for successful implementation of this plan. Our legal system could help by making use of ankle bracelets as an alternative to incarceration where a youth must comply with a court-imposed sanction. This youth-focused transitional aid, while allowing the youth to remain active and connected to the community, will also assure the community that safety can and will be consistently monitored.

FUNDING

We need new funding streams that promote flexibility and the individualization of services. We must make changes to our current payment structure for the provision of services, which focuses on outcomes/results and de-emphasizes compliance with process-oriented regulations. One of our goals is to establish community outcomes with the SPOA/A partners and providers responsible for implementing changes. The government can then begin to contract with these providers or network providers, who will need to join forces with both the child and families to achieve the established community outcomes. Existing resources must also be diverted from re-institutionalization into this new approach to placements.

CANS TRAINING

As we all know, training is essential to ensure consistency in any tool we develop or use. One of the many strengths of the CANS is its ability to be communicative. The more people are trained on the instrument, the better. This communication could be across systems or within the same system. Although the CANS can be administered by anyone, anyone who administers the CANS must be trained. This training provides consistency in assisting in the completion of the assessment. In this regard, the lead person coordinates with others working with the child and family for information to complete the CANS. Attempts to make the assessment comprehensive, accurate, and complete are helpful. However, families only tell so much, or are able to tell only so much, to the person administering the assessment. Having readminstrations of the CANS will eventually capture more and more information as the child and family begin to trust the workers and systems.

In Oneida County, people are trained across systems. More specifically, we train intake workers, therapists, and other clinical staff in the mental health system, caseworkers and supervisors in the child welfare system, juvenile justice liaisons (and would like to train juvenile probation officers) in the juvenile justice system, and psychologists, school social workers, nurses, special education teachers, and individuals who participate in child study team meetings. We also train family advocates. In training these various participants in a child/family team, we are able to divide up the work—for example, the family advocates might complete the family/caregiver section, while a mentor would complete the child strength section and therapist or caseworker the other domains.

CHANGES IN THE RTF SYSTEM

A RTF in the State of New York is the highest level of care provided for children and adolescents. This type of residential placement treats severely mentally ill children and functions like an inpatient hospital, but with an average length of stay of eighteen months. This care is there to be used when other least restrictive care systems are exhausted. The SPOA/A process is there to ensure that families of high-risk children needing access to services that coordinate care systems have priority access to these services.

Oneida County's SPOA/A, in conjunction with families, DSS, probation, and the schools, established a level of local use at RTFs for the county's families. This included establishing a committee in concurrence with mental health regulations on appropriate RTF admissions to access underused resources for a more effective/efficient system approach. The goals of this process were to decrease children's lengths of stay in RTFs, eliminate recidivism, and develop a reintegration program to decrease the number of beds in the future. The vision of SPOA/A was to incorporate the clinician/advocate and family team approach in the process to take into consideration the child and family's strengths and setting their goals.

More specifically, Oneida County has priority access to eleven beds from two facilities. The SPOA/A is set up to work with the RTF administrations and providers to coordinate and oversee discharge planning needs. The SPOA/A developed a process that builds on the strengths and assets of the various child care serving systems. The CANS is used to assess level of risk and protective factors of children on a monthly basis so as to coordinate the current system.

New York State currently has a placement advisory committee model for admitting children to a RTF that Oneida County has adopted in its SPOA/A process. Children referred to this level of service must first have used the Kid's Oneida program and been found beyond its reach.

The discharge process for the RTF pilot included providing a monthly status report on all Oneida County children to the SPOA/A-placement advisory committee. The report included: treatment status, updated CANS assessment, treatment plan, significant incidents, current discharge targeted date, and a detailed discharge plan. The detailed discharge plan must include services needed for a successful discharge in transitioning back into the community with school placement, housing arrangements, and case coordination.

Oneida County put a further vision into operation. It established a four-bed Teaching Families model program and a six-to-eight-bed community residence program. Now, children discharged from a RTF will enter one of these types of RTC models, or Kid's Oneida, based on his or her needs at discharge. Additionally, the SPOA/A-PAC process will monitor the discharge plan for twelve to twenty-four months after the discharge date.

To manage the RTF waitlist, the SPOA/A monitors the children in the RTF on a monthly basis and compares their risk and protective factor levels, through use of the CANS, with those of children waiting for placement. In this way, using the CANS, the children with the highest levels of risk and lowest levels of protective factors whose current treatment and support are inadequate will be prioritized for RTF placements.

A third way is to identify the child who was not initially admitted to a RTF but whose CANS scores are higher than those of an admitted child. If the admitted child's CANS is significantly lower, a discharge will be initiated and supported by an individualized, community service plan for the child and family. Most important, children who need to be medically stabilized and/or pose risk of harming themselves or others would access inpatient services (hospitalization).

If the committee cannot come to a resolution, the Deputy Commissioner of Oneida County Mental Health will hear the appeal. If he is not able to resolve the matter, the decision will be brought before the Commissioner of Oneida County Mental Health, who will make the final decision.

IMPACT OF THE INITIATIVE

As envisioned, SPOA/A and the use of the CANS assessment could potentially have several significant impacts upon all services offered to the community. The first significant impact would be a reduction in the demand for institutional level of care beds. As the partnerships evolve, a stronger trust will develop between families, providers, and governmental purchasers of services. This will be supported by more focused, individualized services rather than the current one-size-fits-all approach to program delivery.

At the local level, the CASSP values and principles will be the guiding force to assist the partners and providers to change the focus from control to one of a supportive movement to ensure a brighter and more productive future. We can begin to create an environment that promotes and supports change. Youths and families will begin to feel secure and connected with the partners and providers to achieve the goal of community connection and support required to maintain the same.

At the state level with the systematic and regulatory reform changes made, partners and providers can begin to open up different, nontraditional ways for service delivery. This can create an energy that may be the motivating force for other communities to make some changes into these types of services. Replication is a strong possibility as we begin to demonstrate how change can better assist our families, children, and communities from a quality of life and fiscal point of view.

References

Child and adolescent needs and strengths methodology: An information integration tool for children and adolescents with mental health challenges (CANS). Copyright © 1999 Buddin Praed Foundation.

Hawkins, J. D. & Catalano, R. F. (2007). *Investing in your community's youth: An introduction to the communities that care system*. Washington, DC: U.S. Department of Health and Human Services, Substance Abuse and Mental Health Services Administration.

New York State Office of Mental Health (OMH) (2001). *Progress report on New York State's public mental health system*. Albany, NY: Author.

Single point of access/accountability program (SPOA/A) (2001). Albany, NY: New York State Office of Mental Health.

Stroul, B. & Friedman, R. (1993). *Systems of care for children and adolescents with severe emotional disturbances: What are the results?* Washington, DC: National Technical Assistance Center for Children's Mental Health, Child and Adolescent Service System Program, Georgetown University Center for Child and Human Development.

Chapter 5

A Statewide Implementation of an Information Management and Decision Support System for Children and Families in New Jersey

by Julie Caliwan, M.S.W. and Susan Furrer, Psy.D.

INTRODUCTION

New Jersey is the nation's most densely populated state, containing the tenth largest population of children and youth in the country. The state's Department of Human Services is currently undertaking a total transformation of its children's mental health system. This effort, which began services in January 2001, addresses a very broad population of children, including children with serious emotional disorders and those at risk. It covers children whose private insurance will not cover the services they need and children eligible for public health insurance programs. Medicaid and Family Care, New Jersey's State Children's Health Insurance Program, has carved out behavioral health services from physical health care services and has coordinated the benefit packages. This system transformation was designed with the values and principles of Stroul and Friedman's (1986) system of care (SOC) as its operating framework. Its purpose is to ensure that children and their families receive the services and supports they need, when and where they need them, so they can remain at home, in school, and out of trouble.

The state has been creating new infrastructure components, services, and supports, new policies and procedures, and realignments of existing ones. Now integrated within New Jersey's Child Welfare Reform Plan entitled *A New Beginning: The Future of Child Welfare in New Jersey* (2004), this transformation effort operates under the department's new Office of Children's Services (OCS) within the OCS's Division of Child Behavioral Health Services (DCBHS). Like many states, New Jersey's child welfare agency is under a court settlement necessitating numerous child welfare system reforms. New Jersey's plan includes children's behavioral health as a critical component requiring, among other things, the closure of the state's only children's psychiatric hospital. Table 5.1 outlines the set of integrated strategies that were used to establish each component of New Jersey's system reform efforts.

Based on our experience that each child service system (child welfare, mental health, juvenile justice) has its own mandates and priorities and its own set of services, we have found that common vision and language is essential to develop an integrated SOC for youth throughout the state. In New Jersey, we have approached this challenge by developing four versions of the Child and Adolescent Needs and Strengths tool

Table 5.1
System Transformation Through a Set of Integrated Strategies

Component	Objective
Integrated system administration to ensure appropriate and effective service use. Value Options (a privately owned, managed social and behavioral health care company) is the contracted systems administrator (CSA).	To provide a single point of entry, ensure that access is based on need, provide a uniform response to crisis, track and authorize services, coordinate care, and assist DCBHS to manage the SOC and improve the quality of services
Uniform assessment tools addressing multiple life domains essential to community-based, individualized service planning (such as risk behaviors, clinical need, functioning, caretaker capacity, child and family strengths). The tools establish a common language for collaborative, community-based service planning across the child welfare, mental health, and juvenile justice systems.	To facilitate communication, drive service planning, identify outcomes, and improve the quality of care throughout the new system To understand service utilization patterns based not simply on cost, but more important, within the context of the types of children served and the outcomes produced
Partnership with parents and youth	To ensure the system is child-centered and family friendly through local family support organizations (FSOs)
Care management mechanisms to ensure appropriate and effective service use, including the capacity to provide intensive care management.	To organize an intensive and individualized service plan by bringing together clinical services and natural community supports To provide face-to-face assistance to children at a moderate level of need To organize the assessment and service planning process for youth in the family court
Expanded community service options	To provide a full range of clinical care and social supports so children can remain at home, in school, and out of trouble
Integrated financing and payment mechanisms	To ensure access is based on need To mitigate the effects of categorical funding for children with emotional and behavioral disturbances To eliminate a child's need to go on the protective services caseload (relinquish custody) to get residential treatment services and allow for service continuity across eligibility status
Integrate and realign the pre-existing children's mental health services and functions	To ensure existing services are fully integrated with expanded community options To realign old service provision practices within the system of care framework

(CANS) (Lyons et al., 2003) to create a total clinical outcomes management process and infrastructure for our developing SOC. In the New Jersey local parlance, this is referred to as the information management decision support (IMDS) process. The purpose of the IMDS is to implement a systematic process that allows the Department of Human Services to understand utilization patterns, not only based on cost, but within the context of the youth and caregiver needs and the outcome of services. Over time, the ability to link assessment and outcomes data to the development of best practices becomes possible.

The goal of implementing such a shift in visioning of the needs of children and their caregivers and building a data collection and management system statewide is no mean feat. The contracted systems administrator (CSA), which provides a single point of access as well as a single information repository (of the electronic record of the child), warehouses all the IMDS data.

THE CRITICAL ROLE OF ASSESSMENT

Initial Steps

The state recognized the critical role that assessment plays in the development of an effectively functioning children's behavioral health system. A key principal of systems of care is that:

> [S]creening, assessment and evaluation take into account both the child's and his or her family's strengths, resources, and needs. Another key principle is that there should be an integrated, coordinated assessment across child serving systems so that families do not have to undergo multiple assessment processes . . . In addition, system of care principles call for assessments to be comprehensive—encompassing an ecological perspective across life domains—individualized and culturally appropriate. (Pires, 2002, pp. 53, 54)

In May 2000, New Jersey began reviewing the survey of early and periodic screening, diagnostic, and treatment tools (EPSDT). Using the *Issue Brief 3, An Evaluation of State EPSDT Screening Tools* (1997), the Department of Human Services, Division of Mental Health Services, OCS, convened a stakeholder working group to review and adapt these EPSDT screens for use in New Jersey. An instrument was developed and piloted, and a number of shortcomings became apparent. A checklist approach was limited in several ways. It did not meet the state's interest in ensuring a direct tie between assessments and outcomes. It also did not allow the state to directly tie the assessment instrument and the process of planning for care. These limitations would mean the assessment tools would not function well as management tools. In such a large system reform effort, it would be imperative for the state to have such tools available to ensure that the needs of children and families were always kept front and center in the decisions made at all levels of the system.

Abandoning further development of a checklist instrument, in November 2001 New Jersey began working with Dr. John Lyons, the developer of the CANS, to create a "family of tools" for IMDS (see Figure 5.1). With the CANS serving as the foundation tool for assessment, the state needed tools that were relatively simple to

Figure 5.1
Information Management Decision Support (IMDS) Tools

Information Management Decision Support (IMDS) Tools

Crisis Assessment Tool (CAT)	Needs Assessment (Needs)	Strengths & Needs Assessment (SNA)

Features Common to All Three Tools

- Based on communications theory
- Good face validity
- Provide ratings with immediate meaning
- High inter-rater reliability at the item level
- Collect meaningful information about the children and families being served
- Minimal redundancy in the measure — allows for some redundancy in formation collection

Tool-Specific Characteristics

- Administered by the Mobile Response and Stabilization Services (MRSS) staff during a dispatch
- Collects the information needed for MRSS Treatment Planning

- Administered at intake to all children accessing System of Care services
- Collects information that contributes to a level of care determination
- Represents a "base-line" of the needs of the child and the family at intake into the system

- Administered at 90-day intervals throughout treatment
- Indicates changes in child and family needs during treatment
- Provides the information needed to make decisions on changes to treatment plans and level of care

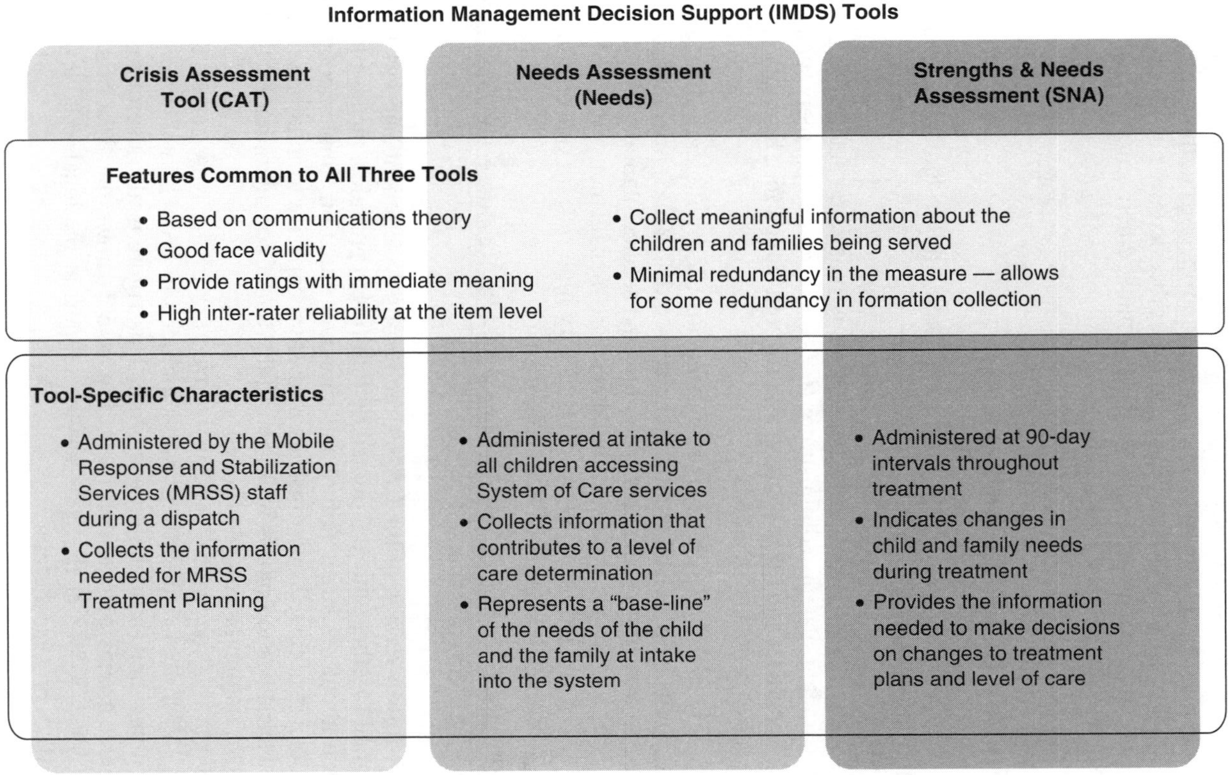

administer and understandable to both providers and families. Parents, youth, and stakeholders from the child welfare, mental health, and juvenile justice systems came together to help develop the tools. Focus groups involving front-line workers across the state also provided input. This effort led to three assessment versions—one for crisis assessment called the Crisis Assessment Tool (CAT), one for initial screening and assessment called the Needs Assessment, and an expanded version of the needs assessment to guide service planning called the Strengths and Needs Assessment (SNA). Use of the tools is increasingly embedded within all of the child-serving systems and is mandated for use by the management entities and providers within the state's SOC.

A Family of IMDS Tools

The IMDS instruments, which encompass similar domains, are designed to build on and inform one another:

1. The Needs Assessment instrument is mandated for use at entry by the contracted systems administrator (CSA), the system partners such as child welfare workers, and the providers, all of whom screen for eligibility and level of intensity of service needed.

2. The SNA instrument is mandated for use by the care management organizations (CMOs), by youth case management (YCM) providers, and by residential treatment providers for individualized service planning. YCM is a distinct type of service separate from intensive care management provided by a CMO. YCM is designed for youth who are at very high risk for out-of-home placement but are not yet involved with a CMO.[1]

3. The CAT is used by the state's Mobile Response and Stabilization Services (MRSS) providers.

A fourth version of the CANS, the Family Assessment Support Tool (FAST), was designed together with and piloted by families to provide a means of integrating information about the larger family and caregiver situation. Implementation of the FAST has not yet occurred due to issues of system capacity to integrate an additional tool. However, a version of this tool is currently under consideration by the OCS as part of a wider, ongoing statewide reform.

Figure 5.2 shows the schematic structure of the New Jersey SOC. Each of the three IMDS tools currently in use is included to show how they provide the basis for communication throughout the system. This figure is also useful for mapping out the different groups of potential users. Figure 5.3 shows the flow of a child and family from lower to higher levels of service support at the local SOC level and the role of the IMDS process therein.

---

[1]New Jersey has provided YCM services for children and adolescents since 1987. Originally state-funded, YCM services are now included in New Jersey's Medicaid Plan in all twenty-one counties. Designed to serve the full range of need complexity for youth with serious emotional disorders, YCM now addresses a moderate level of need, while CMOs address youth with the most complex needs (including juvenile justice). YCM capacity has also increased by approximately 70 percent. YCM remains a significant link in a child- and family-driven, community-based system of care.

Figure 5.2
Schematic Structure of the New Jersey Child Behavioral Health Services System of Care

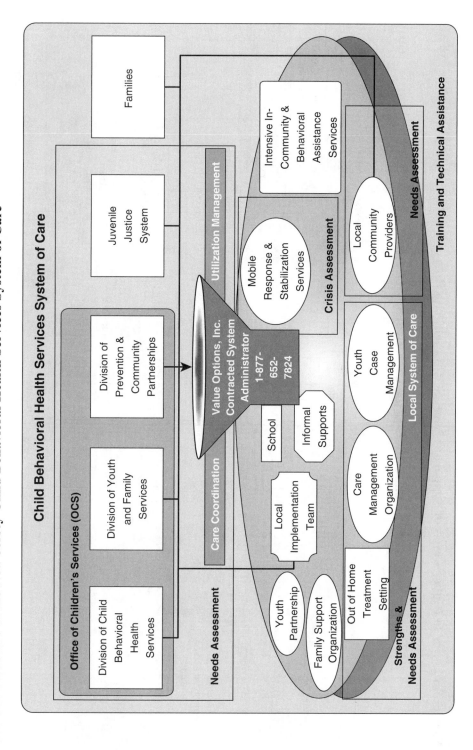

Figure 5.3
Flow From Lower to Higher Levels of Support at Local SOC Level, With Role of IMDS

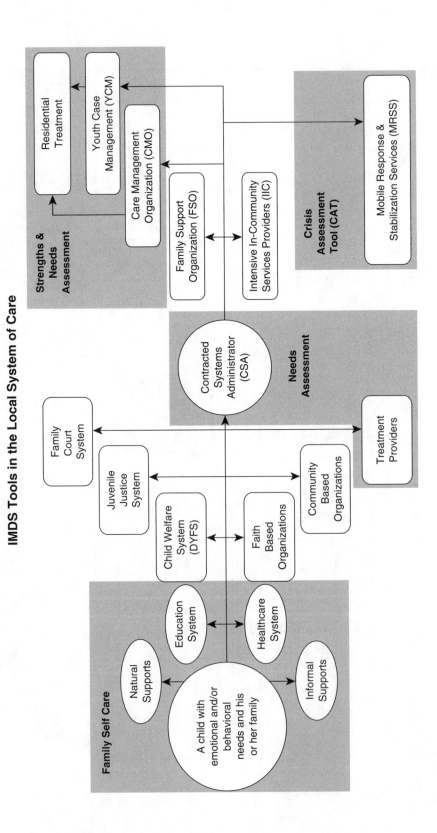

PHASED IMPLEMENTATION

Training the different stakeholders in application and use of the individual tools was fundamental to the implementation of the IMDS process throughout the SOC. The New Jersey DCBHS partnered with the University of Medicine and Dentistry of New Jersey, University Behavioral Health Care's (UBHC) behavioral research and training arm to develop a comprehensive training infrastructure for the entire SOC. Training efforts were enhanced by a close collaboration of the DCBHS, the training and technical assistance program at UBHC, and John Lyons to evolve a training design and delivery process that met the requirements of such a large scale implementation. Because of the IMDS's scope, thousands of people across every child service system would need to know and understand the IMDS tool relevant to their function within the overall system and be able to use that tool reliably.

Training efforts therefore needed to reflect the stakeholders' function relative to the larger system. The training structure and implementation is reflected in the three-stage IMDS implementation process of exposure, initial use, and full use (Lyons, 2004), as described below. (See also Table 5.3 at the end of this chapter, which shows a timeline of the phased implementation of planning/SOC rollout and training.)

Exposure Phase

The exposure phase has two rather distinct components, building consensus and early implementation.

Building Consensus. Together with John Lyons, a sanctioned representative of the SOC started the process of bringing different system partners to the table to discuss the needs of children. We began in late 2000 with this question: What information does the system need to accurately reflect the needs of youth and their caregivers, allocate resources fairly, and meet the needs of different stakeholder groups' mandates? The goal was to identify "factors that inform good decision making within the children's mental health system" (Lyons, 2004, p.131). This process fostered ongoing dialogue, the development of a shared vision that respected the different stakeholder perspectives, and agreement regarding the needs of youth and their caregivers. The product of this phase was the Needs Assessment tool. The other tools—SNA, CAT, and FAST—were subsequently developed as the system needed to add the relevant information management and decision support to the system. The planning and consensus building phase began in mid-2000 and merged into the initial use phase at the end of 2001.

Initial Use/Early Implementation. For the first eighteen months of this phase, John Lyons provided the training for the first IMDS tool (Needs Assessment) to many constituent groups across the state. The approach was, "Here it is, just use it." The initial certification process involved a reliability check that was given at the end of live training. Minimal information such as name and basic contact information was gathered so that the trainee could be notified as to his or her certification status. All this was provided by Dr. Lyons via fax and e-mail. The certification data was maintained on a simple Excel spreadsheet. It quickly became apparent that while this approach worked well for small groups, as the system expanded we needed an integrated and multifaceted training effort.

The early use of the CAT ran almost concurrently with the Needs Assessment, although with a much smaller group of users. The CAT was designed to support decision-making for mobile response services and took the form of a streamlined version of the Needs Assessment, with a focus on risk, symptoms, functioning, and acuity (the time frames were shortened from within the last thirty days to within the last twenty-four hours for many of the items).

By February 2002, residential providers completed needs assessments (DCBHS, 2002) on 1,374 children and adolescents currently in out-of-home settings, including:

- Treatment foster homes

- Group homes

- Psychiatric community residences

- Residential treatment centers (RTCs)

To understand different outcomes, each child was assessed by program staff as he or she presented on admission and current status. In this review, we observed significant differences between children placed in-state versus out-of-state within the RTC level of care:

- In-state had higher *behavioral/emotional* needs, except in psychosis and impulse substance use (SU) categories.

- Out-of-state had *lower functioning*, except in school, developmental, and medical categories.

- Out-of-state had more *dangerous to others* and worse *social behavior* ratings, while in-state had more *other self harm* incidents.

- Out-of-state had higher *caregiver needs*.

Residential treatment facilities (RTFs) began using the SNA in April and May 2003. Joint care reviews began in mid-2003 when SNAs became required as part of the process. CMOs began implementing the SNA process in April and May 2003, with full use of the SNA occurring in early 2004. Until this phase, Dr. Lyons had provided all the training on the IMDS tools. Training reached capacity level during 2003, and two in-state trainers from the UBHC training and technical assistance program became qualified to train on all three IMDS tools. By the end of 2003, the web-based certification system went online and the expectation of certification became more focused.

Partial Implementation

The early implementation part of the exposure phase begun in late 2001 was merged into the partial IMDS implementation in early 2004. The following dates represent the completion of each component of the IMDS tools:

CAT Version 2—July 12, 2002

Needs Manual Version 1.0—August 26, 2002

Needs Manual Version 2.0—October 3, 2002 & training manual—September 17, 2002

SNA Version 1.0—January 17, 2003

SNA Version 2.0—March 5, 2003

The partial implementation phase began in early 2004 and moved into full implementation with the completion of the statewide rollout of the SOC in 2006. Local trainers are doing the bulk of the training, with some consultation and cameo appearances by John Lyons for training in new local SOCs and superuser training.

More stakeholders were folded into the training process in this phase, as residential providers recognized the need for training and certification and began to ask for it. The bar was raised gradually, and certification was encouraged and asked about whenever users submitted an assessment tool to the CSA. The requirement for reliable use of the tool was tightened. To be considered reliable, the user must attain a reliability rating of .7 or higher, a .05 increase from the level required during the early implementation phase. In addition, the training and technical assistance program at UBHC added a full time position to manage the help desk function and support training efforts, in recognition of the additional support needed for the web-based and distance learning applications.

Full Implementation

With all components of the SOC in place by 2006, most potential users of the IMDS tools have had exposure to and/or training in their use. The CSA now requires certification, and reliable use of the tool is tracked via the web-based certification system. Certification is required (rather than recommended) for any user who completes an IMDS tool. This has been an intentionally gradual move over the past three years, so that the goal of tightening the requirement for use does not overwhelm the system. There are no actual consequences for not being able to demonstrate certification, but the expectation is clear. While those who submit IMDS tools when referring a youth and family for services should be using the tools in a consistent and reliable fashion, services are never denied if the person submitting the IMDS information is not certified. In fact, when staff is being interviewed for positions such as a care manager in a CMO or YCM, certification in the SNA has become a requirement of employment.

The training model that has evolved in New Jersey is best described as a combination of three strategies: building a relatively large cohort of certified trainers (a train-the-trainer approach, usually provided by way of a single training for trainers, with some follow-up over time to support consistency in training delivery), using distance learning applications with less focus on the trainer (i.e., the training on CD is provided by an expert), and the use of a limited number of expert trainers. There are advantages and disadvantages to each strategy. One clear advantage of building a cohort of certified trainers is the capacity to train locally. Without follow-up, however, differences in individual style can cause drift over time in how content is presented, which can negatively impact the integrity of the training provided. The distance learning approach was developed to address questions related to cost, accessibility of trainers, and other factors. Expert trainers, while small in number, demonstrate greater consistency in the training delivery process. In New Jersey, we used elements from all three training strategies to maximize the benefits and offset the disadvantages inherent in each.

THE TRAINING PROCESS: USE OF THE THREE IMDS TOOLS

The Needs Assessment tool determines eligibility for intervention. It has the widest use and the largest user group (thousands of users). The SNA is used for decision support in service planning settings. Users of this tool are primarily service providers and include residential service providers, CMO care managers, and YCM case managers. This user group numbers in the hundreds. The CAT is used by MRSS staff. This user group will number in the dozens. (See Chapter 10 for a detailed description of mobile response and stabilization and how responders use the CAT in assessment, decision support, service plan development, and outcomes).

User Characteristics and Implications for Training

The Needs Assessment. Most Needs Assessment users, the largest constituent group, are embedded in the older child serving system whose functions have "metastasized" according to entrenched mandates. They are not part of any new agency or program with a specific service function within the new model of SOC. Therefore, change and information about the SOC takes longer to catch hold with them. The perception of something new, and the additional demands it makes, can be met with a "this too shall pass" attitude rather than one of interest and curiosity.

At first, the purpose of the training venture with this group was primarily to expose as many potential users as possible to the thinking and use of the IMDS tools. We wanted both to expose this group to information and stimulate some interest in the changes to the system. The longer-term goal, of course, was increasingly accurate use of the tools. We needed a long period of exposure to overcome the inertia in this group and to demonstrate that the changes are really going to take place and actually have value. In the early stages of training this group (and in fact all groups), it became obvious that we needed an additional training component that provided users with an orientation to the New Jersey SOC and the IMDS process.

The Strengths and Needs Assessment. Users of the SNA are comprised of a combination of traditional mental health and congregate care providers and the CMO care managers (a newer constituent group in the SOC) and YCM case managers. Users of the SNA tend to split into two subgroups, a mental health provider group (such as in congregate care settings) and a care manager group.

The purpose of the SNA training venture with the mental health provider group was to educate them about the about the new SOC and the accompanying changes in philosophy and practice. We wanted them to understand that the tool was to be used to integrate information and enhance communication, not to make a formal psychometric assessment. The care manager group came to see the relevance and application at the individual child and family service level as well as at the program and system levels. Developing support for accurate use of the SNA was a challenge, however. The mental health provider group tended to struggle initially with application of the rating system—they tended to rate on the high side and were confused about the intent of the tool. The congregate care providers tended to underrate at times, forgetting that the milieu of the placement itself constituted an active intervention (a "setting" effect). CMOs that had been in operation for months at the time the SNA was rolled out had a negative initial reaction. In part this was due to the peremptory way it was implemented at first. Users also feared that the need to collect and integrate this information was antithetical to the child-family team process they had been trained in.

The Crisis Assessment Tool. Crisis assessment users were the smallest group of users and the most eager to learn. They were the easiest to train because use of the CAT was integral to their job function—they were trained to use the tool from the inception of the mobile response and stabilization system. This group easily understood the application of the CAT for decision support, planning interventions, and monitoring outcomes, as they used it on each and every crisis call made.

The Distance Training Model

The idea of creating a distance learning feature of the IMDS training endeavor was prompted by a number of factors. First, with thousands of users, issues of scale needed to be anticipated and addressed. Second, factoring in a fairly steady rate of staff turnover, there would be a continuing need to provide training. We did not have sufficient resources to provide statewide live training in all three IMDS tools on an as-needed basis. Third, accessibility issues arose; live training may not always be geographically or temporally convenient for the potential trainee. Developing the capacity for a distance learning application seemed a good solution to these challenges—the user could receive training anywhere, anytime, with access to a relatively up-to-date (but not state-of-the-art) computer. The expense of travel—both time and cost—would be reduced, and over time the cost of the development of the distance learning application would be offset. Additionally, building a web-based practice and certification system would allow users to practice and become certified online. Such a system would simultaneously provide the capacity to monitor the reliability and certification status of all users.

Development. As the distance learning feature took shape, four compact disk (CD) training modules were developed through the UBHC training and technical assistance program. The first CD provided a generic overview of the IMDS process and a second provided training for each tool (Needs, SNA, and CAT). Given the wide variety of anticipated users with varying levels of computer literacy and comfort, the design of the system needed to be as simple as possible. Trying to find the lowest common denominator to facilitate ease of use, we settled on a combination of training CDs with written instructions and manuals. The user would need Internet access to practice with at least one vignette and then certify as reliable in the use of the tools. The thinking was that if the user could play a CD on the computer and surf the net, he would be able to use the distance learning and certification applications. The design and development took approximately four months. Testing the site before it went live took about two months. The scripting and filming of the materials for the CDs paralleled the website development so that the release of the CDs and website access were simultaneous.

Web-Based Certification—Development and Implementation. The web-based certification system allows the user to create an individualized record, practice rating vignettes, and review and compare his ratings to the recommended ratings. Once the user is confident that he is ready for certification, a randomly selected vignette is presented to be rated, and upon submitting a final rated vignette, his reliability rating is calculated. The user is immediately informed (as is his supervisor by e-mail) of his certification status. If on the first try the user does not achieve a reliability check of .7 or higher, he must take several remedial steps to certify, as outlined in Figure 5.4.

Figure 5.4
Remediation Process Flow Chart

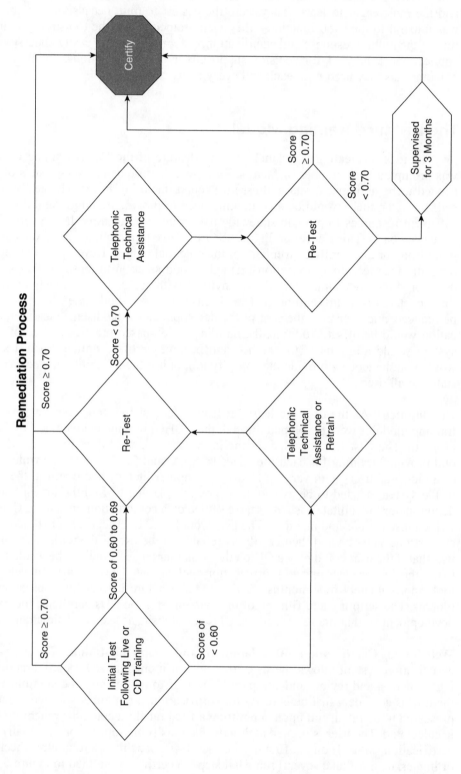

The goal of the remediation process is to support those who did not certify on the first attempt, either through further technical assistance or, in some cases, live training. Users who fail to reach a reliability level of .7 or higher after three attempts are required to wait three months before attempting certification again. During this time, if they are required to complete an IMDS tool as part of their job responsibilities, they must do so under supervision (their supervisor is required to be certified). These steps are not meant to prevent people from certifying, only to ensure that they meet the minimum requirement of training (live or CD) and demonstrate the ability to use the tool reliably.

The electronic capacity was also developed for cumulative tracking and reporting of all certified users and for moving certification information from an excel database created during the initial use phase. Thus, users who were previously certified did not need to recertify; simply by registering in the new system, their certification information would automatically be pulled from a legacy database into the active database (SQL server).

Issues Related to Electronic Training. We quickly discovered that what we hoped would be a fairly straightforward and virtually automated approach to training and certification required a significant amount of troubleshooting and technical assistance by e-mail, telephone, and at times in person. We learned many important and often humorous lessons about distance learning and web-based certification along the way. Perhaps the most gratifying was to receive calls from irate users who had not heeded the warnings on the website that training (live or CD supported) was necessary before attempting to certify. Many of these users were highly trained mental health professionals complaining that there must be a problem with the database, as they were sure they should certify. Upon exploration of the concern, the upshot was that they had not received any training before attempting to certify, either because they did not know they were supposed to or because they tried to circumvent the process. Other users simply did not take the time to follow the directions, did not use the manual, or tried to take short cuts. This highlighted the fact that training really does make a difference and that there is a shift in thinking about and envisioning the needs of children and their families that may not be immediately obvious to traditional mental health providers.

Some groups of users were not comfortable with computers and struggled with the technology, even though they attended live training. These users just needed practice on the website to certify.

We also found differences in learning style to be an important issue. Some users were quite comfortable with the more automated format and were able to certify easily, while others needed live classroom instruction and interaction. In fact, the interaction and discussion that takes place in a small group format in a live training situation, and where the first real application of the IMDS strategy occurs, is hard to replicate in a CD learning situation. Some users reported significant test taking anxiety and would visit the website, practice repeatedly, and not attempt to certify. These people needed some additional coaching on strategies for using the website and reassurance that we would help them to certify. Other users had special needs, including visual impairment, ADHD, and visual processing issues, and required extensive technical assistance by phone and occasionally in person.

Another challenge that occurred with live training was the temporal disconnect between training and certification. Many people who attended training would attempt certification unsuccessfully days or weeks later when the materials were not as fresh, or when they were at work and multitasking or distracted. In live training sessions it was necessary to suggest that those trained should attempt to certify shortly thereafter to avoid this pitfall.

A variety of technical issues also needed to be addressed. Any computer application has certain access requirements. The CD and web-based certification system requires an operating system that used Windows 95, 98, NT, or XP and Internet Explorer 6.0 browser. A high-speed connection is optimal (when is it not?). We found that when Netscape was used, it would at times result in a split screen and freezing of a page in the middle of a certification attempt. We discovered that the entire Child Protection Service division (unfortunately) ran Netscape as its browser. While this can easily be reset, this user group was among the least computer savvy and so was already operating at a disadvantage.

Accurate user and log-on information was another issue. Despite repeated warnings to create only one user identity, users would log on repeatedly and create new identities, either because they had forgotten their password or log-on name or because they had not been able to certify under one log-on and were essentially creating an alias to continue to try to certify. The worst culprit created a total of seventeen different identities! Unfortunately there was no easy fix for this problem other than eyeballing the database and eliminating obvious duplicates where they could be identified. This issue was also addressed in live training; trainees were warned that duplicate identities would be erased if discovered along with certification information. This led to a reduction in this phenomenon, although it does still occur.

Any web-based application can get disrupted or slowed due to a high volume of internet traffic and other gremlins in the system. While these are relatively rare events, they can certainly be frustrating to the individual user. Luckily, when the person staffing the helpdesk was at a loss, we had excellent information technology support available through the UBHC information services department. This department worked in close collaboration with the training and technical assistance program at UBHC in the development and maintenance of the website and online certification system.

The Human Touch. The hope that a CD-enhanced, web-based training and certification system could be virtually automated faded fast. Key to our training effort was the ability to provide easily accessible, friendly, and effective troubleshooting for users. The technical assistance provided covered coaching on content issues and support around remediation and certification. Troubleshooting was initially handled as part of the workload of the training staff, but it quickly became obvious that more help was needed. After about four months of operations, a full time position was created at the UBHC training and technical assistance program to support the training and certification effort. Key functions of this position included:

- The provision of technical assistance;
- Trouble shooting and training;
- Management of the database;
- Interface with information technology personnel around website issues; and
- Enhancements.

Table 5.2 shows how the number of distance learning users has increased since its inception in 2003. The table also shows that many users reported attending live training sessions.

Table 5.2
Distance Learning—Numbers of Users

Database Information	First 9 Months May, 2004	Status May 2005	Status January 2006
Number of registered users	1,139	2,375	3,141
Number of users who attempted certification	810	1,743	2,085
Number of users who practiced only (no certification attempt)	106	308	392
Percentage of users who successfully certified on the 1st or 2d attempt	—	79 percent	—
Number of users who reported attending live training or using the CD	—	1,234 users reported attending live training 609 users reported using CD training	1,419 users reported attending live training 560 users reported using CD training

Lessons Learned About Training From the Initial Implementation

Sometimes the most obvious observations are the ones we forget. One of these is that learning is a process and not an event. What is being taught changes over time as the system evolves, and training efforts need to be responsive to and incorporate these changes. Large systems are generally slow to adapt to change, and resistance is a necessary part of the process. Respecting "the way things are done" is an essential part of the dialogue, as is generating interest about the change wherever possible. Finding the early adapters can support curiosity and a willingness to change that encourages those who are more cautious. Where it seems a heavy-handed approach may work best, it is more important to predict and prepare for negative reactions. As we moved from the early to the partial implementation phase, a change in the atmosphere at scheduled training events was palpable. From wariness, boredom, or skepticism we saw a movement to increased acceptance and curiosity about the assessment tools.

The idea of planned incrementalism (Lyons, 2004) is very helpful to understanding and working the process of change. Large systems tend to respond to change slowly, and the way in which they change will often reflect their history and patterns of operation. Anticipating that the steps of a lasting change are necessarily small and not always linear, it is important to plan for change and sustain the whole effort while looking for windows of opportunity.

Focus on User Concerns. Different styles of implementation produce different reactions. A peremptory approach typically leads to a push-back by those being asked to change. An interesting example of this occurred with the CMOs during their initial implementation of the SNA. An implementation date was set and a training schedule developed. Attendees at the initial training sessions felt that the tool imposed a structure that was disruptive to the child-family team process then in place. Different CMO agencies subsequently reported a variety of concerns and difficulties with the use of the tool, and implementation was delayed.

While a peremptory approach may have succeeded in creating a sense of urgency about getting started with the implementation, the concerns needed to be addressed in a different manner. A team of Dr. Lyons and the key local trainer scheduled visits to every CMO with the express agenda of listening to the concerns and supporting the development of strategies to address them. The concerns voiced reflected a reaction to the required use of the SNA rather than to any specific issue or limitation of the tool itself. This realization evolved through discussions about ways care managers could experiment to make the process work for them. The CMOs were receiving ongoing support and coaching from experts in the child-family team model and individual service planning process, but these experts had no working knowledge of the IMDS process and thus could not support its implementation. The trainers frequently reiterated during this series of meetings that the IMDS tools do not dictate how they are used, as this is left to the creativity of the user. The tools are designed to support youth and family needs and strengths as well as the service planning process.

With subsequent local rollouts of new CMOs across the state, issues about use of the IMDS tools dissipated and the connection with individual service planning became better articulated. Rather than being perceived as an add-on that created more work for the team and distracted it from the process, the IMDS actually helped care managers focus on collecting and understanding key information and issues for the youth and their families. Using the feedback from the visits to support the early use of the SNA by the CMOs, several supportive strategies were developed. These included discussing how the SNA can be used with children and families to gather and integrate information (which was incorporated into the SNA training), developing a family-friendly interview format (in consultation with families and youth) to support care managers who have questions about more challenging areas such as sexual behavior, and developing and then expanding a glossary to address commonly asked questions and clarify common points of potential confusion. Interestingly for the mobile response line staff, the use of the CAT and its connection to service planning and delivery was never an issue, as it was integrated into the training of these workers from the beginning and was seen as central to the information gathering and assessment process. The experience of interfacing with CMO staff around these issues supported the development of superusers as a supportive training function within the system.

With congregate care settings, the use of the SNA was phased in as a part of a new process of quarterly joint care reviews consisting of the treatment plan, a report on the youth's progress, and the SNA. Before implementation, when meetings were held with the senior staff of facilities most often used by New Jersey for placement of youth in need of out-of-home care, the rationale and data presented demonstrated use of the tools as a part of the overall information management and total clinical outcomes management for the state. After implementation of the SNA, periodic meetings with senior staff were held to present the New Jersey data and the trends and patterns that were evolving over time. Initially the reaction was rather cynical, but in some organizations, the potential value of the approach was understood and staff was interested not only in the ability to measure the individual outcomes for youth, but also treatment outcomes for their own organization.

Link Implementation to Existing Organizational Functions. Another lesson learned was to *think* (and wherever possible *plan*) *systemically* and *strategically*. We were implementing a measurement system statewide across all child-serving systems, something never before attempted in New Jersey. Understanding this culture shift is useful in terms of anticipating the varied levels of reception of the idea and, later, its implementation. Paying attention to the process, not only the product, is critical to successful implementation. The response to CMOs who experienced an initial push-back to implementation of the SNA, as noted above, is an example of strategic managing of a situation in which the CMOs felt pressured to use the product, but came around to accept its use and understand its validity.

Working to link implementation to existing organizational functions at the local level can be quite successful and is a worthwhile investment of time and effort in the pre-implementation stage. For example, a decision was made to integrate the Needs Assessment into the juvenile justice system. This required staff at local youth detention centers as well as those in juvenile correctional facilities to learn to use the tool. Juvenile justice staff at the local SOC level had some sporadic training as part of the overall education of system partners, but as yet had not been required to use the Needs Assessment on a consistent basis. In New Jersey, the Juvenile Justice Commission (JJC) system is administered separately from the child mental health child and welfare systems.

Training began to be more focused toward juvenile justice in early 2004. By mid-2004, a series of meetings were held with senior staff of the JJC to review the IMDS tool that they would be using and then to figure out how it could be incorporated into and compliment the JJC's current assessment process. Training sessions were scheduled for fall and held on-site at the convenience of the facility, which acted as host for the training. Senior staff's concerns were addressed regarding the impact and integration of the assessment tool, and the training was adjusted to be meaningful to the audience. Special training vignettes were developed to reflect the population served in the juvenile justice system, and the orientation to the training and the use of the tools was slanted from the juvenile justice perspective. By the time the training occurred, senior staff had spread the word of its value and importance, and line staff was aware that although the training was mandated, it was also sanctioned from within and had value. They were receptive and actively participated in the training.

As the IMDS training and certification became part of the expectation for those in various agencies and components of the SOC, some constituent groups actually began to request training, and resistance noticeably decreased. We welcomed requests for training, as this signaled an increasing recognition of the importance of understanding the tools and accepting the need for their use. Even in some of these situations, however, the targeted trainees were not always receptive. A judge mandated one group of probation staff in one county to receive training in the Needs Assessment, and although they were a small group, they were skeptical of and hostile to the DCBHS staff making the opening comments. The trainees challenged the material being presented every step of the way and repeatedly complained they would not be able to do Needs Assessments with the youth they served. The trainer finally offered to cancel the training and reschedule if the officers did not feel ready or felt they needed further conversation with the judge and other members of their local implementation team. The trainer was fully prepared to hold the group to their decision and to leave then and there, returning when they had resolved whatever the concerns were that appeared to be making it difficult to participate. There was dead silence in the room for a couple of minutes before a brave soul proposed that they should at least "check out what the assessment tool was about," especially if they wanted to argue against its use at the local level. The trainer waited until there was good consensus in the group and then proceeded with the training. Subsequently, the participants shared concerns they had about the possibility that they may not correctly identify serious mental health needs for youth and that this could lead to terrible consequences. Indeed, this county had a history of just such a situation, when a youth whose parents had repeatedly asked for help from both the mental health and juvenile justice parts of the system murdered a boy in his neighborhood. Being sensitive to the culture of a local system can be critical to understanding what can appear only as resistance or skepticism and addressing these concerns as part of the implementation process.

Building Capacity for Ongoing Training and Developing a Learning Community

The Superuser Model. An additional step in the evolution of our training programs was the development of the superuser function and capacity. Clearly, as the SOC rolled out and the implementation of the IMDS family of assessment tools matured, the demand for continuous training and staff certification would only increase. The phenomenon of the relatively short-lived care- or case-manager career is well known, with the average life span of someone in this position being about two years. Thus, there will always be a need for continuing training and support for new learners. Rather than develop a train-the-trainers option that would simply provide the capacity for training in the various tools, we thought that developing a cadre of superusers would have a variety of added benefits, including having them as our ambassadors of the new culture at the local SOC and agency level. These superusers would be able to train new staff in their organizations using the CD coupled with live coaching as well as provide supervison to staff who were having difficulty with the IMDS certification process. This blend of train-the-trainer with distance learning and expert trainer models seemed to provide the best these models had to offer without any of the disadvantages.

We began by targeting key groups of supervisors and quality improvement staff in the CMOs. They could then form a team that covered quality indicators (QI) and implementation. Supervisors from YCM, out-of-home treatment settings, and mobile response were also targeted and invited to participate. We also encouraged staff from the CSA to attend in their role as gate keepers, providing them with additional knowledge and the ability to understand and support users of the IMDS tools.

To become superusers, designated staff members attended an additional two-day training session. The first day included further in-depth information about the development and use of the IMDS process. It also included practice in developing and rating vignettes to deepen their understanding of inter-rater reliability and gain a meta-level of understanding about the IMDS process beyond the mechanics of using the tool and trying to get the right answers. These exercises provide them with the opportunity to discuss the thinking behind a particular rating and the meanings of the anchored definitions as well as the benefits of the IMDS process, which can seem lengthy and at times frustrating to a neophyte. These training strategies translated into an improved ability to teach others who were in earlier stages of using the tools. They reinforced the importance of using the IMDS process as part of supervision and communication with children and families about their needs.

The second day of training provided a review of issues related to the use of the CD-assisted learning modality and the web-based certification system. Superusers were given a crash course on principles of adult learning to help them through the potential challenges of training colleagues and supervisees. Superusers also participated in role-play and presented various sections of the CD-assisted training with feedback from the group to enhance their training and presentation skills. They were given tips and helpful hints about how to use the CD in a discussion in one-to-one or small group reviews of practice vignettes, with staff who were not yet certified or who were having difficulty becoming certified. Superusers were also educated about common technical troubleshooting issues that they could help staff with locally, knowing they could call the help desk if they need assistance beyond their comfort level or if the issue was one they could not manage at the local level. These issues were demonstrated live in the training with instruction on the use of the training CDs and the website.

Superusers receive continuing support and follow-up on a quarterly basis. Meetings focus on issues with learning to use the tool and becoming more fluid in using it with children and families. Other topics include technical issues and training updates. The superuser creates a conduit by which feedback information about decision support thresholds and how they are being used can be provided to line staff within their agency.

There are a variety of hidden benefits to this model:

1. A certain amount of fidelity is assured by the use of the training CD. Thus the drift that can occur once a trainer is considered trained and trains on his or her own is minimized.

2. The superuser role supports the learning process at the local level. Rather than calling a disembodied person for assistance, the supervisor is the first line of assistance and support both in terms of the learning of the mechanics of the tool itself and in its accurate application and reliable use with the children and families. Over time the fidelity of the decision-making process that supports the plan of care can be tracked and used to further the learning of the care manager, supervisors, programs, and the system.

3. The superuser functions as a vehicle for providing feedback about the learning and use of the tools. This can help system users learn and also improve the way the tools are taught. It also ensures the best use of the tools and an operational understanding of the value of the process at the local level. This idea—that the communicators can trust the information being communicated—is crucial to the development of the entire communication system.

Next Steps. New Jersey is moving towards full implementation for the CAT, Needs Assessment, and SNA. Training and implementation of the Needs Assessment took the longest (about three and one-half years) because the scope and number of people needing to be trained was the largest. Training and implementation of the CAT occurred more quickly (about two years) because the trainee group was much more circumscribed and used the tool on every youth that was served. The CAT was also integrated into the training provided to MRSS staff and ongoing feedback loops created early on.

A number of challenges remain. One important goal is to create a learning system, locally and statewide. Information needs to be shared both vertically and horizontally throughout the system so that aggregate data regarding decision-making, algorithms, and trajectories of recovery can be fed back to end users and agencies. This will establish the needed feedback loops that communicate about performance and outcomes and ensure their regular use. Nonlinear & nonhierarchical communication strategies are unusual in a system that is historically hierarchical in its communication patterns. The goal, of course, is to create a focus on learning rather than on liability. The super-user is one part in the building of these loops.

The relationship with the CSA is also critical—it is the entity that manages the data and creates a sense of partnership and information sharing with stakeholders. In some ways this is even more challenging than the training effort because it requires maintaining relationships and communication of the right information at the right level to those receiving it. As algorithms are developed and fed back into the system, we can learn how accurate our decision-making is for children receiving different intensities of care, and also learn about which youth with which constellations of needs tend to do better or worse with which kinds of interventions and durations. Over time, this information will map into best practices for youth in New Jersey. We are in the early stages of building a matrix of mutual accountability. Lyons notes that:

> [W]ithin the concept of outcomes management, accountability should be thought of as nonlinear and multidirectional. In the children's system of care, accountability is a matrix of interlocking relationships in which the actions of one party impact the actions of multiple other parties simultaneously. Thus all partners are accountable to all other partners, but in complex and interlocking ways. (2004, p.207).

EXPANDING USE OF THE IMDS PROCESS IN THE SOC

The IMDS process has a variety of important functions throughout the developing SOC. It provides support for decision making at the child and family level, guides service planning, and facilitates rational service development and reimbursement rates. As a total quality outcomes management approach, it is integral to the management of resources within the SOC and provides a vehicle for embedding quality improvement and opportunities for learning throughout the system.

Assessing Need for CMO Services

At the core of every well-functioning children's behavioral health system is the capacity to answer the question, who should receive what services? This is not so simple, however, in a system culture developed around the principle of scarcity. Every state's children's services department is familiar with legislators' or a governor's referral that instigates admission to the highest levels of care regardless of need. New Jersey sought to replace the advocacy approach to answering the question of who should receive what services with a uniform mechanism to assess need. We believe that this is the most equitable and efficient approach to managing a large system.

New Jersey has developed and continues to develop a number of algorithms to guide service use. One example of implementing an algorithm is the process used to determine appropriateness for a youth and family to receive the intensive case management level of service. Children and families with this profile level would require the highest intensity service response and greatest degree of effort to coordinate their care. The CMOs have a 1:10 ratio of care managers to families. They use a wraparound approach to individualized services planning and thus are designed to respond to this high level of need.

The algorithm for CMO services is at least one 3, or two or more 2s, on emotional/ behavioral needs *and* at least one of the following:

- At least one 3 or two or more 2s on life domain functioning

- At least one 3 or two or more 2s on risk behaviors

- At least one 3 or two or more 2s on caregiver needs and strengths

The first step was to gather data from the Needs Assessment for children identified by the local implementation teams as appropriate for CMOs. Next this data was analyzed and the results presented to the implementation teams for their feedback. The algorithm was then set and put into use by the CSA for assigning children and their families to a CMO.

Service Planning

New Jersey's IMDS process is a strategy that supports the philosophy of the Division of Child Behavioral Health Services, which is to keep the system responsive to the needs of children and families. The only way to do this is to effectively represent youth and families at all levels. The intent of the IMDS approach is to provide a structure that helps at the individual and family levels and that also provides consistent and useful information at the program and state levels. The IMDS process is not intended to replace clinical thinking; its intent is to be consistent with and supportive of child-centered, family-friendly planning.

Representing what children and families need and making decisions regarding those needs are challenges that fall on care managers. The basic idea is that the way information is gathered via the IMDS tool is an individualized process that is sensitive to the situation of the youth and family. As they tell their story, the IMDS tool serves to capture the information in a consistent fashion. The tool reflects the planning in the individual service plan and serves as a check and balance system to make sure that we have looked at all the areas of need across the life domains; it does not drive the individual service plan. When looking at the individual service plan, can the team answer the question, does the plan reflect the moderate and intensive needs (2s and 3s) on the SNA?

The assessment tools do not divine the truth, they serve to identify and communicate about the strengths and needs of the youth and family. The ability to describe belongs to everyone who knows the youth and family, not solely to experts. The role of the care manager is to be the fulcrum of the process that should serve to connect the child, family, and input from the setting that has the most up-to-date information about the youth.

To date, different CMOs have identified three strategies in their use of the SNA:

- The care manager can do the SNA himself and then share it with the family;

- The care manager can talk to the family and, using the information gathered, complete the tool;

- The care manager can do the SNA together with the family—this can be a balance to the individual service plan, helping to keep it on track.

The modal strategy is that the care manager works with the family before the first individual service plan meeting, uses the input of other team members, and then takes the information to the individual service plan meeting. This way the family is empowered and has knowledge about their needs and strengths. In the individual service plan meeting the tools can be used to identify and focus the needs with input from the entire team. The SNA becomes the end product of the information gathering and integration process and helps prioritize the needs to be addressed in the individual service plan, to connect the needs with strengths, and to identify strengths that need to be built.

Contract Management and Rate Setting

New Jersey has also used the CANS to set rates for residential or other out-of-home treatment settings. The DCBHS inherited a rate setting system based on cost reimbursement. Using data on the strengths and needs of children and their families, the DCBHS has been able to establish a rational mechanism for rate setting while in the midst of reorganizing all out-of-home care services. A typical scenario may be: Provider A proposes to serve children as complex as those Provider B serves and, therefore, deserves the same rate as Provider B. By comparing data drawn from assessments done at admissions for both providers, the state can begin to reimburse based on intensity of need.

Quality Improvement and Outcomes Monitoring

The use of the IMDS tools supports the youth/family, care manager, and family team to systematically identify and prioritize the unmet needs and strengths and to track these over time. The IMDS family of tools allows us to look at:

- The percentage of youths' needs that reduce and strengths that increase over time (This information becomes especially important around transition planning.);

- Trajectories of recovery, so we can begin to understand what the expected rates are for youth in recovery; and

- Outcomes at system component levels, such as the CMOs, or congregate care settings.

An analysis of 1,374 New Jersey youth in residential treatment found five clusters (DCBHS internal report, 2002):

- SMI (severe mental illness)

- Disruptive and dangerous

- Disruptive

- Traumatized

- Low need (where residential was a placement alternative)

Lyons notes that preliminary data in Illinois (with the goal of studying both program outcomes as well as individual progress) suggest that residential facilities tend to have a positive impact with high-need youth, but that low-need youth become more symptomatic over time (2004). As the SOC develops and data is gathered, New Jersey will have the capacity to track trajectories and clinical outcomes of youth in the care of various residential facilities as well as CMO and YCM services.

Sizing the System and Planning for Service Development

The New Jersey Child Welfare Reform Plan enforceable elements required the state to identify the level of need by service element from 2005 through 2010 and make a projection of the optimal size of the public behavioral health care system for children in the state over that time. The system needed to be sized to ensure that the other plan requirements would be achieved, including elimination of a waiting period for youth in juvenile detention centers waiting for mental health services throughout the state. The Needs Assessment, completed in March 2005, was critical to this system sizing effort. The state enlisted John Lyons to assist with the following methodology:

1. The population of children and adolescents in New Jersey under the age of eighteen was used to project trends in the size of this population. This estimate was calculated based on United States census data. The most recent estimates were used within the context of any evidence of trends for population growth or decline in the population of children and adolescents.

2. Epidemiological data was used to estimate the number of children and adolescents in New Jersey who have serious emotional or behavioral disorders (SEBD). Several well-done epidemiological studies, such as MECCA (Marshfield Enhanced Charting and Code Acquisition) and Smoky Mountain, were used as a multiplier to estimates based on the findings of step 1, the number of children and youth with SEBD in New Jersey. Population dynamics were then used to project the increase or decrease in this group.

3. The current volume of services was determined using data from the CSA. This included current number of children, number of episodes, and duration of episodes (e.g., sessions or length of stay) for all major program types (e.g., residential treatment, psychiatric hospitalization, care management, YCM).

4. An analysis was conducted to reveal the proportion of youth at each level of care whose needs were appropriate for that level. The decision support algorithms developed for the Needs Assessment were applied to children and adolescents currently served at each level of care. In other words, if there were a substantial number of youth served in residential treatment who could reasonably be served in the community, this analysis would identify the estimated proportion of the population of placed children who could be returned to the community. The current volume of service was adjusted to reflect appropriate service volumes by level of care, based on the clinical status of children and adolescents served in the current system.

5. The results of steps 1 through 4 identified an estimate of the number of youth in the state at need for each level of care. Existing estimates of the durations of episodes were used, along with available outcomes data to estimate the expected duration of services for each level of care. These results were combined to estimate the ideal size of the children's behavioral health system of care.

CONCLUSION—THE PROMISE AND THE CHALLENGE

In building a statewide SOC, a key issue is the ability to advocate for resources based on the actual needs of children, youth, and their families. This has been a significant challenge to traditional child serving systems. To ensure the long-term success of such a venture in terms of cost, quality, and outcomes, an integrated approach to administering a statewide system must ensure fair resource allocation, the ability to measure the relative success of services and interventions, and the development of accountability throughout the system. Critical to maintaining momentum in the developing system of care is the creation and use of information that provides a picture of what actually helps children and families and moves beyond some of the system syndromes and tensions to the creation of a learning culture environment (Lyons, 2004).

Historically, attempts to develop checklists to capture the myriad needs of youth and families have failed to translate into a measurement system that could be useful at the three levels we are attempting to encompass—the individual service level, the local agency/system level, and the larger system level. Clinical outcomes management is not a new concept, but it has failed to be effectively embedded into the mental health service delivery system for a variety of reasons, not least of which have been technological limitations, measurement constraints, resistance among providers, lack of understanding by administrators, lack of funding, and the evaluator's dilemma—the latter being the agency's or program's dilemma of measuring whether or not its services work. If services work well, then that is why you were funded in the first place; if they do not, then you as an agency will look bad and be at risk to lose funding (Lyons, 2004, pp.128, 129). It has been acknowledged that:

> [T]here is a lag in the dissemination of evidence-based practices and in their incorporation into clinical practice . . . [and] . . . many interventions have not as yet been tested on the highly diverse population of children with multiple needs, problems and co-occurring conditions who are typically served within public systems. . . . The challenge is promoting not just the interventions in an effective manner but also their implementation with fidelity. (Huang et al., 2005, p. 621)

Daleiden et al. (2006) have provided leadership in the SOC arena with an approach that builds "specifically empirically supported programs" and pursues "incremental improvement of current care towards evidence-based ideals" (p.750) with monitoring of outcomes, thus beginning to address the science to service gap in the delivery of clinical interventions within a SOC. A next step in the development of the New Jersey SOC will be to use IMDS data to assist the tracking and monitoring of clinical outcomes and interventions.

The strength of a total clinical outcomes management approach is that it serves to keep the focus of the entire service system on the people whom everyone working in that system has agreed to serve (Lyons, 2004). The communications measurement model, a marriage of clinimetrics and psychometrics (Lyons, 2004; see discussion in Chapter 1), provides hope in bridging the gap between clinical research and working in the trenches by providing just enough information when it is needed and having the capacity to track outcomes at the individual, program, and system levels. This is the promise and the challenge for us as we move into statewide implementation.

Table 5.3 below shows the timeline for exposure, training, and implementation of the IMDS.

Table 5.3
Implementation Timeline for IMDS System for Children and Families in New Jersey

2000 Exposure Phase: mid 2000–end 2001	
January to June Planning & Implementation	**July to December**

• In 5/00, reviewed EPSDT instruments (surveyed by Bazelton); developed a stakeholder group to review & adapt EPSDT screens for New Jersey. These attempts were unsuccessful in achieving the development of a uniform assessment tool that would provide needed information at all levels of the system to all users.	• 7/11/00 Pilot application of CANS-CW to a sample of randomly selected case records of children aged 6+ in three New Jersey counties indicates significant trends regarding need, service utilization and placement pathways. Study recommends expanding use of CANS statewide.
	
	• 10/25/00 Proposal for design of an information system and infrastructure submitted by Lyons. Proposed steps included:
	
	  1. Identification of key decision functions in the system;
	
	  2. Identification of information needed for each decision;
	
	  3. Identification of data collection responsibilities;
	
	  4. Development of workflows for collecting data; and
	
	  5. Development of software/data entry.
	
	• 11/8/00 Proposal for development of a Screening & Assessment Tool (CAT).

Training	
• None	• None
2001 Building Consensus	
January to June Planning & Implementation	**July to December**
• 1/01 First 3 CMOs began operations. • 2/01 Crisis Assessment Tool finalized development & review by system partners, incorporation of input.	• 7/01 First stage of statewide CANS application—the Crisis Assessment Tool (CAT)—field tested and refined.

(Continued)

Table 5.3 (Continued)

• 2-3/01 Development of system referral mechanism (CSA), including support indicators. • 3-4/01 Regional forums to review system referral and crisis assessment. • Mid-year snapshot of 90 youth in CMOs (using the Needs Assessment). • 6/01 Incorporation of CAT in to CSA MIS.	
Training	
• 4/01 Identify pilot training materials & audience. • 5/01 Reliability of crisis assessment piloted with 11 providers around the state; used an N of 88 to develop a threshold for admission.	• 12/01-1/02 CAT training as part of first round mobile response training.
2002 Initial Use/Early Implementation January to June Planning & Implementation	July to December
• 1/02 Second set of 3 CMOs began operations. • 2/02 First MRSS programs on line (used the CAT). • 3/02 CSA began operations. • 4-5/02 Review of residential treatment records. • 4/02 Presentation to residential providers. • 5/02 Monmouth MRSS became operational.	• 10/02 Burlington MRSS expanded services to cover Cape/Atlantic Counties. • 12/02 Presentation to residential providers.
Training	
• 2/02 Ongoing support re: use of CAT in three New Jersey counties with supervisory level staff to ensure consistent use of the tool and promote feedback regarding its use. • 4/02 Provided training to new MRSS program in Monmouth.	• 8/02-10/02 Enhancements to training manual. • 10/02 Presentation to residential providers.

Table 5.3 (Continued)

2003 Initial Use/Early Implementation

January to June	July to December
Planning & Implementation	
• 1/03 Implementation of SNA planned to occur; inadequate preparation of user groups (CMO & residential providers).	• 7/03 Next CMO became operational (Hudson).
• 1/03 Development of Family Assessment & Support Tool (FAST) began.	• 11/03 Next CMO operational (Middlesex).
• 4/03 Care management organizations began implementation of use of the SNA.	
• 4/03-5/03 Residential treatment facilities implemented using the SNA.	
• 4/03 YCM became statewide with expanded population served.	
• 4/03 Burlington MRSS expanded services to cover Gloucester/Cumberland/Salem Counties.	
• 5/03 MRSS initial report on decision-making outcomes using the Crisis Assessment Tool.	
Training	
• 2/03 Training provided for SNA by CMOs and residential treatment providers, with immediate utilization of the SNA, replacing the Needs Assessment by these groups. Began with training without using the modules immediately.	• 4/03 – 7/03 Filming & production of CD-based distance learning components: Overview of IMDS tools in the NJ SOC, Needs Assessment, and Strengths & Needs Assessment completed to coincide with launching of the certification web based application.
• 3/03-8/03 NJ IMDS training capacity of two trainers in three IMDS tools was reached.	• 8/03 Follow-up done with CMOs around implementation experiences and ways to incorporate the use of the tool with youth and families and to address additional training needs.
• 3/03 Planning for the development of a web based IMDS certification system was begun.	• 9/03 CD learning and web-based certification launched for all three tools.
• 3/03 Planning for the development of IMDS distance learning feature was begun (CD based).	

(Continued)

Table 5.3 (Continued)

• 3/03 Began development of an IMDS train-the-trainer process. • 4/03 Two-day train-the-trainer pilot program.	• 9/03 Continued development of the train-the-trainer process delayed until the distance learning and web based applications were launched and in operation for about six months. • The train-the-trainer process was changed to incorporate a superuser model that used these materials and learning modalities to promote fidelity of training.

2004 Partial Implementation

January to June	July to December
Planning & Implementation	
• 2/04 Newark and Camden CMOs became operational. • 2/04 Newark and Camden MRSSs became operational.	• 8/04 Hudson MRSS became operational. • 9/04 Middlesex MRSS became operational. • 12/04 Passaic MRSS became operational.
Training	
• 1/04 MRSS training for two new counties. • 3/04-4/04 Targeted training for community-based providers as in-community use of Needs Assessment rolls out. • Help desk feature for the IMDS web-based certification added (a full time person).	• 7/04 Superuser training of supervisory level staff in CMOs and YCM. • Ongoing train-the-trainer to expand superuser capacity (added support for web-based practice and certification, CD-assisted training). • 12/04 Joint superuser training with John Lyons, targeting all CMO supervisory level and QA/QI level staff, with NJ trainers taking the lead.

2005 Moving Towards Full Implementation

January to June	July to January 2006
Planning & Implementation	
• 1/05 Passaic CMO operational. • 3/05 Ocean County MRSS became operational.	• 7/05 Ocean, Gloucester/Salem/Cumberland CMOs became operational. • 9/05 Mercer MRSS became operational. • 10/05 Gloucester/Salem/Cumberland Counties MRSS became operational (had been delivering services under the auspices of Burlington County MRSS since 4/03).

Table 5.3 (Continued)

	• 1/06 Cape/Atlantic Counties MRSS became operational (had been delivering services under the auspices of Burlington County MRSS since 4/03). • 1/06 Final groupings of CMOs and MRSSs became operational (Sussex/Morris and Hunterdon/Somersest/Warren Counties).
Training	
• Translation of all tools manuals and glossary into additional languages (Spanish). • Filming and producing of Version 2 for all of the tools (CAT, Needs Assessment, and SNA) incorporating updates. • Develop and add the FAST to the online certification website • 3/05 Worked with Middlesex County Mobile Response to translate Crisis Assessment Tool into Spanish version. • 5/05 Created the FAST materials (manual, vignettes) and created the certification web-based capacity for certification. • 6/05 - Launched Version 2 of the CD assisted trainings for all of the tools.	• Training provided to MRSSs about one month before beginning operations. • 9/05 0-4 CANS on the online certification system ready to go live, but not yet operational. • 11/05 Held another train-the-trainer and incorporated CMO, YCM, and residential facilities (out of state) supervisory and QA/QO level staff and new counties to the SOC as statewide rollout ends. • 12/05 Accomplished training at all of the regional diagnostic centers on the SNA. • Early 2006 0-4 CANS training pilot planned (OCS focus).

EPILOGUE

In January 2006, the newly elected Corzine administration appointed a new Commissioner of the Department of Human Services (DHS), and as a result the top level executive management of the DCBHS was replaced. In July 2006, the division was split off from DHS and combined with the Child Protective Services agency to form a new Department of Children and Families. The purpose of the split was to enable the new organization to focus on the effort to reform child welfare services. An independent assessment of New Jersey's children's behavioral health care system was conducted by the Louis de la Parte Florida Mental Health Institute of the University of South Florida (Armstrong et al., 2006). The assessment found that "There is tremendous value in having statewide, uniform assessment tools and an IMDS process. Used wisely, these processes can balance individual responses with objectivity and inform decision-making with best practice guidance" (p. 69). It also found that "the CANS was consistent with goals of the Children's Initiative and was well suited to New Jersey's high need for flexibility and a common language to effectively serve youth in all child serving systems" (p. 69). The long-term effects on the implementation of the system of care reform effort in New Jersey are still unknown; however, the new administration continues to use the IMDS tools. The potential of the IMDS tools and process remains as a mechanism to support decision-making for children and their families and to improve the effectiveness of services and the quality of the overall system.

References

Armstrong, M. I., Blasé, K., Caldwell, B., Holt, W., King-Miller, T., Kuppinger, A., Obrochta, C., Policella, D. N. & Wallace, F. (2006). *Final report: Independent assessment of the New Jersey's children's behavioral health care system.* Tampa, FL: The University of South Florida, Louis de la Parte Florida Mental Health Institute.

A new beginning: The future of child welfare in New Jersey (2004). New Jersey Child Welfare Agency, Child Welfare Panel.

Daleiden, E. L., Chorpita, B. F., Donkervoert, C., Arensdorf, A. M. & Brogan, M. (2006). Getting better at getting them better: Health outcomes and evidence-based practice within a system of care. *Journal of the American Academy of Child and Adolescent Psychiatry, 45,* 749-756.

New Jersey Department of Human Services, DCBHS internal document (2002). Needs assessments completed by residential providers: An analysis.

Issue Brief 3, An Evaluation of State EPSDT Screening Tools (1997). Washington, DC: Bazelon Center for Mental Health Law.

Huang, L., Stroul, B., Friedman, R., Mrazak, P., Friesen, B., Pires, S. & Mayberg, S. (2005). Transforming mental health care for children and their families. *American Psychologist, 60,* 615–627.

Lyons, J. S. (2004). *Redressing the emperor: Improving our children's public health system.* Westport, CT: Praeger.

Lyons, J. S., Griffin, E., Fazio, M. & Lyons, M. B. (2003 rev.). *Child and adolescent needs and strengths: An information integration tool for children and adolescents with mental health challenges: CANS-MH manual.* Winnetka, IL: Buddin Praed Foundation.

Pires, S. A. (2002). *Building systems of care: A primer.* Washington, DC: National Technical Assistance Center for Children's Mental Health: Georgetown University Center for Child and Human Development.

Stroul, B. & Friedman, R. (1986). *A system of care for children and youth with severe emotional disturbances.* Washington, DC: National Technical Assistance Center for Children's Mental Health, Child and Adolescent Service System Program, Georgetown University Center for Child and Human Development.

Chapter 6

Managing Treatment Foster Care With Decision Support and Outcomes

by Stacey Hirsch, M.S.W., Murielle Elfman, M.S.S., L.S.W., and Angelica Oberleithner, M.S.

HISTORY AND BACKGROUND OF
TREATMENT FOSTER CARE REFORM IN PHILADELPHIA

In October 2001, the City of Philadelphia Department of Human Services (DHS) took the first step toward redesigning treatment foster care (TFC). Enhancing and increasing the availability of TFC for Philadelphia's children, youth, and families was one of many initiatives the DHS had undertaken as part of its *Blueprint for Reform: Roadmap for Excellence* (2001). Successful implementation and sustainability of TFC reform in Philadelphia reflect the DHS's ongoing commitment to improving outcomes for children, youth, and families and to achieving the goals of safety, permanency, and well-being for all children who become involved with the DHS.

The DHS forged a relationship with a local nonprofit organization, PMHCC (formerly the Philadelphia Mental Health Care Corporation), to create the Best Practices Institute (BPI). BPI became one of PMHCC's core programs, charged with accelerating reform of Philadelphia's child welfare system through research, evaluation, program development, training, and technical assistance. BPI started to play a key role in identifying research-based best practices in child welfare and working with local stakeholders to implement those solutions in Philadelphia. The local consultants from BPI managed the project in all phases, from the initial needs assessment to program planning and development to implementation, data collection, and evaluation.

To assist with carrying out the DHS's strategic plan for reform, with its renewed focus on permanency, BPI was asked to examine potential service delivery options for children discharged from residential treatment facilities (RTF). After researching the literature,[1] BPI presented the National TFC Program Standards developed by the Foster Family Treatment Association (FFTA, 2002) to the leadership team of Philadelphia's child welfare and behavioral health systems (DHS/BHS), a forum for collaborative decision-making that has met at least twice a month since January 2000. In January 2002, this leadership team decided to adopt the FFTA standards, with some local modifications, for Philadelphia's contracted TFC providers.

The City of Philadelphia sought to define placement options for children and youth who were leaving residential placements and were either unable to return home or were placed in congregate care because general foster care providers did not feel equipped to handle these youth based on their age, placement history, and described and reported behaviors. The DHS was looking for a program service to fill the gap between congregate care and general foster care. The existing intensive foster care services (foster care mental health and mental health step-down) had proven unsuccessful in meeting the department's needs.

The FFTA describes TFC as:

> a distinct, powerful and unique model of care that provides children with a combination of the best elements of traditional foster care and residential treatment centers. In TFC, the positive aspects of the nurturing and therapeutic family environment are combined with active and structured treatment. Treatment Foster Care Programs provide, in a clinically effective

---

[1]Many articles that were reviewed are now described in *Treatment Foster Care: A Cost-Effective Strategy for Treatment of Children with Emotional, Behavioral or Medical Needs*, Brad Bryant, July 2004, FFTA.

and cost-effective way, individualized and intensive treatment for children and adolescents who would otherwise be placed in institutional settings.[2]

TFC in Philadelphia is designed as an intensive level of family-based foster care and as a community-based step-down from higher levels of care such as residential treatment facilities (RTF), community host homes, or other institutional placement. Children placed in TFC have identifiable needs that cannot be met in their own homes or in general foster care but are not severe enough to warrant placement in a residential setting.

Initial Stages in the Reform Process

To reconfigure the existing levels of care, the DHS asked the BPI to develop and manage a request for qualifications (RFQ) process for the existing mental health foster care providers. All applicants went through a careful selection process, with a review team that consisted of a diverse group of professionals.

The DHS had to assure prospective TFC providers that under the new requirements, the DHS would refer only children and youth who required this level of care. The DHS decided to strengthen its assessment capability by adopting a new decision support tool, the Child and Adolescent Needs and Strengths (CANS). In addition, the DHS developed a new TFC rate structure to meet the advanced requirements of the new TFC program. In the TFC program manual, which was developed and distributed at the time of implementation, the national FFTA program standards were adapted to the local needs, the strengths of providers, and the community. The new standards also included the DHS mandate that providers implement the use of an approved behavior management model in which both TFC agency staff and TFC parents would be trained. It was the first time in the DHS's history that such a requirement was included in the program standards.

In the first year, the selection process determined which existing mental health foster care providers appeared capable of redesigning their programs to meet the new standards. An enormous amount of work was done with both DHS staff and contracted providers. Implementing the redesigned program went hand-in-hand with training for TFC providers and DHS staff on the philosophy, goals, and expected outcomes of a revised TFC model, a behavior management model (ABC model of behavior management[3]), and a parent training curriculum. In addition, a TFC steering committee was formed led by BPI staff that included DHS, the behavioral health system, and TFC provider representatives.

Within the DHS, a program analyst was appointed to specialize in TFC and its operations citywide. Weekly phone conferences were held with TFC program directors and regular e-mail communication was established. Technical assistance site visits were held whenever indicated or requested by the providers, and internal meetings were held with the DHS's central referral unit to troubleshoot and coordinate the referral process.

A monthly administrative data report (MDR) was implemented to gather data to analyze TFC performance outcomes on both a system level and individual agency level, and to help TFC providers with self-monitoring. The MDR requires that providers collect and report various administrative data (e.g., census, entries, exits,

---

[2]This definition was approved by the Foster Family-based Treatment Association's Board of Directors in 2001 and is derived from the work of Gerald Bereika, Ph.D.

[3]The ABC Model curriculum, developed by People Places, Inc., provides behavior analysis and in-home intervention planning for staff and foster/adoptive parents.

permanencies). BPI developed a database with mechanisms in place to analyze the data regularly and to share the outcomes with the DHS leadership and the providers. In addition to the quantitative analysis of self-reported provider data, BPI and DHS periodically analyze and then compare the MDR data with DHS administrative data. BPI also conducts various qualitative evaluations such as foster parent surveys and provider training surveys.

The involvement of several key stakeholders and system partners was required to make this reform initiative efficient and successful. Stakeholders include local child welfare system partners, the behavioral health system, contracted providers, university partners (Dr. John Lyons of Northwestern University), and nationally recognized experts on TFC in the research and practice field.

Four years into this effort, with management of TFC and CANS operations resting with the DHS, discussions and planning meetings are ongoing at the DHS with BPI involvement. The TFC steering committee meeting is held with provider representatives and behavioral health system representatives at least every two months. Meetings with all contracted TFC providers take place each quarter.

Anticipated Goals and Outcomes

The primary goal of reforming TFC has always been to ensure that children and youth with significant behavioral and mental health needs are placed at the least restrictive level of care by providing them an intensive, family-based placement option. By redesigning the system to create a more consistent and rational program model that could be evaluated and monitored, and by collaborating with various partners in a citywide effort to increase permanency and step-down for children and youth, Philadelphia has succeeded in providing TFC as a viable option for its high-end children and youth.

Stepping children and youth down to TFC from higher levels of care and eventually bringing them back to Philadelphia from out-of-state placements into local TFC placements was another DHS goal. A step-down process was developed and implemented over the course of a year. The CANS has been instrumental in identifying when children need placement in TFC, in guiding the development of goals for the child and family, and in determining who is ready to be stepped down to a lower level of care. As part of the step-down process, it was necessary to include incentives for TFC parents to opt for permanency. That is, TFC parents worried that agency and system supports for children would not continue to the same degree after an adoption. Older children sometimes did not want to be adopted, and thereby lose contact with birth families. While a substantial increase in permanency and step-downs was achieved, this also led to providers' concerns about the increased need for parent recruitment, as there were many children who achieved permanency with their current TFC parent.

IMPLEMENTATION

Introduction of the CANS in Philadelphia

In the spring of 2002, the DHS began conducting research with BPI on assessment tools used by child welfare systems that support the decision-making of out-of-home placements. This research revealed several advantages of the CANS over other assessment tools. The CANS includes a broader conceptualization of child capacities than other instruments; for example, it includes an assessment of strengths such as talents/interests and spiritual/religious involvement. Particularly notable is its effectiveness as an inter-agency communication tool—CANS information can be used as a common language for all agencies dealing with children and adolescents. The CANS is also versatile. It can be administered *prospectively*, as a tool for decision support, or *retrospectively*, to review or design service systems. The CANS can also be modified for use in different settings without jeopardizing its validity and reliability.

For Philadelphia, the CANS represented an opportunity to establish a common assessment framework with inter-agency involvement for children and adolescents in the child welfare system. Implementation of CANS assessments by the DHS was intended to support the development and design of comprehensive services for children, adolescents, and their families.

Several key features of the CANS tool were particularly salient to the DHS:

- The CANS takes the subjectivity out of child welfare assessments and placement decisions. The CANS-CW can be used to ensure that children are placed into the appropriate level of care (general foster care, TFC, congregate care, etc.).

- The CANS allows the system to collect and manage data in order to advance system reform.

- The CANS assesses strengths (e.g., talents and interests, community involvement).

- The CANS can be used as common language for the public and private child welfare systems, the behavioral health system, the court system, and community advocates.

- The CANS is a means of integrating all known and available information about the child (including information from other assessment and evaluation instruments, if available), and putting it all in one place. The CANS does not replace clinical evaluations, but it does help put clinical results in a language that multiple systems (medical, psychological, child welfare, behavioral health, courts) can understand.

- The CANS can be easily modified for local use without jeopardizing its reliability or validity. In Philadelphia, for example, some items were added about school achievement and school attendance, and "fire-setting" was added to the section on risk behaviors.

Conceptualization

In the summer of 2002, the DHS used the CANS in a pilot project to assess selected groups of children and adolescents placed in various foster care settings. Researchers reviewed a few hundred DHS case files using the CANS and looking at two points in time: (1) when the child entered the TFC program and (2) the child's status at the time of the case file review. As a result of the study's findings, and to plan for the use of the CANS in Philadelphia, the DHS decided to move forward with contracting with an external, community-based agency to coordinate a CANS assessment unit. The primary role of the contracted agency was to administer the CANS in the community.

Collaboration

A variety of partners, internal and external, collaborated to develop the localized version of the CANS-CW instrument: the DHS and local behavioral health care system, the Office of Behavioral Health and Mental Retardation Services, consultants from the PMHCC BPI, and John Lyons, Ph.D. Several inter-agency meetings were held over the course of a few months in which management and clinical staff reviewed the standard child welfare version of the CANS supplied by the Buddin Praed Foundation (2002). The outcome of the discussions was the localization of the tool to reflect the issues specific to children living in an urban setting.

Setting the Threshold for TFC

In Philadelphia, there are several levels of out-of-home placement: general foster care, TFC, congregate care (group home or institution), and supervised independent living. To support rational level of care decision-making, specifically for TFC, the inter-agency management group developed a set of thresholds to determine which children were appropriate for TFC. Several factors contributed to the development of these thresholds that distinguish whether or not a child would benefit from general or treatment foster care.

First, the reform and standardization of TFC led to a well-defined scope of services for children entering this level. Second, Philadelphia recently implemented a performance-based contracting model for general foster (and kinship) care with defined parameters for who was eligible. Third, there were several defining factors, generally accepted by the DHS, that distinguished the children most likely to be placed in a residential setting (group home and institution), such as children with a high risk of running away and/or children needing an on-grounds school. DHS staff making placement referrals generally considered these factors. Thus the first set of thresholds were developed in Philadelphia in the spring of 2003, to distinguish between general and treatment foster care. Later threshold development included a set of thresholds to distinguish between TFC and residential care (group home or institution).

Identifying the Primary CANS Partner

In the fall of 2002, the DHS released a Request for Qualifications (RFQ) to solicit proposals from community-based organizations interested in contracting with the DHS for the administration of all child welfare CANS. The purpose of the RFQ was to give organizations the opportunity to demonstrate their interest and capacity to enter into a contract with the DHS to administer the CANS to children and youth in the child welfare system. It was important that the external provider agency have expertise in behavioral health services to administer the CANS.

The DHS contracted with Philadelphia Health Management Corporation (PHMC) to staff the CANS administration team (CANS unit). The CANS unit is composed of master's level professionals with child welfare and/or behavioral health backgrounds. It is supervised by a master's level professional with an extensive background in education and family therapy as well as supervision and program management.

A new DHS staff position, the CANS coordinator, was created to oversee and manage all activities related to the CANS, both internally at the DHS and externally with the contracted partner. The CANS coordinator receives all requests to assess a child with the CANS to determine the appropriate level of residential care. The CANS coordinator refers all requests to the PHMC CANS unit, which then administers the CANS.

Staffing and Training

The original RFQ specified that the contracted provider hire CANS unit staff with specific skills and experience. The rationale for requiring advanced degrees, in addition to at least three years of mental health or child welfare experience, was that professionally trained staff would better comprehend, interpret, and synthesize information from psychiatric and psychological evaluations. A limited number of children in the TFC system have current evaluations (i.e., conducted within the past sixty days). Staff proficient in DSM-IV (1994) diagnostic criteria can review a child's current behaviors described in the case file by the TFC parent or worker in relation to the latest diagnoses and determine (specific to CANS scoring purposes) whether the behaviors continue at the diagnostic level (the difference between the actionable and non-actionable CANS scores).

The CANS team (both the contracted CANS unit and internal DHS staff) was trained by Dr. John Lyons on both the history and administration of the CANS. In addition to the CANS training, the CANS specialists learned the DHS acronyms, procedures, and policies so they could extract as much information as possible from the files. They were also provided with an overview of the placement process at the DHS by the DHS CANS coordinator.

Initial Implementation

The planning team prepared and distributed information to DHS staff about the impending changes to the TFC admission process in the weeks prior to launch. During this time, the CANS coordinator presented the new process to meetings of administrators, supervisors, and executives to ensure that management staff understood and could instruct line staff on the process.

Recognizing the inevitable response by operations staff to another layer of process to obtain a TFC placement, it was crucial to plan for an effortless move into the CANS phase of the central referral unit's (CRU) overall procedure and a smooth, timely transition back to the CRU for completion of the placement process. To that end, the CANS referral form was limited to only the most essential information: the child's basic identifying information and current location (this enabled the CANS unit to set priority for turnaround time).

Initially, DHS staff was reluctant to adapt to the new placement decision-making process. The decision to place a child in TFC had always been made solely by a DHS worker, and the new process shifted one of the key decision-making elements to a centralized unit of operation with a standardized tool.

A primary responsibility of the DHS CANS unit in the referral process in Philadelphia involves the unit's management of DHS case files. The PHMC CANS specialist accesses case material through them. The meticulous management of the DHS files and the ease of referral eventually proved to be the most effective means of creating acceptance for the CANS process by operations staff. At this writing, four years after implementation, the CANS unit has handled more than 9,000 files without misplacing any.

CANS Summary Report for Case Planning

With the CANS instrument offering a wealth of information in snapshot form, it seemed important to format the report of CANS scores in a way that would be useful for case planning. The suggested CANS reporting format is a score sheet limited to item numbers and numerical scores. The lack of text and justification for how a score

Table 6.1
"Anger Control" Sample Summary Report

Item: 20
Item Description: Anger Control
Score: 2
Justification: Youth has angry outbursts, and her anger escalates quickly; periodic low frustration tolerance. She has tantrums (stomps, yells, and slams doors once monthly) over not getting her way at home. She has angry affect and gives intimidating looks to others. Others are aware of her anger potential. Foster brother, who is FP's biological son, does not trust this youth in his home due to her outbursts. Youth is verbally abusive to others. Little to no physical altercations are present.
Source of Information: Provider Intake evaluation 10/04; Case note 12/13/04; CANS 12/04-provider worker notes 11/29/04; Int. with provider caseworker, 2/15/05

was chosen, while allowing the instrument to be scored quickly, did not seem to capitalize on the opportunity to communicate with and educate end users on the CANS's value in individualized planning. A new report format was designed to maximize the usefulness of the CANS information.

The CANS summary report was formatted into the database so that as information and scores for each item are collected in the appropriate fields, the database will automatically generate a document that is readable and easy to understand. The summary report lists each item, and the reviewer makes notes on specific information that leads to an actionable versus a non-actionable score and includes notes on the source of the information that provided the basis for that score. An example of one item on the summary report is shown in Table 6.1.

For this sample item—anger control—the information included in the justification supports the score chosen. The source information identifies the documents reviewed and the party interviewed to obtain the information used to score. The format of the CANS summary report has been well received, particularly by contracted provider staff, who routinely refer to it to inform their individual service plan (ISP) reviews.

Internal Logistics

With the new TFC program in place and a contracted provider selected to administer the CANS, the DHS began the implementation process in earnest to determine eligibility for TFC placement. The DHS initially planned for one staff position solely dedicated to managing the CANS initiative and anticipated 1,100 CANS referrals during the first year of implementation. The plan included the eventual development of a CANS data system to track and manage the referral process between the DHS and PHMC.

Several steps occur before a CANS is administered. The DHS worker prepares a placement referral form and meets with a screening worker, who reviews the case file and the referral form and makes an initial level of care recommendation. If the recommended level of care is higher than general foster care, the referral is directed to the CANS unit for a review. The CANS review is completed, thresholds are applied, and the CANS summary report is distributed to appropriate parties.

Referrals for entry into TFC also come from contracted foster care agencies who believe that a child requires more intensive services (step-ups) than are available at the lower level of care and from contracted providers of higher levels of care (RTFs, hospital inpatient units, group homes, and institutions) who make referrals for TFC as a step-down resource.

The CANS process is also designed to evaluate the continued appropriateness for a child to remain at the TFC level of care. A CANS review is completed on every child in TFC twice each year, synchronized with the DHS accept-for-service date, at which time the family service plan (FSP) and the child's individual service plan (ISP) are reviewed and revised. This review differs from the entry evaluation because the CANS specialist travels to the TFC provider agency to read the case file. The provider should be available to discuss the child's current functioning and behaviors. The CANS reviews are done on a schedule that allows the results to be available to the DHS worker for service planning purposes.

Within the first month of operation, it became clear that additional internal DHS capacity was needed. The average number of referrals quickly reached eight to ten per day. The time required to retrieve and return the DHS files to operations staff proved to be a barrier to timely processing of the referral process to the PHMC. Contracted provider agencies delivering services at all levels within the system called with questions. The CANS coordinator requested an additional position to assist with file management and the referral process in general. A data services support clerk position was approved and filled by the end of the second month of implementation. Adding this position was critical to the success of the project.

Concurrent with implementing the process, the planning team (DHS, PHMC, and BPI) continued to develop a data system to support the project. The DHS expanded the contract with PHMC to include purchase of MIS services to support CANS database development.

Database Development and Data Collection Strategies

The placement of children and youth could not be delayed, so timely turnaround of the CANS process was required. Rather than rely on paper referrals and reports, the DHS decided to create a database to manage referrals, collect data, and generate reports. Its original intention was to develop an in-house data system. Planning of the database began in earnest three months before implementation, but it became apparent that the DHS information systems team did not have the capacity to operate the database in the interim. The PHMC had previously used an ACCESS database to manage referrals for various DHS programs. With that general model as a starting point, the PHMC systems staff designed the CANS database.

The collaboration of program staff with systems staff resulted in a design that allowed for immediate access by the PHMC CANS team to referral information. Remote access via an Internet website allowed the DHS staff to input referral data, track the status of referrals, electronically approve completed CANS, view CANS scores for any referral, and communicate in real time with PHMC staff.

The PHMC uses the database to assign individual referrals to specific staff who can also access the database from remote locations and to create invoices, track staff time logs, and generate management reports.

To minimize data entry errors, the PHMC and DHS arranged a daily data transfer of DHS administrative data, demographic, case management (placement goal, length of stay in placement, etc.), and case contact information for every child referred. The transfer includes the universe of children in placement through the DHS. There are occasions when a referred child's data are not included in the data transfer, such as when a child new to the DHS has not been entered into the administrative database. In that situation, the referral information is added to the system and is automatically updated by the data transfer when the child is entered into the DHS system.

The CANS was programmed into the database, along with TFC threshold algorithms. The reviewers enter each score into the database, along with justifications and source information for each score. They are able to tag items to appear in the final summary report format (see Table 6.1) that is later distributed to DHS case workers, supervisors, and TFC provider staff to guide case planning.

A child's individual scores are collected for multiple CANS administrations. The resulting data can be sorted by child for individual outcomes, by TFC agency for TFC provider outcomes, and in the aggregate for program/system outcomes. Data analysis by other external partners is possible through export of data sets via remote desktop access.

The CANS database is expandable, to include multiple versions of the CANS (e.g., child welfare, juvenile justice), along with multiple, complex algorithms for decision making within each unique application. Currently, the PHMC-managed CANS database includes two separate CANS data systems: the child welfare system (originally the TFC program) and the juvenile justice application. Plans to expand the database to accommodate the family assessment and services tool application are in the works.

CHALLENGES TO IMPLEMENTATION

First Six Months

Large bureaucratic agencies inherently resist change. When the proposed change effectively reduces one's discretionary decision-making, the resistance increases dramatically. Although we anticipated some push back, the level of resistance initially demonstrated from multiple quarters (TFC providers, DHS operations staff, child advocate attorneys, judges) was considerably more intense than we expected.

Later Implementation

Four years after implementation, the CANS process has been accepted for the most part by DHS providers and by DHS operations staff. Some Family Court judges value the CANS, some are indifferent, and some disregard the CANS as useful. The most longstanding and forceful opposition remains the child advocate attorneys. Despite targeted trainings and conferences to explain CANS use and methodology, and the impact that CANS makes on informing individualized service planning, the child advocate attorneys refuse to accept the CANS's value and actively oppose its use in case planning and level-of-care decision making in Philadelphia.

Table 6.2 presents some of the operational and systemic challenges to implementation, along with the solutions developed and lessons learned from each obstacle.

In addition, we had to deal with larger system challenges related to implementation, which are detailed in the sections below.

Table 6.2
Challenges and Solutions to Initial Implementation

Internal Capacity		
Challenges:	*Solution/Effort:*	*Recommendations:*
• Managing the retrieval/return of DHS files was complicated. • No backup for CANS coordinator (vacation, sick leave, etc.).	• Addition of data services support clerk in the second year. • No resolution of this until second year of operation.	• Assess system regarding the availability, cost, and willingness to add staff as needed to support project. • Consider CANS team staff's federal/state/local reimbursement rate. • Assess consequences of understaffing on flow of work.
Acceptance by Staff		
Challenges:	*Solution/Effort:*	*Recommendations:*
• Despite pre-implementation information, operations staff demonstrated high level of resistance. • Internal system partners frequently bypassed new procedure.	• Recognized that an additional layer of process needed to place a child would create resistance. • Repeated reinforcement of the need to follow procedures; scheduled monthly meetings with staff to answer questions related to CANS process. • Frequent check-ins with PHMC staff.	• Anticipate a high level of resistance to any change in procedure. • Recognize that use of an instrument will be viewed as "impersonal" by operations staff. • Recognize that any perceived (or real) loss of autonomy in case management will create dissension.
Bypassing the System		
Challenges:	*Solution/Effort:*	*Recommendations:*
• Placement of child into TFC without a CANS to evaluate TFC eligibility. • Placement of child into TFC on "emergency basis" without a CANS, when child did not meet threshold and had to be stepped down when placement provider had accepted child at the TFC level. • Placement of child into a higher level of care despite CANS recommendation for TFC level. • Family Court judges who ordered placement of a child into TFC with untrained kin and/or without a CANS determination for TFC.	• Ongoing meetings with CRU administration; tracking entries into TFC through the DHS's internal data system, FACTS [Family & Children Tracking System]; feedback to CRU administration. • Addressed intervention through TFC providers; they cannot accept an emergency until a referral for a CANS has been made and verified. • Production of regular reports identifying children placed in a level of care higher that the CANS recommendation. • Ongoing education of family court judges, including a special training by Dr. Lyons; court improvement initiative; training for DHS court representatives; DHS attorneys; child advocate attorneys; continues to be an issue.	• When implementing the use of CANS, try to anticipate system partners or internal staff who may feel threatened/challenged by the new process. • Identify places where the new process can break down. • Develop the capacity to track and monitor the universal application of the process.

(Continued)

Table 6.2 (Continued)

HIPPA		
Challenges:	**Solution/Effort:**	**Recommendations:**
• Unanticipated challenge regarding sharing of confidential information (particularly related to inpatient hospitalization) with CANS reviewers. • Regulations related to electronic transfer of confidential information via email/website.	• The DHS consulted with its legal team to understand privacy requirements related to CANS process. • Legal consultants specializing in HIPAA law drafted a letter to private agency providers and hospitals naming PHMC as a legal agent of the DHS. • CANS database created to comply with HIPAA law's security levels.	• Anticipate implications of federal, state, or local restrictions on sharing client information.
Quality Assurance		
Challenges:	**Solution/Effort:**	**Recommendations:**
• Variation in quality and quantity of information provided by CANS reviewers. • Despite qualifying reliabilities, some disparity among reviewers in scoring. • Tendency for some reviewers to use CANS to advocate for what they perceived was the right outcome.	• Each CANS summary report was read by the CANS coordinator and feedback was given to the PHMC supervisor to streamline or expand justifications where needed. • Regular recertification was scheduled during the first year of operations (quarterly); reviewers who could not maintain acceptable level of reliability were coached or eventually terminated; recertification now occurs every six months. • Regular team meetings with DHS CANS coordinator and PHMC team to underscore need for objectivity.	• Know the system's primary and other goals for implementation. • The instrument is only effective when the scorers maintain reliability. • Recognize that depending on the reviewer, certain items may appear on the instrument (e.g., a reviewer with a background in education may be more sensitive to items related to that area); be alert for evidence in work product.
Threshold Adjustment		
Challenges:	**Solution/Effort:**	**Recommendations:**
• Thresholds for TFC eligibility were based on an extensive record review; however, it became apparent that the thresholds were too low. • Occasionally a youth did not meet the threshold but presented a clear need for the higher level of care.	• By reviewing each completed CANS summary, the CANS coordinator identified one item (school achievement) as qualifying a youth who would not otherwise meet threshold; data analysis verified this finding; thresholds revised. • By reviewing each completed CANS summary, the CANS coordinator identified a small percentage of youth who did not technically meet the threshold but who had an overall presentation that required an override. Overrides of the CANS thresholds are rare.	• Maintain a clear picture of the system goal when implementing the CANS instrument for decision support. • Build capacity for data analysis to determine how youth are qualifying for specific levels of care and to understand the profiles of meeting/not meeting the threshold. • Program features should support the needs identified for a specific level of care population.

The Step-Down Process

Introducing change into an existing system may have several effects. Before the CANS initiative was implemented, youth placed in TFC rarely stepped down to lower levels of care; they either aged out of the system at that level or stepped up to a higher level. The reason for this upward drift was that levels of care were largely determined by the contracted providers who would look at a youth's behaviors and history and agree to place a child conditionally: "we have a home, but we can only serve this child at the TFC level." If foster parents had concerns about a child's behavior and/or challenged the appropriateness of a placement, then the DHS staff would raise the level of care to TFC to avoid having to move the child. At the higher level of care (with the higher per diem for the foster parent and the agency), there was no review of the placement decision or of whether the child's needs continue to justify TFC services. With the CANS implementation, TFC-level decisions are based solely on a youth's needs, not on the fiscal needs of the placing agency or the foster parent.

The DHS was faced with a conundrum of how to reduce the placement per diem rate when a child's level of need decreased, allowing for step-down from TFC to the regular foster care level. The DHS developed a step-down process designed to reverse upward drift of children in the system and increase permanency. At the six-month CANS review, where a child no longer meets the threshold for TFC, the CANS coordinator notifies the TFC agency. At that point, the administrative rate to the agency decreases, as the agency is no longer under contract to provide the TFC level of service to the child. The per diem to the TFC parent, however, remains in effect for thirty days to allow the parent time to consider her willingness to become a permanency resource for the child. Permanency options include reunification, adoption, or permanent legal custodianship. At the end of the thirty-day period, if the TFC parent opts to become a permanency resource, the TFC per diem rate to the TFC parent continues for an additional six months to allow completion of the permanency plan (finalizing a pending adoption or completing the PLC process).

In Pennsylvania, the adoption subsidy for foster parents is determined by the rate of foster care reimbursement for the thirty-day period immediately preceding the finalization. Therefore, if a TFC parent moves forward with an adoption within seven months of a step-down, the adoption subsidy would be set at the TFC rate even though the child no longer meets the threshold for TFC. If the TFC parent chooses not to proceed with permanency, the child is either moved to another TFC home in which the parent is open to permanency or stepped down to a general foster care home. The TFC parent may also opt to remain the caregiver at the lower per diem for regular foster care.

Throughout the first year of implementation, this policy was strongly contested by TFC agencies on behalf of their foster parents. It was interpreted as punishment for doing a good job. The DHS, intending the policy to be a bonus for a job well done and to encourage permanency, considered other options, but the step-down process remains in effect at this writing. Despite the objections from providers and caregivers, there have been no instances of TFC parents requesting a child be moved on the basis of a lowered per diem rate.

The Step-Up Process

Within days of the CANS project implementation, a higher than expected number of referrals arrived from agencies that provided both general foster care and TFC for youth to step-up to TFC. The CANS coordinator notified DHS executive staff of this trend and the DHS commissioner implemented a step-up policy. Agencies making referrals for a step-up from general foster care to a higher level of care were required to demonstrate that every effort had been made to maintain the youth at the lower level of care. The CANS coordinator was responsible for determining whether the agency had exhausted other means of meeting a child's needs before accepting a step-up referral. With the new policy in place, the step-up requests from foster care agencies decreased by approximately 70 percent, and in the fall of 2005 averaged two per month. By spring 2007, the average was three and one-half per month.

The agencies were required to document the following:

- Increased challenging behaviors within the sixty-day period preceding the request

- Current evaluation (psychiatric, psychological, bio-psycho-social assessment)

- Detailed documentation of services sought to meet the child's increased needs

- Detailed documentation of services sought by the general foster care provider but not accessed, and reason (e.g., waiting list)

- Explanation of the use of "stabilization funds" (A $16 per day flexible funding option available to agencies with PBC contracts for foster care, this funding is designed to support maintaining a child at the lower level of care typically used by agencies for additional home visits by staff.)

Kinship Care

The DHS promotes the value that children should be placed with kin whenever possible. Before the CANS, DHS-contracted providers who delivered case management services to kinship foster families had a long-standing difficulty of a higher rate of noncompliance with foster care training requirements, visitation by case management staff, and home safety standards among kinship foster families than among non-kin caregivers. With the implementation of the new TFC program standards and the use of the CANS tool, TFC agencies and the DHS found a higher level of liability related to the Child and Family Services Review (CFSR) outcomes. If the CANS finds that a child needs TFC and the CANS summary report in the child's file indicated so, then the DHS and the contracted provider are responsible to provide that level of service (as defined by the DHS TFC Program Standards) (DHS, 2002). TFC caregivers receive substantially more training than general foster caregivers receive, and the TFC parents were required to maintain daily behavior logs as part of the ABC Model of Behavior Management system (1986).

Six-month review CANS summary reports in fact revealed a higher level of noncompliance with the TFC program standards among kinship TFC caregivers than among non-kin. The tension between meeting a child's needs as identified in the CANS review versus the preference for relative care poses a system challenge. One possible solution that has been proposed but not yet implemented is for the DHS to place the TFC-eligible child who is about to be discharged from inpatient hospitalization with a certified, non-kin TFC parent. Potential kin caregivers will be asked to begin the TFC certification process while maintaining a close relationship with the child and non-kin caregiver. Once the relative is fully certified, a move to the kinship home may occur.

EVALUATION AND OUTCOMES

The CANS is used to track program outcomes in the Philadelphia TFC program. On the *individual level*, the CANS is used to track a child's ongoing behavioral health needs and determine whether TFC is still the appropriate level of care, or whether the child can be stepped down to general foster care or achieve permanency (adoption, reunification, permanency legal custodianship).

On the *system level*, CANS data are used to analyze system performance in providing services that are timely and appropriate and that facilitate permanency whenever possible. The DHS works with Northwestern University to track the rates of entry into TFC, discharge from TFC, and moves to permanency. The DHS utilizes the CANS as one of several criteria in monitoring TFC programs annually.

Lessons Learned

Our experience to date has been positive. The lessons learned from the beginning of the implementation process to the present have provided guidance and opened a new realm of understanding in the DHS's care and placement of children and youth.

CANS Is an Effective Communication Tool on Multiple Levels. On the individual child level, the CANS is a user-friendly, quantifiable system to identify child and adolescent needs and strengths. By collecting multiple CANS reviews for a child over time, individual child outcomes can be measured, and the information provided in the CANS can inform highly individualized case planning.

CANS data also allow the DHS to track TFC provider agency outcomes. By sorting scores by agency the DHS has learned, for example, that one particular TFC provider was more successful at reducing needs in school attendance than any other agency. By knowing the methods this provider employs to encourage school attendance, the methods can be adopted elsewhere. On a system-wide level, aggregate CANS data reveal program deficits and strengths. For example, the TFC program features were designed to address externalized behaviors. Review of the CANS data shows that 62 percent of the children in the TFC level of care score at an actionable level on adjustment to trauma or attachment. These data motivated the DHS to explore in partnership with the Behavioral Health System in Philadelphia new therapeutic interventions to address trauma and attachment vulnerabilities in our child clients.

CANS Stops the Upward Drift Into Child Welfare. CANS is an effective tool to interrupt upward drift of children in the child welfare system. With one of the nation's highest percentages of youth placed in congregate care, Philadelphia has had a long tradition of moving youth to higher, more restrictive levels of care and leaving them at those levels until they aged out of the system. Introduction of the CANS to support placement decisions based on a youth's individual needs and strengths, rather than system needs, immediately resulted in more youths' being referred to lower levels of care. Age was no longer the primary factor considered when a youth required placement. By closely monitoring the actual placements made after a CANS recommendation was available, and by requiring an explanation for not following the CANS recommendation, bias in the system to place youth over age twelve in congregate care was revealed.

CANS Meets Specific Needs of Youth. CANS enables a system to design programming to meet specific needs of specific populations. The TFC application and, to a greater extent, the congregate care pilot study highlighted program deficits for specific populations. Youth in congregate care settings, typically teenagers, scored high needs for independent living items. Clearly, with a population that faces a looming need for self-sufficiency, the existing programming does not adequately address those needs. The data provided by the CANS reviews, when aggregated, allows a system to understand what is working and what is not. Contracts for service providers can pinpoint program requirements that address the most common areas of needs for a specific population. Ongoing CANS reviews allow the system to quantifiably gauge the success of program revisions.

CANS Facilitates Proper Placement. CANS enables placement planning to be based on a child's or youth's needs, not the system's needs. An historical tension existed between the private providers needing higher reimbursement for placement services and the DHS's need to place youth at the least restrictive setting. The DHS's need to place youth in a safe setting created a de facto provider-driven system. Providers often refused to place youth at lower levels of care due to "increased behaviors" in the children in need of placement. As a result, providers often felt compelled (due to liability and staffing needs) to place youth at higher levels to obtain higher reimbursements. The DHS, the consumer of placement services, responded by accepting the providers' assessment that youth behaviors required higher, more restrictive settings, contributing to the upward drift of the children served. Prior to the implementation of CANS, there was general consensus in Philadelphia that any youth over age thirteen could not be effectively managed in a family-based setting.

Use of the CANS has refocused the placement process on the needs and strengths of the specific child. By doing so, more acute tension within the system has emerged. The DHS, armed with data on child needs, is attempting to reverse the upward drift by requiring providers to attempt to meet child needs in a family-based setting, where permanency resources are more available. Thus, some behaviors once determined to require a higher level of care will no longer meet the higher level threshold.

CANS Allows for Independent Scorers. During the planning stage, TFC providers were concerned that the DHS would deny the higher level of care as a cost-saving measure. The behavioral health partner anticipated that the DHS would move too many children into TFC. In an effort to provide the most objective ratings of need for children and youth in DHS care, the decision was made to hire an external partner with no fiscal interest in the outcomes of CANS scores. The primary advantage is that an independent CANS scoring allows a fresh look at the child's current situation from an objective perspective. In addition, the privately contracted CANS team is able to develop expertise in CANS scoring because it does not have additional case management responsibilities.

A practical challenge has been achieving a balance between referrals made and staffing the PHMC. The original RFQ specified five full-time reviewers, with a supervisor and an administrative assistant. As demand grew (and, on occasion, ebbed, typically in late summer), the PHMC found it helpful to hire part-time CANS specialists when the number referrals was high. This has proved to be a successful adaptation to the original staffing plan.

For approximately six months, the DHS worked with TFC provider staff to have them conduct the six-month reviews of children in their TFC programs. The inherent conflict of interest in that plan resulted in inaccurate scoring and delays in CANS reviews. The loss of cost containment (in the form of delayed step-downs) exceeded the projected savings from reduced fee for service payments to PHMC. After a six-month trial, the DHS abandoned this effort.

CANS Helps Establish a Threshold Model for Congregate Care. In the spring of 2004, the DHS contracted with BPI to conduct a case record review of youth in congregate care (group homes and institutions) and supervised independent living (SIL) settings. Using the CANS tool, 159 cases were chosen for the review. The DHS's goal was to develop a better understanding of the needs and strengths of older youth and to establish a threshold model for the rational assignment of children to congregate and SIL levels of care. One key finding was that youth in institutions had higher levels of need than those in group homes. Based on the existing TFC threshold and CANS data on more than 1,000 children and youth collected by the DHS in fiscal year 2004, a congregate care threshold was developed. In addition, several recommendations were made that have already been implemented or soon will be.

The BPI's first recommendation was to implement a congregate care threshold for all new entries to support decisions about appropriate placement into congregate care settings. This means (1) the establishment of a rational pathway into congregate care based on a youth's characteristics and (2) the DHS's ability to ensure that efforts to place a youth into general or TFC are attempted first. In the spring of 2005, the DHS began administering CANS for all new entries.

Second, the researchers recommended that the DHS administer the CANS for all youth currently placed in congregate care to guide service planning, provide the DHS with additional information for thoughtful, system-wide program development and resource planning, and to support the DHS in reassessing the youth's continued eligibility for, and appropriateness of, a congregate care placement. As of fall 2005, the DHS was in the planning process.

The third recommendation was to institute a step-down process for youth currently placed in congregate care. About one-quarter of the youth currently in congregate care placement have very limited behavioral health needs based on the results of the congregate care review. These youth should be the priority of any step-down process. To implement a successful step-down process, the researchers recommended that the DHS create a team of step-down specialists to implement the step-down and permanency process. They also recommended the incorporation of six additional items into the CANS, specific to older youth, and use of the case record review findings for planning and program development efforts.

Following the congregate care pilot project, the DHS made plans to implement a CANS process for congregate care. While planning was underway, the Secretary of the Pennsylvania Department of Public Welfare issued a mandate, instructing local behavioral health entities to fund all mental health placements for youth in the child welfare system. The existing integration of the DHS with Behavioral Health Services-Community Behavioral Health (BHS-CBH) enabled this shift in funding to occur at an accelerated pace. Any youth who warranted a mental health level of care placement would, under the new protocol, be placed into a CBH-funded placement. The traditional residential treatment facility level was expanded to include two step-down levels requiring medical necessity, known as residential continuum of treatment services (RCTS). CBH would manage the movement of youth among the three mental health levels.

After careful consideration, the CANS-CW was accepted as the preliminary means by which a youth could be accepted into the RCTS levels of care. Upon admission to the CBH-funded level of care, the youth would receive a psychiatric evaluation. The DHS and CBH partnered to develop program expectations of providers delivering services to these youth so that mental health treatment (in addition to child welfare issues) was thoroughly addressed. Use of the CANS-CW in the RCTS process was implemented May 2005.

Threshold algorithms for additional levels of care were developed based on the congregate care pilot project, in consultation with CBH, around medical necessity criteria. After four months of operation, the threshold algorithms were adjusted slightly to divert some group home youth in general levels to TFC. The additional levels are as follows:

- DHS-funded placements: group home—general; institutional—general

- CBH-funded placements: group home—mental health; institution—mental health

In late 2005, the DHS began conducting CANS reviews for youth who have resided in a general-level placement group home for twelve months or longer, with six-month follow-up CANS reviews until the youth are eligible for step-down or reunification (patterned after the TFC model). Projections were that the group home, general-level population would shrink by up to one-third during the first year of implementation. After one year of administering the CANS reviews, we found that we could place 77 percent of these youth at lower levels of care while meeting their needs. Now that the CANS is administered before a group home placement, the rate of youth eligible for step-down from group home to lower levels after twelve months has dropped to 64 percent.

Additional System Benefits

Before the CANS implementation, the TFC population averaged 480 children and youth. As of October 2005, the average TFC population was 350. It became apparent after a year of implementation that children placed at the TFC level typically needed at least one year of placement at the higher level before their needs decreased enough to qualify for step-down. As a result, beginning with the second year of the CANS/TFC project, the first six-month CANS review after a child entered TFC was eliminated for most children. Exceptions are made for children who are placed into TFC by means other than the CANS scores (e.g., court order, or CRU override).

Of the 1,400 youth who have entered TFC since CANS was introduced, just eleven remain from the original existing TFC population. The DHS conducted a study of this small group of youth to create a profile of their needs. Clinical reviews by the DHS's behavioral health partner and careful study of multiple CANS scores for these children are expected to yield valuable information to guide DHS in developing appropriate resources for these children, who typically present chronic, severe developmental vulnerabilities.

References

ABC model of behavior management (1986). Staunton, VA: People Places, Inc.

Diagnostic and statistical manual of mental disorders (4th ed.) (DSM-IV) (1994). Washington, DC: American Psychiatric Association.

Philadelphia Department of Human Services (DHS) (2001). *Blueprint for reform: Roadmap for excellence*. Philadelphia: Author.

Philadelphia Department of Human Services (DHS) (2002). *Department of Human Services treatment foster care program standards*. Philadelphia: Author.

Foster Family Treatment Association (FFTA) (2002). *National TFC program standards*. Hackensack, NJ: Author.

Child and adolescent needs and strengths-Child welfare (CANS-CW), Philadelphia version. Copyright © 2002 Buddin Praed Foundation.

Chapter 7

Introducing Outcome Management Measures Where None Exist: The Lake County, Indiana, CANS Implementation Experience

by Thomas W. Pavkov, Ph.D. and Bruce Hillman, M.S.

BACKGROUND

Over each of the past ten years, the child welfare system in Lake County, Indiana has assumed responsibility for the care of between 1,500 and 2,000 "children in need of services," otherwise referenced as CHINS, in the State of Indiana. The second largest county in the state, Lake County is home to the three industrial cities of East Chicago, Hammond, and Gary. With an economy that largely depended on an aging steel manufacturing infrastructure, the poverty rate for children between infancy and age seventeen was estimated in 2005 at 26.4 percent by the United States Census Bureau (2005). The high rates of child poverty that characterize Lake County contribute significantly to the challenges of serving children and families involved in the child welfare system.

Before 2006, the child welfare system was funded through local county tax dollars and administered by employees of the State of Indiana's Family and Social Services Administration, Division of Family and Children—now reorganized as the Indiana Department of Child Services (DCS). In a county with slightly less than 500,000 people, over $60 million of county child and family fund tax dollars were spent to provide services to children and families. The majority of resources were directed toward the care of between 400 to 500 children in residential placement centers. The same funding stream was combined with federal funds to support services such as therapeutic foster care, in-home services, adoption services, and other types of service.

The Lake County Superior Court, Juvenile Division is an integral driving force behind all placement decisions for children and families in the county. With the Honorable Judge Mary Beth Bonaventura and three magistrates presiding, the court maintains a two-day per week schedule of case review. While placement decisions for high-need children are routinely staffed by family case managers (FCMs) from the county DCS office, all final decisions regarding placement are adjudicated by the juvenile court. The juvenile court must rely on information that FCMs, service provider representatives, and court appointed special advocates present to the court.

Before the Child and Adolescent Needs and Strengths (CANS) assessment process was implemented, neither the child welfare nor the juvenile justice department had used Total Clinical Outcome Management (TCOM) methodologies, nor did the county use a single point of access (SPOA) or a single process of access for purposes of assessing the mental health needs of children entering the child welfare system. The county had no uniform screening/assessment process, no decision support methodology, and no mechanism to monitor the outcome of treatment. The screening and assessment process was largely the responsibility of the FCM, who had no specified screening process or tool for gathering information on the child and family. Most FCMs had limited clinical training and made their treatment decisions on the basis of personal preference or experience. FCMs provided the court with supporting information and could request a psychological evaluation to advise their decisions.

For a child in a highly restrictive placement who was being transitioned to a less restrictive placement (e.g., from a psychiatric hospitalization to residential care), the FCM would staff the case with a residential placement committee. The committee, comprised of supervisors and division managers, gave the FCM treatment recommendations before the case was presented in juvenile court. A child who had had inpatient psychiatric treatment would usually have his or her case presented to such a committee, which provided residential treatment options. Children who did not respond to community-based interventions were also presented for consideration before the residential placement committee. Before the CANS assessment was implemented, the court was not provided with a uniform template of information because there was no standardized assessment process to generate it.

RESIDENTIAL TREATMENT CENTER EVALUATION PROJECT

Process Evaluation

In the fall of 2001, the Lake County Office of Children and Families, under the leadership of Director Bruce Hillman, committed adequate resources to invest in a formative evaluation process designed to assess the services delivered to seriously emotionally disturbed children being treated in residential treatment settings in Lake County and beyond. The decision to evaluate these processes emerged as a function of the high costs (over $40 million annually) associated with residential treatment, anecdotal evidence related to the poor care children receive in these settings, and the inability of the county child welfare office to monitor the quality of services in congregate settings. Named the Residential Treatment Center Evaluation Project, the evaluation process by faculty from both Purdue University Calumet and Indiana University Northwest used a randomized case study approach as the primary means of data collection (Pavkov & Hug, 2006). This case study approach was designed to examine all aspects of the treatment process, beginning with the initial assessment of children referred to congregate care settings through the treatment and aftercare processes.

From the quality assurance data generated by the evaluation project emerged the county's realization that it needed a uniform screening and assessment process. Based on the evaluators' review of over 150 cases in 2001 and 2003, it became apparent that:

- Placement recommendations were not being made on the basis of a systematic and unbiased decision support mechanism;

- Based on the characteristics of each case, many placement recommendations were inappropriate;

- Poor placement decisions were resulting in increased costs for county taxpayers; and

- The quality of psychological assessments used by the FCMs was both questionable and of limited utility.

Decision to Adopt the CANS Assessment Tool

In April 2003, the evaluation project staff facilitated a series of work-group sessions to focus on the assessment issue. Much of the information presented at the sessions came from presentations given at the 2003 Children's Mental Health Research Conference in Tampa, Florida, which focused on the child welfare population. Through the sessions, the Lake County Department of Child and Family Services and the Lake County juvenile court probation staff became familiar with the research related to the epidemiology of mental health need among children in foster care (Burns et al., 2004) and best practices related to screening and assessment (Leslie et al., 2003), and they gained a familiarity with the tools used to assess children in foster care.

The work-group reviewed a number of specific assessment tools, including:

- The Mental Health Screening Tool (MHST) (California Institute for Mental Health, 2002);

- The Child and Adolescent Functioning Assessment Scale (CAFAS) (Hodges, 1994);

- The Child Behavior Check List (CBCL) (Achenbach, 1991);

- The Massachusetts Youth Screening Instrument-2 (MAYSI-2) (Grisso & Barnum, 2003);

- The Child and Adolescent Level of Care Utilization System (CALOCUS), now renamed the Child and Adolescent Service Intensity Instrument (CASII) (American Academy of Child and Adolescent Psychiatry, 1998); and

- The CANS assessment tool (Lyons et al., 1999).

The work-group narrowed its preferences to the CALOCUS and the CANS. Work-group members heard presentations by the authors of both instruments. The process of evaluation ended in July 2003 with the work-group recommending the use of the CANS as the primary assessment tool to be used in Lake County.

The decision to adopt the CANS as the assessment tool was based on the following criteria:

- The CANS incorporates the strengths of the traditional psychometric approach, the clinimetric approach (as used in the field of medicine), and communication theory.

- The CANS provides a method of decision support that the placement committees need to improve their efficiency and quality of decision.

- The CANS assessment provides a comprehensive assessment of family strengths and needs that will inform the planning of services for families involved with the Indiana DCS.

- The CANS tool easily maps to both child welfare case plans and provider treatment plans.

- The CANS assessment provides the information needed to monitor both the progress of children receiving services and the overall effectiveness of those services.

- The CANS tool compliments the DCS's approach to quality assurance and provides a capacity to efficiently audit the treatment experiences of children and families receiving services.

- The CANS tool provides the information needed to complete a baseline study of children and families involved with the DCS, to better understand the service population's needs relative to the capacity of the present system-of-care.

The decision to commence with CANS implementation was made for a variety of reasons. First, a plethora of evaluation data suggested the need for a comprehensive assessment strategy to support child welfare placements. Second, the county director recognized the need for a uniform assessment process and was willing to commit resources to the project. Third, the juvenile court agreed that a common assessment tool was required for adjudicated delinquents and viewed the CANS as that potential tool.

CANS IMPLEMENTATION

Phase I: Training

Once the CANS was chosen as the primary assessment tool, the county director made the determination that all county child welfare workers must be trained on use of the CANS tool. The county's rationale was twofold. First, it was decided that CANS implementation would start with a focus on cases being presented before the residential placement committee, so FCMs would need to be trained to effectively present their cases. Second, the long-term goal of using the CANS as an ongoing communication tool required that FCMs acquire a working knowledge of how to use it.

Two evaluation staff and one child welfare staff trainer attended the train-the-trainer session convened at Northwestern University in July 2003. On completion of the CANS training, a training schedule was developed for all FCMs in the Lake County office. Throughout the fall of 2003, all FCMs attended training sessions. Training was completed by December 2003, with 85 percent of the FCMs meeting the required level of proficiency.

The training developed for FCMs in Lake County was a joint effort on the part of the evaluation project staff and child welfare staff. All training teams included a child welfare staff person and a member of the evaluation team. The training content provided (1) a context for the use of the CANS in Lake County, (2) a brief discussion of the epidemiology of mental health needs among children in the child welfare system, (3) a brief discussion of measurement, including the clinimetric properties of the CANS, and (4) an overview of the Phase I assessment process that would be implemented in Lake County in January 2004.

While 85 percent of FCMs successfully completed the CANS training and were certified to use it, a small number were resistant to the instrument training. On balance, however, most FCMs recognized the value of using the CANS. The clinical psychologist serving as the CANS trainer made the following observations:

- FCMs showed a wide range of understanding related to mental health needs of children served in the child welfare system.

- A small percentage of FCMs were openly opposed to the notion of using the assessment tool, believing that it represented another layer of redundant paperwork. Most, however, were relieved that the tool provided quality information with a minimum of time investment.

- A number of FCMs were also skeptical about long-term use of the CANS. Much of their skepticism was rooted in their previous experiences with prescribed changes being implemented in the state child welfare bureaucracy.

- A number of FCMs also indicated skepticism related to localized CANS implementation. Some expressed concern that contradictory policies and procedures might be developed at the state level.

- Most FCMs found the CANS training and certification process to be informative and thought provoking. Most FCMs understood the utility of the tool.

Phase I of CANS implementation was limited to assessing the cases coming to the residential placement committee for placement recommendations, as noted earlier. Beyond the trainer observations noted above, a quality review of the CANS completed by the FCMs showed that they completed the CANS correctly. Most cases reviewed indicated that the FCMs were taking the assessment process seriously and putting thought into their ratings. In fact, most ratings were observed to be consistent in most sub-domains.

A number of challenges related to the ratings were also observed. Reviewers noted that about 40 percent of cases reviewed reflected an inadequate understanding of psychiatric symptomatology. Similarly, about 40 percent were in error regarding the symptomatology of depression and anxiety. Fifty percent reflected an inadequate understanding of adjustment to trauma, and 40 percent under-identified past trauma. These observations were taken into consideration as preparations were made for Phase II CANS implementation.

Phase II: Screening and Assessment

A 2003 national study of child welfare departments (Leslie et al., 2003) found that only one-half of child welfare departments at the county level had delineated procedures for mental health screening and assessment of children coming into the child welfare system. Of those who did have a procedure, only a small proportion of counties followed it. Most screening and assessment activity was completed on a serendipitous basis.

The Department of Health and Human Services (DHHS) found that the child welfare system in the State of Indiana was no different. The DHHS's completed Child and Family Services Review (2002) found that screening and assessment were a significant deficiency in the Indiana child welfare system for both children and families.

To address the deficiencies, in late 2003 the Indiana Department of Child Services articulated a new screening process. The primary goal was to pilot a screening tool in five of ninety-two counties starting in July 2004, with full implementation of the screening process to be rolled out in all ninety-two counties by December of that year. The screening process was administered by both the Indiana Division of Mental Health and Addictions and the Division of Family and Children, now reorganized as the Department of Child Services. State administrators chose the MHST for use in the screening process, and Lake County was chosen as one of the five pilot screening sites.

The local CANS implementation was conjoined with the MHST implementation statewide. Subsequent training of both staff and service provider personnel included an extensive segment related to the use of the MHST screening tool and its relevance to the overall screening/assessment initiative in Lake County.

Assessment Providers. A prolonged series of meetings was convened over the course of 2004 related to the initiation of CANS Implementation Phase II. These meetings were designed to engage the provider community as it related to use of the CANS in Lake County. Given Indiana's screening initiative, using community mental health agencies across the state as the primary source of assessment services became a priority. This decision was based on the fact that these agencies were the sole providers of Medicaid rehabilitation option (MRO) services throughout the state. While this strategy seemed logical from a fiscal perspective, the process was not entirely consistent with system of care principles—it precluded many well-established providers of therapeutic foster care, residential treatment, and in-home services from participating as assessment providers. This situation became a barrier to CANS implementation and is discussed later in this chapter.

It is important to understand the context in which Phase II took place. The choice of a tool for use in the screening/assessment process was driven by the needs of the placing agencies (child welfare and juvenile court) and was supported by three factors:

1. Formative evaluation data;

2. Use of the CANS tool in Phase I; and

3. A comprehensive review of assessment tools by personnel from both child welfare and the juvenile court. (Inasmuch as these agencies were paying for the assessment services, administrators from placing agencies felt strongly that it was their prerogative to choose the assessment tool.)

Resistance to CANS. A cross-section of providers was chosen to participate as assessment providers. These included three community mental health centers, a residential service provider, and a home-based service provider. All agencies were located in Lake County. The choice of providers was based on the ability of each provider to bill either the Medicaid clinic option or the Medicaid rehab option for assessment services. Beginning with the initial meeting in Phase II implementation, two of the three community mental health providers were highly resistant to the notion of CANS implementation. These providers attempted to subvert the implementation process. They dominated the course of discussion in planning meetings. They generated misinformation related to the context and direction of statewide screening and assessment implementation. They also advocated the use of other assessment tools. The remaining providers were willing to work through a process of CANS implementation even though the method of funding the assessments and the related return on investment for assessment providers was unclear. Vocal resistance by two community mental health centers' staff diminished following the county child welfare director's reaffirmation of the use of the CANS as well as other informal communication between the director and community mental health administrators.

As Rosen and Weil (1996) have described, resistant behaviors can arise when computerization is introduced into the context of behavioral health care. Some staff members at the community mental health center were true CANS resistors, and only the child welfare director's intervention, in the form of meetings with the executive directors of their organizations, brought about cooperative behavior.

Resistance to CANS implementation was driven by two factors. First, it was generated by the centers' negative experiences using the Division of Mental Health and Addiction's required assessment tool, called the Hoosier Assurance Plan Instrument: Children and Adolescents (HAPI-C). The HAPI-C (Newman et al., 2003) was developed for use in the Hoosier Assurance Plan to determine eligibility of youth receiving state-funded mental health services and to hold providers accountable for changes in behavior. Mental health center personnel found the tool both cumbersome and time consuming. Second, frustration with the HAPI-C was compounded by the fact that mental health centers did not have access to HAPI-C data for evaluation purposes, so it was of little use in treatment planning.

Integrating CANS and MHST in the Screening/Assessment Process

Given the context of the state screening initiative and the local CANS implementation, the screening assessment process was designed to integrate the two complementary processes. The state screening initiative required use of the screen on the following child welfare populations:

- All children for whom a CHINS petition had been filed, and

- All children placed in out-of-home care.

The implementation process involved intake and screening by FCMs from the investigations unit. The FCMs collected pertinent documents and attempted to complete the background information form (Form DCS L166). After completing as much of the form as logistically possible, FCMs completed the MHST. Depending on the characteristics of the case, the FCM arranged for services for the children immediately.

If the MHST indicated that a child was likely at risk for needed mental health services, the FCM compiled an assessment referral package for transmittal to the assessment providers. The FCM sent the MHST to the assessment provider within five days, and the provider transmitted it back within ten days. The FCM then forwarded the assessment referral information to DCS administrative support staff for inclusion on the Screening/Assessment Tracking Tool. We developed this tool to monitor the progress of assessment referrals and augmented reports generated by the Indiana child welfare information system; it was designed to monitor screening completion by FCMs of children entering that system.

All FCMs in Lake County participated in the Phase II training developed by members of the Residential Treatment Center Evaluation Project and Lake County DCS's unit managers. This five-hour training session had a three-prong focus: (1) the screening/ assessment process; (2) use of the MHST, especially with young children; and (3) a review of developmental indicators of mental health need.

Indiana First Steps, an early intervention services provider for infants and children through age three who have developmental problems, participated in training planning. Discussions with the First Steps administrator revealed low levels of referrals from FCMs. It was hypothesized that many FCMs lacked knowledge related to the developmental challenges of many young children entering the child welfare system. The training team developed a quick reference guide to help FCMs use the MHST in a developmentally appropriate manner. Developmental specialists also participated in the FCM training section that focused on screening practices for young children and the First Steps referral process.

When an FCM completed a child's screening process, DCS administrative support staff took the information provided and logged both negative and positive screens on the Lake County Screening/Assessment Tracking Tool. Positive screens were logged with the contact information of the assessment provider to whom the positive screen was referred. The support staff used the logged information to determine whether referred screens were in a "pending" or "completed" status. This allowed child welfare staff to follow-up on any outstanding assessment referrals that were not returned as completed within the specified period of time.

FCMs were responsible for assembling referral packages and contacting the assessment provider for all positive screens. The FCM faxed the referral assessment package to the assessment provider contact person. Providers were selected based on their geographic service area and ability to return a completed assessment in a timely manner. For children under age three, a referral was made to Indiana First Steps, noted above. The assessment referral package included the following information:

- MHST screening form
- Referral form
- Blanket consent form
- Form L166 (brief social history)
- Placement history
- Service history
- Previous psychological assessments
- Current/previous educational documents (e.g., individualized education plans, or IEPs)

Figure 7.1
Process for Assessment

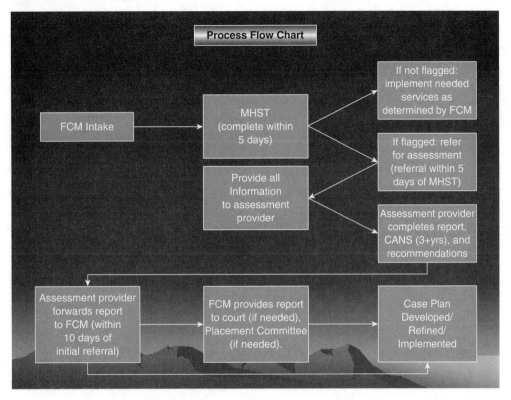

The assessment provider completed the assessment and transmitted the completed report back to the Lake County DCS's point person within ten working days of obtaining the assessment referral. The flowchart in Figure 7.1 outlines the assessment process.

For children under age three, the referral process was quite similar to that developed for older children, as shown in Figure 7.2. The children identified as in possible need of mental health services were referred to First Steps for evaluation. The First Steps referral form required the FCM to note concerns related to the child's development and included any of the following areas:

- Physical/motor (including gross and fine motor)

- Social/emotional

- Thinking/cognitive

- Self-help

- Language/communication

As with the assessment referral package given to assessment providers for children age three and older, the DCS and First Steps referral form was faxed to First Steps

Figure 7.2
Process for Children Age 0-3 (First Step Referrals)

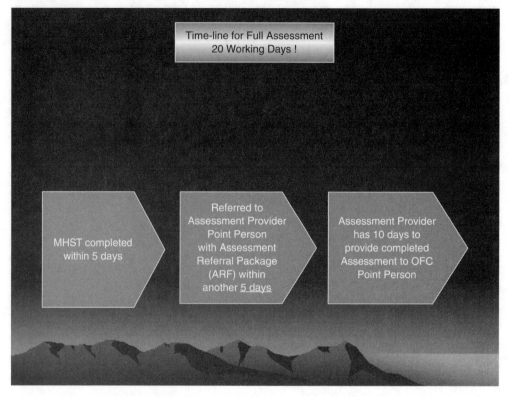

(along with the L166, placement history, and other pertinent documents). On receipt, a First Steps intake coordinator was assigned who completed intake procedures within ten days. The eligibility/assessment team visited each home within another ten days and completed the assessment within two days of the home visit. The treatment team, FCM, and family met and developed a service plan within two days of completed assessment. The service plan was forwarded to relevant parties and implemented within one week. Children were reevaluated on a yearly basis and service plans were reviewed at six-month intervals.

CONTENTS OF COMPLETED ASSESSMENT

All CANS assessments were completed by a master's-level, trained qualified mental health professional (QMHP). All assessment providers were required to meet with both the children and their families. The DCS forwarded a letter of notification to each family informing them that the FCM was required to make an assessment before the assessment provider visited with the family. If the FCM failed to provide school information in the assessment referral package, the assessment provider was strongly encouraged to obtain this information from the child's school. The FCM provided a blanket consent form for the provider to help facilitate access to needed background information. The assessment provider's completed assessment report included a completed assessment summary form that articulated treatment recommendations. A completed CANS assessment was also included.

PEER REVIEW FOR UNIFORM ASSESSMENT QUALITY

Lake County child welfare and juvenile justice administrators expressed concerns related to the ability of assessment providers to provide timely and high quality assessment services. The quality of the psychological assessments was uneven, and the administrators were also receiving mixed formative evaluation findings from the Residential Treatment Center Evaluation Project.

In their initial attempt to ensure the quality of assessment services, the administrators developed an assessment quality assurance form that included an evaluation of how the CANS was completed by assessment service providers. The form was to be completed on a random sample of completed assessments. This first strategy was eventually discontinued, however, in lieu of a second strategy that was born of the contentious series of meetings in 2004 related to Phase II implementation. Over the course of these meetings, service providers agreed that they would like to adopt a peer-review process. The process eventually adopted was completed during scheduled monthly meetings in which one provider's completed assessment were critiqued by peer providers. This process had a secondary benefit of increasing the communication between assessment providers and child welfare staff as well as increasing the trust levels of all who were involved in the Phase II implementation process.

BARRIERS TO CANS IMPLEMENTATION

A number of barriers existed to implementing the CANS in Lake County, at both the state and local levels. In an ideal world, bureaucracies would remain stable and their institutional memories would remain intact. Given the political realities of government, however, little has proven predictable in the context of CANS implementation.

CANS implementation was a county-level initiative that seemed sensible at the time of its inception. County child welfare directors enjoyed considerable autonomy as related to the development of services, the development of service contracts, and the administration of fiscal resources needed to pay for those services. Each county existed as an autonomous potpourri of service providers and placing agencies. At the state level, little attention was paid to the fragmentation of services and to how poorly systems actually worked in many cases. It is no surprise that survey results of stakeholder ratings of both service providers and system performance in each of the ninety-two Indiana counties was mostly negative (Pavkov, 2004).

The dominant barrier to CANS implementation in Lake County remained the lack of a coherent set of state priorities for serving the needs of the child welfare system. In the context of CANS implementation, the lack of a coherent set of policy priorities resulted in poor communication between local and state administrators. In Phase I, this was characterized by the state's skepticism toward the training of FCMs to complete CANS assessments and by its inability to delineate a reasonable response to the statewide assessment dilemma. In Phase II, it was characterized by the state's introduction of a screening/assessment initiative that lacked both financing for screening and assessment procedures and a set of uniform standards for screening and assessment quality.

Gains and Reforms

Much is currently being done statewide to centralize and provide strong leadership in the area of child welfare. Reform efforts have resulted from a change in state administrations, new child welfare legislation, and consequent reorganization. While these new developments are warranted, little attention has focused on the significant gains realized through the process of CANS implementation in Lake County.

Before the CANS was implemented, the child welfare system was also the beneficiary of a Center for Mental Health Services, Child Mental Health Initiative award to support a system of care for children and families in Lake County. The Circle Around Families initiative, funded in 1999, was designed to provide wraparound services to children with serious emotional disturbances through the development of a system of care for children and families. While ideally the initiative was the perfect strategy to develop uniform assessment processes for children coming into the child welfare system, the administration of grant funds was closely held by an administrative services organization owned by two of three community mental health centers serving Lake County. As such, CANS implementation could not occur in a context that was not controlled by the payers of services (i.e., child welfare and juvenile justice). Circle Around Families has embraced the concept of the CANS initiative, however, and much of the credit for this must reside with the honorable Judge Boneventura, who has required the community mental health centers to use the tool.

Statewide Momentum

Similarly, the CANS implementation process has spawned much interest in other parts of the state. Over the course of 2004 and 2005, administrators and services providers from Lake County participated in a statewide assessment advisory committee. Information generated from Lake County and provided in the form of presentations to the committee has created both interest and excitement about the use of the CANS tool. The committee unanimously recommended the use of the CANS tool statewide and this recommendation was included in a comprehensive child mental health plan developed by policymakers for adoption in 2006-2007.

Simultaneous to the state-level assessment committee's work, momentum for use of the CANS has grown as a result of contractual requirements to use the CANS in both residential and therapeutic foster care agencies serving children from Lake County. Quality assurance reviews conducted by the Residential Treatment Center Evaluation Project of both agency types have reinforced this requirement (Pavkov & Hug, 2006). The Evaluation Project has also collaborated with the Circle Around Families child mental health initiative to provide CANS train-the-trainer training for providers across the state. A number of agencies commenced with the use of the CANS prior to the statewide implantation anticipated for 2007.

NEXT STEP: CREATION OF A MULTIDISCIPLINARY TREATMENT DECISION SUPPORT TEAM

In his book titled *Redressing the Emperor: Improving Our Children's Public Mental Health System*, John Lyons (2004) describes a three-phase process of implementation that characterizes many system change initiatives similar to the introduction of the CANS in Lake County. The phases are the "exposure phase," the "initial use phase," and the "full use phase." Implementation of the CANS in Lake County is beyond the exposure phase. Most service providers have now completed CANS training; the juvenile court is initiating use of the CANS in the community transition program; and child welfare has incorporated the CANS into some aspects of its business process. Changes in state government and in the administration of child welfare have also mediated further implementation of the CANS and TCOM technologies locally. As of this writing, local momentum related to CANS implementation has grown into the larger prospect of CANS use statewide.

Regardless of the how the CANS is used statewide, implementing and operating TCOM methodologies using the CANS will eventually take place at the county/regional level throughout the state. The paragraphs that follow describe the methodologies that were planned for Lake County before statewide implementation.

Given the clinical skills of many child welfare FCMs, CANS implementation required the support of a multidisciplinary team to support the treatment decision-making process. The DCS planned a multidisciplinary committee, designated as the treatment decision support team, comprised of child welfare division managers, supervisors, and clinical consultants (e.g., clinical psychologist, psychiatrist). The team would consider the assessment provider's treatment recommendations as presented by the assigned FCM and make a treatment intensity decision using a tool created for Lake County called the Treatment Intensity Decision Support Tool. This tool was designed to objectify the treatment intensity decision-making process, but it was not intended to impose a treatment requirement should circumstances indicate otherwise. Furthermore, the use of this decision support tool was intended to guide treatment decisions in the context of existing treatment options. The treatment decision support team as proposed reflected systems-of-care principles (Stroul & Friedman, 1994). The composition of the team was designed to (1) facilitate cross-system communication and collaboration related to individual cases, (2) provide quality assurance related to the screening assessment process, and (3) monitor the ongoing screening/assessment process.

The intensity decision support tool developed for Lake County took information from the CANS tool and used it to make an objective decision about the intensity of services that a child and family may require. Inasmuch as referrals for services clear guidelines, this tool was designed to provide a "decision standard" for services being provided for children and families.

The intensity decision support tool consists of a set of algorithms that are mapped to a continuum of treatment intensity. Appendix 7.1 details the decision rules associated with the algorithms. The algorithm is rooted in nine evaluative criterion that include: (1) diagnosis, (2) risk to self (risk A), (3) risk to others (risk B), (4) service needs, (5) school behavior and performance, (6) caregiver capacity, (7) strengths, (8) social ecology, and (9) developmental functioning. Each evaluative criterion is assessed using a combination of individual CANS items. The decision support tool was designed to yield a treatment intensity "recommendation" based upon the raters' consideration of the nine evaluative criteria.

The levels of treatment intensity correspond with differing combinations of evaluative criteria. For instance, Level 7 is the most treatment intense of the 7 levels of intensity and a recommendation for services at Level 7 are largely influenced by severity of diagnosis and risk. As a rater considers youth with less challenging presenting symptoms, the evaluative criterion of diagnosis and risk will exhibit less impact on the treatment recommendation. For instance, a child presenting without extreme risk to self or others will likely be evaluated more closely on the school and caregiver capacity criterion than on the diagnosis and risk criterion. As such, various evaluative criteria may be referenced in the treatment recommendation as a function of the acuity of symptoms and need for service.

The preferences of the development group were influenced by their review of the CALOCUS's treatment intensity levels. By defining levels of treatment intensity, the tool more readily conforms to the availability of locally present treatment options, changes to treatment options as the continuum of care continues to develop, and the availability of the levels across Indiana's counties. The "levels of treatment intensity" stated in Appendix 7.2 represents an adaptation of CALOCUS levels of treatment intensity (American Academy of Child and Adolescent Psychiatry & American Association of Community Psychiatrists, 1998) and is specifically influenced by the realities of locally available programmatic options. For instance, the Lake County version includes an additional level of intensity at the intensive end of the continuum (Levels 6 and 7). Furthermore, the level descriptions were aligned with local vernacular as it related to mental health services in Lake County. Modifications such as these were intended to facilitate the adoption of the tool along with providing a useful paradigm for use in staff training and supervision processes.[1]

The developers of the intensity decision support tool also felt that treatment intensity levels should be linked to very detailed description of how services might "look and feel" at each intensity level. The levels of treatment intensity as shown in Appendix 7.2 describe a number of different service types and combinations that would be appropriate for each level. Driven by the notion that each child should receive care in the least possible restrictive environment, some intensity levels describe both congregate and community-based care options that might be chosen depending on the service options available at the local level. When put into operation, the treatment intensity levels would also serve as a basis for payment for levels of treatment intensity.

CONCLUSION

TCOM has arrived in Lake County, Indiana. While not realizing its full potential, many of the rudimentary concepts related to the sophisticated world of managing by outcomes have arrived. Many of the individuals responsible for running the day to day operations of child welfare and the court have received some exposure to the fact that managing using real data rather than anecdotal evidence is possible.

---

[1]Detailed descriptions of CALOCUS treatment intensity levels are available online for reference at: http://www.comm.psych.pitt.edu/finds/CALOCUSv15.pdf.

One poignant illustration reveals the progress that has occurred over the course of two years of work-group meetings, placement committee meetings, and an ambitious program of training. The lead author was discussing the progress of screening and assessment in Lake County with a child welfare manager who was expressing some displeasure with the progress being made during a time when the office was without a director. Specifically, the child welfare manager was frustrated with FCMs who were bypassing the initial screening process for children entering the system. Our conversation ranged from the usual frustration of why the number of screenings appeared to be lower, to the uneven quality of CANS assessments coming from providers, to the need to use the CANS data more effectively. A meeting was scheduled to attempt to identify the source of the problem. During the course of the meeting, I asked the manager whether the information system used by the state generated a report to monitor the completion of screenings. After an inventory of the available reports on the computer system, I identified two reports that specifically pertained to the screening process and generated the reports. The reaction of the supervisor was telling; he indicated that he had never explored the reporting capability of the state's multimillion dollar computer system. In fact, he was never informed that the reports existed, much less encouraged to explore the system for himself. At the end of the meeting, the supervisor was excited about the prospect of using the reports for management purposes.

The above illustration suggests that progress has occurred in terms of understanding the basic utility of outcomes management through the use of the CANS and other methods. It also reveals a significant amount of work ahead, however. When will the dream of full implementation be realized? The dream will only be realized through consistent, uninterrupted leadership that understands and embraces the notion of managing by data and outcomes. Unfortunately, most of our professional training programs do not prepare human service workers from this perspective, and many managers are not conditioned to use management by outcomes. Unfortunately, most managers *are* heavily involved in a "cover myself" set of management priorities, and TCOM as a measure of performance threatens the culture within many human service organizations.

For Lake County, full implementation is now a function of how state policy-makers respond as the state is under new management. Many state policy-makers have indicated their interest. Time will tell. Whether or not the CANS is fully implemented, providing key stakeholders a glimpse of the TCOM dream has resulted in significant progress. The real payoff is realizing the benefits for children.

References

Achenbach, T. (1991). *Manual for child behavior checklist/ 4-18 and 1991 profile*. Burlington, VT: University of Vermont.

American Academy of Child and Adolescent Psychiatry and the American Association of Community Psychiatrists (1998). *Child and adolescent level of care utilization system (CALOCUS)*. Pittsburgh: American Association of Community Psychiatrists.

Burns B., Phillips S., Wagner H., Barth R., Kolko D., Campbell Y. & Landsverk, J. (2004). Mental health need and access to mental health services by youths involved with child welfare: A national survey. *Journal of the American Academy of Child & Adolescent Psychiatry, 43*, 960–970.

Mental health screening tool: 5 years to adult (MHST) (2002). Sacramento, CA: California Institute for Mental Health.

Child and family services review: Final report–Indiana (2002). Washington, DC: U.S. Department of Health and Human Services, Administration for Children and Families.

Grisso, T. & Barnum R. (2003). *Massachussetts youth screening instrument—Version 2: User's manual and technical report.* Sarasota, FL: Professional Resource Press.

Hodges, K. (1990, 1994 rev.). *Child and adolescent functional assessment scale.* Ypsilanti, MI: Eastern Michigan University, Department of Psychology.

Leslie K., Hurlburt, M., Landsverk J., Rolls J., Wood, P. & Kelleher, K. (2003). Comprehensive assessments for children entering foster care: A national perspective. *Pediatrics, 112,* 134–142.

Lyons, J. (2004). *Redressing the emperor: Improving our children's public mental health service system.* Westport, CT: Praeger.

Lyons, J., Almeida, C., Rautkis, M. & Lyons, M. (1999). *Child and adolescent needs and strengths—CW Manual.* Winnetka, IL: Buddin Praed Foundation.

Newman, F., McGrew, J., Deliberty, R., Anderson, J., Smith, T. & Griss, M. (2003). Psychometric properties of the HAPI-child: An instrument developed to determine service eligibility and level of functioning in a state mental health and substance abuse service system. Unpublished manuscript.

Pavkov, T. (2004). *Indiana 92-county system of care assessment.* Hammond, IN: Institute for Social and Policy Research at Purdue University, Calumet.

Pavkov, T. & Hug, R. (2006). *Residential treatment center evaluation project: Final Report.* Hammond, IN: Institute for Social and Policy Research at Purdue University, Calumet.

Rosen, L. & Weil, M. (1996). Easing the transition from paper to computer-based systems. In T. Trabin (Ed.), *The computerization of behavioral healthcare.* San Francisco: Jossey Bass.

Stroul, B. & Friedman, R. (1994). *A system of care for children & youth with severe emotional disturbances.* Washington, DC: National Technical Assistance Center for Children's Mental Health, Child and Adolescent Service System Program, Georgetown University Center for Child and Human Development.

Appendix 7.1
Summary Algorithms

LEVEL 7:
Must meet the requirements of:

- Criterion 1 AND
- Criterion 2

LEVEL 6:
Must meet the requirements of:

- Criterion 1 AND
- Criterion 2 OR Criterion 3

LEVEL 5:
Must meet the requirements of:

- Criterion 1 (Diagnosis) AND
- Criterion 2 (Risk A) OR Criterion 3 (Risk B) AND
- Criterion 4 (Service Needs) AND
- Criterion 5 (School) OR Criterion 6 (Care Giver Capacity) OR Criterion 8 (Social Ecology)

LEVEL 4:
Must meet the requirements of:

- Criterion 1 (Diagnosis) AND
- Criterion 2 (Risk A) OR Criterion 3 (Risk B) AND
- Criterion 4 (Service Needs) AND
- Criterion 5 (School) OR Criterion 6 (Care Giver Capacity) OR Criterion 8 (Social Ecology)

LEVEL 3:
Must meet the requirements of:

- Criterion 6 (Care Giver Capacity) OR Criterion 7 (Strengths) AND
- Criterion 5 (School) OR Criterion 8 (Social Ecology)
- Criterion 1 (Diagnosis) AND
- Criterion 2 (Risk A) OR Criterion 3 (Risk B) AND
- Criterion 4 (Service Needs)

LEVEL 2:
Must meet the requirements of:

- Criterion 6 (Care Giver Capacity) OR Criterion 7 (Strengths) AND
- Criterion 5 (School) OR Criterion 8 (Social Ecology)
- Criterion 1 (Diagnosis) AND
- Criterion 2 (Risk A) OR Criterion 3 (Risk B) AND
- Criterion 4 (Service Needs)

LEVEL 1:
Must meet the requirements of:

- Criterion 6 (Care Giver Capacity) OR Criterion 7 (Strengths) AND
- Criterion 5 (School) OR Criterion 8 (Social Ecology)
- Criterion 1 (Diagnosis) AND
- Criterion 2 (Risk A) OR Criterion 3 (Risk B) AND
- Criterion 4 (Service Needs)

Lake County Department of Children's Services Decision Support Guidelines Based on Use of the CANS Instrument

Criterion	Area	Rating	CANS Item
1. Diagnosis	Presence of symptom areas associated with a serious emotional/ behavioral disorder		
Level 7	Two symptom areas are *very acute*.	3	17. Psychosis
Level 6	Two symptom areas *are acute*.	2 or 3	18. Attention Deficit/ Impulse Control
Level 5	Two symptom areas are present, persistent, but not acute	2 or 3	19. Depression/Anxiety 20. Anger Control
Level 4	Two symptom areas require attention	1 or 2	21. Oppositional Behavior
Level 3	Same	1 or 2	22. Antisocial Behavior
Level 2	Same	1 or 2	23. Adjustment to Trauma
Level 1	Symptom areas possibly present or in remission	0 or 1	24. Attachment 33. Severity of Substance Abuse
2. Risk A			
Level 7	Serious risk behaviors in at least one these areas	3	
Level 6	Same	2 or 3	
Level 5	Notable risk behaviors in at least one these areas	1 or 2	29. Danger to Self 31. Runaway
Level 4	Same	1 or 2	
Level 3	Possible risk behaviors in at least one of these areas	0 or 1	
Level 2	Same	0 or 1	
Level 1	Same	0 or 1	

Criterion	Area	Rating	CANS Item
3. Risk B			30. Fire Setting
Level 7	N/A	N/A	32. Social Behavior
Level 6	Serious risk behaviors in at least one of these areas	2 or 3	38. Seriousness of Criminal Behavior
Level 5	Notable risk behaviors in at least one these areas	1 or 2	40. Violence
Level 4	Same	1 or 2	41. Sexually Abusive Behavior
Level 3	Possible risk behaviors in at least one these areas	0 or 1	
Level 2	Same	0 or 1	
Level 1	Same	0 or 1	
4. Service Needs			
Level 7	Service needs which require urgent and intensive attention in one or both of these areas	3	
Level 6	Same	2 or 3	46. Monitoring
Level 5	Same	2 or 3	47. Treatment Intensity
Level 4	Same	2 or 3	
Level 3	Service needs which require notable attention in one or both of these areas	1 or 2	
Level 2	Service needs which require possible attention in one or both of these areas	0 or 1	
Level 1	Same	0 or 1	
5. School			
Level 7	Serious impairment in school functioning in one or more of these areas	3	9. School Achievement
Level 6	Same	2 or 3	10. School Behavior
Level 5	Same	2 or 3	11. School Attendance
Level 4	Same	2 or 3	
Level 3	Possible inadequacies in school functioning in one or more of these areas	0 or 1	
Level 2	Same	0 or 1	
Level 1	Same	0 or 1	

Criterion	Area	Rating	CANS Item
6. Caregiver Capacity			50. Physical/Behavioral Health
Level 7	N/A	N/A	
Level 6	N/A	N/A	51. Supervision
Level 5	Serious weaknesses in care giving capacity in at least two of these areas	2 or 3	52. Involvement with Care
Level 4	Notable weaknesses in care giving capacity in at least two of these areas	1 or 2	53. Knowledge
			54. Organization
Level 3	Same	1 or 2	55. Resources
Level 2	Possible weaknesses in care giving capacity in at least two of these areas	0 or 1	56. Residential Stability
Level 1	No weaknesses noted.	0	
7. Strengths			57. Family
Level 7	N/A	N/A	58. Interpersonal
Level 6	N/A	N/A	59. Relationship Permanence
Level 5	Serious deficits in two or more of these areas	2 or 3	
Level 4	Notable concerns in two or more of these areas	1 or 2	60. Educational
			61. Vocational
			62. Well Being
Level 3	Same	1 or 2	63. Talent/Interests
Level 2	Possible concerns in two or more of these areas	0 or 1	64. Spiritual/Religious
			65. Inclusion
Level 1	Possible but minimal concerns in these areas	0 or 1	
8. Social Ecology			13. Abuse
Level 7	N/A	N/A	14. Neglect
Level 6	N/A	N/A	15. Permanency
Level 5	Serious environmental problems in at least two of these areas	2 or 3	16. Exploitation
Level 4	Notable environmental problems in at least two of these areas	1 or 2	36. Peer Involvement in Substance Use
			37. Parental Involvement in Substance Use
Level 3	Possible environmental problems in at least two of these areas	0 or 1	
Level 2	Same	0 or 1	42. Peer Involvement in Crime
Level 1	Environmental problems are minimal	0	43. Parental Criminal Behavior
			44. Environmental Influences

Criterion	Area	Rating	CANS Item
9. Functioning			1. Motor
Level 7	Serious impairment in functioning in at least one area	3	2. Sensory
Level 6	Same	3	3. Intellectual
Level 5	Notable impairment in functioning in at least one area	1 or 2	4. Communication 5. Developmental
Level 4	Possible impairment in functioning in at least one area	0 or 1	6. Self Care/Daily Living Skills 7. Physical/Medical
Level 3	Same	0 or 1	
Level 2	Minimal impairment in any of these areas	0 or 1	
Level 1	Same	0 or 1	

Appendix 7.2

Brief Descriptions of Levels of Intensity

LEVEL 7: SECURE, 24-HOUR PSYCHIATRIC MONITORING

Type of Care
- Psychiatric inpatient unit

LEVEL 6: SECURE, 24-HOUR SERVICES WITH PSYCHIATRIC MANAGEMENT

Types of Care
- Residential programs attached to a psychiatric hospital program
- Closed and locked residential facilities
- Specialized and intensive treatment programs which are locked and staff secure

LEVEL 5: NON-SECURE, 24-HOUR SERVICES WITH PSYCHIATRIC MONITORING

Types of Care
- Open residential settings with on-grounds school
- Intensive wraparound services
- Treatment foster care

LEVEL 4: INTENSIVE INTEGRATED SERVICES WITHOUT 24-HOUR PSYCHIATRIC MONITORING

Types of Care
- Therapeutic foster care—Level 3 as delineated in the Therapeutic Foster Care Level of Care Workbook
- Intensive wraparound
- Day treatment
- Transitional independent living with intensive support
- Open residential treatment

LEVEL 3: INTENSIVE OUTPATIENT SERVICES

Types of Care

[As the intensity of mental health and related support services are the critical issue at this level, any child in one of the arrangements below could benefit from services at the Level Three intensity]

- Therapeutic foster care—Level 2 (as delineated in the Therapeutic Foster Care Level of Care Workbook
- Wraparound
- Intensive case management
- Foster care with day treatment
- Living at home—With day treatment
- Independent Living
- Living at home—With in-home services

LEVEL 2: OUTPATIENT SERVICES

Types of Care

- Therapeutic foster care—Level 1(as delineated in the Therapeutic Foster Care Level of Care Workbook)
- Outpatient services
- Foster care without day treatment
- Home/relative foster care
- Independent living
- Living at home—With in-home services

LEVEL 1: RECOVERY MAINTENANCE AND HEALTH MANAGEMENT

Types of Care

- Maintenance
- Case management
- Regular (and non-problematic) foster care
- Living at home
- Independent living (with acquired self-sufficiency and socialization skills)

Chapter 8

History of Placement Control and Utilization Management in Los Angeles County

by Michael Rauso, Psy.D., M.F.T. and Mitch Mason, M.S.W.

BACKGROUND

Los Angeles County is one of the largest Counties in the nation, with just over ten million people (Children's Scorecard, 2004). Of those ten million, there are an estimated 2.8 million children and youth—more than the population of seventeen individual states, including Kansas, Utah, Nevada, and New Mexico, and larger in size than Rhode Island and Delaware combined. The overwhelming majority (80 percent) of Los Angeles County's children are of color, and almost one-half of the county's children live in low-income families. In 2002, the Los Angeles County Department of Children and Family Services (DCFS) provided child welfare services to over 50,000 children. One of every twenty children ages infant to five years living in the county were referred to the DCFS and subsequently received emergency response services based on reports of abuse and neglect (County of Los Angeles Budget Addendum, 2004). For children placed in foster care, the DCFS experienced a 35 percent decrease between 1998-1999 and 2001-2002, from approximately 50,000 to 32,000 children. Although the DCFS was reducing the number of children in foster care, there remained a significant concern about the historical and current use of congregate care.

The concern about overusing congregate care placements for children and youth has been an integral part of the Los Angeles County Department of Children and Family Services' culture since its formation in 1984. Although the use of congregate care is not a new concept to child welfare, Los Angeles has struggled over the years with using its congregate care placements appropriately. The struggle Los Angeles is currently experiencing is understandable once you have tracked the history of how congregate care became so widely used.

From Orphanages to Congregate Care

Los Angeles opened its first formal orphanage approximately 125 years ago. As a safe haven for children who no longer had parents to care for them, it was a place to learn, heal, and thrive under the watchful eye of matrons, nuns, priests, and teachers. Although the first orphanage was established in the 1700s by Ursuline nuns to care for children whose parents were killed in an Indian massacre, the original intention was the same: children were protected and provided a safe place to grow under the caring eyes of adults.

Over time and as societal values and beliefs changed, so too did the use of large facilities. Institutions once used as orphanages changed from safe havens to primarily residential treatment, shelter, or correctional facilities. In the early 1930s, the belief started to take hold that placing needy children in such institutions made the streets safer. About this time, Los Angeles County's oldest orphanage also shifted from being a refuge to being a place that primarily cared for children whose parents were unable to care for them—essentially, a facility for foster care children.

Over many decades, as the number of foster children in Los Angeles kept increasing, so too did the number of facilities to serve them. The increase in the number of foster children placed in congregate care facilities was accompanied in time by protests against the "warehousing" of children, which is how the practice of placing foster children in large congregate settings was viewed. This view eventualy led to the movement for deinstitutionalization. Although the movement peaked in the mid-1970s, the concern about appropriate placement of foster children in congregate care facilities never left.

Short-Term and Private Shelters

An alternative to placing children in congregate care facilities was to place them in short-term shelters, a solution seen as temporary and for assessing the best and most appropriate setting for the youth. When the Department of Children and Family Services was created, it assigned the responsibility of running the county's shelter facility. MacLaren Children's Center, the County's emergency shelter for dependent children, was used to provide short-term respite while a more appropriate placement could be secured. Unfortunately, the population of the shelter exploded from 100 children to 300 as a result of the increase in use of illegal drugs, subsequent increases in children's removal due to parental substance abuse, and the difficulty in placing the children. One-third of these children were infants and toddlers, and the county's ability to recruit an adequate number of county-licensed foster homes and relatives was severely taxed. As a result, the department worked to develop several infant-toddler nurseries that were run by private operators.

Soon the private shelters were filled to capacity. The department recognized the need to control the flow of infants and toddlers to the facilities, as well as to screen to ensure that foster and relatives' homes were used first whenever possible. The department set up a "special placement unit" to focus on removing children from MacLaren and getting them placed in foster homes and congregate care facilities.

Early Assessment and Placement Strategies

As a result of the development of congregate care facilities for infants and young children, a new belief developed that the early placement of children in congregate care may be a desirable service strategy. Over the next ten years, from 1985 to 1995, the focus at MacLaren was on the development of an assessment center where children's health, mental health, and behavioral needs were identified and appropriate placement matches made. The thought was that early identification, assessment, and treatment of these children's specialized needs would greatly benefit them and increase their stability in placement. The idea was to get the children early treatment, stabilize their behavior, and then step them down to less intense levels of care.

But this idea was never fully realized. In fact, when the population at MacLaren would explode, the center would contact large group homes to remove some of the children. These large group homes would frequently "cherry pick" children, taking those with less intense treatment needs. Those left behind would be placed in smaller, six-bed facilities that did not have the rigorous program or on-site social work or mental health staff to deal with the children's needs. Thus, there were more frequent placement disruptions and return trips to MacLaren. While MacLaren's stated purpose was emergency placement, its actual purpose devolved into housing the more "hard to place" children and teens.

In the early 1990s, MacLaren's population had dropped to approximately 220 children. Infants and toddlers were now rarely housed there. Most of the children were adolescents or older latency age (nine to twelve years old). These children were assessed to have extreme mental health needs and behavioral issues. Many were admitted to MacLaren from psychiatric hospitals; others were admitted as the result of seven-day notices from group homes when their behavior was not acceptable.

As a result of the focus on the shelter care/assessment center concept, more staff from the county's Department of Health Services (DHS) and Department of Mental Health (DMH) were assigned to MacLaren to collaborate and develop comprehensive assessments of the residents. In 1996, the DCFS decided to implement the Resource Utilization Management Section (RUM), whose goal was to divert children with complex needs and those who were hard to place from being admitted to MacLaren. RUM became the gatekeeper for MacLaren admission. The RUM staff would work with the line social workers to put together placement packets with extensive information on the youth. This information was forwarded to congregate care providers to assist them in improved matching of children's needs and services.

The target population for the new MacLaren assessment program were at-risk children and youth who may need group home placement primarily due to disruptive behavior in relatives' homes, foster homes, and Foster Family Agency (FFA) homes. It was believed that FFA homes would reduce the number of children in need of congregate care because the FFA homes provided on-staff social workers and access to mental health services. From the beginning of their use, however, more and more young children (under age six) were being placed in FFA homes. These children had few if any mental health treatment needs. The incentives for using FFA homes were that sibling groups could be kept together; the FFA assisted with family visitation; and the weekly visits by FFA social workers provided a sense of increased safety and an extra set of eyes and ears monitoring the children's placement.

With the implementation of RUM came team conferencing, a precursor to family-to-family team decision-making conferences. The RUM staff would ask the county social worker, staff from the current placement, and the potential new placement to attend the team meetings. This process showed dramatic results almost immediately.

Wraparound and Team Decision-Making

The idea of better decision-making was not new for people familiar with the "wraparound" philosophy, with its emphasis on individualized service planning through the use of child-family teams. In 1998, Los Angeles County started the Wraparound 10 Child Pilot at MacLaren, staffed by county employees and enrolling only children at MacLaren. The pilot began an intensive community-based services program for children with severe emotional problems.

With the positive results of the initial pilot, the DMH awarded the Wraparound contracts to two non-profit providers and expanded the referral criteria to any child in, or at risk of, a rate classification level (RCL) of 12 or above. The levels of the RCL program are established by the California Department of Social Services. The program classifies group homes into one of fourteen levels based on a number of important variables (such as the training and professional levels of staff).

The implementation of Wraparound and the expansion of the referral criteria were believed to be the answer to reducing the reliance on large congregate care facilities, but it was found to be only a partial answer to a much larger question. The Los Angeles County Board of Supervisors made the decision to close MacLaren in 2002, after a class action lawsuit was filed against the state and the county alleging that children in the county's foster care system were not receiving the mental health services to which they were entitled. With the center's pending closure and the emphasis on more community-based placements, it was not clear why the population in the RCL 12 facilities was not decreasing. More specifically, the larger question was, what firewalls were in place to prevent ongoing inappropriate placement of children to congregate care facilities?

The DCFS identified two specific strategies to remove children from MacLaren, based on its previous positive experience with the team decision-making process and the wraparound model. A new group of providers were contracted, bringing the total number of Wraparound providers to twelve. For the team decision-making process, each regional administrator was tasked with creating a regional placement review team (RPRT) to review all of their children in MacLaren and the crisis situations that might result in an emergency placement change. The RPRT consisted of a high-level administrator from the impacted office, the case worker, a supervisor, and any potential service providers to review each child's social history and expedite planning for family reunification, placement with relatives, placement with siblings, or adoption. The team identified the child's points of attachment and barriers to achieving permanency. The team also used services from existing resources available in each office—RUM, the Independent Living Program (ILP), Family Group Decision-Making, or System of Care (SOC)/Wraparound—to help achieve permanency. Very quickly, the RPRT became more than just a strategy to remove children from MacLaren; it was also used to identify and proactively respond to conditions that resulted in children being placed or replaced on an emergency basis.

Yet as successful as the RPRTs were in removing children from MacLaren and discussing scenarios for subsequent emergency situations, it again highlighted the question, how do we as a county make placement decisions uniformly and objectively? The RPRT process was a partial answer to this question, but when MacLaren closed, many of the RPRT meetings stopped. This was due to several reasons, but a major one was the fact that most of the RPRTs were run differently and had different processes, further exposing our need for a consistent, objective assessment process to make appropriate placement decisions.

In 2004, the Board of Supervisors instructed the DCFS to create a work-group composed of our county partners, community stakeholders, group home providers, and youth and parent advocates to look at group home utilization and ensure the appropriateness of group home placements. A driving force behind the directive from the board was that about seventy group homes had closed in the past ten years, and one of the county's first orphanages (i.e., Hollygrove) planned the closure of its group home in the coming year. Additionally, the number of children in RCL 12 placements was decreasing, and the community, concerned about the number of group home closures, wanted to ensure that there was a larger plan for children who needed that level of support. To address that concern and to answer the larger question of how the county makes appropriate placement decisions, the work-group focused its efforts on looking at implementing a placement-level decision-making process.

Focus on the CANS

One of the first tasks was to collect all existing placement level tools and do an assessment of their validity, reliability, ease of use, cost, and other factors for replication in Los Angeles County. After several discussions and reviews, the work-group adopted the Child and Adolescent Needs and Strengths tool (CANS, 1999; Lyons, 2004). The CANS is designed for use at two levels—for the individual child and family and for the system of care. The CANS provides a structured assessment of children along a set of dimensions relevant to service planning and decision-making. It also provides information regarding the child's and family's service needs for use during system planning and quality assurance monitoring. It is designed to be used as a prospective assessment tool for decision support during the process of planning services, and as a retrospective assessment tool based on the review of existing information for use in the design of high-quality systems of services.

This flexibility allows for a variety of innovative applications. The CANS can be used for retrospective file reviews for planning purposes. Retrospective review of completed CANS allows for a form of measurement audit to facilitate the reliability and accuracy of information (Lyons et al., 1999). The next task was to use the CANS to review Los Angeles' current placement system. Results of this review are discussed below.

CANS STUDIES CONDUCTED ON CHILDREN AND YOUTH IN PLACEMENT IN LOS ANGELES COUNTY

In 2004, Dr. John Lyons, the Director of the Mental Health Services and Policy Program at Northwestern University in Chicago and developer of the CANS, was asked to come to Los Angeles to make a presentation of the CANS tool and to discuss his findings from a group home review he conducted earlier that year.

In late 2004, the DCFS contracted with Dr. Lyons to conduct a study of 200 children placed in congregate care facilities. The case review was held in February and March 2005. Case records from two offices (Covina and South County) were reviewed. Because a high number of children age twelve and younger were in the facilities (483 as of October 31, 2004), the sample was split; the reviewers studied 100 case records of children age twelve and younger, and 100 of youth thirteen and older. Significant findings included:

- 78 percent of the children and youth had experienced three or more prior placements, with 16 percent having experienced ten or more placements.

- 42 percent of the children and youth had a case plan goal of long-term foster care/planned permanent living arrangement. An additional 16 percent had a case plan goal of emancipation.

- 54 percent of the children had been in their current placement for less than one year.

- 70 percent of the children and youth were on psychotropic medications.

After reviewing the case records using the CANS tool, Dr. Lyons compared the ratings to studies done in two other jurisdictions, Philadelphia and New York State. He found that 50.6 percent of the Los Angeles youth would have been eligible for group home admission and 20 percent eligible for institutional placement according to the Philadelphia decision model. Los Angeles County group home youth were comparable to youth admitted to residential treatment facilities in New York.

He also found that Los Angeles County youth significantly improved on all of the CANS dimensions after group home treatment. Improvements in mental health status were particularly pronounced; however, youth also improved functionally, in school, and there was evidence of strength identification and strength building while in placement.

Dr. Lyons found that Los Angeles County had a relatively low percentage of children served in group homes relative to national averages and that most of these children had significant behavioral health needs. However, due to their improvements in behavior after their stays in congregate care, they did not have the types of functional impairments or risk behaviors that indicated current congregate care placement. They appeared trapped in congregate care and would be better served in specialized foster care environments that were tailored to address their emotional and behavioral needs. Dr. Lyons made several recommendations:

- Expansion of Wraparound services to move children to permanent homes or lower levels of care;

- Implementation of a decision support process to guide group home placement and utilization;

- Development of a uniform assessment strategy to improve the match between the needs of specific children and the programs available;

- Development of benchmarking to understand which children are best served and likely to improve in different congregate care facilities; and

- Increased oversight of the use of psychotropic medications in group homes.

As a result of this study, the DCFS's executive team raised the question: if not group home care, where? The most logical alternative for stepping down these children and youth to a lower level of care would be to FFA-certified homes, which are reimbursed at a treatment foster care rate by the county. To find out more about the current population of children in FFA homes and the ability of FFAs to meet children's special needs, a second case review study was conducted.

Due to the large number of children in FFA care (over 6,000 in May 2005), the sample size for the second case review was set at 600 children and youth of all ages. To determine whether differences existed in how individual DCFS offices made placement decisions regarding FFA homes, the sample was pulled from all seventeen DCFS offices. The review was held in July 2005. Significant findings included:

- More than one-third of the FFA placements involved children age five and younger, and 75 percent involved children age twelve years and younger;

- This was the first placement following removal from parents for 43.5 percent of the children;

- 42.7 percent of the children had a case plan goal of reunification with a parent; 19.5 percent had a case plan goal of placement with a relative; and 25.5 percent had a case plan goal of adoption.

These findings suggested to Dr. Lyons that in Los Angeles County, FFA placements are functioning in a role similar to that of regular foster homes.

Following review using the CANS tool, Dr. Lyons applied the criteria used by Philadelphia for its treatment foster care (TFC) eligibility model and found that only 10.6 percent of the children in FFA care in Los Angeles County would be eligible for TFC in Philadelphia. Dr. Lyons believed that this number was surprisingly low until the large number of infants and toddlers in FFA care in Los Angeles County was considered. When broken down by age, over 35 percent of older teens (ages sixteen and seventeen) and nearly 20 percent of ten- to fifteen-year-olds would be eligible for TFC using Philadelphia's model.

When DCFS offices were compared to each other, reviewers found a wide variance in how FFA placements were used. The percentage of children who were "TFC eligible" ranged from zero (0) to 25.0 percent between different offices, indicating that placement decision-making varied dramatically across different parts of the county.

The subset of seventy-two children who were TFC eligible were assessed to see if they had improvements in their level of functioning as a result of placement in FFA care. Dr. Lyons found that their behavioral indicators upon placement to FFA care were comparable to children and youth placed in group homes. These children experienced significant improvement in symptoms and risk behaviors. Thus, Dr. Lyons found that FFA placements can successfully serve children and youth who have a level of need similar to those placed in group homes in Los Angeles County.

Dr. Lyons made several qualitative observations as a result of the FFA study:

- Los Angeles County had a large number of absolutely outstanding FFA foster parents who are very committed to the children who live with them. The quality of foster parenting was quite high.

- The rate of payment for FFA placement is a deterrent to permanency. In a number of case files, there was documentation that adoptions and/or legal guardianship was refused by FFA foster parents as they would suffer income loss.

- There was a substantial variation in the level and quality of services provided by different FFA agencies and there was infrequent evidence of actual treatment services other than regular social work visits by FFA social workers.

- There was substantial movement of children within the FFA agencies among different foster parents. In most cases this was to move sibling groups in to the same home. On some occasions, moves were made to improve the match between the children's needs and foster parents' ability and willingness to work with children with these special needs.

Dr. Lyons made five recommendations as a result of the FFA study:

- Reduce the number of newborns, infants, and toddlers placed in FFA homes.

- Encourage step-down placements from group homes as a component of the redesign of the Los Angeles County group home system.

- Implement a decision support model with a centralized monitoring unit to encourage a better match between children's needs and FFA placement.

- Create incentives for regular foster homes to accept sibling groups.

- Initiate discussions with the State of California, which sets placement reimbursement rates, around payment models that would keep high-quality foster parents in the system even if their homes were no longer supported through the FFA.

Subsequent to the completion of this second study, Dr. Lyons conducted a comparison between the reimbursement made by Los Angeles County to FFAs for treatment foster care and that paid by other large jurisdictions. He found that rates paid for treatment foster care vary dramatically across the country, as does cost of living. Thus the straightforward comparison of rates across jurisdictions is complicated. However, to provide a context for Los Angeles County's FFA program, the treatment foster care rate paid in Philadelphia is $107 per diem. Of this, at least $40 to $45 goes to the treatment parents. In Illinois, specialized foster care has an average rate of about $101 for mental health expenses and $97 for medical expenses. All of these rates are substantially higher than even the highest current Los Angeles County FFA rate, which ranges from $1,589 to $1,685 per month depending on the age of the child.

NEXT STEPS

In 2003, the DCFS identified three critical outcomes: improved permanence, improved safety, and reduced reliance on detention. It identified five key strategies to support the three outcomes: points of engagement (POE), permanency planning process (P3), concurrent planning, structured decision-making (SDM), and team decision-making (TDM). All five strategies support, complement, and strengthen each other. They also create a continuum of care that emphasizes family, community, best practice, permanency, and respect. Specifically, by implementing these strategies, the family, community, and DCFS are partners in ensuring support for our children and their future.

TDM is the process of bringing together all family members, family supports, informal and formal caregivers, community representatives and the DCFS to make a placement decision. It is an open process that emphasizes respect for each other, listening, an open and honest conversation about the safety factors present, and making the best decision based on all the information. TDM was the logical place to establish the CANS recommendations for placement. In 2005, there were approximately 3,000 TDM recommendations completed, but due to the lack of staff not all were made mandatory. In 2006, a request for a large number of additional TDM facilitators was submitted and granted, which gave the county a capacity for sixty-four TDM facilitators. At the same time, there was a strong push to secure staff to conduct the CANS before the TDM for all children experiencing their third move and for children who were being recommended for their first group home placement. The team would be given the results of the CANS and would use the developed algorithm to make the best possible decision about the level of placement. This new process is viewed as the "front door" for children experiencing placement instability and children being considered for group homes. Again, TDM brings together different parties to make the best decision and to bring all available resource knowledge to the table. This provides the caseworker the ability for better case planning and for better resource options.

As one can imagine, this process has increased the pressure on group homes and other out-of-home service providers. No longer can a caseworker send a child to a group home without a process to explore every option available to the child. It is expected this new process will not only significantly improve the outcomes for our children, but also help define the future needs and services of our community partners.

As mentioned earlier, Los Angeles County has a strong history of using congregate care, and for the culture to change, there must be buy-in and support at every level, from the grass roots community leaders to the county's political leaders. In addition, the ability to get federal and state support would bolster the idea that this is not a new emphasis, but rather a new way of doing business. In Los Angeles County, the ability to gain local support started with helping the community to understand the DCFS's new goals and expected outcomes. Working directly with all the current service delivery providers will start to change the conversation.

In 2005, the DCFS invited all existing group home providers to a meeting to discuss the future of congregate care in Los Angeles. At the meeting, providers expressed concern about their future role, a reaction to the DCFS's mission that was both anticipated and understandable. Volunteers were asked to join a subcommittee to discuss issues in more detail and then submit a group home recommendation to the Board of Supervisors. The group originally comprised a wide representation of group home providers, community stakeholders, and county departmental staff from the mental health and probation departments. As the group progressed, the "wait and see" expectations became reality when word came that some group homes were going out of business and others were seriously struggling to stay in business. The group soon joined forces with a state group that was working on legislation to restructure group home financing. In the proposed legislation, the first change was to the name, to emphasize the new shift in philosophy: "residentially based services" (RBS) was suggested as the new name for group homes.

The philosophy and approach shifted to more short-term, behavior-specific interventions, with a strong emphasis on family involvement and transition and aftercare services. The new RBS legislation was partially influenced by a pilot study in Los Angeles called Residential Wraparound, which infused the principles of Wraparound with group homes. The pilot study was very successful at reducing the length of stay of children in group homes, and it also maintained good outcomes over the long-term. The emphasis on bringing the family and community sooner into group home service plans and building on strengths was something with which all of the members of the group agreed.

On March 31, 2006, the State of California was granted authority to waive certain provisions of Title IV-E of the Social Security Act in order to establish a demonstration project to use Title IV-E funds more flexibly. The state has agreed to accept a capped allocation of Title IV-E funds in order to expand the services that can be claimed under this title. Up to twenty counties expressed interest, but only Los Angeles County and Alameda County entered the waiver on July 1, 2007. The goals of the waiver are to:

- Enhance the array of services provided to children and families;

- Increase child safety without relying primarily on placing children in out-of-home care;

- Improve timelines to permanency, including family reunification, adoption, guardianship, and placement with relatives; and

- Improve the quality of life and well-being of children in foster care.

Funding for new preventive, intensive, and after-care services will come from current Title IV-E funds that can be redirected from savings in traditional IV-E expenses. To realize these savings, Los Angeles will need to continue to divert children from entering placement, when safely possible, by providing in-home preventive services, reducing the length of stay in out-of-home care through expeditious reunification and other forms of permanency, and using the most expensive levels of out-of-home care for the shortest duration necessary.

The reliance on the use of the CANS as not only a screening tool for the appropriate level of care, but also as a monitoring tool to assess the continued need for higher levels of care, will be a critical element in managing our use of congregate care.

References

Child and adolescent needs and strengths methodology: An information integration tool for children and adolescents with mental health challenges (CANS). Copyright © 1999 Buddin Praed Foundation.

Children's scorecard (2004). County of Los Angeles, Children's Planning Council (internal document).

County of Los Angeles budget addendum (2004). County of Los Angeles Board of Supervisors (internal document).

Lyons, J. S. (2004). *Redressing the emperor: Improving our children's public mental health system.* Westport, CT: Praeger.

Lyons, J. S., Yeh, I., Leon, S. C., Uziel-Miller, N. D. & Tracy, P. (1999). Use of measurement audit in outcomes management. *Journal of the American Academy of Child and Adolescent Psychiatry, 38*, 305–310.

Part 3

Managing Single Programs Across Systems

Chapter 9

Understanding Psychiatric Hospital Admissions and Outcomes

by Scott C. Leon, Ph.D.

INTRODUCTION

Efforts to monitor and manage access to inpatient services began in the adult private sector in the 1970s. The primary goal of these efforts was to reduce the number of inpatient admissions and bed days as a means of controlling the costs of this most expensive form of mental health care. The strategies employed to accomplish this goal varied but typically included managed care practices such as prospective and current review, capitation, and greater use of lower levels of care. Research has supported these strategies by demonstrating that they lead to greater overall access to the full range of mental health care and cost containment (e.g., Goldman et al., 1999). Evidence also suggests that managed behavioral health care strategies offer the potential for improved outcomes (e.g., England, 1999; Olfson et al., 1999).

The management of inpatient utilization in child welfare proved more complicated for several reasons. First, an unfortunate historical reality of the children's mental health system is that relative to the admittedly imperfect adult system, a majority of youth who need care do not receive it (Knitzer, 1982; Huang et al., 2005). In this environment, preventive and/or less restrictive therapeutic care is often lacking, creating greater demand for unnecessary inpatient services. Second, behavioral health care decisions in the child welfare system are often made against a backdrop of myriad extra-clinical forces. For example, hospitalization has been used by foster families to provide respite, by caseworkers to reduce the pressure of stressful caseloads, and by government representatives to head off the potential negative consequences of graphic media cases. Finally, in a per diem, state-funded, Medicaid environment, no direct financial incentives exist to limit the use of psychiatric hospitalization among the individuals who make health care decisions.

ILLINOIS' INPATIENT SYSTEM FOR YOUTH IN SUBSTITUTE CARE

Consent Decree Mandates Changes

Illinois' child welfare system, like most, was not immune to these challenges and the potential for misuse of inpatient admissions. In the early 1990s, several troubling trends began to emerge about Illinois' system, which suggested that mental health decisions were being fueled by provider and system incentives and not in the best interests of youth outcomes. For example, growing numbers of youth were being served out of state and inpatient lengths of stay lasting several months at a time were common. This breakdown of the system led the American Civil Liberties Union (ACLU) in 1991 to bring a lawsuit against the Illinois Department of Children and Family Services (IDCFS), *B.H. v. McDonald*, charging the IDCFS with neglecting the children it was supposed to protect. The consent decree that emerged as a result of this case mandated several dramatic changes to Illinois' mental health system for youth in substitute care. Many of these changes reflected the prevailing thinking regarding mental health care organization and delivery, represented primarily by the Child and Adolescent Service System Principles (CASSP) model (Stroul & Friedman, 1986), which calls for treatment that is least restrictive, community-based, and family-centered.

As a result of the *B.H.* litigation and consent decree, the IDCFS was required to put systems in place that would match the needs of youth to appropriate services in their local communities, in compliance with the least restrictive environment philosophy. This proved to be a substantial undertaking that developed over more than a decade and is still evolving. One thing was clear from the outset of the *B.H.* Consent Decree: system change would require an aggressive, comprehensive, centralized effort involving all service systems and their various stakeholders. New services would be required as well as a large statewide evaluation to monitor utilization performance.

Screening Assessment and Supportive Services

The Screening Assessment and Supportive Services (SASS) program began in 1992 as the primary new service entity designed to be the gatekeeper for hospital referrals. In keeping with the *B.H.* Consent Decree, the main purpose of SASS is to "assure clients referred for acute inpatient psychiatric hospitalization are appropriate for admission and that appropriate and less restrictive service options have been fully explored and ruled out" (DCFS, 2005, p. 3). For a referral to be appropriate for hospitalization, at least one of the following criteria must be met:

Aggressive and/or dangerous behaviors which are likely to cause harm to self or others, even if that is not the intent; or

Aggressive behaviors with a plan and/or means to carry out the plan; or

Suicidal/homicidal ideation with plan and/or means to carry out the plan; or

Psychotic or dissociative behaviors which are likely to require hospitalization in order to stabilize and/or prevent harm to the child or others. (SASS Program Plan § 11.1, p. 17)

SASS agencies attempt to uphold this purpose through a variety of services. Foster parents and residential care providers concerned about the safety of the wards they serve can make referrals to SASS, which is responsible for a psychiatric screening within four hours of a referral. This screening ultimately leads to a decision on admission (hospitalize or deflect). If the child is hospitalized, SASS is required to deliver a number of services intended to ensure that children are not hospitalized beyond medical necessity. SASS's responsibilities include: choosing the most appropriate hospital, attendance at seventy-two-hour staffings, assessing the viability of the pre-hospital placement, monitoring the discharge date, continuing assessment, treatment planning, and discharge planning. These services are intended to ensure that lengths of stay are appropriate and that placement stability is maintained (SASS Program Plan §§ 12.0, 13.0).

If hospitalization is not considered appropriate for the child and the psychiatrist agrees, a variety of deflection services can be implemented, including crisis stabilization services to resolve the crisis, education to the child and caregiver regarding the hospitalization decision and the psychiatric crisis, respite, case management, and a variety of other Medicaid-reimbursable services (SASS Program Plan § 14.0). A majority of SASS workers are Masters-level social workers.

STATEWIDE EVALUATION OF ILLINOIS' SASS SYSTEM AND INPATIENT UTILIZATION

Development of Standardized Tool

Early anecdotal feedback about the SASS program was positive. However, the IDCFS was cognizant of the need to formally evaluate the benefits of the program in the effort to reduce unnecessary hospitalizations. To accomplish this, IDCFS administrators began in 1993 to work with Dr. John Lyons from Northwestern University to develop a comprehensive statewide evaluation of hospital decision and utilization practices. The first task in the evaluation process was to develop a reliable and valid standardized tool with items appropriate to psychiatric hospital decisions. Standard principles of tool development were employed in this task, including the use of extensive focus groups with multiple stakeholders, the development of comprehensive assessment domains, item development with concrete anchoring on an interval (0 to 3) scale, and several rounds of item writing and refinement. An early version of the Children's Severity of Psychiatric Illness (CSPI) tool was developed as a result of these efforts.

The researchers conducted a pilot test to determine the reliability and validity of the new tool. They used samples of youth psychiatric charts to develop reliability estimates that were consistently above .85 (Lyons et al., 1997). Items that failed to achieve consistent reliability were amended or deleted. The final version of the CSPI contained twenty-five items across the following five dimensions:

- Symptoms

- Risk factors

- Functioning

- Comorbid factors

- Placement/system factors

In 1995, the CSPI was formally validated with a sample of wards of the state presenting for hospitalization. The researchers randomly selected 330 closed youth charts of youth from Cook County, Illinois for participation. Youth in the sample were either hospitalized (n=155) or deflected (n=173). Using logistic regression, Lyons and colleagues (1997a) were able to predict decision to admit or deflect using variables appropriate to admission such as suicide risk and dangerousness to others. A significant model emerged, accurately classifying close to 70 percent of all cases; this indicated that the tool was successful in predicting the criterion of interest, admission decision. Further, results indicated that inappropriate admissions (actual decision = hospitalize; predicted decision = deflect) could be further differentiated from appropriate admissions (actual decision = hospitalize; predicted decision = hospitalize) using several of the CSPI variables putatively unrelated to an admission, such as emotional problems, posttraumatic stress disorder (PTSD), or the presence of learning disabilities. Finally, rates of inappropriate admissions varied intuitively by placement. For example, residential treatment referrals were inappropriate in only 26 percent of cases, presumably reflecting its greater capacity to create a structured environment to manage acute behavior. On the other hand, home-of-relative referrals were inappropriate at a rate of 60 percent. Overall, these findings indicated that the CSPI was a reliable and valid measure of psychiatric hospital decision-making, and the IDCFS determined that the CSPI was ready for use on a statewide basis to manage inpatient utilization.

SASS Evaluation Roll-Out

Beginning in early 1997, all SASS workers participated in CSPI trainings. Workers were required to achieve reliability scores above .70 to be certified as CSPI raters. After statewide training, SASS workers were required to complete CSPIs and a demographics cover page for all wards screened for hospitalization. SASS workers completed the CSPI and a range of demographic information upon completion of their crisis evaluations. The CSPI and demographic data were sent to Northwestern University for data entry and analysis. SASS workers completed the CSPI and other data for *all* youth, whether they were hospitalized or deflected. This allowed us to investigate differences between these two samples of youth as a means of exploring hospitalization appropriateness.

By the end of fiscal year 1998 (FY98), SASS workers had screened 2,180 youth with the CSPI. The stage was set for a full statewide evaluation of the SASS program and its commission to ensure appropriate hospitalization for wards of Illinois. This represented the first effort to conduct such a comprehensive review of a state's hospitalization decisions for a specific population of youth (Leon et al., 1999). The primary goal of the statewide evaluation was to explore the extent to which specific CSPI variables would predict hospitalization decision. In keeping with the SASS program plan, our hope was that variables such as suicide risk, dangerousness to others, and psychosis would play the largest role in predicting whether youth would be hospitalized or deflected. Variables unrelated to admission decision, such as the presence of emotional and behavioral disorders, should not predict decision to admit to a psychiatric hospital. In the current behavioral health care environment, these presentations are best treated in community and residential treatment settings.

Evaluation Findings

Logistic Progression Analyses. To explore differences between deflected and hospitalized youth, we employed logistic regression analyses, a popular statistical technique used to find differences between values of a binary independent variable (hospitalize versus deflect). Logistic regression analyses also allow for the creation of a classification table containing numbers (*ns*) and percentages of correctly and incorrectly classified cases. We entered a total of twenty-five dependent variables into the logistic regression model predicting hospital decision, ranging from clinically appropriate variables such as suicide and dangerousness to inappropriate demographic variables such as race and region of placement (e.g., Southern versus Central region). Variables were entered in hierarchical blocks, or stages. In the first block, CSPI variables were entered, and in the second, demographic variables. In the final block, interactions were entered and tested based on the findings from the first two blocks. This allowed us to test the extent to which CSPI variables independently predicted admission decisions, and to test the extent to which non-clinical variables predicted admission decision after first controlling for clinical variables.

Figure 9.1 presents the variables that emerged as statistically significant predictors of decision to admit or deflect. A total of eight variables predicted decision to admit. We were pleased to discover that suicide, dangerousness to others, and psychosis were all strong predictors of decision to admit, with odds ratios of 2.7, 2.5, and 2.1 respectively. These are the variables that reflect the SASS program plan language for an appropriate hospitalization. Further, behavioral problems, a composite of conduct disturbance and oppositional behavior, predicted decision to deflect. This finding was welcome due to anecdotal reports before the SASS implementation that youth were being hospitalized to manage difficult but nonrisky externalizing behavior.

The regression statistics in a logistic regression are conveyed in terms of odds ratios, along with confidence intervals. Relatively higher odds ratio variables indicate greater power in predicting decision to admit. For example, in the FY98 model,

Figure 9.1
FY98 Predictors of Hospitalization Decision

Variable	Odds Ratio	Confidence Interval
Psychosis	2.5	1.7–3.6
Emotion	2.2	1.5–3.2
Impulsivity	2.2	1.5–3.3
Suicide	2.7	2.0–3.5
Dangerousness to Others	2.1	1.5–2.8
Behavior Problem	.8	.77–.93
African-American	1.5	1.2–2.0
Hispanic	2.0	1.2–3.3

suicide risk had the highest odds ratio, at 2.7. This indicates that as a youth's suicide risk increases one point, for example from 0 (no risk) to 1 (past risk), the odds of being hospitalized versus deflected increase almost threefold. Odds ratios of less than 1.0 indicate a greater probability of deflection.

The Baseline: Fiscal Year 1998 Results. Figure 9.2 presents the classification table for the FY98 analyses. The overall model accurately predicted 79 percent of all hospitalizations and deflections, which easily outstripped the base rate of 62 percent (percentage of deflections). However, for all youth who were actually hospitalized, they were correctly predicted to be hospitalized (sensitivity) in 68 percent of cases. Actual deflections were accurately predicted (specificity) in 87 percent of cases. This suggests that the model was better at capturing deflections than hospitalizations. It also suggests that in 32 percent of cases, hospitalizations present similarly to deflections, a statistic offering room for system improvement.

Examining specific CSPI predictors of admission decision tells a more nuanced story of admission decision that again provides direction for future system evolution. For example, our findings suggested that the CSPI variables emotional disturbance and impulsivity also predicted decision to admit. These clinical presentations are challenging, but again, do not in and of themselves warrant hospitalization. It might be, however, that these variables operate in conjunction with suicide risk, dangerousness to others, and psychosis to produce greater risk of harm to self and/or others, therefore possibly warranting justification as an acceptable predictor of psychiatric hospitalization. This possibility was tested in the original model through the use of statistical interactions. Both impulsivity and emotional disturbance were multiplied by suicide risk, dangerousness, and psychosis to create and test interactions. Interestingly, none of these interactions were significant, again suggesting that these variables operate independently, and presumably inappropriately, in predicting decision to admit.

The most disheartening results regarding admission decisions appear to be reflected in the race and ethnicity findings. Both African-Americans and Latino(a)s in FY98 had a greater chance of being hospitalized after controlling for the clinical variables

Figure 9.2
Classification Accuracy for FY98 Prediction of Hospitalization Decision

Observed		Predicted		
		Hospitalize	Deflect	Percent
Observed	Hospitalize	562	270	68%
	Deflect	179	1169	87%
Percent		76%	81%	79%

of impulsivity and emotional disturbance (which were entered after the clinical CSPI variables). The fact that race and ethnicity predicted decision to admit after controlling for clinical variables indicated that Illinois' system varied in its decision appropriateness in FY98; African-American and Hispanic youth presumably experienced higher probabilities of being hospitalized compared to European-American youth, clinical risk held constant. These findings suggested the existence of institutional racial and ethnic disparities and the need for system improvement in this domain.

Overall then, the FY98 results offered some evidence of appropriate hospital use, evidenced by acceptable admission decision classification accuracy (80 percent). Accurate differentiation of level of care decisions is a necessary condition for the conclusion that service utilization is rational. Further, the primary predictors of admission decision were clinical variables indicative of danger to self or others. Behavioral problems such as conduct disturbance and oppositional behavior, which anecdotally predicted admissions decisions in years prior to the onset of SASS, actually predicted decision to deflect in the FY98 model. This indicates that hospital referrers were attempting to use hospitalizations under the previous framework but were being stopped by SASS gatekeepers.

However, these findings provide diagnostic evidence of some system dysfunction. For example, despite the high overall accuracy, hospital accuracy—at 68 percent—was lower than the 87 percent deflection accuracy. Further, variables such as impulsivity and emotional disturbance predicted decision to admit independent of danger to self and others, indicating that they were inappropriately influencing hospital decisions. Finally, race and ethnicity were predicting decision to admit above and beyond clinical and other demographic variables. This troubling finding indicated that admission decisions were more appropriate for European-Americans versus African-Americans or Hispanics.

The FY98 findings provide a context for admission decision that sets the stage for ongoing system improvement. Continuous quality improvement (CQI) models recognize that health care systems are not and never will be perfect. In lieu of perfection, CQI attempts to provide ongoing feedback that offers benchmarks, goal-setting, recommended areas for change, and additional evaluation to ensure that expected evolution is realized. In keeping with this value, the IDCFS, SASS, and Northwestern University remain committed to continuing evaluation and working together to monitor and understand hospital utilization. To realize this goal, evaluations similar to the FY98 SASS statewide study are conducted with regularity. Over four fiscal years, Illinois' inpatient system, through the SASS program, experienced continuous changes, as described below.

POSITIVE CHANGE OVER TIME: 1998-2001

The same variables used to predict hospitalization decision in FY98 were used to predict hospitalization decisions in FY99, FY00, and FY01. Classification accuracies using logistic regression for each of these years are presented in Figure 9.3, along with deflection base rates. The figure suggests that overall, accuracy remained constant, ranging from 79 percent to 81 percent, and always showing an improvement over the base rate. This indicates an overall constancy in the ability of these variables to predict who will be deflected and who will be hospitalized. Indirectly, this suggests that the system is broadly functioning in much the same way over the four fiscal years.

However, additional analyses point to changes in Illinois' psychiatric hospital system indicative of positive growth. The overall accuracy statistics presented in Figure 9.3 can be disaggregated into two component accuracies, hospital accuracy (sensitivity) and deflection accuracy (specificity). Hospital accuracy is the probability of being predicted hospitalized for all actually hospitalized cases. Deflection accuracy, on the other hand, is the probability of being predicted deflected for all actual deflections. Figure 9.4 presents hospital and deflection accuracies across the four fiscal years, revealing system changes not seen in the overall analyses presented in Figure 9.3. These analyses reveal a clear trend of increasing hospital accuracy and decreasing deflection accuracy. It appears that hospitalization decision-making became more accurate but that deflection decision-making became less accurate.

Stated differently, Figure 9.4 suggests that across time, fewer actual hospitalizations were predicted to be deflected and more actual deflections were predicted to be hospitalized. This situation would occur in an environment where only acute, severe youth are hospitalized and greater numbers of higher risk youth are deflected. It is reasonable to see how higher numbers of acute youth being hospitalized is a sign of a positive evolution in the system; however, it is less clear how to interpret the finding that greater numbers of deflected youth are higher risk. One possibility is that due to the implementation of SASS, an entity designed not only to screen youth but to work with youth and families to manage acute distress, higher acuity behavior is being safely managed at lower levels of care. A typical example occurs when a youth threatens suicide without a clear plan or means. Prior to SASS, the indication of self-harm would lead to an immediate hospitalization. However, with the implementation of SASS, clinical resources are devoted to understanding the suicidal ideation. In the process of understanding sources of distress, it is common for youth and families to see that the verbalization of threat to self-harm is actually a communication of anger over frustrated needs. Therefore, while still warranting a higher rating on the suicide risk variable of the CSPI due to verbalization of suicidal ideation, a positive clinical intervention with contracting and ongoing support can prevent hospitalization while still maintaining safety. Further support for this hypothesis comes from evidence that re-screening rates remain constant over the years of the study.

Further evidence of system evolution can be found in the study of changes in the impact of non-clinical variables in predicting admission decision across the four fiscal years. In FY98, race and ethnicity findings suggested that both African-Americans and Hispanics had higher rates of hospitalization even after controlling for clinical variables. Positive system evolution would therefore be indicated by a decrease in the importance of these variables over time. Figure 9.5, based on research from Rawal and colleagues (2003), provides evidence of just such an evolution. This figure shows rates of presumably inappropriate referrals across five years, 1998-2002. To determine the appropriate

Figure 9.3
Classification Accuracies Versus Base Rates (Deflections) From FY98 Through FY2001

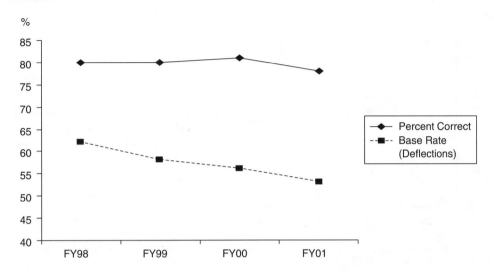

Figure 9.4
Percentages of Hospital and Deflection Accuracy Across Four Fiscal Years

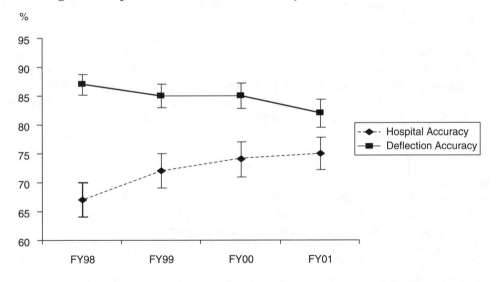

versus inappropriate referrals, the researchers first used the logistic regression strategies presented above. But instead of examining classification accuracies, which represent agreement between actual and predicted decisions (e.g., predicted = hospitalized; actual = hospitalized), these researchers explored rates of misclassification over time (e.g. predicted = hospitalized; actual = deflected). The numbers presented in Figure 9.5 are rates of youth predicted to be deflected but actually hospitalized over time. As such, they represent rates of inappropriate hospitalizations.

Figure 9.5
Percentages of Inappropriate Hospital Referrals for Caucasians,
African-Americans, and Hispanics, FY98–FY02

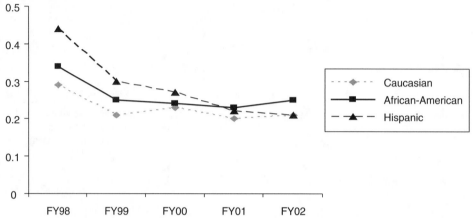

Reproduced from paper presented by Rawal, Romanksy, and Lyons at the American Health Services Association
Conference (2003). Reprinted with permission.

As Figure 9.5 demonstrates, rates of inappropriate hospitalizations varied significantly between racial and ethnic groups in 1998. Close to 45 percent of all hospital admissions for African-Americans were inappropriate in 1998, compared to less than 35 percent for Hispanics and less than 30 percent for Caucasians. However, this discrepancy decreased dramatically over the course of five years. In 2002, rates of inappropriate referral rates across the three racial and ethnic groups varied by less than 5 percentage points: 25 percent for African-Americans, and 21 percent for Hispanics and Caucasians. Therefore, these findings provided evidence of improved system functioning as demonstrated by reduced racial and ethnic disparities.

Further evidence of positive system evolution can be seen in Figure 9.6. This figure compares the odds ratios for the CSPI variables impulsivity, emotional disturbance, suicide risk, and dangerousness to others across the four fiscal years. As we noted above, impulsivity and emotional disturbance played a significant role in predicting decision to admit in FY98. The fact that in FY98 impulsivity and emotional disturbance did not interact with self and other risk variables to further predict admission decision suggested that they operated independently and inappropriately in predicting utilization. However, Figure 9.6 demonstrates that the influence of these variables appears to have decreased over time, from odds ratios of over 2 in FY98 to 1 in FY01. While impulsivity and emotional disturbance appear to have decreased in importance, suicide risk and dangerousness to others remained constant in their roles as predictors of admission decision.

The overall findings indicate that Illinois' system is generally functioning well and is improving with time. Most of this success can be attributed to the SASS program, the major service entity change from prior years. However, it took a statewide evaluation to unearth SASS's success and provide definitive evidence of Illinois' improved hospital utilization performance. Despite the generally positive results, however, they appear to have provided the most benefit to higher-level system administrators concerned with

Figure 9.6

Odds Ratios Predicting Strength of Decision to Admit to Hospital for Four CSPI Clinical Variables, FY98–FY01

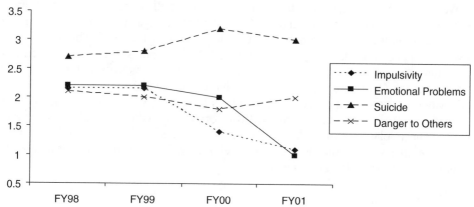

the overall success of the SASS program and appropriate utilization of psychiatric hospitalization. While all stakeholders in the system presumably benefited from such global information, these findings were still of limited value to individual agencies and hospitals, workers, and their supervisors because they only provided limited direct guidance for improved service delivery. Lyons' Total Clinical Outcomes Management (TCOM) system (Lyons, 2004) recognizes this inherent limitation in the typical focus of evaluation. In response, TCOM advocates for an approach to outcomes management that provides useful feedback to parties at all levels in the system. In keeping with this philosophy, the next sections provide examples of how we attempted to use data to provide support for ongoing improvement for multiple entities in the system.

USING EVALUATION FINDINGS FOR SYSTEM IMPROVEMENT

As noted earlier, predicting hospital admission decisions led to a 2×2 table and four decision categories, as shown in Figure 9.2. When actual decisions agree with predicted decisions, we can imply that the decision was appropriate, or at least consistent with the typical child in the state. However, when actual decisions fail to align with predicted decisions, the case is inconsistent with the norm for the state. As argued above, this can ostensibly happen for both positive and negative reasons. For example, a hospitalization predicted to be deflected might occur where a SASS worker is concerned about maintaining the placement; without clinical justification, this is a negative explanation for decision-prediction dissonance. On the other hand, a deflection that was predicted to be hospitalized might occur if a SASS worker is able to help a youth with acute symptomatology and his family manage the crisis with exceptional clinical intervention.

Not long after we developed our first prediction models, we began to use data on predicted versus observed admission decisions to help individual SASS workers and agencies better understand their utilization practices and improve their clinical work. At the end of every month, we used the hospital prediction formula developed from the logistic regression to develop hospital and deflection predictions. We then created documents unique to each SASS agency that listed the youths they served in that month.

Next to each youth's name were two additional columns: one for actual decision and one for predicted decision. Each agency was then able to see how often its decisions aligned with what was predicted based on the statewide prediction model.

We offered SASS agencies the opportunity to use these reports to better understand reasons for classification inaccuracies. We then suggested that supervisors use the reports in their meetings to help create dialogue among their staff about their clinical work and decision-making. We also invited SASS agencies to document their case discussions and report back to us at Northwestern the reasons they had uncovered for a misprediction. Over a period of eight months, we received 150 narratives containing SASS worker case descriptions and hypotheses for why a statistical misclassification occurred. A team of reviewers from Northwestern examined the narratives and developed four basic classes of misclassification reasons. The reviewers then double-rated a sample of charts and achieved acceptable reliability. The four reasons for misprediction could easily be coded as follows:

- Positive treatment factors
- Non-clinical factors
- Measurement issues
- Other clinical factors

Figure 9.7 presents the rates of each of these factors for the sample, broken down by cases that were actually hospitalized but predicted to be deflected (mispredicted hospitalizations) and cases that were actually deflected but predicted to be hospitalized (mispredicted deflections).

Positive Treatment Factors

Positive treatment factors occurred exclusively for mispredicted deflections, representing 43 percent of such cases. In these cases, deflections were made possible due to the implementation of intensive clinical services such as contracting and effective respite. For example, one SASS worker was able to take a highly agitated youth out of his foster home for lunch and to the music store to help him relax and help the foster parents achieve respite. To avoid reinforcing decompensatory behavior, the worker created a contract with the youth at lunch that made future outings contingent on healthy expression of emotion and appropriate self-soothing. The SASS worker reported that no further hospital referrals had been made at discharge from SASS, forty-five days after opening the case.

Non-Clinical Factors

Non-clinical factors occurred exclusively for mispredicted hospitalizations, representing 53 percent of such cases. In these cases, extenuating, non-clinical factors such as placement decisions were driving the decision to hospitalize in the absence of acute and dangerous clinical presentations. For example, one SASS worker reported that he received a call from a caseworker seeking a referral for a youth who had become

Figure 9.7
SASS Worker Coded Reasons for Actual Versus Predicted Hospital Decision Discrepancies

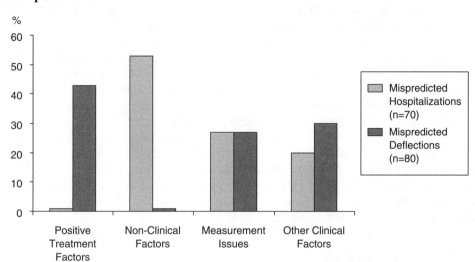

a media case. The youth was recently removed from a foster mother who had beaten and malnourished him for several years. The SASS worker was reluctant at first to hospitalize but changed his mind after receiving a phone call from a high-level IDCFS administrator indicating that the youth should be hospitalized to avoid media coverage that implied the youth was denied services.

Non-clinical reasons for a hospitalization can also be justified based on concern for a youth's long-term placement stability. Hospitalizations are thus seen as unfortunate but necessary opportunities for caregiver respite. In these circumstances, it is often quite understandable for caseworkers and SASS workers to want to preserve the placement, especially if it is a permanency placement. However, the desire to use a hospital for this purpose often speaks to dysfunction in the service system, such as a lack of services or poor provider communication; it further begs the question as to why an urgent hospitalization was required to manage a tense family situation that had most likely been building over time.

Measurement Issues

Measurement issues reflect an inaccurate coding or administration of the CSPI. Figure 9.7 shows that 27 percent of all mispredicted hospitalizations and mispredicted deflections are due to measurement issues. In one example, a strong ten-year-old girl had recently become angry and hit her foster sister over the head with a solid wooden cutting board, knocking the girl unconscious. This should have been rated a 3 on dangerousness to others because the cutting board led to "imminent danger of harm" to another. Instead, it had been mistakenly rated a 2 on this scale. The realization of a measurement error has the benefit of reminding SASS workers to pay close attention to the CSPI anchorings and the general importance of reliability.

Other Clinical Factors

SASS workers' intuitive clinical judgments in decision-making reflect other clinical factors as well. Since tools such as the CSPI cannot measure intuition, the CSPI profile in these cases is less accurate in predicting a decision. Other clinical factors occurred in 20 percent of mispredicted hospitalizations and 30 percent of mispredicted deflections. The most common reason for an "other clinical factors" classification in a mispredicted hospitalization occurs when a SASS worker believes that while the youth is not currently at risk, an increase in his or her psychiatric distress is imminent and a future hospitalization is guaranteed.

These preemptive admissions are tempting and are often grounded in the best clinical interests of the youth. However, there are two major problems associated with the use of clinical intuition. First, research suggests that clinical intuition is fraught with error, leading to such mistakes as misdiagnosis and wrong prognoses (e.g., Grove et al., 2000). Second, clinical intuition could conceivably be used to justify any mental health decision, opening the door to the type of misallocation of resources seen in the early 1990s in Illinois and elsewhere.

PROVIDER OUTCOMES

Quality outcomes are made possible by a system that is healthy at multiple levels. So far, the evaluation described in this chapter makes evident that sound policy at the highest state administrative level led to a program (SASS) that appears responsible for improved allocation of hospital resources. Further, we found evidence of sound clinical work at the level of the individual SASS worker and evidence for variability across workers in quality. Below is a description of efforts to understand variability in outcomes at another level in the system, the institutional provider of services. Recent evidence suggests that institutional providers directly and indirectly play a role in creating workplace cultures that impact mental health outcomes (Glisson & Hemmelgarn, 1998). It is therefore imperative to understand variability across providers in utilization and quality as part of a future effort to find those institutional environments that support the best youth outcomes.

Inpatient Hospital Performance

So far, this chapter has discussed the prediction of hospital admission as an indicator of the appropriateness of the IDCFS's mental health care utilization. Another indicator evaluators use is length of stay (LOS). If admission decision is a method for exploring appropriateness of level of care, LOS has historically been used to study appropriateness of "dose of care." The methods for exploring appropriateness of LOS are similar to methods used to study admission decision. The evaluators first use clinical variables, and after controlling for the clinical variables, they use non-clinical variables to further predict LOS. In a healthy system of care, clinical variables are the primary drivers of LOS, and non-clinical variables have a limited role in accounting for variability in LOS.

In a recent study, we used the same data set described earlier, the SASS referrals from FY98-FY01 and selected cases that were screened and hospitalized. We were able to predict LOS using the CPSI variables discussed so far and a range of non-clinical variables (Leon et al., 2006). Overall, 30 percent of the variance in LOS was predicted using ordinary least squares regression, a typical finding in the LOS literature (Pavkov et al., 1999; Pottick et al., 1999, 2000). Further analysis revealed that clinical variables such as suicide and dangerousness predicted just 7 percent of the variance in LOS, while non-clinical variables predicted over 20 percent of variance. Interestingly, the primary determinant of LOS was hospital provider.

Figure 9.8 demonstrates the significant variability that exists across hospitals in LOS. The figure presents unstandardized beta weights and standard errors of six hospitals in the state. The numbers represent the average number of days youth at these hospitals stay longer or shorter than the mean number of days, controlling for clinical variables. As the table indicates, some hospitals actually predict a lower LOS after controlling for clinical and non-clinical variables, while others predict a higher LOS. For example, youth at Hospital *A* stayed five fewer days on average than the typical youth in the state; and youth at Hospital *F* stayed five days longer.

Overall, the LOS findings indicated that bed day utilization is less appropriate and rational than admission decision. Future remediation of this problem might involve focusing evaluation resources on understanding practice pattern variations at the hospital level. It is possible that these efforts will lead us to discover significant variability in clinical models, organizational culture and climate, and a range of other hospital-level variables that act as moderators of observed differences in LOS. These efforts could lead to the enhancement and solidification of hospital best practices.

Residential Treatment

In another provider study (Leon et al., 2000), we explored the frequency of inappropriate hospital referrals received from residential treatment providers. Residential treatment centers (RTCs) are expected to provide an array of intensive services to youth with the most serious emotional disturbance. Therefore, they should be able to manage high-risk behavior and make hospital referrals only when all the resources at their disposal have been exhausted and frontline staff can no longer manage safety risk. To determine referral appropriateness, we placed youth referred from ten RTCs in Cook County, Illinois into one of two categories: high-risk and low-risk. High-risk youth displayed a 2 or a 3 on any of the following CSPI variables: suicide risk, dangerousness to others, or psychosis.

The ten residential providers in the sample could easily be classified into one of the two risk categories. The first category appeared to have high rates of low-risk referrals. Providers in this group made low-risk referrals at a rate ranging from 35 percent to 50 percent. The second group of RTCs made low-risk referrals at a much lower rate; rates for this group ranged from 0 percent to 15 percent. The low-risk referral group not only had higher rates of inappropriate referrals but also had significantly higher rates of hospitalizations compared to the latter group. In an effort to further understand the characteristics of these providers, we then compared the two groups across a range of provider CSPI variables. Our findings indicated that the group with higher rates of low-risk referrals and eventual hospitalizations were rated by SASS workers as displaying poorer supervision of their clients. These three findings coalesced to suggest significant variability in the quality of services across the ten RTCs. As with the LOS study and hospital findings, these results provided a method for understanding variability in quality across providers as a catalyst for improvement in Illinois' RTC community.

Figure 9.8
LOS Hospital Beta Weights, FY98-FY01

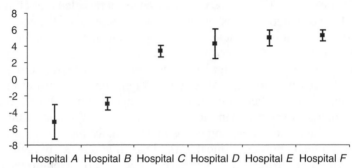

Hospital *A* Hospital *B* Hospital *C* Hospital *D* Hospital *E* Hospital *F*

[*Note:* Each hospital's number of days above or below the mean for the state are presented (with standard errors) corrected for clinical and other demographic factors.]

CONCLUSION

The evaluation described here is affirming of the IDCFS' work over the past thirteen years to improve the rationality of its inpatient utilization. Admissions decisions are made primarily based on risk. Further, the system has evolved in a positive direction over time by lessening the impact of variables that should not bear on admission decision. Racial and ethnic disparities have decreased, inappropriate clinical variables have become less potent, and it appears that higher risk youth are being effectively served at lower levels of care. Subsequent explorations of the data provided opportunities for improved services among SASS clinicians and the potential for enhanced provider accountability at hospitals and RTCs.

The evaluation was made possible through buy-in at the highest administrative levels to monitor adherence to a consequential consent decree. The tool developed to monitor decision-making, the CSPI, was created with adherence to the principles of measure development and achieved acceptable reliability and validity. Results from the evaluation were provided as feedback to system administrators with the expectation of system improvement (e.g., CQI). In this way, the evaluation of Illinois' inpatient system is consistent with typical evaluation approaches.

Addressing Weakness in Evaluation Models: TCOM

Traditional models of evaluation still have weaknesses, however, that the current approach attempts to mitigate. For example, when choosing a measure, typical evaluation practices focus almost exclusively on reliability and validity. While reliability and validity are crucial to evaluation, a sound psychometric tool must also be user friendly for all system stakeholders. The tool must serve not just to provide data, but to enhance communication and treatment planning. A second, related weakness of traditional approaches is that they endeavor to operate invisibly in an attempt to limit data contamination. A consequence of evaluator invisibility, however, is limited communication and threatened trust, which can hurt psychometric reliability through provider nullification—the intentional rigging of report tools to prevent untoward consequences. Third, these approaches focus their feedback on the highest-level stakeholders (e.g., the IDCFS) in the system and spend less time providing feedback to direct care providers and the institutions in which they work.

Lyons (2004) addressed these weaknesses through what he Calls Total Clinical Outcomes Management. TCOM begins with traditional approaches to evaluation by advocating for rigorous methodological strategies and regular feedback to system providers. However, TCOM moves beyond these approaches by seeking to use evaluation to become an active, integrated partner in service delivery, treatment planning, supervision, and ongoing improvement. TCOM accomplishes these goals primarily through its reliance on effective communication at all stages and with all stakeholders in the evaluation process. Below is a brief discussion of how TCOM was used to improve the quality of the evaluation through its emphasis on what Lyons terms communimetrics.

Communimetrics in Illinois' Statewide Hospital Utilization Evaluation

A typical item on a behavioral health measure contains three to five response options. The options are anchored at several points along the scale, differentiated primarily by problem severity (e.g., "Not at all a problem," "Severe problem") or frequency (e.g., "Never," "Always"). The CSPI used here anchors its items using typical severity descriptors, but it also anchors on need for services, a strategy somewhat unique to the CSPI and all measures in the Child and Adolescent Needs and Strengths (CANS) (1999) collection. For example, a 0 rating indicates that no action is necessary on the domain (e.g., caregiver problems providing supervision to a youth). A 1 indicates that no intervention is currently necessary but that "watchful waiting" is warranted to prevent an escalation in problems on the domain. A 2 indicates that intervention is necessary and a 3 indicates that immediate or intensive action is necessary.

Considering that a primary purpose of all communication is to express need, the CSPI's use of clinical need as an anchoring strategy goes a long way towards helping providers first communicate to themselves and then to others their sense of the client's service requirements. This process sets the stage for the crucial phase of service prioritization. Once clinical need and its associated service requirement are articulated, providers are immediately accountable for service implementation.

An actual case example illustrates these points. At a SASS meeting, two workers were discussing a case and disagreed on the most appropriate post-hospitalization disposition. The youth was an eleven-year-old boy who had begun to demonstrate symptoms of conduct disorder. He lived with his grandmother, who was beginning to experience significant cognitive and physical decline. He had been referred for hospitalization by the principal of his school after a fight in which he attacked a classmate with scissors.

One SASS worker believed that the youth needed referral to a residential placement facility upon discharge from the hospital, while the another believed he needed another chance in the community. The worker advocating for residential treatment argued that the youth was physically aggressive at school, in the neighborhood, and at home. This was represented by his 2 rating on the CSPI variables contextual consistency of symptoms, school functioning, and peer functioning, and a 3 rating on the variable dangerousness to others. However, the second worker noted that the youth's current environment was not conducive to his well-being due to his grandmother's decline, leading to a 2 rating on caregiver supervision. The worker also noted a relative lack of available community services to support the youth, leading to a rating of 2 on the CSPI variable wrap-capacity. Taken together, these ratings indicated to the second worker that more could be done to structure the youth's environment and connect him to community resources such as mentoring, after-school programming, and respite.

Clearly this was a complicated case that required great care and attention. Post-hospital placement decisions require some of the most thoughtful clinical consideration because of the import these decisions have for a youth's well-being. Imagine leaving a hospital after attacking someone with scissors to find that you are not moving back home to your grandmother, but to a group home in another community. In this case, the supervisor stepped in to decide that the youth should be given a second chance in the community. One could not help but notice that his decision was made after simultaneously looking at all the CSPI ratings and with special consideration of the grandmother's lack of supervision and the community's lack of support. He realized that these issues, by virtue of being rated a 2, reflected a pressing need that had never been addressed in the youth's service plan.

As this example illustrates, the CSPI is more than just decision support; it also serves to enhance what might be called communication support. Supporting communication across stakeholders serves to do what all good communication does—expresses need and perspective as a point of departure for compromise, shared understanding, and the force of group action. Encouraging others to quantify and categorize the communication of need in the service of this process is what Lyons (2004) terms communimetrics. And despite all of the important work that goes into data collection and analysis, evaluation, report writing, and publication, enhanced communication and the broader goals of TCOM will likely be the ultimate legacy of the evaluation described here.

References

Agency for Health Care and Policy Research (AHCPR) (1993). *Using clinical practice guidelines to evaluate quality of care. 2. Methods.* Rockville, MD: Author.

B.H. v. Macdonald, also known as *B.H. v. Suter*, *B.H. v. Johnson*, and *B.H. v. Ryder*, 128 F.R.D. 659 (N.D. Ill. Dec. 19, 1989), 715 F.Supp. 1387 (ND Ill. May 30, 1989), 49 F.3d 294 (7th Cir. 1995), *reh'g and reh'g en banc denied* (Apr. 7, 1995).

Child and adolescent needs and strengths methodology: An information integration tool for children and adolescents with mental health challenges (CANS). Copyright © 1999 Buddin Praed Foundation.

Children's Severity of Psychiatric Illness (CSPI) (2005). Buddin Praed Foundation. Retrieved March 18, 2005 from: http://www.buddinpraed.org/form/cans-mhman.asp.

Department of Children and Family Services (DCFS) (2005). *Overview of the Illinois child welfare system.* Available online at: http://www.state.il.us/dcfs/index.shtml.

England, M. J. (1999). Capturing mental health cost offsets. *Health Affairs, 18,* 91–93.

Glisson, C. & Hemmelgarn, A. L. (1998). The effects of organizational climate and interorganizational coordination on the quality and outcomes of children's service systems. *Child Abuse and Neglect, 98,* 401–421.

Goldman, W., McCulloch, J., Cuffel, B. & Kozma, D. (1999). More evidence for the insurability of managed behavioral health care. *Health Affairs,* 18, 172–181.

Grove, W. M., Zald, D. H., Lebow, B. S., Snitz, B. E. & Nelson, C. (2000). Clinical versus mechanical prediction: A meta-analysis. *Psychological Assessment, 12,* 19–30.

Huang, L., Stroul, B., Friedman, R., Mrazak, P., Friesen, B., Pires, S. & Mayberg, S. (2005). Transforming mental health care for children and their families. *American Psychologist, 60*, 615–627.

Knitzer, J. (1982). *Unclaimed children: The failure of public responsibility to children and adolescents in need of mental health services*. Washington, DC: Children's Defense Fund.

Leon, S. C., Uziel-Miller, N. D., Lyons, J. S. & Tracy, P. (1999). Psychiatric hospital service utilization of children and adolescents in state custody. *Journal of the American Academy of Child and Adolescent Psychiatry, 38*, 305–310.

Leon, S. C., Lyons, J. S., Uziel-Miller, N. D., Rawal, P., Tracy, P. & Williams, J. (2000). Evaluating the use of psychiatric hospitalization by residential treatment centers. *Journal of the American Academy of Child and Adolescent Psychiatry, 39*, 1496–1501.

Leon, S. C., Snowden, J., Bryant, F. B. & Lyons, J. S. (2006). The hospital as predictor of children's and adolescents' length of stay. *Journal of the American Academy of Child and Adolescent Psychiatry, 43*, 322–328.

Lyons, J. S., Rawal, P., Yeh, I., Leon, S. & Tracy, P. (2002). Use of measurement audit in outcomes management. *Journal of Behavioral Health Services & Research, 29*, 75–80.

Lyons, J. S., Kisiel, C. L., Dulcan, M., Cohen, R. & Chesler, P. (1997). Crisis assessment and psychiatric hospitalization of children and adolescents in state custody. *Journal of Child and Family Studies, 6*, 311–320.

Lyons, J. S., Howard, K. I., O'Mahoney, M. & Lish, J. (1997). *The measure and management of clinical outcomes in mental health*. Wiley: New York.

Lyons, J. S. (2004). *Redressing the emperor: Improving our children's public mental health system*. Westport, CT: Praeger.

Olfson, M., Sing, M. & Schlesinger, H. J. (1999). Mental health/medical care cost offsets: Opportunities for managed care. *Health Affairs, 18*, 79–90.

Pavkov, T. W., Goerge, R. M. & Czapkowicz, J. G. (1997). Predictors of length of stay among youths hospitalized in state hospitals in IL. *Journal of Child & Family Studies, 6*, 221–231.

Pottick, K. J., Hansell, S., Miller, J. E. & Davis, D. M. (1999). Factors associated with inpatient length of stay for children and adolescents with serious mental illness. *Social Work Research, 23*, 213–224

Pottick, K. J., McAlpine D. D. & Andelman, R. B. (2000). Changing patterns of psychiatric inpatient care for children and adolescents in general hospitals, 1988-1995. *American Journal of Psychiatry, 157*, 1267–1273.

Rawal, P., Romansky, J. & Lyons, J. S. (June 2003). *Reducing racial disparities in psychiatric hospital admissions of children*. Paper presented at the American Health Services Association, Nashville, TN.

Stroul, B. A. & Friedman, R. M. (1986). *A system of care for severely emotionally disturbed children and youth*. Washington, DC: National Technical Assistance Center for Children's Mental Health, Child and Adolescent Service System Program, Georgetown University Center for Child and Human Development.

Chapter 10

Building a Mobile Response and Stabilization System

by Susan Furrer, Psy.D. and
Joan Mechlin, M.A., M.S.N., A.P.R.N.B.C.

OVERVIEW

In the New Jersey Children's System of Care (SOC), the mobile response and stabilization system (MRSS) is the vehicle for delivering crisis intervention to children, youth, and their families when escalating behavior puts a child at risk of losing his or her current living arrangement. Mobile response and stabilization is provided in the home, community, or wherever the crisis is occurring. It is an integrated, comprehensive system using time-limited, focused, clinically based interventions. Mobile response is available immediately, twenty-four hours a day, seven days a week, for up to seventy-two hours. The goal of mobile response is to diffuse the targeted behavior, assess the child or youth, and develop a plan for safety. The mobile responder may decide that a worker should stay with the child and family to diffuse and manage the situation within the seventy-two hours, or within that time frame the responder's team may plan for interventions to continue stabilizing the targeted behavior for up to eight weeks. Together with the youth and caregiver, the mobile response team will develop and manage an individual crisis plan focusing on the behavior that put the child at risk, and the stabilization network will implement the plan.

The team obtains assessment information through use of the Crisis Assessment Tool, or CAT, which is a version of the Child and Adolescent Needs and Strengths (CANS) tool adapted for crisis situations. Interventions are done in the community, and targeted outcomes are identified and tracked according to an individualized crisis plan. Most important, the goal is to maintain the child or youth in his or her home or present living arrangement.

In 2000, the New Jersey Department of Human Services (DHS) initiated a major, statewide restructuring of the system that delivers services to children and their families experiencing emotional and behavioral challenges. Critical issues addressed included the frequent movement of children in the care of the Department of Youth and Family Services (DYFS), New Jersey's child protective service, from one placement to another; overcrowding in the state hospital for children awaiting placement in residential facilities; and the inappropriate hospitalization of children due to a lack of community-based resources. One change was the design and implementation of the Children's MRSS. This component of SOC development was new; it was designed as a network of new programs within separate mental health provider agencies and was not an add-on to any other emergency or crisis services that existed.

MODEL BASED IN CRISIS THEORY

The design for the MRSS practice model has its basis in crisis theory, which posits that a psychological crisis "refers to an individual's ability to solve a problem . . . that he cannot readily solve by using the coping mechanisms that have worked before" (Aguilera, 1994, p.3). Crisis situations or behavior can occur periodically during the normal life span. One author has summed up the heart of crisis theory and practice in a few basic statements:

> They [crisis situations] are often initiated by a hazardous event. This may be a catastrophic event or a series of successful stressful blows which rapidly build up a cumulative effect. The impact of the hazardous event disturbs the individual's homeostatic balance and puts him in a vulnerable state. If the problem continues and cannot be resolved, avoided or redefined, tension rises to a peak, and a precipitating factor can bring about a turning point during which the self-righting devices do not work and the individual enters a state of disequilibrium . . . [an] active crisis. (Golan, 1978, p.8)

Caplan (1964) and others (Roberts, 2000) concur that people cannot remain indefinitely in a state of psychological turmoil and survive, and that in a typical crisis state, equilibrium will be restored in four to six weeks. While crisis behavior tends naturally to stabilize in four to eight weeks, this period provides just a beginning for learning new coping skills and resources to use in the future. Mobile response and stabilization is the process of working through the crisis event so that the child and his or her caregivers can understand what causes the behaviors to escalate and what works for them at that time.

The model is also based on the fundamental principle that children and adolescents have the greatest opportunity for normal, healthy development when they maintain their ties to community and family while being helped. Philosophically and practically, the development of MRSS is based on four key SOC values, which are that the care must be:

- Child-centered and strength-based;
- Community-based;
- Culturally competent; and
- Collaborative across child-service systems.

Key Program Functions

In planning the development and implementation of the New Jersey MRSS (Lyons, 2008), the DHS's Division of Mental Health Services (DMHS) developed a work group consisting of providers of crisis services as well as in-home services to explore different models. Using the crisis theories outlined above and assessing the effectiveness of existing home-based crisis programs and its own experiences, the team developed and presented a model crisis intervention program to the Children's Initiative work group and to the directors of children's services in New Jersey. The DMHS-Office of Children's Services (OCS) decided to allow MRSS to be a stand-alone service within already existing mental health agencies in each county, through a request for proposal (RFP) process. Typically, MRSS services were the first of the new SOC components that became operational at the local level.

The mobile response agency would develop a network of stabilization interventions from existing agencies that were willing to deliver in-home services and have those services managed by the mobile response agency. The agency would provide services for up to seventy-two hours to diffuse the behavior and then develop a plan and refer the child for stabilization, or decide that the behavior was sufficiently stabilized and required no further intervention. The stabilization agency would provide services for up to eight weeks. The mobile response agency would manage the individual crisis plan that directed the interventions by the agency providing stabilization. The interventions would be based on identified, targeted behaviors that had put the child and family in crisis and the use of a uniform assessment tool that would support level-of-care and level-of-need decisions.

A contracted system administrator (CSA) would function as the single entry-level point for access to mobile response and stabilization. All referrals to MRSS would go to the contracted systems administrator, who would triage the calls and then call mobile response. The CSA would also collect information and maintain the database for mobile response.

Critical to the development and viability of this practice model is the ability to collect meaningful information that can be used at the individual, programmatic, and system levels. The CAT, one of the family of Information Management and Decision Support (IMDS) tools, became part of the New Jersey SOC's Total Clinical Outcomes Management (TCOM) process (see Chapter 5).

Initial Development and Implementation

We planned to begin implementation of the new MRSS model in four counties that represented rural, urban, and suburban demographics, and then develop across the state as the budget allowed. We began with a gradual implementation so we could learn from and build on our experience. We were concerned that we would be unable to provide the service to the entire population of children and youth exhibiting crisis behaviors, so we limited the population to children and youth experiencing a behavioral/emotional crisis. As CAT and service utilization data were collected from the very beginning of the implementation of the MRSS, we were able to identify and address any programmatic or data collection issues as they occurred.

Initially, the number of referrals was small. We identified two areas needing improvement. First, we opened the program to all children, youth, and their families experiencing escalating behaviors. Second, we recognized that the word *crisis* limited referrals, so we expanded the target population to include *all* children whose escalating behaviors put them at risk of losing their present placement or needing a higher level of care. Funding new programs became an issue, so the DMHS-OCS made a decision to develop MRSS services in other counties and, where possible, to use an existing mobile response agency as an administrative hub to service multiple counties.

THE NEW JERSEY MRSS PROGRAM

Program Description

The program consisted of two components, response (the first seventy-two hours) and stabilization (up to eight weeks). The flow chart in Figure 10.1 shows the relation of these components.

Mobile Response. This aspect of the program is responsible for delivering services to children and maintaining their current living arrangement or level of care. The response is immediate; the worker must be at the site within one hour of the phone call from the CSA, whose office provides a statewide, single point of access for the entire MRSS. The response includes immediate therapeutic interventions to control and diffuse the crisis situation and can last up to seventy-two hours.

During this phase, the worker collects key information regarding the child's crisis behavior, risk factors, and family strengths and needs. The information, which is integrated by the use of the CAT, supports the development of the individual crisis plan, which is behaviorally oriented and indicates the need for, and required intensity of, crisis stabilization services. When appropriate, the child/youth may be referred for a higher level of care such as hospitalization.

In some cases the target behavior is diffused by the crisis response, and additional services are not required. As part of the seventy-two-hour crisis response, a staff person may remain with the youth and family for up to twenty-four hours. Alternatively, a youth could be placed in a crisis bed for up to seven days if one is available; the crisis bed functions as a respite for the child and family when hospitalization is not needed. Unfortunately, it has been a challenge to develop sufficient crisis bed capacity in most counties to make this a routinely available service option. The individual crisis plan is managed by the local mobile response agency and is monitored by the supervisor of that program. Should the child and family require further intervention regarding the target behavior that resulted in the crisis call, the next stage is stabilization.

Figure 10.1
Mobile Response and Stabilization Services Flow Chart

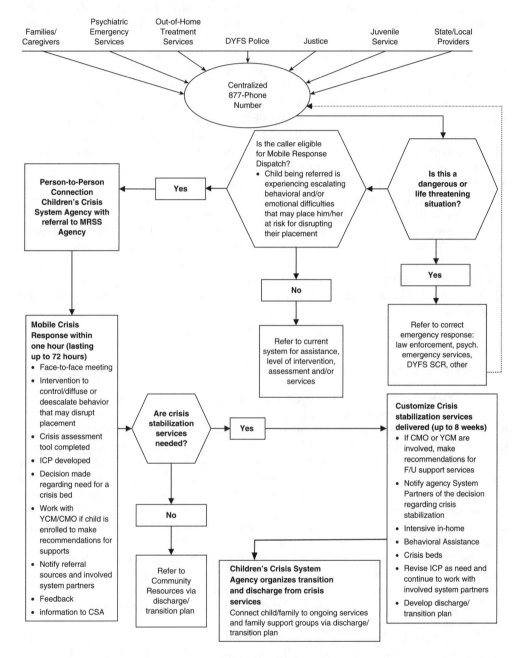

Stabilization. Intensive in-community interventions are based on an individual crisis plan developed by the response worker. This plan, using information collected with the CAT, identifies the behaviors and level of risk that support the stabilization intervention which may prevent hospitalization or require referral to a higher level of care. Stabilization interventions are delivered in the community by experienced, trained staff and can be provided for up to eight weeks.

Therapeutic interventions include behavioral assistance and in-home therapists. Behavioral assistants provide clinically driven, time-limited, therapeutic behavior management interventions for behavior that has been identified as challenging. In-home therapists are master's level licensed mental health professionals, who provide short-time behavioral-focused interventions to the youth and family. The intensive in-community services are driven by the individual service plan that has been developed using the CAT to provide information about the needs of the youth and family.

As target behaviors become stabilized and expectations for outcomes are met, the intensity of intervention is decreased. The stabilization worker, together with the caregiver(s), will then identify challenging behaviors and the triggers to those behaviors, as well as positive coping skills that can be used and/or developed. A second CAT is completed at the end of stabilization. This information is used to develop an at-risk crisis plan for the family to use if and when another crisis occurs. The mobile response and stabilization agency coordinates and manages the transition of the child and caregiver(s) to community-based agencies and makes referral recommendations for continued care through the contracted systems administrator.

The expected outcomes from mobile response and stabilization interventions include (1) reductions in movement from one home to another and (2) improved permanency in community placements. Providing appropriate interventions supported by individual crisis plans has led to decreased admissions to acute psychiatric hospital settings, improved management of risks, and less disruption in the child's home and community.

Use of the Crisis Assessment Tool

To reflect crisis behaviors, the CAT modified the typical CANS time frames to address acuity, shortening periods from thirty days to twenty-four hours in key areas such as risk, symptomatology, and behavior. The CAT facilitates the collection of critical data about the dispositions of children and youth based on their profiles with respect to risk, behaviors, symptoms, functioning, and caregiver capability. Through the use of its action levels for each item and algorithms developed from initial experiences, the CAT identifies the intensity of interventions needed to keep youth in the community. It also identifies service and support gaps in the community. Using the CAT, we can manage mobile response and stabilization at the individual planning level, manage and identify needs at the program level, and manage needs at the system level.

The CAT helps identify behavior profiles of youth being served in each MRSS. By identifying specific behaviors and corresponding needs, we can identify best practice interventions and improve and refine program development at the program and system levels. Thus, our own data may be used as practice-based evidence of decision-making processes and outcomes.

We used the CAT as a basis of support in making decisions about service planning and the level of need for and intensity of interventions in the stabilization process. The next step in decision support was to develop algorithms for mobile response and stabilization. A decision algorithm is "a logical set of criteria that describes the clinical characteristics of children and families that would be best served by the available decision options relevant to the algorithm" (Lyons, 2004, p. 158). The first algorithm within the SOC, the decision support criteria and thresholds, was developed for mobile response. Table 10.1 outlines our completed initial decision support model.

Table 10.1
CAT Decision Support Model for Service Planning

CAT Decision Support Model

1. Two or more of the following risk behaviors rated as 3:

   a. Suicide risk
   b. Self-mutilation
   c. Other self harm
   d. Danger to others
   e. Sexual aggression
   f. Runaway
   g. Judgment
   h. Fire setting
   i. Social behavior

2. One or more of the following risk behaviors rated as 3:

   a. Suicide risk
   b. Self-mutilation
   c. Other self harm
   d. Danger to others
   e. Sexual aggression
   f. Runaway
   g. Judgment
   h. Fire setting
   i. Social behavior

3. Three or more of the following risk behaviors rated as 2 or higher:

   a. Suicide risk
   b. Self-mutilation
   c. Danger to others
   d. Sexual aggression
   e. Runaway
   f. Judgment
   g. Social behavior

4. Two or more of the following risk behaviors rated as 2 or higher:

   a. Suicide risk
   b. Self-mutilation
   c. Danger to others

   d. Sexual aggression
   e. Runaway
   f. Judgment
   g. Social behavior

5. One or more of the following risk behaviors rated as 2:

   a. Suicide risk
   b. Self-mutilation
   c. Other self harm
   d. Danger to others
   e. Sexual aggression
   f. Runaway
   g. Judgment
   h. Fire setting
   i. Social behavior

6. One of more of the following symptoms rated as a 3:

   a. Psychosis
   b. Impulsivity
   c. Depression
   d. Anxiety
   e. Adjustment to trauma

7. Two or more of the following symptoms rated as 3 or higher:

   a. Psychosis
   b. Impulsivity
   c. Depression
   d. Anxiety
   e. Oppositional
   f. Conduct (antisocial behavior)
   g. Adjustment to trauma
   h. Anger control
   i. Substance abuse

8. Three or more of the following symptoms rated as 2 or higher:

   a. Psychosis
   b. Impulsivity

(Continued)

Table 10.1 (Continued)

c. Depression

d. Anxiety

e. Oppositional

f. Conduct (antisocial behavior)

g. Adjustment to trauma

h. Anger control

i. Substance abuse

9. Two or more of the following symptoms rated as 2 or higher:

   a. Psychosis

   b. Impulsivity

   c. Depression

   d. Anxiety

   e. Oppositional

   f. Conduct

   g. Adjustment to trauma

   h. Anger control

   i. Substance abuse

10. Criterion 9 OR at least one of the following symptoms rated as a 3:

    a. Impulsivity

    b. Adjustment to trauma

    c. Substance abuse

11. One of the following symptoms rated as a 3:

    a. Oppositional

    b. Conduct (antisocial behavior)

12. One of the following symptoms rated as a 3:

    a. Psychosis

    b. Impulsivity

    c. Adjustment to trauma

13. Two or more of the following caregiver needs or strengths rated as 2 or higher:

    a. Health

    b. Supervision

    c. Involvement

    d. Social resources

    e. Residential stability

14. One or more of the following caregiver needs or strengths rated as 2 or higher:

    a. Health

    b. Supervision

    c. Involvement

    d. Social resources

    e. Residential stability

EVALUATION OF INITIAL OUTCOMES

We included a total sample of 846 unique children in our analysis of the initial period of operation of all MRSS programs (Lyons, 2003). Data from these cases were used to develop an understanding of the needs profile across service dispositions. Of the sample, 312 had follow-up CAT assessments within ninety days of the initial screening. We focused on this group to study initial outcomes resulting from the MRSS implementation.

Levels of Risk Behaviors

Table 10.2 presents the percentage of children in each of the four primary disposition categories who were rated 2 or 3 on the risk behavior and behavioral/emotional needs items from the CAT.

Table 10.2
Percentage of Children With Actionable (2) and Immediately Actionable (3)
Levels of Risk Behaviors and Behavioral/Emotional Needs With Each Initial
Disposition Option in the MRSS Program

Risk Behavior	Outpatient N=283		In-Home N=492		Crisis Bed N=48		Hospital N=23	
	2	3	2	3	2	3	2	3
Suicide risk	12.0	3.5	19.3	2.0	10.4	2.1	4.3	39.1
Self-mutilation	3.9	0.7	7.3	0.4	2.1	0.0	4.3	8.7
Other self harm	5.3	1.1	9.8	23.2	10.4	2.1	26.1	4.3
Danger to others	10.3	3.8	15.7	2.5	17.0	14.9	9.1	27.3
Sexual aggression	2.1	0.0	1.2	0.2	2.1	2.1	8.7	4.3
Runaway	8.5	2.1	13.0	5.7	8.3	22.9	13.0	21.7
Judgment	40.3	4.9	49.2	7.9	60.4	8.3	39.1	52.2
Fire setting	3.6	0.0	3.9	0.0	2.1	2.1	4.3	4.3
Psychosis	1.4	0.0	1.2	0.6	4.2	0.0	1.7	13.0
Impulse/Hyper	28.3	4.9	35.6	6.3	41.7	8.3	39.1	26.1
Depression	25.1	1.4	36.4	2.8	41.7	2.1	47.8	8.7
Anxiety	9.5	1.4	25.2	2.2	20.8	2.1	30.4	8.7
Oppositional	42.0	6.4	51.0	9.3	54.2	22.9	56.5	21.7
Conduct (Antisocial)	22.6	2.8	23.4	1.6	37.5	10.4	21.7	17.4
Adj to trauma	18.4	1.8	29.3	3.7	18.8	2.1	30.4	13.0
Anger control	46.6	7.1	39.1	8.5	50.0	22.9	39.1	21.7
Substance use	4.9	1.4	4.5	1.0	10.4	0.0	17.4	13.0

Table 10.3 shows the percentage of children rated 3 (immediate/intensive action) on each risk behavior and behavioral/emotional need item; the children were placed in one of the four initial dispositional categories as shown. Review of these tables provides a clear elaboration of the differences in clinical presentation across the four common dispositions.

In general, children referred to outpatient services were at low risk (e.g., not engaged in any high-risk behaviors) and did not have acute symptomatology. Many of these youth did not require MRSS services. No child referred to outpatient services had an acute risk of sexual aggression or fire setting, or dangerous levels of symptoms of psychosis. However, as seen in Table 10.4, simply having one acute risk was not always associated with a higher level-of-care disposition. Nearly one-third of children rated as having high suicide risk were treated on an outpatient basis.

Table 10.3
Percentage of Children With an Immediate/Intensive Level (3) of Risk Behavior or Behavioral/Emotional Needs, Placed in Each of the Four Initial Dispositions

Risk Behavior	N	Percentage (%)			
		Outpatient	In-Home	Crisis Bed	Hospital
Suicide risk	33	30.3	30.3	3.0	27.3
Self-mutilation	7	28.6	28.6	0.0	28.6
Other self harm	9	33.3	22.2	11.1	11.1
Danger to others	38	26.3	31.6	18.4	15.8
Sexual aggression	4	0.0	25.0	25.0	25.0
Runaway	58	10.3	48.3	19.0	8.6
Judgment	78	17.9	50.0	5.1	15.4
Fire setting	2	0.0	0.0	50.0	50.0
Psychosis	6	0.0	50.0	0.0	50.0
Impulse/Hyper	61	23.0	50.8	6.6	9.8
Depression	24	16.7	58.3	4.2	8.3
Anxiety	20	20.0	55.0	5.0	10.0
Oppositional	90	20.0	51.0	12.2	5.6
Conduct (Antisocial)	27	29.6	29.6	18.5	7.4
Adjust to trauma	30	16.7	60.0	3.3	10.0
Anger control	84	23.8	50.0	13.1	6.0
Substance use	16	25.0	31.3	0.0	18.8

Children referred to the in-home crisis stabilization program generally are not at acute risk, with the exception of children exhibiting the risk of other self-harm. These youth tend to be more likely to exhibit internalizing symptoms (e.g., depression, anxiety, and adjustment to trauma). However, children with dangerous levels of oppositional behavior and conduct problems also were most commonly referred for in-home crisis services. This may reflect perceived caregiver characteristics that influence the decision for in-home stabilization; there are also few crisis bed slots, so bed availability likely influences this decision as well.

Among the children placed in crisis beds, runaway and danger to others are fairly common acute risks. These children have significant levels of externalizing behavior as seen through the percentage of children rated a 3 on oppositional behavior, conduct, and anger control. Crisis beds were comparable to hospitalization for children with acute issues of sexual aggression and fire setting. Children with acute suicide risk were generally not placed in crisis beds.

As expected, the children admitted into a psychiatric hospital are in much higher need than those served in other programs. These data demonstrate that more than one-third of all hospitalized children have an acute level of suicide risk and more than one quarter are at acute risk of violence against others (danger to others). However, as Table 10.4 shows, a significant number of children with acute risk are served below the hospital level of care. Thus the decision-making for these dispositions is more complicated and does not appear to be based on the presence of a single risk factor.

A significant model can be generated using a discriminant function analysis to predict the four primary dispositions with all of the CAT rating variables. The model is accurate in classifying 77.3 percent of all hospital admissions. The remaining children who were hospitalized were predicted to be served either in crisis beds (n=3, 13.6 percent) or in-home crisis stabilization (n=2, 9.1 percent).

The in-home crisis program served forty-four children who, based on their CAT ratings, were predicted to be admitted to the hospital. The hospital deflections represent 9.6 percent of all intensive, in-home cases. Another 20.5 percent were predicted to be placed in the crisis bed program. Only 24 percent of cases served by in-home services were predicted to be outpatient referrals. These data suggest that the intensive in-home program is targeting a fairly high-need group of children, as intended.

Only four children (9.8 percent) placed in a crisis bed were predicted to receive outpatient services only. An additional four children were predicted to be hospitalized. Of the remaining thirty-three children, two-thirds were predicted for the crisis bed program while the other one-third were seen as more similar to the intensive in-home program.

Follow-Up of Reassessed Cases

Table 10.4 presents the change in CAT scores from screening to follow-up for cases that were reassessed. On average, children improved on all the CAT dimension scores. However, some differences were observed based on initial disposition. As expected, hospitalized children were rated much higher on the CAT dimension scores at screening. These children demonstrated reductions in risk behaviors and functioning problems, but no change in symptom levels. Interestingly, the caregivers of these children demonstrated some improvements in capacity over time.

Outpatient referrals demonstrated positive improvements in symptoms, risk behaviors, and functioning, but no change in caregiver capacity. The intensive in-home children demonstrated a similar but more dramatic impact of the intervention. Again, there was no evidence of impact on caregiver needs. Children placed in crisis beds initially demonstrated symptom improvement and reductions in risk behaviors but did not demonstrate improved functioning.

For the children with a follow-up CAT assessment within ninety days of initial screening, only 2.5 percent of children initially referred to outpatient services were later hospitalized. Only 1.2 percent of children treated in the intensive in-home program were hospitalized. No children placed in crisis beds who were followed up ninety days later were hospitalized during the ninety-day period.

These initial data suggest the following conclusions:

1. A clear clinical rationale seems to exist for the use of the four primary dispositions within the MRSS program. Outpatient services are used for those children with the lowest needs. Intensive in-home services are directed primarily toward moderate-risk children with internalizing disorders, although some disruptive children receive these services as well. Disruptive behavior with problems of runaway or violence characterizes the children who are placed

Table 10.4
Change in Clinical Status During Treatment Episode by Initial Disposition

	Symptoms Initial/Follow-Up		Risk Behavior Initial/Follow-Up		Function Initial/Follow-Up		Caregiver Initial/Follow-Up	
Outpatient	7.5	6.6	4.2	3.5	3.7	3.1	2.3	2.2
In-Home	8.0	6.1	4.4	3.1	4.0	3.4	3.4	3.2
Crisis Bed	10.5	8.9	7.0	5.8	4.3	4.5	3.9	4.2
Hospital	12.8	12.5	10.8	9.7	6.0	5.3	5.7	4.8

in crisis beds. Psychiatric hospitalization is reserved for the very high-need, clinically complicated child.

2. Initial outcomes data suggest that each program is effective, particularly in controlling and reducing high-risk behaviors. Improvements in symptoms and functioning occur in some services but not others. Improvement in caregiver capacity is not common.

3. Outpatient, intensive in-home, and crisis bed services all appear to reduce the risk of psychiatric hospitalization of the children served.

Thresholds to Support Level-of-Care Decisions

We developed criteria and thresholds to support level-of-care decisions needed for youth with certain profiles. The criteria incorporated information to indicate whether high, medium, or low intensity interventions were needed. Table 10.5 outlines the criteria and thresholds for three levels of intervention intensity. These thresholds help the system managers learn how MRSS matches needs to interventions and answer the question "what is working for whom?" This informational loop is also used as part of a quality improvement process for both mobile response and stabilization. Once identified, important issues are addressed via targeted technical assistance for workers and trainers.

Other uses of the CAT are measuring program outcomes, contrasting decision-making and outcomes across provider agencies, assessing and supporting supervisor functions, and developing profiles of behavior that will indicate particular interventions and their intensity.

MRSS Assessment

The initial data we collected also gave us information about how MRSS was working. The data reinforced the concept that immediate interventions would keep more children in their present living arrangement; in the first two years, 95 percent of youth were maintained in their current living situation. In the beginning, we identified the areas we felt were important in measuring how MRSS was meeting our goals. Using data from the CAT, we were able to identify how well the goals were met and where service gaps in the system occurred.

Table 10.5
CAT Criteria and Thresholds

Thresholds for Crisis Assessment Tool

I. High Intensity—Consider the following:

Outcome deflection/de-escalation
Intensive use of wraparound services
Monitor safety
Intensive in-home services, such as behavior assistance for up to twenty-four hours
Crisis intervention therapy (brief directed to de-escalation)
Crisis bed with supports
Inpatient

Child/youth meet following criteria:

Criterion 1
Criteria 8 and Runaway rated 3
Criteria 3 and 7
Criteria 3 and 11
Criterion 5 and living situation rated 3
Criterion 11 and living situation rated 3
Caregiver Involvement rated 3

II. Intermediate Intensity—Consider the following:

In-home stabilization phase
In-community therapy 2-3 x per week and tapering over the remainder period
Behavioral assistance – less time and focused on stabilizing behavior
Use crisis bed shorter time and probably for a family break/respite

Child/youth meet the following criteria:

Criteria 1 and 6
Criteria 1 and 8
Criteria 5 and 9 and 14
Criterion 12
Criterion 2
Criterion 2 & 7

III. Low Intensity—Consider the following:

Minimal support for brief time—may consider in home for a brief time
Outpatient
Youth case management
More office-based
May need transportation or financial support if there are barriers for getting to outpatient services
Need to define barriers

(Continued)

Table 10.5 (Continued)

Child/youth meet the following criteria:
Criterion 4
Criteria 10 and 13
Criteria 10 and residential Stability rated 2 or 3
Criteria 10 and Involvement rated 2 or 3

For each of the counties providing mobile response and stabilization, we wanted to know how many children were stabilized in their present living arrangement and remained there. We compared levels of risk behaviors and symptoms across crisis dispositions and then compared CAT dimension scores across dispositions. Of 661 children and families served:

- 33 percent of mobile responses resulted in initiating stabilization interventions across counties;

- 95 percent of children and youth served remained in their current living arrangement;

- 60 percent were placed in a crisis bed;

- 2 percent were hospitalized.

Youth rated 3 in risk behaviors, symptoms, judgment, and functioning received a high intensity of intervention, usually hospitalization. Youth rated 2 and 3 in risk behaviors, symptoms, and judgment, and a 2 in functioning, usually received intensive in-home services. High ratings in judgment and functioning influenced the use of hospitalization with a 2 or 3 rating in risk behaviors and symptoms.

We developed a profile of behaviors of the children we were serving. Using our criteria and thresholds, we began to identify best practices and develop interventions that were appropriate. It should be noted that in New Jersey we currently have two service delivery systems for children in crisis, the mobile response system described in this chapter and the preexisting mental health screening system (essentially screening to determine the need for psychiatric hospitalization). The data set being described does not include the subset of children screened and admitted through the preexisting system, or the subset screened and not admitted, if they were not subsequently referred for mobile response.

One advantage of an integrated assessment like the IMDS process is the opportunity to collect data on the children not included in the mobile response data set, and then compare their need and behavior profiles. It is anticipated that the children who are hospitalized would have higher risk factors and would be more symptomatic.

Reviewing the data, we identified youth who were and were not hospitalized when they met the criterion for an intense level of care. We discovered that the difference between the hospitalized children versus the unhospitalized had to do with their level

Table 10.6
Percentage of Children With Actionable Needs Rated 2 or 3

Risk Behavior	Percentage
Oppositional	56.9%
Living Situation	54.4%
Anger Control	54.1%
Judgment	53%

of functioning and the impact of their behaviors on caregivers, the community, and the schools.

In 2002, the first year of operation, as part of outcomes management, we identified the actionable needs (ratings of 2 or 3 on the CAT) of the youth and their families we were serving. Table 10.6 shows the percentages of children with actionable needs in these ranges.

EVOLUTION OF TRAINING STRATEGIES

The development and evolution of training strategies and information taught as MRSS expanded and evolved over time. In large part, the developments mirror the learning and the increasing sophistication of the system. We are indebted to the enthusiasm and ongoing honest feedback of the trainees and their supervisors. The team that developed the training quickly formed a close working relationship, so initial implementation, training, and support for training went hand in hand and we could learn as we went along. The training team consisted of the training liaison from the DMHS-OCS and the university-contracted training coordinator and staff.

Building a Course of Study

When we began, there was no existing model to build on. New Jersey has regional psychiatric screening units, but their focus is primarily on adults and the decision of whether the person screened requires psychiatric hospitalization. Children are also screened, but as the goal of the MRSS system was to work with children who did not need acute psychiatric hospitalization, we needed to adapt the training model. The immediate goal of the MRSS training curriculum was to have an efficient and effective way to prepare crisis workers for their jobs. The long-term goal was to refine the training curriculum into a certification process for the MRSS worker as the SOC matured.

We studied the experiences of the existing service delivery model and came away with a number of goals for MRSS certification:

- Workers who go into the community must understand key concepts regarding their own personal safety and that of the children and families they will be interacting with;

- Crisis response must be within the context of a wraparound SOC;

- Workers must be able to assess behavior and psychiatric symptomatology and risk factors, and to engage the family/caregivers in developing a plan to support the management of the crisis; and

- The CAT is central to this training and certification and will be the assessment tool that informs the decision-making process.

New Jersey began with three MRSS programs. Once the RFPs were submitted and approved, we met with agency chief executive and chief operating officers to begin a process of acculturation to the new model and discuss the early phases of implementation, such as setting up the program structures and hiring supervisory staff who then became integral to the process of clarifying core competencies and hiring line staff. In part because of delays to the initial actual start-up and the fact that the first three MRSS programs had already hired staff, the DMHS-OCS had the unusual luxury of more time than we expected.

The intent of the first phase of training was to give the supervisors and the new staff an orientation to systems of care, the model of mobile response and stabilization, and to provide a foundation for system change. Using the resources of the Substance Abuse and Mental Health Services Administration monograph on training (SAMHSA, 1999), we identified core competencies for staff working with youth and families in a SOC and then reached out to Trinity Program in Vermont for a detailed listing of their core competencies for wraparound workers, and adapted both of these resources to the MRSS model. These competencies were then used to guide training and skill development as well as to inform hiring and supervision so that the program model and staffing remained congruent. The new MRSS program directors helped to design the course of training; they were present with their new staff throughout the training and could subsequently support their staff in implementing what they were trained to do.

In introducing our first MRSS training, we were fortunate to garner the support of one family who agreed to share its experiences regarding both positive and negative interactions with the traditional crisis responses their child had received. The parents' voice provided a poignant introduction to the training series and served as a reminder to all of us of how we would like to be treated should it be us or our child in crisis.

The first wave of training was an initial, comprehensive eighteen-day course of study. Topics included an orientation to the values and principles of the New Jersey SOC, an overview of crisis theory, actuarial and clinical risk assessment strategies, diagnostic issues, developmental issues, how this information applies to assessing a child and family in a variety of environments, developing a crisis plan, understanding the meaning and function of behavior, and use of the CAT. While this initial intensive training course was rated positively by the participants, we learned by way of follow-up questionnaires from trainees and feedback from supervisors that while the information was good, the training did not provide the practical mechanics and how-to's that come with learning in the field. These mechanics included how to sequence entering the home while assessing the situation for key personal safety issues and simultaneously engaging the child and caregiver(s), and ensuring that all the important information is elicited so that it can be captured and communicated by the CAT. We also needed to develop a crisis plan.

After the first wave of training, the implementation group transitioned from the CEOs and COOs to continuing meetings with program directors during at least the first year to problem solve, troubleshoot, and hold to the model (by way of supervision and additional training as needed), all of which were essential to reinforce early success and promote consistent implementation.

Skills Development

For the second phase of MRSS implementation, we modified the training effort by applying lessons learned. In retrospect, our early training for initial implementation, with its emphasis on classroom-style learning, was overkill. There had been too much abstract information, all at once, which didn't help the actual application in the field. The initial training effort did create a common vision and understanding of the model, however, and a culture of learning and camaraderie that was very helpful in the early stages of implementation. From here on, we focused more on refining the essential elements of the job and less on theory. Together with one of our national consultants, Mary Grealish, M.Ed., we developed a task analysis of the job, which helped us get a more realistic sense of the day-to-day work realities and the anatomy of a crisis response. With this information, we could tailor the training to mirror the actual flow and functions of the work. We developed a training sequence of "just enough" information to enable the worker to start, followed by further training components to build on early experience and consolidate knowledge and skill development.

Procedural Protocol

By the third and fourth iterations, the training model really began to gel. The model included a step-by-step procedural protocol that defined and sequenced the functions of crisis response and integrated use of the CAT and development of a rudimentary planning process. Vignettes and role-plays were used to illustrate the procedures. We realized that the structure of the CAT actually provides the architecture for the skill set needed to do the job. We deconstructed the CAT into the basic categories of assessment, adding basic listening skills, the fundamentals of risk assessment and describing and understanding behavior, and safety training. This has provided the best template for training to date.

The design of the MRSS, with close collaboration between the new MRSS programs and the OCS, training and implementation support, and the integral use of the CAT from inception, created the infrastructure for developing informational feedback loops and supporting continued use of the IMDS/CAT in decision-making and service planning.

Consolidation and Certification

The next step in the evolution of the program is to consolidate the measurement of the MRSS skill set with the goal of a comprehensive certification process that will be based on the following criteria, with the method by which the information would be assessed:

1. Attendance at required MRSS training series and documentation by on-line registration.

   Method of assessment: Attendance reconciled with sign-in and -out sheets.

2. Self-assessment on essential knowledge and skills.

    Method of assessment: Quarterly completion of self-assessment questionnaire (skill-based).

3. Supervisory performance evaluation report, including meeting of standards regarding: fidelity to wraparound/care manager practice model based on supervision, direct observation of crisis response, ability to work collaboratively.

    Method of assessment: Report card completed by supervisor.

4. Documentation adequately reflects integration of CAT data, crisis intervention, and ICP process.

    Method of assessment: Random electronic record audit (by MRSS, QA [quality assurance] & contracted systems administrator).

5. Client feedback, including client satisfaction. Was the family voice heard? Was the family treated with respect? Was the response timely?

    Method of assessment: Client satisfaction data (gathered by the contracted systems administrator).

6. 75 percent pass rate on written proficiency examination.

    Method of assessment: Multiple choice, vignettes, and written ICP.

7. IMDS tool (CAT) reliability check/recheck.

    Method of assessment: Use IMDS tool with sample vignette (annually or biannually).

To date, we have successfully developed a training and certification process for the CAT that is part of the overall IMDS certification process.

Lessons Learned

Goldilocks was right—asking for feedback from the end user, at both the supervisor and the line staff level, and on a continuous basis, helps find the best fit (once you knew what you are doing). Ongoing meetings with program managers provided the forum for sharing what was learned, incorporating lessons from what was learned, and redesigning training to make it more user friendly. Over time, the supervisory staff from the more experienced MRSS programs became integral to developing and implementing new MRSS programs and providing ongoing support.

CONCLUSION

This chapter describes the initial development and implementation of the MRSS component of the New Jersey SOC. A number of key strategies, described below and used together, produced a relatively smooth implementation process (Fixen et al., 2005).

1. Commitment of leadership to the implementation process is critical to success. Leadership must build a case for change, show that change is possible, communicate explicit goals, reinforce persistence, reconcile conflicts with other goals, and help create details of activities and processes to implement policies. The RFP process laid out a clear model for MRSS and expectations for the services to be developed. Leadership within the organizations awarded the contracts and within the New Jersey Division of Child Behavioral Health Services facilitated a collaborative process that became the template for subsequent implementation efforts.

2. Resources must be available to support the system change process, especially time for training and building expertise both within and across the developing system. A staged rollout of both the population of youth to be served and the geographic areas to be covered by new contracted MRSS services was gradually expanded, so that expansion was balanced by an understanding of the conditions and existing resources at the local level.

3. Involvement of the stakeholders and key players in planning and service delivery development is essential for success. Involvement was achieved by regular meetings first with the program staff at the higher level agencies awarded the contracts in the initial planning stages, and then with the supervisory staff who were provided with training and consultation about the model before line staff were hired. Staff members were trained together to ensure that everyone understood the model and could implements it as a team in collaboration with the Division of Child Behavioral Health Services. Troubleshooting meetings allowed issues and concerns to be addressed collaboratively, in a consistent and timely fashion. Thus, shared information in terms of planning, implementation and data, especially CAT data, were integral to the process from the outset. From the outset, CAT data was gathered and presented regularly as part of the implementation meetings. Supervisory staff was challenged to understand and refine the use of the data in the development of algorithms and decision-making as a part of the supervisory process. The distinct advantage of this approach was that everyone understood and agreed on the need for and use of the data to support decision-making and manage the system.

4. A commitment to continuing resources and support for providing time for coaching, planning, evolution of teamwork, and generating data locally is integral to the process. Such resources were integral to both the initial rollout and subsequent MRSS implementation within the developing SOC. Because of the close linkage of the MRSS rollout with training and technical assistance efforts, the continual focus on providing time-limited intervention, and the use of CAT and resulting data, the MRSS component rapidly demonstrated its effectiveness. This was a first for the child-serving system in New Jersey in terms of having meaningful and useful decision support and outcome data for youth and families.

The mobile response and stabilization programs have been implemented in fifteen service areas for the past two years. Current data reports show that a total of 1,393 youth and their families were served in the third quarter of 2007 and 90 percent were maintained in their residence (New Jersey Department of Children and Families, 2007). As the New Jersey SOC system matures, the initial conditions described above have contributed to the continued effectiveness of MRSS, as the current data supports, to de-escalate children in crisis, preserve placement, and prevent psychiatric hospitalization.

References

Aguilera, D. C. (1994). *Crisis intervention, theory and methodology* (6th ed.). St Louis: Mosby.

Caplan, G. (1964). *Principles of preventive psychiatry.* New York: Basic Books.

Fixsen, D. L., Naoom, S. F., Blase, K. A., Friedman, R. M. & Wallace, F. (2005). *Implementation research: A synthesis of the literature.* Tampa, FL: University of South Florida, Louis de la Parte Florida Mental Health Institute, The National Implementation Research Network (FMHI Publication No. 231).

Golan, N. (1978). *Treatment in crisis situations.* New York: Free Press.

Lyons, J. S. (2008) *Mobile response and stabilization system. Initial report on the decision making and outcomes using the crisis assessment tool.* Trenton, NJ: New Jersey Division of Mental Health Services, Division of Child Behavioral Health Services.

Lyons, J. S. (2004). *Redressing the emperor: Improving our children's public mental health system.* Westport, CT: Praeger.

New Jersey Department of Children and Families (2007). *Child behavioral health.* This report is available online at: http://www.state.nj.us/dcf/home/childdata/behavioral/#6

Pires, Shiela A. (2002). *Building systems of care: A primer.* Washington, DC: National Technical Assistance Center for Children's Mental Health, Georgetown University Center for Child and Human Development.

Roberts, A. R. (2000). *Crisis intervention handbook: Assessment, treatment and research.* 2d ed. New York: Oxford University Press.

Promising practices in children's mental health, vol. V (1998 series). Washington, DC: Center for Effective Collaboration and Practice, SAMHSA.

Training strategies for serving children with serious emotional disturbance and their families in a system of care (1999). Part of the 1999 annual report to Congress on the evaluation of the comprehensive community mental health services for children and their families program. Washington, DC: U.S. Department of Health and Human Services, SAMHSA, Child, Adolescent and Family Branch.

Chapter 11

Illinois's Mental Health Juvenile Justice Initiative: Use of Standardized Assessments for Eligibility and Outcomes

by Inger Burnett-Ziegler, M.A., Jason Brennen, B.A., and Crystal Jackson, M.A.

BACKGROUND

On any given day, approximately 107,000 youth younger than age eighteen are incarcerated in the United States (Austin et al., 2000). More troubling is the fact that each year the number of juveniles in custody steadily climbs (Sickmund, 2004). It is also evident that a considerable proportion of these youth have significant mental health needs (Lyons et al., 2001). A 2002 Chicago-based study funded by the National Institutes of Mental Health (NIMH) (Abram et al., 2002) found that nearly two-thirds of male and three-quarters of female juvenile detainees had a diagnosable psychiatric condition. Disruptive behavior and substance abuse made up the majority of these disorders, with 14.5 percent of males and 17.5 percent of females having oppositional defiant disorder, 37.8 percent of males and 40.6 percent of females having conduct disorder, and 50.7 percent of males and 46.8 percent of females exhibiting a substance abuse disorder. However, approximately 15 percent of the total population was believed to have a major mental illness, such as major depressive disorder or psychosis. In many instances, this was due to a failure to have successfully identified a youth in the past as having mental health issues, or a youth's or caregiver's noncompliance with treatment (Scott et al., 2002). Recent evidence suggests, however, that if youths in detention were properly identified and successful linkage with appropriate service providers occurred, this would prove effective in preventing further delinquency for this population.

OVERVIEW OF EFFECTIVE INTERVENTIONS

A number of models have achieved some success to this end, namely multisystemic treatment (MST), mental health courts, and the wraparound treatment in line with the system of care (SOC) philosophy.

Multisystemic Treatment

MST targets those factors in each youth's social network that are contributing to his or her antisocial behavior. Interventions typically aim to improve caregiver discipline practices, enhance family affective relations, decrease the youth's association with deviant peers and increase it with prosocial peers, improve school or vocational performance, engage the youth in prosocial recreational outlets, and develop an indigenous support network of extended family, neighbors, and friends to help caregivers achieve and maintain such changes. Specific treatment techniques used to facilitate these gains are integrated from empirically supported therapies including cognitive-behavioral, behavioral, and pragmatic family therapy, all provided in the natural environment (home, school, community).

MST has been shown to be effective in numerous studies over the years involving detained youth (Curtis et al., 2004). In working with violent and chronic juvenile offenders, MST has reduced long-term rates of rearrest by 25 to 70 percent, in comparison with control groups (Borduin et al., 1995; Henggeler et al., 1992). However, MST is intensive, expensive, and demands that workers maintain small case loads (between two to six families). Furthermore, although MST has demonstrated effectiveness in treating behavioral disorders related to conduct, oppositional, and sexual offenses, there has been less evidence to support serving offenders with serious mental illness, such as those with psychotic or affective disorders.

Mental Health Courts

Specially designed mental health courts, sensitized to mental health issues of defendants, have demonstrated some success in increasing court defendants' access to mental health services (Boothroyd et al., 2003). However, although defendants from a mental health court are more likely to be linked to services, there has been little data demonstrating that linkage to treatment results in positive changes in clinical status (Boothroyd et al., 2005). Moreover, most mental health courts have limited access to new resources or the reallocation of current community-based resources, including housing and basic health services, for the treatment of mental illness and co-occurring disorders. The length of time from referral to diversion has been shown to be much longer in mental health courts than in other types of diversion programs (Steadman et al., 2005). Lastly, the primary or secondary referent is either a court magistrate or the public defender, who will less characteristically use detention center staff or probation/parole officers in the referral process citation.

Wraparound Model

The wraparound model, which provides intensive and comprehensive community-based mental health services, is currently used in a wide variety of service contexts, including those related to special education, developmental disabilities, child welfare, and juvenile justice. Recently, much attention has focused on children's mental health, where the wraparound approach has become a primary strategy for planning and coordinating community-based care for children with severe emotional and behavioral disorders. Numerous individual wraparound programs have gained impressive reputations built on program evaluation and more formal studies (Burchard et al., 2002).

Among these programs, the most notable example is Wraparound Milwaukee (2002), which was cited in the President's New Freedom Commission on Mental Health's *Interim Report* (2003) as a model program. The Center for Mental Health Services (CMHS), part of the Substance Abuse and Mental Health Services Administration (SAMHSA), characterized the available research as providing "emerging evidence" for the effectiveness of the approach (CMHS, 1999).

Fundamental to this approach is a move away from service systems with an over-reliance on a limited set of choices, particularly on inappropriately restrictive care. A fully implemented wraparound model can offer a diverse array of mental health, social, educational, juvenile justice, recreational, vocational, health, substance abuse, and informal community supports. The SOC philosophy is based on the wraparound approach. In particular, the wraparound strategy defines its practices based on a number of important tenets:

- Strength-based approach to children and families
- Family involvement in the treatment process
- Outcome-focused approach
- Needs-based service planning and delivery
- Integration of formal and informal service systems
- Individualized service plans

THE MENTAL HEALTH JUVENILE JUSTICE PROGRAM

In Illinois, the tenets underlying the system of care/wraparound approach form the basis of the Mental Health Juvenile Justice (MHJJ) program. The primary purpose of the program is to identify, screen, refer, and case monitor juveniles in detention who are identified as having either a psychotic or an affective disorder. Juveniles with disruptive behavior disorders (e.g., conduct disorder) are excluded unless the behaviors are comorbid with a psychotic or affective disorder. In line with the SOC philosophy, the MHJJ provides wraparound care to the youth in a community-based setting. The service period of community reintegration and service linkage is intended to last six months, with extension periods considered on a case-by-case basis.

Because length of service is only six months, it is imperative that the program expedite its role in setting up services in a timely and responsive manner. Apart from improving behavioral and functional outcomes, the principle goal is to reduce the recidivism of involved youth. In addition, program staff also play a strong advocacy role for the SOC philosophy by strengthening the linkages among courts, probation, detention, schools, health care, mental health, and other community-based agencies.

IMPLEMENTATION OF MHJJ PROGRAM

Starting Out

In early 2000, the Illinois Department of Human Services (DHS) initiated a pilot of the MHJJ program at seven agencies, across seven counties in the state. These agencies included both urban areas, such as Cook County composing the Chicagoland region and Sangamon County composing the Springfield city region, as well much more rural counties downstate, such as Madison county, to test the program's applicability to various settings across the state. Preliminary data from the first year of the pilot showed that participating youths from both urban and rural areas improved significantly on behavioral and functional outcomes by the time of transition from the MHJJ (although there were no specific analyses comparing rural/urban differences). Moreover, less than one-half of the children enrolled in the MHJJ initiative were rearrested during the period of service. This finding was substantially lower than the average juvenile recidivism rate with no interventions in Illinois (Olsen & Dooley, 2003) and is comparable to more expensive and intensive MST results. In response to this promising evidence, the DHS authorized statewide expansion of the project to include seventeen agency grants across sixteen counties in late 2001. There are now nineteen detention centers across the state of Illinois, of which there are twenty attached community mental health agencies that service the program.

Staffing and Staff Responsibilities

The primary clinical staff involved with the MHJJ at each agency are known as liaisons. Liaisons are all master's level clinicians with a history of case management and counseling in the community provider arena. Liaisons with the MHJJ do not actually provide direct therapy to enrolled clients, however. Their fundamental role is more that of a case manager; their primary tasks in the program process are screening for eligible youth, assessing for needs-based services, devising individualized treatment plans, and then linking clients to various outside providers or services within the agency. Other key responsibilities that make up their everyday responsibilities include advocacy in the youth's ongoing judicial process, relating to the client's family, and reintegrating the client back into the community at large.

In addition to these liaisons at the staff level, the DHS allocates additional flex fund dollars annually to be spent towards other needed personnel at each agency site. The most common use of the flex funds is to retain case managers to support the role of the liaison in client management responsibilities. Many sites have also used flex funds to hire youth mentors, interns for special psychological screenings, and parent/family advocates.

Procedural Design

Referral. Referrals can be issued from a number of different sources in the judicial process, which is a key advantage for ensuring proper identification of youths needing the program. Referral sources include:

- Court personnel (judge, state's attorney, public defender);
- Probation officers;
- Correctional officers; or, alternatively,
- Any SOC professionals who suspect that a youth exhibits symptoms.

To validate appropriate and reliable referrals from these sources, the program relies heavily on the liaison's ability to educate and advocate court and correctional personnel about the MHJJ program's eligibility criteria. To this end, the program's referral form, which is readily available to all judicial and correctional personnel, was designed as a simple screening tool for use by non-clinical staff. The referral form is essentially a checklist that includes indicators of the primary target conditions, such as symptoms of depression and psychosis, but it also includes indirect indicators to maximize the sensitivity of the screen, such as psychotropic medication use or psychiatric hospitalization history.

Juveniles do not require a previous diagnosis of a mental illness disorder to be eligible for referral. However, beyond the actual presence of symptoms, the criteria for referral are: (1) involvement with a juvenile center program some time during the past six months and (2) being between ages ten and seventeen. Juveniles with disruptive behavior disorders are excluded, unless these disorders are comorbid with psychotic or affective disorders. Youths who are wards of the Illinois Department of Children and Family Services (DCFS) or who are sentenced to the Illinois Department of Corrections (DOC) are also not eligible for the MHJJ program.

Eligibility Screening. The liaison uses an assessment tool known as the Childhood Severity of Psychiatric Illness (CSPI) to determine a child's actual enrollment qualification. Although not a diagnostic assessment, the CSPI is a decision-making tool designed to assess immediate and current needs of the youth. Many Illinois community agencies are familiar with this tool because it is used by clinicians in the DCFS. Developed by John Lyons, the CSPI parallels the child and adolescent needs and strengths tool, or CANS, in its outline of specific needs-based measures and scoring criteria. The basic design is that a score of 0 reflects no evidence of a particular dimension, a rating of 1 reflects a mild degree of the dimension, a rating of 2 reflects a moderate degree, and rating of 3 reflects a severe or profound degree.

The MHJJ version of the CSPI focuses on three main clusters: symptoms, risk factors, and functioning. Program eligibility is determined by a score of 2 or higher on either measure of "neuropsychiatric disturbance" or "emotional disturbance" under the symptoms section. The "neuropsychiatric disturbance" dimension is used to rate symptoms such as hallucinations, delusions, unusual thought processes, strange speech, or bizarre/idiosyncratic behavior. "Emotional disturbance" refers to depressed mood, social withdrawal, anxious mood, sleep disturbances, weight/eating disturbances, and loss of motivation.

Service Provision

CANS Assessment. Multiple versions of the CANS tool exist and are in use in varying service programs across the nation. Providers and systems planners adjust the domains and dimensions comprising the CANS to fit the needs of their organization or region. The MHJJ uses the mental health version (CANS-MH), the methodology of which is described below. The dimensions and objective anchors used in this version were developed by focus groups with a variety of participants, including families, family advocates, representatives of the provider community, and mental health case workers and staff. The strengths of the measurement approach are that it is face valid and easy to use; it provides comprehensive information regarding the clinical status of the child or youth; and it is significantly reliable across reviewers (Rawal et al., 2004; Anderson et al., 2003).

Table 11.1
Sections of the CANS-MH

SECTIONS OF THE CANS–MH

A. Problem Presentation
Psychosis
Attention Deficit/Impulse Control
Depression/Anxiety
Oppositional Behavior
Antisocial Behavior
Substance Abuse
Adjustment to Trauma
Situational Consistency of Problems
Temporal Consistency of Problems

B. Risk Behaviors
Danger to Self
Danger to Others
Runaway
Sexually Abusive Behavior
Social Behavior
Crime/Delinquency

C. Functioning
Intellectual/Developmental
Physical/Medical
Family
School Achievement
School Behavior
School Attendance
Sexual Development

D. Care Intensity & Organization
Monitoring
Treatment
Transportation
Service Permanence

E. Caregiver Needs and Strengths
Physical
Supervision
Involvement with Care
Knowledge
Organization
Residential Stability
Resources
Safety

F. Strengths [of the Youth]
Family
Interpersonal
Relationship Permanence
Education
Vocational
Well-being
Optimism
Spiritual/Religious
Talents/Interest
Inclusion

Once a child is determined eligible for the MHJJ program, the liaison administers the CANS-MH to assess service needs. By using this tool, the MHJJ establishes an assessment framework based on a common clinical language for collaboration with other agencies in the provider SOC. The CANS-MH assessment builds on the methodological approach of the CSPI but expands the assessment to include a broader conceptualization of needs and the addition of an assessment of strengths.

CANS Methodological Overview. Given at initial intake, mid-point (three-months), and closing of the case, the CANS is intended to capture the current profile of the needs and strengths of both the youth and his or her family. For most measures, "current" translates to the last thirty days before administration. The general sections of the CANS-MH assessment are set out in Table 11.1.

Each domain of the CANS-MH is comprised of individual dimensions that are based on a 4-point (0 to 3) anchor scale. A rating of 0 reflects no history of or presence of a particular problem or behavior. A rating of 1 indicates a history of particular problem or behavior and/or watchful waiting or monitoring if a problem may emerge. A rating of 2 reflects a problem of moderate intensity requiring intervention; on many of the dimensions in the symptoms/mental health needs domain, a rating of 2 indicates the presence of a diagnosable disorder. A rating of 3 indicates a problem of severe intensity requiring immediate and/or intensive action. The last two categories of dimensions, caregiver needs and strengths as well strengths of the youth, are rated in a reverse logical manner. A rating of 0 is seen as a *positive*, centerpiece strength, a rating of 1 indicates useful strength, a rating of 2 reflects an identified strength, and a rating of 3 indicates a not yet identified strength. Thus, in all cases, *a low rating is positive.*

Dual Role of CANS: Service Planning and Outcomes Assessment. The MHJJ implementation of the CANS illustrates two applications of the tool:

- *Service planning*—As a decision-making tool, the CANS outlines an individualized and wraparound treatment plan to address the needs and strengths of the client and family.

- *Outcomes assessment*—Equally, as a retrospective tool, the CANS serves as an outcomes measure for the individual client as well the program as a whole.

For service planning, the agency team itself (supervisor, liaison, case manager, other support staff) as well as interagency staff in the system of care use the common language of the CANS to address needs-based planning. Among the system of providers (court staff, counselors/therapists, medical practitioners, educators), the CANS identifies relevant issues that might relate to a specific domain (e.g., mental health) or a particular setting (e.g., school or home). The treatment plan, also known as *action plan*, is formulated directly from the initial CANS assessment and adjusts every time there is a follow-up CANS assessment to reflect the current needs of the youth and family. The action plan addresses every actionable needs measure scored on the CANS (a score of 2 or higher).

The action plan focuses equally on services to leverage the identified strengths of the client and caregiver that can be used advantageously. Each actionable CANS measure is addressed by an individual service intervention type (e.g., individual therapy, substance abuse evaluation, case management, mentoring). In many instances, clinicians select more than one service type for a specific actionable measure. For instance, to address an actionable need for the depression/anxiety measure, a clinician might choose (1) individual therapy, (2) psychiatric medication evaluation/medication maintenance, and (3) family therapy as service interventions.

As an outcomes assessment tool, the CANS provides a retrospective evaluation of the juveniles currently in care and the functioning of the current system in relation to their and their families' needs and strengths. On the case level, the clinician's review of the CANS assessments over the course of the treatment period provides information as to the appropriateness of the individual plan of care and whether individual goals and outcomes were achieved. In addition, the tool can be used by site supervisors and regional contract managers as a quality assurance/monitoring device for their caseloads. As a program-wide evaluation tool, it clearly points out service gaps in the current provider system as well as differences among individual site provider agencies. Thus, the CANS provides key oversight reporting to the DHS to ensure program efficiency and effectiveness standards.

Providers also complete monthly reports on services provided and basic school, community, and juvenile justice outcomes for all open cases within their programs. These reports allow for monitoring of basic outcomes and provide necessary data to perform cost effectiveness analyses of the MHJJ programs at each site. Information regarding continued service linkage as well as school and community statuses is collected at times of intake, active month-to-month service periods, and transition of the case.

Services Offered Via Linkage Process. The following services are offered by MHJJ:

- Case management and support
- Court advocacy
- Counseling/therapy linkage
- Psychiatric services linkage
- Psychological assessment
- Medical services
- Respite care
- Educational advocacy/tutoring
- Job training linkage
- Recreational facilities/activities linkage
- Mentoring
- Transportation
- Vocational training
- Flex fund assistance

Funding. Where needed services (e.g., therapy, psychiatric services) are not covered by public or private insurance, the MHJJ program offers a flexible spending fund to pay for them. Flex funds can also be used to address any other component of the treatment plan that cannot be covered by insurance, including transportation needs, involvement in extracurricular activities, testing vocational interests, and securing emergency housing for the family. Flex funds are managed through a private foundation that facilitates staff requests for such funds. The foundation tracks individual service usage trends. In fiscal year 2005 (FY05), MHJJ used $721,343 of flex fund assistance monies for program youth (Brennen & Lyons, 2005).

BARRIERS TO IMPLEMENTATION

This section addresses a number of programmatic and research barriers that existed in the MHJJ and the interventions implemented to fix them.

Referral Sources—Education and Advocacy

Reliable use of the referral form by court and detention staff ensures that the system refers appropriate youth to the program, based on the suspicion of psychotic or affective symptoms covered in the lay language of the referral form's checklist. MHJJ program staff need continuous communication with referral sources not only to ensure that referral measures are reliable, but to manage the staff's efficiency/workload in the screening process. In the program's early years, the screening process itself mandated a significant portion of the staff's workload. This took away from time needed for basic case management and service linkage duties. The evaluation team and agency supervisory staff put efforts in place to strengthen communication channels between program staff and referral sources in the courts and detention. They made presentations about the MHJJ program to court audiences, had court and detention staff participate in MHJJ meetings, distributed program brochures, and had MHJJ liaisons maintain a continued presence in court and detention facilities, all of which played out as key strategies to reinforce the referral process.

Based on these efforts, each year the program became more efficient in its referral and screening processes. In FY05, 82.9 percent of referred youth were found to have symptoms of a psychotic or affective disorder that were serious enough to meet qualification for the program. This is in comparison to earlier years, in which the efficiency of referral and screening was much less reliable: in FY02, only 53 percent met referral criteria; in FY03, 72 percent; and FY04, 71 percent. The high percentage of youth currently meeting qualification for the MHJJ program also demonstrates that the CSPI is an appropriate and efficient tool for determining eligibility. However, this is in large part due to continuing effort on behalf of MHJJ staff to educate court and correctional staff on the proper usage of the program referral form.

Staff Training for Application of Screening Tools

To ensure the reliability of program assessments (CSPI, CANS) by provider staff, all clinical staff members undertake mandatory initial training. Relevant personnel—liaisons, case managers, supervisors—are brought together at regional training sessions to maximize the consistency of use of these measures by peer provider staff and to build a dialogue among those who will be using the measures. Specific training sessions are scheduled monthly and are offered in four regional sectors of the state: Cook County (Chicago), Northern, Central (Springfield), and Southern. The training provides an overview of the purpose of the measures, a review of the specific items used by the measures, and group practice rating several vignettes followed by a review of vignettes and scores with the trainer. Staff members who complete the training must demonstrate significant reliability before using the screening and assessment instruments in the field. While they often show competence to apply these tools immediately following initial training, reliability tends to deteriorate over time. This lessened reliability can be further exacerbated by a staff member's tendency to advocate for program involvement by individual youth above recommendations based on the CANS ratings.

In anticipation of and to counteract these tendencies, liaisons from different sites follow up on group training, reviewing the purpose and design of the measures and redistributing vignettes for individual scoring and group discussion. Continuous training and auditing of the use of the screening and assessment tools is maintained to keep individual liaison reliability above 0.70 (interclass correlation) throughout the duration of the MHJJ program evaluation. As a further means to make training and retraining more efficient, an interactive CANS training website helps provide successful mastery of the instruments via the Internet. The website allows staff to view interactive video presentations by trainers, review training vignettes, ask follow-up questions, and test on the tools at their own pace and time availability.

Accurate and Timely Client Assessment; Oversight Monitoring

Given the numerous amount of assessments and reports involved in screening, service planning, and case monitoring for MHJJ youth (see Figure 11.1), it became imperative to design a system that could capture and maintain the vast amounts of clinical information needed for outcomes management. After two years of program service statewide, the DHS and Northwestern University proposed that the university design an online system to accomplish this task. By implementing an online system that would allow for onsite, digital submission of relevant forms at each agency site, the paperwork would be drastically reduced, and the further step of inputting relevant research data into a separate database later on by oversight staff would be eliminated. Equally important, an online system would allow for oversight capabilities of ensuring accurate and prompt submission of time-sensitive reports and assessments.

Starting in mid-2003, the program began using the web-based data system. Several dimensions of security were put into place to ensure the privacy and protection of child and agency data, including a secure user name/password sign-on and a sophisticated firewall put in place by the hosting website company. Since inception, the website has substantially enhanced the oversight staff's ability to monitor and assess the program's effectiveness. The system has a variety of programs available to help manage the timing of follow-up assessments for each youth. Data is compiled and reported based on a summary of descriptive statistics for each site, and distributed to program liaisons and supervisors for feedback. The website also has reporting capabilities on the site itself that allow DHS staff, agency supervisory staff, and clinicians to understand county and statewide trends for any particular time frame in areas such as referrals, number of screenings, number of eligible youth, and youths served. Lastly, the site captures clinical information based on the submission of assessments such as the CANS and client tracking forms that will be used in analyzing outcomes measures. Staff feedback has been substantially positive from this web-based transition in terms of both a case management tool and an efficient data management solution.

PROCESS AND OUTCOMES EVALUATION

The process evaluation data is reported to the DHS to ensure performance standards levels in line with operational goals set forth in each agency's program grant. The outcomes evaluation entails analyzing the clinical, functional, and forensic outcomes of youth in the program to ensure appropriate dispositions and service referrals.

Figure 11.1
Evaluation and Assessment Within MHJJ

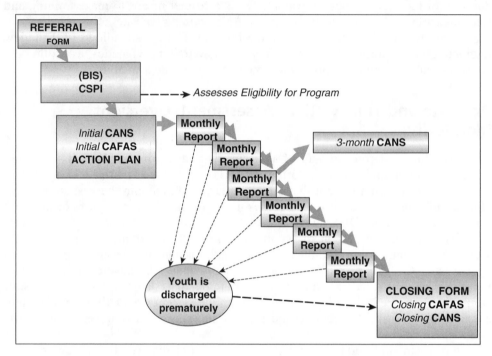

Process Evaluation

The process evaluation of the MHJJ initiative was set up to capture the percentage and nature of youth who meet each of the six stages of the MHJJ process, as follows.

1. Referral

2. Eligibility

3. Initiation of service

4. Dose of services

5. Engagement

6. Completion and clinical improvement

Referral of youth to the MHJJ program is through identification by court staff. Referrals are evaluated to determine the degree to which each county (1) is able to achieve the target number of referrals and (2) is able to achieve appropriate referrals (the rate of eligible cases compared to all referrals).

Eligibility is determined through application of the CSPI screening tool to referred youth. For youth deemed eligible via the CSPI, the assessment determines the nature of their needs as well as how timely and reliably the referred youth receive the eligibility assessment. Needs are monitored to identify any shifts in the complexity of referrals relative to the target population of youth with affective or psychotic disorders. All analyses are accomplished at both a state and county level.

Initiation of service commences once the initial CANS assessment is completed, following eligibility determination. Initiation of service is evaluated by studying the number of eligible youth who receive an intake CANS assessment. A set of prediction models has been developed to identify whether specific characteristics of youth served predict whether a CANS is completed.

Dose of services begins the successful engagement in treatment (at least seven sessions). Doses of services are evaluated in several ways. First, the frequency of various service uses are documented statewide and by county. Then, prediction models are created to identify which children receive more or fewer services, by type of service. Finally, dose response curves are generated for each service type to study the impact of each service type on outcomes (e.g., functional improvement and rearrest).

Outcomes Evaluation

Developed by Dr. John Lyons of Northwestern University's Mental Health Services and Policy Program, the outcome evaluation model (Lyons, 2004) was created to address the following four basic questions.

1. Can youths with affective or psychotic disorders who are in juvenile detention centers be reliably identified and recruited for mental health treatment by the MHJJ?

2. Can these youths effectively be linked to community-based treatment?

3. Does this linkage result in an improvement in these youths' mental health?

4. Do these youths become less likely to be rearrested or detained in the future?

The answer to these specific questions relies on analysis of clinical, functional, and forensic outcomes. Clinical outcomes consist of improvements in symptoms and risk behaviors assessed using the CANS. Functional improvements are evaluated using the functioning items, the caregiver items, and the strengths items from the CANS. Forensic outcomes include rearrest and re-detention outcomes, along with DOC placement outcomes.

Analyses of outcomes data have been undertaken using a variety of statistical approaches, from t-tests (statistical tests) of simple change to hierarchical linear regression models for establishing recovery curves. In addition, prediction models are used to determine which youth have better or worse outcomes based on initial assessment findings.

Results

The following statistics are based on the fifth fiscal year analysis of the program, July 1, 2004 through June 31, 2005.

Crimes Resulting in Detention. Youth are typically arrested and detained for crimes such as battery, theft, probation violations, property offenses, drug offenses, and sex

Figure 11.2
Breakdown by Crime Type, 2003

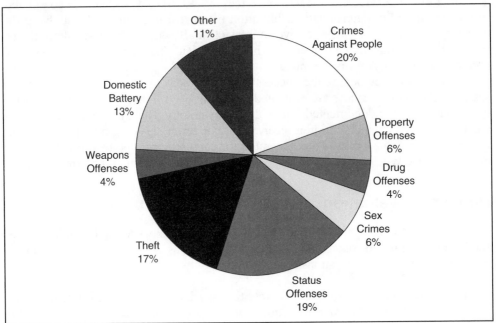

offenses. As a baseline, Figure 11.2 shows an analysis of program data in 2003, broken down by crime type.

Referral, Screening, and Eligibility. With each fiscal year, MHJJ liaisons and detention staff become increasingly adept at identifying youths with psychotic or affective disorders. In FY05, 1,222 youths were referred for screening; of those, 82.9 percent were found to have symptoms of a psychotic or affective disorder serious enough to meet qualification for the MHJJ program. Youths are eligible if they report symptoms consistent with an affective or psychotic disorder, but the majority met the eligibility criteria because they had an affective disorder. Among eligible youths, the mean CSPI score on the affect item was 2.06 on a 0 to 3 scale, versus 0.36 on the psychosis item. Youths who qualified because of an affective or psychotic disorder also demonstrated higher scores on the conduct, oppositional, and impulsivity items (CSPI scores of 1.45, 1.54, and 1.53 respectively). Among youths who enrolled in the program, 89.6 percent reported symptoms of depression and anxiety and 7.8 percent reported psychotic symptoms on their initial CANS measure. Consistent with the symptom endorsement on the CSPI measure, 57 percent also indicated attention difficulties and impulsivity and 57 percent reported oppositional behavior.

Demographics of Youths Served. In the MHJJ program in FY05, slightly more than one-half of the youths served were Caucasian (51.8 percent), 38.4 percent were African-American, and 7.0 percent were Hispanic. The majority of the youth were male (71.3 percent), between ages ten and seventeen, with a mean age of 15.4. Less than one-fifth

(18.3 percent) had been mandated by the court to participate in the MHJJ program. Most were living at home (84.1 percent) and enrolled in school (87.7 percent) when they were arrested. A small fraction (13.1 percent) had previously been placed in a group home or residential treatment center. Slightly more than one-half of the sample (54.9 percent) had a history of special education services, and most (70.0 percent) had a history of mental health services; however, only 37.8 percent were taking psychotropic medications. Additionally, 27.4 percent had a history of substance abuse treatment, a 4 percent increase from FY04, and a nine percent increase from FY03.

Service Planning. In FY05, program liaisons indicated a need for case management services (88.7 percent) and individual therapy (95.9 percent) for the majority of clients. Liaisons also frequently identified a need for other services, including community programs (53.9 percent), mentoring (56.7 percent), psychiatric mediation evaluations (67.3 percent), and family therapy (75.3 percent). Liaisons spent an average of 3.52 hours per month on each case. An additional 2.14 hours per month per youth were spent by the system's flex-funded staff (e.g., case manager, parent advocate). Cumulatively, approximately 5.66 hours were allocated by staff per client per month. Of these hours, 3.54 hours were spent in direct contact with the client or their family. Youths received an average of 1.5 home visits and 4.26 outpatient visits monthly. This demonstrates a substantial increase in outpatient visits over the past few years; there was an average of 1.94 monthly outpatient visits in FY04 and an average of 3.64 monthly outpatient visits in FY03. Although about 90 percent of youths received outpatient services, it is likely that even more are linked to services as this figure does not reflect missed appointments. More than two-thirds (70.8 percent) of MHJJ clients received individual counseling services; about one-half (51.3 percent) received psychiatric medications; and slightly less than one-half (46.9 percent) received case management services beyond liaison linkage. Additionally, about one-third (33.9 percent) received family therapy and one-quarter (24.2 percent) received school consultations.

Behavioral and Functional Outcomes. The CANS measure is critical in assessing the outcomes of youth who have participated in the MHJJ Initiative. The FY05 data demonstrate that the youth improved significantly (p<0.01) on their final CANS scores from their initial CANS scores on all of the six dimensions of the CANS: problem presentation, risk behaviors, functioning, care intensity and organization, caregiver needs & strengths, and youth strengths. They also had significant improvements on the total measure score. In general, youth had fewer symptoms of mental health disorders, engaged in fewer risk behaviors, functioned at higher levels, and had greater strengths. Table 11.2 compares youths' scores on the dimensions of their initial and final CANS. Figure 11.3 displays this information graphically.

Rearrests. The MHJJ Initiative continues to become more adept at reducing recidivism among youth participants, as shown by the gradual decline in rearrest rates over the past three years (see Figure 11.4). Only 23.1 percent of youth who received MHJJ services in FY05 were rearrested, compared to 25.7 percent in FY04 and 42 percent in FY03. It is clear that there has been a significant drop in rearrest rates since the inception of the program to the present among participants. Since the MHJJ initiative began, it has had a substantially lower rearrest rate than the 72 percent rearrest rate for all juveniles detained in the state of Illinois.

Table 11.2
Pre- and Post-CANS Scores of MHJJ Youth

Pre- and Post-CANS Scores of MHJJ Youth			
Dimension	Initial	Final	Level of Significance
Problem presentation	11.55	10.24	0.00
Risk behaviors	5.12	4.45	0.00
Functioning	4.05	3.55	0.00
Care intensity and organization	3.28	2.97	0.00
Caregiver needs and strengths	6.96	6.51	0.00
Strengths	13.03	12.14	0.00
Total Score	44.00	39.89	0.00

Figure 11.3
Change in CANS Domain Scores From Enrollment to
Transition Out of Services

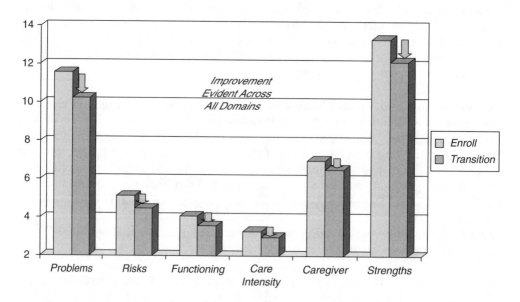

Predictors of Rearrest at Program Entry. Youth who are rearrested tend to have different clinical characteristics than those who are not. Rearrested youth report a unique set of symptoms and behaviors on their baseline CANS, including oppositional behavior, antisocial behavior, situational consistency of problems, and temporal consistency of problems on the problem presentation dimension of the CANS. On the risk

Figure 11.4
Rearrest Rates, Fiscal Years 2002–2005

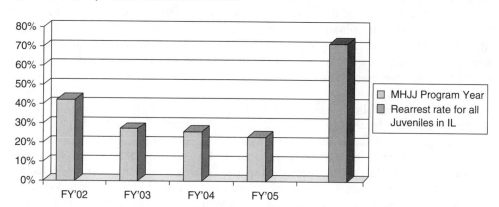

behaviors dimension, rearrested youth are more likely to report having runaway more often and crime/delinquency behaviors. On the functioning dimension, they are more likely to report increased difficulties with school functioning and family functioning. On the care intensity dimension, they are more likely to report increased monitoring needs. On the family/caregiver needs and strengths dimension, they have reduced family involvement and poorer residential stability. On the strengths dimension, they reported fewer interpersonal strengths, talents and interests, vocational skills, reduced optimism, and family strengths. Those with sexual development problems are less likely to be rearrested. In general, recidivism is likely to be higher among youths who have fewer total hours of service and who have fewer home visits and less direct contact with MHJJ staff.

Service Predictors of Rearrest. The type of services received while in the MHJJ program is also correlated with rearrest rates. Youth who are rearrested receive fewer total hours of services and fewer home visits, but *more* hours of direct services by program staff. This is explained by the fact that as more time is spent with MHJJ staff, less time is being spent on service linkage towards service providers.

Services Associated With Improvement. There are a number of significant predictors of outcomes based on service intervention. For example, individual counseling improves family/caregiver needs and strengths; school-based services improve family/caregiver needs and strengths and items on the functioning dimension; and case management services improve strengths. Community programs improve a youth's strengths; transportation services improve school performance; substance abuse treatment improves school performance; and increased flex-funding improves functioning and school performance.

Transition. The MHJJ program is designed to serve its clients for six months, although many drop out before then and others continue beyond six months. Forty-one percent of MHJJ clients completed six months of the program and 11 percent closed early due to noncompliance by the youth or family. Seventy-five percent of the clients were linked with services when they terminated their involvement with MHJJ. However, those who completed all six months were significantly more likely than those who closed early to be connected with ongoing treatment. Among youth whose only reason for closing was the end of the six-month period, 85.6 percent were connected to continuing treatment at termination. For the majority of services, linkage remains higher for clients who stayed in the program for the full six months. Overall, the most common services that remained linked were individual therapy, family therapy, psychiatric treatment, and case management.

Racial Disparities. There was a notable disparity between the number of African-American and Hispanic youth in juvenile detention in need of mental health care versus how many were enrolled in the MHJJ program (Burnett-Ziegler, 2005). This may suggest a bias in referrals into the MHJJ program in favor of Caucasian youth; it may also represent a failure to detect mental health needs in African-American and Hispanic youth. Within the program, race was a predictor in which youths become enrolled, linked, and engaged in services. However, once the juveniles were engaged in services, there were negligible differences by race in who completed the MHJJ program and showed improvement on the CANS-MH.

Caucasians demonstrated greater improvement than African-Americans on the CANS-MH before enrollment, but afterwards these differences diminished. Although the majority of enrolled youth benefited from a breadth of services, analysis of data in FY04 reveals that minority youth received significantly less of almost every type of service. The most striking difference was found in referrals to individual and group substance abuse programs, psychiatric medication evaluations, and individual and family counseling. This may be partly due to the limited availability and poor quality of services offered in low-income communities where many minorities reside.

The rearrest rates for African-American youth increased at a consistent rate while they were in the program and were higher than rearrest rates for Caucasian youth for the duration of program involvement. Rearrest rates decreased for Caucasian youth engaged in the program. There are few racial differences in the reasons why youth are rearrested. Engaging youths in the MHJJ initiative is crucial, as it marks the point where they begin to demonstrate positive outcomes as a result of their participation in the program. Future improvements to the program should focus on ways in which to engage more youth.

CONCLUSION

Screening for eligible youths has improved: 83 percent of those screened were found to qualify for the program. Prevention of rearrest has also improved: only 23.1 percent of MHJJ youth were rearrested, significantly lower than the 72 percent rearrest rate for Illinois delinquents who did not receive treatment (Olson & Dooley, 2003). Involvement in MHJJ led to significant behavioral and functional improvements as evaluated by the CANS. Youth exhibited fewer symptoms of mental health disorders, engaged in fewer risk behaviors, functioned at higher levels, and had greater strengths than they did previously. Longer length of stay ensures better outcomes by remaining linked to services. Seventy-five percent of the clients were linked to continuing services; for those who stayed through the entire six-month program, 88 percent remain linked.

Other chapters in this volume have discussed the relation of Total Clinical Outcomes Management (TCOM) to successful implementation of the CANS. By imbedding the TCOM philosophy into our program design, we have been able to engender the use of the CANS-MH to support treatment planning. The tenure of MHJJ liaisons has been relatively short at most agencies, averaging a little over one year. The program's procedural design, therefore, emphasizes assessments that drive eligibility and service planning, and supports ongoing training and smooth transitions to new liaisons. The web-based system further aids in this effort and provides comparative data across sites. Each year we award a liaison of the year for the individual who has served the most youth. Many liaisons track these numbers closely on the web system.

With the strong outcomes data available to policy-makers, the MHJJ program has become a model in the state of Illinois. As such, extensions are being considered. A pilot program is underway of extending the approach to youth who are transitioning from the DOC back to their communities. Adding youth with disorders of impulse, such as attention deficit hyperactivity disorder, is being considered for the next fiscal year.

The MHJJ program is an excellent example of a statewide program that has seamlessly implemented the CANS as a communication tool into its service delivery process to support good clinical decision-making while setting the stage for monitoring and managing outcomes. That the program has been so successful is in large part a testimony to the hard work of the good people who become liaisons. However, the TCOM strategy has allowed this program to demonstrate the value of this hard work to a variety of system partners.

References

Abram, K. M., Teplin L. T., McClelland, G. M. & Dulcan, M. K. (2002). Comorbid psychiatric disorders in youth in juvenile detention. *Archives of General Psychiatry, 59,*1133–1143.

Anderson, R. L., Lyons, J. S., Giles, D. M., Price, J. A. & Estle, G. (2003). Reliability of the child and adolescent needs and strengths—mental health (CANS-MH) scale. *Journal of Child and Family Studies, 12,* 279–289.

Austin, J., Johnson, K. D. & Gregoriou, M. (2000). *Juveniles in adult prisons and jails: A national assessment.* Washington, DC: Office of Juvenile Justice and Delinquency Prevention. Available online at: www.ncjrs.org/pdffiles1/bja/182503.pdf.

Boothroyd, R. A., Mercado, C. C., Poythress, N. G., Christy, A. & Petrila, J (2005). Clinical outcomes of defendants in mental health court. *Psychiatric Services, 56,* 829–834.

Boothroyd, R. A., Poythress, N. G., McGaha, A. & Petrila, J. (2003). The Broward County mental health court: Process, outcomes, and service utilization. *International Journal of Law and Psychiatry, 363,* 55–71.

Borduin, C. M., Mann, B. J., Cone, L. T., Henggeler, S. W., Fucci, B. R., Blaske, D. M. & Williams, R. A. (1995). Multisystemic treatment of serious juvenile offenders: Long-term prevention of criminality and violence. *Journal of Consulting and Clinical Psychiatry, 63,* 569–578.

Brennen J. & Lyons, J. S. (2005). *The evaluation of the mental health juvenile justice initiative: Results from the fifth year of a statewide demonstration project, fiscal year 2005.* Northwestern University.

Burchard, J. D., Bruns, E. J. & Burchard, S. N. (2002). The wraparound approach. In B. J. Burns & K. Hoagwood (Eds.), *Community treatment for youth: Evidence-based interventions for severe emotional and behavioral disorders.* New York: Oxford University Press, 69–90.

Burnett-Ziegler, I. (2005). *Racial disparity in the mental health juvenile justice initiative, second year project.* Illinois Department of Human Services.

Center for Mental Health Services (1999). *Annual report to Congress on the evaluation of the comprehensive community mental health services for children and their families program.*

Washington, DC: U.S. Department of Health and Human Services, Substance Abuse and Mental Health Services Administration. Available online at the SAMHSA Web Center for Mental Health Services, at: http://mentalhealth.samhsa.gov/publications/allpubs/CB-E199/default.asp.

Curtis, N. M., Ronan, K. R. & Borduin, C. M. (2004). Multisystemic treatment: A meta-analysis of outcome studies. *Journal of Family Psychology, 18*, 411–419.

Henggeler, S. W., Melton, G. B. & Smith, L. A. (1992). Family preservation using multisystemic therapy: An effective alternative to incarcerating serious juvenile offenders. *Journal of Consulting and Clinical Psychology, 60*, 953–961.

Interim report of the President's New Freedom Commission on Mental Health (2003). Available online at: http://www.mentalhealthcommission.gov/reports/Interim_Report.htm.

Lyons, J. S. (2004). *Redressing the emperor: Improving our children's public mental health system.* Westport, CT: Praeger.

Lyons , J. S., Baerger, D. R., Quigley, P. & Griffin, G. (2001). Mental health service needs of juvenile offenders: A comparison of detention, incarceration, and treatment settings. *Children's Services: Social Policy, Research, and Practice, 4*, 69–85.

Olson, D. & Dooley, B. (2003). *Report to the Illinois Criminal Justice Information Authority.* White paper. Springfield, IL.

Rawal, P, Romansky, J., Jenuwine, M. & Lyons, J. S. (2004). Racial differences in the mental health needs and service utilization of youth in the juvenile justice system. *Journal of Behavioral Health Services and Research, 31*, 178–188.

Scott, M. A., Snowden, L. & Libby, A. M. (2002). From mental health to juvenile justice: What factors predict this transition? *Journal of Child and Family Studies, 11*, 299–311.

Sickmund, M. *Juveniles in Corrections* (2004). Washington, DC: Office of Juvenile Justice and Delinquency Prevention, National Report Series, June 2004. Available online at: http://www.ncjrs.gov/pdffiles1/ojjdp/202885.pdf.

Steadman, H. J., Redlich, A. D., Griffin, P., Petrila, J. & Monahan, J. (2005). From referral to disposition: Case processing in seven mental health courts. *Behavioral Sciences and the Law, 23*, 215-226.

Stiffman, A., Hadley-Ives, E., Dore, P., Polgar, M., Horvath, V. E., Striley, C. & Elze, D. (2000). Youths' access to mental health services: The role of providers' training, resource connectivity, and assessment of need. *Mental Health Services Research, 2*, 141–154.

Wraparound Milwaukee (2002). Milwaukee County Behavioral Health Division, Child and Adolescent Services Branch, Annual Report.

Part 4
Program-Level TCOM

Chapter 12

Implementation of Total Clinical Outcomes Management in an Acute Care Pediatric Inpatient Setting

by Lise M. Bisnaire, Ph.D. and Stephanie L. Greenham, Ph.D.

INTRODUCTION

Serious mental health problems, including psychiatric disorders, are prevalent among Canadian children and youth. A significant number of "mainstream" youth ages thirteen to eighteen surveyed as part of the Canadian Youth Mental Health and Illness Survey reported that they struggle frequently with feelings of stress (51 percent), depression (43 percent), or suicidal thoughts and behaviours (19 percent) (Davidson & Manion, 1996). Results of the Ontario Child Health Study (Offord et al., 1989) indicated that the six-month prevalence of conduct disorder, hyperactivity, emotional disorder, or somatization in children ages four to sixteen was 18.1 percent. Comorbid psychiatric diagnoses were observed for 68.2 percent of these children, indicating severe and complex mental health needs. Furthermore, children and youth with psychiatric disorders were almost four times more likely to receive mental health or social services than children and youth without such disorders (Offord et al., 1987). Similar trends have been reported in the United States (Pumariega & Glover, 1998; Zimmerman, 1990) and worldwide, with 15 percent to 25 percent of children and youth in developed and developing countries suffering from a psychiatric disorder (Davidson & Manion, 1996).

Despite an increased emphasis on community-based mental health services for children and youth with serious mental health problems (Lourie et al., 1998), there continues to be a need for specialized mental health services such as hospitalization during times of crisis or acute risk (Lyons, 2004). Since the 1980s, increased clinical need combined with funding restraints has imposed a shift in the focus of hospital-based inpatient psychiatric and mental health services for children and youth. Inpatient care has changed from long-term treatment to brief intervention directed primarily at crisis stabilization and assessment. Acute psychiatric care is currently seen as an intensive care service (Blanz & Schmidt, 2000). Thus, the goals of hospitalization are:

1. To serve the most acute, severe, and complex cases;

2. To emphasize crisis stabilization and risk reduction;

3. To provide interdisciplinary assessment and diagnosis (where indicated); and

4. To facilitate connections in the community where treatment can be provided in a less-restrictive environment (Atlas, 1994; Doherty et al.,1987; Gold et al., 1992).

Acute care inpatient psychiatric settings have historically been, and remain, a critical component of the system of care for child and youth mental health. Over the last three decades, inpatient services have experienced significant change; in fact, change is a given. This is a reality in all domains, and mental health and the delivery of mental health services in the acute care setting is no exception. Being the most expensive and restrictive service on the continuum of care, acute care services have the utmost obligation to be responsible and accountable at all levels—patient, provider, service agency, community, and funding agency. An outcomes management approach, more specifically Total Clinical Outcomes Management (TCOM; Lyons, 2004), is a framework that can provide for accountability within this complex, ever-changing system. This chapter describes the design and development of an outcomes management approach that has led to the adoption of TCOM in the delivery of acute care psychiatric services to children and youth in a tertiary care pediatric hospital. It describes the current implementation of TCOM and outlines plans for future development.

BACKGROUND AND CONTEXT FOR CHANGES TO THE MODEL OF ACUTE CARE SERVICES

Redesign at Full System Level

The Children's Hospital of Eastern Ontario (CHEO) is a tertiary care pediatric teaching hospital with a catchment area of approximately 600,000 children and adolescents in the Eastern Ontario region of Canada. The inpatient psychiatry program at CHEO includes a ten-bed child unit and a fifteen-bed adolescent unit. Both units provide crisis stabilization, assessment, and transitional care, services delivered by interdisciplinary teams. The focus is on acute care hospitalization with a targeted average length of stay of fourteen days. Since 2000, the inpatient psychiatry program has undergone significant changes in its model of service delivery and philosophy of care. A number of independent change processes occurred at different levels to set the stage for the development and implementation of an outcomes management approach within the inpatient psychiatry program. These changes occurred at the provincial, community, and hospital levels.

In the mid- to late 1990s, the two provincial government departments responsible for the provision of mental health services to children and youth in Ontario separately undertook the task of examining the redesign of the model of service delivery across the province. This process resulted in the publication of policy frameworks by both the Ministry of Health and the Ministry of Child and Family Services. These provincial initiatives were among the factors that contributed to the development of a health services restructuring commission, which in 1997 gave directives at a regional level to provide specialized psychiatric and mental health services for children and youth in CHEO's catchment area.

A concomitant process of change at the community level was occurring between two hospitals in the region that provided mental health services to children and youth, namely CHEO and the Royal Ottawa Hospital (ROH). A consolidated and integrated system was planned to improve access to psychiatric emergency services for the region. This led, also in 1997, to the creation of the Regional Psychiatric Emergency Service for Children and Youth (RPESCY), which designated CHEO as the single point of entry for psychiatric emergencies in the Eastern Ontario region. This prompted the development of a team of crisis intervention workers and psychiatry staff and residents to assess children and youth presenting to the CHEO emergency department with acute mental health needs.

Parallel to these community-level processes, significant internal changes within CHEO as a whole to the delivery of health care services reflected a more integrated, patient-based model. In 1996, CHEO moved from a department-based model to a program management model of care. The new design included nine patient service units in which the focus of care was interdisciplinary and driven by patient needs (e.g., rehabilitation, oncology, and pediatrics). Mental health services, including inpatient psychiatric services, were now consolidated under the mental health patient service unit (MHPSU).

Historically, the inpatient psychiatry unit at CHEO was a twelve-bed unit for adolescents that provided a milieu-based therapeutic approach, and where length of stay was six to eight weeks on average. Overflow admissions to psychiatry were typically admitted to medical units where neither the milieu approach to psychiatric service nor the treatment team was available. The combination of a milieu-based inpatient program with a long length of stay on the one hand, and the increasing number of adolescents admitted in crisis under RPESCY on the other, resulted in a bottleneck for admissions to the inpatient psychiatry unit. The bottleneck caused more adolescents to be admitted to medical units with minimal interdisciplinary support from the inpatient psychiatric unit. An increase in the acuity of risk for this patient population was observed that was challenging to manage on medical units. As an interim solution, a small number of inpatient beds were protected for brief crisis admissions to allow for a better flow of patients through the unit and to reduce the number of admissions to medical units. CHEO eventually recognized that a greater number of inpatient psychiatry beds was needed to manage the increasing demands on the service. This resulted in a proposal in 1999 to the Ministry of Health and Long-Term Care for additional funding to increase the number of inpatient beds at CHEO.

CHEO's request for increased beds came at a time when provincial directives from the Heath Services Restructuring Commission compelled CHEO and the ROH to jointly plan an integrated mental health service system for children and adolescents in Eastern Ontario. Out of this directive, a decision was made for CHEO to take the lead in the overall provision of specialized psychiatry services to children and youth who present with severe, complex, and persistent mental illness. For inpatient services this meant specifically a shift of resources, both staff and beds, from the ROH to CHEO. CHEO's independent request to the Ministry for an increase in the number of inpatient psychiatry beds was in keeping with the proposed regional redesign of services and was ultimately successful. The increase in beds and the change in mandate toward specialized services created an opportunity to design an inpatient psychiatry program that was in keeping with current best practice and fulfilled our obligations to be responsible and accountable to patients, program, hospital, community, and system needs.

Redesign at Program Level

Changes to the structure and model of inpatient service at CHEO occurred incrementally over a period of five years. In 1999, in preparation for the redesign in the model of service, interdisciplinary working groups developed the framework based on a review of the literature and focus groups comprised of community stakeholders. The resulting proposal supported a dramatic shift from the milieu-based approach to a brief-stay crisis stabilization, assessment, and transitional care model. In 2000, under this new model of care, the number of inpatient beds increased from twelve to eighteen, with an average length of stay of fourteen days. With CHEO now being the single point of entry for psychiatric emergencies in the region, more children under age thirteen were being admitted to the inpatient unit.

Within the new model of service in the inpatient psychiatry program, children and adolescents in crisis were admitted to a safe, supportive, and highly structured inpatient environment with a team that provided crisis intervention and management during periods of high risk or psychiatric instability. The interdisciplinary team consisted of nurses, child and youth counselors, social workers, occupational therapists, teachers, psychologists, psychiatrists, and a case coordinator. Risk assessment was continuous throughout hospitalization. All families and caregivers were offered ongoing support by the social worker on the team. The unit had the capacity to offer highly specialized, interdisciplinary assessments and preliminary diagnostic evaluations if deemed necessary. Short-term interventions based on individual needs (e.g., anger management, problem-solving, stress management) were also available in individual, group, and family modalities. Transitional care services were initiated following a period of crisis stabilization and/or assessment for cases in which there were more complex needs or in which other factors made further inpatient intervention necessary before a successful discharge (e.g., response to medication). Treatment recommendations and post-discharge planning were initiated early in the admission process and the team strived to liaise with community providers to facilitate the youth's return to community-based resources as quickly as possible.

In keeping with the provincial directives to relocate all specialized psychiatric and mental health services for children (under age sixteen) from the ROH to CHEO, the number of inpatient beds at CHEO was increased from eighteen to twenty-five. In 2003, CHEO developed a separate ten-bed inpatient unit with a similar model of care and goals for children age twelve and younger, resulting in the original inpatient unit reverting to a fifteen-bed adolescent unit. However, the model of service delivery and goals remained the same. A new component of the inpatient psychiatry program, after-care, now referred to as transitional care, was added in 2004. This component provides immediate follow-up contact for all discharged inpatients from both inpatient units and their families to ensure that the discharge plan is implemented. Furthermore, short-term support is offered to patients for whom outpatient services are not yet in place immediately at discharge but who continue to need interim support.

DESIGN AND DEVELOPMENT OF THE OUTCOMES MANAGEMENT APPROACH

When developing any new service that has as one of its core principles responsiveness to changing needs, it is essential to create a philosophy of care that provides the direction to these changes. An outcomes management approach was included among the core principles of the philosophy of care of the CHEO inpatient psychiatry program.

Planning Phase

With the development and redesign of the new inpatient psychiatry program came the unique opportunity to adopt an outcomes management approach that was fully embedded in the clinical service. This also addressed the expectation from the Ministry level that the inpatient service incorporate an evaluative component. Outcomes management as it was conceptualized in the early implementation of the new model incorporated the following core principles as articulated by Lyons and colleagues (1997):

- Define the key goals of the acute care service and identify relevant and feasible clinical measures that allow for evaluation of these goals.

- Incorporate appropriate clinical measures that will allow identification of child, youth, and family needs from their particular perspectives.

- Choose established measures, whenever possible, that are standardized and psychometrically sound.

- Ensure that the appropriate clinician assesses the needs of the patients.

- Ensure measurement at predictable time points, including at admission and discharge.

Although outcomes management has been applied to a variety of settings, such as residential treatment, foster care, and juvenile justice (e.g., Lyons et al., 1998), there is no evidence that this approach has been integrated into an acute care inpatient setting. In late 1999 and early 2000, the outcomes management approach was operationalized as a comprehensive program evaluation plan for the inpatient unit at CHEO. In keeping with the core principles outlined above, the process included a comprehensive review of outcome literature in acute care settings, mapping outcomes onto the program goals, selecting appropriate informants and standardized measures, and establishing time points for assessment.

Existing Literature on Acute Care Outcomes. Specifically, the literature review was an important first step in providing a survey of current practice and outcomes of various models of pediatric inpatient psychiatric care. Review of the scant literature that described outcomes for inpatient psychiatry programs dealing with acute crisis stabilization and assessment revealed serious limitations. In one report (Doherty et al., 1987), the discussion of outcomes was limited to level-of-care dispositions at the time of discharge. Furthermore, this report contained no information about standardized assessment at admission, discharge, or follow-up. A Canadian study of an acute care inpatient program for youth (Bradley & Clark, 1993) included a retrospective chart review that incorporated standardized measures of treatment outcome and satisfaction; results showed that both parents and service providers were satisfied with the program. Those most satisfied also tended to indicate that home-based problems were addressed during hospitalization. However, treatment outcome was restricted to parents' assessments of their children's behavioral functioning and was measured only at the follow-up time point, which ranged from one to seventy-six days after discharge. The average length of stay in both of these acute care programs ranged from twenty-eight to forty-two days.

Overall, the existing outcomes research had a number of limitations (Blanz & Schmidt, 2000; Cornsweet, 1990). Many studies were qualitative and descriptive without presenting empirical outcomes data; others were retrospective. Few used appropriate comparison groups, standardized and psychometrically sound outcome tools, or baseline assessments of functioning and level of severity of presenting complaints. There was no consensus on which components of outcome were important to assess. With the evolution of acute inpatient services, the need exists for clinically relevant measures designed specifically to be sensitive to mental health outcomes in these settings.

The information obtained from this review highlighted the need to take a prospective, systematic approach to assessment that was fully integrated within the delivery of the clinical service and included the perspective of multiple informants. Practically speaking, this meant gathering standardized clinical information from the child, the family, and the interdisciplinary team members at different time points during the patient's admission.

Buy-In From All Program Participants. In the planning phase, we recognized that buy-in from all team members, including administration, was imperative to successfully implement the evaluation plan. Only overall buy-in would ensure active and meaningful participation in the outcomes approach. Several critical elements would enhance staff buy-in, including a proper explanation of the rationale behind the approach and its link to patient care and staff training in the use of specific outcome tools. It was particularly helpful to have an expert in the field who was external to the organization present both the rationale and the training. This provided an additional perspective and enhanced the credibility of the new outcomes approach, which was a significant departure from the previous approach to care.

Initial Implementation Phase

In January 2000, the initial implementation of the program evaluation plan occurred with the launch of the redesigned inpatient service from a milieu to a crisis assessment unit. The goals of the new inpatient psychiatry unit were:

- To provide valid assessments of risk severity and acuity from multiple sources of information, including patient, parent/guardian, and staff;

- To provide risk reduction and crisis stabilization by providing a safe environment;

- To provide a comprehensive interdisciplinary assessment of needs and strengths and provisional diagnosis (if warranted);

- To provide a treatment plan and mobilize resources involving family and community;

- To provide brief, individualized, goal-focused interventions (if warranted) and;

- To accomplish these goals within a short length of stay.

We selected appropriate clinical measures that would allow us to evaluate these goals. At the time, self-report and parent-report measures of emotional and behavioral functioning were completed at the time of admission, and the information was then used in the clinical assessment process. We selected additional measures, including one more specific to outcome, but they required staff training to implement; these measures include the Childhood Severity of Psychiatric Illness Scale (CSPI) (Lyons, 1998a) and the Childhood Acuity of Psychiatric Illness Scale (CAPI). The ratings on the CSPI are based on the thirty-day period before admission, whereas the ratings on the CAPI are based on the previous twenty-four hours. The CAPI, a tool designed specifically to monitor change resulting from involvement in mental health services, was well suited for completion by the front-line staff (nurses and child and youth counselors) to assess acuity of risk at both admission and discharge, given their daily interaction with the patients on the unit. The CSPI was well suited for completion by clinicians on the inpatient team (psychologists, psychiatrists, social workers, and occupational therapists) given that their assessments involve the integration of historical information from different sources. This distribution of responsibility among different team members allowed for shared participation in the clinical assessment and the evaluation approach. In June 2000, Dr. Lyons served as the external expert to provide training to staff. After establishing inter-rater reliability among members of the inpatient team, the CSPI and CAPI were included as part of the standard assessment at admission.

Full-Time Evaluation Coordinator. It quickly became evident that to fully implement and oversee the evaluation plan, we needed an individual with protected time to assume these responsibilities. In July 2000, a full-time, post-doctoral fellow in psychology with clinical, research, and teaching responsibilities filled this role. As the evaluation plan evolved, the following activities were accomplished:

- Relevant variables were identified;
- A data base was developed;
- Documentation was created to systematically collect clinical information; and
- An iterative process was identified for sharing the standardized assessment information with the clinical team at daily rounds.

Mechanism for Regular Communication. We also recognized that we needed a forum for regular communication and exchange of ideas on how best to make use of the clinical information at both the individual patient and program levels. To this end, we created a formal team with key role membership, including inpatient management. This team met regularly to identify and facilitate such activities as ongoing staff training in the use of outcome tools and presentations of data updates at regular intervals to the inpatient team, the hospital, and externally.

Contact With Providers From External Sites. To facilitate ongoing review of the evaluation plan, we developed and maintained contacts with key individuals from external sites who embraced a similar evaluation philosophy. This provided opportunities to learn about current approaches and measures. For example, through ongoing consultation with Dr. Lyons, the inpatient team became aware of the Child and Adolescent Needs and Strengths–Mental Health tool (CANS-MH; Lyons, 1999) as an alternative to the CSPI. The CANS-MH was seen as providing a means to assess not only needs, but strengths. This was a key facet of a comprehensive inpatient assessment that had not been included in the original program evaluation plan. As a result, the CANS-MH replaced the CSPI in 2002, and the clinicians who were to complete the tool received training.

Current Implementation Phase—TCOM Framework

Program evaluation as a means to operationalize the outcomes management approach evolved over time. What began as a concrete way of measuring outcomes was now more broadly understood as a framework for the use of clinical information to better assess and understand child and adolescent needs, to provide individualized treatment recommendations, and to monitor the inpatient program as a whole. This iterative use of clinical information builds in a process for responding to change.

Dr. Lyons articulated his TCOM strategy (2004) concurrent with the CHEO inpatient program's broader conceptualization of outcomes. TCOM, as noted earlier, is a comprehensive strategy for outcomes management that garners accountability at all levels of the system. Its central premise is that decision-making at every level—individual child/adolescent, program, agency, network, and full system—is informed by the clinical needs *and strengths* of children and their families. With its broad scope, TCOM provided the conceptual framework for the changes already implemented in the inpatient program and direction for maximizing the existing outcomes approach.

Individual Level. Within the current phase of implementation, the focus has been on the individual and program levels within TCOM, which map onto the acute care setting in a number of ways. The first and most important level addresses the clinical needs and strengths of the individual children, adolescents, and their families who are seen in the inpatient psychiatry program. As indicated, this clinical information is collected systematically and incorporated into the clinical assessment and decision-making for each patient. For example, a key component of the outcomes management approach is the CANS-MH (Lyons, 1999). The CANS-MH is a forty-two-item information integration tool designed to identify a profile of mental health needs and strengths for children and adolescents. This tool can guide and structure a clinician's assessment and provide support for clinical decision making for the individual child. Within the inpatient program at CHEO, a team clinician completes the CANS-MH early in the patient's admission, and this information is discussed at daily team rounds to inform the development of a treatment plan. Additional assessment measures, such as the CAPI and other standardized self-report measures, guide the process in a similar way. The primary use of these tools is clinical in nature, and this clinical information is central to the TCOM approach.

Program Level. The program represents the second level within TCOM. In the acute care setting, this would be the inpatient psychiatry program as a whole. An example of how clinical information has guided the choice of assessment and treatment approaches can be drawn from the children's inpatient unit. Data from the first year of service indicated that the vast majority of children presented with, among other problems, moderate to severe disruptive behavior including impulsive and oppositional behaviors (Bisnaire & Greenham, 2004). In many acute care settings, these behaviors often result in the use of physical or pharmacological restraint. The inpatient psychiatry program, however, had adopted the principle of least restraint as a core value within its philosophy of care, and it incorporates an evidence-based approach to the assessment and management of difficult behavior. As a result, inpatient teams were trained in collaborative problem solving (Greene & Ablon, 2005), an approach that provides alternative means to manage explosive and oppositional behaviors.

Clinical information also guides decision-making at the program level through the iterative use of clinical data at an aggregate level. That is, the information gathered using the standardized clinical tools is regularly reviewed for the inpatient population as a group, and this data further informs decision-making. For example, the selection of standardized tools may be adjusted or changed based on the utility of information they provide. A related project undertaken at the program level was a survey of inpatient team members regarding the utility of the various clinical tools and measures currently used in the program (Scoular, 2005). These included standardized measures, care plans, and other documentation on the medical chart. The purpose of this survey was to identify ways to optimize the use of these tools and the perceived barriers to optimization. This was in keeping with the commitment to continually respond to changing program needs.

Inpatient Hospital Setting. The third level in TCOM is the agency, which in the acute care setting is the hospital. Planning for the new model of inpatient service included a commitment to build-in a process of frequent review of how services are delivered, based on patients' continually changing needs. This review process allows us to regularly present the clinical outcome data to different hospital groups. To date, these data have been shared at CHEO with outpatient mental health services, the quality management council, the accreditation team, and the board of directors. These presentations give us a forum to demonstrate to the hospital that inpatient services are delivered in a responsible and accountable manner that is true to the initial commitment. In addition, the value of having a transparent and accountable process is reflected in the level of support the hospital provides to the program in terms of resources allocated to sustain the outcomes management approach.

The Hospital Within the Community. The fourth level of TCOM extends to the broader community the hospital serves. A tertiary acute care setting is reserved for acute and complex cases, and it must partner with its community to successfully meet this mandate, even when community needs and partners change. This has become particularly relevant in light of the significant shift in focus of the inpatient service from treatment to crisis stabilization and assessment, and the resulting decrease in the length of psychiatric hospitalization. Currently, partnerships include formal liaisons with community mental health centers, private practitioners, and school boards. To date these connections have focused mainly on the process by which patients flow within the broader system of care. In addition, for individual patients, community providers are active participants throughout the hospital admission and discharge feedback meeting.

The Broader System of Care. The fifth and final level within TCOM is the full system. For the acute care setting, this represents the relationships developed beyond the local community level. Inpatient psychiatry is an inherent part of the broader system of care and must assume its responsibility within the continuum. Further, the inclusion of inpatient psychiatric services provides an opportunity to reduce the stigma associated with hospitalization for mental health needs. This full system includes those sectors that also provide services to the children and adolescents who are admitted to the inpatient psychiatry program such as education, juvenile justice, residential care, and child welfare. These broader systems impact beyond the local community, at a minimum at the provincial level, and potentially at the national level. At present, the full system level is at an early stage of development for the acute care setting.

Next Steps for Implementation

The progress to date, as described above, has primarily focused on developing TCOM at the individual and program levels. Progress has been made to a lesser extent at the hospital and community levels, using the existing resources made available to support the inpatient program. However, to fully optimize TCOM at all levels in a timely and effective manner, additional resources and support are necessary. Such support must be secured both internally and externally to the program.

External funding was granted to the inpatient program through a provincially funded Centre of Excellence for Child and Youth Mental Health to provide the necessary resources and support for fully realizing the outcomes management approach. The primary objectives of the grant are to more fully articulate the process of strengthening and further developing TCOM from the individual to full system levels. These funds are being used to employ a clinical research associate and to facilitate ongoing training and consultation with external partners.

At the individual child and adolescent level, several goals have been identified. First, the content of the CANS-MH will be adapted for use in an acute care setting. In collaboration with Dr. Lyons, additional items or sections will be added or substituted to capture the unique needs and strengths of children and adolescents admitted to the inpatient program. Second, the clinical information gathered using standardized measures will be more directly translated for use in developing individual care plans. The goal is to be more systematic in mapping identified needs and strengths onto treatment goals and discharge plans. The ultimate goal is to incorporate outcomes management into the post-discharge transitional care services to ensure that these individual treatment goals and discharge plans are implemented.

At the program level, the goal is to strengthen the process for regular monitoring and review of aggregate clinical data. This will ensure that changes in the population needs are reflected in services provided. For example, changes in patient needs may warrant the adoption of new assessment tools or interventions. By reviewing the data regularly and systematically, the program can respond in a timely and clinically meaningful way.

At both the hospital and community levels, the goal is to more fully develop integrated care between the inpatient program and its mental health service partners. For example, at the hospital level, many inpatients are admitted through the crisis intervention program in the emergency department. We have made efforts to streamline and consolidate the assessment tools used by the crisis and inpatient teams, both to allow for clear and more efficient communication of patient needs upon admission and to establish a common language by which to understand identified needs and strengths. Optimizing TCOM at this level will also enhance monitoring of the appropriateness of level-of-care decisions. At the community level, a common outcomes management approach is currently under development with the hospital's outreach services. Outreach teams of clinicians from CHEO travel to outlying regional communities within the catchment area to work collaboratively with community agencies to deliver specialized mental health services.

Other partnerships will be formalized with local agencies and organizations external to CHEO that provide services to children, such as community mental health agencies, school boards, residential care providers, and juvenile detention centers. The purpose of establishing these partnerships will be to facilitate a common outcomes management approach. The development of these partnerships, or local networks, within and external to CHEO will serve to establish the common outcomes management approach that ensures continuity of care within an integrated system driven by the needs of the individual children, adolescents, and families.

Research funding has been obtained in part to develop a provincial systems network that would include all of the aforementioned sectors but at the full system level. At the full system level, government is a crucial stakeholder and must be an active participant. The network would include all hospital-based acute care sites in the province and would interface with all other sectors that provide services to children and youth. This network will strengthen communication and collaboration within the system of care that is inclusive of acute care settings. The support and active participation of government in this systems network is necessary to ensure the development of a mental health policy and programming. To this end, developing collaborative relationships with key individuals in the various sectors and at the government level is a crucial first step.

CHALLENGES TO IMPLEMENTATION

Accepting a Culture That Embraces Change

Implementation of an outcomes management approach in an acute care setting is actually a process of continuing change. Change in and of itself is a core component of the model and brings with it many challenges. One of the most significant and necessary requirements is a fundamental shift in the system towards recognizing the central role of the needs and strengths of children, youth, and their families. Traditionally, decisions about the development of mental health services were made at a government, agency, or program level where the actual needs of individual patients and families are often far removed from the process. As a result, changes to programs or services occur at a much slower pace and are more focused on the needs identified by the agency or organization. In fact some services, such as inpatient psychiatry programs, have gone unchanged for years.

By virtue of children's and adolescents' continuing physical, emotional, cognitive, social, and behavioral development, their needs are always evolving. Families are also a dynamic system. Never has this been more evident than in today's society, with its increase in the number of single and working parents and blended families. In making the individual needs and strengths core to the development of mental health services, the full system becomes not only accountable to these individuals but also responsive in addressing their changing needs over time. The challenge in facilitating this fundamental shift in the full system is to foster at all levels a culture that embraces change as an ongoing reality.

Building a culture of change in any setting starts with the ability to recognize and act upon opportunities for change. Opportunities may be externally driven (e.g., change in government) or internally driven within the agency or program (e.g., new director). The key is to seize, or create, opportunities in order to provide a context for change. For some individuals, this context is often necessary to explain or justify the rationale behind the proposed changes. Such justification increases the likelihood of acceptance.

Opportunities for change to the inpatient psychiatry program at CHEO originated from both internal and external circumstances. As noted earlier, internal pressures on the demands for inpatient services necessitated a shift in the model of service delivery at the same time that restructuring of mental health services was occurring at a regional level. These internal and external demands provided the necessary context for staff to understand the need for change. Having staff participate in the conceptualization of the new model further enhanced acceptance of change.

An additional consideration in building a culture of change is to introduce change in incremental steps (Lyons, 2004). This planned approach, which introduces new concepts in a step-wise manner, allows individuals to accommodate change at a less threatening and more manageable pace. Furthermore, incremental change provides the necessary conditions for the iterative process to develop. Each incremental step provides the opportunity to review the clinical needs and adjust the program accordingly.

Understanding the Importance of TCOM to Service Delivery

One of the primary challenges to implementing an outcomes management approach in any setting is to secure buy-in, or acceptance of the importance of this approach, to clinical service delivery. To fully realize TCOM, which is systemic by definition, it is essential that buy-in is secured at all levels. In the acute care setting, one of the most important keys to securing buy-in from patients, families, inpatient team members, and program and hospital administrators is to fully embed outcomes management into the daily delivery of clinical services. To do this, it is imperative to use measurement tools that provide clinically meaningful information about the patients' and families' needs and strengths. In the inpatient setting, the clinical information is available early in the admission and discussed at daily rounds. This information then directly informs treatment planning decisions and recommendations. Buy-in from both patients and staff is more achievable when it is apparent that the information is meaningful and has a direct impact on the delivery of care.

Another key to securing buy-in is to be mindful of the burden placed on patients, family, and staff in completing the measurement tools. The assessment tools should be targeted, efficient, kept to a minimum in number, while still capturing the pertinent information. In addition, the process of collecting information should be systematized as much as possible so that it is seamless with the delivery of routine clinical care. For example, in the acute care setting, tools are incorporated into the package of information introduced at the time of admission to the inpatient unit by the staff responsible for completing the admission. This eliminates the need for a separate staff member to administer these measures.

To maintain the buy-in from staff and administration, it is important to develop a process to regularly share clinical data at an aggregate level. This process provides the forum by which all participants maintain an active role in reviewing and revising the program. Having input in the decision-making process facilitates a sense of ownership and ongoing commitment to the approach.

Securing Key Staff

A significant challenge to implementing an outcomes management approach in an acute care setting is securing committed key staff. Such a large undertaking requires at the outset a commitment by one or more individuals to conceptualize TCOM and to provide direction for implementing this approach. Once the stage has been set for change and buy-in is secured, the need continues for one or more people with protected time to assume responsibility for overseeing and monitoring the process of day-to-day management of clinical information, including scoring, sharing of data at daily rounds, data entry, and analysis. An ongoing training program is needed for new staff members, and regular monitoring of inter-rater reliability on assessment tools is required. These responsibilities are central to maintaining the importance of an outcomes management approach that is embedded within the delivery of clinical care.

Securing Financial Resources

In addition to human resources, significant financial resources are often required. For example, there are a number of expenses related to the systematic collection and use of standardized assessment measures, from purchasing the questionnaires to storing the data, either electronically or physically. Cost reduction is possible through judicious selecting of targeted and clinically relevant tools. A number of these tools are available in the public domain (e.g., the CANS-MH) which can help offset or reduce the cost of implementation. Most importantly, an outcomes management approach that is delivered in a clinically responsible way can diminish any added financial burden associated with such an initiative. In other words, if the clinical information driving the outcomes management approach is the information required for the delivery of clinical service, there is little need to invest in resources beyond those required for clinical care.

CONCLUSIONS

All those involved in the design and delivery of mental health services, from providers to administrators to funding agencies, have an obligation to be responsive to the needs of the children, youth, and families they serve. TCOM provides a mechanism to respond to the needs of those who receive mental health services in the acute care setting. The same could be said for any type of mental health service. Furthermore, an outcomes management approach such as TCOM, grounded in patient needs, allows for mental health service providers to respond in a flexible manner to these needs that change or evolve over time. Changes in patient needs result in corresponding changes at other levels of the system, including agency, community, and full system levels. This, in turn, creates a system that is able to be more directly responsible and accountable to the children and families that rely on these services.

Designing and implementing an outcomes management approach to the delivery of acute care inpatient services has been a process of incremental change that continues to occur over time. This process has required a common vision and a long-term commitment to change from a large number of individuals and stakeholders at all levels. Key to the successful implementation of an outcomes management approach in any setting is recognizing or creating opportunities for change in the service delivery model that places central importance to the needs of children and families. It is essential to create and foster a culture of change that further ensures acceptance by program staff and agency and government administration.

The outcomes management approach is more likely to be successfully implemented if it is embedded directly into the delivery of clinical care and the clinical relevance is made highly salient. Finally, the importance of adequate human and financial resources must be addressed. At the end of the day, success is defined by a system that is directly responsive to the changing needs of children, adolescents, and families. The onus is not on the needs of children and families to be appropriate for the available mental health services, but rather on the mental health system to deliver services that are appropriate to meet the needs of children and families.

Author's Note

We would like to acknowledge the collaboration and significant contributions of the interdisciplinary teams and the management committee of the Inpatient Psychiatry Program at CHEO. Thank you for your unwavering commitment to the children, youth, and families that we serve and for embracing this outcomes management approach to care. This endeavor would not be possible without the ongoing support and confidence of Karen Tataryn and Simon Davidson, operations and medical directors of the Mental Health Patient Service Unit. We also appreciate the commitment to this work of Susan Richardson, vice-president of Patient Services and Allied Health at CHEO. We acknowledge the generous financial support of the Provincial Centre of Excellence for Child and Youth Mental Health at CHEO, the CHEO Psychiatry Research Fund, the CHEO Research Institute and the CHEO Foundation.

References

Atlas, J. A. (1994). Crisis and acute brief therapy with adolescents. *Psychiatric Quarterly, 65*, 79–87.

Bisnaire, L. & Greenham, S. L. (2004). *Use of the CANS-MH with children and adolescents admitted to acute care inpatient psychiatric services.* Presented at the First Annual CANS conference, Chicago, IL.

Blanz, B. & Schmidt, M. H. (2000). Practitioner review: Preconditions and outcome of inpatient treatment in child and adolescent psychiatry. *Journal of Child Psychology and Psychiatry*, *41*, 703–712.

Bradley, E. J. & Clark, B. S. (1993). Patients' characteristics and consumer satisfaction on an inpatient child psychiatric unit. *Canadian Journal of Psychiatry*, *38*, 175–180.

Cornsweet, C. (1990). A review of research on hospital treatment of children and adolescents. *Bulletin of the Menninger Clinic*, *54*, 64–77.

Davidson, S. & Manion, I. G. (1996). Facing the challenge: Mental health and illness in Canadian youth. *Psychology, Health & Medicine*, *1*, 41–56.

Doherty, M. B., Manderson, M. & Carter-Ake, L. (1987). Time-limited psychiatric hospitalization of children: A model and three-year outcome. *Hospital and Community Psychiatry, 38*, 643–647.

Gold, I. M., Heller, C. & Ritorto, B. (1992). A short-term psychiatric inpatient program for adolescents. *Hospital and Community Psychiatry*, *43*, 58–61.

Greene, R. W. & Ablon, J. S. (2005). *Treating explosive kids: The collaborative problem-solving approach.* NY: Guilford.

Lourie, I. S., Stroul, B. A. & Friedman, R. M. (1998). Community-based systems of care: From advocacy to outcomes. In M. H. Epstein, K. Kutash & A. Duchnowski (Eds.), *Outcomes for children & youth with behavioral and emotional disorders and their families: Programs & evaluation best practices*. Austin, TX: Pro-Ed.

Lyons, J. S. (1998). *The severity and acuity of psychiatric illness scales: An outcomes-management and decision-support system—Child and adolescent version* (*manual*). San Antonio, TX: Psychological Corp.

Lyons, J. S. (1999). *Child and adolescent needs and strengths—Mental Health manual.* Chicago: Buddin Praed Foundation.

Lyons, J. S. (2004). *Redressing the emperor: Improving our children's public mental health system.* Westport, CT: Praeger.

Lyons, J. S., Howard, K. I., O'Mahoney, M. T. & Lish, J. D. (1997). *The measurement and management of clinical outcomes in mental health.* New York: Wiley.

Lyons, J. S., Mintzer, L. L., Kisiel, C. L. & Shallcross, H. (1998). Understanding the mental health needs of children and adolescents in residential treatment. *Professional Psychology: Research and Practice, 29,* 582–587.

Offord, D. R., Boyle, M. H., Fleming, J. E., Blum, H. M. & Grant, N. I. (1989). Ontario child health study. Summary of selected results. *Canadian Journal of Psychiatry, 34,* 483–491.

Offord, D. R., Boyle, M. H., Szatmari, P., Rae-Grant, N. I., Links, P. S., Cadman, D. T., Byles, J. A., Crawford, J. W., Blum, H. M., Byrne, C., et al. (1987). Ontario child health study: II. Six-month prevalence of disorder and rates of service utilization. *Archives of General Psychiatry*, *44*, 832–836.

Pumariega, A. J. & Glover, S. (1998). New developments in service delivery research for children and adolescents and their families. *Advances in Clinical Child Psychology*, *20*, 303–343.

Scoular, D. (2005). *Inpatient mental health unit survey of the utility of the clinical measures: A survey of team members' perceptions.* Unpublished manuscript.

Zimmerman, D. P. (1990). Notes on the history of adolescent inpatient and residential treatment. *Adolescence*, *15*, 9–38.

Chapter 13

Implementing Total Clinical Outcomes Management in a Program for Individuals With Substance Abuse and Chronic Homelessness

**by Renanah K. Lehner, Ph.D.
and Elizabeth M. Durkin, Ph.D.**

INTRODUCTION

The demand for clinical outcomes management strategies in behavioral health care has grown as an increasing focus on treatments, known as evidence-based treatments, has been shown to be effective. This interest in understanding how treatments interact with consumers of behavioral health care started in the 1960s with federal requirements for program evaluation (Lyons, 2004). Although the federal requirement was never fully realized, in the ensuing decades outcomes research has become more common in service delivery programs. Insurers, government funding sources, private and public organizations, and consumers all have demanded greater evidence of the beneficial impact of treatment to justify the cost of care and demonstrate the utility of interventions (Martin & Kettner, 1996).

This focus on outcomes has prompted the inclusion of an outcomes management component in many newly developed service delivery programs. The design of outcomes management strategies for collaborative start-up programs can present unique challenges, however. Many challenges start during the program's planning phase and can stem from a lack of knowledge about the service population, changes to the service delivery program, and the need to attend to unexpected delays and program problems. Challenges to outcomes management in interagency collaborations also may arise from the typically diffuse leadership structure that can result when multiple stakeholders create a new entity. This chapter will describe a new collaborative service program and its organizational structure, and our own experiences implementing our clinical outcomes management plan. In addition, we provide a summary of lessons learned that can guide future efforts in establishing clinical outcomes management with start-up programs.

THE PROGRAM: ASSERTIVE COMMUNITY TREATMENT RESOURCES FOR THE CHRONICALLY HOMELESS

Homeless advocates in Chicago have long recognized that few housing and social services existed for homeless individuals on the city's South Side. In response to this service gap, a collaboration of public and private agencies developed a program called the Assertive Community Treatment (ACT) Resources for the Chronically Homeless, known as ARCH. These agencies represent multiple service delivery systems, including mental health, substance abuse, Department of Veterans Affairs (VA), and housing services.

ARCH provides ACT and permanent housing to chronically homeless individuals who have mental health and/or substance abuse disorders and who reside in one of twenty-two neighborhoods on Chicago's South Side. The ARCH team is staffed by a full-time nurse, a part-time psychiatrist, five case managers, and a team leader. Each team member is employed by a different partner agency in the collaboration, thus bringing together the expertise of multiple service systems. In accordance with typical ACT protocol, ARCH uses a shared caseload model wherein team members have joint responsibility for all program participants (Stein & Santos, 1998).

Housing First

ARCH team members engage eligible participants on the streets, in shelters, or in local social service agencies. Once engaged by the team, ARCH consumers move to permanent housing within a short time period using HUD Shelter Plus Care housing vouchers. The relatively swift transition to permanent housing reflects the ARCH program's adoption of a "housing first" model (Tsemberis et al., 2004). Housing first proponents argue that individuals can better address their treatment needs once their basic needs for stable housing are met. ARCH consumers reside either in scattered site apartments operated by private landlords, or in one of two clustered-site settings run by local social service agencies. In either case, the ARCH consumer holds the lease for his or her own residence and in return agrees to participate in ongoing social and/or health services. In keeping with a housing first approach, ARCH consumers face no demands to maintain abstinence nor to enter treatment for their substance abuse and mental health disorders. Instead, ARCH workers employ motivational interventions to encourage both treatment engagement and the resolution of problems in other functional domains (e.g., vocational, interpersonal, financial) (Miller & Rollnick, 1991).

ACT originated as a treatment model for individuals with serious and persistent mental illness (Stein & Santos, 1998). ARCH diverges from that model in that a majority of program consumers report primary substance abuse disorders, although many also have co-occuring mental health disorders. The ARCH program thus serves as an innovative adaptation of ACT to a new group (chronically homeless persons with substance disorders), but one whose complex constellation of needs resembles that of the original ACT target population.

ARCH Program Organization

The ARCH program, along with eleven other programs nationwide, received initial funding through a special initiative of the federal government's Interagency Council on Homelessness. This initiative promoted collaborative local efforts to address chronic homelessness by combining funds from three cabinet agencies—HUD, the VA, and the Department of Health and Human Services (DHHS). Two specific agencies within the DHHS, the Substance Abuse and Mental Health Services Administration (SAMHSA) and the Health Resources and Services Administration (HRSA), had designated roles in the initiative. The structure of the initiative required local applicants to submit separate applications to each federal partner, along with a combined comprehensive plan for the collaboration.

In Chicago, organizations with distinct areas of expertise took the lead on each of the four applications. The City of Chicago's Department of Human Services (CDHS), which serves as the HUD grantee, also acts as lead grantee for the entire collaboration. The Division of Alcoholism and Substance Abuse (DASA) within the State of Illinois' Department of Human Services (IDHS) serves as the SAMHSA grantee, while Heartland Health Outreach, a local provider of health care for the homeless programs, receives the HRSA funding. Finally, the VA funnels its resources through the homeless outreach program of Chicago's Jesse Brown VA Medical Center.

Representatives of each of these four grantee agencies serve on the ARCH project management team, along with a representative of IDHS's Division of Mental Health, researchers involved in the local evaluation team, and the ARCH team leader. The project management team is a consensus-driven body that provides oversight of the ARCH team, develops policies and procedures, ensures compliance with the various funding agencies' reporting and service delivery regulations, and monitors stakeholders' fidelity to program practices. In addition, a project advisory group brings together representatives from the five private agencies (Community Mental Health Council, Cornell Interventions, Habilitative Systems, Salvation Army, and Thresholds) that staff the ARCH team through subcontracts with DASA and the two agencies (Catholic Charities and YMCA) operating the clustered-site housing. These agencies provide members of the ARCH project management team with stakeholder feedback and with expertise regarding their respective service delivery systems.

At the invitation of the project management team, Northwestern University's Mental Health Services and Policy Program joined with the Illinois Mental Illness/Substance Abuse (MISA) Institute to design and implement a continuous quality improvement plan for the ARCH program. This plan combines a focus on fidelity to the evidence-based practices used by ARCH (the ACT model and motivational interviewing) with a Total Clinical Outcomes Management (TCOM) (Lyons, 2004) approach to program evaluation. We discuss the rationale for adopting a TCOM approach and the critical TCOM components used in ARCH's continuous quality improvement program in greater detail below.

TOTAL CLINICAL OUTCOMES MANAGEMENT

TCOM is an approach to data collection and outcomes measurement that can help structure services so as to directly address consumers' needs and strengths (Lyons, 2004). In contrast to more traditional approaches that prioritize data collection for external accountability or for research purposes, TCOM focuses on capturing information about consumers that can translate directly into service delivery decisions at multiple levels (consumer, program, and service system). Used retrospectively or with existing programs, TCOM provides information about the needs and strengths of current service populations, the match between consumers and the services provided, and changes in consumer needs and strengths over time. When used prospectively during the development of interventions, TCOM also allows for the needs and strengths of the people being served to facilitate the design of the service delivery system. The feedback from TCOM informs clinicians and administrators about the ways that their services are meeting consumers' needs and incorporating their strengths; it also finds their unmet needs and missed opportunities to use their strengths.

ARCH TCOM IMPLEMENTATION PLAN

A Multi-Component Treatment Structure

We incorporated a prospective TCOM design into the ARCH program from its inception. The goals of the ARCH TCOM strategy include:

1. To provide the ARCH team with consumer-level data to inform strengths-based treatment planning;
2. To monitor the fidelity of treatment planning and services to the ARCH model; and
3. To provide outcomes data to assess program effectiveness.

There are four interrelated components to the ARCH TCOM strategy:

1. Periodic assessment of the consumers, at the point of initial engagement and throughout the course of treatment;

2. Development of treatment plans directly tied to the needs and strengths identified via the periodic assessment process;

3. A review of ARCH's fidelity to strengths-based treatment planning and service delivery; and

4. The monitoring of consumer outcomes as measured by changes in the assessment ratings across time.

This multi-component structure allows us to provide feedback about various aspects of the ARCH program at set intervals throughout ARCH service delivery.

Adult Needs and Strengths Tool

The assessment component of the ARCH TCOM strategy involves the rating of consumer needs and strengths at intake and every ninety days thereafter. This systematic approach to consumer assessment allows for the tailoring of service delivery to individual consumers' needs and encourages the use of consumers' strengths as a positive resource for promoting behavior change. ARCH team members use the Adult Needs and Strengths Assessment (ANSA) (Lyons & Anderson, 1999) as their primary assessment tool. The ANSA, a strengths-based evolution of the severity of psychiatric illness tool (SPI, Lyons, 1998), has well-established reliability and validity and has been used in behavioral health care research (Anderson & Lyons, 2001; Lyons et al., 1995; Lyons et al., 1997(a); Lyons et al., 1997(b); Mulder et al., 2005). The ANSA instrument has known clinimetric properties (as distinguished from psychometric properties). It is a forty-item measure that assesses five domains of need:

- Presenting problems

- Risk behaviors

- Functioning

- Intensity of services

- Caregivers' capacity to provide care

Feinstein (1999) describes six concepts that distinguish clinimetric from psychometric measures: clinically-based items, unweighted items, heterogeneity of items, ease of use, face validity, and observational ratings. Clinimetric measures use items for their clinical relevance rather than items selected for their significance based on statistical calculations, as with psychometric measures. Psychometric measures also typically have items weighted based on statistical calculations, whereas clinimetric measures typically use ordinal ratings that are easy to understand and use in the clinical field.

Another important difference between clinimetric and psychometric measures involves the diversity of items. Clinimetric scales aim to describe the varied aspects of a clinical presentation or construct, while many psychometrically developed scales aim to describe a unidimensional or homogenous construct. As a result, psychometric scales are often carefully calibrated to exclude statistically extraneous or duplicative variables, while clinimetric scales are developed to include a range of items that describe a construct broadly enough to be considered clinically informative. Clinimetric scales also typically have face valid items and can be completed via observation. As a result of these distinct characteristics, clinimetric scales can be completed and understood by clinicians in the field.

The ANSA strengths domain includes items such as interpersonal and relational skills, work and education, interests, spirituality, community involvement, and well being. All items on the ANSA are rated on a four-point scale, with lower scores on the needs items indicating the absence of a problem or need and higher scores indicating the presence of a problem or need. For strengths items, a lower score indicates the presence of a strength and a higher score indicates that a strength has not been identified.

The structure of the ANSA rating scale translates to four levels of action for service providers:

0 = No need for action

1 = Need for monitoring or minor intervention

2 = Need for intervention

3 = Need for immediate and intensive intervention

Strengths ratings translate into actions levels in parallel fashion to needs, so lower scores indicate that a strength should be used as a centerpiece in strengths-based treatment planning and higher scores indicate that a strength needs to be developed or identified before it can be used in strengths-based planning. The treatment planning component of the ARCH TCOM plan calls for team members to develop a written treatment plan that addresses all ANSA needs items rated 2 or 3 and all ANSA strengths items rated 0 or 1. Team members briefly update these treatment plans with ninety-day ANSA reassessments and produce entirely new treatment plans on an annual basis. The ARCH team completes the treatment plan documents in collaboration with consumers so as to encourage the definition of needs and strengths that both consumers and ARCH team members recognize and use.

Fidelity to Strengths-Based Treatment

The third component of the ARCH TCOM strategy consists of a chart review designed to evaluate fidelity to strengths-based treatment. The fidelity review examines each chart's treatment plan documents and progress notes. Using the treatment fidelity index (TFI) developed for ARCH and shown in Table 13.1, a Northwestern TFI reviewer rates the charts on three fidelity items relevant to needs and problems. For each ANSA need item rated 2 or 3, the rater assesses the degree to which (1) treatment plans and updates focus on the need; (2) the progress notes discuss the need; and (3) the notes indicate that services were rendered to address the need.

Similarly, for each ANSA strength item rated 0 or 1, the reviewer rates the degree to which (1) the treatment plans and updates incorporate the strength; (2) progress notes discuss the strength; and (3) the notes indicate that the strength was incorporated into the services rendered. Once the TFI is completed for all items, a score can be tallied to determine the degree of program fidelity to a strengths-based treatment model. The chart review component of the TCOM plan helps identify discrepancies between the intent of the ARCH program and its actual implementation. We can detect fidelity problems across the program overall, as well as at the level of individual needs or strengths items that the ARCH team might fail to address appropriately.

Table 13.1
Excerpt From the ARCH Treatment Fidelity Index

ARCH TFI
MENTAL HEALTH

1. Enter all the ANSA ratings for the dimension.
2. For every ANSA item identified as a 2 or a 3, circle the number in each column that provides the best description of the chart contents.
3. Add all the ratings across rows to get the TFI rating for that item.

Key: M = Mostly   P = Partially   R = Rarely

ANSA Rating	Dimension: MENTAL HEALTH	Consumer needs were a focus of tx plans?			Consumer needs were discussed in progress notes?			Documentation indicates that services were rendered to address this need?			TFI Rating Add items across rows.
		M	P	R	M	P	R	M	P	R	
	Psychosis	2	1	0	2	1	0	2	1	0	0 1 2 3 4 5 6
	Impulse Control	2	1	0	2	1	0	2	1	0	0 1 2 3 4 5 6
	Depression/Anxiety	2	1	0	2	1	0	2	1	0	0 1 2 3 4 5 6
	Antisocial Behavior	2	1	0	2	1	0	2	1	0	0 1 2 3 4 5 6
	Substance Abuse	2	1	0	2	1	0	2	1	0	0 1 2 3 4 5 6
	Stage of Recovery	2	1	0	2	1	0	2	1	0	0 1 2 3 4 5 6
	Adjustment to Trauma	2	1	0	2	1	0	2	1	0	0 1 2 3 4 5 6
	Personality Disorder	2	1	0	2	1	0	2	1	0	0 1 2 3 4 5 6

TFI Ratings: Ratings can range from 0 to 6 for each item in a domain. Higher ratings indicate better fidelity to a needs and strengths-based treatment model. Scores of 0 to 2 = poor fidelity to the model; 3 to 4 = fair fidelity; 5 to 6 = good fidelity.

Consumer Outcomes

The final component of the ARCH TCOM strategy monitors consumer outcomes by analyzing change over time in ANSA item ratings. This analysis then informs the ARCH workers and management regarding the impact of their interventions and enables them to further refine their work with consumers.

BARRIERS TO IMPLEMENTING TCOM

During the first two years of implementing TCOM for ARCH, we encountered a variety of barriers across all four components of the plan—assessment, treatment planning, fidelity review, and outcomes management. Barriers encountered with the assessment process included issues related to team composition, frequency of scheduled ANSA assessment, and unanticipated characteristics of the service population. These problems then had repercussions for the outcomes management component, because that component relied on the assessment data to analyze change over time. Barriers impeding treatment planning and fidelity review were centered on problems with documentation and training. The emergence of these barriers required us to restructure both the TCOM procedures and our role within the ARCH program so as to maintain progress toward our identified TCOM goals. We turn now to a discussion of these barriers and describe our responses to them.

Barriers Impeding Assessment

Diverse Team Member Backgrounds. ARCH team members came from diverse agencies and work backgrounds, and many lacked formal training as mental health clinicians. Team members varied greatly in their perceptions of mental illness and in their ability to recognize signs and symptoms of mental illness. This variability in perspective and training proved challenging for the assessment component of the TCOM plan, as team members did not have a uniform method for screening consumers for mental illnesses.

Team members also had varying views on the stigma and importance of undiagnosed mental illnesses. In team training sessions, some team members agreed that while consumers appeared to have symptoms of mental illness, they did not want to label them by rating them as such on the ANSA. Team members without significant mental health training also lacked the clinical confidence to rate consumers on mental health ANSA variables. They relied solely on the formal documentation of a psychiatric diagnosis made by a mental health professional to make their ANSA ratings on these items. These barriers in the assessment phase threatened the validity of the ANSA data as well as the treatment planning process. Because some team members did not accurately document consumers' mental health needs, the ANSA data did not reflect the consumers' true level of need, and the program ran the risk of not adequately planning to address those needs.

We detected this discrepancy in training and assessment styles after observing unexpected variation in assessment ratings. Our strategy for resolving this problem involved meeting with the ARCH team to address the variability in mental illness conceptualization and assessment. We invited team members to share how they thought about, assessed, and rated the mental illness symptoms of the ARCH consumers. Based on this information, we clarified several important issues related to use of the ANSA, including that ratings on the ANSA mental illness items can be made by a trained rater, even in the absence of a professional mental health diagnosis. We also educated the ARCH team about the importance of overcoming concerns regarding stigma, because improvements in documenting and communicating actual needs would lead to better treatment planning and more effective service delivery. To reinforce our message, we showed the ARCH team preliminary ANSA data that portrayed the program's consumers as being relatively high functioning. This proved an effective training technique, because the ARCH team expressed surprised that they had not adequately communicated the high levels of need that ARCH consumers experience.

Infrequent ANSA Assessments. The infrequency of scheduled ANSA assessments presented another barrier to the assessment component of TCOM. The ARCH program serves about fifty people, each of whom receives an initial ANSA rating and follow-up

ANSAs every ninety days. At maximum enrollment, the five ARCH team members are each responsible for completing ANSAs for approximately ten consumers. It is often the case that ARCH team members do not complete an ANSA for several weeks at a time. In the months after being trained and certified as reliable on the ANSA, infrequent opportunities to administer the instrument prevented some team members from maintaining their ANSA rating familiarity. Those workers who frequently returned to the ANSA manual to guide their ratings tended to become overly reliant on the manual itself. This resulted in undue focus on the illustrative examples found in the text of the manual rather than on the action levels those examples were designed to represent.

Across the ARCH team members, the development of idiosyncratic methods for rating some ANSA items threatened the integrity of the TCOM data and the treatment planning process. We addressed this issue by holding an ANSA review session. We educated the team members about shifting their focus to the action levels (no action needed; watchful waiting/minor action; action; immediate action) associated with each of the ANSA ratings. We worked with the ARCH team to revise some ANSA items that were confusing or contradictory for the dually diagnosed and homeless population that ARCH served.

Special Problems of the Homeless. The final barrier to the TCOM assessment component stemmed from the chronically homeless nature of the population ARCH serves. Accurate completion of the ANSA requires in-depth knowledge of individuals' needs and strengths. Because ARCH consumers tended to have spent years disconnected from formal service providers, referral sources usually provided only scant information about their health and social histories. During their initial engagement period, consumers were often reluctant to trust ARCH team members with personal details about their mental health history and frequently attempted to hide the degree of their substance use. The presence of this barrier to the assessment component of TCOM became apparent to us through our conversations with ARCH members during the ANSA review trainings, as well as through our own comparison of the ANSA with similar tools used in programs serving other, less transient populations. Although we could not change the nature of the ARCH target population, we did encourage the ARCH team members to carefully gather as much pertinent information as possible during their initial assessment interviews and to continue to incorporate new personal, social, and health information into future ANSA ratings as they acquired it.

Barriers Impeding Treatment Planning and Fidelity Review

Communication between team members was a paramount concern. To communicate efficiently, the ACT model adopts a shared caseload approach to service delivery, with ACT teams commonly employing systematic documentation of treatment plans and detailed charting of progress notes. Both the treatment planning and the fidelity review components of the ARCH TCOM plan rely on the existence of documentation that reflects the strengths-based treatment model incorporated into the ARCH design. When we began to prepare for our first annual fidelity review, however, we became aware that the ARCH documentation did not contain elements clearly related to the needs and strengths identified during the periodic assessments, with respect to either the planned treatment or the services rendered. This disconnect left the ARCH team members with little guidance on how to develop strengths-based treatment plans, and left us with little data for the fidelity review component of our TCOM plan.

To respond to this unexpected barrier, we met with the team leader to develop new treatment planning materials and to discuss the importance of uniform charts for all consumers enrolled in the ARCH program. In collaboration with the ARCH team, we developed treatment planning materials that allowed the team to link needs and strengths identified on the consumer's initial ANSA with concrete plans for service delivery. At the request of the team leader, we also designed an abbreviated treatment plan update form to be used in conjunction with every ninety-day ANSA assessment. To counter team member resistance to the introduction of new documentation procedures, we designed both of these instruments to maximize communication around consumers' primary need and strengths. We also created the documents as templates that team members could complete directly on their computers. The documents contained check boxes for items routinely used, which cut down the need to type long narratives. To allow the treatment plans to be sufficiently individualized, we included additional sections in which team members and consumers could add narrative as needed. A modified example of the treatment planning material is shown in Table 13.2.

After we developed the new treatment planning materials, we turned our attention to improving the quality of consumer charts and their capacity to reflect a strengths-based service approach. We first conducted a chart review to provide feedback to the ARCH team regarding the contents and quality of their charts. We checked charts for the presence of initial evaluations, referral information, progress notes, treatment plans, and ANSA evaluations. We then provided feedback to the team to assist them in improving their documentation and treatment plan completion. Having provided that guidance, we then allowed for six months of charting under the new procedures before conducting our planned fidelity review.

Barriers Impeding Outcomes Management

Problems encountered in earlier phases of TCOM impacted our ability to collect and analyze data for the outcomes management component of our plan. We needed reliable ANSA data from initial and ninety-day review assessments that would provide the necessary feedback to the ARCH team and stakeholders regarding how our clients' needs and strengths were changing. The earlier problems with idiosyncratic data collection threatened our ability to accurately analyze the consumers' changes over time and report on clinical outcomes. Much to our surprise, our initial analyses indicated that the chronically homeless and substance abusing population served by ARCH was actually quite functional and free of mental health needs.

Given that this data suggested ARCH was serving a low-need population, we could not expect to find much change in needs or strengths over the course of ARCH's service delivery. Team members' reports were not consistent with these findings, and we suspected that this initial data did not reflect consumers' true needs. After meeting with the team our suspicion was confirmed. The team agreed that initial findings were a result of measurement error rather than a functional and healthy service population. Once the assessment issues were addressed with the team, future ANSA data better reflected the true needs and strengths of the ARCH consumers.

LESSONS LEARNED FROM THE ARCH PROGRAM

This chapter's review of the barriers encountered in the ARCH program and our responses provide two main lessons regarding TCOM implementation. First, start-up

Table 13.2
Modified Excerpts From the ARCH Integrated Treatment Plan

ARCH INTEGRATED TREATMENT PLAN

Consumer's Name:

Program Start Date: Initial Treatment Plan Date: New Treatment Plan Due (1 year):

ANSA Date: Treatment Plan Update Due (3 mos.): Referral Source:

Problem #	Problem List	Related ANSA Items
1	☐ Mental Wellness/ Symptoms	Psychosis, Impulse Control, Depression/Anxiety, Antisocial, Danger to Self or Others, Personality Disorder, Adjustment Trauma, Motivation for Care, Knowledge
2	☐ Productive Use of Time	Employment/ Education
3	☐ Care of Self and Home	Living Skills, Residential Stability, Physical/Medical, Self-Care, Medication Compliance
4	☐ Social/Relationship Issues	Relationship Permanence, Social Behavior, Family Functioning
5	☐ Alcohol/Drug Use	Substance Abuse, Stage of Recovery
6	☐ Problems with Police/Courts	Crime, Sexually Abusive Behavior
7	☐ Strengths	All Strengths

History of Medical Procedures & Psychiatric Hospitalizations	
Current Medications & Dates	
Allergies/Drug Allergies & Reactions	

Motivational Interviewing Areas	Stages of Change Assessment (check one)				
Housing	☐ Precontemplation	☐ Contemplation	☐ Preparation	☐ Action	☐ Maintenance
Substance Abuse	☐ Precontemplation	☐ Contemplation	☐ Preparation	☐ Action	☐ Maintenance
Mental Health	☐ Precontemplation	☐ Contemplation	☐ Preparation	☐ Action	☐ Maintenance

(Continued)

Table 13.2 (Continued)

Problem/Focus	Goals/Behavioral Objectives	Interventions/Modalities
1: Symptoms/ Mental Wellness **Primary Diagnosis:** ☐ Primary Symptoms ☐ **ANSA Items and Scores** Psychosis Impulse Control Depression/Anxiety Antisocial Adjustment Trauma Personality Disorder Motivation for Care Danger to self or others Knowledge	**Symptoms:** ☐ Monitor and discuss symptoms, triggers, and medication side-effects ☐ Identify thoughts, feelings, behaviors, and events that trigger symptoms ☐ Maintain/Increase ability to manage symptoms through medications ☐ Maintain/Increase ability to manage symptoms through skills and lifestyle changes ☐ Maintain/Increase ability to reduce impact of symptoms on daily functioning ☐ Maintain or improve daily functioning despite symptoms **Medication/Treatment issues:** ☐ Learn how medications and treatment can help ☐ Discuss views of medications and treatment with staff ☐ Arrive at agreement on treatment and medications ☐ Understand and accept illness ☐ Work with nurse to manage medications effectively **Thoughts of harm to self/others:** ☐ Monitor and assess suicidal and homicidal ideation ☐ Inform ARCH staff of potential for harm ☐ Call psychiatric emergency department ☐ Learn to identify triggers ☐ Identify dynamics of violent impulses ☐ Develop investments and ties to life ☐ Learn ways to manage violent impulses ☐ OTHER:	**Educate about symptoms and treatment of illness through:** ☐ Case management ☐ Individual counseling ☐ Individual therapy ☐ Medication counseling ☐ Medication management ☐ Motivational interviewing ☐ Medication monitoring ☐ Couples/family counseling or couples/family therapy ☐ Coordinate with outside provider(s): Referred for: (if other, list intervention: Name: Phone: Relationship: Referred for: (if other, list intervention: Name: Phone: Relationship: ☐ Communication with outside provider(s) about risk of harm Name: Phone: Relationship: OTHER:

Table 13.2 (Continued)

Problem/Focus	Goals/Behavioral Objectives	Interventions/Modalities
6: PROBLEMS: POLICE/ COURTS **ANSA Items and Scores** Sexually Abusive Behavior Crime Legal Issue	☐ Clarify any court requirements with ARCH Team ☐ Comply with court mandates ☐ Communicate with courts ☐ Work towards getting court record sealed/ expunged ☐ OTHER:	**Educate about legal issues through:** ☐ Case management ☐ Individual counseling ☐ Individual therapy ☐ Medication counseling ☐ Medication management ☐ Attend court dates ☐ Aid in court record process ☐ Motivational interviewing ☐ Communicate with court/case worker: ☐ Name: ☐ Phone: ☐ Relationship: ☐ OTHER:
7: STRENGTHS: **ANSA Items and Scores** Family Interpersonal Relationship Permanence Vocational/Educational Well-Being Spiritual/Religious Talents/Interests Inclusion	☐ Maintain/increase contact with family ☐ Include family in planning ☐ Maintain/increase contact with friends ☐ Utilize vocational/educational abilities ☐ Remain/become active in faith community ☐ Incorporate/maintain prayer or personal spiritual activities into daily life ☐ Explore talents and interests and find a way to become active with them. Talent/ Interest: ☐ Develop positive relationships ☐ Increase opportunities for community involvement through organizations, neighbors, activities ☐ OTHER:	☐ Educate about the role of strengths in promoting wellness through: case management, individual counseling, individual therapy, medication counseling, medication management, motivational interviewing ☐ Encourage and facilitate contact with family and include in planning ☐ Encourage and facilitate contact with friends ☐ Assist consumer to utilize vocational/educational abilities ☐ Aid consumer to remain/become active in faith community of their choice, remain non-judgmental of their faith choice ☐ Discuss role of faith in consumer's life, recovery, and mental health ☐ Support consumer in his/her use of prayer or personal spiritual activities ☐ Assist consumer in exploring talents and interests and find a way to become active with them. Talent/Interest: ☐ Assist consumer in finding opportunities for community involvement through organizations, neighbors, activities ☐ OTHER:

programs present unique challenges to successful TCOM implementation. Second, multi-agency collaborations often create complex organizational issues that can in turn influence TCOM implementation.

The development of efficient TCOM procedures benefits from access to accurate information about the program's consumers, staff, and services. With existing programs, TCOM planners have such access to necessary information about the program's consumers and services. Even with the best of planning, however, start-up programs often modify their program model once services are underway. These modifications can have a detrimental effect on the ability to implement TCOM, particularly when program components essential to TCOM are altered or eliminated. With ARCH, the initial program design included (1) hiring staff with more clinical training and (2) serving more consumers with mental illness. These changes impacted the nature of the program and the data collection. To lessen the impact of programmatic changes, it is important to remain in communication with administrators regarding the program components that are essential to the TCOM plan, and to be aware that the TCOM plan will need enough flexibility to adapt to unexpected delays and changes to program design.

Ideally when implementing a TCOM plan prospectively, an extended planning phase will allow for the development of all necessary tools and procedures. During this period, program management will also have time to develop a clear understanding of how the TCOM process will be incorporated into the project. Start-up projects, however, are frequently rife with delays that can impact TCOM implementation. In the case of the ARCH program, delays in obtaining computers, office space, and personnel either directly or indirectly impacted our ability to implement a TCOM plan. In addition, delays specific to the TCOM procedures themselves can complicate matters, such as the need to obtain approval from institutional review boards or other higher level authorities.

With a start-up program, timely data analysis is essential to successful TCOM. Early analysis can help identify programmatic problems or unanticipated challenges in the TCOM process. In the case of ARCH, we experienced delays in data collection, which in turn delayed the identification of data integrity problems in the assessment and outcomes management components of the TCOM plan. The underestimation of problems with implementing the TCOM procedures was exacerbated by our inattention to the preliminary data we did have. Had we begun analysis earlier, we likely would have detected the deviation between the design of the ARCH program and its implementation. Advance planning that establishes set time lines for preliminary data analysis and feedback could have led to earlier identification of some of these problems and better data collection earlier in the program. Even with the best of plans, however, a start-up will have difficulty adhering to a pre-established data analysis time line.

The second lesson learned, as noted above, is that multi-agency collaborations demand additional time and management skills from those responsible for implementing a TCOM plan. Multi-agency collaboration is increasingly favored by funding sources and can be a desirable component of project proposals. This type of collaboration can bring together the varied stakeholders who are involved in service provision in an effective effort to better serve consumers. It is, however, an added challenge in the TCOM process for several reasons. In general, people responsible for implementing the TCOM plan must aim to ensure that project leaders understand and support the steps necessary to carry out a successful TCOM strategy. Multi-agency collaborations often result in a diffuse leadership structure and sometimes lack a clearly identified project director. This diffusion of ownership can leave a project without a guiding authority (1) to make decisions when conflicts arise and (2) to keep the various agencies on task and on time with project goals. Often during our initial implementation of the ARCH program, the focus of the project management team shifted to managing unexpected complications such as transportation risk management concerns, staffing issues, and computer and phone problems. These issues diverted attention away from ensuring the efficient implementation of the ARCH TCOM procedures and at times even contributed to a discounting of the feedback we provided from our data analyses. We therefore modified our perspective on our role in the program and began exerting greater leadership in the design of charting and documentation materials. Staying aware of deadlines and making changes to accommodate the evolving ARCH program allowed the data collection to proceed with modifications.

Multi-agency collaboration adds a diversity of knowledge and perspective, but can also result in increased demands and management complexities in coping with differing views and interests of the stakeholders and their varied needs for information. The many grantees involved in a collaborative project inevitably face demands for information stemming from unique internal and external reporting requests. This was the case with ARCH, and we needed to balance the ongoing data needs of the collaborators with the desire to minimize the burden of data collection on staff and consumers. Gathering information about data expectations early in the design of the data collection can mitigate this challenge for TCOM evaluators. Although unexpected data requests are bound to emerge, soliciting collaborators for examples of typical reports and expected data needs will minimize additions to the data collection. TCOM evaluators also need to find ways to keep the data collection as simple and streamlined as possible. Three tactics can assist in this goal of developing a useful yet unobtrusive data collection. First, motivate collaborators to prioritize their data needs by creating lists of essential and desired information. Second, look for areas of duplication in data needs, as multiple reports often can be served by the same data. Third, when responding to information requests, consider alternate analyses that do not increase the burden of data collection. When data collection becomes too burdensome for consumers and staff, compliance is likely to waver and data integrity can suffer.

CONCLUSIONS

Program evaluation plays an important role in the development process for new service delivery programs. By quantifying and describing program achievements and areas for improvement, TCOM can guide program development, help to keep the program focused on consumers, and identify program drift. The employ of TCOM strategies for program evaluation has the potential to provide critical information to a developing program. To insure this information is used, TCOM evaluators must facilitate communication to create a flexible TCOM plan that is useful and informative for the service delivery program and ultimately for the consumers.

To successfully implement TCOM, evaluators need to build relationships that will facilitate communication with individuals on several operational levels, including program leadership and collaborators, service delivery staff, and external stakeholders or funding sources. It is essential for evaluators to have a clearly defined role within the program to facilitate the development of productive relationships. Frequent access to leadership as well as the staff members providing direct service is a key part of relationship building for TCOM evaluators, who run the risk of being viewed as external to the program. Having access to and influence with program leadership encourages information gained through TCOM to be used to facilitate the necessary changes and adaptations in the service delivery program. This can be achieved by becoming active and integral members of the planning and operating teams. Moreover, being present at service delivery planning meetings and being visible within the treatment milieu are two ways to develop relationships and maintain communication with service delivery staff. Evaluators have the unique role of bridging the potential communication gap between leadership and service delivery staff. A productive and positive relationship with direct service providers facilitates gaining accurate and useful information about the implementation process, which can then be used in the TCOM process. This relationship also impacts the likelihood that service providers will be open to the changes that may be necessary to respond to issues brought to light by TCOM.

TCOM plans and evaluators need to be flexible to adapt to inevitable program changes and to respond to the context of the service delivery program. Evaluators who anticipate this need for flexibility will be more effective and prepared to manage within an evolving program. It is also useful to retain a focus on the TCOM process without becoming wedded to procedures that have become cumbersome or are no longer possible due to programmatic changes. The role of clinical outcomes evaluator requires particular flexibility when barriers to implementation become evident. In addition to the anticipated activities of data collection and analysis, TCOM evaluators may be called on to assess needs, train staff, monitor the quality and content of work product, hold staff focus groups, or participate in logistical problem solving. Many of these activities have an indirect impact on the TCOM process and may be necessary to maintain the progress of the program. If TCOM evaluators view their role as serving the organization based on its changing needs and growing competencies, the organization will be better equipped to serve its consumers based on their needs and strengths.

References

Anderson, R. L. & Lyons, J. S. (2001). Needs-based planning for persons with serious mental illness: The severity of psychiatric illness of persons residing in intermediate care facilities. *Journal of Behavioral Health Services & Research, 28,* 104–110.

Feinstein, A. R. (1999). Multi-item "instruments" vs. Virginia Apgar's principles of clinimetrics. *Archives of Internal Medicine, 159,* 125–128.

Lyons, J. S. (1998). *The severity and acuity of psychiatric illness manual. Adult version.* San Antonio, TX: Psychological Corp.

Lyons, J. S. (2004). *Redressing the emperor: Improving our children's public mental health system.* Westport, CT: Praeger.

Lyons, J. S. & Anderson, R. L. (1999). *Adult needs and strengths assessment. An information integration tool for adults with mental health challenges. Manual.* Winnetka, IL: Buddin Praed Foundation.

Lyons, J. S., Colletta, J., Devens, M. & Finkel, S. I. (1995). Validity of the severity of psychiatric illness rating scale in a sample of inpatients on a psychogeriatric unit. *International Psychogeriatrics, 7,* 407–416.

Lyons, J. S., Kisiel, C. L., Dulcan, M., Cohen, R. & Chesler, P. (1997a). Crisis assessment and psychiatric hospitalization of children and adolescents in state custody. *Journal of Child & Family Studies, 6,* 311–320.

Lyons, J. S., Stutesman, J., Neme, J., Vessey, J. T., O'Mahoney, M. T. & Camper, J. (1997b). Predicting psychiatric emergency admissions and hospital outcomes. *Medical Care, 35,* 792–800.

Martin, L. L. & Kettner, P. M. (1996). *Measuring the performance of human service programs*, vol. 71. Thousand Oaks, CA: Sage.

Miller, W. R. & Rollnick, S. (1991). *Motivational interviewing: Preparing people to change addictive behavior*. New York: Guilford.

Mulder, C. L., Koopmans, G. T. & Lyons, J. S. (2005). Determinants of indicated versus actual level of care in psychiatric emergency services. *Psychiatric Services, 56,* 452–457.

Stein, L. I. & Santos, A. B. (1998). *Assertive community treatment of persons with severe mental illness*. New York: W.W. Norton & Co.

Tsemberis, S., Gulcur, L. & Nakae, M. (2004). Housing first, consumer choice, and harm reduction for homeless individuals with a dual diagnosis. *American Journal of Public Health, 94,* 651–656.

Chapter 14

Finding the Balance in an Evolving Service Sector: The Role of Measurement in Matching Treatment Need to Service Delivery in an Adult Prison

by Rachel L. Anderson, Ph.D.

In a given field of human endeavor, progress sometimes may be measured not so much by the problems it has solved, as by the new types of problems it produces.
—Albert Deutsch, *The Mentally Ill in America*

INTRODUCTION

This chapter describes an Iowa initiative that used the Adult Needs and Strengths Assessment (ANSA) (Lyons et al., 1997a) tool to understand the match between psychiatric clinical needs of offenders across Iowa's state prisons and the levels of care necessary to address those needs. This effort was in response to a legal decision to improve the mental health services for offenders, particularly offenders with more severe and persistent disorders. This chapter will discuss this initiative, its historical and political context, how Iowa addressed the legal mandate involved, changes in the overall system in response to the initiative, lessons learned, and future plans.

BACKGROUND AND CONTEXT FOR THE INITIATIVE

Lack of Prison Mental Health Policies

The assessment, diagnosis, and treatment of psychiatric disorders among prison populations historically has been a complex phenomenon, defined by differing philosophies, legal decisions, and changing social attitudes (Lamb & Weinberger, 1998; Ogloff et al., 1994; Sigurdson, 2000). The National Institute of Corrections has reported that a growing number of offenders in state prisons experience psychiatric difficulties and are in need of treatment (NIC, 2001). While research has varied with regard to methodology for determining prevalence of psychiatric disorders among prison populations, findings over the past decade document higher rates as compared to community samples (Diamond et al., 2001). The Bureau of Justice has estimated that 16 percent of offenders in state prisons have a psychiatric condition (Ditton, 1999).

While the U.S. Department of Health and Human Services increasingly recognizes that psychiatric disorders among offenders are a major public health concern (DHHS, 2005), many offenders receive no mental health treatment. The Bureau of Justice has estimated that 60 percent of male offenders with psychiatric disorders in state prisons reported the use of mental health services (Ditton, 1999). The dilemma regarding proper assessment and treatment is worsened by the fact that we have no national mental health policy in the United States (World Health Organization, 2005). Mental health policy is an organized set of values, principles, and objectives to improve mental health and reduce the burden of disease. A national mental health policy is critical, as it defines a vision and mission for the future and assists in establishing a model for action and service delivery.

The prison system does not intentionally harm offenders with mental illness through a policy of providing inadequate mental health care. Given the federal government's historic lack of involvement in providing guidance regarding the care of people with psychiatric illnesses, and given the ideals of federalism (i.e., the devolution of health care policy and delivery to the states), it is the states that have become responsible for protecting basic human rights, particularly of the most vulnerable in our communities. Unfortunately, tight fiscal budgets, lack of expertise, and the powerful burden of stigma have all contributed to the failure of public officials to fulfill their responsibilities toward the mental health of our growing offender population.

Our research and subsequent follow-up of legislative mandates suggests that what is lacking in prison mental health services is not knowledge about what is needed or the necessary resources, but the commitment to it. Sparked by court-ordered mandates and fueled by funding that has not kept pace with an increasing number of offenders, the emphasis placed on the delivery of mental health care to offenders in state prison systems is growing (Osofsky, 1996). The landmark decision *Estelle v. Gamble* (1976) highlighted the need for the correctional community to be more accountable to offenders who require psychiatric services (Jones & Connelly, 2002). This case established offenders' Eighth

Amendment right to treatment for medical conditions, and it has influenced lawmakers to pay closer attention to the provision of mental health care in prisons.

Iowa's Mandate and Response

Iowa has nine state prisons. According to the Iowa Department of Corrections (IDOC), there are about 8,700 offenders in Iowa state prisons (IDOC *Daily Statistics*). The 1997 Iowa case *Goff et al. v. Harper et al.* made clear that Iowa's offenders with psychiatric disorders fared no better than those in other states. In *Goff*, presiding Senior U.S. Judge Donald O'Brien ordered major changes in Iowa's prison facility operations and in the way the state responds to offenders with mental illness. The Iowa State Penitentiary (ISP), also known as Fort Madison, contains Cellhouse 220, a maximum-security unit that housed forty-eight of the state prison's worst behaving inmates, including some with severe and persistent mental illnesses. Judge O'Brien criticized state officials for the shameful conditions in Cellhouse 220, where some offenders shouted and screamed at all hours of the day and night, and urinated and defecated almost everywhere. O'Brien's 118-page ruling faulted conditions inside Cellhouse 220 and agreed with expert opinions that conditions in the cellhouse violated the offenders' rights, including unconstitutionally inadequate mental health treatment, under both the Due Process Clause and Eighth Amendment standards.

Under due process, the *Goff* court found that the extraordinarily long lockup sentences violated substantive due process rights. The three Eighth Amendment violations were inadequate mental health treatment received by offenders with psychiatric disorders; deprivation of exercise for inmates in lockup during the winter months; and lack of safety and security for mentally stable offenders who had to endure pandemonium and bedlam because they were intermingled with the mentally-ill offenders who either could not or would not control their behavior.

In 1997, Judge O'Brien ordered the IDOC to improve treatment for offenders with mental illness. The state's plan in response to this ruling was not accepted until the third submission two years later. Part of the state plan was to propose the design and implementation of a 200-bed special needs unit located at the ISP (see Figure 14.1), in order to place a greater priority on offender mental health issues.

The state also responded to O'Brien's ruling by forming a partnership with the College of Public Health at the University of Iowa to assess the match between level-of-care needs and service utilization for offenders across all state prisons. While the research literature presented a consistent picture of the prevalence of psychiatric illness among the prison population, there was insufficient research examining the level-of-care needs among offenders with psychiatric problems. Understanding and attending to level-of-care needs was required to address Judge O'Brien's ruling; diagnostic and therapeutic concerns had to be understood and addressed correctly so as not to potentially overwhelm available services or jeopardize existing security needs.

The research task was to inform service delivery by documenting the resources required to provide essential mental health services for offenders. At the time, there were few options in terms of levels of care for offenders with chronic psychiatric illnesses or who had experienced acute episodes associated with their disorder. The Oakdale Medical Assessment and Treatment Facility, the reception center for all sentenced offenders, had twenty-three beds designated as psychiatric beds. However, even those limited beds were not actually available for treatment because they were used almost exclusively for unsentenced forensic cases. For mental health treatment,

Figure 14.1
Iowa State Penitentiary 200-Bed Special Needs Unit: Site Plan

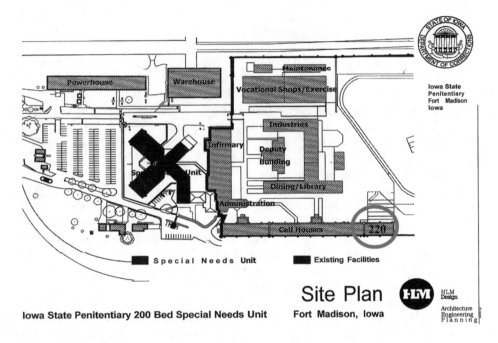

Site Plan

Iowa State Penitentiary 200 Bed Special Needs Unit   Fort Madison, Iowa

offenders were sent first to the Oakdale facility and then disbursed throughout the system; the most difficult to manage were assigned to the Special Housing Unit at Fort Madison—Cellhouse 220.

DESCRIPTION OF THE INITIATIVE

The research initiative focused on assessing the match between psychiatric clinical needs and level of care received by male offenders across eight state prisons from January 1999 to June 2000. To specifically address the decision by Judge O'Brien, we were particularly interested in understanding the mental health service utilization by offenders with severe and chronic psychiatric disorders. To that end, we assessed the clinical and service needs of offenders that entered the IDOC with a psychiatric diagnosis (n = 289) and those that did not have a diagnosis upon entry but used mental health services at some point during the first year of their incarceration (n = 277). Further, we were interested in identifying unmet clinical needs among offenders and subsequently drew a random sample across all prisons of offenders who did not have a psychiatric diagnosis and did not use mental health services during their first year of incarceration (n = 442). We identified each group using the IDOC administrative database, and validated the findings from chart review.

Adult Needs and Strengths Assessment

We used the ANSA to assess clinical need across several dimensions, including psychiatric problems, risk behaviors, functioning, and strengths/supports. Lyons and colleagues developed the ANSA as an evolution of the Severity of Psychiatric Illness

(SPI) tool (Lyons et al., 1997a). The authors determined the need to include the measurement of strengths and supports in reaction to research that had shown both strengths and psychopathology to be independently related to functioning and risk behaviors (Lyons et al., 2000).

We chose the ANSA for several reasons. First, despite little published information on its reliability and validity, the validity of the SPI both as a predictor of service use and outcomes and a case severity adjustment tool had been demonstrated (Lyons et al., 1997b; 1997c; Anderson & Lewis, 1999). Second, the published work on the use of the SPI as a retrospective data collection tool, and our prior experience using the ANSA retrospectively, showed high inter-rater reliability (Anderson et al., 2003). Having a measure that showed adequate validity and reliability as a retrospective data collection tool was critical because this project was designed to inform legal and legislative decisions in a timely manner. Third, it was important to identify a tool that did not rely solely on diagnosis, but rather on a comprehensive clinical profile so that we could better inform the development of treatment options for offenders. Reliance on diagnostic criteria alone to model mental health services has generated little success (Allen et al., 1987; Goldman et al., 1990; Mezzich & Coffman, 1985; Zwanziger et al., 1991). Findings from this research have demonstrated that simply the presence of a diagnosis may not constitute sufficient reason for receiving care. Similarly, the absence of a diagnosis may not constitute sufficient reason for not receiving care.

Interviews With Stakeholders

We also conducted 116 semi-structured interviews with various stakeholders across all nine prisons, including wardens and deputy wardens, administrative staff, correctional officers, mental health personnel, medical personnel, pharmacists, legal council, treatment directors, and unit managers. We felt this would help us better understand the process of education around mental health issues, the balance of rehabilitation versus security issues, and the availability and training of mental health personnel. Findings from stakeholder interviews suggested very little mental health training of the workforce and a primary focus on safety issues.

EVALUATION

Matching Psychiatric Needs and Treatment

With the ANSA, we were able to cast a wider net and include cases that presented with no formal diagnosis but with some level of treatment need associated with psychiatric problems. Because of its focus on functional impairment separate from symptomatology, the ANSA can clarify the impact of illness, identify targets for treatment, and determine service needs. Table 14.1 shows the differences in relying on chart diagnoses versus functional assessments associated with symptomatology. For offenders entering the IDOC, the table compares chart diagnosis and ANSA assessment as methods for assessing need for treatment and mental health service utilization at some point during the first year of incarceration.

This table provides several points to consider. First, based on the information at entry into prison, 763 offenders were identified with psychiatric problems in need of treatment using the ANSA. In fact, of the 442 offenders we randomly selected to identify unmet need, 200 of them—or 45 percent—were identified as needing mental health

Table 14.1
Need for and Use of Treatment by Chart Diagnosis vs. ANSA Assessment

		Mental Health Treatment	
Chart Diagnosis		Use	No Use
Chart diagnosis at entry:	289	274	15
No chart diagnosis, but used mental health services in first year of incarceration:	277	277	0
No chart diagnosis, and no use of mental health services in first year of incarceration:	442	0	442
Total:	*1,008*	**551**	**457**
ANSA Assessment			
ANSA need for treatment at entry:	763	456	307
No need for treatment, but used mental health services in first year of incarceration:	95	95	0
No need for treatment, and did not use any mental health services in first year of incarceration:	150	0	150
Total:	*1,008*	**551**	**457**

treatment but did not receive a diagnosis or treatment in their first year of incarceration. While casting a wider net has important implications for illness prevention and early intervention, it also has direct fiscal implications for any service sector. Determining the magnitude of these costs most certainly would require a comprehensive economic evaluation. Second, consistent with the Bureau of Justice reports, 40 percent of offenders with mental health treatment needs identified on entry to prison had not received any services within the first year of incarceration.

Standard clinical criteria for hospital admission in community-based settings include the presence of a profound level of severity in symptoms and/or the presence of a safety risk (harm to self or others) (Hillard et al., 1988; Lansing et al., 1997; Marson et al., 1988; McNiel et al., 1992; Mezzich et al., 1984; Prunier & Buongiorno, 1989). Most important for our research effort, we identified 139 offenders as having profound symptom severity and/or as being an immediate safety risk based on information available on entry. In using the ANSA, this group was identified as needing an intense level of care because they presented with a profound level of symptom severity (a rating of 3 on psychosis, impulsivity, depression/anxiety, antisocial behavior, oppositional behavior, or adjustment to trauma) and/or as an immediate safety risk to self or others (a rating of 3 on either danger to self or others). Table 14.2 demonstrates this level of service need based on ANSA criteria. For example, a moderate degree of symptom severity in the presence of an immediate safety risk would suggest an appropriate admission to the hospital. However, in the absence of an immediate safety risk, a moderate degree of psychiatric symptoms does not necessitate a stay in the hospital (Leon et al., 1999).

While 139 offenders were identified with profound symptom severity and/or were a safety risk on entry, only 17 percent (n = 24) received inpatient care during their first year of incarceration.

Table14.2
Inpatient Service Need Based on ANSA Criteria

	Safety Risk (Danger to self or others)			
Symptom Severity (Presenting Problems)	No evidence or history (0)	History of self-injurious or aggressive behavior-none in past 30 days (1)	Self-injurious or aggressive behavior within past 30 days (2)	Self-injurious behavior within past 24 hours or dangerous level of aggression that posed an immediate risk to others (3)
No evidence (0)				Inpatient
Mild (1)				Inpatient
Moderate (2)				Inpatient
Profound (3)	Inpatient	Inpatient	Inpatient	Inpatient

Relation of Treatment to Custody Level

We examined why some offenders with need for intense levels of care received that care and others did not. Our analyses suggested that the receipt of inpatient treatment was not driven by offenders' clinical needs. Offenders who needed and received inpatient care were similar in the severity of their clinical needs to those who needed inpatient care but did not receive it. Rather, the receipt of inpatient care was determined by non-clinical factors. First, prior use of community mental health services was associated with the receipt of inpatient care. This difference might indicate that these offenders are more willing to accept care in the prison treatment setting.

However, custody level was one other important factor. Table 14.3 provides a comparison of the custody levels reached between offenders with a mental health treatment need and offenders without a treatment need. This table shows that offenders with mental health treatment needs were more likely than offenders without treatment needs to have been placed into a higher level of custody at some point during their incarceration. Each group had a similar number of offenders placed from a minimum custody level to a higher custody level. The difference between these groups is that offenders with mental health treatment needs were more often placed to maximum custody level as compared to offenders without mental health treatment needs.

Custody level was an important service delivery issue for offenders with more profound psychiatric conditions. The special needs unit at the Oakdale facility was not equipped to handle the violent, aggressive, or high-risk inmates and, for the most part, rejected them when they were referred for transfer to that unit. This included most of the inmates at the state penitentiary. "We don't want them and don't need the aggressive or high-risk inmates who are also mentally ill" (*Goff et al. v. Harper et al.*, p.15). One reason offenders with mental illness more often ended up in maximum security was the scant review of psychological records of inmates before disciplinary sentences were issued. As such, the kind of behaviors consistent with an acute episode of psychosis (e.g., yelling or reaching out at a correctional officer) would lead more often to being placed in lockup and spending more time in higher levels of security. The catch-22 was that the more severe your psychiatric symptoms, the more likely you

Table 14.3
Comparison of Number of Transfers and Custody Level Reached Between
Inmates With and Without a Mental Health Treatment Need

Average Number of Transfers and Custody Level Reached While at DOC	Inmates Identified by ANSA-DOC as Needing Mental Health Treatment at Entry into DOC (n = 763)	Percent Change in Custody Level from Entry	Inmates Without Mental Health Treatment Needs at Entry into DOC (n = 245)	Percent Change in Custody Level from Entry
Number of Transfers	4		4	
Custody Level Reached Minimum	137 (18%)	-29%	66 (27%)	-37%
Medium	488 (64%)	-4%	154 (63%)	+21%
Maximum	99 (13%)	+50%	12 (5%)	+31%

were to be placed in lockup without adequate access to services that might assist in stabilizing your symptoms.

While it is critical to address the treatment needs of offenders with less severe psychiatric symptoms in order to prevent a decline in health status, service priority to the least well off (i.e., individuals with the most severe symptoms and impaired functioning) is most critical and in harmony with a set of values regarding society's obligation to vulnerable populations.

NEW CLINICAL CARE UNIT

The special needs unit at the ISP, officially termed the clinical care unit, opened in September 2002 and housed 134 offenders with mental health problems. Our research assisted in getting the Iowa state legislators to approve funding for an additional 200-bed special needs unit located at the Oakdale Medical Assessment and Treatment facility, the reception center for all sentenced offenders. The Oakdale facility opened in September 2007.

A consultant from the NIC was contacted to conduct a comprehensive evaluation of Fort Madison's clinical care unit due to several recent suicides at the unit. The report, issued in February 2005, called for urgent and decisive steps to be immediately taken to address problems in the provision of care in Fort Madison's Clinical Care Unit (White, 2005). A number of recommendations were provided; however several of them focused on the lack of service provision and mission.

CONCLUSIONS

Prisons as Warehouses for the Mentally Ill

Prisons have become warehouses for a large proportion of the country's mentally ill (Fellner & Abramsky, 2003). What this means is that for some offenders, prisons provide little more than a custodial environment in which few treatment services are offered and those most in need are significantly under-treated. These adults are trapped in a new world of custodial care that again depends on state financing and state care-giving.

Two issues need further consideration. The first is whether current custodial care derives from the nature of the illnesses or from the nature of the society in which we live. Current economic, ideological, and political realities focus on ensuring the allocation of state resources in ways that will maximize utility or satisfy the principle of the *greatest good for the greatest number*. Efforts directed toward offenders and/or people with mental health and substance use challenges have considerable trouble satisfying those standards.

Second, fiscally, the state's continuing desire for federal reimbursement and cost-shifting has stifled the development and innovation of community-based services for persons with mental illness (Frank & McGuire, 1996). Chairperson Michael Hogan, in his cover letter of the final report of the President's New Freedom Commission on Mental Health, noted that it is widely accepted that the result for community-based care has been a "patchwork relic—the result of disjointed reforms and policies" (*Achieving the Promise*, 2003, cover letter, p. 1). At some point the state must take responsibility for developing and coordinating its fragmented mental health care system (Torrey, 1997). Ignoring mental illness and its associated suffering will not make it go away; indeed new types of problems will arise as individual needs and service sectors evolve.

Need for Global Assessment and Common Vision

Globalized assessment is a necessary first step in understanding the match between an individual's treatment needs and the level of resources necessary to address his needs in a cost-efficient and effective manner. Guesswork is no longer an acceptable approach. We need to pay only for those levels of care people require, but we must understand that some people will require intense levels of care. As David Ellwood (1988) stated, America must decide what role it wants social policy to play. If the goal of the current correctional system of care is to relieve some of the burden caused by the general failures and misfortunes of both society and poor policy development, then perhaps our system has not done a great deal of damage. However, if our hope is that social policy will address some of the real causes of fragmentation, recidivism, and inadequate care; if the goal is to use social policy as a tool for integrating health and social sectors to aid persons with mental illness to become more independent and responsible, then the current system must be judged more harshly.

Again, we must share a common vision about health care delivery for persons with mental illness. Among mental health care professionals at the IDOC there tends to be extreme variation in the definition of health and illness, eligibility for care, and treatment versus safety approaches (White, 2005). As Deutsch astutely stated more than fifty years ago:

> It is a significant commentary on the backwardness and general inflexibility of our legal mechanisms that, though life and death frequently hinge on the proper understanding of insanity in its relation to law, one finds only chaos and contradiction where one has every right to expect precise definition. The interpretation of insanity, or unsoundness of mind, varies greatly in different jurisdictions, and often enough within a single jurisdiction. (Deutsch, 1949, p. 383)

One thing is clear, however: the structures of prison mental health systems continue to be focused on a medical model of health care delivery, and mentally ill offenders are cast into the chaos of the general population until they require crisis intervention. Even then, offenders with mental illness, particularly in a rural health care delivery system, continue to confront a paucity of qualified staff who can evaluate their illness, develop and implement effective treatment plans, and monitor their symptoms and conditions.

We must remember that prisons were not designed as mental health facilities. As states invariably disregarded their responsibility for people with mental illness during the process of dehospitalization, prisons have become by default a principal in the business of mental health service delivery. However, the future need not be so dim. Several states have taken leadership, in collaboration with the private sector, with regard to the provision of care to persons with psychiatric difficulties.

Fragmented Funding and Service Delivery

A serious problem in the management of mental health care arises from the fragmentation caused by the existence of multiple funding streams and service-delivery systems; such fragmentation is exacerbated by differences between various programs' eligibility criteria. The costs of a fragmented, inefficient system are significant and contribute to the administrative problem of cost-shifting. Savings said to have been realized through cost-shifting are not real. The traditional fuzziness of the boundaries of mental health care must therefore be addressed anew in a shift to managed care.

The lack of accountability bridging corrections and mental health systems has created a policy dilemma reported on by the Bazelon Center for Mental Health Law (*Effective Public Management of Mental Health Care*, 2000). Policies to alleviate the prevalence, incidence, and suffering of mental illness have often been presented as a set of hopeless tradeoffs and dilemmas with the underlying message that nothing much can make a difference. If we are willing to decide what is expected of our nation and citizens, look carefully at how we define health, and set up a coordinated mental health service delivery system that will reinforce our values, then our system of support and treatment for persons with mental illness can be something more than a holding ground and can be the basis of hope (Ellwood, 1988).

References

Achieving the promise: *Transforming mental health care in America* (2003). Rockville, MD: The President's New Freedom Commission on Mental Health. Available online at: http://www.mentalhealthcommission.gov/reports/FinalReport/downloads/FinalReport.pdf.

Allen, J. G., Coyne, L., Beasley, C. & Spohn, H. (1987). A conceptual model for research on required length of psychiatric hospital stay. *Comprehensive Psychiatry*, *28*, 131–140.

Anderson, R. L. & Lewis, D. A. (1999). Clinical characteristics and service use of persons with mental illness living in an intermediate care facility. *Psychiatric Services*, *50*, 1341–1345.

Anderson, R. L., Schultz, S. K., Buckwalter, K. C. & Schneider, J. E. (2003). Clinical characteristics of older adults admitted to an inpatient psychiatric unit: Implications for resource allocation. *Journal of Mental Health and Aging*, *9*, 211–221.

Effective public management of mental health care: *Views from states on Medicaid reforms that enhance service integration and delivery* (2000). Milbank Memorial Fund & Bazelon Center for Mental Health Law. Available online at: http://www.milbank.org/reports/bazelon/bazelon.html

Deutsch, A. (1949). *The mentally ill in America: A history of their care and treatment from colonial times.* New York: Columbia University Press.

Diamond, P. M., Wang, E. W., Holzer III, C. E., Thomas, C. & des Anges, C. (2001). The prevalence of mental illness in prison. *Administration and Policy in Mental Health, 29,* 21–40.

Ditton, P. M. (1999). *Mental health and treatment of inmates and probationers.* Washington, DC: U.S. Department of Justice, Office of Justice Programs, Bureau of Justice Statistics.

Ellwood, D. T. (1988). *Poor support: Poverty in the American family.* New York: Basic Books.

Estelle v. Gamble, 429 U.S. 97 (1976).

Fellner, J. & Abramsky, S. (2003). *Ill-Equipped: U.S. prisons and offenders with mental illness.* NY: Human Rights Watch.

Frank, R.G. & McGuire, T. G. (1996). Health care financing reform and state mental health systems. In R. F. Rich & W. D. White (Eds.), *Health policy, federalism, and the American states.*

Goff et al. v. Harper et al., No. 4-90-CV-50365 (S.D. Iowa, 1997). Testimony of Lowell Brandt, treatment Director at the Iowa Department of Corrections' Medical and Classification Center, 15.

Goldman, H. H., Pincus, H. A. & Morton, T. (1990). Predicting length of hospital stay for psychiatric inpatients. *Hospital and Community Psychiatry, 41,* 149–154.

Hillard, J. R., Slomowitz, M. & Deddens, J. (1988). Determinants of emergency psychiatric admission for adolescents and adults. *American Journal of Psychiatry, 145,* 1416–1419.

Iowa DOC. *Daily statistics.* Available online at: www.doc.state.ia.us/DailyStats.asp.

Jones, G. & Connelly, M. (2002). *Mentally ill offenders and mental health care issues: An overview of the research.* College Park, MD: Maryland State Commission on Criminal Sentencing Policy.

Lamb, H. R. & Weinberger, L. E. (1998). Persons with severe mental illness in jails and prisons: A review. *Psychiatric Services, 49,* 483–492.

Lansing, A. E., Lyons, J. S., Martens, L. C., O'Mahoney, M. T., Miller, S. I. & Obolsky, A. (1997). The treatment of dangerous patients in managed care. Psychiatric hospital utilization and outcome. *General Hospital Psychiatry, 19,* 112–118.

Leon, S. C., Uziel-Miller, N. D., Lyons, J. S. & Tracy, P. (1999). Psychiatric hospital utilization of children and adolescents in state custody. *Journal of the American Academy of Child and Adolescent Psychiatry, 38,* 305–310.

Lyons, J. S., Howard, K. I., O'Mahoney, M. T. & Lish, J. D. (1997a). *The measurement and management of clinical outcomes in mental health.* New York: Wiley.

Lyons, J. S., O'Mahoney, M. T., Miller, S. I., Neme, J., Kabat, J. & Miller, F. (1997b). Predicting readmission to the psychiatric hospital in a managed care environment: Implications for quality indicators. *American Journal of Psychiatry, 154,* 337–340.

Lyons, J. S., Stutesman, J., Neme, J., Vessey, J. T., O'Mahoney, M. T. & Camper, H. J. (1997c). Predicting psychiatric emergency admissions and hospital outcomes. *Medical Care, 35,* 792–800.

Lyons, J. S., Uziel-Miller, N. D., Reyes, F. & Sokol, P. T. (2000). Strengths of children and adolescents in residential settings: Prevalence and associations with psychopathology and discharge placement. *Journal of the Academy of Child and Adolescent Psychiatry, 39,* 176–181.

Marson, D. C., McGovern, M. P. & Pomp, H. C. (1988). Psychiatric decision making in the emergency room: A research overview. *American Journal of Psychiatry, 145,* 918–925.

McNiel, D. E., Myers, R. S., Zeiner, H. K., Wolfe, H. L. & Hatcher, C. (1992). The role of violence in decisions about hospitalization from the psychiatric emergency room. *American Journal of Psychiatry, 149,* 207–212.

Mezzich, J. E. & Coffman, G. A. (1985). Factors influencing length of hospital stay. *Hospital and Community Psychiatry, 36*, 1262–1270.

Mezzich, J. E., Evanczuk, K. J., Mathias, R. J. & Coffman, G. A. (1984). Symptoms and hospitalization decisions. *American Journal of Psychiatry, 141*, 764–769.

Prunier, P. & Buongiorno, P. A. (1989). Guidelines for acute inpatient psychiatric treatment review. *General Hospital Psychiatry, 11*, 278–281.

National Institute of Corrections (NIC) (2001). *Provision of mental health care in prisons.* Washington, DC: U.S. Department of Justice.

Ogloff, J. R. P., Roesch, R. & Hart, S. D. (1994). Mental health services in jails and prisons: Legal, clinical and policy issues. *Law & Psychology Review, 18*, 109–135.

Osofsky, H. J. (1996). Psychiatry behind the walls: Mental health services in jails and prisons. *Bulletin of the Menninger Clinic, 60*, 464–479.

Sigurdson, C. (2000). The mad, the bad and the abandoned: The mentally ill in prisons and jails. *Corrections Today, 62*, 70–76.

Torrey, E. F. (1997). *Out of the shadows: Confronting America's mental health crisis.* New York: Wiley, 106.

U.S. Department of Health and Human Services (DHHS) (2005). *Healthy People 2010* (conference ed., 2 vols.). Washington, DC: Author.

White, T. (2005). Consultant report to the Iowa Department of Corrections. Washington, DC: National Institute of Corrections, Prison Division. Accessed online on 09/27/05, at: http://www.doc.state.ia.us/publications/DrWhitesFindings.doc.

World Health Organization (2005). Mental health atlas–2005. A project of the Department of Mental Health and Substance Abuse, WHO, Geneva. Accessed online on 09/027/05, at: www.who.int/mental_health/evidence/atlas/index.htm.

Zwanziger, J., Davis, L., Bamezai, A. & Hosek, S. D. (1991). Using DRGs to pay for inpatient substance abuse services: An assessment of the CHAMPUS Reimbursement System. *Medical Care, 29*, 565–577.

Part 5

Treatment Management
for Special Populations

Chapter 15

Integrated Care for the Complex Medically Ill With the INTERMED Method

by Frits J. Huyse, M.D., Ph.D., Friedrich C. Stiefel, M.D., Ph.D., Wolfgang Söllner, M.D., Joris P. J. Slaets, M.D., Ph.D., John S. Lyons, Ph.D., Corine H. M. Latour, C.N.S., R.N., Nynke van der Wal, A.N.P. and Peter de Jonge, Ph.D.

INTRODUCTION

Health care systems in developed countries share a common feature, which has been accentuated over the last decade. These health care systems are fragmented due to (1) medical (sub)specialization, (2) the split between general health care and mental health care, and (3) the rupture between primary and secondary health care settings. Such fragmented health care systems are often unable to deliver either what patients need or the recommended standards of care. This chapter stems from a recently published book, *Integrated Care for the Complex Medically Ill*, published in the Medical Clinics of North America (2006). Benjamin Druss states in the Foreword:

Comorbidity and complexity are increasingly the rule rather than the exception in clinical care. Society's success in treating acute illnesses has resulted in longer lives but also rising prevalence, burden, and costs of chronic conditions. Chronicity, in turn, is invariably associated with high levels of comorbidity. However, clinical training, reimbursement, and research funding all remain organized around discrete clinical conditions. The result is a growing disconnect between the health system, which focuses on single diseases, and patients' clinical needs, which often span multiple providers, disciplines, and systems of care.

He continues:

[T]his book seeks to understand how better to deliver care for the "complex medically ill," patients with multiple medical, mental, psychosocial, and/or functional problems. Rather than focus on specific comorbidities, it addresses the broad themes regarding the identification, assessment, and management of these vulnerable patients. . . . The recently-released IOM report *Improving the Quality of Health Care for Mental and Substance Use Conditions* (2006) found that deficits in quality of care for persons with behavioral conditions were as great or greater than the problems faced by persons with other medical problems. Many of these gaps result from fragmentation within the general- and behavioral health system, and between the behavioral health and general medical systems.

The important groups of patients who suffer from these splits in our current health care systems—resulting in either their under-use or excessive use—are the frail elderly, the chronically ill with multiple morbidities, including psychiatric morbidity, and patients with persisting functional complaints. We will refer to these patients as the complex medically ill. For the care of these patients, a report by the Committee on Quality of Health Care of the Institute of Medicine (IOM) in the United States, entitled *Crossing the Quality Chasm: A New Health System for the 21st Century* (IOM, 2001), is most relevant. The report states, "Quality problems occur typically not because of failure of goodwill, knowledge, effort or resources devoted to health care, but because of fundamental shortcomings in the ways care is organized. Trying harder will not work; changing systems of care will." These reports are complemented by a series of publications on complexity and clinical care in the *British Medical Journal* (Wilson & Holt, 2001; Plesk & Wilson, 2001). Both underline the need for a change within medical care. The complex medical patients are the most vulnerable to the deficiencies of a fragmented health care system and most in need of these new rules.

Over thirty years ago in the journal *Science*, George Engel (1977) called for the biopsychosocial model of disease, which integrates somatic, psychological, and social aspects of disease, as opposed to the medical model. The relevance of the biopsychosocial model is acknowledged and supported by an impressive body of evidence. It is also reflected in the above-mentioned series of articles in the *British Medical Journal* on complexity science (Wilson & Holt, 2001; Plesk & Wilson, 2001):

> Human beings can be viewed as composed of and operating within multiple interacting and self-adjusting systems (including biochemical, cellular, physiological, psychological and social systems). Their illness arises from dynamic interaction within and between these systems, not from failure of a single component. (Engel, 1977)

Psychiatric and somatic morbidity often coexist; and functional limitations, psychological state, social support, and health care utilization are interrelated. In addition, confounding variables, such as depression or socioeconomic status, have been proven to influence morbidity and mortality of somatic diseases (Demyttenaere et al., 2004; Ansseau et al., 2004; Fink et al., 2003; Polsky et al., 2005; Kessler et al., 2003; Hansen et al., 2001; Silverstone, 1996; Katon, 2003; Regier et al., 1993). Engel's vision influenced the care of patients with chronic and life threatening diseases and resulted in disease-management programs, which integrate psychologists, social workers, and paramedics in the treatment of patients suffering from diabetes, Parkinson's disease, organ failure, or cancer. However, disease management is lacking a specific patient-tailored approach, and "complex patients" don't fit these programs.

In addition to the classical disease-oriented approach, this chapter focuses on a generic approach based on the concept of case complexity and care complexity (de Jonge et al., 2001a; de Jonge et al., 2001b; Huyse et al., 2001a; de Jonge et al., 2006). Basic to such an approach is the notion that illness clusters in persons. The coexistence of dementia and deliria in the frail elderly is well known. However, the increased prevalence of depression, anxiety, and substance use disorders among patients with physical disorders is less well known and requires additional attention. The disorders not only coexist but also interfere with one another. Recent findings underscore the pertinence of these interactions. For instance, patients with depression and diabetes report more serious physical manifestations of their diabetes, compared to diabetes patients without depression, even after controlling for the variation in their HbA1c (glycosylated hemoglobin, and the fraction of hemaglobin to which glucose has non-enzymatically attached in the blood stream; Ludman et al., 2004). At the same time, depressed diabetes patients are less compliant with the treatment of their diabetes (Ciechanowski et al., 2000). Such patients also report a lower quality of life and use medical resources more frequently (Egede, 2004a; Egede, 2004b).

Despite these arguments, the biopsychosocial model of disease has not been implemented in standard general health care, resulting in under-treatment of psychiatric and psychosocial comorbidities (Kessler et al., 1999; Penn et al., 1997; Goldman et al., 2000; Hirschfeld et al., 1997; Wells et al., 2002). Although several attempts have been made to operationalize the biopsychosocial model of disease and to develop related assessment instruments, efficient methods for use in general clinical care are still lacking (Leigh et al., 1980; Huyse, 1997). The issue of how to approach biopsychosocial morbidity thus remains an important challenge. The IOM report, *Improving the Quality of Health Care for Mental and Substance-Use Conditions: Quality Chasm Series* (IOM, 2006), provides a blueprint for integrating mental health and general health in the service of improving the quality of all health care. This report, in combination with a series of other recent reports, all have as a focus paving the way towards an integration of physical and mental health for those in need (IOM, 2006; Bazelon Center for Mental Health Law, 2005). As such, it is the right time for the introduction of an operationalized biopsychosocial model.

In this chapter we describe the INTERMED method, which aims to operationalize the biopsychosocial model of disease and to fill the gap between general medical and mental health care. The INTERMED is an interview-based instrument to assess case complexity. It is an action-oriented decision support tool offering a visualized risk profile and an outline for multidisciplinary treatment planning (Huyse et al., 1999; Stiefel et al., 1999; Huyse et al., 2001b).

THE INTERMED

Method—Operationalizing the Biopsychosocial Model of Disease

The INTERMED project was initiated to develop an instrument to assess biopsychosocial case complexity. In contrast to the patient grouping methodologies, the INTERMED was not designed to collect diagnostic data, since this information is often not available at the beginning of the process of care delivery and often explains only a limited amount of variance with regard to use of health care services. Also, in contrast to other methodologies assessing complexity, the INTERMED could not rely on existing data, since many of the relevant psychosocial patient characteristics are not routinely collected in general health care. To start developing a method to assess biopsychosocial case complexity and to define related integrated treatment plans, we therefore first relied on clinical experience with the format of life charts, as introduced by Querido (Boenink & Huyse, 1997), and on similar approaches (Leigh et al., 1980; Nurcombe & Gallagher, 1986), as shown in Table 15.1.

This format has been used for many years to analyze and supervise complex medical cases in multidisciplinary conferences by drawing the patient's situation on white boards (see the blank schema in Table 15.2 used for this purpose). The life chart offers a structured approach to organize clinical data with regard to biological, psychological, social, and health care related aspects in a context of time. As such, the life chart provides an opportunity to develop an integrated treatment plan.

Table 15.1
Examples of Life-Charts

(Querido) (Boenink & Huyse, 1997)	Physical	Psychological	Social
Time-axis			

(Nurcombe-Gallagher, 1986)	Predisposing Factors	Precipitating Factors	Maintaining Factors
Biological			
Psychological			
Health care system			
Social system			

(Leigh, 1980)	Current State	Recent Events	Background
Biological			
Psychological			
Health care system			
Social system			

Table 15.2
Blank Schema

	Facts Time-axis ⟶	Interventions
Biological		
Psychological		
Social System		
Health Care System		

Table 15.3
Variables of the INTERMED Schema

	History	Current State	Prognoses
Biological	Chronicity Diagnostic dilemma	Severity of symptoms Diagnostic challenge	Complications and life threat
Psychological	Restrictions in coping Psychiatric dysfunctioning	Resistance to treatment Psychiatric symptoms	Mental health threat
Social	Restrictions in integration Social dysfunctioning	Residential instability Restrictions of network	Social vulnerability
Health Care	Intensity of treatment Treatment experience	Organisation of care Appropriateness of referral	Coordination

Copyright © Huyse, Lyons, Stiefel, Slaets, de Jonge; reprinted with permission by Elsevier. First appeared in Huyse, F. J., Lyons, J. S., Stiefel, F. C., Slaets, J. P. J., Lobo, A., Guex, P., De Jonge, P., Fink, P., Gans, R. O., Guex, P., Herzog, T., Lobo, A., Smith, G. C. & van Schijndel, R. S. (1999). INTERMED: A method to assess health service needs. I. Development and first results on its reliability. General Hospital Psychiatry, 21, 39–48.

We selected a pool of variables to develop the INTERMED based on clinical experience with the life chart and epidemiological literature on the characteristics influencing patients' treatment response and health care utilization. In 1995, Lyons and colleagues (1997) introduced the communimetric approach for assessment instruments for the mental health field, and a first version of the INTERMED was integrated in a research project funded by the European Union for the European Consultation-Liaison Workgroup. The main objective of this project was to develop an instrument to detect patients with complex care needs; based on this project, Huyse and colleagues developed the COMPRI (care complexity prediction instrument) (Huyse et al., 2001a). Thereafter, an international multidisciplinary group consisting of consultation-liaison psychiatrists, psychologists, and colleagues from different somatic disciplines continued to elaborate on the INTERMED. This resulted in the grid and the variables shown in Table 15.3.

The INTERMED describes the biological, psychological, social, and health care characteristics of the patient in a time perspective consisting of his or her history, current state, and prognoses. It is structured to organize information into the twelve cells in the above table. We selected two pertinent variables from the variable pool for each cell of the History and Current State columns and one variable for each cell of the Prognoses column. The selection of these twenty variables was discussed and validated (face validity) by a panel of researchers and clinicians.

History Variables

Information collected in the history domains includes the following:

1. *Biological domain.* In the biological domain, information is collected about the chronicity of a given illness (chronicity) and about prior episodes of diagnostic uncertainty (diagnostic dilemma). The distinction between acute and chronic diseases has proven to be helpful for the conceptualization of somatic diseases

and the patient's care needs, especially in the elderly. It is also an indicator for the risk of a comorbid psychiatric disturbance, since the prevalence of psychiatric disturbances is increased in chronic medical illnesses (Fink, 1990; Covinsky et al., 1997). Diagnostic uncertainty, especially when reflected in multiple testing and contradictory medical diagnoses, indicates possible episodes of depressive, anxiety, or somatoform disorders, known to increase case complexity and health care utilization and to diminish response to medical treatments. It may indicate also the existence of a rare or complex physical disease (Beitman et al., 1989; Jones et al., 1989).

2. *Psychological domain.* In the psychological domain, information is collected about past coping resources (restrictions of coping) and psychiatric history (psychiatric dysfunctioning). Both are known to increase case complexity and health care use, to diminish treatment response, and to enlarge the expression of functional physical symptoms. As a result, patients with such disturbances have increased health care needs (Fink, 1990; Saravay & Lavin, 1995; Browne et al., 1990; Katon et al., 1990). As psychiatric morbidity has a tendency to become chronic, the two variables are predictive for the patient's current and future adaptation to disease and therefore for prospective care needs. In contrast to the other variables, which are assessed over the last five years, the variable psychiatric dysfunctioning is assessed as a life-time variable, since it is known that psychiatric disorders—even when they occurred many years ago—can reflect psychiatric vulnerability when facing current medical stressors (Fink, 1990).

3. *Social domain.* In the social domain, information is collected about social integration in terms of having a job and leisure activities (restrictions of integration) and the patient's capacity to maintain relations (social dysfunctioning). Being socially embedded has been proven to influence adaptation to somatic illness; this domain thus reflects the patient's social needs. Moreover, it has been demonstrated that social isolation is associated with an impaired prognosis of somatic illnesses, such as cardiovascular disease (Berkman et al., 1992; Johnson et al., 1992).

4. *Health care domain.* In the health care domain, information is collected about intensity (intensity) and adequacy of prior care (treatment experience). Health care use during prior illness episodes and the quality of past relationships with health care providers are likely to influence current and future care needs. Patients with negative experiences, such as missed medical diagnoses or conflicts with staff, are likely to be suspicious or distrustful in future relations with clinicians and therefore may be associated with unnecessary second opinions and doctor shopping (Kessler et al., 1987).

Current State Variables

The following information is collected for the current state variables:

1. *Biological domain.* In the biological domain, information is collected about the severity of physical symptoms and related physical impairment (severity of symptoms), and about complexity of the medical diagnosis (diagnostic challenge). Both variables are related to current therapeutic medical/nursing needs (Horn, 1981).

2. *Psychological domain.* In the psychological domain, information is collected about the level of cooperation of the patient with the recommended treatment (resistance to treatment) and current psychiatric disturbances (psychiatric symptoms). Compliance and psychiatric comorbidity, such as in cognitive impairment, substance abuse, and depression, are interrelated, and both influence the outcome of medical illness (Fink, 1990; Haynes et al., 1979).

3. *Social domain.* In the social domain, information is collected about patients' current living situation (residential instability) and supportive social relations, such as family, friends, or colleagues (restrictions of network). These variables influence adjustment to disease and the organization of care (Berkman et al., 1992; Johnson et al., 1992).

4. *Health care domain.* In the health care domain, information is collected about the organizational complexity in terms of number and types of health care providers involved in the care before referral or admission (organization of care). This information reflects both the intensity and complexity of the care that will have to be delivered. Here also the appropriateness of transitions of care such as referral and hospitalization is evaluated (appropriateness of referral). These variables assess the complexity of care and the possible splits and fragmentations within the system (i.e., primary versus secondary or general versus mental health care) having negative effects on care (IOM, 2001).

Prognoses Variables

The following information is collected for the prognosis variables:

1. *Biological domain.* In the biological domain, information is collected about the anticipated outcomes of the disease such as impairments, complications, recurrence of disease, or life threat. All are of major importance for the future medical needs of a patient and related treatment planning.

2. *Psychological domain.* In the psychological domain, information is collected about the anticipated mental health threat and related psychological needs that may result from the current illness episode or past psychiatric history.

3. *Social domain.* In the social domain, information is collected about the anticipated social needs with regard to the social integration of the patient. This is most important for patients with changes in the physical and psychological status resulting in social disintegration, such as physical dependence or social isolation that might require adjustment of care, such as the provision of additional support at home or (temporary) admission to a facility (Berkman et al., 1992).

4. *Health care domain.* In the health care domain, information is collected about anticipated health care needs in terms of intensity and complexity of its organization. The health service needs on the different system levels (biological, psychological, social) are accumulated and, depending on their mutual interference, the degree of the need to integrate health services is evaluated. Additional efforts may be needed to organize care, either by means of multidisciplinary case conferences, known as horizontal coordination of care, or initiation and monitoring of longitudinal care trajectories by means of the introduction of a case manager, known as vertical coordination of care.

Table 15.4
Uniform Scoring of the Variables of the INTERMED

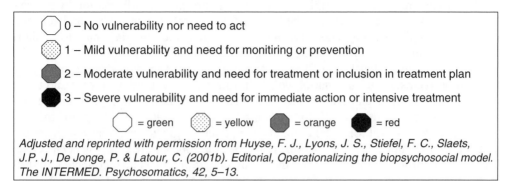

○ 0 – No vulnerability nor need to act

◉ 1 – Mild vulnerability and need for monitiring or prevention

⬣ 2 – Moderate vulnerability and need for treatment or inclusion in treatment plan

⬣ 3 – Severe vulnerability and need for immediate action or intensive treatment

○ = green   ◉ = yellow   ⬣ = orange   ⬤ = red

Adjusted and reprinted with permission from Huyse, F. J., Lyons, J. S., Stiefel, F. C., Slaets, J.P. J., De Jonge, P. & Latour, C. (2001b). Editorial, Operationalizing the biopsychosocial model. The INTERMED. Psychosomatics, 42, 5–13.

SCORING OF THE INTERMED

In Chapter 1 of this book an argument was made for a communimetric approach to develop action-oriented, clinical decision support systems, specifically for the management of patients with complex needs who are cared for in complex medical systems, in which appropriate and efficient communication between health professionals becomes crucial. In contrast to psychometric methods, which were basically developed for research and have limited meaning for clinical work, communimetric assessment instruments are geared toward clinical decision-making and management. The mixed psychometric, clinimetric, and communimetric approach (see discussion of scientific evaluation of the INTERMED later in this chapter) used in developing the INTERMED resulted in an action-oriented decision support tool for the management of complex medical cases. The universal scoring and the uniform colors of the variables to indicate risks and need for action (traffic lights: green, yellow, orange, and red—see Table 15.4) facilitate the integration of the INTERMED in clinical practice (Huyse et al., 2001b).

For each variable, specific clinical anchor points are defined to facilitate reliable scoring. The scores on the variables can be summed up to a total score ranging from 0 to 60, reflecting the level of complexity of the case (see Appendix 15.1, INTERMED Variables and Their Clinical Anchor Points, at the end of this chapter.)

Data Collection and Clinical Interview

Data collection with the INTERMED depends on the profession of the assigned user and the setting. For example, a trained physician is able to conduct the full interview and obtain scoring, while a trained nurse will be able to assess almost all variables with the exception of the variables diagnostic challenge and the biological prognosis, for which the treating physician needs to be consulted. When used in an outpatient setting for selected cases identified by red flags or identifiers, a separate appointment for such an assessment can be made with the patient.

The patient is guided through the different domains in a coherent and emotionally acceptable and supportive way. This is crucial to establish a relationship and foster mutual understanding of the problems to be faced. Fourteen leading questions help the patient provide the relevant information (see Appendix 15.2, Leading Questions for the INTERMED Interview). The sequence of the fourteen questions does not follow an absolute rule; once familiar with the INTERMED interview, raters can use their own style and adjust to the specific information provided by the patient (Huyse et al., 2001b).

Before the interview, the clinician should evaluate existing information by reviewing the patient's medical history, the reason for referral or admission, and relevant psychosocial information. When starting the interview, the clinician may use a short introduction, such as: "Now that we know about your medical situation, I would like to get a better idea what kind of person you are and how are you dealing with your medical problems. This information will help to organize you medical care and tailor it to your individual needs. As we have to discuss several issues, I might interrupt you sometimes when I know enough for a comprehensive overview of your problems."

After covering the biological domains, the patient is given a summary of the available information and asked if this information seems appropriate from his perspective. The specific information concerning the health care domains is then collected. A shift is then made toward the social domains, and finally the variables of the psychological domains are explored. At the end of the interview, the interviewer underlines the importance of the information provided by the patient and summarizes and verifies the most relevant information. The interviewer asks whether pertinent issues have been missed, and the patient is invited to express how he or she feels about the interview. Finally, the patient will be informed how the information will be handled and the next steps to expect. Our clinical experience is that the overwhelming majority of medical patients are satisfied with the interview, with the occasional exception of patients with severe somatization, feeling threatened by questions concerning their psychological state. We often hear patients saying: "You are the first clinician who is not only interested in my illness, but also in me as a person who has to deal with the illness." With regard to the question whether pertinent issues have been missed, most patients do not think so. A not yet published scientific evaluation of patients has demonstrated that patients are generally very satisfied with the INTERMED interview.

INTERMED Interview in Specific Patient Populations

In elderly patients or in patients with indications of cognitive disturbances, a series of questions are asked to evaluate cognitive impairment. Such questions, derived from cognitive screening tests, could include: Can you tell me why you are here? And if not, Can you tell me what kind of person I am? Can you tell me where you are? Or, Can you tell me what date it is? In case of incorrect answers, one might decide to interview a partner or someone else close to the patient, including professionals who care or cared for the patient.

In patients who are very anxious, depressed, or emotionally disturbed, one might consider asking a consultation-liaison psychiatrist, a psychologist, or a psychiatric nurse to conduct the interview, or it might be important to wait until the patient agrees to provide information about sensitive issues, such as social integration. Especially with these patients, it is important to obtain such information, since it is most likely to influence the current illness episode.

Patients suffering from severe somatization may be reluctant to provide information about their psychological state and the history of their social integration; this may be due to alexithymia or a fear that the clinician will see their symptoms as linked to psychological factors and not be taken seriously. If patients can not be assured that their symptoms are taken seriously or if they seem not to be able to express their emotional state, the lacking information in the INTERMED grid should alert the clinician to reflect on the case and to consider a psychiatric disturbance, such as somatization.

A case is presented in detail below from available information, from the interview through the process of scoring, followed by the organization of the written information and a plan for treatment.

EXAMPLE OF AN INTERMED INTERVIEW: MR. GLOVER

Huyse and colleagues (2001b) provide the following INTERMED interview. Available information at admission showed that Mr. Glover was a fifty-five-year-old, married real estate salesman who attended the emergency room after having been pressured by an employee of his firm to consult a physician. He had symptoms indicating a possible myocardial infarction; he already was hospitalized for a first myocardial infarction six months earlier. The investigations in the emergency room confirmed the diagnosis. While in the emergency room, the patient developed ventricular fibrillation requiring cardio-version, sedation, and admission. The patient was admitted on a cardiology ward where an emergency admission is a red flag (indicator) for an assessment with the INTERMED.

The next day, a trained nurse conducted the interview after the patient was physically stabilized and had some rest. The cardiologist informed the nurse about the diagnosis and physical status. The diagnosis was a second myocardial infarction of a person known to have arterial hypertension without evident signs of pump failure. The patient, whose circulation was stabilized after the cardio-version, was confined to his bed and was later to have a cardiac work-up. According to the protocol, this required standard cardiology follow-up and a post discharge rehabilitation program. It was expected that the patient would be slightly limited in his physical activities (New York Heart Association classification 1-2). Mr. Glover, who did not see his wife in the last month, asked that only his sister be informed about his condition. The sister was living in another state and seemed very concerned when she heard what happened, and she announced to the nurse that she would visit Mr. Glover the next day.

Interview Questions and Answers

After a stable night during which the patient slept well with hypnotics, the nurse started the INTERMED interview. She began with the opening question: "*I heard you have been admitted for a myocardial infarction and that your situation has stabilized since yesterday. To be able to provide the best treatment, we would like to know a little bit more about who you are and how it is for you to be here. Now, first of all, how do you feel physically?*"

The patient reported that he did not have pain or other physical complaints. He knew he did not feel well the day before. He remembered having visited the emergency room and that the doctor informed him he had suffered a myocardial event, but he still could not believe it. He thought the physical symptoms he experienced before admission were related to a bad night's sleep. The nurse informed Mr. Glover that although he is currently stable, he must stay in bed for a while. She then stated, "*I will tell you what I know about the reason for your admission and your current state. You should correct me when I am wrong,*" and provided the information described by the cardiologist. She informed him that she would like to know more about the circumstances of this current illness episode: "*Now I would like to know, how did you feel emotionally during the last week?*"

Mr. Glover answered he had been feeling tense; he did not sleep well at all and felt blue during the last weeks. To try to get to sleep and to cheer himself up, he had been drinking several whiskies in the evenings. When asked, he said that he did not presently feel tense from not having alcohol, but he would not mind having something to smoke. When the nurse asked him whether feeling blue was related to the problems with his wife, the patient confirmed. The nurse told Mr. Glover that this was important information and that she would come back to this issue, and she then continued, "*I would like to have some more information concerning the physical illnesses and treatments of the past five years.*" Mr. Glover informed the nurse that he had a myocardial infarction about six months ago for which he was admitted. For more than fifteen years he has suffered from uncomplicated hypertension for which he had been taking medication (Captopril); there hadn't been any other reasons to see a doctor.

The nurse then asked, "*Who have been the doctors that took care of you in the last five years?*" A primary care physician had treated Mr. Glover's hypertension. After his first cardiac infarction, he had seen a cardiologist twice. The cardiologist had pointed to his lifestyle and suggested to the patient that he see a psychologist to discuss his attitude towards work. As he was too busy and anxious about keeping up with his new job, he did not follow these recommendations. The nurse continued, "*Have you ever seen a psychiatrist in your life or have there been periods that you have been anxious, depressed, or confused?*" Mr. Glover stated that he was "depressed" once, a long time ago, when his first wife divorced him. It resulted in a period of one-half year that he became very passive and was not able to work. He consulted a psychiatrist and was treated with antidepressants. He stopped his medication and psychiatric follow-up when he moved to another state.

Currently, he didn't know—he might be depressed again. His new job was stressful and he was again in conflict and without the support of his wife; living in a hotel room for the past few weeks had been tough. The nurse stressed the importance of this information. She said that she will come back to this issue. Then she continued and asked him to specify: "*Now, who are the doctors, nurses, social workers, or psychologists who are currently taking care of you?*" Mr. Glover answered that there had been no time for consultations; the last time had been tense and busy. He should have seen his cardiologist, but failed to do so. Maybe he should have seen a psychologist too, he said.

Upon the nurse's question, "*Have there been issues with doctors during the last five years that have given you a bad feeling to such an extent as to interfere with your trust in doctors?*" Mr. Glover told her that at the end of his previous cardiac admission the patient next to him died unexpectedly during the night. Afterwards he heard that the hospital had organizational problems for which it had been sued. In addition, during his last visit to the cardiologist, when he mentioned that he and his wife were in conflict concerning his current job, the cardiologist did not react and continued to focus on his cardiac condition. These events changed his view of doctors. "*You cannot simply rely on them,*" he stated. The nurse confirmed that she too thought this was important information, as trust in your doctor is crucial. She continued: "*I would like to know how you follow your doctor's recommendations. Are you a person who is, generally speaking, inclined to do what doctors say?*" Mr. Glover answered that concerning his medication, for years he had been a regular user. During the last month it was a mess; it was impossible to keep up with the regimen.

"*Now I would like to change the subject and ask you how you currently live,*" the nurse stated. The patient reported that his wife did not want to follow him to the new job. There had been quarrels concerning the interference of his work with their marriage. When Mr. Glover insisted on changing his job and moving, his wife said that she did not want to see him for a while. This happened about one month ago. Consequently, he was living in a hotel room, looking for an apartment. Besides seeing a colleague, whom he met once a week, he worked late and ate in restaurants. The nurse confirmed that she saw the problem and continued, *"Now I would like to know what kind of person you are. Generally speaking, are you an easy going person?"* The patient replied that his wife would say that he is a difficult person to live with, but he doesn't think so. He does not need many people as long as he can work. For him, it is important to be successful. *"That's not an easy job,"* he said.

The last few weeks, he had the feeling that he was not fully in control of the situation. The nurse asked him whether everything was an effort and whether he felt blue or hopeless about the future, and the patient confirmed. She asked whether he had given up or wanted to die, and Mr. Glover, who seemed distressed, ignored this question. The nurse told Mr. Glover that after she talked with the cardiologist she would consider appropriate psychiatric consultation and would confirm such consultation soon after the interview. *"Now, coming to the end of the interview, I would like to ask you about your smoking and drinking habits and their relation to the current problems,"* the nurse continued. The patient informed her that he had been drinking up to six whiskies an evening in the last month. He has had earlier periods of heavy drinking. In such periods he also was smoking; lately he only smoked cigars. When asked, he told the nurse that he never suffered from symptoms of withdrawal.

The nurse thanked the patient for all the relevant information he provided in such a short time. She emphasized that she understood that he has had a difficult time, that he did not function well, and that this situation would be taken in consideration in the treatment plan. Mr. Glover ignored the question, *"Do you think we missed any pertinent information?"* and the nurse continued, *"I finally would like to know how you have experienced this interview. Do you think that this will be helpful information or do you think this was inappropriate?"* The patient replied that he felt somewhat relieved and thought the questions were appropriate and helpful.

As you can see, these guiding questions do allow the interviewer to develop rapport. The issues evolve from "normal" medical to more personal. The more internalized the interview becomes and the more skilled the interviewer is, the easier it is to develop one's own interviewing style. It is most helpful to visualize the schema in Table 15.3 with the variables and mentally scan it during the interview for the completeness of information. On wards in which the method has been implemented, the variables have been integrated in the existing nurse-chart based on nurse processing techniques for treatment planning (Gordon, 1994).

Scoring the Glover Case

Scoring of the variables is based on the matching of the clinical data with the clinical anchor points described in the manual. Where the clinical information concerning a specific variable does not exactly match the information provided by the anchor points, or in case of doubts, the rater will estimate by comparison with the anchor points how the given information influences the complexity of the patient and the need for action. In scoring Mr. Glover, the anchor points to which we refer in the text are described in Table 15.3. The goal of this scoring example is not to discuss all reflections concerning different scoring options, but to provide the reader with a "flavor" of how the INTERMED works and how Mr. Glover would be scored.

Biological

1. *Chronicity.* Chronicity is scored as 3 since the hypertension and the myocardial infarction are seen as two separate medical diagnoses. Although one could argue that the patient has two expressions of the same illness, the myocardial infarction being a complication of the hypertension, both conditions are chronic and the prognosis of the combination is worse than that of hypertension alone. Consequently this makes the patient more complex, which is reflected in the highest score on this item.

2. *Diagnostic dilemma.* Diagnostic dilemma is scored as a 1 since about six months ago the patient had a myocardial infarction, for which the diagnosis was immediately obtained.

3. *Severity of symptoms.* Severity of symptoms is scored as 2. In Mr. Glover's case, it is not the patient who provides information on the severity of symptoms and the related functional capacity. Even if he had been able to walk around, the cardiologist decided that he had to stay in bed for the first days after his admission and he was not allowed to perform any functional activities. He therefore scores 2. In most other cases, this item is scored on the basis of the information provided by the patient. For example, if it would concern a patient who is a wheelchair dependent somatizer, he would be scored as 2 (moderate to severe symptoms that interfere with current functioning).

4. *Diagnostic challenge.* Diagnostic challenge is scored as 0, since the findings are, without doubt, consistent with a myocardial infarction. For example, if this patient had been diagnosed as not having had an infarction and the pain had been considered to be possibly related to anxiety, this variable would have been scored as a 3 (complex differential diagnosis, in which no diagnosis is to be expected from a biological perspective).

Psychological

5. *Restrictions in coping.* Restrictions in coping is scored as 2 since the patient has impaired coping skills. Although he has had a serious illness (myocardial infarction) and both his cardiologist and his wife confronted him about being a workaholic, he was not able to face adequately a new job offer, nor had he been able to control his drinking and smoking behavior.

6. *Psychiatric dysfunctioning.* Psychiatric dysfunctioning, in contrast to all other variables, is scored from a lifetime perspective. As the patient has been previously depressed and unable to function for some time, the score is 2.

7. *Resistance to treatment.* Resistance to treatment is scored as 2 since the patient did not follow the recommendations provided by the cardiologist, including the suggestion to see a psychologist; in addition, he was not able to follow his medication schedule during the last month. Finally, he was not willing to initiate a medical consultation despite his chest pain and had to be convinced by a colleague. These are serious expressions of noncompliance, which surpass the anchor point (some ambivalence, but willing to cooperate with treatment).

8. *Psychiatric symptoms.* Psychiatric symptoms is scored as 2; Mr. Glover is not just a bit tense or having problems concentrating, but there is evidence of significant depressive symptoms. In addition, he has a problem with substance abuse, both smoking and alcohol. Since he shows no symptoms of withdrawal, he only scores 2.

Social

9. *Social integration.* Social integration is scored as 1 since Mr. Glover qualifies as "having a job without having leisure activities." For example, patients who are retired or who do not have a job but actively take care of their household, and patients who are studying, are scored as those who have work.

10. *Social dysfunctioning.* Social dysfunctioning is scored as 1 since the patient reports quarrels and disagreement with his wife.

11. *Residential instability.* Residential instability is scored as 3 since the patient has an unstable living situation; the score reflects that action is needed. However, it is assumed that a solution can be found with the help of his sister.

12. *Restrictions of network.* Social network is scored as 2 since Mr. Glover has social restrictions in two areas, but there is still a sister and a colleague who are concerned.

Health Care

13. *Intensity of treatment.* Intensity of treatment is scored as 2 since the patient was hospitalized about one-half year ago. A score of 3, for example, would be given if the patient had stayed for a longer time on an intensive care unit during his last admission due to serious complications.

14. *Treatment experience.* Treatment experience is scored as 1 since Mr. Glover had mentioned negative perceptions of health care providers on two occasions (negative experiences with health care providers, self, or relatives). Even a score of 2 could be considered, since the patient reported that he had consequently stopped his contact with the cardiologist (requests for second opinions or changing contacts with doctors). This is an example in which scoring may at times slightly differ between interviewers; still, inter-rater reliability for the global INTERMED score was always satisfactory.

15. *Organization of care.* This variable rates the number of health care providers involved and, thereby, the potential complexities in communication. Mr. Glover's organization of care is scored as 0, since he was not treated by different medical specialists. In his case, a cardiologist and a psychologist should have treated him, but he did not follow these recommendations. The fact that he was not compliant increases his complexity, but this fact has already been reflected in the two variables, restrictions in coping and resistance to treatment.

16. *Appropriateness of referral.* Appropriateness of admission or referral is scored as 1 since this was an emergency admission (unplanned referral or admission). For example, if Mr. Glover had been readmitted after a week in a state of self-neglect and heavily drinking, a score of 2 (able to plan a strategy for treatment, yet not capable to provide optimal care) would be appropriate.

Prognoses

17. *Biological prognosis.* Biological prognosis is scored as 2 since the patient has a chronic condition and/or permanent substantial limitations in activities of daily living. For example, if the cardiologist had indicated the myocardial infarction was complicated by a serious risk of dying, a 3 would be appropriate.

18. *Psychological prognosis.* Psychological prognosis is scored as 2 since the patient has a current depressive episode, complicated substance abuse, work-related problems, a marital conflict, and a serious physical condition with noncompliance. These associated problems indicate that the depression, as well as the associated psychiatric and psychosocial problems, may persist for quite some time (moderate psychiatric disorder requiring psychiatric care).

19. *Social prognosis.* Social prognosis is scored as 2 since there is a serious risk of admission to a facility until a new housing situation can be found with the help of his sister (temporary admission to facility/institution).

20. *Health care.* Prognosis of health care is scored as 3 because of the various risks in different domains and the high scores with regard to prognoses; this requires intensive action including initiation of a multidisciplinary case conference and long-term coordination of care by a case manager.

INTERMED Total Score

Mr. Glover's total score on the INTERMED is 34, which belongs to the high range and supports the argument made for coordination of care and a case manager. Figure 15.1 illustrates the visual representation of the risks.

Written Organization of the Glover Case Vignette

The clinical data related to the scoring can also be organized as shown below. This may be helpful, for example, when the patient should be referred to a different facility. In the electronic version, the clinical information presented is computer-entered and automatically organized.

- *Biological risks.* Mr. Glover is a fifty-five-year-old male who has been admitted through the emergency room to a cardiac ward for a myocardial infarction complicated by a ventricle tachycardia; the cardiac condition requires immobilization. Mr. Glover suffers from a chronic disease (hypertension), recently complicated by another chronic condition (heart disease due to a myocardial infarction). There have not been other episodes of physical illness in the last five years.

- *Social risks.* Over the last five years, work has dominated his life to such an extent that it has negatively influenced the relationship with his wife; they have lived separately for a month. The patient is currently living alone in a hotel room. Beyond a sister and a colleague, he does not have people who may support him, nor does he have time for or interest in leisure.

- *Psychological risks.* From a psychological perspective, Mr. Glover has denied his cardiac condition and tends to reduce tension with smoking and drinking. His history indicates an earlier episode of mood disorder and impaired coping

Figure 15.1
Mr. Glover

Problem: Pain on the breast
Sex M   **Age** 55

	PAST		CURRENT		PROGNOSES
Biological	CHRONICITY	●	SEVERITY	◉	◉
	Dx DILEMMA	◌	Dx CHALLENGE	○	
Psychological	COPING	◉	RESISTANCE	◉	◉
	FUNCTIONING	◉	SEVERITY	◉	
Social	INTEGRATION	◌	INSTABILITY	◉	◉
	FUNCTIONING	◌	NETWORK	◉	
Health care	INTENSITY	◉	ORGANISATION	○	●
	EXPERIENCE	◌	REFERRAL	◌	

IM score: 34   **Indicator:** Emergency admission

○ = green	◌ = yellow
◉ = orange	● = red

Adjusted and reprinted with permission from Huyse, F. J., Lyons, J. S., Stiefel, F. C., Slaets, J.P. J., De Jonge, P. & Latour, C. (2001b). Editorial, Operationalizing the biopsychosocial model. The INTERMED. Psychosomatics, 42, 5–13.

after the separation from his first wife. Currently he presents substance abuse problems with tobacco and alcohol and a depressive disorder. This psychological state interferes with his compliance with medical treatment as reflected in the recent inability to take medication on a regular basis and his behaviour, which represents a risk for his cardiac condition.

- *Health care risks*. In the last five years Mr. Glover has been admitted for a first myocardial infarction and has been treated by a primary care physician and a cardiologist. At the moment he does not see any medical or other caretakers. His trust in doctors has been negatively influenced by two earlier incidents.

Prognoses

The report gives the following prognoses for Mr. Glover.

- *Biological prognosis*. The patient suffers from a chronic condition and might in the future be subjected to permanent substantial limitations in activities of daily living.

- *Psychological prognosis*. The patient has a psychiatric disorder requiring psychiatric care; he suffers from depression, which is complicated by various other conditions, such as substance abuse, social isolation, and a serious medical illness.

- *Social prognosis*. Due to his current physical condition and social situation, the patient has a serious risk of a temporary admission to a facility.

- *Health care*. Taking into account the various risks factors in the various domains, the patient has to be considered as complex, requiring different specialist consults and care coordination, including mental health care.

Treatment Plan

Table 15.5 shows the INTERMED treatment plan for Mr. Glover, providing the following diagnostics and proposed treatment plan. (In *Integrated Care for the Complex Medically Ill*, the authors provide additional cases for training in Chapter 12, Appendix III, Huyse & Stiefel, 2006).

- *Biological level*. Depending on the stabilization of the circulation in the first twenty-four hours, the patient's cardiac condition will be evaluated according to protocol. The cardiologist regards his post-discharge functional prognosis to be in the range of New York Heart Association classification 1-2. For the first twenty-four hours the patient should be monitored for physical symptoms of alcohol withdrawal by observing his sleeping patterns, although the risk seems relatively low. Given the overall situation, a low dosage of benzodiazepines will be prescribed for three to five days to prevent distress, which could negatively influence his cardiac condition. After stabilization, the patient should be referred to a cardiac rehabilitation program, followed by regular medical appointments.

- *Psychological level*. A psychiatric consultant should assess the patient and evaluate the interrelation between coping, compliance, substance abuse, and depression. As a result of this assessment, it should be decided who should initiate treatment, at what time, and what kind of treatment. As compliance with treatment is crucial in this patient, the primary focus of the intervention should be to motivate the patient to accept psychological treatment. Depending on the results of the contacts with his sister and his wife, the integration of these persons in the psychiatric treatment plan should be considered.

- *Social level*. The patient's wife should be invited to explore further his social and relational situation. Based on the results of this exploration, the outcome of his physical condition and the results of the psychiatric assessment, decisions on the location of post-discharge treatment planning should be made: psychiatric transfer, rehabilitation clinic, or ambulant treatment.

- *Health care level*. A multidisciplinary case conference should be organized in the next days to integrate the results of the different consultants (rehabilitation, psychiatry, and social work); later an assigned case manager should coordinate the treatment program.

SCIENTIFIC EVALUATION OF THE INTERMED

Classical Test and Items Response Theories

There are different approaches to developing and evaluating measurement instruments. The essence of classical test theory is that the measure of any construct involves

Table 15.5
Treatment Plan

Patient Identification   **Diagnostics and Treatment**

Date	:
MD	:
Nurse	:

	Diagnostics	☑	Treatment	☑
BIOLOGICAL	Cardiac monitoring		Cardiac protocol	
	Withdrawal monitoring		R/ Oxazepam 10-25 mgr ttd	
	Sleep monitoring		R/ Oxazepam 25-50 mgr AN	
			PM:	
			• R/ antidepressants	
			• Cardiac rehabilitation	
			☐ **Restrictions of Treatment**	
PSYCHOLOGICAL	Monitor mood and suicidal thoughts		Motivational intervention to secure	
	Psychiatric assessment :		psychological Tx for coping,	
	• substance abuse, depression		compliance, substance abuse, and	
	• compliance and coping		depression	
	Assessment of relation with wife		Consider participation of wife	
SOCIAL	Assessment of housing situation		Plan discharge management	
			based on findings of consultants	
	Participants		**Activities**	
HEALTH CARE GEZONDHEIDZORG	Psychiatrist		Case conference after initial consults	
	Rehab specialist		Assign casemanager	
	Social worker			

the use of all possible items that can be identified to accurately measure the target construct. Item analysis evaluates the degree to which items in a given set correlate; a correlation between 0.30-0.60 is desirable, items measuring a similar construct without being redundant (Nunnally, 1976). Factor analysis identifies the underlying structure of relationships among sampled items and evaluates whether the items share a common construct. Reliability and validity (especially construct validity based on statistical evidence) testing complements this evaluation. In contrast to classical test theory, items response theory approaches the problem by evaluating whether the measurement has the ability to distinguish between different people reliably, all along a continuum. Its goal is to identify a set of items that allows for the precise measurement of an individual on the latent continuum or trait. However, from a pragmatic perspective, classical test theory and items response theory value measures that have a large number of items and measure a single dimension, leading to longer, one-dimensional measures.

These two traditional approaches to developing and evaluating psychometric measurement instruments thus share the problems that (1) their usefulness is limited in clinical practice, since most clinical conditions and also outcomes have more than a single dimension; (2) there is little time and motivation to implement one-dimensional and long measures; (3) they are diagnostic instruments with limited relevance for decision-making and treatment planning; and (4) they have been produced for research purposes and have not been developed under real world conditions. For these reasons, one can easily imagine that the objectives of the INTERMED, a biopsychosocial assessment instrument for case complexity, which serves as a decision support and treatment planning tool, cannot be based solely on classical test theory and items response analysis, but has to be complemented by the so-called clinimetric and communimetric approaches.

Clinimetrics and Communimetrics

Clinimetrics, in contrast to psychometrics, aims to convert "intangible clinical phenomena into formal specified measurement" (Feinstein, 1999); for clinimetric measures, items are selected on clinical rather than statistical criteria; scoring is simple and readily interpretable; variables are heterogeneous; and face validity is required. The Global Assessment of Functioning Scale is an example (Endicott et al., 1976). Clinimetric instruments tend not to be sensitive to change and are usually unable to embrace the complexity of a given clinical state. Communimetrics aims to integrate in a measure elements that facilitate easy and accurate communication of relevant results; this requires that communimetric measures have a high face validity, high inter-rater reliability, high concurrent and predictive validity, and results that immediately can be used for decision-making, treatment planning, and outcome measurement. As described in the introduction of this chapter, the INTERMED shares the objectives of clinimetrics and communimetrics, but its development and scientific evaluation draw also on classical test theory relevant for psychometric measurements. In the following section, the scientific aspects of the INTERMED are summarized. For a detailed description, the reader is referred to the existing literature referenced in the text.

Face Validity

Initially, an item pool characterizing biopsychosocial case complexity was selected on the basis of face validity and evidence from the literature that a given item is known to increase case complexity and associated health care utilization. Chronicity (history, biological domain) was selected to the INTERMED item pool because it reflects an important variable when describing biopsychosocial case complexity. The distinction between acute and chronic diseases has proved to be helpful in conceptualizing somatic diseases and the patient's care needs, especially regarding the elderly. Chronic illnesses cannot be treated based solely on a standardized, scientific evidence approach. They must be complemented by adjustments in treatments goals that are realistic for individual patients. For example, management of diabetes in an elderly man who in his youth suffered consequences of the Second World War, and who is now depressed after the death of his wife, cannot follow the same lines as the management of diabetes in a young school teacher who performs sports on a regular basis. In addition, chronic diseases, in contrast to acute illness episodes, increase the risk of having a comorbid psychiatric disturbance, since the prevalence of psychiatric disturbances is increased in chronic medical illnesses. With chronicity an important variable, initial development of the INTERMED followed a combination of a psychometric and clinimetric approach, favoring the selection of clinically meaningful and face valid items that can be easily used in clinical practice.

Concurrent Validity With Other Tools

Subsequently, the INTERMED item pool was reduced and validated by means of correlations with existing, longer, and one-dimensional instruments (Nunnally, 1976; Crocker & Algina, 1991). No gold standard for assessing case complexity existed. In evaluating concurrent validity, we compared the INTERMED with other instruments that were valid for some dimensions of the INTERMED, such as the biological domain (SF-36 physical health component score), the psychological domain (SF-36 mental health component score; hospital anxiety and depression scale, or HADS), and the social domain (compared with scales measuring characteristics, such as social support and social isolation) (Stiefel et al., 1999; de Jonge et al., 2003c). This approach was based on a psychometric evaluation of concurrent validity. In contrast to a purely clinimetric approach, items reflecting subjective data were not excluded, since complaints perceived and expressed by the patient are relevant for the assessment of case complexity and especially for health care utilization.

Inter-Rater Reliability

With regard to reliability, the evaluation of the INTERMED again followed psychometric approaches by testing internal consistency, inter-rater, and test-retest reliability (Crocker & Algina, 1991). Following the first inter-rater reliability study with the INTERMED (Huyse et al., 1999), a final version was developed and tested in a sample of patients with varying somatic illnesses. Patients were double scored by two raters, a psychologist and a psychiatric nurse, based on a review of the medical chart and a patient interview conducted by one in the presence of the other. The two raters showed high agreement, as indicated by a Kappa of 0.85 (de Jonge et al., 2002). Temporal stability of the INTERMED was assessed in outpatients with multiple sclerosis, with one year between the two assessments and without a specific intervention other than care as usual (de Jonge et al., 2004). The correlation between the two assessments was moderate to good (indicated by a Kappa of 0.60), reflecting the fact that the INTERMED is a rather stable measure.

As in classical test theory, data from several of the INTERMED studies in different somatic patient populations were pooled to evaluate internal consistency (de Jonge & Stiefel, 2002). In the total sample (n=1104), Cronbach's alpha was 0.87 (95 percent confidence interval: 0.86-0.89), while for the individual samples, alphas ranged from 0.78 to 0.94. The findings gave sufficient support for the reliability of the INTERMED and the usefulness of the total score to describe biopsychosocial case complexity.

Predictive Validity

Predictive validity is required of an instrument meant to provide clinically meaningful information (clinimetric approach). To study predictive validity, we selected relevant outcome variables in several specific patient populations (for a summary, see Table 15.6). In patients admitted to a general medical ward, those classified by the INTERMED as having a high degree of case complexity were found to have a doubled length of hospital stay and increased use of medications, nurse interventions, and specialist consultations (de Jonge et al., 2001c). The findings were replicated later (de Jonge et al., 2003a); in addition, poorer quality of life at discharge was documented for the complex patients. In patients with diabetes, INTERMED scores correlated with HbA1c values, assessed six months before and three and nine months after the INTERMED interview (Fischer et al., 2000). In a sample of low back pain patients who participated in a three-week functional rehabilitation program or who applied for disability compensation, INTERMED scores were significantly higher in those applying for disability compensation (Stiefel et al., 1999). In patients undergoing dialysis, INTERMED scores were associated with low quality of life at one-year follow-up (de Jonge et al., 2003c), which in turn was unrelated to severity of illness at baseline. In multiple sclerosis outpatients, INTERMED scores were associated with measures of disability and with the number of disciplines proposed in the multi-disciplinary treatment plan (Hoogervorst et al., 2003). In patients suffering from rheumatoid arthritis, INTERMED scores predicted—in contrast to other measures evaluating severity of illness—health care utilization on follow-up (Koch et al., 2001). These data confirmed the ability of the INTERMED to detect complex patients at risk for decreased treatment response and increased health care utilization.

As a criterion for detecting complex cases in general medical wards, we identified a cut-off point of 20/21 (de Jonge et al., 2003a) based on an optimized prediction of patients with poor outcomes at discharge from the hospital. The identification of a cut-off point is contrary to the statement that the instrument to assess case complexity should result in a continuous score. In addition, any cut-off point of a continuous score is to a certain extent arbitrary; it can result in bias (Babyak, 2004) and, with regard to the INTERMED, should depend on the specific case mix of the sample and the available resources to deal with complex patients. Therefore, if INTERMED cut-off scores seem reasonable to use in a specific clinical practice, we recommend basing a cut-off score on empirical grounds.

Other Communimetric Elements

While the characteristics we have described above—face validity, inter-rater reliability, and concurrent and predictive validity—are key communimetric elements of the INTERMED, they are not the entire communimetric spectrum. The relevance of the INTERMED for patients is an important communimetric property. Patients have

Table 15.6
Overview of INTERMED Validation Studies (49)

	N	Poor outcome defined as	Area under the curve	P	Prevalence of poor outcome	Sensitivity	Specificity	Odds ratios ¥	95% CI	P
Internal medicine	152	SF-36 <50 #	0.69	<0.0001	51%	0.58	0.76	4.45	2.22-8.94	<0.0001
Multiple sclerosis	72	EDSS > 4 $	0.75	<0.0001	53%	0.65	0.94	8.89	1.85-42.63	<0.0001
Dialysis	46	SF-36 <50 ^	0.76	0.002	50%	0.61	0.74	4.41	1.26-15.41	0.02
Low back pain	102	Applying for disability compensation §	0.89	<0.0001	50%	0.94	0.45	13.14	3.62-47.76	<0.01
Diabetes mellitus	55	HbA1c >8.3 ¶	0.65	0.06	51%	0.71	0.52	2.32	0.76-7.08	0.14

Assessed at discharge (INTERMED at admission)

$ Cross-sectional designs

^ Assessed at one-year follow up

§ Cross-sectional design

¶ Mean HbA1c over three-, six-, and nine-month follow-ups

¥ Odds for a poor outcome for patients with INTERMED score beyond cut-off criterion (20/21)

Reprinted with permission from De Jong, P., Huyse, F. J., Slaets, J. P., Sollner, W. & Stiefel, F. C. (2005). Operationalization of biopsychosocial case complexity in general health care: The INTERMED project. Australian and New Zealand Journal of Psychiatry, 39, 795–799.

expressed satisfaction with the interview (unpublished data) and the simple manual with the described anchor points, and they have helped clinicians find a common language when using the INTERMED in daily clinical practice and multidisciplinary case conferences. The feasibility of conducting a multi-center study involving different European countries (Ludwig et al., 2005) demonstrates communimetric characteristics. The INTERMED's communimetric elements also make possible the objective that results can be used directly for decision-making and treatment planning. Randomized clinical trials are currently being conducted to evaluate the INTERMED as a decision support and treatment planning tool (Stiefel et al., 2004). In addition, the INTERMED is implemented in two different clinical settings—a university clinic (internal medicine ward at University Medical Center Groningen, and neurology ward at Vrije Universiteit Medical Center in Amsterdam, both in the Netherlands), and a regional rehabilitation clinic for accident victims of the Swiss national insurance company SUVA in Sion, Switzerland (Luthi et al., under review).

Improved Outcome for the Complex Medically Ill

Whether implementation of the INTERMED leads to improved outcome of the complex medically ill has been addressed in two earlier studies. In the first study, we investigated the effects of implementing psychiatric interventions on a general medical admission ward by means of a stepped detection and treatment strategy, conducted by a consultation-liaison nurse, to see how a reduced length of hospital stay and improved quality of life at discharge compared to usual care. We found a significant effect of the intervention on quality of life, and in patients age sixty-five or older, a reduction in median length of hospital stay from sixteen to eleven and one-half days. These data suggest that screening for risk of increased health care needs might improve outcomes in general medical inpatients. Because of the design of the study—including a historic control group—these findings should be considered preliminary and to be confirmed in a larger, multi-center, randomized controlled trial (de Jonge et al., 2003b). In a second study, patients discharged home after hospitalization in the general hospital were randomly assigned to usual care or a nurse-led, home-based case management intervention, based on a health needs assessment with the INTERMED. No significant differences were found on re-hospitalizations, care utilization, quality of life, and psychological functioning after twenty-four weeks of follow-up. The primary reason for the lack of effectiveness in this trial is that the case manager implemented the intervention in relative isolation, which hampered its effectiveness, instead of being fully integrated with the existing health care delivery (Latour et al., 2006).

Recently, the value of the INTERMED approach has been addressed in a randomized, controlled trial involving inpatients admitted to a rheumatology ward and diabetic outpatients. The hypothesis was that an early multidisciplinary intervention targeted at complex patients identified with and based on the INTERMED is superior to care as usual (Ludwig et al., 2005). Comparative epidemiological studies evaluating health care benefits of implementing the INTERMED will complement the randomized clinical trials conducted up to now (Latour et al., 2006; Kathol et al., 2005).

In addition to the scientific evaluation above, the INTERMED can be used in research protocols, for example to control for case mix or for stratification of populations with different degrees of case complexity (see Table 15.7). Integration of the

Table 15.7
Research Applications of the INTERMED

- Inclusion and exclusion criterion for intervention studies, using either the total score (cut-off) or combinations of variable scores

- Stratification

- Prediction of outcomes measures such as mortality, morbidity, quality of life, etc.

- Reduction of unexplained variance in RCTs (case-mix measure) leading to an increase of the power of the study and a smaller sample required to reach significance

- Control for possible confounders in RCTs leading to a better estimation of the effect-size

- A standardized procedure to design an individualized patient-oriented integrated intervention, such as in case management studies

---

INTERMED in scientific projects could be of great help to interpret outcome and to identify patients who benefit most from a given intervention.

WHEN TO USE THE INTERMED: INDICATORS

Though complex patients may constitute an important group, their proportion varies depending on the specific population. Pre-selection through indicators is almost a *conditio sine qua non* for effective treatment. Arguments have been made to screen for psychiatric disease, specifically depression, in patients with unexplained physical complaints or a chronic disease such as diabetes (Kroenke et al., 2001; 2003). A decade ago our group presented a complementary approach—not a disease-specific approach identifying psychiatric morbidity per se—to screen for case complexity related to multimorbidity, including psychiatric disorders (Huyse, 1997). Therefore, a method for both detection and assessment of case complexity able to direct clinical care was needed. Such a method, however, should be used with defined indications. Table 15.8 presents a list of potential indicators.

Fragmented Care

The most important factor to influence use of the complexity factors is recognition, by the medical team and others, that fragmented care for a subgroup of patients—the complex medically ill—does not deliver adequate services. Without recognition there is no integrated care, and without appropriate reimbursement there is no integrated care. It is therefore of utmost importance that all clinicians, politicians, health care policy-makers, health plans (insurance companies), providers, and patients—the parties mentioned in the *Chasm* report of the Committee on Quality of Care (IOM, 2006)—become aware of the need to develop high quality integrated care

Table 15.8
Potential Indicators

Clinical Identifiers of Complexity

Illness
 Disease (stage)
 Clinical parameter(s)
 Negative health behavior
 Non-compliance
 Persisting unexplained physical complaints

High intensive and demanding treatments
 Intensive cancer treatment
 Hemodialysis
 Transplantation

Organization of care
 Number of participating healthcare professionals and institutions
 Health care utilization (missed or excess)
 Conflicts/miscommunication

Instruments to Assess Complexity

 Complexity Prediction Instrument (COMPRI)
 Groningen Frailty Index (GFI)
 The INTERMED method

Clinimetric
 Patient Health Questionnaire 9   (Kroenke et al., 2001)
 Patient Health Questionnaire 2   (Kroenke et al., 2003)
 Distress thermometer   (Jacobson et al., 2005)

for complex patients (2001). Local insurers and providers should decide the specific populations on which to focus (Bazelon, 2005). Such plans should use indicator-based integrated care for complex patients, which could become part of chronic disease management programs (Wagner et al., 1996) (e.g., for diabetes or chronic heart failure). This method can also be used by general internal medicine, for instance, where the staff is aware of the limited benefits of their services for the large number of patients seen for unexplained complaints. This should lead to a flexible and operational framework for health service delivery, adjusted to the individualized needs of this growing group of complex patients. It should also include appropriate reimbursement, which together with the awareness of the medical team, is the second driving force behind the development of integrated care.

Population Characteristics

Population characteristics, such as extent of psychiatric comorbidity or level of frailty, contribute to complexity. The proportion of complex patients depends on the type of patients seen (e.g., patients with diabetes or cardiac disease) and the type of services delivered by the provider (e.g., primary care or a general hospital acute admission ward). For instance, in a transplant population, one might assume that about one-half of the population will have additional physical morbidities; moreover, the risk of psychological distress or psychiatric morbidities in this group is high (Trzepacz et al., 2000), making all such patients candidates for complexity assessment. The medical team can formulate patient-oriented care plans in a highly stressed population with somatic and psychiatric comorbidities, reduce unpredicted events and negative outcomes, and thereby reduce staff stress and increase staff satisfaction. For the transplant population, the planned transplantation would be the identifier, or red flag, for complexity assessment. In other populations, such an assessment might be desirable but not feasible or cost-effective for the whole population.

Screening Levels

Another factor to consider is the relation between screening and prevention. As primary prevention, health screening can identify risk factors for an illness; as a secondary prevention, it can detect early signs or pre-symptomatic stages of a disease; and as a tertiary prevention, it can identify factors that modulate the development of disease (Rimes & Salkovskis, 2000). Screening for complexity fits the criteria of tertiary prevention, as its main purpose is to prevent negative effects on quality of life and outcomes of care. However, when "complexity" becomes a more integrated concept in the practice of health care, complexity screening might expand to the other levels of prevention. Secondary prevention screening could help detect early signs and pre-symptomatic stages of complexity. For instance, early signs of noncompliance in patients with diabetes could be defined by means of HbA1c levels, and could be an early identifier of complexity. So could missed appointments, excess doctor visits or hospital admissions, and excess use of medical services such as repeated consults for unexplained physical complaints, all of which may signal depression and somatization of illness.

IMPLEMENTATION OF THE INTERMED IN CLINICAL PRACTICE

Integrated Team Approach

The primary step towards integrated medicine is the medical/nursing team's awareness that integrated medicine benefits the complex patient. Implementing the INTERMED method is similar to initiating a quality management procedure (the details of which are beyond the scope of this chapter). Most important, implementing the INTERMED in clinical practice is based on teamwork and requires an assigned group to guide and evaluate the process. As the team changes its approach from a classical disease-oriented focus to an integrated approach, the team members' focus will become concentrated on the needs of the patients—which implies, for example, the need to integrate a mental health specialist. In hospitals, there should be contracts between different services and departments; in primary care, arrangements with mental health organizations are needed, most of which will agree to integration of the INTERMED. The integrated care teams should identify the symptoms that indicate a need for assessment and interventions, and target the interventions they will focus on.

A team could start by conducting a cohort study to identify the proportion of complex patients, their specific needs, and indicators that identify patients; it could then decide on which competencies to integrate in the team. A next question is who should be responsible for assessment. For inpatients, primary care patients, and those using outpatient clinics, higher-trained nurses may be best suited to do such assessments, in collaboration with the physicians. However, in some settings—depending on local and cultural circumstances—physicians may themselves conduct INTERMED interviews. The most important aspect of the implementation of the INTERMED method is interdisciplinary collaboration; differing professional perspectives should be aired and interdisciplinary communication should be stressed. That is, the "chasms" described in the IOM Report (2001) need to be counteracted not only on the level of communication between departments or institutes, but also on the level of interdisciplinary communication within a team. Integration of the collected information and its analyses in the admission/referral process is crucial where it becomes the driving force to guide the therapeutic process. With multidisciplinary meetings as part of the health service structure, care will shift from a professional to a patient perspective.

INTERMED in Practice

The clinical implementation of the INTERMED method began in 2003; it is currently used in several settings and a variety of teams in several countries are working on implementation. It was first implemented in the admission department of general internal medicine of the University Medical Center in Groningen (UMCG), the Netherlands. All patients admitted to this ward are screened with the INTERMED and discussed in daily multidisciplinary rounds. During these rounds, the team designs an outline of the treatment plan based on the results of the INTERMED, including decisions on discharge within forty-eight hours or a longer admission with related transfer to a specialized ward. Transfers are accompanied by the INTERMED treatment plan. As the INTERMED method is part of the clinical management system, all data are accessible at any time. Consultants such as psychiatrists, geriatricians, and social workers add pertinent information to the electronic INTERMED module to ensure completeness of information. Reports can be printed for the transfer of individual patients or to provide an overview.

In the UMCG the implementation, as part of a pre-assessment clinic for elective surgery, is currently considered as a means to decrease peri-operative complications. In the neurological department of the Vrije Universiteit Medical Center, a similar procedure is followed. In contrast to its use in the department of internal medicine in Groningen, the INTERMED method drives a weekly multidisciplinary meeting. Only those patients with a score above a cut-off point of 20/21 are discussed in this meeting. This procedure has reduced the duration of the meeting from ninety to forty-five minutes. On both the internal medicine and the neurological wards, the INTERMED data collection became an integrated part of the nurse chart (Gordon, 1994). In Switzerland, the INTERMED is used in the Clinic of the Swiss National Accident Insurance Fund for admission screening and related ongoing research (Luthi et al., under review). Responsible physicians report that the implementation of the INTERMED has changed their practice, enhanced interdisciplinary communication, speeded up specialists' consultations, and improved staff satisfaction. A primary care (home practitioner or general practitioner) project has been initiated in a lower socioeconomic area of the city of Utrecht, the Netherlands, with a high level of uninsured persons; here the aim is to have a better idea of their specific treatment needs. A European multi-center outcome prediction study in transplant patients is currently underway; its aim is to evaluate the benefits of an implementation of the INTERMED in this complex field. In the United States, interest in the INTERMED has been raised on the level of health plans, pharmacy monitoring, and primary care.

HOW TO KNOW MORE ABOUT THE INTERMED

The manual with the clinical anchor points is now available in English, French, German, Dutch, Italian, Spanish, and Turkish. The English, French, German, and Dutch versions were developed in close collaboration with the founders of the INTERMED project. Subsequently, the Italian, Spanish, and Turkish versions were developed according to the professional standard of forward and blind backward translations. These manuals can be printed from the following website: www.INTERMEDfoundation.org. A Japanese version is in process of validation. Multi-language, web-based clinical and training facilities are in development to support clinical practice and (multi-center) research. This information technology application includes a medical problem list, the option to enter the clinical data collected during the interview in addition to the scoring, and the option to detail the treatment plan. Related to these data entry facilities are report functions, including a letter function in which the information is presented as it is organized in the case-vignette of Mr Glover, described earlier.

FUTURE DEVELOPMENT

The INTERMED method provides a conceptual framework and a basis for operationalizing effective and integrated multidisciplinary treatment targeted at the complex medically ill. As such, it is relevant for health care providers, policy-makers, hospital managers, insurance companies and, most important, for complex patients with psychosocial comorbidities that may diminish response to medical treatments. Preliminary results of ongoing randomized trials confirm the benefits of implementing the INTERMED and driving a multidisciplinary treatment plan based on its results. There are still many steps to take to make the INTERMED method more accessible and to increase its implementation. For example, a web-based training using INTERMED interviews of simulated patients should help future users to learn how to use the method. We hope that the INTERMED project will foster a paradigm shift from a specialty-oriented to a patient-centered model of interdisciplinary care and enable comprehensive assessment and treatment of the complex medically ill, thus helping to fulfill the six aims and ten new rules as formulated by the IOM for the future of integrated care for the complex medically ill (2001).

References

Ansseau, M., Dierick, M., Buntinkx, F., Cnockaert, P., De Smedt, J., Van Den Haute, M. & Vander Mijnsbrugge, D. (2004). High prevalence of mental disorders in primary care. *Journal of Affective Disorders, 78*, 49–55.

Babyak, M. A. (2004). What you see may not be what you get: A brief, nontechnical introduction to overfitting in regression-type models. *Psychosomatic Medicine, 66*, 411–421.

Bazelon Center for Mental Health Law (2005). *Integration of primary care and behavioral health*. Report on a roundtable discussion of strategies for private health insurance. Washington, DC. Available online at: www.bazelon.org.

Beitman, B. D., Mukerji, V., Lamberti, J. W., Schmid, L., DeRosear, L., Kushner, M., Flaker, G. & Basha, I. (1989). Panic disorder in patients with chest pain and angiographically normal coronary arteries. *American Journal of Cardiology, 63*, 1399–1403.

Berkman, B., Walker, S., Bonander, E. & Holmes, W. (1992). Early unplanned readmissions to social work of elderly patients: Factors predicting who needs follow-up services. *Social Work in Health Care, 17*, 103–119.

Boenink, A. D. & Huyse, F. J. (1997). Arie Querido (1901-1983), a Dutch psychiatrist. His views on integrated health care. *Journal of Psychosomatic Research, 43*, 551–557.

Browne, G. B., Arpin, K., Corey, P., Fitch, M. & Gafni, A. (1990). Individual correlates of health service utilisation and the cost of poor adjustment to chronic illness. *Medical Care, 28*, 43–58.

Ciechanowski, P. S., Katon, W. J. & Russo, J. E. (2000). Depression and diabetes: Impact of depressive symptoms on adherence, function, and costs. *Archives of Internal Medicine, 160*, 3278–3285.

Covinsky, K. E., Fortinsky, R. H., Palmer, R. M., Kresevic, D. M. & Landefeld, C. S. (1997). Relation between symptoms of depression and health status outcomes in acutely ill hospitalized older persons. *Annals of Internal Medicine, 126*, 417–425.

Crocker, L. & Algina, J. (1991). *Introduction to classical and modern test theory*. New York: Holt, Rinehart & Winston.

Demyttenaere, K., Bruffaerts, R., Posada-Villa, J., Gasquet, I., Kovess, V., Lepine. J. P., Angermeyer, M. C., Bernert, S., de Girolamo, G., Morosini, P., Polidori, G., Kikkawa, T., Kawakami, N., Ono, Y., Takeshima, T., Uda, H., Karam, E. G., Fayyad, J. A., Karam, A. N., Mneimneh, Z. N., Medina-Mora, M. E., Borges, G., Lara, C., de Graaf, R., Ormel, J., Gureje, O., Shen, Y. C., Huang, Y. Q., Zhang, M. Y., Alonso, J., Haro, J. M., Vilagut, J., Bromet, E. J., Gluzman, S., Webb, C., Kessler, R. C., Merikangas, K. R., Anthony, J. C., Von Korff, M. R., Wang, P. S., Alonso, J., Brugha, T. S., Aguilar-Guixola, S., Lee, S., Heeringa, S., Pennell, B. E., Zaslavsky, A. M., Ustun, T. & Chatterji, S. (2004). Prevalence, severity, and unmet need for treatment of mental disorders in the World Health Organization World Mental Health Surveys. *Journal of the American Medical Association, 291*, 2581–2590.

Druss, B. (2006). Foreword. In F. J. Huyse & F. C. Stiefel (Eds.), Integrated care for the complex medically ill, *Medical Clinics of North America* (special issue). Philadelphia: Elsevier.

Egede, L. E. (2004a). Diabetes, major depression, and functional disability among U.S. adults. *Diabetes Care, 27*, 421–428.

Egede, L. E. (2004b). Effects of depression on work loss and disability bed days in individuals with diabetes. *Diabetes Care, 27*, 1751–1753.

Endicott, J., Spitzer, R. L., Fleiss, J. L. & Cohen, J. (1976). The global assessment scale. A procedure for measuring overall severity of psychiatric disturbance. *Archives of General Psychiatry, 33*, 766–771.

Engel, G. L. (1977). The need for a new medical model: A challenge to biomedicine. *Science, 196*, 129–136.

Feinstein, A. R. (1999). Multi-item "instruments" vs. Virginia Apgar's principles of clinimetrics. *Archives of Internal Medicine, 159*, 125–128.

Fink P. (1990). Mental illness and admission to general hospitals: A register investigation. *Acta Psychiatrica Scandanavia, 82*, 458–462.

Fink, P., Hansen, M. S., Sondergaard, L. & Frydenberg, M. (2003). Mental illness in new neurological patients. *Journal of Neurology, Neurosurgery and Psychiatry, 74*, 817–819.

Fischer, C. J., Stiefel, F. C., de Jonge, P., Guex, P., Troendle, A., Bulliard, C., Huyse, F. J., Gaillard, R. & Ruiz, J. (2000). Case complexity and clinical outcome in diabetes mellitus: A prospective study using the INTERMED. *Diabetes Metabolism, 26*, 295–302.

Goldman, H. H., Rye, P. & Sirovatka, P. (2000). *A report of the surgeon general*. Washington, DC: DHHS.

Gordon, M. (1994). *Nursing diagnosis: Process and application* (3d ed.). Philadelphia: Elsevier.

Hansen, M. S., Fink, P., Frydenberg, M., Oxhoj, M., Sondergaard, L. & Munk-Jorgensen, P. (2001). Mental disorders among internal medical inpatients: Prevalence, detection, and treatment status. *Journal of Psychosomatic Research, 50*, 199–204.

Haynes, R. B., Taylor, D. W. & Sackett, D. L. (1979). *Compliance in health care*. Baltimore: Johns Hopkins University Press.

Hoogervorst, E. L. J., de Jonge, P., Huyse, F. J. & Polman, C. H. (2003). The INTERMED: A screening instrument to identify multiple sclerosis patients in need of multi-disciplinary treatment. *Journal of Neurology, Neurosurgery and Psychiatry, 74*, 20–24.

Horn, S. D. (1981). Validity, reliability and implications of an index of patient severity of illness. *Medical Care, 19*, 354–359.

Hirschfeld, R. M., Keller, M. B., Panico, S., Arons, B. S., Barlow, D., Davidoff, F., Endicott, J., Froom, J., Goldstein, M., Gorman, J. M., Marek, R. G., Maurer, T. A., Meyer, R., Phillips, K., Ross, J., Schwenk, T. L., Sharfstein, S. S., Thase, M. E. & Wyatt, R. J. (1997). The national depressive and manic-depressive association consensus statement on the undertreatment of depression. *Journal of the American Medical Association, 277*, 333–340.

Huyse, F. J. (1997). Editorial, From consultation to complexity of care prediction and health service needs assessment. *Journal of Psychosomatic Research, 43*, 233–240.

Huyse, F. J., Lyons, J. S., Stiefel, F. C., Slaets, J. P. J., Lobo, A., Guex, P., de Jonge, P., Fink, P., Gans, R. O., Guex, P., Herzog, T., Lobo, A., Smith, G. C. & van Schijndel, R. S. (1999). INTERMED: A method to assess health service needs. I. Development and first results on its reliability. *General Hospital Psychiatry, 21*, 39–48.

Huyse, F. J., de Jonge, P., Slaets, J. P., Herzog, T., Lobo, A., Lyons, J. S., Opmeer, B. C., Stein, B., Arolt, V., Balogh, N., Cardoso, G., Fink, P. & Rigatelli, M. (2001a). COMPRI—An instrument to detect patients with complex care needs: Results from a European study. *Psychosomatics, 42*, 222–228.

Huyse, F. J., Lyons, J. S., Stiefel, F. C., Slaets, J. P. J., de Jonge, P. & Latour, C. (2001b). Editorial, Operationalizing the biopsychosocial model. The INTERMED. *Psychosomatics, 42*, 5–13.

Huyse, F. J. & Stiefel, F. C. (Eds.) (2006). Integrated care for the complex medically ill, *Medical clinics of North America* (special issue). Philadelphia : Elsevier.

Institute of Medicine (IOM) (2001). *Crossing the quality chasm: A new health system for the 21st century.* Washington DC: National Academies Press.

Institute of Medicine (IOM) (2006). *Improving the quality of health care for mental and substance use conditions: Quality chasm series.* Washington, DC: National Academies Press.

Jacobson, P. B., Donovan, K. A., Trask, P. C., Fleishman, S. B., Zabora, J., Baker, F. & Holland, J. C. (2005). Screening for psychological distress in ambulatory cancer patients. *Cancer, 103*, 1494–1502.

Johnson, J., Weissman, M. M. & Klerman, G. L. (1992). Service utilization and social morbidity associated with depressive symptoms in the community. *Journal of the American Medical Association, 267*, 1478–1483.

Jones, P. W., Baveystock, C. M. & Littlejohns, P. (1989). Relationships between general health measured with the sickness impact profile and respiratory symptoms, physiological measures, and mood in patients with chronic airflow limitation. *American Review of Respiratory Diseases, 140*, 1538–1543.

de Jonge, P., Huyse, F. J., Slaets, J. P., Herzog , T., Lobo, A., Lyons, J. S., Opmeer, B. C., Stein, B., Arolt, V., Balogh, N., Cardoso, G., Fink, P., Rigatelli, M., van Dijck, R. & Mellenbergh, G. J. (2001a). Care complexity in the general hospital: Results from a European study. *Psychosomatics, 42*, 204–212.

de Jonge, P., Huyse, F. J., Herzog, T., Lobo, A., Slaets, J. P., Lyons, J. S., Opmeer, B.C., Stein, B., Arolt, V., Balogh, N., Cardoso, G., Fink, P. & Rigatelli, M. (2001b). Risk factors for complex care needs in general medical inpatients: Results from a European study. *Psychosomatics, 42*, 213–221.

de Jonge, P., Huyse, F. J., Stiefel, F. C., Slaets, J. P. J. & Gans, R. (2001c). INTERMED—A clinical instrument for biopsychosocial assessment. *Psychosomatics, 42*,106–109.

de Jonge, P., Latour, C. & Huyse, F. J. (2002). Inter-rater reliability of the INTERMED in a heterogeneous somatic population. *Journal of Psychosomatic Research, 52*, 25–27.

de Jonge, P. & Stiefel, F. C. (2002). Internal consistency of the INTERMED in patients with somatic diseases. *Journal of Psychosomatic Research, 54*, 497–499.

de Jonge, P., Bauer, I., Huyse, F. J. & Latour, C. H. (2003a). Medical inpatients at risk of extended hospital stay and poor discharge health status: Detection with COMPRI and INTERMED. *Psychosomatic Medicine, 65*, 534–541.

de Jonge, P., Latour, C. & Huyse, F. J. (2003b). Implementing psychiatric interventions on a general medical ward: Effects on patients' quality of life and length of hospital stay. *Psychosomatic Medicine, 65*, 997–1002.

de Jonge, P., Ruinemans, G. M. F., Huyse, F. J. & Ter Wee, P. M. (2003c). A simple risk score predicts poor quality of life and non-survival at one year follow-up in dialysis patients. *Nephrology Dialysis Transplantation, 18*, 2622–2628.

de Jonge, P., Hoogervorst, E. L. J., Huyse, F. J. & Polman, C. H. (2004). INTERMED: Temporal stability in a sample of MS patients. *General Hospital Psychiatry, 6*, 147–152.

de Jong, P., Huyse, F. J., Slaets, J. P., Sollner, W. & Stiefel, F. C. (2005). Operationalization of biopsychosocial case complexity in general health care: The INTERMED project. *Australian and New Zealand Journal of Psychiatry, 39*, 795–799.

de Jonge, P., Huyse, F. J. & Stiefel, F. C. (2006). Case and care complexity in the medically ill. In F. J. Huyse & F. C.Stiefel (Eds.), Integrated care for the complex medically ill, *Medical Clinics of North America* (special issue). Philadelphia: Elsevier.

Kathol, R. G., McAlpine, D., Kishi, Y., Spies, R., Meller, W., Bernhardt, T., Eisenberg, S., Folkert, K. & Gold, W. (2005). General medical and pharmacy claims expenditures in users of behavioral health services. *Journal of General Internal Medicine, 20*, 160–167.

Katon, W. J., VonKorff, M., Lin, E. & Lipscomb, P. (1990). Distressed high utilizers of medical care. DSM-III-R diagnoses and treatment needs. *General Hospital Psychiatry, 12*, 355–362.

Katon, W. J. (2003). Clinical and health services relationships between major depression, depressive symptoms, and general medical illness. *Biological Psychiatry, 54*, 216–226.

Kessler, L. G., Burns, B. J., Shapiro, S., Tischler, G. L., George, L. K., Hough, R. L., Bodison, D. & Miller, R. H. (1987). Psychiatric diagnoses of medical service users: Evidence from the epidemiologic catchment area program. *American Journal of Public Health, 77*, 18–24.

Kessler, D., Lloyd, K., Lewis, G. & Gray, D. P. (1999). Cross sectional study of symptom attribution and recognition of depression and anxiety in primary care. *British Medical Journal, 318*, 436–439.

Kessler, R. C., Ormel, J., Demler, O., Stang, P. E. (2003). Comorbid mental disorders account for the role impairment of commonly occurring chronic physical disorders: Results from the National Comorbidity Survey. *Journal of Occupational and Environmental Medicine, 45*, 1257–1266.

Koch, N., Stiefel, F., de Jonge, P., Fransen, J., Chamot, A. M., Gerster, J. C., Huyse, F. J. & So, A. K. (2001). Identification of case complexity and increased health care utilization in patients with rheumatoid arthritis. *Arthritis & Rheumatism, 45*, 216–221.

Kroenke, K., Spitzer, R. L., Williams, J. B. W. (2001). The PHQ-9; Validity of a brief depression severity measure. *Journal of General Internal Medicine, 16*, 606–613.

Kroenke, K., Spitzer, R. L., Williams, J. B. (2003). The patient health questionnaire–2: Validity of a two-item depression screener. *Medical Care, 41*, 1284–1289.

Latour, C. H. M., de Vos R., Huyse F. J., de Jonge, P., van Gemert, E. A. M. & Stalman, W. A. B. (2006). Effectiveness of post-discharge case management in general medical outpatients; randomized controlled trial. *Psychosomatics, 47*, 421–429.

Leigh, H., Feinstein, A. R. & Reiser, M. F. (1980). The patient evaluation grid: A systematic approach to comprehensive care. *General Hospital Psychiatry, 2*, 3–9.

Ludman, E. J., Katon, W., Russo, J., Von Korff, M., Simon, G., Ciechanowski, P., Lin, E., Bush, T., Walker, E. & Young, B. (2004). Depression and diabetes symptom burden. *General Hospital Psychiatry, 26*, 430–436.

Ludwig, G., Michaud, L., Berney, S., Amann, S., Skacel, J., Lobo, E., Ferrari, S., de Jonge, P., Stiefel, F. & Söllner, W. (2005). The biopsychosocial screening of transplant patients by means of the INTERMED. *Journal of Psychosomatic Research, 59*, 38.

Luthi, F., Deriaz, O., Stiefel, F., Roth, C., Russell, A., Gobelet, C. & Rivier, G. (under review). Biopsychosocial "case complexity" and treatment outcome after musculoskeletal injuries: A prospective study utilizing the INTERMED.

Lyons, J. S., Howard, K. I., O'Mahoney, M. T. & Lish, J. D. (1997). *The measurement and management of clinical outcomes in mental health*. New York: Wiley.

Nunnally, J. (1976). *Psychometric theory*. New York: Wiley.

Nurcombe, B., Gallagher, R. M. (1986). *The clinical process in psychiatry: Diagnosis and management planning*, Chs. 14, 15, 19. Cambridge, UK: Cambridge University Press.

Penn, J. V., Boland, R., McCartney, J. R., Kohn, R. & Mulvey, T. (1997). Recognition and treatment of depressive disorders by internal medicine attendings and housestaff. *General Hospital Psychiatry*, *19*, 179–184.

Plesk, P. E. & Wilson, T. (2001). Complexity, leadership, and management in healthcare organizations. *British Medical Journal*, *323*, 746–749.

Polsky, D., Doshi, J. A., Marcus, S., Oslin, D., Rothbard, A., Thomas, N. & Thompson, C. L. (2005). Long-term risk for depressive symptoms after a medical diagnosis. *Archives of Internal Medicine*, *165*, 1260–1266.

Regier, D. A., Narrow, W. E., Rae, D. S., Manderscheid, R. W., Locke, B. Z. & Goodwin, F. K. (1993). The de facto U.S. mental and addictive disorders service system. Epidemiologic catchment area prospective 1-year prevalence rates of disorders and services. *Archives of General Psychiatry*, *50*, 85–94.

Rimes, K. & Salkovskis, P. (2000). Health screening programs. In M. G. Gelder, J. J. Lòpez-Ibor & N. C. Andreasen (Eds.), *New Oxford textbook of psychiatry*. New York: Oxford University Press.

Saravay, S. M. & Lavin, M. (1995). Psychiatric comorbidity and length of stay in the General Hospital. A critical review of outcome studies. *Psychosomatics*, *3*, 233–252.

Silverstone, P. H. (1996). Prevalence of psychiatric disorders in medical inpatients. *Journal of Nervous and Mental Disorders*, *184*, 43–51.

Stiefel, F. C., de Jonge, P., Huyse, F. J., Guex, P., Slaets, J. P. J., Lyons, J. S., Spagnoli, J. & Vannotti, M. (1999). "INTERMED": A method to assess health service needs: II. Results on it validity and clinical use. *General Hospital Psychiatry*, *21*, 49–56.

Stiefel, F. C., Bel Hadj, B., Zdrojewski, C., Boffa, D., de Jonge, P., Dorogi, Y., Miéville, J. C., Ruiz, J. & So, A. (2004). A randomised psychiatric intervention in complex medical patients: Effects on depression. *Journal of Psychosomatic Research*, *56*, 578–579.

Trzepacz, P. & Dimartini, A. (2000). *The transplant patient. Biological, psychiatric and ethical issues in organ transplantation*. Cambridge, UK: Cambridge University Press.

Wagner, E., Austin, B. & VonKorff, M. (1996). Organizing care for patients with chronic illness. *Milbank Quarterly*, *74*, 511–544.

Wells, K. B., Miranda, J., Bauer, M. S., Bruce, M. L., Durham, M., Escobar, J., Ford, D., Gonzales, J., Hoagwood, K., Horowitz, S., Lawson, W., Lewis, L., McGuire, T., Pincus, H., Scheffler, R., Smith, W. & Unutzer J. (2002). Overcoming barriers to reducing the burden of affective disorders. *Biological Psychiatry*, *52*, 655.

Wilson, T. & Holt, T. (2001). Complexity and clinical care. *British Medical Journal*, *323*, 685–688.

Appendix 15.1

INTERMED Variables and Their Clinical Anchor Points

Note:

1. The INTERMED assesses complexity. Complexity is defined as interference with standard care by coexisting conditions, be they biological, psychological, social, or concerning the health care system, which require a shift from standard care to individualized care. Whenever a variable is rated, in addition to the clinical anchor points as defined below, one should keep in mind this question: "Will this information result in interferences with the standard care?"

2. All variables of History concern a time frame of the last 5 years. There is one exception; the variable Psychiatric Dysfunctioning. This variable covers a lifetime perspective.

BIOLOGICAL HISTORY

Chronicity[1]

0   Less than 3 months of physical dysfunctioning

1   More than 3 months of physical dysfunctioning or several periods of less than 3 months

2   A chronic disease

3   Several chronic diseases

Diagnostic Dilemma

0   No periods of diagnostic complexity

1   Diagnoses and the aetiology was clarified quickly

2   Diagnostic dilemma solved, but only with considerable diagnostic effort

3   Diagnostic dilemma; not solved despite considerable diagnostic efforts

---

[1]A good indicator for chronic illness is chronic use of drugs; psychopharmaca use excluded.

CURRENT BIOLOGICAL STATE

Severity of Symptoms

0   No symptoms or symptoms reversible without intensive medical efforts

1   Mild but notable symptoms, which do not interfere with current functioning

2   Moderate to severe symptoms, which interfere with current functioning

3   Severe symptoms leading to inability to perform any functional activities

Diagnostic Challenge

0   Clear diagnosis

1   Clear differential diagnosis

2   Complex differential diagnosis, in which a diagnosis from a biological perspective is to be expected

3   Complex differential diagnosis, in which no diagnosis is to be expected from a biological perspective

PSYCHOLOGICAL HISTORY

Restrictions in Coping

0   No restrictions in coping: ability to manage stress adequately, no impairment of medical treatment

1   Mild restrictions in coping, which causes mild to moderate distress in patient and/ or relatives or health care providers (such as complaining behavior)

2   Moderate restrictions in coping, which causes severe emotional distress in patients and/or relatives or health care providers (such as aggressive behavior or substance abuse without negative biopsychosocial effects) and/or impairment of medical treatment (such as prolonged denial)

3   Severe limitations in coping, which produces serious psychiatric symptomatology (such as substance abuse with negative biopsychosocial effects, self-mutilation or attempted suicide) and impairment of medical treatment

Psychiatric Dysfunction

0   No psychiatric dysfunction

1   Psychiatric dysfunction without clear effects on daily functioning

2   Psychiatric dysfunction with clear effects on daily functioning

3   Psychiatric admission(s) and/or permanent effects on daily functioning

CURRENT PSYCHOLOGICAL STATE

Resistance to Treatment

0   Interested in receiving treatment and willing to cooperate actively

1   Some ambivalence though willing to cooperate with treatment

2   Considerable resistance, such as noncompliance, hostility, or indifference towards health care professionals

3   Active resistance against medical care

Psychiatric Symptoms

0   No psychiatric symptoms

1   Mild psychiatric symptoms, such as problems concentrating or feeling tense

2   Psychiatric symptoms, such as anxiety, depression, or confusion

3   Psychiatric symptoms with behavioral disturbances, such as violence or self-inflicting behavior

SOCIAL HISTORY

Restrictions in Integration

0   A job (including housekeeping, retirement, studying) and having leisure activities

1   A job (including housekeeping, retirement, studying) without leisure activities

2   At least 6 months unemployed, with leisure activities

3   At least 6 months unemployed, without leisure activities

Social Dysfunctioning

0   No social disruption

1   Mild social dysfunctioning, interpersonal problems

2   Moderate social dysfunctioning, such as incapability of initiating or maintaining social relations

3   Severe social dysfunctioning, such as involvement in disruptive social relations, or social isolation

CURRENT SOCIAL STATE

Residential Instability

0   Stable housing situation, fully capable of independent living

1   Stable housing situation with support of others, such as an institutional setting or home care

2   Unstable housing situation, change of current living situation required

3   Unstable housing situation, immediate change required

Restrictions of network[2]

0   Good contacts with family, work, and friends

1   Restrictions in one of the domains

2   Restrictions in two of the domains

3   Restrictions in three of the domains

HISTORY of HEALTH CARE

Intensity of Treatment

0   Less than 4 contacts with physicians per year

1   4 or more contacts with physicians per year or one specialist

2   Different specialists or an admission

3   Several hospitalizations or stay on intensive care, complex surgery or rehabilitation unit

---

[2]Persons with sickness leave are scored as working. Those with disability compensation are scored as having no work. Those who study and those with unpaid labor are scored as having labor.

Treatment Experience

0   No problems with health care professionals

1   Negative experience with health care providers (self or relatives)

2   Requests for second opinions or changing contacts with doctors

3   Repeated conflicts with doctors, or involuntary admissions

CURRENT STATE OF HEALTH CARE

Organization of Care

0   One specialist (general health care or mental health care)

1   Different specialists from the general health care system

2   Both general and mental health specialists

3   Transfer from another hospital

Appropriateness of Referral

0   Regular referral or planned admission

1   Unplanned referral or emergency admission

2   Able to plan a strategy for treatment, yet not capable to provide optimal care

3   Unable to plan a strategy for treatment

PROGNOSES

Complications and Life-Threat

0   No limitations in activities of daily living

1   Mild limitations in activities of daily living

2   Chronic condition and/or permanent substantial limitations in activities of daily living

3   Severe physical complications and functional deficits, serious risk of dying

Mental Health Threat

0   No psychiatric disorder

1   Mild psychiatric disorder, such as adjustment disorder, anxiety, feeling blue, sub-
    stance abuse or cognitive disturbance

2   Moderate psychiatric disorder requiring psychiatric care

3   Severe psychiatric disorder requiring psychiatric admission

Social Vulnerability

0   No changes in the living situation, no additional care needs

1   No changes in the living situation, but additional home (nursing) care or social
    work facilities

2   Temporary admission to facility/institution

3   Permanent admission to facility/institution

Coordination of Health Care[3]

0   No problems in the organization of care

1   Minor efforts needed to organize care: multidisciplinary care which is easy to
    organize

2   Moderate efforts to organize care: multidisciplinary care which is difficult to
    organize

3   Severe efforts needed to organize care: need for case conference and/or coordination
    of care

---

[3]This item is rated taking the organization of the current health care system in account

Appendix 15.2

Leading Questions for the INTERMED Interview

Leading questions for the INTERMED interview:

1. Now, first of all, I would like to better understand how you feel physically?

2. I will tell you what I know about the reason for your admission and your current state. You should correct me when I am wrong.

3. Now I would like to know how you felt emotionally during the last week?

4. I would like to have some more information concerning physical illnesses and treatments in the past five years.

5. Who have been the doctors who have been taking care for you in the last five years?

6. Have you ever seen a psychiatrist in your life or have there been periods that you have been anxious, depressed, or confused?

7. Now who are the doctors, nurses, social workers, or psychologists who you are currently seeing and who take care for you?

8. Have there been issues with doctors during the last five years, which gave you a bad feeling to such an extent that it might interfere with your trust in doctors?

9. I would like to know how you follow your doctor's recommendations. Are you a person who is, generally speaking, inclined to do what doctors say?

10. Now I would like to change the subject and ask you how you currently live?

11. Now I would like to know what kind of person you are. Generally speaking, are you an easygoing person?

12. Now, coming to the end of the interview, I would like to ask you about your smoking and drinking habits and their relation to the current problems?

13. Do you think we missed any pertinent information?

14. Finally, I would like to know how you have experienced this interview. Do you think that this will be helpful information or did you think this was inappropriate?

Chapter 16

Use of the CANS-SD in the Treatment and Management of Juvenile Sexual Offenders

by John A. Hunter, Ph.D. and Keith Cruise, M.L.S., Ph.D.

INTRODUCTION

The effective management of juvenile sexual offenders continues to represent a challenge for mental health and legal professionals across the country. On a case-by-case basis, critical disposition and intervention decisions must be made that not only potentially affect the lives of the adjudicated youth and his family, but also his victim(s) and the public at large. Legally, there are issues of dangerousness and risk for reoffending that must be considered in determining whether the youth should be committed to corrections or managed in the community or an alternative residential environment. Clinically, treatment plans must be formulated and benchmarks developed for assessing treatment progress. The effective management of the population therefore requires an overall understanding of the nature of juvenile sexual offending—the motivations of youth who engage in sexually abusive behavior, and their developmental and psychiatric characteristics. Furthermore, professionals working in the field must have at their disposal decision-support tools to help them systematically evaluate individual youth and determine their specific intervention and level-of-care needs. This chapter provides a review of the clinical research literature on the characteristics of juvenile sexual offenders and the process and methods of their clinical evaluation. The Child and Adolescent Needs and Strengths—Sexual Development (CANS-SD) (Lyons, 2001) tool is discussed as a new assessment tool to help formulate comprehensive and effective clinical and legal management plans.

BACKGROUND

Offense Characteristics and Legal Trends

Each year, juveniles account for approximately one-fifth of arrests for rape in the United States and about one-fourth of arrests for other sexual crimes (excluding prostitution)(Uniform Crime Report, 2001). The majority of offenses are committed by adolescent males, although adolescent females and prepubescent children of both sexes have been identified as engaging in sexually abusive behaviors. Adolescent females represent about 2 percent of arrests for rape and 8 percent of arrests for child sexual molestation (Uniform Crime Report, 2001). While some prepubescent children have been observed as engaging in sexually abusive behaviors, youth within this age group are generally less likely to be prosecuted except in cases of flagrant and aggressive sexual offending.

Juvenile-perpetrated violent crime, including sexual offending, peaked in the mid-1990s and has been in decline since then. As discussed by Hunter and Lexier (1998), this rise in serious juvenile crime provided impetus for an array of new legislation designed to "get tough" on juvenile crime and hold juvenile offenders more accountable within the judicial system. Substantive changes were made in legal statutes, or regulatory policy, in over 90 percent of the states. This reform included change related to the following: juvenile court waivers, sentencing guidelines, record confidentiality, community notification, registration requirements for sex offenders, and correctional programming. The number of delinquency cases waived to the adult criminal courts increased by 44 percent between 1985 and 2002 (OJJDP, 2005). In general, imposed sanctions within the juvenile court system have become more severe. As an example, the number of adjudicated delinquency cases resulting in formal probation increased by 103 percent between 1985 and 2002, and the number of adjudicated cases resulting in residential placement increased by 44 percent (OJJDP, 2005). At the end of the 2003 legislative session, thirty-two states required adjudicated juveniles to register as sex offenders under Megan's Law. Only seven of these states exempted juveniles from community notification laws (Szymanski, 2003).

The above trend toward tougher sanctions represents a major shift in legal policy from the early 1980s, when juvenile sexual offender work first began. During the early years of clinical practice, in many communities across the country, the courts were reluctant to become involved in all but the most serious cases of juvenile sexual offending. After passage of the new legislation, clinicians were faced with having to make recommendations to the courts that had far-reaching legal and clinical consequences.

Etiological and Developmental Considerations

Clinicians have had a long-standing interest in understanding the developmental antecedents of sexually abusive behavior in juveniles, as insight into these developmental processes offers guidance on the development of both effective intervention and prevention programming. Much of the study of the etiology of juvenile sexual offending has centered on the role of prior child maltreatment, including both physical and sexual abuse experiences. A reported history of physical abuse has been found in 20 to 50 percent of sampled adolescent sexual offenders, and of sexual abuse in approximately 40 to 80 percent (Hunter, Figueredo et al., 2004; Worling, 1995; Kahn & Chambers, 1991). In contrast, approximately 5 to10 percent of the normal (non-offender) population of males in the United States were sexually victimized as children (Finkelhor, 1994). Rates of physical abuse and sexual victimization have been found to be even higher in samples of prepubescent and female youths who have engaged in sexually abusive behaviors (Gray et al., 1997; Matthews et al., 1997). Research suggests that age of onset, number of incidents of abuse, period of time elapsing between the abuse and first report of it, and perceptions of familial response to awareness of the abuse are all relevant in understanding why some sexually abused youths go on to sexually perpetrate and others do not (Hunter & Figueredo, 2000).

Hunter and Figueredo (2000) found that male youths who cycled from childhood sexual victimization experiences to adolescent sexual perpetration were distinguished from those who did not on the basis of four characteristics: (1) they were younger than the comparison group at the time of first sexual victimization; (2) they were sexually abused more frequently; (3) they waited a longer period of time to report the abuse to others; and (4) they perceived their families as being less supportive of them after they divulged their victimization. These findings are consistent with theory and clinical observation that the younger the youth at the time of psychological trauma, and the more extensive and severe the trauma, the greater is its potential negative developmental impact (Trickett et al., 1997; Nelson & Carver, 1998; Black & DeBlassie, 1993). Furthermore, the findings regarding the importance of early intervention and family support parallel those from other studies of child sexual abuse and maltreatment (Kendall-Tackett et al., 1993).

The influence of maltreatment experiences is thought to be multifaceted and may include effects related to both posttraumatic stress disorder (PTSD) and modeling (Freeman-Longo, 1986; Kendall-Tackett et al., 1993). PTSD symptomatology has been observed in a number of youths with sexual behavior disorders—especially children (under age thirteen) and females. These symptoms include recurrent and intrusive recollections of the traumatic event and increased psychophysiological arousal (e.g., irritability and outbursts of anger). Youths who have directly experienced or witnessed sexual abuse may imitate the behavior of the role model(s) in their interactions with others. Hunter et al. (2003) found that 75 percent of the sample of adolescent male sexual offenders reported a history consistent with sexual abuse; 63 percent reported a history of physical abuse by a father or stepfather. Reported nonviolent sexual abuse by a non-relative male was associated with sexual perpetration against a male child. Reported physical abuse by a father or stepfather was associated with depression and anxiety.

In addition to maltreatment experiences, study of etiology has focused on the effects of exposure to domestic violence and male-modeled antisocial behavior. Hunter et al. (2003) found that 75 percent of the referenced sample of adolescent male sexual offenders reported having witnessed a male relative beat a female; observation of males engaging in illegal and antisocial behavior was reported by 90 percent of these youth. Nearly one-half of the youth in the study had viewed a male relative threaten another male with a weapon. Exposure to violence toward females was found to be associated with psychosocial deficits and engagement in non-sexual violence and delinquency. In a subsequent analysis, it was also found to be associated with reduced emotional empathy (Hunter et al., 2007). Observation of male-modeled violent and antisocial behavior was associated with higher dominance scores and engagement in non-sexual violence and delinquency. Other etiological influences studied include exposure to pornography and substance abuse (Ford & Linney, 1995).

Psychiatric Characteristics

Adolescent males and females who engage in sexually abusive behavior have been found frequently to manifest other forms of psychological and emotional maladjustment in addition to their psychosexual disorder. Depression and anxiety appear to be particularly prevalent in populations of such youth. An array of mood disorders are manifest in samples of studied teenage male perpetrators, including dysthymic disorder, major depression, bipolar disorder (both Type I and II), ADHD, learning disabilities, and conduct disorder. One study (Fago, 2003) found evidence that 82 percent of studied adolescent male sexual offenders in community-based programming met diagnostic criteria for ADHD or showed evidence of other neurodevelopmental disorders associated with deficits in executive function. Furthermore, 44 percent of this sample of youth had documented histories of a specific learning disability or showed evidence of school failure. Nearly one-half of juvenile sex offenders in community-based programming have been found to meet diagnostic criteria for conduct disorder (Kavoussi et al., 1988). This rate is likely to be even higher in residential samples. The detected high prevalence of general conduct disorder in these youth is supported by observation that non-sexual recidivism rates in these youth are typically two to four times higher than sexual recidivism rates (Becker, 1998). Thus, these youth often engage in a variety of antisocial behaviors, and intervention and deterrence programming must be holistically focused to be effective.

Rates of psychiatric comorbidity are even higher in samples of adolescent female sexual offenders. Matthews and colleagues (1997) found that over one-fourth of the female sexual offenders in a mixed sample of community-based and residentially treated youth had a substance abuse problem, nearly one-fourth were learning disabled, and one-third had a history of being a runaway. Nearly 40 percent had experienced suicidal ideation or made a suicide attempt, and over 70 percent had previously received mental health treatment. Especially prevalent in residential samples of juvenile female sexual offenders are mood disturbances and PTSD. In a recent survey of residentially placed adolescent females with sexual behavior problems, over 90 percent had an affective disorder diagnosis, and over 53 percent a diagnosis of PTSD (Hunter & Lexier, 2003). These psychiatric diagnoses are consistent with the previously discussed extensive maltreatment and exposure to violence experiences of many of these youth during their childhood and early adolescence. As discussed by Hunter et al. (2006), these experiences often appear to be the focus of recurrent nightmares and intrusive thoughts and may engender self-injurious behavior and aggressive and sexual acting-out. Like their adolescent male counterparts, many of these females also meet diagnostic criteria for conduct disorder and ADHD and have engaged in other forms of delinquent and antisocial behavior, such as lying, stealing, and physical assault. Prepubescent youth who have engaged in sexually abusive behavior likewise show high incidences of these comorbid psychiatric disorders.

Heterogeneity of the Populations

Each population of adolescent (male and female) and prepubescent youth who engage in sexually abusive behavior reflect considerable intragroup diversity. Hunter and colleagues are conducting ongoing research directed at identifying and understanding salient subtypes of adolescent male sexual offenders. Initial research has focused on comparing youth who sexually offended against a peer or adult female with those who target children. The former group was found less likely to be related to the victim and to commit the offense in the victim's home or their own residence, as opposed to another setting. They were more likely to have been arrested for a non-sexual crime and to use force, and a higher level of force, than offenders of children. Additionally, they were more likely to use a weapon in the commission of the sexual offense and to be under the influence of alcohol or drugs at the time of the offense (Hunter et al., 2003).

Subtypes of Adolescent Male Offenders. In his current research, Hunter is exploring three prototypic subtypes of adolescent male sexual offenders: (1) life-course persistent (LCP) youth, (2) adolescent-onset/non-paraphilic youth, and (3) early adolescent-onset/non-paraphilic youth. This research builds on Moffitt's (1993) typology research and explores hypothesized differences between the identified groups on psychological and offense characteristics, amenability to treatment, and risk of sexual and non-sexual recidivism.

Consistent with Moffitt's theoretical predictions, the first group is believed to represent youth who begin to engage in oppositional and aggressive behaviors early in life and continue such behavior into adolescence and adulthood. They are like Moffitt's LCP group in that they are believed to possess underlying character pathology (i.e., psychopathy and impulsivity) that fuels antisocial behavior. However, those that sexually offend against peer or adult females are believed also to score high on the construct of hostile masculinity. This construct represents a negative, pejorative view of females as controlling and rejecting and has been found to predict sexual aggression (Malamuth, 1998).

The second prototypic subtype, adolescent onset/non-paraphilic, describes youth who engage in transient sexual offending. Their behavior is thought to stem from either adolescent experimentation or deficits in social competency that impair their ability to form and maintain healthy, age-appropriate relationships. It is hypothesized that the majority of these youth sexually offend against prepubescent or same-age females. Their prognosis is believed to be good if they do not become ensnared in drug and alcohol abuse or negative peer affiliations.

Early adolescent onset/paraphilic youth are believed to be in the process of developing, or to have already developed, pedophilia, or a pronounced and sustained sexual interest in and arousal to children. Thus, the sexual offending of this group of youth is thought to primarily emanate from deviant sexual interests and arousal. Based on previous research (Hunter et al., 1994; Hunter & Becker, 1994; Marshall et al., 1991) suggesting an earlier age of onset to same gender pedophilia, it is predicted that these youth will have more prepubescent male victims than the above two subtypes. Furthermore, and by virtue of the chronic nature of this disorder, these youth are believed to be at higher risk for continued sexual offending into adulthood.

Preliminary research supports the presence of the described subtypes in samples of adolescent male sexual offenders in corrections-based treatment programs. Prospective research is underway to assess whether hypothesized differences between subtypes on offense characteristics, treatment response, and longer-term psychosexual adjustment are confirmed.

Subtypes of Female Sexual Offenders. As discussed by Hunter and colleagues (2006), the relatively low numbers of adolescent female sex offenders found in clinical and legal settings limit the conduct of large-scale and more formal typology research on the population. Hypothesized differences amongst these youth primarily stem from clinical impression. Matthews et al. (1997) have offered a description of three groups of adolescent female sexual offenders seen in clinical settings. The first is termed naïve/experimenters and consists of youth who have engaged in limited sexual offending and who have not used physical force or threat in the commission of their offenses. As implied, these youth appear to be devoid of major psychopathology or sexual maladjustment and, instead, appear to have engaged in transient sexual offending out of curiosity and naiveté. A number of these girls seem rather fearful or anxious about sexuality, but as a group they do not appear to be at high risk for continued sexual acting-out or antisocial behavior.

The second group represents those who have engaged in more extensive sexual behavior with one or more children. Many of these girls have a preceding history of sexual victimization or were observed as sexually offending during a period wherein they were being sexually victimized. Thus in many cases, the perpetrating behavior of these youth parallel their own victimization experiences. These adolescent females typically manifest a higher level of psychopathology than the first subtype and typically have few age-appropriate sexual experiences. Depression and identity disturbances are particularly common, as are family dysfunction and conflict. As noted by Hunter et al. (2006), the treatment prognosis for these youth is generally good; however, their treatment needs are more extensive and complex than those in the first subtype.

The third group of adolescent female sexual offenders Matthews et al. (1997) describe have more chronic, and greater, psychosexual and psychiatric disturbances. Not only is their sexual offending longer-standing, and at times involving multiple victims, but they often meet diagnostic criteria for conduct disorder, PTSD, and/or major affective disorders. In addition to mood regulatory and impulse control problems, a number of these girls manifest thought disturbances and have histories of intermittent psychosis. Their developmental histories are marked by a higher level of trauma and upheaval than the first two subtypes, and their course of treatment is longer and more complicated. Medical management typically plays a prominent role in the treatment of these youth, and it may require inpatient or residential placement.

Sexually Aggressive Prepubescent Youth. Limited study has been conducted in support of the development of a typology of sexually aggressive prepubescent youth. The most comprehensive to date was conducted by Pithers and colleagues (1998), whose research focused on male and female children between ages six and twelve who had exhibited problematic sexual behaviors. The researchers used theory-driven cluster analysis to identify five subtypes: (1) sexually aggressive, (2) nonsymptomatic, (3) highly traumatized, (4) rule breaker, and (5) abuse reactive. The sexually aggressive subtype had an overrepresentation of males, the highest percentage of children with a diagnosed conduct disorder, and the greatest percentage who engaged in highly aggressive sexual misbehavior. Furthermore, the sexually aggressive children manifested the lowest trait anxiety of any child type and showed the poorest response to sex offender-specific treatment.

ROLE OF ASSESSMENT IN INTERVENTION PLANNING

Assessment provides a foundation for intervention planning and helps establish critical benchmarks for the subsequent evaluation of attained treatment progress. Thus, conducted assessments must be both comprehensive and holistic and include an evaluation of the youth's amenability to treatment and required intensity of care. Such assessments should also identify salient treatment goals and objectives, and provide an estimation of the youth's risk for sexual and non-sexual reoffending. To avoid legal and ethical complexity (see Hunter & Lexier, 1998, for a full discussion of these issues), it is generally recommended that the initial psychosexual assessment not be focused on issues of innocence or guilt, and be conducted post-adjudication and before sentencing. In addressing the specified areas of focus, it is recommended that assessments include evaluation and/or measurement of the following domains: the youth's and family's acceptance of his responsibility for the sexual misbehavior, the youth's motivation for change and willingness to cooperate with clinical and legal directives, the youth's intra- and interpersonal functioning, and the cultural and community influences on his behavior. Each of the referenced assessment domains are briefly reviewed below.

Multidisciplinary Approach

Effective management of juvenile sexual offenders requires the coordinated, and preferably integrated, effort of legal and clinical professionals. Coordination should begin with the assessment process. Court agents can facilitate a youth's and family's cooperation with an evaluating mental health provider by providing them with an understanding of the purpose of the assessment and how the court will use the information the assessment generates. Probation and parole officers can play a more direct role in pre- and post-adjudication evaluations, including participating in the interviewing of youth and families and the administration of risk and needs assessment instruments. Some model community-based programs have specially trained probation and parole officers who participate in joint in-home assessments of youth and families with the clinical professionals (Hunter, Gilbertson et al., 2004). Probation and parole officers are an integral part of the clinical team in such programs, and they help formulate recommendations to the court regarding the youth's service needs. Parole officers can also play an important role in preparing for a youth's return to the community following residential placement. This includes participating in treatment team meetings before the youth is discharged from the facility, administering risk and needs assessment instruments to the youth in support of discharge planning, and helping to determine the most appropriate living environment for the youth upon his return to the community.

Accountability for Sexual Offense

Most clinicians agree that a youth's acceptance of responsibility for his sexual offending behavior and his stated willingness to comply with treatment directives are prerequisites for successful completion of sex offender-specific treatment programs. Research supports the belief that youth who are steeped in denial are more likely to be noncompliant with therapeutic directives and to fail to successfully complete prescribed programs (Hunter & Figueredo, 1999). Denial may be linked to adjudication status, with adjudicating youth tending to show less denial than youth not under court supervision. Acceptance of responsibility for offense is closely linked to sexual attitudes and cognitions, and may reflect overall personality adjustment and capacity for empathy.

While a youth's full acceptance of responsibility for behavior is a primary treatment goal, it should be remembered that it is common for youth to be in full or partial denial at the time of initial evaluation. Evaluating clinicians should help them and their families understand the importance of acknowledging the behavior and should try to identify any barriers to doing so. This includes exploring the parents' attitudes about the offense and their willingness to support the youth in a full disclosure of events surrounding the offense. The evaluator must take into consideration cultural and peer group influences. Clinical experience has shown that it is unusual for a youth to remain in denial when his parents are fully supportive of disclosure. Such parental support helps allay anxiety about familial rejection for acknowledging the offending behavior. Assessment in this domain typically relies on the clinical interview and record review, although there are some psychometric measures, such as the Multiphasic Sex Inventory-II (Nichols & Molinder, 2007), that tap into attitudes of denial and minimization.

Intrapersonal Functioning

The intrapersonal domain includes an offender's personality and psychosexual interests and attitudes. Assessment of an offender's manifest level of psychopathy and tendency to disregard social norms is critical to this assessment. How willing is the youth to use aggression to resolve interpersonal conflicts and gratify needs? What is the youth's mood and level of social self-esteem; for example, is there

Table 16.1
Domain-Specific Assessment Measures

Interpersonal Functioning

- *Youth Self-Report* (overall personality functioning) (see Achenbach & Dumenci, 2001)
- *Antisocial Process Screening Device* (youth psychopathy) (see Frick & Hare, 2001)
- *Adolescent Sexual Interest Cardsort* (sexual interests) (see Hunter et al., 1995)
- *Adolescent Cognition Scale* (distorted sexual cognitions) (see Hunter, Becker, Kaplan, & Goodwin, 1991))
- *Multiphasic Sex Inventory-II* (adolescent male and female versions) (Nichols & Molinder Assessments, Inc., 2007)

Intrapersonal Functioning

- *Family Adaptation and Cohesion Scales-III* (family adaptability and cohesion) (see Olson, 1986)
- *Parenting and Peer-Affiliation Scales* (see Loeber et al., 1998)

evidence of depression or social anxiety and avoidance? There should also be a focused assessment of the youth's sexual interests and attitudes, including whether there is the presence of paraphilic sexual arousal and interests and negative, stereotypic attitudes toward females that the offender believes justify the use of sexual coercion or force. Assessment in this realm typically consists of a combination of record review, clinical interviewing, and psychometric assessment. The latter includes both measures of overall personality functioning and measures specific to relevant personality constructs (e.g. psychopathy) and psychosexual interests and attitudes. Table 16.1 provides examples of instruments in this assessment domain.

Interpersonal Functioning

The interpersonal domain includes the youth's family system and living environment, and his peer affiliations and relationships. Understanding these influences is important to both treatment and discharge planning. Many youth come from families in which antisocial, violent, and abusive behavior is modeled by paternal figures. Marital strife may be high and there may be few positive socialization experiences. Some youth lack effective social skills and positive self-esteem and are socially isolative. Others identify and affiliate with negative and delinquent peers. Either condition may increase the risk of reengagement in sexual and non-sexual delinquent behavior, making assessment in this domain critical to understanding the youth's intervention needs. As with intrapersonal functioning, assessment in this realm includes a combination of record review, clinical interviewing, and administration of focused psychometric instruments like the ones listed in Table 16.1.

Cultural and Community Influences

A youth's behavior is influenced not only by family and peer relationships, but by larger cultural and community influences. Culture helps shape a male's sense of masculinity, his sexual attitudes and values, and his approach to interpersonal conflict. The community environment in which he lives may or may not afford ample opportunity for positive socialization, vocational/educational, and recreational pursuits. Unfortunately, there are few measures that help clinicians evaluate cultural and community influences on a youth's behavior, so clinicians must primarily rely on interviews of the youth and his family to glean an understanding of these issues.

Risk for Reoffending

Risk assessment of juvenile sexual offenders is in its relative infancy. There are several validated actuarial measures for assessing risk for sexual reoffending and violence in adult males, but no measures presently exist in the juvenile sexual offender field that permit statistical calibration of risk for sexual reoffending. While research is underway, the development of actuarial risk assessment measures for juveniles is complicated by virtue of low base rates of sexual reoffending in the population. Such low rates make it difficult to empirically establish reliable and valid predictors of reoffense risk. Secondly, data show that juvenile sex offenders generally have higher rates of rearrest and conviction for general delinquency than for sexual offending per se (see Righthand & Welch, 2001; Caldwell, 2002). Furthermore, most of the convictions for general delinquency are for nonviolent crime. This suggests that assessment of risk in juvenile sexual offenders must take into consideration risk for general delinquency as well as for sexual and violent crime—with the latter being difficult to reliably predict.

Evidence suggests that specialized treatment reduces risk for future sexual offenses (Bourdin & Schaeffer, 2001; Worling & Curwen, 2000). Worling and Curwen (2000) reported recidivism data comparing a small sample of adolescent offenders who completed twelve months of treatment with a comparison sample who did not complete treatment. Recidivism rates for treated offenders (5.2 percent sexual, 18.9 percent violent non-sexual, and 20.7 percent nonviolent) were lower than for nontreated offenders (17.8 percent sexual, 32.2 percent violent non-sexual, and 50.0 percent nonviolent). Unfortunately, this research did not identify which specific risk factors were reduced through the treatment process. Further, this study used broad categories (i.e., treated versus nontreated) that ignored the heterogeneity found among sexually offending youth. As noted earlier, current research by Hunter and colleagues suggests it may be possible to identify unique subtypes of juvenile sex offenders based on a combination of offense, background, and personality factors. Furthermore, it is thought that these subtypes reflect differential offense risk trajectories and levels of amenability to treatment (see Hunter, Figueredo et al., 2003; Hunter, Figueredo et al., 2004). Such research has potential implications for the design of risk assessment measures.

Risk assessment for reoffending typically involves identifying an overall level of risk as well as the presence of specific risk factors that increase the likelihood of an identified negative outcome. The field recently has made advancements in this area (see Miner, 2002; Prentky et al., 2000; Witt et al., 2003; Worling, 2004; Worling & Curwen, 2000) through the development of specialized risk assessment instruments that are modeled after the structured professional judgment approach (see Borum, 2000; Borum et al., 2005). This approach involves the systematic review and coding of risk factors that have demonstrated an empirical association with relevant external criteria (e.g., general or sexual recidivism). The new generation of adolescent risk assessment instruments (e.g., the Juvenile Sex Offender Assessment Protocol II, or J-SOAP-II, and the Estimate of Risk of Adolescent Sexual Offense Recidivism, or ERASOR) typically includes a combination of static (historical) and dynamic (proximal short-term states, or stressors, that are contextual and/or amenable to change) factors. Benefits of these instruments include anchored risk ratings that promote consistent coding across raters, and organization of risk factors into static and dynamic scales. Assessors can organize risk-relevant information into scales that describe the history and severity of past behavior problems, and factors that may attenuate or exacerbate a youth's risk of reoffending. However, these instruments are limited by a dearth of independent research regarding their construct and predictive validity. Furthermore, they lack scoring schemes by which to prioritize treatment targets and generally do not permit the comprehensive review of mental health, family, and environmental factors that require therapeutic attention.

Needs Assessment

In addition to risk assessment, the comprehensive evaluation of juvenile sexual offenders should involve assessment of their overall intervention needs. This includes a review of pertinent parameters of individual and family functioning, taking into consideration the impact of ecological (environmental) factors and circumstances. As such, needs assessment should encompass consideration of the nature of the youth's sexual behavior problem, his other manifest psychiatric and substance abuse problems, his family system, and his supervisory needs. Ideally, needs assessment should identify both strengths and weaknesses/needs in the youth, his family, and ecological systems. As to the latter, professionals should aim to develop intervention plans that capitalize on individual and family competencies and maximize existent environmental supports. Research suggests that intervention models that emanate from an understanding of social-ecological and family system issues (e.g. multi-systemic therapy) produce superior clinical outcomes with delinquent and behaviorally disordered youth (Henggeler et al., 2006).

Case Management. For adjudicated youth, needs assessment should play an integral role not only in clinically conducted psychosexual evaluations, but in the development of probation and parole case management plans. The latter form the basis of the legal supervision of the youth and can include special terms or conditions of probation or parole that help minimize the risk of sexual recidivism. Needs assessment should be viewed as a continuous endeavor, with treating clinicians and supervising probation and parole officers conducting periodic reviews of the youth's progress in treatment and attainment of specific treatment goals. Conducted in this manner, more formal and systematic needs assessment can provide guidance in the revision and updating of treatment and case management plans based on professional observation and new assessment data.

Discharge Planning. It is especially important to conduct formal needs assessment in support of discharge planning. Not surprisingly, many youth experience difficulty transitioning from structured residential treatment environments to community-based care. Even those who have done well in residential care and have successfully completed court-prescribed programs sometimes flounder and regress when faced with the demands and temptations of living in the community. As such, it is imperative that discharge planning be based on a thorough review and careful consideration of the youth's individual strengths and needs, and available familial and environmental supports. In this regard, conceptualization of a plan for the youth's successful community reentry should not be limited to a review of his intra-psychic problems, but should include an understanding of the multiple systemic influences on his behavior. In particular, it should reflect an understanding of the interrelatedness of his sexual behavior problem with his other emotional, behavioral, and educational/vocational issues and needs. The discharge plan should therefore be holistic and broadly focused. An inadequately construed or poorly implemented discharge and aftercare plan places the youth at heightened risk for treatment failure.

Determining the most appropriate living environment for the youth is a critical element of needs assessment and post-residential discharge planning. Many youth cannot return to their families and homes of origin for a multitude of reasons. These may include the presence of a victim (or potential victim) in the home and the continuing risk of emotional or physical harm to that person, family dysfunction/conflict, inadequate supervision, and the youth's chronological age and related educational/vocational programming needs. Circumstances may necessitate the availability of alternative placements such as therapeutic foster/group homes and independent living programs. The latter are especially appropriate for youth who are eighteen years or older when they complete a residential program and need help with attaining an independent living status. Placement usually involves help finding a job or vocational training and the teaching of life skills (budgeting money, using public transportation, and the like.). Again, needs assessment should play a pivotal role in identifying the youth's aftercare needs and the most optimal environment for his post-discharge placement.

The Child and Adolescent Needs and Strengths—Sexual Development (CANS-SD) assessment instrument, discussed below, is a new generation, juvenile sex offender-specific needs assessment tool. It was designed to provide a comprehensive, ecologically sensitive, and holistic assessment of the intervention needs of youth with manifest sexual behavior problems. As such, it offers considerable promise as a tool that can aid clinicians, court officers, and social services workers in critical treatment planning and disposition decision-making.

THE CANS-SD INFORMATION INTEGRATION TOOL

The CANS-SD (Lyons, 2001) is one of several needs assessment instruments that comprise the CANS system. As noted above, its overarching strength is its inclusion of individual, familial, and social-ecological dimensions that facilitate prioritization of treatment targets and intervention needs. Users familiar with the CANS-MH (Lyons, 1999) will find that the CANS-SD and CANS-MH are similar in terms of structure, items, and scoring format. The CANS-SD has been designed for use in developing service delivery plans for youth with identified sexual development and behavior problems. Here we provide an overview of the CANS-SD, highlighting its unique aspects and potential use in the comprehensive assessment of juvenile sexual offenders.

The CANS-SD is comprised of fifty items, organized into seven unique dimensions. All CANS-SD items use the same scoring format as those used with other CANS system instruments: 0 = no need for action; 1 = need for watchful waiting or monitoring; 2 = need for action; 3 = need for immediate or intensive action. Ratings of 2 or 3 on individual items are viewed as "actionable" items that warrant higher priority in terms of treatment planning (Lyons, 2001). The first three CANS-SD dimensions—functioning, risk behaviors, and mental health needs—resemble the first three dimensions of the CANS-MH and provide a review of individual needs related to the emotional and behavioral functioning of the youth. The next two dimensions—care intensity and organization, and caregiver capacity—provide a review of familial and social contextual needs that affect the level and intensity of the youth's treatment needs, and the family's capacity for responding to the same. Similar to other measures in the CANS system, the next CANS-SD dimension—strengths—provides a systematic review of relevant competencies of the youth, his family, and his social and spiritual/religious affiliations. The final CANS-SD dimension—characteristics of sexual behavior—is unique to the CANS-SD and includes ten items that communicate information about the history, type, frequency, and severity of problematic sexual behavior. Items on this domain allow users to better understand the nature of the youth's sexual behavior problem and identify treatment needs and issues related to past sexual victimization and prior specialized sexual offender treatment.

Uses of the CANS-SD

Used prospectively, the CANS-SD provides a common metric by which clinically relevant information can be communicated between treatment providers and legal personnel. As part of legal management planning, rating the CANS-SD post-adjudication and before legal disposition can provide valuable information to legal decision-makers in crafting a disposition strategy that includes placement decisions. For example, legal personnel such as juvenile probation/parole officers can review actionable items across all domains and initiate appropriate treatment referrals based on the identified intervention needs of the youth and family. Such decisions could be based on locally established minimum dimension thresholds, such as average dimension score and/or number of actionable items. Key problem areas that could impact supervision and/or response to supervision could also be identified (e.g., school functioning, crime/delinquency, monitoring, transportation).

Sex offender treatment providers can also use the CANS-SD prospectively to prioritize individual intervention efforts. For example, in establishing an initial treatment plan for a sexually offending youth, actionable items on "danger to self" and "depression/anxiety" items require immediate attention and intervention; that is, emotional instability and recent suicidal gestures/behavior would potentially place the youth in danger and interfere with his ability to engage in specialized sexual offender programming. Information about family strengths and support is often critical at the beginning of treatment, as this relates to the family's capacity to support specialized intervention and supervision. Treatment providers could also include readministration of the CANS-SD at regular intervals during the treatment process, so as to measure improvements in functioning and identify emerging treatment needs.

The CANS-SD can also be used retrospectively as a quality assurance and program development/evaluation tool. For example, retrospective chart reviews of prospectively completed CANS-SD profiles can be compared to patterns of delivered care to determine whether a youth's treatment needs were adequately addressed. Such reviews could also help determine whether measured changes in dimension and item functioning reflect commensurate changes in service delivery plans across time. Retrospectively reviewing CANS-SD profiles on an aggregate basis can also assist in identifying systemic service delivery gaps (see Anderson, 2003). For example, aggregating CANS-SD results across all youth served within a single system of care may identify gaps in service provision and promote the development of new services or intervention programs.

Psychometric Properties

Recently the authors conducted an archival, chart-review study to investigate the psychometric properties of the CANS-SD (Cruise et al., 2006). Intake mental health records and legal history information were reviewed on eighty adolescent male offenders who were court-ordered into a large secure custody facility following adjudication for a sexual offense. The youth ranged in age from thirteen to eighteen years (M = 15.54, SD = 1.37) at the time of admission. The sample was comprised of approximately the same percentage of Caucasian (51.3 percent) and African-American (45.0 percent) youth. CANS-SD profiles were coded by chart review, with a small subset of cases (n = 21) independently coded by two reviewers in order to establish inter-rater reliability. Basic psychometric properties were calculated and concurrent validity was investigated by comparing dimension scores to scales on the J-SOAP-II (Prentky & Righthand, 2003).

Results from this study suggested variable but acceptable reliability estimates. Dimension internal consistency (Cronbach's alpha) ranged from .45 to .70. Average corrected item-total correlations ranged from .24 to .41. These estimates reflect the heterogeneity of problems or needs organized under individual dimensions. The average item-total correlations indicate that CANS-SD items demonstrate an acceptable association with the overall dimension score. Inter-rater reliability was investigated by calculating intraclass correlation coefficients (ICC) and percentage agreement for each dimension. Intraclass correlations ranged from .73 to .88 across six of the seven dimensions. The exception was the "strengths" dimension, which had an average ICC of .42. Percentage agreement ranged from 64.9 percent to 84.1 percent across all dimensions. With the exception of the strengths dimension, all estimates of inter-rater reliability were acceptable and comparable to similar estimates found for the CANS-MH (see Anderson et al., 2003).

The concurrent validity of the CANS-SD was investigated by comparing average dimension scores, as well as the total number of actionable items per dimension, to static scales on the J-SOAP-II. Both scoring approaches resulted in statistically significant relationships between CANS-SD dimensions and conceptually similar J-SOAP-II scales. For example, the CANS-SD "characteristics of sexual behavior" dimension demonstrated significant positive correlations with the J-SOAP-II Sexual Drive Preoccupation scale (r = .62 and .58, across the two scoring approaches respectively). CANS-SD "functioning," "other risk behavior," and "mental health needs" all demonstrated significant positive associations with the J-SOAP-II Impulsive/Antisocial Behavior Scale (r ranging from .61 to .76 and .53 to .77, respectively). While preliminary, these results provide positive evidence of the CANS-SD's concurrent validity with an established risk assessment procedure designed for use with juvenile sexual offenders.

As noted above, the CANS-SD can provide guidance to clinicians, probation officers, and social services workers in the development of comprehensive treatment and management plans for individual youth. As adolescent male sexual offenders are a diverse and heterogeneous clinical population, we provide two case examples below that represent contrasting intervention needs.

PROSPECTIVE TREATMENT PLANNING—CASE EXAMPLE 1

Ralph is a fourteen-year-old male who was referred for psychosexual evaluation following adjudication for sexually molesting his six-year-old sister. The molestation occurred when Ralph was babysitting for his parents, who had gone out for the evening. The sexual molestation consisted of fondling and having his sister perform oral sodomy on him.

According to the sister's report, Ralph asked her if she wanted to play an "adult sex" game. When she hesitated, he allegedly called her a baby and said he was going to send her to bed early that evening. As further incentive, he told her that she could play with his *Game Boy* (electronic video game) if she complied with his request. Afterwards, he told her not to tell their parents and that if she did, he would deny it and never play with her again. Apparently, the sister kept the incident a secret for two weeks, but confided in their mother after the latter informed her that Ralph was going to baby-sit her again the coming weekend. Although shocked and confused, the parents eventually decided to report the incident to the police after consulting their pastor.

Ralph initially denied the allegation but confessed during the police interrogation. He told the police that he had heard friends talking about oral sex and had recently viewed a sex video depicting this and other sexual acts at a friend's house. He said, "I had been thinking about it (asking his sister to perform oral sex on him) for a couple of weeks—then just went ahead and did it when I had the chance." He went on to explain that he was very embarrassed by the incident and wished that he had never done it. However, he seemed to have little empathy for his sister and commented, "I'm sure she is o.k., she never has any real problems." Ralph's parents both work full time. Ralph generally provides after-school supervision for his sister until his parents return home around 6 p.m. He has also been baby-sitting on weekends for the past six months, and before the sexual abuse incident had spoken to his parents about offering baby-sitting services to neighbors. The family attends church on a regular basis and is active in many church-related activities.

Ralph's history is notable for diagnosis of a learning disability in reading at age eight and a 50 percent hearing loss in his left ear since birth. The latter necessitates wearing a hearing aid—something that he apparently is embarrassed about. His mother described him as a shy youth who never made friends easily. He apparently had never had a real "girlfriend," although he has talked from time to time about girls at school that he liked. Ralph has one or two male acquaintances with whom he occasionally socializes after school. However, he spends most of his time away from school playing with his *Game Boy* or watching television. According to his parents' report, he is generally behaviorally compliant at home and school. They did report that he has historically complained that he did not like school, and went through a period a few years earlier in which he resisted getting up in the morning to go to school. School records also indicate that he skipped school three times in the last year and has been absent or tardy on four occasions during the current semester. Ralph states that he likes to build things and shows some mechanical aptitude. He sometimes helps out his father, who operates a furniture repair shop. Ralph's CANS-SD results are shown below.

Scoring

Ralph's scores on the CANS-SD identified three actionable items: school (presence of a learning disability and school avoidance), relationship (evidence of clear sexual victimization of his sister), and age differential (Ralph was fourteen and his sister was six). In addition, a number of items scored a 1, indicating a mild degree of dysfunction. Scoring of the CANS-SD suggested that Ralph was a mildly developmentally delayed youth with a hearing impairment and learning disability. Furthermore, he showed evidence of social avoidance and anxiety and having difficulty forming age-appropriate peer relationships. These deficits may contribute to a sense of dysphoria, anger, and frustration. While his sexual acting-out appears serious enough to warrant intervention, it may be compensatory in nature. Overall, he appears to be a good candidate for

CANS-SD Results—Ralph

Functioning	0	1	2	3	U
Intellectual	X				
Developmental		X			
Physical/Medical		X			
Attachment					
Family		X			
School			X		
Risk Behaviors					
Danger to Self	X				
Violence	X				
Crime/Delinquency		X			
Runaway	X				
Social Behavior		X			
Mental Health Needs					
Psychosis	X				
Attention Deficit/Impulse	X				
Depression/Anxiety		X			
Anger Control		X			
Oppositional		X			
Antisocial	X				
Substance Abuse	X				
Adjustment to Trauma	X				
Care Intensity and Organization					
Monitoring		X			
Treatment		X			
Transportation	X				
Service Permanence	X				
Caregiver Capacity					
Physical/Behavioral Health	X				
Supervision		X			
Involvement with Care	X				

Knowledge		X		
Organization	X			
Resources	X			
Residential Stability	X			
Safety		X		
Strengths				
Family	X			
Interpersonal			X	
Relationship Permanence		X		
Educational			X	
Vocational		X		
Well-being			X	
Spiritual/Religious		X		
Talents/Interests		X		
Inclusion			X	
Characteristics of Sexual Behavior				
Relationship			X	
Physical Force/Threat	X			
Planning		X		
Age Differential				X
Type of Sex Act		X		
Response to Accusation		X		
Temporal Consistency of Behavior		X		
History of Sexually Abusive Behavior	X			
Severity of Sexual Abuse	X			
Prior Treatment	X			

community-based treatment. The CANS-SD profile would suggest that the intervention plan should address his monitoring needs and include a parental education component. Positively, the family appears to be loving and invested in the children. Furthermore, the family appears to receive social and spiritual support from their local church.

Assisted Disposition Planning

Ralph was placed on twelve months' community probation and referred to an outpatient juvenile sex offender treatment program. Arrangements were made for him to live with his maternal grandparents until significant progress had been made and it was deemed by the court, treating clinicians, social services, and family that it was safe for him to return home. The grandparents, who resided in the community, agreed to provide ongoing supervision and participate in his treatment. Arrangements were made for his sister to be evaluated at the local mental health center and provided with supportive counseling. Ralph's treatment includes individual and group therapy once a week, and family therapy once every two weeks. The treatment plan includes a focus on teaching social skills and the promotion of positive peer relations and social self-esteem. It also includes addressing his experienced social anxiety and underlying dysphoria. Family therapy sessions are initially to be conducted with Ralph, his parents, and his grandparents. The plan calls for his sister to join these sessions when she and her therapist feel that she is ready, and Ralph has progressed to the point that he is able to meaningfully apologize and read an "empathy letter" to her and the family. The initial focus of family therapy sessions will be on helping Ralph accept responsibility for his behavior and make a commitment to positive change. They will also be directed at educating Ralph and his parents about the nature of adolescent sexual behavior problems and their effective treatment and management. The latter will include identifying situations that would place Ralph at risk for future sexual offending (e.g., babysitting) and discussion of his emotional and social support needs.

Also addressed in the treatment plan is the need for alternative after-school supervision plans for both Ralph and his sister. It was decided that Ralph would participate in a variety of after-school programming that includes a one-day-per-week mentoring program offered by his church, a one-day-per-week community service program sponsored by the local juvenile court, and one afternoon per week helping out in his father's furniture shop. Arrangements were also made for private tutoring and school-based counseling, directed at helping him address his educational difficulties and issues that lead to school avoidance. The parents have made plans for an adult female friend of the family to provide after-school supervision for Ralph's sister. The developed plan is to be reviewed in three months and revised as needed.

PROSPECTIVE TREATMENT PLANNING—CASE EXAMPLE 2

Billy is a sixteen-year-old male who was referred for psychosexual evaluation following adjudication for sexually molesting two neighborhood boys, an eight-year-old and his six-year-old brother. The molestations occurred in Billy's house on four occasions over the course of six months. On the first occasion, Billy invited the youth in to watch a video while his parents were away and then proceeded to play a pornographic tape on the VCR. Billy told the youth that he would give them money and video games if they did to him what was shown on the tape. This molestation consisted of fondling and having the boys perform fellatio on him. On subsequent occasions, Billy fondled and orally sodomized the youth and attempted anal sodomy on the younger of the two brothers. Each time he would bribe the youth by giving them money, video games, and candy. He warned the boys not to tell anyone about the molestations and stated that they would all get in "a lot of serious trouble" if anyone found out. After the attempted anal penetration of the younger brother (which involved holding the child down), the boys told their parents. The parents then reported the matter to the police.

Billy initially denied the allegations but agreed to cooperate with police after talking with his parents. He admitted to police that he had planned the first and each subsequent molestation. He went on to say that he had initially targeted the two boys because they were new to the neighborhood and seemed "impressionable." He spoke of the sexual abuse in a matter-of-fact manner and did not express remorse or sensitivity to the potential harmful impact of his behavior on the children. A review of Billy's criminal record showed that he had been investigated, approximately one year earlier, for allegedly fondling a four-year-old boy for whom he had baby-sat. Billy had denied the allegation and no charges were filed, primarily because the child's parents were reluctant to have him testify in court. Billy's history is notable for his own sexual victimization at age three by a male baby-sitter. Apparently, there were several incidents of fondling and oral sodomy over a period of six to nine months. Billy apparently did not receive counseling for this victimization. Billy is in the eleventh grade and makes average to above average grades. He reportedly is not a behavior problem at school. While he gets along reasonable well with peers, he prefers to spend most of his time in solitary pursuits and is especially fond of video games and Internet "surfing." Billy lives with his mother, who works full time in a local restaurant as a cook. His parents divorced when he was three and he seldom sees his father. According to the mother, his father was an alcoholic and frequently beat both her and Billy.

Scoring

Billy's scores on the CANS-SD identified thirteen actionable items, including family (a history of child abuse, domestic violence, and divorce), treatment (indication of the need for daily parental care), supervision (the absence of consistent supervision because the mother is a single parent and works full time), resources (limited familial and social support resources), and safety (the present placement represents a moderate level of risk for the youth to get into trouble because of the absence of consistent parental monitoring). In addition, the characteristics of sexual behavior dimension scores suggest that Billy's sexual behavior problem is serious and long-standing in nature. This includes evidence that he has been clearly sexually abusive of more than one child, has engaged in well-planned acts of sexual abuse that were invasive and occasionally coercive, and shows little remorse for his behavior or empathy for his victims. Furthermore, there is evidence that he himself was severely sexually victimized as a young child and did not receive treatment or supportive counseling for it. Overall, these results suggest a moderate to high level of risk for sexual reoffending and the need for intensive treatment in a secure and structured environment.

Assisted Disposition Planning

Comprehensive psychosexual assessment of Billy confirmed that his sexual behavior problem was serious and relatively long-standing. In particular, interview and psychometric data indicated a sustained sexual interest in young male children. Billy acknowledged that he frequently fantasized about young males and was often sexually aroused in their presence. He reported a sexual interest in boys his own age, but stated that he had minimal sexual interest in females of any age. He also acknowledged having spent a considerable amount of time after school and on weekends searching on the Internet for sites that offered sexually provocative or explicit pictures of male children. He reportedly had been engaging in such behavior over the past two years.

Billy was given a suspended commitment to juvenile corrections and placed in a nearby twenty-four-hour residential treatment program for adolescent male sexual offenders. The placement decision was based on two things, the risk he represented for sexual recidivism in a community setting and the intensity of his treatment needs. The

CANS-SD Results—Billy

Functioning	0	1	2	3	U
Intellectual	X				
Developmental	X				
Physical/Medical	X				
Attachment					
Family			X		
School	X				
Risk Behaviors					
Danger to Self	X				
Violence	X				
Crime/Delinquency		X			
Runaway	X				
Social Behavior	X				
Mental Health Needs					
Psychosis	X				
Attention Deficit/Impulse	X				
Depression/Anxiety	X				
Anger Control	X				
Oppositional	X				
Antisocial	X				
Substance Abuse	X				
Adjustment to Trauma	X				
Care Intensity and Organization					
Monitoring		X			
Treatment			X		
Transportation	X				
Service Permanence	X				
Caregiver Capacity					
Physical/Behavioral Health	X				
Supervision			X		
Involvement with Care		X			
Knowledge		X			

Organization		X			
Resources			X		
Residential Stability	X				
Safety			X		
Strengths					
Family			X		
Interpersonal		X			
Relationship Permanence			X		
Educational		X			
Vocational				X	
Well-being		X			
Spiritual/Religious			X		
Talents/Interests			X		
Inclusion			X		
Characteristics of Sexual Behavior					
Relationship				X	
Physical Force/Threat			X		
Planning				X	
Age Differential				X	
Type of Sex Act				X	
Response to Accusation			X		
Temporal Consistency of Behavior		X			
History of Sexually Abusive Behavior			X		
Severity of Sexual Abuse				X	
Prior Treatment	X				

decision took into consideration the predatory nature of his sexual offending and his monitoring needs. The residential treatment plan places an emphasis on further assessing and treating his age-inappropriate (i.e. pedophilic) sexual interests and arousal. With confirmation of the diagnosis of pedophilia (nonexclusive), treatment is to include educating Billy and his mother about the nature of the disorder and its effective, long-term therapeutic management. Relapse prevention planning will stress the importance of avoiding situations, thinking patterns, and behaviors that place him at risk for future sexual offending (e.g., frequenting settings that cater to children) and the importance of forming age-appropriate social and sexual relationships. Billy will also receive therapeutic attention for his history of sexual victimization; this will include exploring its potential influence on his current behavior. The residential treatment plan also focuses on the development of a long-term educational and/or vocational plan for Billy, and stresses the importance of collaboration between the local court and residential facility in formulating an effective after-care plan. The latter would include intensive outpatient treatment, enrollment in a variety of age-appropriate social and vocational activities, and strict court monitoring and supervision.

RETROSPECTIVE PROGRAM REVIEW AND PLANNING

The CANS-SD can also provide guidance to system administrators and supervisors who review service delivery (e.g., quality assurance) and identify aggregate treatment needs presented by the youth served. As noted earlier, use of the CANS-SD in this manner involves conducting a retrospective review of prospectively completed CANS-SD aggregated across youth served within a system. As an example, aggregate CANS-SD results from the eighty CANS-SD profiles coded from the sample of adjudicated adolescent sexual offenders are noted on the table that follows (see Cruise et al., 2006). All CANS-SD profiles were coded based on intake information and therefore create an aggregate profile of the needs and strengths presented by this population.

Reviewing the CANS-SD results across each dimension provides the following information about the service delivery needs of this population. Within the functioning dimension, 62.4 percent (score of 2 or 3) of youth were identified with moderate to severe school-related problems. A smaller percentage was identified with intellectual (9.1 percent) and developmental (7.8 percent) issues. This pattern of results suggest that service planning for this population needs to address the behaviors that are compromising the youths' daily functioning in the school environment, with particular attention to the approximately 10 percent of youth who are likely in need of specialized educational services due to limited intellectual functioning or other developmental delays.

Review of the risk behaviors domain indicates that 62.3 percent of youth were identified with actionable needs related to violence and 79.2 percent with crime/delinquency needs. This level of endorsement is expected given the nature of the setting (e.g., secure custody juvenile facility). However, the high level of endorsement on the violence item indicates that the aggression identified by these youth has resulted in significant injury to others, therefore heightening the importance of supervision and monitoring in a closed treatment environment. It further suggests the need for quick implementation of aggression management strategies and clinical programming directed at impulse control and anger management.

Juvenile sex offenders have a variety of mental health needs, and the profile noted within the mental health needs dimension reflects this finding. Consistent with the risk behavior findings, 64.9 percent were identified with moderate to severe anger control problems; similar percentages of youth were identified on the antisocial (76.6 percent) and oppositional (53.2 percent) behavior items. The needs identified within this section also suggest that comprehensive service delivery should include substance abuse treatment services, as 39.0 percent of youth were identified with moderate to severe problems in this realm. Although less frequent, the presence of mood disturbance (11.7 percent) and attentional problems (9.1 percent) were also noted.

Disruptions in service delivery and family organization and engagement scores identified needs across both the care intensity/organization dimension and the caregiver capacity dimension. Reflecting the fact that youth in this sample were transferred to different juvenile justice institutions, 53.3 percent were identified as having recent

Percentage CANS-SD Endorsements

Functioning	0	1	2	3
Intellectual	61.0	29.9	9.1	0.0
Developmental	37.7	54.5	7.8	0.0
Physical/Medical	81.8	15.6	2.6	0.0
Attachment	83.1	6.9	0.0	0.0
Family	24.7	16.9	9.1	49.4
School	18.2	19.5	18.2	44.2
Risk Behaviors				
Danger to Self	67.5	24.7	7.8	0.0
Violence	27.3	10.4	59.7	2.6
Crime/Delinquency	2.6	18.2	64.9	14.3
Runaway	89.6	7.8	1.3	1.3
Social Behavior	36.4	18.2	45.5	0.0
Mental Health Needs				
Psychosis	94.8	3.9	1.3	0.0
Attention Deficit/Impulse	63.6	27.3	7.8	1.3
Depression/Anxiety	55.8	32.5	11.7	0.0
Anger Control	2.4	11.7	55.8	9.1
Oppositional	13.0	33.8	51.9	1.3
Antisocial	5.2	18.2	61.0	15.6
Substance Abuse	35.1	26.0	37.7	1.3
Adjustment to Trauma	85.7	9.1	5.2	0.0
Care Intensity and Organization				
Monitoring	3.9	79.2	15.6	1.3
Treatment	0.0	71.4	26.0	2.6
Transportation	97.4	2.6	0.0	0.0
Service Permanence	45.5	1.3	44.2	9.1
Caregiver Capacity				
Physical/Behavioral Health	74.0	16.9	6.5	2.6
Supervision	28.6	49.4	11.7	10.4
Involvement with Care	5.2	58.4	10.4	26.0

Continues on next page

Knowledge	27.3	23.4	29.9	18.2
Organization	37.7	23.4	33.8	5.2
Resources	58.4	39.0	1.3	0.0
Residential Stability	68.8	28.6	1.3	0.0
Safety	75.3	15.6	9.1	0.0
Strengths				
Family	1.3	68.8	27.3	2.6
Interpersonal	0.0	79.2	13.0	7.8
Relationship Permanence	11.7	14.3	70.1	3.9
Educational	2.6	6.5	44.2	46.8
Vocational	1.3	11.7	31.2	55.8
Well-being	0.0	58.4	39.0	2.6
Spiritual/Religious	0.0	50.6	37.7	11.7
Talents/Interests	3.9	2.4	70.1	2.6
Inclusion	15.6	5.2	41.6	37.2
Characteristics of Sexual Behavior				
Relationship	3.9	2.6	89.6	3.9
Physical Force/Threat	62.3	22.1	15.6	0.0
Planning	20.8	53.2	22.1	3.9
Age Differential	14.3	22.1	5.2	58.4
Type of Sex Act	16.9	27.3	54.5	1.3
Response to Accusation	6.5	31.2	23.4	39.0
Temporal Consistency of Behavior	1.3	85.7	11.7	1.3
History of Sexually Abusive Behavior	48.1	33.8	9.1	9.1
Severity of Sexual Abuse	70.1	22.1	3.9	3.9
Prior Treatment	71.4	5.2	0.0	23.4

disruptions in treatment service delivery. This result suggests that obtaining consistent collateral documentation on the type and quantity of past services will be difficult given the number of changes in service providers prior to admission. Notable findings from the caregiver capacity dimension are reflected in the percentage of actionable scores on the involvement with care, knowledge, and organization items (36.4, 48.1, and 38.2 percent, respectively, scored as actionable). These items suggest that treatment providers working with these youth can expect that at least one-third of the parents/legal guardians of the sexually offending youth may be difficult to engage in service planning, or will require education and assistance in understanding and meeting the service needs of the youth.

Strengths items are reverse-coded with lower scores denoting the item as a relative strength (score of 0 or 1). Identifying common strengths among a group of youth served within the same system of care is important for a number of reasons. First, adjunctive treatment services or activities can be designed that fit with the defined strengths of the majority of the youth. Second, building on and enhancing the protective and coping capacities of the population is consistent with social and ecological approaches to treatment (i.e., multi-systemic therapy) and helps fosters treatment engagement. Within the assessed sample, family (70.1 percent), interpersonal (79.2), and spiritual/religious (50.6 percent) strengths were noted.

A careful examination of the characteristics of sexual behavior dimension provides a clear description of the common sexual behavior problems presented by the offending youth. Approximately 90 percent were sexually abusing at least one other person, with over one-half (63.6 percent) involving a victim five years younger than the offender and penetrative acts (55.8 percent). Taken together, these findings suggest that the vast majority of victims were prepubescent children who were at heightened risk of trauma or injury related to the abuse. Consistent with prior research, 93.6 percent (score ≥ 1 on response to accusation) of the youth were noted as partially or completely denying involvement in the offense, which of course has important implications for treatment engagement. At the time of intake, 71.4 percent (score of 0 on prior treatment) had no record of receiving specialized intervention for problematic sexual behavior. Also consistent with previously cited research, approximately 30 percent (score ≥ 1 on severity of sexual abuse) of youth were noted to have been sexually victimized. The latter would suggest that treatment services should incorporate a trauma-focused intervention component.

SUMMARY AND DIRECTIONS FOR FURTHER ENHANCEMENT OF THE CANS-SD

The CANS-SD is a promising new needs assessment tool for use with youth with identified sexual behavior problems. The instrument can be used prospectively to aid in treatment and legal intervention planning, and retrospectively as a tool for conducting program evaluation and review. Like other CANS instruments, the CANS-SD reflects sensitivity to the importance of understanding a youth's intervention needs from a holistic, social-ecological perspective. In this regard, the instrument's focus extends beyond a youth's demonstrated sexual behavior problem and includes a review of his overall psychological, social, and physical functioning. Furthermore, the instrument is intended to encourage professionals to carefully assess the youth's environmental support and monitoring/supervision needs in the course of placement decision-making. Finally, the instrument reflects an understanding of the importance of assessing not only individual youth, but their families and caretakers, and of developing intervention plans that build on existent youth and familial strengths, talents, and interests.

Beyond its thoughtful construction, the CANS-SD offers a number of other helpful advantages to potential users. First, prior research with the CANS-MH suggests that both treatment and paraprofessionals can be trained to rate youth and families with an acceptable level of accuracy (see Lyons et al., 2004), with these results translating to the CANS-SD given the similar structure, items, and scoring on both instruments.

Thus, the instrument is user friendly, does not require extensive training to employ, and potentially gives professionals with different levels of training and background a common framework and metric for evaluating youth and families and discussing their intervention needs. Second, the CANS-SD lends itself to repeated measurement over time, so both service providers and quality assurance reviewers can gauge whether implemented treatment plans are adequate and when they are in need of revision. Third, data from the instrument can be viewed on an individual basis or in aggregate form. As previously discussed, the latter provides a basis for macro-level system of care review and service system planning.

Further Revision and Study

While the CANS-SD is comprehensive, versatile, and easy to use, the authors would like to identify areas where it may benefit from further study, and perhaps revision. The characteristics of sexual behavior dimension is helpful in identifying domains of offending behavior and psychosexual functioning that clinicians should evaluated. However, it should be noted that the identified domains are not exhaustive or inclusive of all relevant issues that require assessment. For example, the instrument does not direct clinicians to assess a youth's expressed sexual interests and attitudes. Thus there is no basis for evaluating whether the youth appears to be predominantly sexually interested in peers, younger children, or adults, or whether he may have distorted sexual cognitions that contribute to his sexual acting-out. As we discussed earlier, such considerations are important both diagnostically and in planning for the effective treatment and management of this population.

As it relates to perpetrator modus operandi, the instrument does not provide a firm basis for identifying how a youth may have approached or gained the cooperation of the victim—other than through physical force. Thus issues of bribery, trickery, and deception are not addressed. Other areas within this realm that receive little or no attention include parental attitudes about the offense and level of expressed support for the youth in addressing his demonstrated sexual behavior problem, degree of victim empathy (as distinguished from remorse), and pattern of sexual offending. The latter would include assessment of whether there was evidence of progression of the problem over time, as well as target victim characteristics (e.g., young boys).

Risk of Offending and Response to Treatment

Neither the characteristics of sexual behavior dimension as presently constructed, nor the CANS-SD in its entirety, provides an adequate basis for assessing either risk of sexual offending or response to sex offender-specific treatment. As to the former, users are advised to not confuse risk and needs assessment, but instead view them as separate and complimentary assessment endeavors. While the CANS-SD identifies some issues that have relevance in risk assessment (e.g., number of incidents and victims), it does not provide for a comprehensive and systematic review of all such dynamic and static factors. Nor is there a way to statistically quantify risk. The characteristics of sexual behavior dimension also does not provide for a comprehensive review of all issues related to evaluating a youth's response to treatment and readiness for step-down in level of care. For help in assessing risk of reoffending with juvenile sexual offenders, readers are encouraged to utilize the J-SOAP-II (Prentky et al., 2000) or ERASOR

Table 16.2
Guidelines for Assessing Readiness for Step-Down in Level of Care and Termination of Services

---

Criteria for "Step-down" in Level of Care or Supervision

- Youth (and parents where applicable) has attended all scheduled therapy sessions (except for excused absences) and has demonstrated a positive attitude toward treatment.

- Youth (and parents where applicable) has been fully compliant with therapeutic directives and is judged to be making good progress in the attainment of treatment goals.

- Youth acknowledges all sexual offenses of which he was convicted and takes full responsibility for his behavior.

- Youth appears remorseful for his sexual offending and has empathy for his victim(s).

- Youth has a well-developed relapse prevention plan and has a good understanding of his sexual offense cycle and high-risk factors. Offender has not engaged in high-risk behaviors or thinking patterns for a minimum of ninety days.

- Youth has been fully compliant with all court orders and terms/conditions of his probation/parole.

- In the case of residential placement, the youth has completed the treatment program in its entirety and has a viable aftercare plan. The latter should include a safe and supportive living environment and enrollment in follow-up outpatient therapy.

Criteria for Termination of Legal and/or Clinical Services

- Offender takes full responsibility for his sexual offending and acknowledges all behaviors for which he was convicted.
- Offender appears genuinely remorseful for his sexual offending and has empathy for his victim(s)
- Offender was fully cooperative with his therapist(s) and compliant with therapeutic directives.
- Offender successfully completed the prescribed treatment (and aftercare) program in its entirety.
- Offender understands his sexual offense cycle, including the thoughts, feelings, and events that lead to his sexual acting-out.
- Offender sufficiently understands his risk factors for re-offending, and can identify and successfully employ coping and management skills to maintain control over his behavior.
- All of the offender's psychiatric and behavioral problems were adequately addressed, and he displays overall emotional maturity and behavioral control.
- Offender was fully compliant with all legal directives and prohibitions.
- Offender's living environment is conducive to maintenance of control over his sexual behavior, and other psychiatric and behavioral problems (*Note:* Consider issues of structure/supervision and environmental distance from high-risk factors.).
- Offender is gainfully employed or enrolled in an educational/vocational program that offers the promise of developing competitive job skills.
- Offender has positive peer and familial relationships that support him in maintaining a healthy lifestyle and refraining from future sexual acting-out and delinquent behavior.

(Worling, 2004). For additional support in assessing response to treatment, and readiness for step-down in level of care or termination of services, readers are directed to the J-SOAP-II Clinical Intervention Scale and clinical guidelines developed by Cruise as shown in Table 16.2.

References

Achenbach, T. M. & Dumenci, L. (2001). Advances in empirically based assessment: Revised cross-informant syndromes and new DSM-oriented scales for the CBCL, YSR, and TRF: Comment on Lengua, Sadowski, Friedrich, and Fisher. *Journal of Consulting & Clinical Psychology*, *69*, 699–702.

Anderson, R. L. (2003). Use of community-based services by rural adolescents with mental health and substance use disorders. *Psychiatric Services*, *54*, 1339–1341.

Anderson, R. L., Lyons, J. S., Giles, D. M., Price, J. A. & Estes, G. (2003). Examining the reliability of the child and adolescent needs and strengths-mental health (CANS-MH) scale from two perspectives: A comparison of clinician and researcher ratings. *Journal of Child and Family Studies*, *12*, 279–289.

Becker, J. V. (1998). What we know about the characteristics and treatment of adolescents who have committed sexual offenses. *Child Maltreatment*, *3*, 317–329.

Black, C. A. & DeBlassie, R. R. (1993). Sexual abuse in male children and adolescents: Indicators, effects, and treatments. *Adolescence*, *28*, 123–133.

Borum, R. (2000). Assessing violence risk among youth. *Journal of Clinical Psychology*, *56*, 1263–1288.

Borum, R., Bartel, P. & Forth, A. (2005). Structured assessment of violence risk in youth. In T. Grisso, G. Vincent & D. Seagrave (Eds.), *Mental health screening and assessment in juvenile justice*. New York: Guilford.

Bourdin, C. M. & Schaeffer, C. M. (2001). Multisystemic treatment of juvenile sexual offenders: A progress report. *Journal of Psychology and Human Sexuality*, *13*, 25–42.

Caldwell, M. F. (2002). What we do not know about juvenile sexual reoffense risk. *Child Maltreatment*, *7*, 291–302.

Cruise, K. R., Hunter, J. A., Dandreaux, D. M., Marsee, M. A. & DePrato, D. K. (submitted for publication). Use of the child adolescent needs and strengths scale—sexual development (CANS-SD) in the comprehensive assessment of juvenile sex offenders.

Fago, D. P. (2003). Evaluation and treatment of neurodevelopmental deficits in sexually aggressive children and adolescents. *Professional Psychology: Research and Practice*, *34*, 248–257.

Finkelhor, D. (1994). Current information on the scope and nature of child sexual abuse. *Future of Children*, *4*, 31–53.

Ford, M. E. & Linney, J. A. (1995). Comparative analysis of juvenile sex offenders, violent nonsexual offenders, and status offenders. *Journal of Interpersonal Violence*, *10*, 56–70.

Freeman-Longo, R. E. (1986). The impact of sexual victimization on males. *Child Abuse and Neglect*, *10*, 411–414.

Frick, P. J. & Hare, R. D. (2001). *The antisocial process screening device*. Toronto: Multi-Health Systems.

Gray, A., Busconi, A., Houchens, P. & Pithers, W. D. (1997). Children with sexual behavior problems and their caregivers: Demographics, functioning, and clinical patterns. *Sexual Abuse: Journal of Research and Treatment*, *9*, 267–290.

Henggeler, S. W., Schoenwald, S. K., Swenson, C. C. & Bourdin, C. M. (2006). Methodological critique and meta-analysis as Trojan horse. *Children and Youth Services Review*, *28*, 447–457.

Hunter, J. A., Becker, J. V. & Kaplan, M. S. (1995). The adolescent sexual interest card sort: Test-retest reliability and concurrent validity in relation to phallometric assessment. *Archives of Sexual Behavior*, *24*, 555–561.

Hunter, J. A. & Becker, J. V. (1994). The role of deviant sexual arousal in juvenile sexual offending: Etiology, evaluation, and treatment. *Criminal Justice & Behavior*, *21*, 132–134.

Hunter, J. A., Becker, J. V., Kaplan, M. S. & Goodwin, D. W. (1991). The reliability and discriminative utility of the adolescent cognition scale for juvenile sexual offenders. *Annals of Sex Research*, *4*, 281–286.

Hunter, J. A., Becker, J. V. & Lexier, L. (2006). The female juvenile sex offender. In H. E. Barbaree & W.L. Marshall, *Juvenile Sex Offender*, 2d ed. New York: Guilford.

Hunter, J. A., Goodwin, D. W. & Becker, J. V. (1994). The relationship between phallometrically measured deviant sexual arousal and clinical characteristics in juvenile sexual offenders. *Behaviour Research & Therapy*, *32*, 533–538.

Hunter, J. A., Gilbertson, S. A., Vedros, D. & Morton, M. (2004). Strengthening community-based programming for juvenile sexual offenders: Key concepts and paradigm shifts. *Child Maltreatment*, *9*, 177–189.

Hunter, J. A. & Lexier, L.J. (1998). Ethical and legal issues in the assessment and treatment of juvenile sex offenders. *Child Maltreatment*, *3*, 339–348.

Hunter, J. A. & Lexier, J. J. (2003). *A survey of residentially treated juvenile female sexual offenders*. Unpublished manuscript.

Hunter, J. A. & Figueredo, A. J. (1999). Factors associated with treatment compliance in a population of juvenile sexual offenders. *Sexual Abuse*: *Journal of Research & Treatment*, *11*, 49–67.

Hunter, J. A. & Figueredo, A. J. (2000). The influence of personality and history of sexual victimization in the prediction of offense characteristics of juvenile sex offenders. *Behavior Modification*, *24*, 241–263.

Hunter, J. A., Figueredo, A. J., Malamuth, N. & Becker, J. V. (2004). Developmental pathways in youth sexual aggression and delinquency: Risk factors and mediators. *Journal of Family Violence*, *19*, 233–242.

Hunter, J. A., Figueredo, A. J. & Malamuth, N. M. (2003). Juvenile sex offenders: Toward the development of a typology. *Sexual Abuse*: *Journal of Research and Treatment*, *15*, 27–48.

Hunter, J. A., Figueredo, A. J., Malamuth, N. M. & Becker, J. (2007). Non-sexual delinquency in juvenile sexual offenders: The mediating and moderating influences of emotional empathy. *Journal of Family Violence*, *22*, 43–54.

Kahn, T. J. & Chambers, H. J. (1991). Assessing reoffense risk with juvenile sex offenders. *Child Welfare*, *70*, 333–345.

Kavoussi, R. J., Kaplan, M. & Becker, J. V. (1988). Psychiatric diagnoses in adolescent sex offenders. *Journal of the American Academy of Child and Adolescent Psychiatry*, *27*, 241–243.

Kendall-Tackett, K. A., Williams, L. M. & Finkelhor, D. (1993). Impact of sexual abuse on children: A review and synthesis of recent empirical studies. *Psychological Bulletin*, *113*, 164–180.

Loeber, R., Farrington, D. P., Stouthamer-Loeber, M., Moffitt, T. E. & Caspi, A. (1998). The development of male offending: Key findings from the first decade of the Pittsburgh youth study. *Studies on Crime & Crime Prevention*, *7*, 141–171.

Lyons, J. S. (1999). *Child and adolescent needs and strengths—Mental health manual.* Chicago: Buddin Praed Foundation.

Lyons, J. S. (2001). *Child and adolescent needs and strengths: An information integration tool for children and adolescents with issues of sexual development.* Chicago: Buddin Praed Foundation.

Lyons, J. S., MacIntyre, J. C., Lee, M. E., Carpinello, S., Zuber, M. P. & Fazio, M. L. (2004). Psychotropic medications prescribing patterns for children and adolescents in New York's public mental health system. *Community Mental Health Journal*, *40*, 101–118.

Malamuth, N. M. (1998). The confluence model as an organizing framework for research on sexually aggressive men: Risk moderators, imagined aggression, and pornography consumption.

In R.G. Geen & E. Donnerstein (Eds.), *Human aggression: Theories, research, and implications for social policy*. San Diego: Academic Press.

Marshall, W. L., Barbaree, H. E. & Eccles, A. (1991). Early onset and deviant sexuality in child molesters. *Journal of Interpersonal Violence, 6*, 323–335.

Matthews, R., Hunter, J. A. & Vuz, J. (1997). Juvenile female sexual offenders: Clinical characteristics and treatment issues. *Sexual Abuse: Journal of Research & Treatment, 9*, 187–199.

Miner, M. H. (2002). Factors associated with recidivism in juveniles: An analysis of serious juvenile sex offenders. *Journal of Research in Crime and Delinquency, 39*, 421–436.

Moffitt, T. E. (1993). Adolescence-limited and life-course-persistent antisocial behavior: A developmental taxonomy. *Psychological Review, 100*, 674–701.

Multiphasic sex inventory-II— adolescent male version (2007). Nichols and Molinder Assessments, Inc. Available online at www.nicholsandmolinder.com.

Nelson, C. A. & Carver, L. L. (1998). The effects of stress and trauma on brain and memory: A view from developmental cognitive neuroscience. *Development and Psychopathology, 10*, 793–809.

Office of Juvenile Justice and Delinquency Prevention (2005). *OJJDP statistical briefing book*. Washington, D.C.: U.S. Dept. of Justice, OJJDP.

Olson, D. H. (1986). Circumplex Model VII: Validation studies and FACES III. *Family Process, 25*, 337–351.

Pithers, W. D., Gray, A, Busconi, A. & Houchens, P., (1998). Children with sexual behavior problems: Identification of five distinct child types and related treatment considerations. *Child Maltreatment, 3*, 384–406.

Prentky, R. & Righthand, S. (2003). *Juvenile sex offender assessment protocol-II* (unpublished test manual).

Prentky, R., Harris, B., Frizzell, K. & Righthand, S. (2000). An actuarial procedure for assessing risk with juvenile sex offenders. *Sexual Abuse: A Journal of Research and Treatment, 12*, 71–93.

Righthand, S. & Welch, C. (March, 2001). *Juveniles who have sexually offended: A review of the professional literature*. Washington, DC: Office of Juvenile Justice and Delinquency Prevention.

Szymanski, L. (2003, update). *Megan's law: Juvenile sex offender registration age limits*. NCJJ Snapshot 8(5), Pittsburgh, PA: National Center for Juvenile Justice, 2003.

Trickett, P. K., Reiffman, A., Horowitz, L. A. & Putnam, F. W. (1997). Characteristics of sexual abuse trauma and prediction of developmental outcomes. In D. Cicchetti and S. L. Sheree (Eds.), *Developmental perspectives on trauma: Theory, research, and intervention*, vol. 8, 289–314, U. of Rochester Press.

Uniform Crime Report (2001). *Crime in the United States*. Washington, DC: U.S. Department. of Justice, Federal Bureau of Investigation. Available online at: http://www.fbi.gov/ucr/01 cius. htm.

Witt, P. H., Bosley, J. T. & Hiscox, S. P. (2003). Evaluation of juvenile sex offenders. *The Journal of Psychiatry & Law, 30*, 569–592.

Worling, J. R. (1995). Sexual abuse histories of adolescent male sex offenders: Differences on the basis of the age and gender of their victims. *Journal of Abnormal Psychology, 104*, 610–613.

Worling, J. R. (2004). The estimate of risk of adolescent sexual offense recidivism (ERASOR): Preliminary psychometric data. *Sexual Abuse: A Journal of Research and Treatment, 16*, 235–254.

Worling, J. R. & Curwen T. (2000). Adolescent sexual offender recidivism: Success of specialized treatment and implications for risk prediction. *Child Abuse & Neglect, 24*, 965–982.

Chapter 17

Treating Children with Traumatic Experiences: Understanding and Assessing Needs and Strengths

by Cassandra Kisiel, Ph.D.,
Margaret E. Blaustein, Ph.D., Jason Fogler, Ph.D.,
Heidi Ellis, Ph.D., and Glenn N. Saxe, M.D.

INTRODUCTION

Assessment of childhood trauma is a challenging task that must take into account the history of trauma exposures, current status and functioning of the child across a range of domains and diagnostic categories, the status and functioning of the caregiving system, and the larger social context. The complexity of presentation and needs of this population point to the utility of a comprehensive assessment instrument that can be used in a range of settings in a flexible manner.

This chapter describes the background and development of the Child and Adolescent Needs and Strengths—Trauma Exposure and Adaptation (CANS-TEA), an assessment tool designed to specifically address the range of adaptations and relevant contextual factors for children exposed to traumatic experiences. This comprehensive assessment strategy will be discussed in terms of the process of development, its clinical utility and application, and its ability to meet an important need in the field of child trauma.

NATURE OF THE PROBLEM: TRAUMA EXPOSURES AND OUTCOMES

The experience of trauma has historically been viewed as an overwhelming event falling "outside of the range of normal human experience" (DSM-III, 1980); however, epidemiological studies within the United States indicate that a significant number of children are at risk for exposure to potentially traumatic experiences. In epidemiological studies, as many as one in four children report previous exposure to high-magnitude stressors (e.g., Costello et al., 2002), and in one retrospective study surveying over 17,000 adults, over one-half of the respondents report having had at least one adverse childhood experience (Felitti et al., 1998).

The term "trauma" is used to encompass a wide range of stressful exposures extreme enough to elicit feelings of "fear, helplessness, or horror" (DSM-TR, 2000). Traumatic experiences may range from acute events, such as accidental injuries and natural disasters, to chronic, interpersonal exposures, such as childhood abuse and neglect or witnessed familial violence. These experiences vary widely in their circumstances, yet can be conceptualized in dichotomous terms: chronic versus acute time frame, events masked in secrecy versus those that are widely public, social support versus denial of experience, close relationship to perpetrator versus a stranger, early developmental onset versus later occurrence, and interpersonal versus natural or accidental exposure. Not surprisingly, the preponderance of evidence links chronic and/or multiple adverse experiences to earlier onset of difficulties and increasingly complex outcomes (van der Kolk et al., 2005).

Despite the multi-layered nature of trauma exposure and outcome, there remains only a single diagnosis designed specifically to capture the phenomenological aftermath of trauma. Posttraumatic stress disorder (PTSD), as defined in the DSM-IV (1994), involves exposure to a defined traumatic event and a constellation of three symptom clusters: reexperiencing of the event through intrusive thoughts, imagery, or behaviors; avoidance of traumatic reminders and/or numbing of emotions; and hyperarousal. Originally conceptualized to capture the constellation of symptoms displayed by combat veterans (e.g., Grinker & Spiegel, 1945), there is a growing awareness that PTSD fails to fully capture the array of difficulties experienced by survivors of trauma (Ballenger et al., 2000; Miller, 2003, 2004), particularly of early-onset, chronic, traumatic stress.

Adults diagnosed with PTSD rarely meet criteria for PTSD alone; rather they routinely meet criteria for other Axis I and Axis II disorders, with as many as 80 percent carrying comorbid diagnoses (Solomon & Davidson, 1997; Kessler et al., 1995). This risk for complex outcomes appears to increase with trauma exposures that begin early in life. In the DSM-IV field trials, for instance, individuals with trauma exposure in childhood were significantly more likely than those with adult-onset exposure to experience a range of difficulties beyond the PTSD criteria, including altered ability to regulate emotional experience, difficulties with interpersonal relationships, alterations in attention due to dissociative coping, impaired sense of self and identity, changes in systems of meaning, and somatic complaints (van der Kolk et al., 1996). With exposure to multiple childhood adversities, the risk increases exponentially for outcomes such as depression, alcohol and substance abuse, health risks such as obesity and cigarette smoking, and high-risk behaviors such as promiscuity and violent relationships in adulthood (Dube et al., 2003; Edwards et al., 2003; Whitfield et al., 2003).

Awareness of the distinction between acute exposures and more chronic, interpersonal forms of childhood trauma has led to the description and study of *complex trauma*. Complex trauma encompasses both the experience of multiple or chronic adverse events, often within the caregiving system that should be the source of safety and stability, and the multi-layered impact of these events on immediate and long-term outcomes across domains of development (Cook et al., 2005).

Exposure to complex trauma may be one of the driving forces behind use of mental health services in childhood. Across studies, children exposed to chronic interpersonal stressors such as physical or sexual abuse, neglect, or domestic violence have been found to be at increased risk for a range of diagnoses including depression, oppositional defiant disorder, attention deficit/hyperactivity disorder, generalized anxiety disorder, simple phobias, and conduct disorders (Putnam, 2003; Ford et al., 1999). In fact, PTSD is rarely found to be the most common diagnosis among children exposed to trauma given the various symptom manifestations that children may present (Ackerman et al., 1998). Beyond diagnosis, these children have increased academic difficulties and failure (Ackerman et al., 1998; Cahill et al., 1999; Leither & Johnson, 1994; Kurtz et al., 1993); impairments in executive function skills, attention, and concentration (Mezzacapa et al., 2001; Beers & de Bellis, 2002); difficulty regulating emotional experience (Rogosch et al., 1995; van der Kolk et al., 1993); difficulties with peer relationships (Shapiro & Levendosky, 1999; Trickett, 1993; Schneider et al., 2001); and altered physiological and neuroanatomical development (DeBellis, 2001). Recognition of the multi-layered impact of early trauma exposure across multiple domains of functioning has led to a call for increased representation of these posttraumatic outcomes in our diagnostic system (van der Kolk, 2005).

The Challenge of Assessment

Assessment provides a structured framework for understanding the range of needs of children and families. When children present for treatment or other services with a single diagnostic picture or difficulty, assessment may be fairly routine. For a child presenting with a simple phobia, for instance, assessment may focus on measuring the intensity of the anxiety symptoms, gaining an awareness of onset and course, and evaluating current level of functional impairment. For children with early trauma exposure, however, clinical assessment and prioritization of service needs is significantly more challenging for several reasons.

Five important issues arise in assessing complex trauma in children. First, trauma is an etiology, not an outcome. Overwhelming evidence points to the variable nature of symptoms, developmental challenges, and social-contextual needs across children and families coping with traumatic stress (e.g., Anda et al., 1999, 2001, 2002a, 2002b;

Arnow, 2004; Dong et al., 2004). Measurement of a single diagnostic category or symptom profile would therefore fail to capture significant aspects of the experience of traumatized children.

Second, children and families exposed to trauma often present with an array of significant needs. For instance, a child may be referred who is currently failing in school, engaging in self-harmful behaviors, failing to form appropriate peer relationships, and exhibiting oppositional behaviors with caregivers. Children may also exhibit a range of strengths and positive coping behaviors that have the potential to mediate their symptoms, functioning, and adaptation to trauma. Previous studies have suggested the importance of child and caregiver strengths in the provision of mental health services (Lyons et al., 2000) and in the process of recovery from trauma (Briere & Spinazzola, 2005). Prioritizing service needs and optimally leveraging the family's strengths are therefore essential. However, there are few focused instruments that adequately capture intensity, onset, course, and level of impairment across multiple diagnostic categories and domains of functioning, while taking into account individual and familial strengths.

Third, children who experience trauma may present very differently across settings or time. They may dissociate; there may be changes in their ability to self-regulate, the impact of traumatic triggers may increase their stress levels; and they may show developmental variations in expression. Evaluators must capture and integrate an often-changing symptom presentation and variable information from caregivers, school personnel, and their own clinical observations. It is not uncommon, for instance, to encounter children who function very well in a regulated state but who become highly dysregulated to the point of needing emergency services when triggered by reminders of their traumatic experience (e.g., Saxe et al., 2006).

Fourth, childhood trauma often takes place within an important social and contextual environment. By definition, complex trauma involves to some degree the child's caregiving system, and there is significant evidence that caregiver response plays a significant role in child recovery and symptom course (e.g., Cohen & Mannarino, 2000). Therefore, assessment of childhood trauma should capture not just the experience and functioning of the child, but that of the caregiving system.

Fifth, children who have experienced trauma often are referred for services not because of their trauma exposure but because of their most prominent difficulty (e.g., behavioral or academic problems). It is helpful to view the implications of this through the prism of a pediatric visit for childhood fever. In and of itself, a fever is a surface symptom, the body's response to an underlying illness. The source may range from a simple cold to a more serious illness such as chicken pox or a bacterial pneumonia. If the pediatrician focuses simply on the presenting symptom, he or she may miss significant underlying conditions. The initial fever might be treated, but a failure to recognize and treat the root cause would lead to at best a temporary solution, and at worst significant complications for the child's health.

Trauma may be conceptualized in a similar manner. Often the distressing symptoms, behaviors, and challenges that affected children manifest are simply surface demonstrations of more complex difficulties. Treating the surface symptom without an understanding of the larger picture may ultimately lead to significant complications and worsening outcomes over time. It is imperative, therefore, that assessment of the needs of traumatized children captures their individual and familial history, challenges, and strengths.

Currently available evaluation measures are of limited use, however. While a variety of assessment and research tools exist for child trauma, many are too general, or too specific, or too limited to a particular symptom or cluster of trauma-related symptoms, without assessing for trauma-specific symptoms (Gilbert, 2004). There are no assessment tools to date that gather information on the multiple dimensions related to trauma adaptation *and also* yield information that can be readily translated into clinical practice. In fact, within existing child trauma tools, there is a notable absence of assessment of various strengths dimensions. A comprehensive evaluation system that addresses the multifaceted needs and strengths of children and families exposed to complex trauma is required, as discussed below.

A Comprehensive Model for Child Trauma Assessment

There is abundant evidence within child mental health services that appropriate determination of service and placement needs depends on assessing a range of dimensions related to both the child's overall functioning (including strengths) and the functioning of his caregiver system (Lyons et al., 2000). Emerging evidence within the child trauma field highlights the importance of comprehensive and clinically useful assessment strategies to address identified gaps and provide important advances to existing child trauma assessment practices (Briere & Spinazzola, 2005). Comprehensive assessment strategies are critical (1) to identifying the specific needs and resources of traumatized children across a range of domains, (2) to gathering information on the multiple dimensions relevant to adaptation from trauma from a range of important perspectives, and (3) to providing a rational framework for interpreting this information and using it in clinical decision-making. By assessing and documenting the range of needs of traumatized children and their families, we will be better able to match these specific needs with the specific services required to treat them. This information may get collected in various clinical settings, through various sources, but a better assessment strategy would integrate such a range of information to provide an efficient and useful framework for understanding the complex effects of trauma. Where such an assessment strategy is embedded in the process of treatment planning, it can serve as a mechanism for establishing a common language to guide and integrate the work of service providers across different systems. This is especially important given the variety of treatment approaches used and the multiple settings in which traumatized children often present (e.g., mental health, schools, juvenile justice).

CANS-TEA METHOD AND SCORING SYSTEM

Purpose and Unique Features

The CANS-TEA assessment tool is designed with four overall purposes:

1. To document a range of traumatic experiences and their level of severity;
2. To document the range of difficulties and complex adaptations exhibited by traumatized children that cut across current diagnostic classifications;
3. To describe the contextual factors and systems that can support a child's adaptation from trauma; and
4. To assist in the management and planning of services for children and adolescents with exposure and adaptation to traumatic experiences.

Table 17.1
The CANS-TEA Scoring System

0 = an area of strength or no evidence of impairment = *no need for action*
1 = a mild degree of difficulty = a need for *watchful waiting* to see whether action is needed (i.e., flag it for later review to see if any circumstances change) or prevention planning
2 = a moderate level of difficulty = *a need for action*
3 = a severe level of difficulty = a *need for either immediate or intensive action*
9 = unknown

The CANS-TEA uses a flexible, easy-to-understand format that yields clinically useful information and addresses some important gaps and challenges in child trauma assessment. Whereas several existing tools assess different domains of psychiatric symptomatology (e.g., depression, anxiety) (Foa et al., 2001) or functional impairment (Bolton et al., 2004), there is no single measure at present that integrates information on both strengths and impairment following trauma, much less one that incorporates information from multiple informants or reports. The CANS-TEA is designed to integrate information from a variety of sources in order to meet the needs of children who have been exposed to multiple or chronic traumas.

Information gathered during an open-ended clinical interview, collateral reports, direct observation, and other structured assessment tools (e.g., self-report questionnaires) can be summarized using the CANS-TEA's clinically useful four-point scoring system. As shown in Table 17.1, scores are assigned to domains of interest based on two criteria: (1) the degree of strength or impairment and (2) the degree of urgency for intervention. Hence, a unique feature of the CANS is that ratings are readily translated into "action" planning in service settings. Table 17.1 shows the CANS-TEA scoring system.

Using these scores, a clinical team can efficiently prioritize a child's difficulties in order of greatest severity and most emergent need while also attending to those strengths and resources in the child's life that might act as a buffer. For instance, it is quite likely in clinical practice with traumatized children that an intake may be streamlined to attend to emergent issues, such as ongoing abuse or suicidality. To accommodate these commonly occurring scenarios, clinicians are able to assign "unknown" ratings on the CANS-TEA as placeholders for information to be updated over the course of working with a family.

When integrating information from multiple sources, the scenario may arise where discrepant or conflicting information is provided through the range of reports from children, various caregivers, and other informants, as well as from the different techniques used. In such cases, the decision can be made to establish different ratings on a particular dimension based on these reports, and then either average the discrepant ratings across reporters or identify whether a particular report/rating is clearly more accurate and should be considered over the other perspectives based on clinical judgment. The decision for how to handle such ratings can be addressed within a given service setting based on specified practices within that setting or determined on a case-by-case basis. This flexibility in usage is an important defining feature of the CANS approach, which has helped to establish its utility in a range of settings and fills an important need in terms of more readily translating assessment data into clinical practice.

Background

The CANS-TEA is based on prior work in modeling decision-making for psychiatric services using the Childhood Severity of Psychiatric Illness (CSPI) (Lyons, 1998) tool. The CSPI was developed to measure dimensions crucial to good clinical decision-making with respect to appropriate use of psychiatric hospitalization and residential treatment services. The CSPI has been used to guide reforms in the decision-making process for residential treatment (Lyons et al., 1998) and to improve crisis assessment services (Lyons et al., 1997; Leon et al., 1999). The CSPI was found to be face valid and easy to use, while providing comprehensive information regarding a child's clinical status. The CANS approach was built upon prior work with the CSPI and added a strengths-based assessment, which is a critical component of working with children and adolescents.

The promising results of the CANS led to the development first of the CANS-MH (mental health) and then, with increasing recognition of the need for a similar measure tailored to trauma-specific child mental health services, the CANS-TEA. Both CANS measures focus on multiple areas of strength and difficulty, but for the CANS-TEA, we reconfigured many items into new category descriptions based on our evolving conceptualization of how children adapt to trauma. In addition, we developed several new items related to traumatic experiences, trauma-specific responses, and contextual factors hypothesized to moderate children's adaptation to trauma.

Dimensions and Items

The overarching dimensions, specific items, and scoring anchors used in the CANS-TEA were developed through a systematic process of item selection, development, and pilot testing. Several clinicians with expertise in child trauma at the Trauma Center in Boston and Boston Medical Center initially developed a list of relevant items, and we held interviews or focus group discussions with other experts in the field, mental health clinicians and caseworkers, other providers, and family representatives. These individuals helped identify the clinically relevant constructs that modeled the existing thinking and decision-making practices in actual child trauma service settings. Several individuals became primary contributors in the overall development and refinement of the CANS-TEA (Kisiel et al., 2002). The constructs reflect a careful review of the child trauma literature, which covers the range of trauma exposures in childhood, the variety of potential responses and outcomes across development and areas of functioning (emotional, behavioral, cognitive, interpersonal, physiological), and the factors that may moderate those outcomes. We identified the following dimensions: trauma history, traumatic stress symptoms, regulation of emotions, regulation of behaviors, other behavioral health concerns, attachment difficulties, problem modifiers, stability of social environment, child strengths, functioning, and acculturation. We conceptualized these dimensions based on the assessment framework outlined above, to fully capture the crucial components necessary to understand, plan for, and implement services for traumatized children and their families.

After initially identifying the dimensions, we determined the specific items and item descriptions corresponding to different levels or degrees of each need and strength identified. We brainstormed our criteria within smaller groups of providers, including clinicians, administrators, and psychology or social work trainees within child trauma clinic settings. We based the anchor descriptions (associated with 0 to 3 ratings) on clinical definitions and relevant case examples identified by clinical staff and associated with different levels of severity or strength in each area. To be immediately relevant for service planning, we worded items in terms of the level of intervention needed as noted in the scoring system in Table 17.1. For example, a rating of 3 on the item "reexperiencing" captures a child's showing of "trauma-specific reenactments that include sexually or physically traumatizing other children or sexual play with adults," or "persistent flashbacks, illusions or hallucinations that make it difficult for the child to function"; this rating indicates a need for an immediate focus on such behavior in the treatment plan.

As a next step, the primary contributors asked clinicians to pilot test the CANS-TEA on a subset of their child trauma cases and to provide direct feedback about the relevance of the items—whether the range of responses to trauma was captured through this tool, whether other items needed to be added or deleted to make it more relevant to their range of cases, its ease of use, and its usefulness in service settings. Caseworkers and clinicians were asked to provide similar feedback on the dimensions and their item descriptions through focus groups during initial trainings on how to use the CANS-TEA. The organizing framework and dimension descriptions went through a corresponding process of review and revision based on the input of child trauma experts contacted through the National Child Traumatic Stress Network. Feedback from this pilot testing and review process was incorporated into a revised version of the CANS-TEA for subsequent cycles of testing; this process took place over several iterations, including implementation in different settings, before a final version was developed. The final list of dimensions, items and descriptions of the CANS-TEA were determined based on the review, feedback, and consensus of child trauma providers in a range of settings. Table 17.2 shows the CANS-TEA final list of dimensions and items.

The trauma history dimension contains items that assess a wide range of traumatic experiences, from accidental injuries to natural disasters to interpersonal traumas. The trauma types included within this dimension parallel the trauma types identified through the National Child Trauma Stress Network, which outlines the range of potential trauma exposures in childhood. The traumatic stress symptoms dimension assesses posttraumatic stress reactions outlined in the PTSD diagnostic criteria, while the other dimensions (i.e., regulation of emotion, regulation of behavior) assess other symptomatic manifestations, functioning variables, child strengths, caregiver needs and strengths, and other contextual variables that can mediate the impact of trauma exposure on children's functioning. As trauma impacts an entire system that includes the child and his or her caregiver, we included dimensions that assess the caregiver and social environmental system. The stability of social environment dimension assesses both the strengths and difficulties of the caregiver system, given the vital role this system has in supporting or hindering a child's recovery from trauma (Saxe et al., 2005). The overall goal was a comprehensive yet practical measure of whether the caregiver system can manage and support the traumatized child in the context of his or her symptoms and current functioning. Using this system, any additional service needs or resources required to support the child's recovery from trauma can be prioritized as areas for intervention quickly and systematically based on the level of severity.

Table 17.2
CANS-TEA Dimensions and Items

Trauma History

Sexual Abuse
Physical Abuse
Emotional Abuse
Neglect
Medical Trauma
Witness to Family Violence
Community Violence
Natural or Manmade Disasters
Traumatic Grief/Separation
War
Terrorism
Intervention

Traumatic Stress Symptoms

Reexperiencing
Avoidance
Numbing

Regulation of Emotions

Anxiety
Depression
Affect Disregulation
Dissociation
Somatization
Attention/Concentration

Regulation of Behavior

Suicide Behavior
Self-Harm
Physical/Verbal Aggression
Sexually Aggressive
Sexually Provocative
Runaway
Behavioral Regression
Impulsivity

Functioning

Intellectual/Developmental
Physical/Medical
School/Day Care
Social Functioning
Sexual Development
Sleep Disturbance

Other Behavioral Health Concerns

Eating Disturbances
Substance Abuse

Oppositional Behaviors
Conduct Problems

Attachment

Attachment Difficulties

Problem Modifiers

Temporal Consistency of Trauma-Related
Symptoms
Time Between Trauma & Victim/Witness to
Criminal Activity

Stability of Social Environment

Caregiver Physical Health
Caregiver Depression
Caregiver Posttraumatic Reaction
Caregiver Substance Abuse
Caregiver Isolation
Caregiver/Marital Violence/Monitoring/
Supervision
Knowledge
Organization
Safety
Resources
Residential Permanence
School
Peer Group
Neighborhood
Situational Consistency of Problems

Child Strengths

Interpersonal
Relationship Permanence
Vocational
Psychological
Spiritual/Religious
Talent/Creative Interest
Community Involvement

Acculturation

Language
Identity
Ritual
Cultural Stress
Racism

Prospective and Retrospective Uses

The CANS-TEA is designed for use at two levels—the individual child and family, and the system of care (e.g., school, community). It provides for a structured assessment of a traumatized child along a set of dimensions relevant to service planning and decision-making, and it provides information about the child's and family's service needs during system planning. With its modular design, the tool can be adapted for local applications without jeopardizing its psychometric properties. In other words, selected categories of the CANS-TEA (instead of the entire tool) may be used separately or in combination, based on their relevance or the needs of a particular agency.

The CANS-TEA's flexibility allows for a variety of innovative applications. As a *prospective* assessment tool, it allows for a structured assessment along a set of dimensions relevant to post-traumatic adaptation and trauma-specific treatment planning. Information about the child's and family's mental health needs is used to develop the individual plan of care. The staffing process is structured in *strengths-based* terms for the clinicians, other providers, and the family. This is a unique feature that makes information gathered through the CANS-TEA readily translatable into service planning; this separates the CANS-TEA from other trauma-based assessment tools that focus more specifically on symptoms.

As *a retrospective* assessment tool, the CANS-TEA allows for assessment of the children and adolescents currently in care and of how well the current system functions in relation to the needs and strengths of the child and family. It clearly points out service gaps in the current services system. This information can then be used to design and develop the community-based, family-focused system of services appropriate for the target population and the community. When working with child trauma populations this becomes particularly important, as there is a range of potential domains of impairment that are not always readily addressed given the limitations of staff expertise and resources in particular areas. For instance, a systems-level assessment might indicate that there are several current cases with difficulties in the area of dissociation; however, there may be few staff resources or little expertise in this area. This may point to a need for enhancing the level of clinical expertise or appropriate clinical consultation in this area to better meet the needs of the presenting client population.

Providers and supervisors can also use the CANS-TEA as a quality assurance monitoring device. Review of a case record in light of this assessment tool will provide information as to the appropriateness of an individual plan of care and whether individual goals and outcomes are being achieved. Retrospective review of prospectively completed CANS allows for a form of measurement audit to facilitate the reliability and accuracy of information (Lyons et al., 2002).

Profile Rating

After initial intake or follow-up interview, routine service contact, or following the review of a case file, the four-point CANS-TEA ratings are generally made based on the time frame of the past thirty days to capture the child's most recent functioning. These ratings are designed to be clinically useful and assist with decision-making by highlighting areas of particular need, resources or strengths on which to build, and gaps in understanding that may deserve further attention within the child and caregiver system (Lyons, 2004). There are a few exceptions to the thirty-day rule, including the trauma history category, which assesses lifetime exposure to trauma, and the regulation of behavior category, which documents the lifetime history of risk-taking behaviors as an important predictor of future high-risk behaviors.

All of the items in the CANS-TEA are meant to be descriptive rather than explanatory. Ratings are intended to describe how the child or caregiver system is functioning at the time of assessment, based on the current evidence, to give an accurate profile of the particular case. However, while there may be a tendency to elevate a child's rating in a particular dimension (e.g., trauma history or emotional responses) without direct evidence in order to potentially justify or provide explanation for particular internalizing or externalizing behaviors, ratings are intended to capture what is currently happening for the child. This is where the action levels can become useful: if there is no current evidence but there is a suspicion of a trauma exposure or a certain level of difficulty, the CANS ratings can be used to capture this type of information.

In other words, the CANS-TEA is designed to provide a profile of the needs and strengths of the child and family exposed to trauma, rather than a total score. While a total score would provide an indicator of relative severity or urgency, its sole use would obscure the tool's ability to prioritize specific treatment targets or identify areas of strength. Therefore, items within a dimension (e.g., functioning in school or social settings) can be used separately to indicate individualized areas of impairment or strength, or changes in functioning over time (i.e., with baseline and follow-up ratings). Alternately, item scores can be totaled within a particular dimension to indicate current functioning or changes within broader domains of child or caregiver functioning (e.g., regulation of emotions). When used in a retrospective review of cases, the CANS-TEA is designed to give an overall profile of the system of services and the gaps in the service system, not an overall score of the current system. Used as a profile-based assessment tool, it gives the clinician, the family, and the agency valuable and reliable information for use in the development and/or review of an individual plan of care and case service decisions.

CANS-TEA IMPLEMENTATION

Pilot Testing and Preliminary Psychometric Properties

Clinicians in the Department of Child and Adolescent Psychiatry at Boston Medical Center provided CANS-TEA ratings for 128 children (eighty-two boys, forty-six girls) with histories of trauma and who were seeking services for a wide range of difficulties between August 2003 and February 2006 (see Table 17.3). Over one-half of the children (53.5 percent) were African-American, 15.7 percent Latino, 6.3 percent African-Caribbean, and 5.5 percent Caucasian. Table 17.3 shows the demographics of all of the children in the pilot study and the types of traumas experienced. As the table shows, the mean age was twelve years and ranged from four to twenty years. The children endorsed experiencing an average of 2.4 traumas, and twenty-nine children (22.6 percent) experienced three or more traumatic events. The most frequent forms of trauma experienced by these children were traumatic grief and separation (40.4 percent), physical abuse (38.3 percent), witnessing community violence (36.7 percent), and neglect (35.2 percent). Fifteen children in the sample were refugees from African and Latin countries (e.g., Somalia, Honduras), and all but one of these children endorsed war-related trauma ($n = 14$, 10.9 percent).

Table 17.3
Demographics of Pilot Sample (*n* =128)

Gender (n, %)	46 female (35.9%), 82 male (64.1%)
Age (M, SD)*	11.98 (4.30)
Ethnicity (n, %)	African-American (68, 53.5%) Latino (20, 15.7%) African-Caribbean (8, 6.3%) Caucasian (7, 5.5%) Biracial (6, 4.7%) Asian (3, 2.4%) African refugee groups (e.g., Somali, Nigerian, Liberian: 12, 9.4%) Latino refugee groups (e.g., Honduran: 3, 2.4%)
Types of Trauma Experienced (n, %)**	Traumatic grief/separation (52, 40.4%) Physical abuse (49, 38.3%) Community violence (47, 36.7%) Neglect (45, 35.2%) Emotional abuse (44, 34.4%) Witness to family (domestic) violence (32, 25.0%) Sexual abuse (24, 18.8%) Medical trauma (19, 14.9%) War (14, 10.9%)

* M = mean score; SD = standard deviation from mean.

** Do not sum to 100 percent, reflecting that children have experienced multiple traumas (*M* = 2.4, *SD* = 1.94); in addition, between 15 and 27 children (11.7 percent to 21.1 percent) were rated as "unknown" across the trauma categories.

CANS-TEA ratings were made after the following intake procedure:

1. A sixty to ninety minute initial clinical interview with the child and caregiver;

2. A multidisciplinary team meeting intended to generate a consensus case conceptualization and treatment plan or additional questions for the family and relevant others;

3. A follow-up meeting with the child and caregiver(s); and

4. Collateral contact with school officials, relevant family members, or outside providers (where applicable).

CANS-TEA ratings were made on average within three weeks of the initial interview. These ratings and analyses were completed using an earlier version of the CANS-TEA which contained sixty-seven rather than seventy items. Three items from the original CANS-MH (impulsivity, oppositional behaviors, and conduct problems) have since been included in the final version of the CANS-TEA and certain items have been reconfigured within the primary dimensions.

Internal Consistency (Cronbach's Alpha)

Cronbach's alpha,[1] overall scale, and scale-if-item-deleted statistics were used to determine the overall internal consistency of the CANS-TEA, as well as the internal consistency of the rationally defined dimensions. The *a priori* dimensions that were tested were designated based on the expected construct coverage of their component items. These included: traumatic stress symptoms, regulation of emotions, regulation of behavior, stability of social environment, functioning, and child's strengths. Trauma history internal consistency was not assessed, as items in this category are used to describe presence of a trauma history rather than to identify an underlying construct. Items related to racial tension and acculturation were not endorsed at a sufficient base rate to pursue further analyses.[2]

The CANS-TEA had an overall high internal consistency (alpha = .94), and acceptable internal consistency on the following *a priori* scales: traumatic stress symptoms (.78), stability of social environment (.74), and child's strengths (.84). Finer grained analyses of scale- and scale-if-item-deleted statistics indicated that the items for regulation of emotions, regulation of behavior, and functioning could be subsumed under a single higher order factor labeled for the purposes of this chapter as "psychiatric and psychosocial functioning," which had an internal consistency of .78.[3] In addition, these analyses suggested that certain items might be better conceptualized within other dimensions. For instance, two items related to temporal consistency of problems and time between trauma and intervention could be subsumed within the child's strengths scale, resulting in an alpha of .90. A more detailed examination of these analyses will be outlined in a separate publication.

Construct Validity (Exploratory Factor Analysis)

Exploratory factor analysis modestly supported a five-factor solution that replicated the internal consistency analyses and accounted for 37 percent of the variance. These results will be detailed in another publication.

Several of the factors showed strong correlations with one another, as Table 17.4 shows. For instance, psychiatric and psychosocial functioning appears to be strongly related to stability of social environment, child strengths, traumatic stress symptoms, and trauma history. One interpretation of these data is that trauma exposure influences multiple domains and that these domains, in turn, affect one another. Of particular note, trauma history was more strongly associated with psychiatric and psychosocial functioning, stability of social environment, and child strengths than with the traumatic stress symptoms factor. This suggests that symptoms associated with PTSD are only one possible outcome of traumatic stress, and those other areas central to child development, such as strengths and the social environment, must be considered when assessing traumatized children.

---

[1] Except where indicated, analyses were conducted in SPSS Version 12.0.

[2] We set a minimum base rate of 20 percent for items to be included in the analyses. These are available by request from JMF. The acculturation-related items and their base rates were: cultural identity (14.3 percent), encounters with racism (15.8 percent), and opportunities to engage in ritual (7.8 percent).

[3] The separate scales' internal consistency ratings were as follows: regulation of emotions (.53), regulation of behavior (.47), and functioning (.71). Combining the two regulation scales was insufficient to achieve acceptable internal consistency (= .55). Hence, we combined the three scales.

Table 17.4
Correlations Among the Five CANS-TEA Factors

	Trauma History	Posttraumatic Stress Symptoms	Psychiatric & Psychosocial Functioning	Stability of Social Environment	Child Strengths
Trauma History	1.0	.29	.51	.43	.40
TSS		1.0	.58	.37	.22
P&PF			1.0	.44	.43
SSE				1.0	.41
Child Strengths					1.0

TSS = traumatic stress symptoms
P&PF = psychiatric and psychosocial functioning
SSE = stability of social environment

Nevertheless, only 37 percent of the variance in the sample has been accounted for with this analysis. While quite impressive for data collected over the course of a two-session intake interview, clearly more than the CANS-TEA factors are accounting for the observed clinical phenomena in these children. Observer or reporter inaccuracies, as well as unmeasured factors such as genetic contribution to mental health, may contribute to the incomplete explanation of variance.

Clinical Utility (Trauma Systems Therapy Assessment Grid)

The CANS-TEA was piloted in a clinical setting that used an intervention model in which the CANS constructs are highly relevant. This model, called Trauma Systems Therapy (Saxe et al., 2006, 2005), is designed to remediate both environmental instability and emotional/behavioral dysregulation, including traumatic stress symptoms. Interventions provided using this model included intensive, crisis stabilization services for forty-six children (35.9 percent); traditional office-based therapy focused on learning cognitive-behavioral- and mindfulness-based emotion regulation skills for fifty-nine children (53.9 percent); and trauma-focused cognitive processing for thirteen children (10.2 percent).

To test the clinical utility of the CANS, the saved factor scores from our exploratory factor analyses were (nonparametrically) correlated with these summary clinician ratings. Clinicians' ratings were distilled into an ordinal scale corresponding to increased stability and less intensive need for services, so that crisis-stabilization was scored 1, office-based skills-building was scored 2, and trauma-focused processing was scored 3. Significant correlations were found between this ordinal scale and Factors 1 (trauma history, Spearman's $Rho = -.48$, $p < .001$) and 3 (psychiatric and psychosocial functioning, Spearman's $Rho = -.41$, $p < .001$). As one might expect, having higher scores on these CANS-assessed factors, corresponding in this case to having more and more severe traumatic events and to having more pervasive and severe psychiatric and psychosocial impairment, was associated with greater clinician-assessed need for intensive, crisis stabilization services. Correlations with the remaining CANS factors did not approach statistical significance, although correlations with Factors 2 (posttraumatic stress symptoms, $Rho = -.11$, n.s.) and 4 (stability of social environment, $Rho = -.12$, n.s.) meet Cohen's (1988, 1992) threshold for small effect size (i.e., $r = .10$) and suggest that a larger sample may have provided enough statistical power to observe meaningful relationships between clinicians' ratings and these factors as well.

SUMMARY AND CONCLUSION

This chapter outlines the need and rationale for the development of a comprehensive assessment strategy designed to assess children exposed to chronic and multiple traumatic experiences who exhibit a range of complex adaptations. The CANS-TEA was developed to address this need as a flexible and easy-to-use assessment tool with direct and practical applications for service usage.

Assessment is critical as a first step in any intervention, but particularly in understanding and addressing the complex needs of traumatized children and in providing services that specifically target these needs. This is especially significant given the high measured prevalence of children in this country exposed to traumatic experiences (e.g., Costello et al., 2002). The multidimensional needs of this population can fluctuate over the course of children's development or as they present within different settings, and these difficulties can become even more serious if not treated appropriately in earlier stages. It is important to address the range of problem areas that these children are exhibiting, but it is equally essential to assess strengths or positive coping responses that may mediate their adaptation to trauma. A comprehensive assessment approach that assesses both needs and strengths can be easily translated and adapted in clinical settings, used over the course of treatment as a part of routine practice, and consulted to determine whether additional services or resources must be put in place based on current needs of the child and family. The CANS-TEA has the potential to serve these functions and offer a useful contribution to the field of child trauma given its previous applications in a range of service settings (Lyons et al., 2000).

The development of the CANS-TEA was multifaceted, combining the established framework of the CANS methodology, the expertise of trauma specialists, and the frontline experience of community clinicians and caseworkers. The resulting assessment instrument is well-grounded in theory and empirical research with immediate clinical application for the trauma practitioner. Future steps will be to continue to evaluate the psychometric properties of the CANS-TEA as well as to examine its utility across a range of service settings with traumatized children.

References

Ackerman, P. T., Newton, J. E. O., McPherson, W. B., Jones, J. G. & Dykman, R. A. (1998). Prevalence of posttraumatic stress disorder and other psychiatric diagnoses in three groups of abused children (sexual, physical, and both). *Child Abuse and Neglect, 22,* 759–774.

Diagnostic and statistical manual of mental disorders (3d ed.) (DSM-III) (1980). Washington, DC: American Psychiatric Association.

Diagnostic and statistical manual of mental disorders (4th ed.) (DSM-IV) (1994). Washington, DC: American Psychiatric Association.

Diagnostic and statistical manual of mental disorders (4th ed. rev.) (DSM-TR) (2000). Washington, DC: American Psychiatric Association.

Anda, R. F., Croft, J. B., Felitti, V. J., Nordenberg, D., Giles, W. H., Williamson, D. F. & Giovino, G. A. (1999). Adverse childhood experiences of and smoking during adolescence and adulthood. *Journal of the American Medical Association, 282,* 1652–1658.

Anda, R. F., Felitti, V. J., Chapman, D. P., Croft, J. B., Williamson, D. F., Santelli, J., Dietz, P. M. & Marks, J. S. (2001). Abused boys, battered mothers, and male involvement in teen pregnancy. *Pediatrics, 107,* E19.

Anda, R. F., Chapman, D. P., Felitti, V. J., Edwards, V., Williamson, D. F., Croft, J. B. & Giles, W. H. (2002a). Adverse childhood experiences and risk of paternity in teen pregnancy. *Obstetrics and Gynecology, 100,* 37–45.

Anda, R. F., Whitfield, C. L., Felitti, V. J., Chapman, D., Edwards, V. J., Dube, S. R. & Williamson, D. F. (2002b). Adverse childhood experiences, alcoholic parents, and later risk of alcoholism and depression. *Psychiatric Services, 53,* 1001–1009.

Arnow, B. A. (2004). Relationships between childhood maltreatment, adult health and psychiatric outcomes, and medical utilization. *Journal of Clinical Psychiatry, 65,* 10–15.

Ballenger, J., Davidson, J., Lecrubier, Y., Nutt, D., Foa, E., Kessler, R. & McFarlane, A. (2000). Consensus statement on posttraumatic stress disorder from the international consensus group on depression and anxiety. *Journal of Clinical Psychiatry, 61,* 60–66.

Beers, S. & DeBellis, M. (2002). Neuropsychological function in children with maltreatment-related posttraumatic stress disorder. *American Journal of Psychiatry, 159,* 483–486.

Bolton, D., Hill, J., O'Ryan, D., Udwin, O., Boyle, S. & Yule, W. (2004). Long-term effects of psychological trauma on psychosocial functioning. *Journal of Child Psychology and Psychiatry, 45,* 1007–1014.

Briere, J. & Spinazzola, J. (2005). Phenomenology and psychological assessment of complex posttraumatic states. *Journal of Traumatic Stress, 18,* 401–412.

Cahill, L., Kaminer, R. & Johnson, P. (1999). Developmental, cognitive, and behavioral sequelae of child abuse. *Child & Adolescent Psychiatric Clinics of North America, 8,* 827–843.

Cohen, J. (1988). *Statistical power analysis for the behavioral sciences* (2d ed.) New York: Lawrence Erlbaum Associates.

Cohen, J. (1992). A power primer. *Psychological Bulletin, 112,* 155–159.

Cohen, J. A. & Mannarino, A. P. (2000). Predictors of treatment outcome in sexually abused children. *Child Abuse and Neglect, 24,* 983–994.

Cook, A., Spinazzola, J., Ford, J., Lanktree, C., Blaustein, M., Cloitre, M., deRosa, R., Hubbard, R., Kagan, R., Liautaud, J., Mallah, K., Olafson, E. & van der Kolk, B. (2005). Complex trauma in children and adolescents. *Psychiatric Annals, 35,* 390–398.

Costello, E. J., Erkanli, A., Fairbank, J. A. & Angold, A. (2002). The prevalence of potentially traumatic events in childhood and adolescence. *Journal of Traumatic Stress, 15,* 99–112.

DeBellis M (2001). Developmental traumatology: The psychobiological development of maltreated children and its implications for research, treatment, and policy. *Development and Psychopathology, 13,* 539–564.

Dong, M., Anda, R. F., Felitti, V. J., Dube, S. R., Williamson, D. F., Thompson, T. J., Loo, C. M. & Giles, W. H. (2004). The interrelatedness of multiple forms of childhood abuse, neglect, and household dysfunction. *Child Abuse and Neglect, 28,* 771–784.

Dube, S. R., Felliti, V. J., Dong, M., Giles, W. H. & Anda, R. F. (2003). The impact of adverse childhood experiences on health problems: Evidence from four birth cohorts dating back to 1900. *Preventive Medicine, 37,* 268–277.

Edwards, V. J., Holden, G. W., Felitti, V. J. & Anda, R. F. (2003). Relationship between multiple forms of childhood maltreatment and adult mental health in community respondents:

Results from the adverse childhood experiences study. *American Journal of Psychiatry, 160,* 1453–1460.

Felitti, V. J., Anda, R. F., Nordenberg, D., Williamson, D. F., Spitz, A. W., Edwards, V., Koss, M. & Marks, J. (1998). Relationship of childhood abuse and household dysfunction to many of the leading causes of death in adults: The adverse childhood experiences (ACE) study. *American Journal of Preventive Medicine, 14,* 245–258.

Foa, E. B., Johnson, K. M., Feeny, N. C. & Treadwell, K. R. H. (2001). The child PTSD symptom scale: A preliminary examination of its psychometric properties. *Journal of Clinical Child Psychology, 30,* 376–384.

Ford, J., Racusin, R., Daviss, W. B., Ellis, C. G., Thomas, J., Rogers, K., Reiser, J., Schiffman, J. & Sengupta, A. (1999). Trauma exposure among children with oppositional defiant disorder and attention deficit-hyperactivity disorder. *Journal of Consulting and Clinical Psychology, 67,* 786–789.

Gilbert, A. M. (2004). Psychometric properties of the trauma symptom checklist for young children (TSCYC). *Dissertation Abstracts International: Section B: The Sciences and Engineering, 65,* 478.

Grinker, R. & Spiegel, J. P. (1945). *Men under stress.* Philadelphia: Blakiston.

Kessler, R. C., Sonnega, A., Bromet, E., Hughes, M. & Nelson, C. B. (1995). Posttraumatic stress disorder in the national comorbidity survey. *Archives of General Psychiatry, 52,* 1048–1060.

Kisiel, C. L., Lyons, J. S., Saxe, G., Blaustein, M. & Ellis, H. (2002). *Child and adolescent needs and strengths: Trauma exposure and adaptation version (CANS-TEA) manual.* Winnetka, IL: Buddin-Praed Foundation.

Kurtz, P., Gaudin, J., Wodarski, J. & Howing, P. (1993). Maltreatment and the school-aged child: School performance consequences. *Child Abuse and Neglect, 17,* 581–589.

Leither, J. & Johnson, M. (1994). Child maltreatment and school performance. *American Journal of Education, 102,* 154–189.

Leon, S. C., Uziel-Miller, N. D., Lyons, J. S. & Tracy, P. (1999). Psychiatric hospitalization utilization of children and adolescents in state custody. *Journal of the American Academy of Child and Adolescent Psychiatry, 38,* 305–310.

Lyons, J. S. (1998). *The severity and acuity of psychiatric illness scales: An outcomes-management and decision-support system—Child and adolescent version (manual).* San Antonio, TX: Psychological Corp.

Lyons, J. S. (2004). *Redressing the emperor: Improving our children's public mental health system.* Westport, CT: Praeger.

Lyons, J. S., Kisiel, C., Dulcan, M., Cohen, R. & Chesler, P. (1997). Crisis assessment and psychiatric hospitalization of children & adolescents in state custody. *Journal of Child and Family Studies, 6,* 311–320.

Lyons, J. S., Mintzer, L. L., Kisiel, C. L. & Shallcross, H. (1998). Understanding the mental health needs of children and adolescents in residential treatment. *Professional Psychology: Research and Practice, 29,* 582–587.

Lyons, J. S., Uziel-Miller, N. D., Reyes, F. & Sokol, P. T. (2000). Strengths of children and adolescents in residential settings: Prevalence and associations with psychopathology and discharge placement. *Journal of the Academy of Child and Adolescent Psychiatry, 39,* 176–181.

Lyons, J. S., Rawal, P., Yeh, I., Leon, S. & Tracy, P. (2002). Use of measurement audit in outcomes management. *Journal of Behavioral Health Services & Research, 29,* 75–80.

Mezzacappa, E., Kindlon, D. & Earls, F. (2001). Child abuse and performance task assessments of executive functions in boys. *Journal of Child Psychology & Psychiatry and Allied Disciplines, 42,* 1041–1048.

Miller, M. W. (2003). Personality and the etiology and expression of PTSD: A three-factor model perspective. *Clinical Psychology: Science and Practice, 10,* 373–393.

Miller, M. W. (2004). Personality and the development and expression of PTSD. *PTSD Research Quarterly*, *15*, 1–7.

Putnam, F. (2003). Ten-year research update review: Child sexual abuse. *Journal of the American Academy of Child & Adolescent Psychiatry*, *42*, 269–278.

Rogosch, F. A., Cicchetti, D. & Aber, J. L. (1995). The role of child maltreatment in early deviations in cognitive and affective processing abilities and later peer relationship problems. *Development and Psychopathology*, *7*, 591–609.

Saxe, G. N., Ellis, B. H. & Kaplow, J. (2006). *Collaborative care for traumatized children and adolescents: The trauma systems therapy approach*. New York: Guilford.

Saxe, G. N., Ellis, B. H., Fogler, J., Hansen, S. & Sorkin, B. (2005). Comprehensive care for traumatized children: An open trial examines treatment using trauma systems therapy. *Psychiatric Annals*, *35*, 443–448.

Schneider, B., Atkinson, L. & Tardif, C. (2001). Child-parent attachment and children's peer relations: A quantitative review. *Developmental Psychology*, *37*, 86–100.

Shapiro, D. & Levendosky, A. (1999). Adolescent survivors of childhood sexual abuse: The mediating role of attachment style and coping in psychological and interpersonal functioning. *Child Abuse and Neglect*, *11*, 1175–1191.

Solomon, S. D. & Davidson, J. R. T. (1997). Trauma: Prevalence, impairment, service use, and cost. *Journal of Clinical Psychiatry, 58*, 5–11.

Trickett, P. (1993). Maladaptive development of school-aged, physically abused children: Relationships with the child-rearing context. *Journal of Family Psychology*, *11*, 134–147.

van der Kolk, B., Pelcovitz, D., Roth, S., Mandel, F., McFarlane, A. & Herman, J. (1996). Dissociation, somatization, and affect dysregulation: The complexity of adaptation to trauma. *American Journal of Psychiatry*, *153*, 83–93.

van der Kolk, B. A., Roth, S. & Pelcovitz, D. (1993). *Complex PTSD: Results of the PTSD field trials for* DSM-IV. Washington, DC: American Psychiatric Association.

van der Kolk, B. (2005). Developmental trauma disorder: A new rational diagnosis for children with complex trauma histories. *Psychiatric Annals, 35*, 401–408.

van der Kolk, B., Roth, S., Pelcovitz, D., Sunday, S. & Spinazzola, J. (2005). Disorders of extreme stress: The empirical foundation of a complex adaptation to trauma. *Journal of Traumatic Stress*, *18*, 389–399.

Whitfield, C. L., Anda, R. F., Dube, S. R. & Felitti, V. J. (2003). Violent childhood experiences and the risk of intimate partner violence in adults: Assessment in a large health maintenance organization. *Journal of Interpersonal Violence*, *18*, 165–185.

Chapter 18

Use of the CANS— Early Childhood in Effecting Change in the Lives of Young Children and Their Families

by Stacey Cornett, M.S.W., L.C.S.W. and Irene Podrobinok, B.A.

INTRODUCTION

Conjure up an image of a twelve-month-old baby girl laughing as her mother engages her in a game of peek-a-boo. Next imagine this same girl lying awake in a crib while her mother sleeps on the couch after a long night of fighting with her boyfriend. Undoubtedly, most people when asked which scenario is the most desirable for this infant would choose the first. Despite this fact, the recognition of how children experience and cope with difficult situations continues to be an area that is misunderstood. Many assume that infants and young children are oblivious to family stressors and that the mental well being of young children is not an area on which to focus concern. Those who accept that young children experience challenges often dismiss their effects with statements such as "she's too young to remember" or "he'll grow out of it." Conversely, the concept that infants and young children may experience cognitive, motor, or language delays is much more generally accepted.

There appears to be a plethora of reasons to resist identifying young children's mental health problems, on the part of both parents and professionals. The stigma attached to a mental health disorder is one factor. Mental health services and diagnosis in young children are often thought of in terms of "irrevocable psychopathology," with parents and some professionals believing that inappropriate "labeling" will do more harm than good (Yoshikawa & Knitzer, as cited in Poulsen, 2005). The emotional responses to seeing this population in distress are also a determinant. Whether it's the helping professional experiencing a visceral response to the absent stare of a depressed toddler, or parents experiencing self-blame when told their infant "has problems," the same thought prevails: *this shouldn't happen at this age*. If advocates for infants and young children are to be successful in overcoming this resistance, opportunities for assessment must value clear communication amongst families and providers. The process of assessment must be educative in and of itself and serve as the gateway to identifying needed interventions.

PREVALENCE OF PROBLEMS AND NEEDS

Decades of research offer us a clearer understanding of issues related to early childhood mental health and its vital relationship to all other developmental domains. Because infants and young children experience the range of human emotions, they are capable of having sound emotional health as well as its converse (Feinberg & Fenichel, 1996). Zero to Three's *Diagnostic Classification of Mental Health and Developmental Disorders of Infancy and Early Childhood* (2005) identifies several areas that may be of clinical concern, including posttraumatic stress disorder, disorders of affect, anxiety disorders, adjustment disorders, and regulation disorders of sensory processing. Infants are brought to clinical attention typically for problems of regulation and failure to thrive. Toddlers are identified more frequently as having behavioral concerns including aggression, defiance, and over-activity (American Academy of Child and Adolescent Psychiatry, 1997).

Early childhood behavioral concerns are typically thought of in terms of the child's internalizing or externalizing of problems. Internalizing problems may stem from a child's experience of unresponsive care giving, and children may appear disconnected, depressed, and withdrawn. Externalizing problems may present as poor self-regulation and may include aggression, tantrums, and extreme noncompliance (Poulsen, 2005). When externalizing problems are left unaddressed, they tend to continue over time (DHHS, 2000). Exposure to trauma in young children has been the focus of many studies that have established that younger children are more vulnerable to trauma and the development of trauma-related symptoms than older children (Pfefferbaum, 1997). Reported prevalence rates of serious behavior concerns in children between ages two and three show a majority of estimates falling between 10 percent and 15 percent (per researchers cited in Carter et al., 2004). Additionally, parent and pediatrician reports for one- and two-year olds show a 10 percent prevalence of emotional and behavioral problems (per researchers cited in Carter et al., 2004). Due to the enormous amount of energy that infants, toddlers, and preschoolers must devote to coping with symptoms of a mental health disorder, their overall development is hindered and in severe cases stalemated. When looking at the overall functioning of infants and young children, it is critical to assess the interrelatedness of development and mental health functioning. Professionals who choose to act on behalf of young children and their families must join with parents to understand this dynamic. We must find ways to empower parents to be the special advocates, the "tellers of the tale," and the decision-makers for what is in their child's best interests.

A CALL FOR ACTION

As more and more young children and their families stepped forward for services and the recognition of the uniqueness of this population grew, the need for a specialized version of the Child and Adolescent Needs and Strengths (CANS) assessment became apparent. The first opportunity for young children and their families to experience the CANS assessment occurred with the development of the Child and Adolescent Needs and Strengths: An Information Integration Tool for Early Development—CANS 0-3 Manual, developed by Lyons and colleagues (Lyons et al., 2000). This tool was later expanded to include four-year-olds. The second development occurred within Indiana. As the state of Indiana moved forward in implementing mental health assessments for all children placed in foster care through the Department of Child Services, the question of what standard for assessment was needed became answered. The state's need of a standard assessment tool for all children in this situation led to the development of an assessment committee composed of staff at the Department of Mental Health and Addictions. A subcommittee of early childhood specialists was formed, whose task was to determine whether the CANS 0-4 could accommodate the needs of Indiana's youngest citizens. After considerable review of various assessment tools, the committee recommended endorsing use of the CANS for mental health assessment of children identified as children in need of services (CHINS) and children in substitute care. The Department of Mental Health and Addictions spearheaded a process to develop both an early childhood version and a version for children ages five to seventeen.

This decision was unique in that the process involved multiple systems that interact with children, including child services, probation, special education, and mental health. The plan for all systems to use the common assessment tool resulted in the development in 2006 of the Child and Adolescent Needs and Strengths: Comprehensive Multisystem Assessment (Birth to 5) (Lyons et al., 2006). This version is currently being used in Indiana primarily by the mental health system. The third development occurred in Pittsburgh, Pennsylvania. Staff in the Systems of Care Initiative within the Allegheny County Department of Human Services' Office of Behavioral Health developed a version of the CANS for their early childhood systems of care. This process took place with the assistance of the early childhood evaluation coordinator with Allegheny County Department of Human Services, Frances Duran, a consultant, Stacey Ryan (Cornett), and parent and provider focus groups. In 2007, the Child and

Adolescent Needs and Strengths: Early Childhood—An Information Integration Tool for Young Children Ages Birth to Eight was completed (CANS-EC) (Cornett, 2007).

YOUNG CHILDREN AND THEIR FAMILIES WITH SPECIALIZED NEEDS

Although all young children and their families may at some point experience distress or a need for intervention, there are some at-risk populations that deserve special attention. Having said this, it is important to acknowledge that the presence of one risk factor is less concerning than the accumulation of multiple risk factors. There are many conditions that can mediate risk, such as environmental supports and positive family interaction patterns. The CANS-EC version appreciates the specialized needs of younger children and the special circumstances that may lead to risk. Some populations that may need preventative activities or intervention are discussed below.

Infants With Disabilities

Certainly, most would agree that children born with developmental disabilities may experience stressors that could lead to mental health challenges. Children with disabilities often experience frustration related to limited abilities and additional challenges in exploring their world. As children with disabilities grow older, they may become aware of differences and at worst feel ostracized or rejected. What can be most challenging to the infant is the parental reaction to the presence of disabilities in their child. Many parents experience grief and need a period of time to accept the reality of their infant's challenges.

Guralnick (1997) identifies four different stressors that may be present for families of children with disabilities. The first is a need for information. Parents may need help understanding the disability, the prognosis, and what appropriate interventions are available. The second stressor is interpersonal and family distress, including the reactions of others in relation to their child's disability. Other family members as well as non-relatives may react in a critical or misinformed manner. The third stressor is a need for resources, reflecting the amount of time, energy, and emotional perseverance that may be needed to support a child with disabilities. The fourth Guralnick refers to as "confidence threats," which may manifest as interference with decision-making and problem-solving skills related to the stress of the experience.

Infants With Parents Experiencing Mental Health Challenges

The primary requirement of infants and young children is parents who are emotionally available, reciprocal in their interactions, and capable of providing for their needs. When a parent experiences difficult symptoms associated with mental health challenges, all of these needs may be poorly or only intermittently met. Much research has taken place regarding how depression in parents affects children. Carter and colleagues (1991) substantiate the disturbances in infants' patterns of regulating affect when they experience parental depression. Murray and Cooper (1997) report that two negative interaction patterns, withdrawn-hostile and hostile-intrusive, have been observed in their research with depressed mothers, and that these two patterns have been demonstrated to interfere with the cognitive and emotional development of their infants. Anxiety or trauma-related challenges in parents also have the potential to cause a number of difficulties for children. Children with parents who are anxious can experience anxiety themselves due to their response to the social cues of their parents or the interference with the care-giving routine.

Infants With Parents Experiencing Substance Abuse Challenges

What typically puts infants with substance-abusing parents at greater risk is the exposure to the multiple risks associated with substance abuse. The effects of substance abuse include parental descent into poverty, disorganized and chaotic lifestyles, stress, and exposure to violence (Lester & Tronick, 1994). As the formation of a secure attachment relationship within the first few years of life is critically important, a young child with substance-abusing parents may be at considerable risk. Research has also shown that a combination of prenatal drug exposure and ongoing substance use in parents puts a child at high risk for learning and behavior problems (Lester & Tronick, 1994; Kaplan-Sanoff, 1996).

Infants With Failure to Thrive

Failure to thrive is a condition in which an infant or child's weight is below the fifth percentile on National Center for Health Statistics (NCHS) growth charts, or in which an infant experiences a decrease across two percentiles in growth or weight (Zeanah, 1993). It is critical to monitor growth and weight because of the potential problems associated with a failure to thrive, including developmental disorders such as oral motor problems, sensory processing disorders, relationship problems, self-regulation problems, or difficult temperament issues. Failure to thrive has also been associated with later cognitive challenges, school problems, attachment difficulties, self-regulation challenges, inability to delay gratification, and various health concerns. Relationship disturbances also arise with failure to thrive, as the growing infant develops a lack of confidence in others, poor self-esteem, or an inability to trust the attachment relationship.

The feeding experience for infants serves functions other than simple caloric intake; through this experience the infant develops a sense of security and source of emotional comfort. Feeding is also an organizing and integrating event in an infant's day. The relevant literature lists numerous causes for failure to thrive due to a lack of caloric intake: a parent's lack of information, parental neglect, an infant's refusal of food, nutritional absorption problems, inappropriate feeding practices, or relationship-based problems centered on feeding challenges. Some of the characteristics of the infant/toddler that can be associated with failure to thrive are listed below. Michael Trout (1987), in his book *Infant Mental Health: A Psychotherapeutic Model of Intervention*, notes the following characteristics of infants and toddlers with failure to thrive:

- Extreme watchfulness
- Bizarre eating patterns (excessive intake, hoarding food, refusing food)
- Protruding abdomen
- Noted improvement in weight gain during hospitalizations
- Poor cuddling or social responsiveness

UNIQUE ASSESSMENT COMPONENTS FOR YOUNG CHILDREN AND THEIR FAMILIES

The many versions of the CANS show that this tool has the ability to be tailored to meet the individualized needs of the children and families it is assessing. The CANS-EC version is similar to other CANS versions in that it is arranged in sections relating to the various dimensions of a young child's and family's life. The sections include child functioning, child problems, risk factors, family needs and strengths, and care intensity and organization; the distinction in CANS-EC sections relates to risk factors. Other versions include risk behaviors that are pertinent to the older age groups to which they refer. Both the State of Indiana and the City of Pittsburgh selected items that varied from the original CANS 0-4 in appreciation of the nuances and needs related to the children served. The various domains and specific assessment needs of young children within those domains are discussed below.

Early Development and Mental Functioning

Numerous infant mental health specialists have attested in various ways that child development and mental health functioning are intertwined. Assessment of a child's developmental status, therefore, requires an additional focus in the CANS-EC on all areas of development. These items include: developmental/intellectual, communication, social/emotional, self-help, motor, and sensory functioning. Because many young children experience challenges with sensory functioning, the manual includes sensory processing within this item. The sensory item includes assessment of a child's ability to fully use his sense of sight, taste, touch, sound, and smell, and to take in these experiences in an organizing fashion. According to Stanley Greenspan (1985), one of the child's major tasks during the first three months of life is to learn to take in sensory information while remaining calm and organized. When this is poorly developed, an infant or young child can do little more than attempt to cope with the sensory experience. The result is an interference in other areas of development and in the capacity to develop and make use of social relationships, which often causes parents to feel poorly able to meet their child's needs and in some cases creates a disturbance in the attachment relationship.

The *Diagnostic Classification of Mental Health and Developmental Disorders of Infancy and Early Childhood, Revised* (DC 0-3R) (Zero to Three, 2005) provides descriptors of how children with sensory processing challenges may react to these types of experiences. The social/emotional item takes into account the importance of a child's demonstrating positive movement in the ability to interact with primary caregivers and others in an appropriate manner. This is an important item to be assessed, as it relates significantly to all other areas of development. A child who is struggling in his capacity to relate to his parents, caregivers, and peers will also struggle to find support for the other areas of development. The importance of the parent-child relationship and the child's capacity to socialize and regulate his emotions gives him the tools to move forward in all other areas. Motivation for challenge, coping with frustration, and the ability to feel good about one's accomplishments all occur through healthy relationships and support further growth.

The interaction between early development and mental health functioning is often clearly demonstrated when a child has communication difficulties. A child's ability to process what is said to him and express his ideas is the foundation for interpersonal relationships and relates strongly to the child's experience of having his needs met. This, of course, impacts the child's ability to develop a sense of trust in caregivers and a core experience of relationships that becomes a foundation for further relationship development. A child frustrated in his capacity to communicate either receptively or expressively usually demonstrates this frustration in a variety of ways. The child may become aggressive, withdrawn, disconnected, hypervigilant, or distrusting of peers and adults. At times, a child may hit himself or other objects in frustration. Head-banging or other self-injurious behaviors sometimes are rooted in poor communication. Self-care/daily living skills refer to tasks that reflect a child's growing ability to take care of his own physical needs and to become responsible for dressing, performing household chores, eating, toileting himself, and preparing for sleeping. Self-care/daily living skills also often reflect cognitive ability. Assessment and monitoring of such skills is most important because when suboptimal, other limitations are placed on the child. Children become excluded from certain environments, and parents face challenges that are often overwhelming. The ability to meet developmental milestones in motor abilities and the presence of coordination, strength, tone, and motor skill are all part of a developmental life skills assessment. Cognitive development is critical to assess as well. A child with impaired cognitive functioning will demonstrate limitations in other areas of development, especially with language and self-help skills.

An additional area in the CANS-EC version is parent-child interaction. Interaction in the parent-child dyad is a critical area to assess and intervene in if necessary. Perhaps nothing has more impact on a child than the way his parents interact with them. Supportive, healthy parent-child interaction allows a child to focus fully on growth and development. It is the foundation for the development of all other social relationships and guides and supports all areas of development. This concept is outlined by Deborah Weatherson and Betty Tableman (2002) in their book *Infant Mental Health Services: Supporting Competencies/Reducing Risks* as a basic principle of infant mental health:

> an impaired or dyssynchronous relationship, or disruption through an extended separation can compromise physical and emotional well-being, impair the ability to trust and relate to others, promote withdrawn or impulsive acting out behavior, delay language development, and constrain the capacity to explore and to learn.

Other versions of the CANS assess a child's school functioning. The CANS-EC modified this item to reflect functioning in day care and early education settings because of the significant amount of time that young children may spend in these environments. There has been a great deal of momentum in the field of infant mental health to promote positive care-giving practices in these settings; Stanley Greenspan and other child advocates have devoted much time in this area. It is clear that the same parenting practices and care-giving techniques that are taught to parents need to be promoted within early care/education settings. These experiences are often critical in supporting growth and development and allowing a child to feel positive about relationships with others outside of the home. Early care and education settings have the potential to impact a child's development, school success, and overall life success. The quality of the day care environment is an important assessment consideration, as is the facility's ability to meet the needs of the individual child within the larger care-giving context. In this regard, infants and young children need to be supported in ways that appreciate their individual needs and strengths. When assessing this item, it is helpful to look for ways that the parent or child can indicate that the child's uniqueness is being accepted and embraced. The following list of important indicators of appropriate early care is adapted from findings from the National Institute of Child Health and Human Development's longitudinal study in 2000 (NICHD, 2000).

Indicators of an appropriate early care/education setting are:

- The infant or child appears happy and content within the environment.
- The environment has adequate space, toys, and materials.
- Accommodations for individual needs can be made.
- Caregivers can offer insight into the child's experiences and feelings.
- There are scheduled times for eating, play, and rest.
- Caregivers provide an appropriate level of supervision and limit setting.
- The child's peer interactions are observed, supported, and monitored.
- Correction is handled in a calm and supportive manner.
- The child is encouraged to learn and explore at his own pace.
- A variety of teaching modalities are used.
- All areas of development are valued and supported simultaneously.
- Group sizes are small.
- There are low child to adult ratios.
- There is a safe and clean environment.
- The early care/education setting provides frequent and open communication with parents.

Child Problems

The CANS-EC reflects differences in the type and significance of needs that may affect young children. A number of items are deleted, added, or modified from earlier CANS versions. Deleted items include psychosis, antisocial behavior, and substance abuse, as these problems are rarely found in very young children and are not typically the focus of intervention with them. Added items include failure to thrive, atypical behaviors, attention, and regulatory problems, which include the ability to develop regular patterns related to sleeping, eating, elimination, and self-control in the areas of sensory reactivity and emotional expression, as described earlier. This area is a developmental task in and of itself and problems in this area often are the root of day care expulsions and parent-child relationship disturbances. Atypical behaviors include head banging, smelling objects repetitively, spinning, twirling, hand flapping, eye blinking, finger-flipping, toe-walking, staring at lights, and making sounds over and over again. This is a most important assessment area because these behaviors are also indicators of pervasive developmental disorders. Modified items include aggression, which is often the reason parents seek assistance for young children. In her research,

Carolyn Webster-Stratton (2003) determined that the need to intervene early with problems of childhood aggression is critical and concluded that "by intervening early, the trajectory of early conduct problems leading to adolescent delinquency and adult antisocial behaviour may be corrected." Aggressive behavior in young children is often associated with other risk factors such as parental stress, parental drug abuse, maternal depression, and single parenthood. The more risk factors that are associated with the aggressive behavior, the more likely the behavior will persist and develop into more serious conduct problems (Webster-Stratton, 2003). Oppositional behavior was modified to be rated only when a child is over the age of three. By age three it is less of a challenge to determine the developmental appropriateness or inappropriateness of oppositional behavior.

Child Strengths

Due simply to age and developmental ability, vocational, well-being, spirituality, and inclusion items do not appear on the CANS-EC. Adaptability and persistence items do appear, however, because they relate to characteristics of temperament. Adaptability is considered one of the original nine temperament characteristics as defined by Chess and Thomas (1959). Temperament characteristics are defined by Chess and Thomas as "the style in which a person does what he or she does." Children who are adaptable are flexible, tolerant of changes and transitions, not bothered by intrusions, and "go with the flow." Adaptability is a protective characteristic for children for a number of reasons. Children exposed to high-risk environments are challenged with multiple stressors, caregivers, and changes in their routine. The ability to cope with such affords them a greater amount of energy to focus on growth and development. Children who are less adaptable often evoke negative reactions from caregivers, authority figures, and even peers, as they manifest increased neediness and changes in behavior. Parents who experience their children as flexible and less demanding overall tend to be more responsive and consistent in their reactions. Parents who are experiencing their own stressors and health or mental health problems typically have less patience to offer their children and are easily overwhelmed.

Manifestations of adaptability in infants and toddlers include:

- Falls asleep easily and remains asleep
- Changes in routine only minimally disrupt sleep
- Accepts new foods easily
- Eats a variety of foods
- Accepts diapering, dressing, and bathing tasks without resistance
- Accepts changes in day care providers or introduction of additional children
- Accepts separations

Manifestations of adaptability in preschoolers and school age children include:

- Transitions from wake to sleep state easily
- Sleep cycle remains unaffected by changes

- Eats a variety of foods and will try new foods
- Accepts control from caregivers and teachers
- Is not excessively needy
- Follows instructions easily
- Can "switch gears" easily
- Makes friends easily
- Tries new activities

Persistence, another of the original temperament characteristics described by Chess and Thomas, refers to the ability to continue an activity that is difficult or unappealing. A persistent child is one who is focused and motivated. This characteristic supports the acquisition of new developmental abilities. In children who are challenged by health or developmental disabilities, this characteristic can prove essential to their well-being. Children that manifest this characteristic show the ability to face challenges physically and emotionally in a more competent fashion.

Manifestations of persistence in infants/toddlers include:

- Attempts tasks related to motor development over and over until mastery occurs
- Will persist in attempting tasks independent of parents
- Plays alone well
- Does not cry or whine easily
- Good attention span
- Sleeps well

Manifestations of persistence in preschool and school age children include:

- Attempts difficult tasks
- Keeps focused and on track
- Motivated internally
- Appears stubborn
- Slow to disengage from activity or task
- Does not quit team sports or play
- Identified as a perfectionist
- Accepts challenges

Playfulness was an added item on the CANS-EC to reflect the importance of this capacity in young children. The experience of play is critical to the child in a number of ways. Play serves as a vehicle to further a child's social, emotional, physical, language, and cognitive development. Table 18.1 lists the benefits of play in five developmental areas.

Table 18.1
Developmental Benefits Facilitated By Play

Cognitive	Emotional	Social	Physical	Language
• Improves attention • Improves problem solving • Enhances imagination • Develops planning and sequencing abilities • Promotes awareness of how items function • Improves concentration	• Facilitates the expression of feelings and experiences in a safe manner • Alleviates anxiety by promoting mastery over stressful situations • Enhances self esteem	• Encourages children to take on a variety of social roles • Develops sharing, cooperating, and compromising abilities • Further develops sense of self • Encourages learning to take the perspective of others	• Enhances fine motor skills • Enhances gross motor skills • Facilitates visual-spatial skills • Develops balance and coordination	• Through interactions learns rhythm, cadence, and pace of speech • Enhances vocabulary acquisition • Develops social conventions of language

Curiosity, also added to the CANS-EC, is another characteristic that can support development and is a useful strength for young children. Curiosity is a characteristic or component of a child's personality that promotes, supports, and enhances development in all areas. This component is often associated with intelligence, as a child's questions and exploration often reflect it. Curiosity serves as a strong motivator and, therefore, results in actions that put a child in a position to learn and develop. Table 18.2 lists the benefits of curiosity in four developmental areas.

We must note again that curiosity is a characteristic considered by some temperament researchers to be reflective of temperament. This means that the characteristic is considered a stable and persistent component of personality, and that while it can be mediated by environmental factors, it is an overall tendency of the child. Assessment occurs by discussion with the caregiver(s) and child depending on age as well as observation of behavior. Table 18.3 lists manifestations of curiosity in infants, toddlers, preschoolers, and school-age children that will help assessors in identifying the characteristic of curiosity as an area of strength.

Caregiver Needs and Strengths

Many caregiver needs and strengths items in the older CANS versions were included in the early childhood version. One of the main characteristics of the CANS-EC is reflection of the importance of the parent-child relationship throughout all of the domains. Empathy is rated in this section. It is considered a critical parental capacity in the formation of a positive parent-child relationship within the first three years, supporting a child's experience of being understood and laying the foundation of developing this

Table 18.2
Developmental Benefits of Curiosity in Children

Motor Development	Cognitive Development	Language Development	Social and Emotional Development
• Initiates attempts to move and explore the environment developing both fine and gross motor skills • Keeps infant/youth motivated to sustain activity and attempts • Curiosity reduces the frustration experienced by attempting new tasks	• Triggers learning by exploring • Encourages children to question • Supports lateral thinking • Develops understanding of causal relationships • Allows the child to enter into new experiences	• Encourages imitation • Encourages interaction both verbally and nonverbally • Places the child in the position to observe social conventions of language	• Encourages learning related to social cues, behavior, and practices • Encourages child to learn to take another's perspective • Challenges the egocentric nature of the child • Supports thinking related to feeling states in relationship to behavior

Table 18.3
Observations of Curiosity in Infants, Toddlers, Preschoolers, and School-Age Children

Observations of Curiosity in Children

Infants

- Turns head to listen to sounds
- Follows activity with eyes or stops movement to watch activity
- Slows breathing and movement when observing new person or occurrence
- Explores with mouth and hands
- Reacts to novelty or change
- Can be enticed to take action
- Spontaneously imitates intonation and words

Toddlers

- Communicates a questioning stance through gestures resulting in parent's explanations of actions or occurrences
- Actively explores new environments
- Frequently imitates others actions
- Is persistent in learning how items work
- Asks questions

Preschoolers/School Age Children

- Requests adults to offer detailed explanations and reasons for behavior
- Searches for relationships between concepts
- Demonstrates ability to categorize
- Demonstrates a tendency to notice details or changes in the environment
- Can relate to others' likes and dislikes

capacity within himself. The CANS-EC also adds social resources as an item to reflect how important it is for caregivers to have a network of support. This item refers to caregivers' need for support from a network of friends, community members, and/or family members who are not paid but are available to them. Some families with young children may need this more than any other service. This item looks at the presence of support available to the caregiver and does not focus on the child's experience of such support.

Risk Factors

It is important to be aware of the child's prenatal and birth experiences. The CANS-EC adds birth weight, exposure to substances, prenatal care, labor and delivery, and maternal availability as items of assessment. Sword (2003) discusses the positive impact of prenatal care on pregnancy outcomes by linking mothers to health and social services that further a healthy lifestyle and social support. All of these factors have relevance to how an infant or child experiences care giving and how they accept parental care and support. This is critical to the development of the attachment relationship.

KEY COMPONENTS TO THE ASSESSMENT OF YOUNG CHILDREN

In *New Visions for the Developmental Assessment of Infants and Young Children*, Greenspan and Meisels (1996) outlined principles of assessment that have become the gold standard for developmental assessment. These standards include the concepts of:

- Never separating the child from his parent(s) for the purpose of assessment;
- Focusing on the parental capacities along with the individual child's capacities;
- Recognizing the interrelatedness of all areas of development;
- Fully including parents in the treatment and support of the child;
- Recognizing strengths as well as needs; and, of primary importance,
- Recognizing that all development occurs within the context of the parent-child relationship.

We find ways to weave all of these conditions into the parent's experience of seeking and accepting help for their child.

One can attest to the importance of all of these elements in the process of assessment, but nothing is more important than the tool itself offering these same assessments. From the moment assessors are introduced to the concepts identified above, they must have the means to ensure that these critical components are part of the assessment process. The use of a tool that will allow for this to happen validates the importance of these concepts for assessors and parents alike. The CANS-EC version offers helping professionals a framework for thinking about early childhood development and mental health. This framework allows for the collaborative experience of identifying needs and strengths from a variety of sources, embracing the interrelatedness of development and mental health, looking at all factors that influence a child, and observing a child within the parent-child relationship. This version supports seeing children within their home environment, as this will often produce the most meaningful information. As all of these conditions are met in the CANS-EC, the end result will be the development of an action oriented treatment plan. The identified needs and strengths and the associated interventions can be shared with all partners involved in the family's care to create a common understanding and language.

ROLE OF PARENTS IN A CANS-EC ASSESSMENT

The Parent-Child Setting

The concept that young children should never be separated from their parents for the purposes of assessment often becomes a pragmatic issue that is argued as being unnecessary or too challenging to arrange. Perhaps more so than any other age group, young children's functioning should never be considered representative of their full potential outside the presence and support of their primary caregivers. Parents also help us to understand what we are seeing, as they may interpret the child's actions and behaviors, their likes and dislikes. Parents serve an organizing function for their children and it is not developmentally appropriate to expect that young children can do this alone or with the help of a stranger (Greenspan & Meisels, 1996). In the past and even to this day, very young children are separated from parents only to meet a stranger who takes them to a strange place. It is no surprise and quite possibly an adaptive skill that a child so placed appears aloof and disengaged. Once staff and policy-makers hear a rationale for not separating the child and parents, they usually embrace it as a necessary condition for assessment. (Of course, some parents may be challenged in supporting their children and may in fact hinder their development, and this is important to understand as well.) Thus, while the CANS-EC can be completed without parents being present through parent interview or chart review, the assessment best occurs within the parent-child setting.

The recognition that the parent is needed to support the child through the assessment process leads to an appreciation for the vital nature of the parent-child relationship. This must be understood, valued, and infused in the assessment and treatment planning process. As stated by Weatherston and Tableman (2002), "Central to an infant mental health perspective is the belief that all children benefit from a sustained primary relationship that is nurturing, supportive, and protective." The attachment relationship itself is the avenue through which physical, cognitive, social, and emotional development occurs. Any challenge to this relationship can impede a child's development, impair the ability to relate to others, and limit the ability to explore and learn. We must use the assessment process to assist in understanding what the infant brings to the relationship, what the parent brings to the relationship, and the environmental and cultural context in which both exist (Weatherston & Tableman, 2002). To do this we spend time both observing the infant, listening to parents' interpretations of their infant's behavior, and observing how the relationship works to support or interfere with a child's development. What the infant brings to the relationship includes his temperament, experiences related to birth, and whether his physical and emotional needs are met. What parents bring to the relationship includes their past experiences of being nurtured as a child, their own beliefs regarding the function of relationships, the status of their current situation, and their level of need and ability to be supported in the parenting role. How these two dynamics fit together must be understood by both the clinician and, ultimately, the parent, for optimum development to occur. The assessment process using the CANS-EC supports this value by including the various domains and educating parents as to its importance.

As with any other field or specialty area, it is human nature to give more focus to one's own area of interest—whether it is mental health, early intervention, or specific areas of dysfunction. As we noted, an assessment tool in and of itself can either support or undermine this way of thinking. Knowledge of developmental issues is important in understanding an older child, but at no other time in life is development so intertwined with mental health and overall functioning than in the early years. When one thinks of an older adult coping with depression, the concept of "shutting down" is often brought to mind. When this same phenomena occurs within young children, we cannot expect anything other than the occurrence of regression in other areas as well. One example is the co-occurrence of speech and language difficulties with social and emotional problems (per researchers cited in Knitzer, 2000). Although developmental issues can occur without the presence of mental health issues, the reverse is much more unlikely. The comprehensive nature of the CANS-EC tool supports this notion and forces clinicians to hold this concept in mind.

D.W. Winnocott's (1965) now famous statement "there is no such thing as a baby" became the foundation for the concept that infants must be viewed within the familial, environmental, and cultural context in which they enter the world. The premise of why home-based services can be effective embraces this concept for all children, but it is of critical importance in the early years because of a young child's high level of dependence on caregivers. Early childhood is a time when parents are needed to meet the needs of their children in a way that supports both optimal brain development and a secure attachment relationship. If caregivers are not able to find their own support system to accomplish this task their ability to do this may be diminished. A lack of resources, parental mental or physical health challenges, and unstable housing can have a profound affect on a parent's ability to be present and available to their children. This is a necessary area to assess with all families and should be tied to intervention strategies whenever a need is identified.

Use of Protective Factors in Assessment and Treatment

Much attention has been given to the importance of focusing on strengths in the assessment process for all ages of children. When a child has well-developed areas of strength, research shows that the child preserves a higher level of functioning and reduces the likelihood for engaging in high-risk behavior (Lyons, 2004). Although the research on protective factors in young children is not extensive, the studies that have been done offer implications for assessment and treatment planning. The protective factors described as low distress, sociability, high vigor and drive, and advanced self-help skills have been replicated in more than one longitudinal study (Werner, 2000). The CANS items of attachment, regulatory problems, developmental/intellectual, curiosity and playfulness relate to these areas and should be given special attention when determining the presence of strengths. Research has informed us that risk factors have less of a direct correlation to dysfunction than protective factors do to ongoing mental health even in the face of adversity. If a child who has numerous strengths is then exposed to a negative home environment, strengths are not extinguished (Anthony, 1987).

The CANS also focuses on the strengths of the parents, not only the child, and again the relationship between parents and children must enter into the assessment. Parents considered good copers were better able to help their children with the problems confronting them (Anthony, 1987). Parents are clearly in the role of mediating the stressors in the environment for children, and the more they are able to focus on this task the better the outcomes for children. Many helping professionals as well as parents have been frustrated with the lack of progress when the focus is solely on deficits. It is much easier to build on something that one already knows how to do than to develop an entirely new skill set. Children, like adults, gravitate toward their strengths. When we apply this understanding to assessment and treatment planning, then professionals, parents, and children experience a greater investment in treatment and movement towards higher functioning.

Throughout the process of assessment, as we are recognizing and using the parent-child relationship to understand the child, we carry this same principle into the interventions that we develop. While it may seem illogical to not include a parent in the treatment of an infant, toddler, or preschooler, this is a concept that is often forgotten. There are many reasons for this. Parents may in fact not want to participate in the treatment of their children. Clinicians often have not been trained in this way of thinking and can be uncomfortable with what they might consider a lack of skill on their part. But the very presence of a clinician where a family relationship or individual child is struggling is of therapeutic value. Clinicians who value this phenomenon and seek reflective supervision open the door for the use of the CANS-EC versions to guide them in ongoing assessment and intervention.

IMPLEMENTATION ISSUES

Professionals in various programs for high-risk youth have recognized the need to improve the assessment and treatment planning process and to have all levels of staff see the value in the chosen assessment. As administrative and supervisory staff were oriented to the philosophy, function, and clinical utility of the CANS-EC, the belief emerged that this version would meet the needs of children and families. The more critical task then became to demonstrate these same concepts to the line staff that would be using the assessment on a regular basis. The clinicians were familiar with the benefits in assessing families from a strength-based perspective and in using the assessment process to develop an action oriented plan. However, there was a need to communicate with families and providers with a common language, and the clinicians felt limited with our current assessment. Although the concepts were universally accepted as beneficial, clinicians needed to understand more fully how the assessment could change the clinical experience for families as well as staff. Just as the infant and toddler must have actual experiences for certain capacities to emerge, so too must clinicians experience a process before investment emerges.

Use of Tool at All Staff Levels

Both bachelor-level and masters-level staff would be using the instrument. Therefore, the assessment had to be one that could be used by all levels of staff and that was not specific to certain disciplines. Staff needed to feel confident that they understood fully what the instrument was assessing and how to reliably score the items. The language and construction of the CANS-EC is not overly complex and results in a comfort level with the process for both families and clinicians. Through the training process, staff became certified in the use of the CANS once they passed vignettes at the needed level of reliability. As a result, all levels of staff had the same understanding and could communicate with one another in a functional way about the needs and strengths of the family. The importance of communication within the various child-serving systems has been emphasized repeatedly within the literature. Zeanah and colleagues

(2005), in their report *Addressing Social-Emotional Development and Infant Mental Health in Early Childhood Systems*, state:

> [T]he take home message is that how state MCH [maternal and child health] programs and their partners communicate about infant mental health deserves considerable discussion during the planning process. We recommend that grantees and their partners adopt a communication strategy that focuses on promoting positive development through positive interactions between caregivers and their children. This focus on prevention may help avoid some audiences' difficulties with the term "mental health" and the idea that infants can suffer from mental illness. Finally, we recommend that the specific communication strategy and terminology used be crafted for the community being addressed. (p. 5)

Staff felt unfamiliar with issues related to young children, however, so we augmented the training with more detail regarding the items, especially those related to child functioning and needs. The staff was given examples of expected capacities within individual areas and ways to determine when there is dysfunction or suboptimal functioning. We also included information on typical development and behavior, normal sequences of development, and how to differentiate the typical from the atypical. Within the Allegheny County Systems of Care Initiative, staff members were assisted through the development of a manual and supplemental guide to support the process of assessment in the various areas (Lyons et al., 2006; Cornett, 2007). Table 18.4 has examples of questions that can be used to elicit information related to the various items.

Importance of Observation and Empathic Skills

Although questioning parents is important and often leads to useful information, the staff were strongly encouraged to use observation of the child and parent/child interaction to guide their rating of the CANS-EC items as well. Clinicians needed support in remembering that families often are at a loss themselves in communicating the concerns or even having an awareness that problems may exist. Parent report alone should not be considered sufficient in rating an item. Ignoring needs because parents cannot see the issue was also discouraged. Staff needed to further develop their observation skills with young children and their parents. The concepts of sensitivity and responsiveness to cues, respect for emerging autonomy, the presence of developmentally appropriate communication and scaffolding are ones that are considered essential in observing infant-parent interaction (Erickson, 2005). Opportunities for observing the child in play interactions, responding to teaching, limit-setting, and feeding routines give valuable information. Staff were encouraged to observe play with the goal of determining whether the play is mutual and reciprocal, sustained, and mutually enjoyable. This has relevance in rating several of the CANS-EC items, especially those related to developmental/intellectual, attachment, and the strength items of interpersonal, curiosity, and playfulness. Observing teaching and limit-setting tasks gives insight into how well a child follows instructions, copes with frustration, and makes use of the parent for assistance in coping, and how well the parent provides support to the child. This has implications for rating the items related to attachment, regulation, developmental/intellectual, caregiver needs and strengths, and the child interpersonal and curiosity strengths items. The combination of parent report, child observation, and parent-child observation allows clinicians to consider multiple factors when assessing CANS items.

Table 18.4
Family Interview Questions

Item	Family Interview Questions
Motor Skills	**Infants** Have you seen a progression of motor skills from month to month? How would you describe your infant's capacity for moving around to explore his or her environment? How would you describe your infant's ability to grasp and handle small objects? **Toddlers** Describe how well your toddler moves around. How would you describe your toddler's skills in activities such as drinking out of a cup or eating with a spoon? Is your toddler becoming more coordinated? **Preschoolers** Does your child appear to enjoy physical activity or become frustrated with certain tasks? Is your child improving his or her ability to move faster and in a more coordinated way? Can your child imitate simple drawings and movements? Have you or anyone else had concerns about your child's motor skills?
Developmental/ Intellectual	**Infants** Has your infant been able to show you that he or she remembers or anticipates your actions? Is your infant aware of what is occurring around him? Does your infant imitate your actions? **Toddlers** Do you feel your toddler remembers things? Does your toddler seem to understand routines, such as a bedtime routine? Does your toddler copy things that he or she has seen you or others do? Does your toddler ask questions? **Preschoolers** Can your child do tasks such as sorting shapes and recognizing colors? Has anyone in a preschool/school setting ever voiced concerns about your child's abilities? How does your child do with self-help activities?
Attachment	**Infants** Do you feel comfortable with your infant? Do you feel special to your baby? How does your baby react to strangers and to separation from you?

Table 18.4 (Continued)

	Are you able to comfort and soothe your infant when he or she is upset? Is it difficult to understand what your infant wants from you? **Toddlers/Preschoolers** How do you feel about you and your child's interaction? Do you feel your child is too clingy? How does your child react to separation and reunion with you? Does your child seek help from you when he or she is hurt or needs something? Does your child choose to be with you when other adults are around?
Anxiety	**Infants** Does your infant ever appear to scan his environment or appear easily startled? Does your infant demonstrate fears or worry in situations that you would not expect? How easily can you comfort your infant when he or she appears distressed? **Toddlers/Preschoolers** Does your child ever appear nervous or worried? Does this keep your child from social interaction or normal routines? Have you needed to put strategies in place to help your child cope with fears or worries?
Regulatory Problems	**Infants** Is your infant in a routine regarding eating and sleeping? Are there certain experiences that over-stimulate or bother your infant? Does your infant have a difficult time calming down when upset? **Toddlers/Preschoolers** Do you have any concerns about your child's ability to control his activity level? Does your child react to frustration or difficult situations poorly? Does your child seem to be in a predictable routine with eating and sleeping?
Adjustment to Trauma	**Infants** Has your infant witnessed or experienced any stressful or traumatic situations within your family or community? Has your infant had to be separated from you? Have you noticed regression in your infant's development? Does your infant appear to be guarded or worried at times? **Toddlers/Preschoolers** Has your child experienced separations from caregivers? Has your child experienced nightmares, night terrors, or regressive behaviors during or after difficult situations? Do certain situations make your child uncomfortable or react in a way that is unusual for him?

Perhaps most important in training was the emphasis placed on creating a positive experience for families. Initially, parents need to be oriented to the process so they know what to expect and can participate fully. Trainers discussed strategies for allowing a family to start at its own comfort level and then sequencing its narrative in a way it chooses. Meetings with parents and young children exposed several scenarios. The most common was that the family believed the child may have some challenges but was confused as to why a mental health clinician was assessing the issues. When such a meeting is a family's first experience of any kind in getting help for the child, the parents are uncomfortable and worried. The story that these parents tell reflects all of these elements in that they don't know where to start, give little information initially, and count on the clinician to support the process. In these scenarios it seems even more critical to have a framework that can be shared with them, so again the tool itself helps them understand the interrelatedness of all domains.

DISCOVERING THE CLINICAL UTILITY OF THE CANS 0-4

The provision of home-based services to high-risk families is often a difficult task that results in staff burnout and turnover. This is particularly distressing to a director of children's services within a community mental health center because maintaining service permanence for families is of utmost importance. Interviews with staff members who left the program turned up complaints of feeling that families won't work with them, that the staff member does not see progress, does not know which interventions work, and provides little variability in types of services. Interestingly, when polling families regarding past and present therapy experiences, there was a parallel in the responses. Families have the same needs as clinicians if there is to be positive feelings regarding the therapy experience. Awareness of this at all levels, from administrative to line staff, is critical in evaluating and supporting the clinical process. The use of the CANS-EC has demonstrated to staff how these types of experiences need not occur.

Assessment must have meaning; it must produce information that can be translated into action for change. Samuel Meisels (2001) cites Hayes, Nelson & Jarrett as defining the meaning of assessment as the ability to contribute to decision-making about practices, interventions, and evaluation of progress. The comprehensive nature of the CANS assessment assures clinicians that they will collect the needed information and therefore inform the treatment planning process adequately. In addition, all CANS versions are designed to collect only the information that is relevant and needed. This eliminates the scenario in which clinicians have information that is documented or placed in the chart only to remain there with no use to treatment planning. When service providers and families have worked in a collaborative fashion to identify needs and strengths, a common mission arises based on an understanding of what will occur in treatment. Engagement is then the product of being heard, being understood from a strength-based perspective, and being poised to use the information to develop a plan.

Once information is gathered through a combination of parent interview, observation, and review of pertinent data, the family and service provider use the results to develop a plan. The expectation for needs and strengths to be included in the plan allows service providers and families both to feel that treatment will meet the array of needs. The decision for how this will occur is a joint effort that looks at traditional as well as nontraditional strategies. The end result is an individualized plan stemming from family input and clinical judgment that allows for everyone to evaluate progress in the same fashion. Families have often expressed their surprise as well as satisfaction in having their strengths recognized. The fact that strengths are used in treatment plans has improved the participation of families in their own treatment, the satisfaction of staff, and outcomes. Engaging families in the assessment and treatment planning process also teaches families how to think about their child's needs and strengths in a way that benefits them long after treatment ends.

Before the CANS was implemented, it was not uncommon for interventions to be determined before there was a common understanding of the issues. Assessment and treatment plans often were not related or used synergistically. Pressure to bring about change was the driving force in the search for creating a new dynamic. Staff have benefited from support in the types of interventions that are promoted in early childhood intervention. Although it is essential that interventions be individualized to the needs of the family, the types of interventions in working with young children have some common threads. Early childhood intervention consists of a variety of strategies to promote the social/emotional well-being of young children, to help families support their children's development, to enhance the non-familial caregivers, and to ensure mental health services to those that need them (Knitzer, 2000). High-risk families often have multiple needs; mental health services should not be delivered without consideration of the child health and developmental services, parenting interventions, and services to support all caregivers (Harden & Lythcott, 2005). The practice of infant mental health (Weatherston & Tableman, 2002) creates the need to provide a range of services, including establishing an alliance, meeting concrete needs, supportive counseling, developmental guidance, teaching coping skills, and infant-parent psychotherapy. All of these interventions should be implemented with the value of the parent-child relationship in mind.

Using the CANS-EC as a Decision Support Tool

The need to determine an appropriate level of care was one that had obvious strong clinical implications. Before use of the CANS, many believed that the families we were serving were not being helped at the needed level of care, resulting in less than optimal outcomes. The assessment process did not effectively guide the level of care determination. The ability to use the CANS-EC as a way to make this determination was one of the most attractive features of the assessment. Research regarding risk factors, protective factors, and interventions guided the rationale for the development of a decision support algorithm. It is often stated that attending to accumulative risk factors is of utmost importance. An individual child may have several risk factors; risk may also be more significant in the parent-child interaction, family relationships, and the environment in which the child lives (Zeanah & Zeanah, 2001). In a 1979 study, children with two risk factors were four times as likely to have a mental health condition as those exposed to one or no risk factors (Rutter, 1979). With this research in mind, the children presenting the greatest concern would be those experiencing risk in multiple areas along with an absence of strengths within both the child and the caregiver. The research regarding protective factors supports the notion that strengths in the caregiver mediate risk in the child. In regards to frequency of services, infants and toddlers at risk benefit from frequent contacts including home visits, phone contacts between sessions, and daily contacts when crisis or extreme distress occurs (Weatherston & Tableman, 2002). In making level-of-care decisions for infants and children to age five, staff at the Community Mental Health Center in Lawrenceburg, Indiana use an algorithm developed in consultation with supervisors to ensure that families needs are being met, as shown in Table 18.5.

Table 18.5
Level of Care Decision-Making Guide

Community Mental Health Center, Inc.
Intensive Youth Services
Level of Care Decision-Making Guide

0-5 years olds

Criterion 1:   One rating of 2, or two or more ratings of 1, on:

         Attachment

         Failure to Thrive

         Anxiety

         Regulatory Problems

         Adjustment to Trauma

Criterion 2:   One rating of 2, or two or more ratings of 1, on:

         Birth Weight

         Prenatal Care

         Labor and Delivery

         Substance Exposure

         Parent or Sibling Behavior

         Abuse/Neglect

         Maternal Availability

Criterion 3:   One rating of 2, or two or more ratings of 1, on:

         Physical/Behavioral Health

         Supervision

         Involvement

         Knowledge

         Organization

         Resources

         Residential Stability

         Employment

         Safety

Systems of Care: Meets first 3 criteria

Intensive Community   Meets 1 and either 2, or 3 Services
(but not all 3):

Outpatient: All others

Enhancing the Supervisory Process With the Use of Outcomes Data

Some of the same research findings that led to the development of the algorithm were used to determine what outcomes would demonstrate success. The value and benefit of relationship-based treatment led to measures that demonstrate improved functioning in this area. In a centrality of relationships paradigm, outcomes consist of qualities of the parent-child interaction, family functioning, parental knowledge, parental confidence and satisfaction, and child adaptive capacities (Weston et al., 1997). With this in mind, the CANS-EC items of family functioning, attachment, knowledge, involvement, and the problem areas are identified as items to be tracked for decreased need and increased strengths. The CANS-EC assessment is administered every ninety days, coinciding with the treatment plan updates. The supervisors use individual and group supervision to build staff's ability to make use of this information in evaluating effectiveness of interventions. Including staff in this evaluation has proven to improve investment in the process as well as the provision of high quality services.

Ensuring Quality Improvement Through Monitoring

The importance of monitoring the use of the CANS-EC led the supervisors in the community mental health center program to identify a process for doing so. Staff were advised of the process and taught the methodology for reviewing completed CANS. Staff members also discussed the benefits of a peer review process that would parallel the supervisory reviews, and this is now being developed. The monitoring process consists of identifying all items identified as 2 or 3 in the needs sections and 0 and 1 in the strengths section, and then reviewing the treatment plans for their inclusion in the plan. The same process is paralleled at the individual family team level. When treatment plans are reviewed, the monitoring of how changes in the CANS items correspond to changes in the types of intervention is noted. This information helps to support the value of recognizing progress and the changes in interventions needed.

SUMMARY

This chapter reviews the issues related to the assessment of infants, toddlers, and preschoolers for mental health and developmental needs. The chapter describes how the use of the CANS-EC supports the core conditions considered necessary in the assessment of young children. As clinicians seek improved outcomes for children and families, the value of using the CANS-EC for the assessment and treatment planning process is described.

References

American Academy of Child and Adolescent Psychiatry (1997). Practice parameters for the psychiatric assessment of infants and toddlers. *Journal of the American Academy of Child and Adolescent Psychiatry, 36,* 21S–36S.

Anthony, E. J. (1987). Risk, vulnerability, and resilience: An overview. In E. J. Anthony & B. J. Cohler (Eds.), *The Invulnerable Child.* New York: Guilford.

Carter, A. S., Briggs-Gowan, M. & Davis, N. (2004). Assessment of young children's social-emotional development and psychopathology: Recent advances and recommendations for practice. *Journal of Child Psychology and Psychiatry, 45*, 109–134.

Carter, S., Osofsky, J. D. & Hann, D. M. (1991). *Maternal depression and affect in adolescent mothers and their infants.* Paper presented at the biennial meeting of the Society for Research in Child Development, Seattle.

Chess, S. & Thomas, A. (1959). Characteristics of the individual child's behavioral response to the environment. *American Journal of Orthopsychiatry, 24*, 791–802.

Cornett, S. (2007). *Child and adolescent needs and strengths (early childhood): A supplemental guide for the comprehensive assessment of young children and their families.* Unpublished manuscript.

Department of Health and Human Services (DHHS) (2000). *Report of the surgeon general's conference on children's mental health: A national action agenda.* Washington, DC: Author. This report is available online at: www.ussurgeongeneral.gov.

Erikson, M. (2005). Using direct observation in prevention and intervention services in infant and preschool mental health: Training and practice issues. In K. M. Finello (Ed.), *The handbook of training and practice in infant and preschool mental health.* San Francisco: Josey-Bass Press.

Feinberg, E. & Fenichel, E. (1996). *Who will hear my cry? Developing a system of care to meet the needs of infants, toddlers, preschoolers and their families.* Washington, DC: National Technical Assistance Center for Children's Mental Health, Georgetown University Child Development Center.

Greenspan, S. I. & Meisels, S. J., with Zero to Three Work Group on Developmental Assessment (1996). Toward a new vision for the developmental assessment of infants and young children. In S. J. Meisels & E. Fenichel (Eds.), *New visions for the developmental assessment of infants and young children.* Washington DC: Zero to Three Press.

Greenspan, S. I. (1985). Comprehensive clinical approaches to developmental and emotional disorders in infants and young children: Emerging perspectives. In *Maternal and child health technical information series.* Rockville, MD: U.S. Department of Health and Human Services.

Guralnick, M. J. (Ed.) (1997). *The effectiveness of early intervention.* Baltimore, MD: Paul H. Brookes.

Harden, B. & Lythcott, M. (2005). Kitchen therapy and beyond: Mental health services for young children in alternative settings. In K. M. Finello (Ed.), *Handbook of training and practice in infant and preschool mental health.* San Francisco: Josey-Bass.

Kaplan-Sanoff, M. (1996). The effects of maternal substance abuse on young children: Myths and realities. In E. Erwin (Ed.), *Putting children first.* Baltimore: Paul Brookes.

Knitzer, J. (2000). Early childhood mental health services: A policy and systems development perspective. In J. Shonkoff & S Meisels (Eds.), *Handbook of early childhood intervention* (2d ed.). New York: Cambridge University Press.

Lester, B. M. & Tronick, E. Z. (1994). Prenatal drug exposure and child outcome. *Special Issue of Infant Mental Health Journal, 15*, 107–120.

Lyons, J. S., Baerger, J. D. & Almeida, M.C. (2000). *Child and adolescent needs and strengths: An information integration tool for early development: CANS 0-3 manual.* Winnetka, IL: Buddin Praed Foundation.

Lyons, J. S. (2004). *Redressing the emperor: Improving our children's public mental health system.* Westport, CT: Praeger.

Lyons, J. S., Ryan, S. & Duran, F. (2007). *Child and adolescent needs and strengths, early childhood: An information integration tool for young children ages birth to eight.* Winnetka, IL: Buddin Praed Foundation.

Lyons, J. S., Ryan, S. & Walton, B. (2006). *Child and adolescent needs and strengths: Comprehensive multisystem assessment (birth to 5).* Winnetka, IL: Buddin Praed Foundation.

Meisels, S. J. (2001). Fusing assessment and intervention: Changing parents' and providers' views of young children. *Zero to Three, 21,* 4–10.

Murray, L. & Cooper, P. (1997). *Postpartum depression and child development.* New York: Guilford.

National Institute of Child Health and Human Development (NICHD), Early Child Care Research Network (2000). Characteristics and quality of child care for toddlers and pre-schoolers. *Applied Developmental Science, 4,* 116–135.

Pfefferbaum, B. (1997). Posttraumatic stress disorder in children: A review of the past 10 years. *Journal of the American Academy of Child and Adolescent Psychiatry, 36,* 1503–1511.

Poulsen, M. K. (2005). Diagnosis of mental health in young children. In K. M. Finello (Ed.), *Handbook of training and practice in infant and preschool mental health.* San Francisco: Josey-Bass.

Rutter, M. (1979). Protective factors in children's responses to stress and disadvantage. In M. W. Kent & J. E. Rolf (Eds.), *Social competence in children.* Hanover, NH: University of New England.

Sword, W. (2003). Prenatal care use among women of low income a matter of "taking care of self." *Qualitative Health Research, 13,* 319–332.

Trout, M. (1987). *Infant mental health: A psychotherapeutic model of intervention.* Champaign, IL: Infant-Parent Institute.

Weatherston, D. & Tableman, B. (2002). *Infant mental health services: Supporting competencies/reducing risks.* Southgate, MI: Michigan Association for Infant Mental Health.

Webster-Stratton C. (2003). Aggression in young children: Service proven to be effective in reducing aggression. In R. E. Tremblay, R. G. Barr & RdeV Peters (Eds.), *Encyclopedia on early childhood development.* Montreal, Quebec: Centre of Excellence for Early Childhood Development,1–6. Available online at: www.excellence-earlychildhood.a/documents/Webster-StrattonANGxp.pdf.

Werner, E. (2000). Protective factors and individual resilience. In J. Shonkoff & S. Meisels (Eds.), *Handbook of early childhood intervention* (2d ed.). New York: Cambridge University Press.

Weston, D. R., Ivins, B., Heffron, M. C. & Sweet, N. (1997). Formulating the centrality of relationships in early intervention: An organizational perspective. *Infants and Children, 9,* 1–12.

Winnicott, D. W. (1965). The theory of the parent-infant relationship. In *The maturational processes and the facilitating environment.* New York: International Universities Press, 37–55.

Zeanah, C. H. & Zeanah, P. D. (2001). Towards a definition of infant mental health. *Zero to Three, 22,* 13–20.

Zeanah, C. H., Jr. (Ed.) (1993). *Handbook of infant mental health.* New York: Guilford.

Zeanah, P. D., Stafford B., Nagle G. & Rice, T. (2005). Addressing social-emotional development and infant mental health in early childhood systems. Los Angeles: National Center for Infant and Early Childhood Health Policy, Building State Early Childhood Comprehensive Systems Series, No. 12.

Zero to Three (2005). *Diagnostic classification of mental health and developmental disorders of infancy and early childhood* (rev. ed.): DC:0-3R. Washington, DC: Zero to Three Press.

Part 6

TCOM Methods

Chapter 19

Needs-Based Planning Using the CANS

by Purva Rawal, Ph.D. and John S. Lyons, Ph.D.

INTRODUCTION

In mental health, as in any health care sector, the goal is to improve client symptomatology and functioning. As managed care has moved into the public behavioral health sector, the need to quantify clinical improvement has become a widespread goal. Efforts to improve treatment quality and to monitor treatment outcomes rely on identifying the needs and characteristics of a population—their symptoms, functioning, sense of well-being, and circumstance, among other factors. Needs-based planning is the primary vehicle in outcomes monitoring efforts. As these efforts progress, data on client needs and strengths yield important information on treatment outcomes (Lyons et al., 1997), and when individual outcomes are aggregated and analyzed, conclusions on the overall effectiveness of a service can be made.

In addition to assessing client change during treatment and determining its overall effectiveness, data on client characteristics provide valuable information on the clinical decision-making process in the service delivery system (Lyons et al., 1997). Clinical decision-making is a key part of the service delivery system, as it directly affects the placement of individuals in services. Needs-based planning plays a pivotal role in improving clinical decision-making by providing data on population characteristics at admission and other key points in service delivery; these data are then used to identify ways to guide clinical decision-making and make it more consistent. Improved placement decisions provide for decreased fiscal spending, more clinically appropriate use of services, and improved treatment outcomes for individuals.

Needs-based planning, clinical decision-making, and treatment outcomes and effectiveness are part of the domain of outcomes management, an expanding sector in mental health. In addition to the changes brought by the introduction of managed care into behavioral health, the United States Congress strongly suggested that the National Institute of Mental Health, among other National Institutes of Health, allocate 15 percent of their funding to health services research (Donenberg et al., 1999). The increased attention to outcomes management and establishment of ongoing systems to collect data and monitor outcomes has occurred in the context of political and health care financing changes.

Needs-based planning is a primary vehicle for establishing outcomes management systems. It is rooted in needs assessment, which occurs daily at the level of the individual client in mental health. When someone presents for treatment, a clinician assesses his symptomatology, daily functioning, treatment needs, hobbies, community involvement, and other strengths. This assessment of individual needs and strengths has been extended to assess the needs of entire service systems. Therefore, needs-based planning approaches use information on client characteristics to provide system-level data regarding those being served. At this level, service providers, administrators, policymakers, researchers, and service consumers receive a broader view of mental health needs at key junctures in the service system.

The success of individual needs assessments, needs-based planning approaches, and large scale outcomes management systems are contingent on the use of structured and reliable measures, such as the Child and Adolescent Needs and Strengths Assessment (CANS) (Lyons et al., 2001). The CANS allows for the retrospective, prospective, and repeated collection of individual data on a variety of symptom, functioning, risk, treatment needs, caregiver capacity, and strengths domains. CANS data are used:

- By service providers in treatment planning for clients;

- In the aggregate, to yield clinical profiles of those in treatment;

- To create trajectories of change in treatment for individuals and groups; and

- To determine predictors of treatment outcome.

The CANS has also been used extensively to support clinical decision-making at multiple levels of care. Multiple versions of the CANS are used in individual needs assessment, needs-based planning approaches, and other outcomes monitoring efforts (Lyons et al., 2003; Lyons, 2004; Rawal et al., 2004). Overall, the CANS has been found to be a reliable measure of clinical and psychosocial needs and to be a reliable outcomes management tool with direct clinical and research utility (Anderson et al., 2003).

The goals for this chapter are four:

- To define needs-based planning approaches,

- To discuss the methodology of needs-based planning,

- To examine the role of needs-based planning approaches in a larger outcomes management effort, and

- To provide illustrations of needs-based planning evaluations using the CANS.

DEFINING NEEDS-BASED PLANNING APPROACHES

Needs-based planning approaches can accomplish two purposes—to assess unmet need within a target system of care, and to assess whether services are being used inappropriately within a service system. These goals can be met through the systematic measurement of the clinical characteristics of a target population. The CANS allows for assessment and use of a variety of needs and strengths, tailored to the requirements of the service system. This section will briefly discuss how to assess unmet need, but the section and chapter will focus primarily on assessing the appropriateness of service use.

Assessing Unmet Need

When assessing unmet need, we must first identify a target population (Lyons et al., 1997). In public mental health systems, this is most commonly a geographic region, or individuals with particular insurance providers (e.g., Medicaid, Medicaid managed care). For instance, a school system may undertake a needs-based planning study to determine the level of clinical need among their students, or a large state public mental health system may want to examine whether the needs of youth in its system are being met. In these cases, the clinical needs and strengths of a population at large are being assessed. Thus, the first step is to clearly identify a target population.

Next, a sampling strategy must be selected (Lyons et al., 1997). A random sampling strategy in which every case in the defined population has an equal chance at selection is optimal. In most cases, a stratified random sampling strategy is used (see below). Samples can be stratified by time period served, age, gender, race, insurance status, region, or socioeconomic factors, among others. Membership lists can be generated within strata, and the desired sample number can be chosen using a computer-generated list of random numbers.

Given that most needs-based planning studies are retrospective, achieving a sufficient amount of power in the sampling size is important to make definitive conclusions about the data. For a threshold of +/- 5 percent precision level, an *n* of approximately 300 cases is sufficient, and for +/- 3 percent, approximately 700 cases is sufficient (Lyons et al., 1997). An *n* beyond 700 is costly and is undertaken for larger planning studies in order to have sufficient sample sizes within service types for statistically meaningful comparisons.

Measurement is the foundation for all outcomes management efforts, including needs-based planning approaches. A variety of measures are used; however, a reliable and versatile measure such as the CANS is the most clinically useful because it directly maps onto criteria in the *Diagnostic and Statistical Manual of Mental Disorders* (DSM-IV, 1994) and onto service provider treatment plans, and it has continuing research and outcomes monitoring capabilities. The use of the CANS in needs-based planning approaches around the country and across child service sectors will be illustrated later in the chapter.

Identifying Inappropriate Service Use

To identify inappropriate use of a service, you first gather data on the clinical characteristics of children and adolescents in a particular level of care and then determine whether their collective profiles are appropriately matched to treatment. The focus, then, is on identifying a target population already being served by an existing treatment program, not on identifying unmet needs and additional service provisions (Lyons et al., 1997).

Again, the first step is to define the target population or the service(s) of interest. Usually, service systems will identify costly services such as psychiatric hospitalization or residential treatment for appropriateness of clinical placement to maximize limited resources. However, as service systems are becoming more nuanced in their approaches to placement, less expensive services such as treatment foster care are also being targeted for investigation. While presently there is little focus on the least expensive services in a child and adolescent system of care (e.g., outpatient services) (Lyons et al., 1997), the same principles would apply.

Stratified Random Sampling. The most optimal approach for identifying inappropriate service use is the stratified random sampling approach. To stratify a sample, a population must be divided into two or more groups, or strata. For most needs-based planning approaches that examine single or multiple services, samples can be stratified by time of service use—for example, the most recent twelve-month period before the start of the review. Samples can also be divided into multiple strata based on other factors, such as race, age, diagnosis, service type, and service provider. A random sample of cases is then taken from each stratum.

There are several factors to consider when deciding to use a stratified random sample. Stratification involves creating a representative sample, just as in simple random sampling. However, the primary concern is creating a sample within the stratum that is homogenous with respect to the characteristics being studied. This must be balanced against the costs of other methods, such as a simple random sample of the entire population, and the level of precision gained with the other methods. We have found that stratified random sampling is the most efficient use of resources for a needs-based planning project and the increased precision is not worth the additional costs of more extensive sampling procedures.

Different proportions of cases can be selected within strata and adjusted to meet the needs of the project. For instance, if the population is stratified by residential treatment providers, the proportion of randomly sampled cases can vary by the number of youth served in each treatment center. Other reasons for adjusting the sampling of proportions within each stratum are to ensure that strata with small numbers of cases are sampled, to ensure a sufficient sample size to perform relevant analyses within strata, and to adjust the proportion with respect to the heterogeneity or homogeneity of a population. For example, if system administrators and service providers know that youth serviced in residential treatment center X all have the same primary diagnosis, then a fewer number of cases may be sampled within this stratum than in residential treatment center Y, which serves youth with a wide range of diagnoses, given the emphasis on homogeneity among the characteristics studied within a stratum. Accounting for the level of variability on the characteristics under study allows for greater precision in measurement of those characteristics.

Stratified random samples are advantageous because they increase the efficiency of sampling compared to a large random sample of a population. The precision gained by using a large random sample should be weighed against the advantages of stratification. Overall, the reasons for using a stratified random sample is that the cost of and resources required for a stratified random sample approach are usually lower than a simple random sample approach, without a significant compromise in measurement precision.

Threshold for Receiving Services. Identifying inappropriate service use requires the evaluator to establish an appropriate level of need, or threshold, for receiving services. For instance, the criteria for psychiatric hospitalization may be dictated by medical necessity or the presence of a significant threat to oneself or others. The criteria to receive residential treatment may be the presence of at least one condition that meets criteria for a diagnosable disorder, and at least one significant functional impairment or one significant risk behavior. This would allow youth with significant mental health symptoms, but with a significant inability to function in at least one life domain or a significant risk behavior (e.g., elopement, self-harm, aggression), to receive non-community-based treatment. The threshold would also prevent youth who do not present with significant needs in at least two out of three of these domains from entering unnecessarily into a highly intensive and restrictive level of care.

The CANS is a reliable measurement tool with the ability to gather data on client characteristics for those already receiving services, to build thresholds for enrollment into services, and to test the validity and utility of the thresholds. The CANS has been used in multiple states to increase appropriate use of services. The majority of the needs-based planning projects undertaken with the CANS have focused on identifying inappropriate service use, as the examples later in the chapter reflect.

METHODOLOGY

For an outcomes monitoring process to be successful, three primary methodology questions must be answered: What targets will be measured? How will they be measured?

When will they be measured? In this section, we will examine the components and goals of each of these questions more closely. We will also examine change analysis, which is the simplest and most direct method for measuring outcomes.

What Targets to Measure

Simple as it may sound, the important first step in measuring targets is to define the goals and objectives of the project. Are the goals to identify unmet need, to assess appropriateness of care, or to identify cases that can be better served by a less restrictive placement? Outcomes of interest should guide the measurement process. There are challenges associated with these efforts, and not all outcomes management projects carefully examine the intended effects of a particular service. The most efficient and effective measurement occurs when you measure only the clinical aspects relevant to the study questions.

Second, outcomes important to key system stakeholders should be considered for maximum positive impact. Families, advocates, service providers, and community leaders can offer useful perspectives and information on local culture and organizational climates; this is integral to successfully executing a needs-based planning project and implementing an outcomes monitoring system. Participation by key stakeholders, especially service providers, increases the likelihood that suggested system changes will be implemented.

Third, you must define the feasibility and scope of the project. If the scope is not clearly defined, competing interests can expand it to a project's detriment. That is, you must harness the perspectives of stakeholders without allowing them to make the project stray from its goals. In considering what to measure, stay focused on the outcomes, measure information directly relevant to only those outcomes, and maintain a reasonable project scope; these are key to increasing the likelihood of successfully completing a needs-based planning evaluation and implementing an outcomes monitoring process.

How to Measure

The foundation of an outcomes management process is measurement. A measure's levels of reliability, validity, and research and clinical utility can cause a project's success or failure. A review of the relevant and existing measurement choices is a necessary first step. Measures with existing databases and norms that can be used as benchmarks for your own sample are ideal; if a measure exists that fulfills your criteria, use it—there is no point in creating an additional measure that does not have an available body of psychometric data.

Deciding how to administer the measure is an important second step. Will data be collected retrospectively? If so, who will collect the data? Which stakeholders can be involved in the training and data collection processes? Are data being collected prospectively? If so, the characteristics of both the services under examination and those being served should drive the data collection. Will retrospective and prospective measurement options be needed at various phases of the project? The next section focuses on the CANS as a measure in outcomes management projects in the context of these questions and considerations.

The CANS in Needs-Based Planning

The CANS, as we have noted, is an information integration tool with the capacity to support both individual treatment planning and the evaluation and planning of service systems (Lyons et al., 2001). Its goal is to provide an assessment framework based on a common clinical language for youth with inter-agency and multiple treatment involvement. As such, it can support service provision commensurate with changing levels of needs. It is a descriptive tool, helpful for prospective clinical uses such as identifying appropriate level of care, treatment planning, and assessing change during the course of treatment. It is also extensively used for research and evaluation purposes such as outcomes monitoring, systems planning, and needs-based planning, for which data are most often gathered retrospectively.

There are multiple versions of the CANS; service providers and system planners adjust its domains and dimensions to fit the needs of their organization or region. This flexibility is integral to needs-based planning efforts, as no two agencies or state mental health systems are alike. Nor are any two adolescent clients alike, making this flexibility a source of meeting their individual needs.

Most versions of the CANS described herein are comprised of the following domains: symptoms/mental health needs, risk behaviors, functioning/functional status, care intensity and treatment needs/care management, caregiver needs and strengths, and child strengths. Each of these domains is comprised of individual dimensions that are based on a four-point anchor scale. A rating of 0 reflects no history of or presence of a particular problem or behavior. A rating of 1 indicates a history of particular problem or behavior and/or watchful waiting or monitoring in case a problem emerges. A rating of 2 reflects a problem of moderate intensity requiring intervention; on many of the dimensions in the symptoms/mental health needs domain, a rating of 2 indicates the presence of a diagnosable disorder. Finally, a rating of 3 indicates a problem of severe intensity requiring immediate and/or intensive action.

The CANS has been used in multiple needs-based planning studies and has been found to be reliable across reviewers (Rawal et al., 2004; Anderson et al., 2003). It has also been used in several needs-based planning projects, including projects in Illinois, New York, and Philadelphia, and it has increased clinical appropriateness of service use across those states' systems (Lyons et al., 1998; Oberleithner et al., 2003; Rawal et al., 2004; Rawal et al., 2008; Lyons et al., 2004).

When to Measure

When to measure depends on the requirements of the selected measure itself. The two driving questions are: when is measurement the most meaningful, and when is it convenient for service providers and organizations? Measurement is usually most meaningful at admission to a new service because it provides critical information on client symptomatology, functioning, and level of treatment intensity required at an acute point in time. Generally, people present with the highest level of symptomatology and need at admission—a time offering the greatest probability of demonstrating significant clinical change—which makes this an ideal time to complete an assessment. Measurement should include those characteristics that you believe are directly affected by the treatment and that may influence treatment outcome.

The decision to conduct follow-up measurements depends on several external factors, such as the availability of data or resources. The best research design would theoretically include multiple measurements over the course of treatment; however, increased numbers of measurements also create an increased burden for respondents and/or those collecting the data. The optimal research design will avoid unnecessarily overburdening the data collection process; this is the key to timing measurement, and also its key challenge.

In needs-based planning studies, assessment at admission is required where the goal is to identify inappropriate service use. For instance, if your goal is to determine whether youth are clinically appropriate for residential treatment, assessment must occur at the time a youth is admitted to the facility. When time, resources, and the research questions permit, it is useful to collect assessment data at regularly timed intervals. However, given that most needs-based planning studies to identify inappropriate service use are retrospective, data can be collected at "current status" or within the last thirty days before the assessment. You can also examine a mix of closed cases and cases that remain open; the second data point can be collected for closed cases at the end of treatment versus at current status for open cases. The open and closed cases can then be compared in aggregate analyses. The comparisons may allow for more complex analyses, such as mapping trajectories of treatment change that can further inform service reform.

Change Analysis

Change analysis is the simplest and the most direct method to approach outcomes management. Change analysis uses client characteristics to assess treatment effectiveness and change over the course of treatment. Data are usually collected at the individual client level and then aggregated in the case of a needs-based planning approach. At the aggregate level, you can make conclusions on the overall appropriateness of service use.

For needs-based planning, retrospective chart reviews are the most direct and cost-effective data collection method. Needs-based planning reviews are usually the starting point of a large outcomes management effort; they allow for the rapid accumulation of enough cases to attain power for reliable analyses. Chart reviews also provide information on other variables that affect service provision, such as prior treatment history of individual subjects, that may not be available from prospective data collection. Given the role of needs-based planning in a larger outcomes management effort, retrospective chart reviews are usually the most practical and efficient data collection method.

However, one of the limitations to this methodology is that data collection is limited to the information in the chart. It is, therefore, important to take this limitation into account when making your conclusions on the available data. When data are collected retrospectively, reliability across those conducting assessments is as important as it is in any other study design. The reliability of the analyses and conclusions resulting from the needs-based planning evaluation are contingent on high levels of inter-rater reliability.

To gain an even clearer understanding of the purposes and effectiveness of needs-based planning, we must examine it in the context of a larger outcomes management effort, as discussed below.

NEEDS-BASED PLANNING IN THE CONTEXT OF AN OUTCOMES MANAGEMENT EFFORT

Outcomes management efforts are comprised of multiple steps. Depending on the complexity and scope of the effort (e.g., number of services targeted for reform, number of youth served by the system, long-term commitment to outcomes management), the steps and the sequence of steps in an outcomes management project can vary. Most of the efforts presented in this chapter use a needs-based planning evaluation as their starting point.

Evaluation

A needs-based planning evaluation using the CANS provides a profile of either youth served within a system or a particular service. The evaluation gives a comprehensive picture of the overall symptomatic, functional, care intensity, and caregiver needs and strengths levels. The resulting profiles provide valuable information on the characteristics of youth at admission into a particular service.

Using the profiles of client characteristics and the input of service providers and other stakeholders, an algorithm with thresholds for placement into specific levels of care can be created. The algorithm provides clinically specific guidelines for appropriate placement into a level of care. In the case of the CANS, guidelines are based on specific CANS dimension scores. For instance, for an algorithm for placement into psychiatric hospitalization, a 3 on danger to self or danger to others would undoubtedly be part of the algorithm. An algorithm for placement into residential treatment might include the presence of at least a 2 on any problem presentation/mental health need dimensions (i.e., a diagnosable DSM-IV mental disorder), plus a 3 on any functioning/functional status dimension *or* a 3 on any risk behavior. Thus, placement algorithms are based on aggregate data from a needs-based planning evaluation, but they can be directly applied to individual cases to make level of care decisions.

Decision Support System

Following data collection and creation of the initial placement algorithm, data are then collected prospectively or retrospectively to validate the algorithm. Based again on the characteristics of youth presenting for treatment, those who are eligible are compared to those who are ineligible to ensure that the algorithm is capturing the clinically appropriate population. At times, the algorithm must be adjusted or modified following the collection of additional data. Once the algorithm is validated, it can be implemented across the system and assumes the role of a decision support system. Thus, the needs-based planning phase and the trial of a decision support algorithm for clinical placement lay the groundwork for decision support systems.

The purpose of a decision support system is to provide clinicians with standardized guidelines for making decisions at keys junctures in the service system (Lyons, 2004) and to promote consistent and high-quality decision-making. For the most part, decisions involve service planning and delivery. Thus, decision support provides a direct link between clinical assessment and decisions regarding level of care for clinicians (Lyons et al., 1996; Rawal et al., 2008).

Existing evidence indicates a strong need for such decision support systems. A study examining psychiatric hospitalization decision-making in a community mental health setting found that treatment staff were confident in their own recommendations for hospitalization, but that practice pattern actually varied widely from one person to the next (Hendryx & Rohland, 1997). Decision support systems have the opportunity to standardize clinical recommendations across clinicians, as our previous work precisely demonstrates. The implementation of decision support systems has resulted in more consistent use of psychiatric hospitalization across providers (Leon et al., 1999) and has even resulted in reduced racial disparities in hospitalization rates (Rawal et al., 2008).

Outcomes Monitoring

After implementing a decision support system, a continuous outcomes monitoring process should be set in place. This process includes systematic and fixed repeated measures for youth receiving particular services. Data are collected over the course of treatment, depending on the mean length of stay or prescribed program duration. For instance, the Illinois Juvenile Justice Initiative, a six-month case management and wraparound program for youth with serious mental illness in detention, collects the CANS-Mental Health version (CANS-MH) at three-month intervals: at admission, at three months, and at six-month termination. The Illinois Residential Treatment Outcomes Study (RTOS) collects CANS and other assessment data quarterly, at admission, for the duration of treatment, and at termination. In these cases, the CANS is used to monitor individual cases for changes over time in treatment. The cases can then be aggregated to make conclusions on the overall treatment effectiveness. The CANS is also used in evaluations, such as in the Illinois RTOS, for ongoing decision support. When youth require more than residential treatment, or demonstrate sufficient improvement to be stepped down to a lower level of care, the CANS can be used to identify these cases.

Creating New Organizational Cultures

When data are regularly collected, predictors of change in treatment and trajectories of change in treatment can be analyzed and used to identify youth most likely to benefit from specific treatments. Overall, a long-term outcomes monitoring process using a tool such as the CANS illustrates the capacities to create organizational cultures focused on feedback, accountability, and quality improvement in mental health.

Needs-based planning efforts are the initial step in this long process. They provide administrators, service providers, and other stakeholders the first snapshot of the needs and strengths of the youth they serve. Inappropriate service use can be identified and system and/or service reform can then be initiated. Figure 19.1 displays a linear chronology of these phases; however, they are often overlapping and can differ based on the individual needs of a project.

A decision support system with a commitment to ongoing outcomes management is driven by the use of a measurement tool such as the CANS, which provides the language and structure for initial data collection on the aggregate characteristics of a population (i.e. needs-based planning), the clinically specific and relevant components of a placement algorithm, the ability to implement a placement strategy on a system-wide scale, and the capacity for ongoing retrospective and prospective outcomes monitoring. Needs-based planning evaluations, implementation, and execution can vary widely from one service system to another, targeting different service systems and yielding different end products. Earlier needs-based planning projects have laid the foundation for the larger outcomes management efforts described below.

Figure 19.1
The Role of Needs-Based Planning in Establishing a Continuous Outcomes Management Process

Needs-based planning →

Development of placement algorithm →

Decision support system →

Ongoing outcomes management

LARGER NEEDS-BASED PLANNING SYSTEMS

New York State Planning Project

The New York Office of Mental Health (OMH) funded a statewide needs-based planning study to determine the needs and strengths of children and families served by its children's public mental health service system (Lyons & Shallcross, 2001). The OMH wanted a complete clinical profile of its service system, with its strengths and weaknesses identified, to guide the evolution of its future service system and investment in resources (Lyons & Shallcross, 2001).

The first step was to identify target services for the project's needs-based planning phase. Administrators chose to focus on ten statewide services and a few single-site demonstration programs. The goal was to gain an understanding of the client characteristics at each of these levels of care. The ten program types included in the reviews and a description of each are listed in Table 19.1.

Sample. The sample consisted of youth ages eight to seventeen years receiving OMH or federal Medicaid funding for mental health services. A stratified random sampling strategy was chosen to select specific programs within each of the ten types of care in each of five state regions. Within the stratified random sample of service providers, cases were further stratified by service date. Using a computer generated list, reviewers randomly selected twenty cases served between January 21, 1998 and January 20, 1999; cases may have been open or closed at the time of the review. They reviewed a total of 1,592 randomly selected (statewide) cases.

Procedure. Reviewers conducted on-site retrospective chart reviews using the CANS-MH. They systematically gathered data from clinical records; for cases with multiple admissions, they used information from the most recent admission data to complete the CANS-MH. Demographic data, current treatment, placement, treatment history, juvenile justice history, school placement, and discharge information were collected from the charts using a standard protocol. The weighted reliability across all reviewers was 0.81.

Table 19.1
Programs Examined in the New York State Needs-Based Planning Evaluation

Program Type	Program Description & Capacity
State-operated inpatient units (SOIP)	The state operated 6 freestanding pediatric psychiatric hospitals (n = 380 beds) and six children's psychiatric units co-located on adult psychiatric center campuses (n = 115 beds).
Residential treatment facilities (RTF)	There were 19 RTFs in operation (n = 520 beds); this was the highest level of care in residential programming, with licensing similar to that of a hospital.
Community inpatient programs (CIP)	125 private or not-for-profit acute hospitals (n = 640 beds) generally serving children in the community were in operation.
Community residences for children and youth (CRCY)	There were 28 community residences, crises residences, and teaching family residences (n = 224 beds) across the state. CRCYs were small congregate care facilities having between 4 and 8 beds.
Day treatment programs (Day Tx)	Day tx focused on children with behavioral health needs and problems with school attendance, behavior, or achievement. Ninety-five programs were operating across the state (n = 3,560 children served per week).
Outpatient clinics (Clinics)	Traditional office-based community clinics were operating in all 57 counties and New York City (n = 30,000 children per week).
Home and community waiver programs (Waiver)	Waiver programs were designed to prevent hospitalizations and residential treatment through the provision of individualized, community-based services to children with active caregiver involvement (13 programs; n = 180 slots).
Intensive case management programs (ICM)	ICM provided a case manager (n = 160) to high needs children and their families when at-risk for residential placement (n = 2200 children and families served).
Family-based treatment programs (FBT)	FBTs were OMH-funded foster care in which professional parents serve a child with significant mental health challenges (n = 19 programs, n = 365 FBT slots).
Home-based crisis intervention programs (HBCI)	HBCI programs (n = 10) provide 6 weeks of crisis response to prevent psychiatric hospitalization (n = 500 families annually). Staff followed a wraparound philosophy with caseloads of two families each.

Results. The New York State needs-based planning evaluation yielded interesting results. Based on the CANS profiles of youth in each program type (see Table 19.1), administrators at the OMH learned that youth could be grouped into two levels of care. One group was consistently served by outpatient community-based services, and the other was served in congregate care (SOIPs, CIPs, RTFs) settings. However, many of the youth served in congregate care settings had similar CANS profiles to those in outpatient community-based services (Rawal, 2005). Therefore, a step-down could occur for large numbers of youth in expensive out-of-home treatments (Rawal, 2005). The needs-based planning evaluation led directly to the identification of inappropriate service use across the state.

Table 19.2
Level of Risk and Corresponding Criteria for Determining Clinical Appropriateness for Residential Treatment

Level	Criteria
No risk	No history or current behavior in suicidality, dangerousness, crime, runaway, crime/delinquency, or sexual aggression.
History of risk	No suicidality, dangerousness, crime, runaway, or crime/delinquency in the past 30 days.
Recent risk	Engaged in at least one of the following behaviors in the past 30 days: suicidality, dangerousness, crime, runaway, or crime/delinquency. However, these youth are not an acute risk.
Acute risk	Currently suicidal, dangerous, or engaging in criminal/delinquent behaviors; includes youth with histories of or recent sexual aggression.

As a result, New York State's OMH allocated increased funding to many intensive community services, including ICM, waiver programs, HBCI, and FBT, to increase its capacity to serve youth who would otherwise have been served in high-end congregate care settings.

Illinois Residential Treatment Evaluation

In 1995, the Illinois Department of Children and Families Services (IDCFS) spent over $450 million, approximately one-third of its annual budget, on mental health services for wards of the state. The problem lay in the fact that $350 million dollars, or 78 percent, of the total spent on mental health services was only for youth receiving long-term congregate care (i.e., residential treatment or psychiatric hospitalization). Many in the state characterized the system as having only one service option—long-term, out-of-home care (Lyons et al., 1998). The lack of community-based treatment options was especially acute in low-income neighborhoods, which were home to over two-thirds of the state wards (Lyons et al., 1998).

Given the state of their expenditures, the IDCFS proposed a needs-based planning evaluation. It targeted residential treatment as the service level for determining whether inappropriate use was occurring. The needs-based planning evaluation sought to determine the characteristics of youth presently served in residential treatment settings and the proportion who may be eligible for a step-down to community-based services. The goal of the evaluation was to decrease the numbers of children in residential treatment and invest the recouped resources to expand the capacities of community-based services.

Methods. Researchers randomly selected seventeen residential providers serving IDCFS wards across the state. Again using a stratified random sampling method, they stratified the programs by service capacity. Using a computer-generated list of numbers, they randomly sampled thirty cases at the larger residential providers, twenty cases at the mid-size programs, and ten to twelve cases at the small programs (Lyons et al., 1998). A total of 333 cases were reviewed, providing a precision level of +/- 5 percent.

Table 19.3
Numbers and Percentages of Youth Served in Residential Treatment by Risk Group

Risk Group	Number of Children	Percentage Served
No risk	44	13.2
History of risk	68	20.4
Recent risk	92	27.6
Acute risk	129	38.7
Total	333	100

All data were collected on-site at residential treatment centers using a retrospective chart review methodology. Trained graduate students and research assistants collected data under the guidance of the project coordinator. A precursor to the CANS, the Childhood Severity of Psychiatric Illness (CSPI) tool was used to collect data on the following domains: symptoms/mental health needs, risk behaviors, functioning/functional status, care intensity needs, and multisystem needs. Demographic data, treatment history, and diagnosis were collected using a standard chart review protocol. Weighted reliability across reviewers was 0.88, indicating high levels of reliability across raters.

Results. Based on the CANS/CSPI data, the reviewers found four levels of risk. These levels and accompanying criteria are listed in Table 19.2.

The study determined the percentage of youth in each of the four levels who were currently being served in residential treatment. Based on these data, the researchers made estimates of youth who could be stepped down to community-based services; Table 19.3 shows these results.

Table 19.3 indicates that about one-third of the IDCFS wards served in residential treatment could be stepped down to community-based services because they fell into either the no risk or history of risk category. When the researchers examined the results by gender, they found that over 41 percent of the 111 females in the evaluation were inappropriately placed (i.e., they fell into no risk or history of risk categories). Almost 30 percent of the males were also inappropriately placed. However, females were 70 percent more likely to be inappropriately placed in residential treatment than males (Lyons et al., 1998).

Since this study was done, the number of residential treatment beds has dropped by over one-third. Concurrently, the capacity for community-based treatments was increased. Therefore, the needs-based planning evaluation, using the CANS/CSPI to gather data on client characteristics and to delineate criteria for residential treatment eligibility, was successful in identifying inappropriate service use within the system. Proper use of these measurement tools has affected change on multiple levels to more appropriately meet the mental health needs of children and families served by the IDCFS.

Philadelphia Department of Human Services Needs-Based Planning Study

In 2001, the Philadelphia Department of Human Services (DHS) sought to restructure its intake, assessment, and referral processes to bring existing services up to date with national best practices standards. The DHS's focus was on improving continuity of care as well as cost-effectiveness within the service system itself. This underscores the significance of reliable measurement tools in meeting the needs not only of individual clients, but of service systems.

While the DHS was undertaking a major service reform, one of its primary goals was to improve the service delivery of a specific program—treatment foster care (TFC). The TFC program was at a key juncture in the city's child and adolescent service system. An important reform goal was to transition a subset of youth served in high-end congregate care services to more cost-effective community-based services like TFC. In an effort to increase TFC bed capacity, the DHS commissioned a needs-based planning study of youth served in the TFC program to determine whether they were currently appropriately placed and served. The DHS adopted large parts of the CANS-MH and other versions, and used its own needs and requirements to create the CANS-child welfare version (CANS-CW) (Lyons et al., 2000), to increase continuity of care throughout its service system.

Methods. All cases receiving TFC through the Philadelphia DHS were reviewed at the time of the evaluation (n = 349). Cases were reviewed using the CANS-CW at two points in time—at admission and current status (i.e., status at the time of the review). The City of Philadelphia tailored the CANS to meet the needs of its population and service system, as noted above. The CANS-CW included the following domains, with multiple dimensions comprising each: functional status, child safety, mental health need, risk behaviors, substance abuse, criminal and delinquent behavior, care management (intensity and level of treatment need), and child strengths. A standard chart review protocol was used to collect the following data: demographic data, current and prior treatment, current and prior placement history, and discharge information (if applicable). Twenty trained reviewers reviewed cases at each site. The weighted reliability across reviewers utilizing the CANS-CW was .81, indicating moderate to high levels of reliability.

After determining that TFC was the target service for the needs-based planning review, evaluators created eligibility criteria for appropriate placement. The criteria for the decision support algorithm were based on CANS-CW domains and dimensions, which are shown in Table 19.4.

The eligibility thresholds considered sufficient for TFC placement were established. Those considered eligible were youth with:

1. At least one mental health need meeting DSM-IV criteria for a mental disorder, *and*

2. Either a significant risk behavior *or*

3. A severe impairment in functional status or severe impairment in school functioning.

The eligibility criteria reflect the clinical utility of the CANS for needs-based planning and decision support purposes, as providers can apply the algorithm to

Table 19.4
CANS-CW Eligibility Criteria and Decision Support Algorithm for TFC in Philadelphia

Criterion	Area	CANS-CW Rating	CANS-CW Dimension
Mental health need	Presence of symptoms associated with a serious emotional/behavioral disorder	2 or 3	Psychosis Attention deficit/Impulse control Depression/anxiety Anger control Oppositional behavior Antisocial behavior Adjustment to trauma Attachment Severity of substance abuse
Functioning	Notable impairment in functioning in at least one area	3	Motor Sensory Intellectual Communication Developmental Self care/Daily living skills Physical/Medical
School and social behavior	Notable impairment in school functioning and social behavior	3	School behavior School attendance Social behavior
Risk	Notable risk behaviors in at least one area	2 or 3	Danger to self Fire setting Runaway Seriousness of criminal behavior Violence Sexually abusive behavior

individual youth. In addition, the criteria can easily be examined in the aggregate for research purposes (e.g., to test the validity of the algorithm, identify those that are inappropriately placed, examine change and outcomes over time).

Results. The DHS used the data from the needs-based planning evaluation to determine the appropriateness of TFC placement for youth currently served in the program across the city. The CANS-CW eligibility criteria determined that approximately 20 percent of youth did not meet eligibility criteria at admission, per the decision support algorithm, for TFC. The CANS-CW data at current status indicated that almost 40 percent of youth were eligible for a step-down to a less intensive, less restrictive service based on their clinical characteristics. Therefore, the needs-based planning review indicated that a significant number of youth could be placed in less intensive and less restrictive services at both admission and after some time in treatment.

The needs-based planning review also indicated that youth improved over time in TFC. Analyses demonstrated that youth who met eligibility criteria at admission demonstrated greater treatment gains at current status. It also showed that one out of every five youth at admission to TFC may have been better served in a less intensive treatment. Therefore, the DHS implemented a step-down strategy to place youth in a lower level of treatment intensity and restrictiveness at both the admission stage and currently. That is, screening for step-down using the CANS clinical eligibility criteria was implemented for new clients at the outset as well as for youth already placed in TFC. In additon, the needs-based planning review data also showed that very few youth presented as clinically too challenging for the TFC level of care.

The Philadelphia TFC needs-based planning review is a useful illustration of a service system undergoing reform and targeting a specific program for a needs-based planning evaluation. TFC was at a key point in Philadelphia's mental health service system to meet the needs of youth with serious emotional and behavioral needs. By increasing the clinical appropriateness of TFC service use, more youth across the service system are being served in the least restrictive and least intensive service setting possible.

CONCLUSIONS

Needs-based planning approaches are the starting point for many larger outcomes monitoring efforts. They assess the needs and strengths of youth unique to different levels of treatment. Often, they are the first attempt at gathering data on the needs and strengths of youth being served in various levels of care. Profiles of cases served provide valuable information on levels of unmet need in a population or how to set thresholds for eligibility criteria for admission to a particular level of care.

When a measure such as the CANS is used in a needs-based planning project, it creates a common language for all stakeholders to use throughout the implementation, establishment, and ongoing management of an outcomes monitoring effort. The measure's clinical and research utility places it in a unique position to facilitate communication across stakeholders and phases of a project.

One of the most powerful and hoped for outcomes from a needs-based planning evaluation is to bring together key stakeholders who often feel they have competing interests or different perspectives on how to improve the clinical status of youth in a public mental health system. A needs-based planning project can open up lines of communication in a service system and can change an organizational climate to increase commitment to accountability and ongoing outcomes monitoring for continual service delivery and quality improvement.

References

Anderson, R. L., Lyons, J. S., Giles, D. M., Price, J. A. & Estes, G. (2003). Examining the reliability of the child and adolescent needs and strengths-mental health (CANS-MH) scale from two perspectives: A comparison of clinician and researcher ratings. *Journal of Child and Family Studies, 12*, 279–289.

Diagnostic and statistical manual of mental disorders (4th ed.) (DSM-IV) (1994). Washington, DC: American Psychiatric Association.

Donenberg, G. R., Lyons, J. S. & Howard, K. I. (1999). Clinical trials versus mental health services research: Contributions and connections. *Journal of Clinical Psychology*, *55*, 1135–1146.

Hendryx, M. S. & Rohland, B. M. (1997). Psychiatric hospitalization decision-making by CMHC staff. *Community Mental Health Journal*, *33*, 63–73.

Leon, S. C., Uziel-Miller, N. D., Lyons, J. S. & Tracy, P. (1999). Psychiatric hospital service utilization of children and adolescents in state custody. *Journal of the American Academy of Child and Adolescent Psychiatry*, *38*, 305–310.

Lyons J. S., Shasha, M., Christopher, N. J. & Vessey, J. T. (1996). Decision support technology in managed mental health care. In C. E. Stout (Ed.), *The integration of psychological principles in policy development*. Westport, CT: Praeger.

Lyons, J. S., Howard, K. I., O'Mahoney, M. T. & Lish, J. D. (1997). *The measurement and management of clinical outcomes in mental health.* New York: Wiley.

Lyons, J. S., Mintzer, L. L., Kisiel, C. L. & Shallcross, H. (1998). Understanding the mental health needs of children and adolescents in residential treatment. *Professional Psychology: Research and Practice*, *29*, 582–587.

Lyons, J. S., Almeida, M. C., Elfman, M. S. & Lyons, M. (2000). *Child and adolescent needs and strengths assessment, child welfare version* (CANS-CW). Available online at: http://www.buddinpraed.org/.

Lyons, J. S. & Shallcross, H. (2001). *The needs and strengths of children and adolescents served by the public mental health system in New York State*. A report to the New York State Office of Mental Health.

Lyons, J. S., Sokol, P. T., Lee, M., et al. 2001. *The child and adolescent needs and strengths for children and adolescents with mental health challenges* (CANS-MH). Available online at: www.buddinpraed.org.

Lyons, J. S., Griffin, E., Jenuwine, M., Shasha, M. & Quintenz, S. (2003). The mental health juvenile justice initiative: Clinical and forensic outcomes for a statewide program. *Psychiatric Services*, *54*, 69–85.

Lyons, J. S. (2004). *Redressing the emperor: Improving our children's public mental health system*. Westport, CT: Praeger.

Lyons, J. S., MacIntyre, J. C., Lee, M. E., Carpinello, S., Zuber, M. P. & Fazio, M. L. (2004). Psychotropic medications prescribing patterns for children and adolescents in New York's public mental health system. *Community Mental Health Journal*, 40, 101–118.

Oberleithner, A., Monahan, K. & Lyons, J. S. (2003). *Use of the CANS-CW in planning treatment foster care in Philadelphia, PA*. Presented at the Foster Family-Based Treatment Association's 17th Annual Conference on Treatment Foster Care, July 2003, Universal City, CA.

Rawal, P. H., Lyons, J. S., McIntyre, J. & Hunter, J. (2004). Regional variation in off-label use of antipsychotic drugs utilized in residential treatment of children and adolescent: A four-state comparison. *Journal of Behavioral Health Services & Research*, *31*, 178–189.

Rawal, P. H. (2005). *Determining level of care in a child and adolescent state public mental health system: Expanding the use of intensive community services*. Dissertation, in print.

Rawal, P. H., Anderson, T., Romansky J. B. & Lyons, J. S. (2008). *Using decision support to address racial disparities in mental health service utilization*. (Manuscript in submission.)

Chapter 20

Service Process Adherence to Needs and Strengths: A Quality Improvement Tool

by Norin Dollard, Ph.D., Mary Beth Rautkis, Ph.D., Keren S. Vergon, Ph.D. and David Sliefert, M.A.

INTRODUCTION

A frequent comment about the Child and Adolescent Needs and Strengths (CANS) tool (Lyons et al., 2004b) is that it is remarkably adaptable. Other chapters in this book have described how it has been used with different populations and for different purposes: to measure outcomes, as a psychosocial assessment, and to determine levels of care. The adaptability of the CANS is due to its roots in communication theory (Lyons et al., 2004b) and the belief that a shared understanding of need, as it relates to functioning rather than description, is the critical measurement issue.

The companion to assessment is implementation. Assessment and implementation often occur on multiple levels—at the child, program, and system levels. Many evaluations have led to inconclusive results because it was never clear whether (1) the implementation occurred and was ineffective; (2) the implementation was incomplete or differed in some critical way from its design; or (3) an appropriate level of measurement was used. Part of this challenge is that there is rarely a systematic way to document and measure the degree of implementation of complex packages of services and interventions (Rosenblatt, 2005).

The Service Process Adherence to Needs and Strengths measurement tool (SPANS) was designed to be used in conjunction with the CANS to determine the degree to which child and family needs and strengths identified in the CANS were being addressed or used in service planning. This chapter describes the development of the SPANS in Alaska, a pilot study of its implementation and application in Pennsylvania, an evaluation of behavioral health services in Florida, and concludes with recommendations for further development of the instrument and future applications.

Fidelity to Wraparound Principles

There is increasing recognition that assessment of fidelity needs to be a regular component of the evaluation of programs, services, and systems (Fixen et al., 2005). This is partly due to the mixed clinical outcomes that have been observed in reports of communities that use a wraparound planning process in framing service delivery (e.g., Epstein et al., 2003). Several measures of wraparound fidelity have been developed to address this. Examples of widely used measures at the team and agency levels include the Wraparound Fidelity Index (WFI) (Bruns et al., 2002) and the Wraparound Observation Form (WOF) (Epstein et al., 1998). Agency and system level research, evaluation, and quality assurance have use the System of Care Practice Review (SOCPR) (Hernandez et al., 2001).

The WFI (Bruns et al., 2002) assesses adherence to wraparound principles through surveys of youth, caregivers, and providers and has been used by more than fifty communities across the United States. Experience has shown that implementations of the wraparound approach have wide variability in fidelity and that supervisors are the most important influence on fidelity (Rast et al., 2005b). A report on a national WFI data set from ten communities indicates that clear differences exist between communities with wraparound programs as compared to those without one, and that wraparound programs with varying levels of support show different levels of fidelity (Leverentz-Brady et al., 2005). The fidelity of the wraparound process has also been shown to correlate with child and family outcomes (Rast et al., 2005a; Rast et al., 2004).

The WOF method of examining a community's adherence to wraparound principles uses child and family team meetings as its primary approach rather than conducting surveys. Using this instrument in a system of care grant community in Tampa, Florida, evaluators determined that fidelity was associated with the number of life domains addressed within a team meeting and the years of experience the team leader has; one other important element was the inclusion of non-clinical domains addressed in the meetings (e.g., cultural/spiritual, social/recreational, financial, and vocational) (Davis et al., 2005).

Like the WFI and the WOF, the SOCPR gathers information at the individual family or "case" level; however, the SOCPR assesses stakeholders' adherence to tenets and principles of the system of care philosophy (Stroul & Friedman, 1986) as well as the systemic context within which wraparound approaches are used. The SOCPR measurement tool examines fidelity to system of care principles through review of case records and interviews with caregivers, formal providers, and youth. This instrument has been used in several federally funded systems of care grant sites that were matched with comparison communities. Reporters have noted that high scores on the SOCPR are correlated with lower symptom levels and impairment scores for children after a year of service receipt (Stephens et al., 2004).

Fidelity to Individual Plan

The measures described above assess fidelity to wraparound and system of care theories and principles, but not necessarily fidelity to an individualized care plan. Some measure was needed to determine the degree to which a bundle of services and supports address the identified needs and strengths of individual children and their families. From this realization arose the development of the SPANS (Rauktis & Sliefert, 2002), as described below.

SERVICE PROCESS ADHERENCE TO NEEDS AND STRENGTHS

The CANS tool (Lyons et al., 2001) is used for assessment and outcomes monitoring, examining both strengths and challenges for the child and family. The modular structure of the CANS provides a platform for looking at child, family, and system needs and strengths.

The SPANS, used in concert with the CANS, is a generic process for assessing the strengths and weaknesses of the service implementation process. The CANS describes the child and family. The SPANS identifies whether a service planning process remains true to the child and family as described by the CANS. In using the SPANS, a chain of evidence is built wherein needs and strengths are identified, services and interventions are proposed and/or implemented to address needs or incorporate strengths, and outcomes are monitored to assess reduction in needs or augmentation of strengths. The SPANS is a tool for reviewing case records to determine whether CANS ratings that indicate moderate to high levels of needs or strengths are being addressed by or incorporated into the services and interventions provided to a child and family.

The CANS and SPANS tools both incorporate system of care and wraparound principles, but use of the latter is not limited to agencies or communities that have adopted a wraparound planning process. The SPANS can be used within the context of evaluating the progress of an individual child and family, at the program or agency level or aggregated to monitor whole systems.

In addition to looking at fidelity at the individual, team, and system levels, the SPANS can also be used as a tool for identifying areas for quality improvement and/or quality assurance. For instance, at the individual child and family level, the SPANS might show that significant child and family strengths are underused in service planning and delivery. At the team level, the SPANS might show that treatment planning needs to be more ecologically diverse to address the needs and strengths of the caregivers as well as of the child. For system activities, the SPANS might suggest that the array of services and supports available to children and families needs more depth and choice. Thus, SPANS findings could be used to design training programs for individual service providers, to help programs and agencies prioritize budget allocations for how service planning and service is performed and, for the community, to identify priority areas for building infrastructure and implementing a philosophy of care.

DEVELOPMENT OF THE SPANS

The need for a measure of wraparound fidelity at the child and system level was identified by two organizations thousands of miles apart—one in Alaska and one in Pennsylvania. The commonality between the two was the use of the CANS and the need for a systematic way to measure whether the services being provided to children and families were appropriate to their identified needs and strengths. Children and youth with serious emotional disturbance require individualized services, which by definition brings up a lack of algorithmic operation— individualization is character-ized by variability and uniqueness. This leads to the measurement problem: detecting variability is essential to determining individualization, but difficult to measure. Yet the need persists for a valid, efficient, and cost-effective method to assess whether services are individualized, responsive, and client-centered.

The Pennsylvania organization, Community Connections for Families (CCF), is a system of care grant program funded through the Comprehensive Community Mental Health Services for Children and Their Families Program, which is part of the Substance Abuse and Mental Health Services Administration (SAMHSA). The program is orga-nized, funded, and administered as part of the Division of Behavioral Health of the Allegheny Department of Human Services in Southwestern Pennsylvania. The goal of CCF is to provide a countywide system of care for children with serious emotional disturbance and their families. While CCF is administered centrally, services are pro-vided in five community site offices in Allegheny County. Like all SAMHSA system of care sites, CCF is a community-based system of care that adheres to the principles of individualization and strengths-based, family-driven, culturally competent care. CCF keeps service provision at the community level and contracts for services and supports with local, grass roots organizations. This allows a level of community-based support tailored to the needs of the child, adolescent, and family. Services are financed through Medicaid and administered through managed care organizations. Financial support and oversight of flexible funds are administered by the central office, along with technical support, training, oversight, and performance improvement and evaluation. The com-munity sites are responsible for planning, implementing, and following up on care.

While decentralization allows for those closest to the child to plan and implement services, CCF experienced the lack of day-to-day financial oversight over actual provi-sion of services as a challenge. CCF management needed a way to accurately assess and monitor how well the systems of care values were embedded in planning and provision of services.

On the other side of the country, David Sliefert and his colleagues were building a system of care in Sitka, Alaska. The community of Sitka is the fourth largest in Alaska and is located on the Baranof Island in Southeastern Alaska. It is a self-contained com-munity, accessible only by plane or boat. Sitka offers myriad social services for a com-munity of less than 9,000 people. Providing an integrated system of care is complicated in regions of Alaska due to the extreme distances between community mental health centers, the added costs of providing services, and the unique environment in which ser-vices are provided. The Alaska Youth Initiative/Island Counseling Service, like the CCF, identified a need for a tool and a process that could reliably guide treatment, monitor the quality of services provided, and assess the development of a system of care. Both groups were using the CANS for planning wraparound services.

Efforts to Extend the Functionality of the CANS

The CANS is an information integration tool that can be used prospectively for planning or decision-making and retrospectively to review treatment decisions, and to assesses needs and strengths of the child and family in multiple functional domains. CANS dimension scores are calculated by summing all items within the dimension; therefore higher scores indicate greater levels of need. Strengths are scored in an opposite manner, with lower numbers indicating greater strengths in the domain. The scoring of the CANS provides a platform that can be used to determine the degree of individualization of services. Used alone, the CANS can be administered at admission and periodically thereafter to determine whether levels of needs are decreasing and strengths are increasing.

However, the CANS does not provide insight into why levels of needs and strengths are changing or not. The two disparate communities above decided they needed modifications or additions to fill this gap. For example, if the CANS identified a high level of need but the need was not addressed in the service plan or plan revisions and documentation, a new fidelity measure would help answer the critical question of whether care and supports were actually being provided. Likewise, if strengths of the child, adolescent, or family member were identified but not included as a centerpiece of a plan, the new measure would indicate that the services were not strengths-based. Could the CANS be further developed to extend its functionality to include measuring the fidelity of treatment delivery? Two pilot studies conducted with the Alaskan and CCH projects began the development of the CANS extension, as discussed below.

Alaska Pilot Study

In the Alaska pilot study in 2001, the effort to add a fidelity of treatment delivery measurement focused on strengths. The goal of the pilot was to create a separate measure to help agencies recognize whether each of the nineteen strength-based dimensions on the CANS was found in individual case records. This measure, to assess adherence to needs and strengths in the service process, eventually became the SPANS.

The Alaska Youth Initiative program serves the approximately 1 percent of Alaskan youth with severe emotional disturbance and incorporates the wraparound philosophy in its service delivery (Burchard et al., 1993). Raters reviewed the files of recipients of the program; two raters reviewed seven cases. Reliability was examined using the Cohen's kappa and "memoing," a qualitative technique, to describe the process of arriving at a SPANS score, as shown in Figure 20.1.

The review process was continuously adapted throughout the study, reflecting input from the raters and group discussion with program stakeholders. The process became simplified in content and a common language developed that was clearly demonstrated through the resolution process at the end of each case, when both raters exchanged their reasons for their choices. On all but a few occasions the raters agreed on a common outcome for each answer—a display of the effectiveness of this type of review, which emphasizes communication and cooperation. Staff were able to attain reliable ratings of 0.8 after review of three to four cases (Sliefert, 2001). This study, though limited in scope, took a solid step towards the creation of a useful, effective SPANS tool.

Figure 20.1
Kappas for File Review

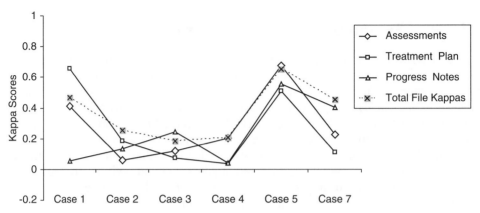

CCF Pilot Results

In 2000, the SPANS was piloted in one CCF site, in which it was used as part of a records audit. This particular CCF site was administered by the local school district, and many of the referrals were from parents whose children attended the elementary schools in the district. Reviewing the most recent CANS records, the reviewers considered needs and strengths to be the target domains that should guide the treatment plans. First they identified needs domains scored as 2 (need for action) or 3 (need for immediate action), and then they identified strengths domains scored as 0 (a strength that can serve as a centerpiece in a treatment plan) or 1 (a strength that can be developed for use in a treatment plan), and noted all of these items on the SPANS. A review of the record followed, focusing on the plans, supporting documentation, and notes that pertained to the target domains. For example, if anger control was scored a 2 on the CANS, then the reviewer would look in the plan for an anger goal and would follow through the record looking for any services and supports that pertained to the goal of helping the youth better manage behavior, such as individual or group therapy to self-monitor affect and control. This included a review of progress notes, correspondence, parent observation, therapy notes, and any other helpful information in the charts. Raters assigned a score from 1 to 5 using the scoring convention displayed in Table 20.1 (Scores were later changed to 0 for *rarely*, 1 for *partially*, and 2 for *mostly* in the Florida study.). In the pilot version, higher SPANS scores indicated that strengths were not being used or needs were not addressed.

Strengths were scored similarly; if a 0 or 1 was scored on any strengths domain in the CANS, the record was reviewed for evidence in the plan and the documentation that the strength was a centerpiece of the plan. For example, if talents/interests was endorsed as a strength on the CANS (scored a 0 or 1), then the reviewer would look for evidence of creative interest planning such as participation in theater or the arts. Using areas of strength as a reinforcement for positive behavior was not rated as positive evidence of developing and strengths in service delivery. For example, using participation in art class as a contingency of good behavior was not counted. Table 20.2 shows an example of SPANS scoring child strengths, along with the Treatment Fidelity Index (TFI) rating for each strength.

Table 20.1
Pilot Study Mental Health Scores

CANS Rating & Dimension (Mental Health)	A Child needs a focus of TX plan	B Services & supports in TX plan	C Needs discussed in progress notes	D Services & Supports in progress notes	E Services & Supports led to positive progress	TFI Rating
Anger Control	M P R	M P R	M P R	M P R	M P R	1 3 5
M		*Mostly*	1 = Two or more *mostly* answers; two of which must be from A & B. No *rarely* answers.			
P		*Partially*	3 = Four or more *partially* answers of which two must be from A & B.			
R		*Rarely*	5 = Four or more *rarely* answers.			

Table 20.2
Sample SPANS Scoring for Child Strengths

CANS Rating & Dimension (Child Strength)	A Child strength used in TX plan	B Child strength in progress notes	C Use of strengths promote progress	TFI Rating
1 Creativity	M P R	M P R	M P R	1 3 5
M *Mostly*	1 = Two or more *mostly* answers; two of which must be from A & B. No *rarely* answers.			
P *Partially*	3 = Two or more *partially* answers, two of which must be from A & B.			
R *Rarely*	5 = Two or more *rarely* answers.			

Figure 20.2 shows results from the first file reviewed. The CANS identified two areas of need for the child, mental health and child risk. These were scored 2 and 3 respectively, but they were not a focus of the child's treatment plan. Child strengths (aggregated in this chart) were also identified and also were not included in the plan or in the supporting documentation. After reviewing the SPANS with the site director, a new plan was created for this child, focusing on finding mental health services and a comprehensive safety plan to address the child's risks.

Figure 20.3 displays the results of another SPANS review. In this record, parent needs were identified in the CANS but not addressed in the plan. This child also had a number of strengths that were not used in planning supports. Supervision included brainstorming with the staff on different ways to help meet parent needs while also building on the child's strengths.

Figure 20.2
First SPANS File Review

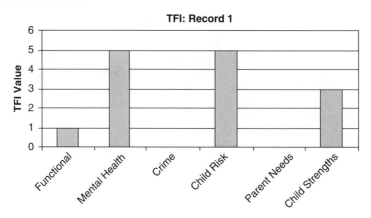

Figure 20.3
Subsequent SPANS File Review

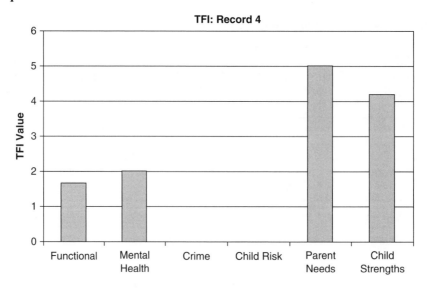

This pilot provided a comprehensive picture of how the site was functioning. In this particular site, the CCF program was well embedded in the community. CCF staff lived in the community and had a vested interest in keeping youth in community schools and at home. However, like many of the communities that CCF operated in, mental health services consisted primarily of traditional outpatient services, and evidence-based practices were not in use. One child psychiatrist served the entire catchment area, hence psychiatric time was limited. The Medicaid managed care system was just starting to be implemented, so the mental health system was in a state of transition. Figure 20.4 gives a snapshot of this site with all of the SPANS results reviewed.

Figure 20.4
All SPANS Results

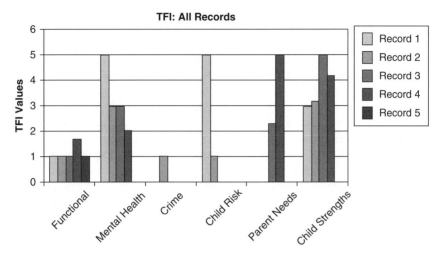

The SPANS results provided evidence that CCF needed to help the community acquire mental health services by working with the managed care company to improve access. This was critical, since a goal of CCF was to divert youth from inpatient care or residential treatment facilities. Access to adequate psychiatric assessment, medication, and effective outpatient treatment was vital if the program was to meet its goal of serving youth in the least restrictive setting (Stroul & Friedman, 1986).

One problem area the SPANS analysis identified was how little strengths were being used within the treatment plans. While the youth had significant challenges, they also had considerable strengths that were not being used to build plans. Thus, there was an unmet training and supervision need on the staff's part that the administration needed to turn its attention to for site performance improvement.

The SPANS also brought light to bear on whether family needs were being met. The results showed that although the CANS had identified parent needs in several areas, the services being provided were not addressing those needs. Helping parents meet their needs so they can care for and advocate for their child is one of the most important aspects of a system of care.

Summary

In summary, although both pilot studies had the limitation of a small sample size, the information obtained using the SPANS provided both the Alaska Youth Initiative/ Island Counseling Services and the CCF with concrete information about performance and, more important, a focus for training, technical assistance, and supervision. For CCF, it also produced evidence that could be used to negotiate with the managed care organization responsible for organizing the network of psychiatrists and therapists in one of the communities. The lessons learned in these pilot studies were applied to studying a larger sample in the State of Florida, as described below.

BEHAVIORAL HEALTH OVERLAY SERVICES IN FLORIDA

Behavioral Health Overlay Services (BHOS) were developed under the Medicaid Community Mental Health Services Program in Florida to allow providers to address, on a child-specific basis, medically necessary mental health and substance abuse treatment needs of children who are placed in group shelters, residential group care settings, or low- to moderate-risk juvenile justice commitment programs. The BHOS rate is "bundled" to include most outpatient behavioral health services under a single payment rate. The bundle structure was originally proposed to increase flexibility in providing individualized services to children and youth while reducing paperwork burdens for provider agencies. The array of covered services was designed to overlay contracted services such as room, board, supervision, and delinquency programming.

Reviewers conducted case record reviews as part of a larger evaluation of BHOS services provided statewide (Dollard et al., 2004). The purpose of reviewing the case files was to determine (1) the amount and types of behavioral services children and youth receive, (2) the types of providers giving these services, (3) the appropriateness of these services, (4) the consistency of services with the youth's treatment plan, (5) the appropriateness of these services, and (6) the outcomes for children and youth served.

Measures

Reviewers in the Florida study used the CANS for two groups, the juvenile justice and child welfare populations. The juvenile justice version (CANS-JJ) was adapted from the CANS version used by the Philadelphia Department of Human Services (as described in Chapter 19); the mental health section was expanded and additional problem related to the specifics of juvenile justice involvement were added, including youth involvement with the drug industry. For the child welfare sample, the CANS-MH version was expanded to describe areas of interest regarding this population, such as permanency and severity of abuse. The majority of items were common to both the juvenile justice and child welfare versions used in the study.

For both groups, the CANS had been administered for the ninety days that preceded admission to either a moderate-level juvenile justice facility or a child welfare group home. The purpose of using the CANS was to determine functioning across life domain areas at admission, to verify diagnoses assigned during the first month youth were in residence, and to identify areas to be addressed in service or treatment plans. All raters were certified for inter-rater reliability at the .70 level, consistent with established CANS training standards.

The SPANS (Rauktis & Sliefert, 2002) process of review was used to determine whether strong needs and strengths areas were addressed in the treatment plans and progress notes. To complete the SPANS, raters identified and noted all of the needs items that were scored as 2 or 3 and all of the strengths items scored as 0 or 1 on the CANS. Raters then identified whether the needs and strengths were addressed or used in the treatment plan and progress notes, and whether progress was observed on the SPANS.

The reviewers' focus on the SPANS was to determine whether, for the following four implementation areas:

1. Client/family needs were a focus of treatment plans;

2. Recommended services and supports were a focus of treatment plans;

3. Client/family needs were discussed in progress notes; and

4. Recommended services and supports were discussed in progress notes.

A fifth area, whether services and supports help to promote positive progress in the specific dimension, was used as the outcome measure in the present analysis. The raters used a three-point scale, reversing the scores for the anchors used in Alaska and Pennsylvania, so that 0 was assigned to ratings of *rarely*, 1 to ratings of *partially*, and 2 to ratings of *mostly*. Raters were also asked to provide substantiation for their ratings in all five areas.

For each of the four implementation areas listed above, the sum of the scores ranged from 0 to 8 for each domain. For example, if a reviewer felt that the needs or strengths were a focus of treatment, were addressed or enhanced through services or interventions in treatment or support plans, and were monitored as evidenced in case notes, the reviewer would assign a 2 for *mostly* in each of the four implementation areas, for a maximum score of 8. Conversely, if needs were not a focus of services, then the rater would assign a 0 for *rarely* in each of the domains, for a total score of 0 for that CANS need or strength area.

As with the Alaska and Pennsylvania pilots, scores between 6 and 8 were considered *mostly or fully* implemented, between 2 and 5 *partially* implemented, and 1 or 0 *low or not* implemented. The scores for the domains were then summed and divided by the number of endorsed items, since the number of items completed would vary depending on the number of items endorsed as 2 or 3 on the CANS to obtain a domain or subscale score. Scores for the outcome measure were similarly calculated and included scores from 0 to 2 as follows:

0 = Services rarely/never contributed to positive outcomes

1 = Services partially contributed to positive outcomes

2 = Services mostly/fully contributed to positive outcomes

The amount of time required to complete the SPANS varied from about forty-five minutes for a record of a youth enrolled in a program six months or less, to two hours for more complex records, such as records of youth involved in multiple systems or who have been enrolled for longer periods of time.

Sample Selection

The study sample was initially stratified by whether the child or youth was in a child welfare group home or in a juvenile justice facility. The second stratification was by size (small, medium, large), in terms of the number of youth the agency had the capacity to serve at any given time. Nine facilities—three from each size group—were randomly selected from facilities statewide. The largest facilities in both the child welfare and juvenile justice groups were purposefully selected because of the high volume of youth served. The sample was further stratified by race and gender to ensure these demographics were reflected in the study. Within each facility, ten youth and a reserve sample reflecting these characteristics were randomly selected. The final sample included 97 youth in child welfare and 101 youth in juvenile justice.

Sample Characteristics

The youth included in the sample came from counties around the state. Consistent with the statewide juvenile justice population and administrative data, youth in the case record review sample were predominantly male and Caucasian. The total number was 101; the number of youth in each category was:

Males—seventy-six (76 percent)

Caucasian—fifty-two (52 percent)

African-American—forty-eight (48 percent)

Haitian—one

Mixed race/ethnicity—two

Latino—thirteen

At the time they entered a juvenile justice facility, they were 15.7 years of age on average; the median age was sixteen years; and the age range was twelve to nineteen years.

The child welfare record review sample included ninety-seven youth from ten facilities statewide. Youth were slightly less likely to be males and Caucasian than their juvenile justice counterparts:

Males—fifty-six (58 percent)

Caucasian—forty-nine (51 percent)

African-American—forty-two (43 percent)

Latino—ten (10 percent)

Other race/ethnicity—one Native American, three multiracial youth, two youth from the Caribbean, and three for whom ethnicity or country of origin was not specified.

At the time they entered a child welfare group home, they were 13.3 years of age on average; the median age was fourteen years; the age range was five to eighteen; and the total number of youth was ninety-seven. The largest proportion—forty-four youth—were twelve to fourteen years old (45 percent), followed by thirty-three youth age fifteen to eighteen (34 percent). The remaining 20 percent of children were eleven years old or younger (see Table 20.3).

Findings

To illustrate how the SPANS was used, the following examples include analysis of one CANS needs domain, substance abuse complications, and one CANS strengths domain, youth strengths. The substance abuse complications domain included five items: severity of abuse, duration of abuse, stage of recovery, peer involvement in substance abuse, and parental involvement in substance abuse. As Table 20.4 shows, the two groups differed significantly on each of the items, with youth in juvenile justice being more likely to be identified as having substance use and abuse issues, peers using substances, and caregivers whose use or abuse of substance suggests the need

Table 20.3
Florida Study—Juvenile Justice and Child Welfare Demographics

		Juvenile Justice N = 101		Child Welfare N = 97	
Gender	Female	25	24%	41	42%
	Male	76	76%	56	58%
Race / Ethnicity	White	52	52%	49	51%
	Black	49	48%	42	43%
	Latino	13	13%	10	10%
	Other	3	3%	11	11%
Age	Med (Med)	SD	Mean (Med)	SD	
	15.7 (16)	1.7	13.3	(14)	2.7

Table 20.4
Substance Abuse Complications—Percentage of Youth With CANS Scores of Moderate or Severe Need

	JJ (n = 101)	CW (n = 97)	Significance
Severity of Abuse	57%	10%	$X^2 = 75.8$ $p < .01$
Duration of Abuse	50%	7%	$X^2 = 103.5$ $p < .01$
Stage of Recovery	55%	10%	$X^2 = 32.9$ $p < .01$
Peer Involvement in Substance Use	50%	9%	$X^2 = 50.7$ $p < .01$
Parental Involvement in Substance Use	53%	41%	$X^2 = 8.0$ $p = <.05$

for further assessment and possible intervention. Children and youth in child welfare, being on average two years younger than their juvenile justice counterparts, were less likely to be using substances; however, there were 10 percent whose severity of use or abuse required further attention.

In examining the degree to which treatment plans addressed identified needs, the reviewers found variation in how well these needs were addressed as well as significant

Table 20.5
Substance Abuse Complications Fidelity

	CW (n = 32)		JJ (n = 73)	
	N	%	N	%
No fidelity	19	59.4%	13	17.8%
Lowe fidelity	3	9.4%	6	8.2%
Partial fidelity	8	25.0%	13	17.8%
Moderate fidelity	0	0	18	24.7%
High fidelity	2	6.3%	23	31.5%

$X^2 = 27.07$
$p < .001$

differences between the child welfare and juvenile justice samples with respect to implementation within the substance abuse domain (see Table 20.5). Youth in the juvenile justice sample were significantly more likely to have identified needs addressed than youth in the child welfare sample ($X^2 = 27.07$; $p < .001$). Whereas 56.2 percent (forty-one youth) in the juvenile justice sample had their needs addressed with moderate to high fidelity, 68.8 percent (twenty-two youth) in the child welfare sample did not have them addressed or had them addressed at a low level. When the outcomes for youth with substance abuse complications were examined for the group as a whole (103 youth), low levels of implementation were associated with poor outcomes and high levels of implementation were associated with more positive outcomes (see Table 20.6).

The youth strengths domain recorded on the SPANS included nine items: family, relationship permanence, vocational, talents and interests, interpersonal, educational, well-being, spiritual or religious, and community inclusion. As noted earlier, the strengths domain of the SPANS was completed only for youth who were rated 0 (a strength that can serve as a centerpiece of a plan) or 1 (a strength that can be further developed).

Table 20.7 shows that in examining the CANS scores for youth strengths, the two groups did not differ in as many areas as they did in the substance abuse domain, although there were differences in several areas. The reviewers identified youth in child welfare as more likely to have strengths in their relationship to their families ($X^2 = 14.2$; $p < .01$), sustained relationships with families or friends ($X^2 = 29.0$; $p < .001$), educational strengths ($X^2 = 27.3$; $p < .001$), and a higher degree of sustained connections to a community or participation in community groups ($X^2 = 14.9$; $p < .01$).

As was found in the CCF pilot, there were relatively few plans that used these strengths in treatment planning (see Table 20.8) Again, lower levels of implementation appeared to be associated with lower degrees of progress towards treatment goal attainment ($X^2 = 12.6$; $p < .05$) (see Table 20.9).

Table 20.6
Relationship of Outcomes and Fidelity in the Substance Abuse Domain (n = 103)

Outcome	Substance Abuse Treatment Fidelity				
	None	Low	Partial	Moderate	High
Services rarely contributed to positive outcomes	28 (27.2%)	4 (3.9%)	5 (4.9%)	1 (1.0%)	0
Services partially contributed to positive outcomes	4 (3.9%)	5 (4.9%)	11 (10.7%)	6 (5.8%)	2 1.9%)
Services mostly contributed to positive outcomes	0	0	5 (4.9%)	11 (10.7%)	21 (22.3%)

$\chi^2 = 88.3$
$p < .001$

Table 20.7
Youth Strengths—Percent of Youth With Strengths That Could Be Used or Developed

	JJ (n =1 00)	CW (n = 70)	Significance
Family	49%	27%	$X^2 = 14.2$ $p < .01$
Interpersonal	43%	38%	*Nsd*
Relationship Permanence	53%	20%	$X^2 = 29.0$ $p < .001$
Educational	21%	49%	$X^2 = 27.3$ $p < .001$
Vocational	25%	20%	*Nsd*
Well-being	19%	23%	*Nsd*
Talents/Interests	35%	41%	*Nsd*
Spiritual/Religious	46%	41%	*Nsd*
Community Inclusion	29%	23%	$X^2 = 14.9$ $p < .01$

Ns varied from 170-198.

Table 20.8
Youth Strengths Fidelity

	CW (n=75)		JJ (n=49)	
	N	%	N	%
No fidelity	21	28.0%	25	51.0%
Low fidelity	8	10.7%	6	12.2%
Partial fidelity	25	33.3%	12	24.5%
Moderate fidelity	15	20.0%	1	2.0%
High fidelity	6	8.0%	5	10.2%

$X^2 = 12.6$
$p < .05$

THE FUTURE

Enhancing the SPANS

Based on the experience in Florida, it is apparent that the SPANS can be enhanced. Measures for caregivers could be added in the areas of parental mental illness and substance abuse, particularly for a child welfare population. As observed in both Pennsylvania and Florida, youth appear to be making progress, but unaddressed issues among caregivers mitigate against youths' ability to make maximum progress and, in child welfare cases, their ability to return to their caregivers.

Implementation codes could be added to the tool to determine whether services are provided with the recommended frequency and intensity, and in cases where services are discontinued before discharge, to determine why. For example, was discontinuation due to youth or caregiver factors, such as a caregiver's request; to staff or agency factors, such as staff turnover; or to system factors, such as changes in funding? Use of such codes is recommended so that barriers to implementation can be systematically captured and reported (1) to an individual staff member, so that his or her work with families might improve; (2) at the agency level, so that staff development efforts can be tailored to the specific needs and strengths of personnel; or (3) to system managers, who must learn when needed services are not in sufficient supply.

Further Development

The analyses presented herein represent an initial effort to identify a means of evaluating implementation of treatment or service plans derived from a commonly used assessment and planning tool, the CANS. Further work will investigate the relationship between outcomes and fidelity using the standardized outcome measure, Child Behavior Checklist (Achenbach & Rescorla, 2001), in a study of residential treatment

Table 20.9
Relationship of Outcomes and Fidelity in the Youth Strengths Domain (n=124)

Outcome	Youth Strengths Treatment Fidelity				
	None	Low	Partial	Moderate	High
Services rarely contributed to positive outcomes	34 (27.4%)	5 (4.0%)	5 (4.0%)	0	0
Services partially contributed to positive outcomes	11 (8.9%)	9 (7.3%)	27 (21.8%)	10 (8.1%)	2 (1.6%)
Services mostly contributed to positive outcomes	1 (0.8%)	0	5 (4.0%)	11 (8.9%)	9 (7.3%)

$X^2 = 87.6$
$p < .001$

options in Florida. Further work is also planned to identify empirically derived cutoff scores for low, partial, and high levels of implementation using the SPANS.

The findings from the two pilots and the larger evaluation were instructive and could be used to provide targeted feedback to agency staff. For example, in the CCF study, a specific finding was that caregivers with behavioral health issues were not getting the services they needed. At the individual family level, such feedback helps provider staff work with the system to obtain services for the family as a whole. At the system or aggregated level, the data could be used to advocate for structural changes to service delivery that addresses the needs of the whole family. In Florida, a specific finding was that some youths with substance abuse issues did not get those issues addressed. An outcomes review using the CANS alone would indicate that their level of need has not changed over time. However, with use of the SPANS to complement the CANS, it became clear that there was no change because the services to meet those needs were not being provided.

In the area of youth strengths, the consistency of the findings in both CCF and in Florida was also instructive. The field of children's mental health holds strengths-based service delivery as a value. In both sites, it appeared that practitioners were able to identify strengths. However, it was also clear that strengths were not part of the treatment planning process and that training in how to use identified strengths in service delivery is needed.

SUMMARY

In sum, the SPANS is a useful tool within the CANS communications framework. At the individual level, it can be used to supervise and train staff in the identification and implementation of services that are appropriate to family needs and strengths. At the program or agency level, the measure has a quality assurance value within the system in that it can identify areas for staff development and training, and thereby expand the array of available services or specific interventions to meet the needs of clients. Just as the CANS can be used to monitor the performance of whole systems (e.g., Lyons et al., 2004a), the SPANS can be used at the system level, as was the case in Florida, where it was aggregated and used to identify areas for improvement and advocacy for system change. Finally, the modular nature of the CANS enables the development of SPANS measurements that are tailored to the characteristics and circumstances of a variety of populations, including very young children and children with developmental disabilities, and across children in multiple systems, such as special education, child welfare, and juvenile justice.

Author's Note

The authors would like to thank Dean Fixsen and Karen Blase of the National Implementation Research Network at the Louis de la Parte Florida Mental Health Institute at the University of South Florida. This work was funded in part through a contract with Florida's Agency for Health Care Administration contract #M0347 and the Center for Mental Health Services and through DHHS Grant #5-HS5- SM52307.

References

Achenbach, T. M. & Rescorla, L. A. (2001). *Manual for the ASEBA school forms and profiles*. Burlington, VT: University of Vermont, Research Center for Children, Youth and Families.

Bruns, E. J., Suter, J. C. & Burchard, J. D. (2002). Pilot test of the wraparound fidelity index 2.0. In C. Newman, C. J. Liberton, K. Kutash & R. M. Freidman (Eds.), *The 15th annual research conference proceedings, a system of care for children's mental health*: *Expanding the research base*. Tampa: University of South Florida, Louis de la Parte Florida Mental Health Institute, Research and Training Center for Children's Mental Health.

Burchard, J. D., Burchard, S. N., Sewell, R. & VanDenBerg, J. (1993). *One kid at a time. Evaluative case studies and description of the Alaska youth initiative demonstration project*. Burlington: University of Vermont.

The child and adolescent needs and strengths for at-risk and delinquent and adolescents— manual. (CANS-JJ). Copyright © 1999 Buddin Praed Foundation.

Davis, C., Vergon, K. S. & Dollard, N. (2005). Tying team and meeting process to wraparound fidelity in the Hillsborough County, Florida THINK program. In C. Newman, C. J. Liberton, K. Kutash & R. M. Freidman (Eds.), *The 18th annual research conference proceedings, a system of care for children's mental health*: *Expanding the research base*. Tampa: University of South Florida, Louis de la Parte Florida Mental Health Institute, Research and Training Center for Children's Mental Health.

Dollard, N., Dailey, K. A. & Dhont, K. (2004). *Behavioral health overlay services*: *Evaluation final report*. Tampa, FL: Louis de la Parte Florida Mental Health Institute, University of South Florida.

Epstein, M. H., Jayanthi, M., McKelvey, J., Frankenberry, E., Hardy, R., Dennis, K. & Dennis, K. (1998). Reliability of the observation form: An instrument to measure the wraparound process. *Journal of Child and Family Studies, 7*, 161–170.

Epstein, M. H., Nordness, P. D., Kutash, K., Duchnowski, A. J., Schrepf, S., Benner, G. J. & Nelson, J. R. (2003). Assessing the wraparound process during family planning meetings. *Journal of Behavioral Health Services and Research, 30*, 352–362.

Fixsen, D., Naoom, S., Blase, K., Friedman, R. & Wallace, F. (2005). *Implementation research*: *A synthesis of the literature.* Tampa, FL: University of South Florida, Louis De La Parte Florida Mental Health Institute. National Implementation Research Network (FMHI Publication 231).

Hernandez, M., Gomez., A., Lipien, L., Greenbaum, P. E., Armstrong, K. H. & Gonzalez, P. (2001). Use of the system-of-care practice review in the national evaluation: Evaluating the fidelity of practice to system-of-care principles. *Journal of Emotional and Behavioral Disorders, 9,* 43–52.

Hernandez, M., Worthington, J. & Davis, C. S. (2005). *Measuring fidelity to wraparound and system of care principles*: *The system of care practice review.* Tampa, FL: University of South Florida, Louis de la Parte Florida Mental Health Institute.

Leverentz-Brady, K. M., Suter, J. C. & Bruns, E. J. (2005). The wraparound process: An in-depth look at fidelity patterns from a national dataset. In C. Newman, C. J. Liberton, K. Kutash & R. M. Freidman (Eds.), *The 18th annual research conference proceedings, a system of care for children's mental health*: *Expanding the research base.* Tampa, FL: University of South Florida, Louis de la Parte Florida Mental Health Institute, Research and Training Center for Children's Mental Health.

Lyons, J. S., MacIntyre, J. C., Lee, M. E., Carpinello, S., Zuber, M. P. & Fazio, M. L. (2004a). Psychotropic medications prescribing patterns for children and adolescents in New York's public mental health system. *Community Mental Health Journal, 40,* 101–118.

Lyons, J. S., Sokol, P. T., Lee, M. et al. (2001). *The child and adolescent needs and strengths for children and adolescents with mental health challenges* (CANS-MH). Available online at: www.buddinpraed.org.

Lyons, J. S., Weiner, D.A. & Lyons, M. B. (2004b). Measurement as communication: The child and adolescent needs and strengths tool. In M. Marinsh (Ed.), *The use of psychological testing for treatment planning and outcome assessment* (3d ed.), vol. 2. Mahwah, NJ: Lawrence Erlbaum Associates.

Rast, J., O'Day, K. & Rider, F. (2005a). A post hoc comparison of child and family outcomes to fidelity of the wraparound process for project MATCH. In C. Newman, C. J. Liberton, K. Kutash & R. M. Freidman (Eds.), *The 18th annual research conference proceedings, a system of care for children's mental health*: *Expanding the research base.* Tampa: University of South Florida, Louis de la Parte Florida Mental Health Institute, Research and Training Center for Children's Mental Health.

Rast, J., Peterson, C., Earnest, L. & Mears, S. (2004). Service process as a determinant of treatment effect—The importance of fidelity. In C. Newman, C. J. Liberton, K. Kutash & R. M. Freidman (Eds.), *The 17th annual research conference proceedings, a system of care for children's mental health*: *Expanding the research base.* Tampa: University of South Florida, Louis de la Parte Florida Mental Health Institute, Research and Training Center for Children's Mental Health.

Rast, J., VanDenBerg, J. D. & Dalder, G. (2005b). Using model development research and fidelity data to guide wraparound curriculum and coaching development. In C. Newman, C. J. Liberton, K. Kutash & R. M. Freidman (Eds.), *The 18th annual research conference proceedings, a system of care for children's mental health*: *Expanding the research base.* Tampa: University of South Florida, Louis de la Parte Florida Mental Health Institute, Research and Training Center for Children's Mental Health.

Rauktis, M. B. & Sliefert, D. (2002). Improving quality in systems of care: Treatment fidelity and the child and adolescent needs and strengths measure. In C. Newman, C. J. Liberton, K. Kutash & R. M. Freidman (Eds.), *The 15th annual research conference proceedings, a system of care for children's mental health*: *Expanding the research base.* Tampa: University of South Florida, The Louis de la Parte Florida Mental Health Institute, Research and Training Center for Children's Mental Health.

Rosenblatt, A. (2005). Assessing the child and family outcomes of systems of care for youth with serious emotional disturbance. In M. H. Epstein, K. Kutash & A. J. Duchnowski (Eds.), *Outcomes for children and youth with emotional and behavioral disorders and their families*: *Programs and evaluation best practices* (2d ed.). Austin, TX: PRO-ED, Inc.

Sliefert, D. (2001). *Developing treatment fidelity measures in a wraparound program for severely emotionally disturbed children using the child and adolescent needs and strengths tool*. Unpublished master thesis, Fairbanks, AL: University of Alaska.

Stephens, R. L., Holden, E. W. & Hernandez, M. (2004). System-of-care practice review scores as predictors of behavioral symptomatology and functional impairment. *Journal of Child and Family Studies, 13*, 179–191.

Stroul, B. A. & Friedman, R. M. (1986). *A system of care for severely emotionally disturbed children and youth*. Washington, DC: National Technical Assistance Center for Children's Mental Health, Child and Adolescent Service System Program, Georgetown University Center for Child and Human Development.

Chapter 21

Recovery Outcomes Management System: Combining the Adult Needs and Strengths Assessment with Consumer and Support Informant Self-Report

by Linda L. Toche-Manley, Ph.D and Grant R. Grissom, Ph.D.

POLARIS HEALTH DIRECTIONS

The Pennsylvania-based Polaris Health Directions develops and markets computer-based clinical decision support, outcomes assessment, and management systems. Its products are used by health care providers, managed care organizations, government agencies, and pharmaceutical companies to improve patient health and reduce treatment costs through evidence-based treatment planning and monitoring of patient progress. Polaris's focus is on the impact of mental health conditions on physical health (e.g., cardiac disease, primary care) and individual welfare (e.g., child welfare, domestic violence, treatment of troubled youths).

In this chapter, we explore the usefulness of consumer self-report when combined with clinician ratings from the Adult Needs and Strengths assessment tool (ANSA) (Lyons, 2004) in a large, regional behavioral healthcare provider in Pennsylvania that serves severely and persistently mentally ill (SPMI) adults. This provider, along with several others in Pennsylvania and Iowa, participated in an NIH-funded study to develop the Polaris Recovery Outcomes Management System (ROMS), a strengths-based, outcome management system that includes the ANSA and consumer self-report assessment among its core components. The ROMS is designed to help adults engage in treatment to achieve more meaningful and satisfying lives, optimal functioning, and community reintegration through more effective care delivery. The system also provides clinical decision support, including level of care determination; facilitates case management and utilization review; and documents outcomes for purposes of accreditation and third-party reporting.

The recovery-empowerment model, which focuses on increased consumer collaboration in treatment planning/monitoring and on identifying consumer strengths, is not consistently applied when serving consumers. All study sites are, of course, committed to using the recovery-empowerment approach to service delivery to improve outcomes. We describe the challenges we encountered in our implementation of the Polaris ROMS, our strategies to deal with them, and the lessons we learned.

Site Description

The large, regional treatment provider highlighted in this chapter has a thirty-year history of providing services with varying levels of structure and support for adults with SPMI and co-occurring disorders. It offers intensive case management, supported employment programming, the use of engagement and peer specialists, psychiatric rehabilitation programs, and programs of assertive community treatment (PACT). It serves more than 20,000 consumers in Pennsylvania, New Jersey, Delaware, and Virginia.

This treatment provider collects various types of outcomes data and uses them to strengthen grant proposals to expanded its services and increase referrals to its facilities from the county and state. The consumer self-report and ANSA assessments from Polaris's ROMS product were intended to support these efforts, while enhancing the role of standardized assessment as a key element of routine clinical practice and quality improvement initiatives.

The Recovery Outcomes Management System

The ROMS, as noted above, is strengths-based and includes the consumer's voice in the treatment planning and monitoring process via self-report of his or her symptoms and strengths. The development of the ROMS was guided by (1) our view that recovery is a process of acquiring the relational, vocational, and emotional skills needed to lead more meaningful lives, with sustained improvement along measurable symptom and strength dimensions; and (2) a conviction that the perspectives of the consumer, clinician, and caregiver are all useful to treatment planning and monitoring. Where these perspectives are consistent, strong confidence can be placed in the shared view. Real or apparent inconsistencies among the reports of these stakeholders often present opportunities for clinical attention and discussion.

The ROMS is a computer-supported system. Its format allows for the multi-informant capability that identifies consumer strengths, assesses the nature and severity of problems, and encourages collaboration in the therapeutic process. In a typical application consumers, clinicians, and caregivers (when available) complete web-based assessments at the program site, or at their homes or offices (ROMS requires access to a computer, but does not require computer literacy.). The response data reside on a Polaris server. The data are immediately analyzed and a real time report is printed at the program site, available for review by the clinician during the treatment session.

Consumer Assessment. The consumer assessment contains measures of problem severity as well as strengths. Symptom and functioning measures include scales from the behavior and symptom identification scale, version 24 (or BASIS-24, a revised version of the BASIS-32) (Eisen & Culhane, 1999). The revised version has been used successfully with over 5,000 consumers in private and public sector mental health settings (Eisen et al., 2004). The BASIS-24 domains included in ROMS are: depression/functioning, interpersonal problems, psychosis, alcohol/drug use, self-harm, emotional lability, and a summary symptom score.

Substance abuse is frequently comorbid with mental illness, and for adults with serious and persistent mental illness, even small amounts of drugs or alcohol are associated with increased violence, hospitalization, and poorer outcomes (RachBeisel et al., 1999). Accordingly, we included the drug and alcohol severity scales from the addiction severity index (ASI) in ROMS. The ASI is the world's most widely used assessment of addiction severity (McLellan et al., 1992), and it is the core component of Polaris CD, the Polaris outcomes management system for chemical dependency (Grissom, 2004). Normative data from Polaris CD are useful to the interpretation of ROMS scores.

Strength-based scales in the ROMS consumer component are: goal directiveness, supports, emotional/relational skills, and resiliency. These strengths are associated with improvement in the consumer's ability to function independently, including finding sustainable employment. For each strength-based scale, a score and specific behavioral indicators are shown on the assessment report.

Clinician Assessment. The clinician assessment in ROMS incorporates the ANSA. The ANSA was chosen because its ratings provide "actionable" information regarding consumer symptomalogy and strengths. The anchors are roughly translated into one of four ratings: *no evidence*, indicating that no action is required; *mild evidence*, suggesting watchful waiting; *moderate evidence*, indicating a need for action; and *severe evidence*, indicating the need for immediate action (Lyons, 1998). Furthermore, the ANSA framework has been widely used in the United States and has been proven to have value for decision-making in residential treatment settings (Lyons et al., 1998) and for quality improvement in crisis assessment services (Lyons et al., 1997; Leon et al., 1999).

Along with the ANSA, ROMS clinician ratings include clinical risk adjusters that Polaris has found to predict improvement in resilience and symptomatology and/or the likelihood of hospitalization. The clinician component of ROMS helps clinicians to focus on the consumer characteristics most important to planning treatment and monitoring progress, and provides care managers with information critical to case review.

Support Informant Assessment. The final component of the ROMS assessment allows informants who are explicitly supporting the consumer in treatment to provide data on consumer strengths and the impact of the consumer's condition on their relationship. The clinical utility of ROMS includes its ability to facilitate the collaboration between the clinician and the consumer when planning and monitoring treatment. A caregiver can provide information, including new strengths, which the consumer or the clinician may not have identified. This third perspective helps the treatment team to reach a more informed understanding of the consumer's developing strengths and progress.

Assessment Process. The assessment process is introduced to consumers and their support informants as an important element of quality care. We start with language like the following:

> For treatment to be successful, you must be an active participant. Our goal is to develop an individualized treatment plan. An initial report is produced that you and your treatment team will discuss during treatment. Throughout treatment you will provide regular updates of this information. To do this we use an assessment called "ROMS" to collect information throughout treatment about your needs and strengths.

Informants (consumer, caregiver, clinician) type in their names to initiate the assessment. Items are presented one at a time. On completion of the assessment, a report is printed that may be reviewed with the consumer during the treatment session. Figure 21.1 shows the ROMS information technology architecture. Respondents complete assessments via the Internet and reports are immediately generated in real time. The organization's administrative staff can access the system to manage the assessment and reporting process; that is, they review assessment dates to identify which consumers are due for an assessment and reprint reports. Polaris personnel having appropriate clearances can access the system to conduct data quality checks and analyses of program-level aggregate data and to produce regular administrative and aggregate clinical reports.

Assessment items are presented one at a time to respondents, as shown in the screen shot. Polaris has found that consumers who take psychotropic medications may have significant eye movements that make it difficult to complete a list of items and may be easily distracted and frustrated by extraneous information. Thus, the ROMS software is designed to present one item at a time, with a minimum of distractions to the user, as seen in the lower part of Figure 21.1. We believe that at least in part, this simplified display design is responsible for our impressive 87 percent assessment completion rate by consumers without staff support.

The use of ROMS requires only a minimal increase in administrative workload; we have found that this is a critical consideration for staff acceptance. Training on the use of the software requires less than one hour and can be completed via webcast.

Assessment Reports. Once the assessments are completed, reports are automatically generated. ROMS produces two types of reports, individual and clinical (ANSA) reports. Individual reports, incorporating consumer self-report symptoms and strengths, are designed to engage consumers and support clinicians and case managers in treatment decisions. The individual report encourages the consumer to participate in

Figure 21.1
Polaris Internet System Design and a Sample Screen Shot

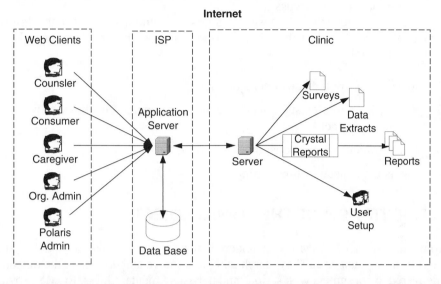

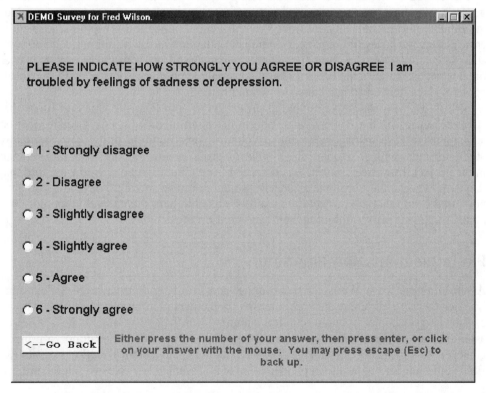

the treatment process; it leads him to begin to understand his behavior, ask questions about building strengths, and receive affirmation over time as he starts to adopt positive thoughts and behavior. It serves as a tool to initiate discussion with the consumer, helping establish a collaborative and supportive relationship. Areas of incongruence among the respondents (consumer, support informant, clinician) or unusual rises or declines in status indicators, including the development of new strengths, are all fruitful areas for collaborative discussion.

ROMS clinical reports help case managers and clinicians answer the following four questions, which reflect the ANSA rating structure and are the foundation of a communimetric tool:

1. How serious are the consumer's problems?

2. What risk factors exist indicating a need for increased clinical involvement with the consumer?

3. How prevalent are the consumer's strengths?

4. How is the consumer functioning?

IMPLEMENTATION OF THE ROMS PROJECT

Implementation of ROMS was undertaken as part of a national study (Toche-Manley) from September 2003 to March 2007 to improve and document the outcome of care delivered to consumers with serious and persistent mental illness. ROMS provides a mechanism to help health care providers to offer (1) *in depth treatment planning*, including reliable information on consumer strengths, functioning and symptoms, as well as critical signs or behaviors requiring immediate attention at the beginning of treatment; and (2) *predictive model treatment management*, based on consumer responses over time, to predict modifiable behaviors and consumer strengths associated with the development of resilience and avoidance of hospitalization.

While ROMS was implemented at programs in both Pennsylvania and Iowa, this chapter focuses on the Pennsylvania program, which included a PACT team location and intensive case management and psychiatric rehabilitation units. Approximately 300 consumers with schizophrenia, bipolar disorder, or severe depression participated in the project. Informed consent was obtained from all participants, who were told that they would complete a computerized assessment at intake and at 90 days and 180 days post-intake, and that the project data would be used to help them develop an individualized treatment plan to monitor their treatment progress.

Pre-Implementation Planning

Assembling the Team. We assessed consumers across different service levels to determine whether there are different or more intensive implementation problems in higher levels of care. Project implementation required planning over the course of six weeks. The site assembled an implementation team consisting of the clinic site administrator, a primary clinician, an information technology (IT) staff member, and a clerical staff representative. Each staff member on the site implementation team assumed key roles within the project.

- *Site administrator*—The site administrator was responsible for conducting discussions with staff on the vision and importance of the project to the program, establishing metrics for success, identifying key members of the implementation team, resolving problems and resistance among staff, and serving as the primary liaison with Polaris on implementation calls to discuss project progress.

- *Primary clinician*—The primary clinician was responsible for creating a strategy to (1) incorporate case reports into the clinical process and (2) monitor completion of assessments by clinicians. The primary clinician was also available to coach clinicians in interpreting report results and discussing these with consumers.

- *IT representative*—The IT representative was responsible for working with Polaris staff to identify optimal computer placement and configuration, manage system installation, and communicate performance to Polaris.

- *Clerical representative*—The clerical representative was responsible for training office staff on the use of ROMS software and eliciting regular input from other staff on operational issues that are conveyed to Polaris in regular check-in conference calls.

Staff Training. Once our implementation team was assembled, we began to train our staff. Training consisted of two two-hour sessions. In the first session, we reviewed the background of the project, the main components of the reports, how both staff and consumers could use the reports to increase engagement and collaboration with providers, how the technology worked, and how the reports were produced. The second portion of the training, completed one week later, used the standardized training protocol for the ANSA. Using this protocol, over fifty clinicians (approximately 80 percent of the clinicians trained) achieved an inter-rater reliability of .7 and were designated as qualified to use the ANSA for the implementation of the project.

Implementation Challenges and Strategy

Despite comprehensive planning and detailed training, we encountered a number of challenges implementing ROMS. These challenges, discussed below, provided an opportunity to strengthen the relationship with the site staff, as we jointly worked to overcome them.

Timely Software Access. We had two IT challenges throughout the implementation of ROMS. The first was to provide all program locations with timely delivery of software and upgrades while conforming to strict corporate IT requirements for outside vendors. The second affected our consumers who had limited transportation and who receive their services in the field. These individuals could not use ROMS software if it were available only at the provider site, so we needed a fundamental change to the technology platform.

Both problems were resolved through development of a web-based version of the software. This allowed for greater flexibility for both consumer and clinician completion of assessments, as they could be completed off-site. The web-based software version provided other benefits as well. It minimized the amount of time that the software was unavailable for use while being upgraded, which led to better system performance and the collection of more data. Polaris staff also could access the system remotely to correct technical problems and resolve many technical inquiries "on the fly."

Change in Staff Compensation. An important organizational change that negatively impacted project implementation was the change in status—from employees to contract workers—that was experienced by case managers, clinicians, and other mental health staff. This change had a dramatic impact on staff expectations and attitudes.

Staff members expected to be paid for time spent completing ANSA ratings and for following up with consumers to make sure that their assessments were completed. Staff were also resistant to making time for training and meetings. The changes prompted frequent and rapid staff turnover throughout the project, which required continuous training of new members.

Turnover had a considerable impact on staff orientation sessions. We had to break the training into separate modules so that case managers and clinicians would be better able to schedule training between their clinical appointments. Remedial training for clinicians who failed to reach the ANSA inter-rater reliability criterion were handled in a similar manner.

Clinic administrators, operational staff, case managers, and other clinical staff discussed ways to provide incentives—for example, rate changes to clinicians for completing ANSA assessments. The focus of discussions changed from operational issues (can this be done?) to staff's questions about the potential value of the project (How do we use these data with consumers?). Implementation problems, including early concerns about the length of time to complete ANSA assessments, were jointly identified and directly addressed, including a major concern of clinicians about the time required to complete their assessments. Experience with the Lyons rating scheme (Lyons, 1999) in other programs indicated that while there was a learning curve, after completing ten to fifteen cases completion times would drop to ten minutes or less. This reassured staff that the ANSA assessments would not consume all of their available time.

Clinical Expectations of Consumer Capacity. Initially, clinicians reported they were unable to get consumers to complete the self-report assessments. Through site visits and discussions with staff, we found that in these cases, clinicians had often ordered the consumer to complete an assessment without explaining the utility of the assessment *to the consumer* (as opposed to the organization). Some clinicians used language that suggested the consumer may not have the capacity to complete the assessment (e.g., "You know, it is ok if you cannot do it—you are seriously ill after all."). Not all clinicians explained that an important goal of the assessment was to improve communication between consumers and providers.

After a candid discussion between Polaris staff and site administrators about staff-consumer communication patterns, we held clinical coaching sessions to role-play positive and negative ways to recruit consumers for the project and to discuss reports. Initially, response was mixed—many clinicians did not see that their habit of ordering consumers to complete tasks was demeaning ("After all, if we don't order them to do something they will just stay in bed."). It took several role-plays to convince clinicians that they could treat consumers respectfully and still have them consent to completing tasks, and that they can feel comfortable allowing consumers to play a significant role in planning their treatment. After the coaching process was fully implemented, sites reported a dramatic decrease in "declines to participate" in the project; less than 5 percent refused to participate compared to more than one-half of consumers who had previously declined. Respectful communication counts.

Evaluation and Lessons

In spite of the challenges, the implementation of ROMS was successful for a majority of consumers and staff. Three out of four consumers (77.1 percent) enrolled in PACT programs and 83.1 percent of consumers receiving intensive case management and/or psychiatric rehabilitation services had no problems understanding or answering items.

ROMS implementation also benefited the PACT program, improving its relationship to its referral sources. Consumers are referred from the county and from a large managed care company. Polaris initiated a series of project open houses with the county and managed care officials to discuss the utility of the consumer self-report and ANSA ratings when providing case-level data, to demonstrate clinical change. The officials were impressed with the capability of the system and the program's commitment to quality improvement.

Our lessons, from an outcomes perspective as well as from the perspective of an organization committed to the recovery-empowerment paradigm, are outlined below.

Include the Consumer in Planning. One important lesson is to include the consumer as much as possible in planning and implementing the project. Much has been written about establishing a culture of measurement, and about the importance of establishing an implementation team, leadership support, and objectively measuring goals (Grissom, 2000). However, as the mental health field shifts its emphasis to fostering self-responsibility and self-resilience in clients, assessment information must include the client's wishes and preferences when implementing a treatment plan. We found that communication respectful of the consumer led to a sharp increase in participation rates, often because consumers told other consumers about "this amazing project where you get to help tell your counselor what you need." Functionally, this may mean including consumer advocates and other consumer/peer specialists in planning meetings regarding services for consumers, which in the past were open only to clinicians and administrators. It also suggests that the fifth person on the implementation team should be the consumer. Unquestionably, it means including the consumer's input during the implementation and treating consumers with respect for their time and expertise.

Provide Clinical Forums for Discussion. It is important for clinicians to have forums during staff meetings and other informal gatherings to discuss the value and use of clinical reports produced by outcome systems. In our implementation of ROMS, the perceived utility of clinical reports, including reports incorporating ANSA ratings, was directly related to the clinician's understanding of them and to the internalization of a schema that allows data to play a significant role in the clinical process.

When reports are considered solely a tool for management, clinicians reflect their ambivalence in unhelpful comments to consumers and other staff. Communications with the consumer are stilted and inauthentic and lack the conviction that the tools will improve the consumer's life. Under-use of the system also reflects a clinician's ambivalence. When clinicians are given opportunities and forums to discuss and internalize the value of the information produced on the consumer self-report and in the ANSA, most will recognize the system's utility.

Provide Flexible Staff Training Options. If staff turnover is high, traditional approaches to staff training may be impractical. Program administrators want maximum flexibility in planning for initial and booster trainings. Polaris intends to build an online training tool in partnership with Dr. Lyons to address this issue with regard to the implementation of ROMS. In the proposed web application, staff will be able to log in to a secure site and view training and test materials. The educational module will feature streaming video of Dr. John Lyons discussing ANSA content. The module will also provide an automated training and testing process that will allow case managers and clinicians to complete vignettes and to receive immediate feedback on their ratings. This tool is now available through Polaris Health Directives. The tool contains materials that allow selected raters to become trainers for their organizations and provides booster vignettes for clinician recertification and remediation.

CONCLUSION

Our project implementing ROMS at a Pennsylvania PACT team site suggests that combining consumer and support informant self-report data with clinical ratings, using computerized assessment, is both practical and well accepted by consumers, clinicians, and administrators. Our experience illustrates the typical challenges that arise when implementing computerized assessment systems with evolving technology. We addressed these challenges with a combination of technology solutions and by coaching clinicians to involve consumers in treatment planning that focused on their strengths (as opposed to weaknesses).

Many of the challenges we encountered were the result of significant changes in service delivery over the past decade, including a shift to serving consumers in their homes and at site locations other than a clinic. The change in staffing from a staff model to a contract model had a negative impact on staff attitudes and retention. It is important to address the continuing need for training when staff turnover rates are high.

An online tool helps alleviate the challenges to training. Use of a web-based tool allows new staff to be trained cost-effectively, with minimal program disruption and acceptable reliability, avoiding any watering down of the original training material. It also allows for metrics to be compiled on staff certification, the need for clinical remediation, and annual checks of clinical skill.

We found it necessary to formally address the misconceptions and transferences that clinicians and case managers often bring to their work with consumers. It is important to address this with sensitivity to the clinicians' level of experience (which may be limited), and with acknowledgment of the stresses and pressures of their work environment. However, most clinicians appreciated the opportunities to participate in role-playing and other exercises. Most do not intend to act in demeaning ways to consumers; on the contrary, they are often transferring onto the consumers their frustrations with having too few resources and the pressure of trying to have consumers perform. One of the underlying messages of ROMS is that recovery is a joint process involving the consumer and the clinician. When clinicians realize this, interactions with consumers are more task-focused and collaborative.

Another significant finding relates to the frequently asked question, "Can consumers report their own symptoms reliably?" Most consumers with serious and persistent mental illness had little difficulty completing assessments using a computer, and they appreciated the opportunity to have their voice considered in their treatment plans. By combining self-report with clinical ratings, a shift towards a stronger focus on teaching consumers to self-monitor their strengths and symptoms becomes possible, thereby reducing reliance on professionals. By adding this third perspective, clinicians also gain additional markers of performance, including congruence/noncongruence with other raters. Reports that present an objective and concrete series of graphs and measures can facilitate consumer-provider communication, highlighting areas of difficulty and affirming consumer progress. Until recently, despite the growing importance of the empowerment-recovery model (Harding, 1991; Fisher, 2004; Anthony, 2000), assessments appropriate to treatment planning and monitoring within a consumer-centered, strength-based paradigm have been lacking. For providers to take full advantage of this model, it is important for the next generation of assessment tools to focus on the measurement of the component skills associated with the development of new strengths and long-term resilience (Grotberg, 1995; Masten, 1994, 2001). Consumers appreciate the opportunity to view their progress, especially as they come to recognize how more effective provider communication can lead to better outcomes. It is our hope that ultimately systems like ROMS will help consumers to pursue the "holy grail" of recovery—independence from the mental health system by learning to self-monitor their mental health status, and reinforcement for positive behaviors, including self-responsibility and achievement of self-directed goals.

References

Anthony, W. (2000). Recovery-oriented service systems: Setting some system level standards. *Psychiatric Rehabilitation Journal, 24,* 159–168.

Eisen, S. V. & Culhane, M. A. (1999). Behavior and symptom identification scale (BASIS-32). In M. Maruish (Ed.), *The use of psychological testing for treatment planning and outcomes assessment.* Hillsdale, NJ: Erlbaum.

Eisen, S. V., Normand, S. L., Belanger, M., Spiro, A. & Esch, D. (2004). The revised behavior and symptom identification scale (BASIS-R). *Medical Care, 42,* 1230–1241.

Fisher, D. (2004). Health care reform based on an empowerment model of recovery by people with psychiatric disabilities. *Hospital and Community Psychiatry, 45,* 913–915.

Grissom, G. R. (2000). The advent of outcomes management and the culture of measurement. In K. M. Coughlin & T. Trabin (Eds.), *Behavioral outcomes and guidelines sourcebook.* New York: Faulkner & Grey.

Grissom, G., Sangsland, S., Jaeger, G. & Beers, T. (2004). PsyberCare CD: An outcomes assessment and clinical decision support system for chemical dependency treatment. In M. Maruish (Ed.), *The use of psychological testing for treatment planning and outcome assessment.* Hillsdale, NJ: Erlbaum.

Grotberg, E. (1995). *The international resilience project: Promoting resilience in children.* Birmingham: Alabama University, Civitan International Research Center (ERIC Document Reproduction Service No. ED383424).

Harding, C. M. (1991). Aging and schizophrenia: Plasticity, reversibility, and/or compensation. In E. F. Walker (Ed.), *Schizophrenia: A life-course developmental perspective.* San Diego: Academic Press.

Leon, S. C., Uziel-Miller, N. D., Lyons, J. S. & Tracy, P. (1999). Psychiatric hospital service utilization of children and adolescents in state custody. *Journal of the American Academy of Child and Adolescent Psychiatry, 38,* 305–310.

Lyons, J. S. (1999). *Adult needs and strengths assessment: An information integration tool for adults with mental health challenges.* Copyright © 1999 Buddin Praed Foundation.

Lyons, J. S., Kisiel, C. L., Dulcan, M., Cohen, R. & Chesler, P. (1997). Crisis assessment and psychiatric hospitalization of children and adolescents in state custody. *Journal of Child and Family Studies, 6,* 311–320.

Lyons, J. S., Mintzer, L. L., Kisiel, C. L. & Shallcross, H. (1998). Understanding the mental health needs of children and adolescents in residential treatment. *Professional Psychology: Research and Practice, 29,* 582–587.

Lyons, J. S. (1998). *The severity and acuity of psychiatric illness scales: An outcomes-management and decision-support system—Child and adolescent version (manual).* San Antonio, CA: Psychological Corp.

Lyons, J. S. (2004). *Redressing the emperor: Improving our children's public mental health system.* Westport, CT: Praeger.

Masten, A. S. (1994). Resilience in individual development: Successful adaptation despite risk and adversity. In M. Wang & E. Gordon (Eds.), *Risk and resilience in inner city America: Challenges and prospects*. Hillsdale, NJ: Erlbaum.

Masten, A. S. (2001). Ordinary magic: Resilience processes in development. *American Psychologist, 56*, 227–238.

McLellan, A. T., Cacciola, J., Kushner, H. & Peters, F. (1992). The fifth edition of the addiction severity index. *Journal of Substance Abuse Treatment, 9*, 199–213.

RashBeisel, J., Scott, J. & Dixon, L. (1999). Co-occurring severe mental illness and substance use disorders: A review of recent research. *Psychiatric Services, 50*, 1427–1434.

Toche-Manley, L. L. (2003-2007). *Recovery outcome management system*. National Institutes of Health Grant No. 7 R44 MH060020.

Chapter 22

Planning and Managing Service System Investments Using Provider Profiles and Clinical Assessments

by Dana A. Weiner, Ph.D.

THE SUPPLY SIDE OF THE BEHAVIORAL HEALTH CARE EQUATION

The chapters in this volume have illustrated the ways in which, using the Child and Adolescent Needs and Strengths (CANS) tool (Lyons, 2004), Total Clinical Outcomes Management (TCOM) can be implemented to improve the appropriateness and effectiveness of behavioral health care. When used within systems that are invested in improving outcomes as well as managing scarce resources for mental health treatment, such approaches have the power to make behavioral health care systems behave more rationally. However, these implementations are often predicated on the assumption that system stakeholders have basic knowledge about the resources that are available.

System administrators' knowledge about the nature of mental health services offered by providers is often vague and general. Providers bill payors within broad categories of services, but these billing classifications are often the most specific information administrators and system planners have about the nature of the services provided.

Billing data have been used to draw conclusions about patterns of use, but these analyses are flawed. They cannot take into account the many factors that influence the "supply" side of the equation, such as barriers to access or quality of services. In fact, they may derive supply-side information from demand data itself—extrapolating the volume, location, and type of providers by examining data about services that were used or paid for. Depending on utilization data to make inferences about supply carries with it the risk of institutionalizing disparities by characterizing need as whatever precipitated supply, which is often skewed in the direction of financial resources, among other factors.

These methods for understanding the supply side of the TCOM equation are inadequate. A complete and detailed understanding of the nature and availability of mental health services is essential to planning for and managing outcomes. Only then can we begin to map the relationships between needs and the services that can effectively address them.

BUILDING A PROVIDER CATALOGUE

Building a provider catalogue requires several things: a common language to use when discussing services and their features, a model for understanding both the structure and content of available resources, the consensus of key stakeholders and users on relevant information, a method for collecting information on the supply of services, and a structure for compiling that information.

A Common Language

The process of building a common language with which to talk about providers is similar to the processes used to develop a common language for the CANS and TCOM. The language must capture the priorities of the system, and it must have relevance both for stakeholders and for providers from whom information will be gathered. Provider interviews reap information about real-world applicability of the language used therein; if providers cannot respond to questions about *modality*, *monitoring*, or *evidence-based practices*, then the system planners must make the effort to translate these concepts into terms that can be understood and responded to meaningfully. For example, when asking providers whether they employ evidence-based practices, we should break down the inquiry into questions the providers can answer, such as: Do you use any approaches that follow a manual, or that require training and certification? Do you perform fidelity checks?

An important aspect of developing a common language is having the terminology to make the structure of provider organizations understandable. That is, your structure should arrange the universe of providers into categories, levels, and dimensions.

Structure and Content of Resources

Provider categories include providers of general behavioral health care, more specialized services (e.g., addressing parenting, domestic violence, or substance abuse), and services that are not clinical in nature but nonetheless essential to meeting the needs of many behavioral health care consumers, such as tutoring, mentoring, and after-school recreation. In addition, providers in most services systems are organized at multiple levels. For instance, the overarching umbrella organization is the agency; the unit providing services is the program; and the interventions provided within the program are the services. Other levels of classification depend on the service system being captured, such as the unit or facility in residential settings. In outpatient settings, programs may be offered at multiple locations, and single locations may offer multiple programs. These relationships are important to understand in preparation for geographic mapping of providers and their availability.

In addition to the hierarchical relationships between agency, program, location, and services, other dimensions must be captured to create an accurate provider classification system. These include level of care (e.g., inpatient, residential, outpatient, intensive outpatient), target population (e.g., sex offender, developmentally disabled) and type of services provided (e.g., group therapy, individual counseling, education). Decisions about how to categorize providers are interwoven with the goals of developing a provider catalogue.

Consensus on Relevant Information

In addition to agreement about terminology and classification, stakeholders and other users must agree on the universe of information that is relevant to include in the provider catalogue. Identifying the target population (e.g., children in the juvenile justice system, children in child welfare) and geographic area that the system will service can facilitate this. The identified target population will determine the providers that will be included in the catalogue. For instance, to include children involved in the juvenile justice system, you will need to include providers who address conduct issues, who may offer varying levels of security, and who may provide courtroom advocacy to youth. A provider catalogue designed to meet the needs of children in custody of child welfare must include service providers who are knowledgeable about the needs of children who experience trauma, domestic violence, or disrupted attachment. Similar considerations are required regarding substance abuse treatment, mental health treatment, and other targeted needs. The target population and system of classification will guide the selection of providers for inclusion in the catalogue.

Collecting Information on Providers and Services

Once relevant information and a system of classification have been agreed upon, you will need a strategy for collecting pertinent information. Certain types of information can be collected at the agency level and will pertain to any program under a given agency, such as the agency's director, number of years the agency has operated, number of sites it operates, and types of programs it delivers. Other information is collected at the program level. Information at the program level often constitutes the bulk of what is required to classify providers, such as the program type, level of care, target population, and also detailed information about intake requirements, monitoring and discharge procedures, personnel, licensing and accreditation, eligibility, and acceptable financing of care. At the service level, detailed information may include the use of specific practices or modalities for treatment, such as cognitive behavioral treatment, and methods of treatment delivery, such as group therapy.

Professional Directories, Referral Lists, and Networks. It can be challenging to identify the universe of providers to be included, even when geographic and clinical boundaries have been agreed upon. It is rarely the case that a comprehensive directory exists; more often than not such directories are piecemeal or exist only in the minds of experienced social workers. Due to a combination of high turnover and low technology among case managers, it is rare that such information is ever "uploaded" to build even the foundation for a centralized database. In lieu of this, other kinds of data can be used to identify relevant providers. Several strategies that can be employed include the use of contract data to identify providers delivering services of interest, directories of services that are put out by broad human service organizations such as the United Way, state hospital outpatient referral lists, and community mental heath networks. In addition to directories that inform data collection strategies, planners can employ a "snowball" strategy to ensure that a comprehensive catalogue is achieved. That is, each provider that is contacted should be asked about other providers to whom referrals are made. Once providers have been identified and interviewing has begun, geomapping (see later discussion in this chapter) can be a useful tool to prioritize and guide data collection strategies, targeting areas with little or no penetration for more extensive searching.

Interviews. The most powerful data collection tools in building a provider catalogue are in-person and telephone interviews. These interviews can facilitate communication about specific programming details, and they have the greatest likelihood of respondent compliance with data collection procedures. The information collected via interviews may be supplemented using interviewer observation, archival data collection, and consumer reports of service receipt and satisfaction.

Interviews are used to collect information at all levels of a provider organization, from the agency level to the smallest unit of analysis—the individual service. The first contact is generally to an agency to develop an understanding of the scope of the agency's programmatic offerings. The information obtained through this initial contact may be supplemented by the agency's website or printed brochure. Relevant programs should be classified by type (e.g., mental health, substance abuse, non-clinical) so that interviewers can select the interview form with the appropriate set of questions for the program type. Interviews must be made by appointment and conducted with a representative of the program.

Selecting the appropriate respondent for a program interview can be challenging. Although usually the program director or assistant director completes the interview, the most desirable respondent is someone who is neither too senior at the agency (and compelled to provide an ideal-world picture of how services should be delivered) nor too junior (and unable to give enough of a big picture of what goes on.) Questions to the respondent should be both broad and detailed enough to learn about several categories of data, including:

- Program and service eligibility
- Service types

- Modalities of treatment

- Geographic catchment area

- Accepted forms of payment

- Methods for documentation and staffing

- Credentials of staff

- Staff to client ratios

- Criteria for discharge

- Provision of wraparound/follow-up services

- Other program features needed for the catalogue

Compiling a Database

Once collected, the information must be complied in a database that can accommodate the relationships between agencies, programs, and services; that can be updated so information remains current; and that can be searched to locate services that match specified child characteristics. Working provider catalogues must be kept current and search tools must be user-friendly. Users, including providers, can keep catalogues current by updating them regularly, which will ensure they are reliable and trusted. Key pieces of information that must be updated regularly to maintain the utility of the catalogue include the waiting list, capacity, and intake information. If need be, a provider database management staff can be employed to maintain the database and make regular updates to pertinent fields at regular intervals.

ILLINOIS DEPARTMENT OF CHILD AND FAMILY SERVICES STATEWIDE PROVIDER DATABASE

Beginning in 2002, as part of a MacArthur Foundation initiative, the Cook County Juvenile Court Clinic (CCJCC) took initial steps toward creating a database, and this effort laid the foundation for the Illinois Department of Child and Family Services (IDCFS) Statewide Provider Database (SPD) (Weiner, 2002, 2004). By 2004, when the IDCFS project was commissioned, the CCJCC database contained several hundred programs in Cook County. The IDCFS project was to incorporate the rest of the state and broaden the focus of the initial project to include services to trauma-affected youth throughout the child welfare system. Initial contact was made at the agency level to identify relevant programs and contact persons. Two interviewers conducted the program interviews, in person or over the phone. The interviews took approximately forty-five minutes to complete and were usually conducted with program directors, assistant program directors, or intake assessors. Instrumentation in use by CCJCC was revised to include questions on the use of evidence-based practices, updated information on service offerings, eligibility requirements, intake procedures, and quality indicators such as staffing, credentials, and documentation. Information was then entered into a related database. The initial design called for a search component that would allow the database to be searched to find services that matched individuals' needs, funding, geographic location, and eligibility information, as well as a resource allocation planning tool in the form of a geomapping application.

Information was kept up to date in several ways. First, as referrals were identified, phone calls were made to providers to confirm key data components. Second, providers who had not been contacted in three months were flagged as requiring "updates"—a subset of questions pertaining to service offerings and intake and eligibility information. Initially, providers were identified using IDCFS contracting data that contained basic, general information (name, address, phone number), along with the "snowball" strategy described above. Later, state hospitals were contacted to obtain mental health network directories, and the state Community Mental Health Association and the Illinois Association for Adult Development and Aging (IAADA) were contacted for lists of providers. Other state agencies' directories were consulted as well.

Uses of the Provider Database

The provider catalogue is a dynamic and flexible instrument that can be used on many levels to enhance service provision and outcomes.

Individual Case Management. For micro-level uses such as identifying appropriate services for an individual, it is first necessary to identify the priority characteristics for matching, such as funding, geographic eligibility, clinical eligibility, and service needs. For a given child, these parameters can be specified when a query of the database is run, so that programs are extracted that match on key characteristics or, within an integrated CANS-based system, are automatically pulled based on the child's most recent assessment. Next, other program details are provided on matching programs to fine-tune matches and facilitate referrals.

Information relevant to a search for services for an individual child may be demographic, clinical, or logistic. One of the most innovative uses of the statewide provider database has been to locate service providers that not only provide the clinical offerings being requested, but also provide supplemental services that address barriers to treatment. These include providers who speak languages other than English, or those who offer transportation assistance, off-site service provision, and childcare for other children in the client's family.

Addressing Barriers to Access and Engagement. For several subgroups of consumers, basic information about accessing services, such as intake phone numbers and required documentation, is not enough to facilitate a referral. Barriers to access and engagement may include cultural factors such as language barriers and provider misperceptions, and logistic impediments such as lack of transportation and childcare.

At the most basic level, culturally competent providers must be able to speak the language of their clients from other cultures. Although some providers approach this issue with the use of interpreters to facilitate treatment with non-English-speaking clients, mental health treatment requires that providers and clients communicate directly with each other in the clients' native language. In addition, culturally competent providers should have an understanding of how their clients' cultural backgrounds will impact the stigma of seeking treatment, ways of relating to authority figures, and family dynamics.

Some providers have the capacity to address logistic barriers as well. Transportation issues can be addressed at several levels: using vouchers for clients who cannot afford public transportation, providing bus or van transportation to and from a mental health center, or providing mental health services in off-site locations such as a client's home or school. The provision of off-site services can also address resistance to treatment and can give the provider information about the context for problematic behaviors that can facilitate engagement. A provider may also offer childcare services for other children in the client's family, or to the client's children.

Use With CANS for Service System Planning. The goals for service system planning are: (1) to provide services where they are needed; (2) to provide services that match the volume and type of need; (3) to make better, more appropriate use of existing resources; and (4) to identify geographic facilitators/barriers.

Considerable discussion has been devoted to our understanding of service providers, including the services they offer, the geographic area within which these services are offered in addition to the actual locations they are provided, who is eligible to receive services, and provider service capacity (i.e., number of children). It is worth mentioning the necessary child-level data for service system planning. Child data for service system planning must include the most basic demographic information as well as the child's location to determine eligibility for service. This includes gender, age, address, and payment information. Clinical assessment results will also be needed to determine the needs of children across the system. CANS data is uniquely suited to this purpose, because of the action implications of CANS ratings. However, there are some additional steps needed to bridge the gap between children and providers at the level of the service system. This can be accomplished using algorithms to map CANS needs to required and recommended services, as discussed below.

Mapping Clinical Need to Services

As described in earlier chapters, the CANS gathers detailed information about the needs and strengths of children. It can be tailored to different clinical foci (e.g., trauma survivors), special populations (e.g., very young children), and specific applications (e.g., Partnership for Children). A noted strength of the CANS is its ability to inform users about the need for action.

Efforts to classify providers at a very detailed level allow us to consider the implications of CANS action levels in a new way. We can map many CANS-identified needs and clusters of needs to service offerings and sets of services. This mapping is performed using a set of algorithms that can be derived clinically or empirically. Clinical methods entail applying clinical knowledge and understanding along with empirical understanding of "best practices" in the field to assign service types to specific CANS elevations. Empirical methods involve analyzing decision-making data about service referrals to arrive at conclusions about which services clinicians most often select to address specific needs. These analyses may also incorporate data on services that result in CANS improvement, as appropriate referrals are more likely to address needs successfully.

Algorithms derived clinically take into account all required services for a given need, as well as services that may be beneficial but are not necessary. For example, where the CANS shows an elevation in needs due to symptoms of psychosis, required services would include consultation with a psychiatrist who could evaluate the appropriateness of psychotropic medication for treating psychotic symptoms. The client would also benefit from receiving services within a mental health program that could provide an array of services that address mental health needs. As psychotic symptoms may compromise one's ability to live independently, an actionable level of need on the psychosis dimension, combined with disruptions in functioning as indicated by the CANS, might justify a recommendation of an intervention to enhance skills for independent living, or a referral to a program at an intermediate level of care such as an intensive outpatient or partial hospitalization program.

To validate such clinical reasoning empirically, one can look to the behavior of a population of treatment providers (if such data is available). Treatment planning documents for individual children who have been assessed using the CANS prior to treatment planning are one source for this information. In the IDCFS project, reviewers analyzed data from the system of care (SOC) program. Using a wraparound philosophy to guide service planning among a broad array of options, the SOC aims to stabilize foster care placements for children at risk of placement disruption. This broad array makes SOC an ideal choice for analyzing provider behavior; case managers have the freedom to choose from a variety of options and act creatively to address needs and strengths using nontraditional interventions. To analyze the behavior of SOC case managers, analysts coded individual plans of care from several hundred cases, using a checklist derived from the categories in the IDCFS statewide provider database.

A comprehensive guide to mapping CANS needs to services can be developed by rating each CANS item against each service type, indicating for each of the action ratings (0, 1, 2, 3) whether a given service is not indicated, is recommended, or is required. This guide can be applied to sets of CANS data to derive a more thorough understanding of the implications of needs aggregated across a population of children.

For the sake of broader illustrations of system need in contrast to provider availability, it may be necessary to conduct analyses to arrive at groups of children with similar clusters of needs. Then algorithms can be developed in the aggregate to assign children with clusters of needs to sets of services addressing the cluster.

Geomapping

One of the most useful tools for displaying system level data is a map. Although tabular reports can contain a great deal of useful information about the volume and type of need and the volume and type of available services, maps are able to illustrate an easily interpretable and readily understood picture of what the service system looks like and where the gaps in services exist when superimposed upon need. When used with provider data alone, maps are useful tools that can illustrate the availability and distribution of providers, along with key factors such as public transportation routes and distances to other community locations (schools, churches, homes). When used with provider and child data, they can become invaluable tools for gap analyses.

There are several different ways that provider data can be prepared, depending on the mapping task for which they are to be used. The four examples that follow were executed using ArcIMS GIS software (ESRI, 2007) along with an ArcView display.

Scenario 1: Mapping Provider Availability. In this scenario, spatial discounting is used to arrive at values for providers distributed across a geographic area. Spatial discounting takes into account the decreasing value of a provider the further a potential client is from the provider's location. If a provider is worth 100 percent of its value to a client who is at its front door, then for each unit (e.g., city block) away from the provider's location, its value is discounted, down to a set value (e.g., 5 percent). Provider values can then be averaged and aggregated by census tracts to arrive at a map that shades areas with greater/lesser density of providers. This process is greatly facilitated by accurate information about each provider's capacity.

Scenario 2: Mapping Child Needs. There are several different methods for mapping child needs for services. At the most basic level, it is possible to map all children within a given service system (e.g., child welfare) by geocoding each child's address (assigning longitude and latitude to each child as a point on the map), and then aggregating children to arrive at a map (similar to that described above for providers) that is shaded darkly for areas with more children, and lightly for areas with fewer children. Such a map gives system planners a sense of where their clients are located, but little sense of exactly what they need. To incorporate the children's needs, you can identify only children with a given need(s) on the map—for example, by creating a map (with superimposed layers) only of children in need of substance abuse treatment, as identified by a 2 or a 3 on the CANS substance abuse item. Another possibility is to conduct a factor analysis to determine common combinations, or clusters, of children based on frequently combined CANS ratings, and then color code the prevalence of children in each of the clusters on the same map. In this way, children in each clinical cluster could be identified by a unique color so that the map illustrates the overlap or distinct distribution of children with different clinical needs.

Scenario 3: Mapping Availability to a Given Need. Once provider availability and child need are mapped, it becomes possible to superimpose one upon the other to easily distinguish areas of gaps in services. Need can be mapped against provider availability for the system as a whole or for a specific type of need. For example, separate maps can be generated for availability gaps in specialists who treat substance abusers and those who treat children with developmental disabilities. Your map can also identify the location of providers (as points on the map) that do not provide the needed services, so that system planners have a better idea of where to reallocate existing resources to providers who might develop capacity to treat the needs of children in their area. In addition, it can pinpoint other important locations, such as community centers, churches, libraries, and schools. This will enable system administrators to assess the availability of satellite locations for implementing services or for providing supplemental services such as outreach, education, and screening in areas where maps indicate needs are prominent.

Scenario 4: Mapping Providers Nearest a Given Child. Among all of these scenarios, probably the most basic is mapping the providers who can meet the needs (geographic, financial, clinical) of a given child. Geomapping used in combination with a searchable provider database can yield information about local providers' services, the transportation to facilitate access to these providers, and the child's distance from both. The child appears as a point on the map, and providers appear as related points. When the cursor scrolls over the points, distance from the child is displayed. At the bottom of the screen, pertinent information about other service offerings as well as intake contact information is displayed to facilitate referrals.

The IDCFS leadership generated a detailed list of other uses for its provider database and geomapping application, including maps of children within twenty minutes and twenty miles of a provider that offers the services they need; maps of children with CANS-defined needs who do not live within twenty minutes or twenty miles of a provider; and reports of needs, received services, and outcomes.

FUTURE DIRECTIONS: OUTCOMES AND CONTINUOUS QUALITY IMPROVEMENT

All of the applications discussed in this chapter are future oriented—toward planning, improved access to services, more rational allocation of resources across systems. The technology and conceptualization of these projects brings us rapidly forward into an era when assessment, case management activities, and system planning can all be accomplished using a central database and web application. The convergence of these different kinds of information in a central platform allows a new kind of monitoring to take place, which in turn can facilitate continuous quality improvement in a more meaningful and empirical way. From the time a child enters the system, we can track assessments, service referrals, and service use. Multiple assessments can yield information about change over time; these data combined with accurate information about the receipt of services can tell us which children with which needs showed improvement after receiving specific services. By examining the outcomes of children who receive different services for different problems, we can begin to develop a different approach to identifying best practices.

As a continuous quality improvement tool, a provider catalogue supports information beyond the relatively static quality indicators such as credentials and staffing plans. It provides, and monitors, more plastic indicators such as the adoption and implementation of evidence-based practices and internalized quality assurance processes. Monitoring these factors can identify areas for targeted intervention at the organizational level, and areas in which capacity can be enhanced to encourage the development of self-sustaining continuous quality improvement systems.

References

Environmental Systems Research Institute (ESRI) (2007). ArcIMS [internet map server], ArcView (computer software). Redlands, CA.

Lyons, J. S. (2004). *Redressing the emperor: Improving our children's public mental health system*. Westport, CT: Praeger.

Weiner, D. A. (2002). Statewide Provider Database (computer software). Chicago, IL.

Weiner, D. A. (2004). CCJCC [Cook County Juvenile Court Clinic] Community Resources Database (computer software). Chicago, IL.

Chapter 23

Applications of Trajectory Analysis in Total Clinical Outcomes Management

by Zoran Martinovich, Ph.D. and Jena H. Stallings, M.A.

INTRODUCTION

Applied research on behavioral health outcomes is often concerned with describing patterns of change across time. In experimental research, the most common focus of change analysis is on comparing a pre-intervention baseline assessment and a post-intervention follow-up. The follow-up typically occurs shortly after the completion of a course of treatment. In applied research oriented toward managing real world outcomes, the relevant time period is less clear, and often varies from person to person as the nature of the intervention is adjusted depending on the unique characteristics of the case at hand. Arguably, the appropriate time period for assessing change in experimental studies is also unclear, and it is merely the cognitive salience of the intervention period that limits the primary analyses to pre-intervention versus post-intervention comparisons. In experimental work, follow-up assessments are sometimes completed, but the time period followed and the number of follow-up assessments appear driven by logistical concerns, since there is rarely an appropriate "naturally occurring" follow-up period. So, in both experimental and applied naturalistic research predicting change, there is rarely a clear prescription for the appropriate number and timing of post-intervention assessments.

Trajectory analysis refers to methods of modeling change that assume an underlying path or trajectory to each person's change over time and have a hierarchical structure (i.e., repeated assessments are nested within each person). These methods are referred to by many names (e.g., mixed regression, hierarchical linear models, random coefficient regression, multi-level models). By reframing the pattern of change in trajectory terms, trajectory models have the unique advantage of allowing the number and timing of outcomes assessments to vary from person to person. In these models, assessment time is treated as a random factor; that is, the particular times assessed are treated as randomly sampled for each person from a range of possible follow-up times. This fact makes trajectory models uniquely useful for behavioral health outcomes evaluation in the real world, since both rational and practical concerns make variable assessment timing inevitable. For example, trajectory analysis has been used to examine treatment outcomes in the areas of individual psychotherapy (Howard et al., 1986), inpatient psychiatric treatment (Lyons et al., 1997a; Lyons et al., 1997b), and partial hospitalization programs (Lyons et al., 1996). Previous research has also examined outcome trajectories of residential treatment facilities for children and adolescents (Lyons et al., 2001; Hussey & Guo, 2002).

Even in experimental studies, whenever follow-up assessment(s) are considered, the more ambitious and informative follow-up studies rarely achieve full compliance with plans for repeated assessments at fixed time points. Although the initial plan may entail multiple assessments (e.g., at three, six, twelve, and twenty-four months), the probability that a case will arbitrarily miss one or more of the follow-up assessments increases as the number of follow-ups in the study design increases. Traditional analytic methods such as analysis of variance (ANOVA) and analysis of covariance (ANCOVA) require assessments at every point, and methods of dealing with missing information (e.g., case deletion, score imputation) are often problematic. Deleting cases with any missing information throws out real data and potentially introduces bias (compromising the internal validity goals of randomization to experimental conditions). Score imputation, or generating "predicted" scores for the missing information, makes efficient use of the existing data but has often been criticized for inflating significance levels by artificially reducing "error" variation estimates. For imputation methods to yield unbiased outcome estimates, common regression or linear interpolation techniques must yield predicted scores that are less variable than the real scores would have been if assessments had been completed. Thus, imputation artificially inflates significance levels.

Ironically, imputation also causes cases with the least data to show the most stable pattern of change across time. Using some analytic strategies, cases with substantial missing assessments would be treated as if their change patterns were more reliable than cases with complete data. Unlike methods relying on imputation, trajectory techniques assign less weight to cases with less complete repeated measures data. Even in experimental studies, trajectory techniques are often useful for dealing with fixed repeated assessment plans that fail in execution.

TRAJECTORY MODELS: THE BASICS

To describe individual case data via a trajectory, we must choose an appropriate model form for that trajectory. For example, a simple linear trajectory would describe each person's outcomes over time with an intercept coefficient plus a slope coefficient multiplied by time in years:

Level 1 Model

$$\text{Outcome} = \text{Intercept} + \text{Slope} \times \text{Years} + \text{Error}_{1-\text{outcome}}$$

or

$$\text{Outcome} = \text{Starting Level} + \text{Rate of Change} \times \text{Years} + \text{Error}_{1-\text{outcome}}$$

"Years" refers to years after the first assessment; "intercept" is the estimated outcome at the first assessment; and "slope" is the rate of change per year. "Error" refers to deviations of each person's outcomes away from the straight-line trajectory. So, one can think of trajectory models as a way of reframing outcomes as a starting level followed by a fixed rate of change.

The model above is referred to as a Level 1 model because person variation in intercepts and slopes may be separated, and each may be modeled as a function of other predictors. The model assessing the relationship between various predictors and these intercepts (i.e., starts) and slopes (i.e., rates) is referred to as a Level 2 model.

$$\text{Level 2 Starting Level model: Start} = \text{Intercept} + \text{Slope} \times \text{Predictor} + \text{Error}_{2-\text{start}}$$

$$\text{Level 2 Rate of Change model: Rate} = \text{Intercept} + \text{Slope} \times \text{Predictor} + \text{Error}_{2-\text{rate}}$$

In the above equations, the two intercept estimates are starting levels for cases scoring 0 on the predictor, and the two slope estimates indicate effects of the predictor on the starting level and rate of change, respectively. These intercept and slope coefficients are referred to as fixed effects. The two error terms refer to deviations of person-level starting levels and rates of change away from expectations based on the predictor. These terms are described by variance estimates, correlated with each other, and referred to as "random effects." If one substitutes the level 2 equations into the level 1 equation, a complete regression equation is obtained with main effects (predictor, years), interaction (predictor x years), and with three error terms. It is possible to augment the model by including additional time-varying predictors at level 1, and additional time-invariant predictors at level 2.

TRAJECTORY MODELS: COMPLEXITIES

Trajectory models are not limited to simple linear trajectories like the ones above. Before completing a trajectory analysis, you must make a decision regarding the trajectory model form. If limited outcome variable scaling properties or historical conventions implicate a particular form, this decision may be determined a priori; however, preliminary empirical evaluation may be needed to identify a model form that yields relatively reliable and unbiased outcome estimates.

Any number of model form modifications may be considered to describe a trajectory appropriate to the problem at hand. For example, trajectories may include rapid break points (e.g., through including additional time-varying predictors at level 1, or partial step-function coding of repeated measures). The time metric can be altered to allow curvilinear patterns (e.g., log-linear time transformations, polynomial functions at level 1). Also, trajectories may be forced to predict known outcome assessment values at specific times (e.g., anchored models eliminating intercept estimation error).

With respect to dependent variable types, trajectory models are not limited to interval-scaled dependent variables (e.g., scale scores as outcomes). Multilevel models may be applied to binary outcomes (success/failure), ordinal outcomes (e.g., four-point CANS items), or other categorical outcomes. Although power is usually better when using reliable multi-item scales with normally distributed error, analyses that reduce the outcome variable to success/failure or to ordinal action-relevant categories are often more useful in applied contexts (e.g., making case management decisions based on the expected success of alternative treatment strategies).

We will consider three diverse examples of trajectory models to illustrate the substantial range of practical applications for these techniques. These examples include experimental and non-experimental data, outcome variables with varied scaling properties (normal, ordinal count data, ordinal 0 to 3 ratings), varied error structures (normal, Poisson, and polytomous logistic), and varied linear and atypical model forms.

Example 1—Predicting Psychotherapy Progress

This example considers a hierarchical model used to predict normally distributed psychotherapy outcomes; a diverse array of person-specific predictors was used to predict rates of change.

The curvilinear "dose-effect" relationship has often been used to describe the relationship between time in psychotherapy and treatment outcome (cf. Howard et al., 1986). Since Howard and colleagues first applied this phrase to psychotherapy outcomes, numerous longitudinal studies of psychotherapy outcomes have demonstrated a curvilinear course, parsimoniously described through a linear relationship with a log-transformed time metric. The present model was used to assist case managers in evaluating the progress of ongoing psychotherapies.

In this example, trajectories on a normally distributed dependent variable are anchored, which means the predicted trajectories are forced to predict starting level at baseline. Because anchoring eliminates the need for a random component for the intercept, all change variance was allocated to the slope term. In addition to simplifying the model, anchoring enhances slope reliability (all reliable change variance is allocated to the slope random component). This indirectly improves statistical power to detect fixed effects, since there is more reliable variation to predict.

Sample Used. In this example, an "anchored" log-linear model was used to predict psychotherapy outcomes in a sample of 2,390 post-intake assessments from 867 cases whose psychotherapy was paid for and managed through a managed care provider. Outcomes were assessed on Polaris's Behavioral Health Status Scale (2000) (a multi-item T-score generated from repeated patient self-report ratings). Cases varied in the number of timing of repeated assessments; 56.5 percent had two assessments (including intake); 23.5 percent had three assessments; and the remainder had four or more assessments. The median number of weeks spanned by repeated assessments was 4.86 (10th pctl = 1.71, 25th = 2.74, 75th = 8.16, 90th = 13.0).

Analysis Strategy: "Anchored" Step-Wise, Log-Linear Model. The analyses were conducted using a hierarchical linear modeling procedure (Raudenbush et al., 2004; Bryk & Raudenbush, 1992). Assuming an underlying log-linear course of recovery, each client's Beck (BHS) T-score was modeled, at hierarchical level 1, as a function of time (measured in weeks after intake date), as follows (Equation 1):

Level 1 (Repeated Measures Level):   (1)

$$BHST_{ct} = \beta_{0c} + \beta_{1c} Log_{10}(Week + 1)_{ct} + e_{ct}$$

$BHST_{ct}$ is the BHS T-score at time t for client c. The β_{0c} parameter (intercept) is the client's expected BHS T-score at the intake assessment. The β_{1c} parameter (slope) is the client's expected change in BHS T-score per log_{10} of "weeks after intake date + 1".

In other words, the slope is the expected change by the end of the ninth week after the intake date, and also the expected change in the subsequent ninety weeks. The random error term, e_{ct}, refers to normally distributed deviations away from expected values for client c at assessment time t.

At level 2, the "client" level, variation in level 1 intercepts and slopes may be modeled as functions of baseline status, as follows:

Level 2 (Client Level):

$$\beta_{0c} = \pi_{00} + \pi_{01} BHST_{0c} + r_{0c}$$
$$\beta_{1c} = \pi_{10} + \pi_{11} BHST_{0c} + r_{1c}$$

Intercepts and slopes at level 2 are modeled as linear functions of client baseline scores. By fixing π_{00} and π_{01} terms at 0 and 1, respectively, the model is forced to predict each patient's actual baseline status on the outcome measure ($BHST_{0c}$) at week 0, and thus, there is no patient-specific "error" term for the β_{0c} intercept parameter. The error term for the slope, r_{1c}, refers to slope variation among clients (after removing variance accounted for by intake BHST). So, the level 2 model reduces to:

Level 2 (Client Level):

$$\beta_{0c} = 0 + 1 \cdot BHST_{0c}$$
$$\beta_{1c} = \pi_{10} + \pi_{11} BHST_{0c} + r_{1c}$$

Finally, the model above may be augmented by including j additional predictors of slope variation. This yields the following level 2 model (Equation 2):

$$\text{Level 2 (Client Level):} \hspace{4cm} (2)$$

$$\beta_{0c} = 0 + 1 \cdot BHST_{0c}$$

$$\beta_{1c} = \pi_{10} + \pi_{11} BHST_{0c} + \sum_{i=1}^{j} \pi_{1i} PRED_{ic} + r_{1c}$$

Twenty additional intake predictors were considered for inclusion via a forward entry stepwise procedure. Each predictor was considered in turn at each step, and the most significant predictor was included, until no significant predictors could be entered.

Substituting Equation 2 into Equation 1, we obtain the full model predicting BHST outcomes from time since intake[1] (Equation 3).

$$BHST_{ct} = BHST_{0c} + \left(\pi_{10} + \pi_{11} BHST_{0c} + \sum_{i=1}^{j} \pi_{1i} PRED_{ic} + r_{1c} \right) Log_{10}(Week + 1)_{ct} + e_{ct} \hspace{0.5cm} (3)$$

Final Model. The final model includes anchored ratings in response to the following questions:

Predictor   *Question addressed*

LONGPRO   How long have you had the current problem?

HOSPE   Have you ever been hospitalized for a psychiatric/emotional problem?

ASKHELP   When I have problems, I go to people who can help me.

COUNS   How much counseling or therapy have you had in the past?

TIMECON   How many times have you been in counseling or therapy before now?

Equation 4 (below) specifies fixed effect coefficients for the final model. Besides Intake BHST, five additional predictors were included. COUNS and TIMECON were included as a sum (thus the same coefficients preceding each predictor). The equation below may be used to generate an expected treatment response (ETR) trajectory anchored to each client's intake BHST score.

---

[1]"Week since intake" is *not* a rounded whole number, but rather a continuous predictor based on subtracting intake and post-intake date stamps. So, 0 refers to a point in time, that is, the intake assessment date and time.

$$BHST_{ct} = BHST_{0c} + \begin{pmatrix} 37.256554 \\ -0.521430BHST_{0c} \\ -0.529566LONGPRO_{0c} \\ -1.630227HOSPE_{0c} \\ +0.715289ASKHELP_{0c} \\ -0.367621COUNS_{0c} \\ -0.367621TIMECON_{0c} \end{pmatrix} Log_{10}(Week+1)_{ct} \qquad (4)$$

Inferential Tests for Fixed and Random Effects. Table 23.1 lists specific inferential tests for fixed effects depicted in Equation 4, and for random slope variance.

As may be expected, substantial reliable slope variation remains unaccounted for in the present model (reliability estimate = 0.417). Overall, slope variance was reduced by 37.9 percent through the inclusion of intake BHST as a predictor (from 45.92 to 28.54). Subsequent predictors further reduced slope variance by 12.1 percent (to 22.99). Approximately 49.9 percent of client slope variance was explained by the present set of predictors.

Although 49.9 percent of client SLOPE variance was explained, this is not the same as the "percent of SCORE variance" explained. The amount of score variance explained is not a constant, but rather decreases as predictions extend away from time 0

Table 23.1
Parameter Estimates and Inferential Tests for Fixed and Random Effects for "Anchored" Log-Linear Model Predicting Behavioral Health Status From Time (Logweek)

Final estimation of fixed effects:

Fixed Effect	Coefficient	Standard Error	t	d.f.	p
For LOGWEEK slope, B1					
NTRCPT2, π_{10}	37.256554	1.875799	19.86	861	0.000
BHST, π_{11}	−0.521430	0.032378	−16.10	861	0.000
LONGPRO, π_{12}	−0.529566	0.147251	−3.59	861	0.001
HOSPE, π_{13}	−1.630227	0.482254	−3.38	861	0.001
ASKHELP, π_{14}	0.715289	0.181273	3.94	861	0.000
PRIORSUM, π_{15}, π_{16}	−0.367621	0.080693	−4.55	861	0.000

Final estimation of variance components:

Random Effect	Standard Deviation	Variance Component	df	χ^2	p
For LOGWEEK slope,					
level 2, r_{1c}	4.79515	22.99345	861	2504.49	0.000
level 1, e_{ct}	4.91546	24.16176			

(i.e., intake). At intake, 100 percent of score variance was explained (the model intercept is anchored on a known intake score), and the percent subsequently decreases. So,
unlike "slope variance explained," the percent of score variance explained is a function of the distribution of assessment times. Specifically, in these data, the correlation
between predicted and observed post-intake BHST scores was 0.607 (i.e., 36.8 percent
score variance explained). However, as should be expected, the correlation becomes
weaker for scores that are further out. Specifically, for predictions after intake but less
than three weeks out, $r = 0.737$; for three to eight weeks, $r = 0.649$; and for predictions
more than eight weeks out, $r = 0.449$.

Example 2—Predicting Response to Treatments for Adolescent Substance Abuse

This example was an experimental evaluation of three treatment strategies for adolescent substance abuse, examining immediate treatment effects and relapse patterns
over four post-treatment follow-up assessments. In this example, the dependent variable was a "count" variable (the number of days using alcohol/drugs in the past ninety
days), and the modeling technique required preliminary work to identify an unbiased
model form that would be able to use all the available data (missing by chance at varied
times for a substantial subset of cases).

The adolescent treatment model (ATM) initiative was a twelve-site, prospective
study designed to evaluate adolescent substance abuse treatment outcomes and to
assess the relative efficacy of the different treatment models (Dasinger et al., 2004).
Sites were classified into three levels of care (LOC): long-term residential (LTR),
short-term residential (STR), and outpatient/intensive outpatient (OP/IOP). Individual
sites and the three levels of care were compared on patterns of change in the number
of days using alcohol or other drugs (AOD) in the past ninety days.

This example illustrates the use of an atypical trajectory model involving a nonlinear pattern with a distinct break between treatment and follow-up periods. Although
the study was experimental, 42 percent of cases did not have available data at one or
more follow-up assessments; thus, a trajectory approach, treating time as a randomly
sampled factor, offered a distinct advantage. As the dependent variable was a skewed
"count" variable, with a distinct mode at zero days using, a Poisson link function was
appropriate, and alternative response models able to capture the distinct break between
treatment and follow-up periods were evaluated for bias before the final model form
was chosen.

Sample Used. The analyses included data collected at 6,616 assessments of 1,504
persons. The number of assessments per person ranged from three to five (3: 18.6 percent; 4: 23.0 percent; 5: 58.4 percent), with all included subjects having been assessed
at baseline. Assessments may have been completed at three months, six months, nine
months, and/or twelve months after baseline.

Analysis Strategy: Poisson Regression Link Function, Atypical Trajectory Form.
A preliminary examination of the data suggested a distinct drop in AOD use between

baseline and three months (the first post-treatment assessment), followed by horizontal or increased use during the period from three to twelve months. To adjust for missing data, various model forms were considered for fitting person-specific response trajectories to data from three to twelve months. A natural log transformation of time (specifically, coding times from three to twelve months as 0, 0.736, 0.914, 1) yielded an optimal fit.[2]

A hierarchical nonlinear model was used to describe the person, site, and LOC differences in AOD use across time.[3] Because the dependent variable was a count variable with a skewed distribution and a lower limit of zero, error variation within any person and time was assumed to be Poisson distributed. For each person, natural log of AOD use in that last ninety days was modeled as a linear function of time and the proportion of time in a controlled environment (PCE).[4] Two time contrasts were included: a step-function contrast (TX), coding time as 0 at baseline and 1 at subsequent times, and the natural log code above (REL), coding time as 0 at baseline and month 3. The level 1 equation below describes the log-link function:

Level 1:

$$\ln(\text{AOD}) = B_0 + B_1\text{TX} + B_2\text{REL} + B_3\text{PCE} + \varepsilon$$

Given the present coding, exponents of the coefficients above are estimates of, respectively:

e^{B_0} Days using at baseline, for someone not in controlled environment in the preceding ninety days

e^{B_1} Days using at three months, expressed as a proportion of days using at baseline, for persons not in a controlled environment

e^{B_2} Days using at twelve months, expressed as a proportion of days using at three months, for someone not in a controlled environment

e^{B_3} Days using at any given time if someone was in a controlled environment throughout the ninety days, expressed as a proportion of days using when not in a controlled environment.

---

[2]Residuals from person-specific regression models predicting ln(AOD use + 1) from time (three to twelve months) were examined to identify whether log-linear, linear, or exponential curved patterns optimally describe change trajectories. A linear time code (0, 1/3, 2/3, 1) was transformed by taking the exponent, then linearly transforming this result to range from 0 to 1. The resulting nonlinear time code was again exponentiated, and rescaled from 0 to 1, and then sequentially exponentiated and rescaled again. Similarly, natural log transformations were applied to the linear code + 1, then rescaled from 0 to 1, and again sequentially log-transformed and rescaled from 0 to 1. Each transformed time predictor was used to estimate change from month 3 (0) to month 12 (1); however, the fifth sequential natural log function yielded an optimal fit, with no significant bias at any given month, and minimizing observed bias at month 12. Thus, the present analytic models predicted natural log of AOD use as a linear function of time, recoded as follows, from month 3 to 12: (0.000, 0.736, 0.914, 1.000).

[3]HLM2L and HLM3L software (version 4.04) was used to conduct the present analyses.

[4]PCE was not included as an exposure variable, but rather as an additional linear predictor, since being in a controlled environment did not prevent AOD use in a substantial minority of cases.

In the tables that follow, exponents of coefficients preceding the TX term are referred to as treatment effects, and exponents of coefficients preceding the REL term are referred to as relapse effects. These values are multiplicative factors by which AOD use declines from pre-treatment to three months post-treatment, and increases from three months to the end of the study period (twelve months), respectively.

Individual differences in the above coefficients were modeled as a function of level 2 predictors. In the present analyses, B_0, B_1, and B_2 coefficients were assumed to randomly vary (across persons), but no random component was included for the B_3 coefficient. Sites (twelve levels) were classified according to three LOC levels (LTR, STR, OP/IOP), Parameter estimates for each LOC were estimated and compared via HLM2L models by including dummy codes for LOC as predictors of the first three level 1 coefficients. For each LOC, estimated treatment effects and relapse effects were evaluated for significance (i.e., "nil" hypothesis t-tests of change within each LOC). In addition, t-tests were conducted comparing each LOC group with the other groups (combined and individually) on baseline status, treatment effects, and relapse effects. With respect to site, baseline, treatment, and relapse, effects were compared by including eleven dummy codes as predictors of corresponding level 1 coefficients and conducting corresponding t-tests.

Person variance and site variance components for each coefficient were estimated by constructing an additional three-level hierarchical model with three random components at the third level describing site variance in baseline, treatment, and relapse effects. In such a model, random components at the second level refer to person variation within site. Thus, variation for each randomly varying coefficient was partitioned into site variance and person variance (within site). Based on these variance components, site variation was estimated as a percentage of person variance for each randomly varying parameter.

Variance Components. Based on the three-level model, patient (within site) variance components for B_0, B_1, and B_2 coefficients were estimated at 1.014, 9.983, and 12.508, respectively. Corresponding site variance estimates were 0.385, 2.034, and 0.108. As a percentage of patient variance, it follows that 27.5 percent of B_0 variance, 16.9 percent of B_1 variance, but only 0.9 percent of B_2 variance was accounted for by site. Although site accounted for a substantial component of baseline AOD and treatment effect variance, site (and therefore LOC) variation in relapse rates was relatively minimal when compared with patient variance within site.[5] After extracting 33 degrees of freedom from two-level models by including a full set of dummy coded site predictors, significant random variation (i.e., person variation) in all three random effects remained present.

Fixed Effects. In the full sample, adjusted to zero days in a controlled environment, estimated baseline status was 57.7 days out of ninety. This rate of use declined by 64 percent to twenty-one days at the third month, then increased by 33 percent to 27.9 days by the twelfth month.

Contrasts of sites and LOC were conducted via two-level models. Table 23.2 lists estimates of site, LOC, and overall model effects with inferential tests based on these models.[6] "Nil hypothesis" tests indicate whether the coefficients deviate significantly

---

[5] 3L model iterations did not converge on a solution when a random component was included for the B_2 coefficient, and were discontinued at macro-iteration 50. No reliable site variation in this component was detected, $\chi^2 (11) = 12.29$, p >.10.

[6] All inferential tests are based on the "population average" model.

Table 23.2
Estimates of Site, Level of Care, and Overall Model Effects with Inferential Tests

Site	Baseline e^{B_0}	Baseline vs ALL t	Baseline vs ALL p	Treatment Effect e^{B_1}	Treatment Nil test t	Treatment Nil test p	Treatment vs ALL t	Treatment vs ALL p	Relapse Effect e^{B_2}	Relapse Nil test t	Relapse Nil test p	Relapse vs ALL t	Relapse vs ALL p	p(Days CE) e^{B_3}	p(Days CE) Nil test t	p(Days CE) Nil test p	n
ALL	57.67			0.36	−25.8	<.001			1.33	6.61	<.001			0.16	−39.8	<.001	1504
LTR	62.51	2.66	.008	0.21	−14.3	<.001	−5.43	.000	1.65	3.94	<.001	1.70	.090	0.17	−37.9	<.001	357
STR	65.84	8.13	<.001	0.31	−21.0	<.001	−3.62	.001	1.45	5.95	<.001	1.77	.076	"			462
OP/IOP	42.45	−11.4	<.001	0.56	−9.13	<.001	8.40	.000	1.16	2.15	.032	−2.70	.007	"			685
LTR: site01	87.95	4.70	<.001	0.03	−9.44	<.001	−4.66	<.001	1.00	0.00	>.10	−0.41	n.s.	0.17	−33.3	<.001	41
STR: site02	79.77	6.81	<.001	0.23	−13.1	<.001	−3.65	<.001	1.68	4.61	<.001	1.60	n.s.	"			137
STR: site03	64.27	3.46	.001	0.38	−12.8	<.001	0.55	n.s.	1.29	2.96	.004	−0.37	n.s.	"			276
LTR: site04	58.43	0.63	n.s.	0.25	−12.4	<.001	−3.48	.001	1.66	3.88	<.001	1.68	.092	"			259
STR: site05	67.80	4.15	<.001	0.29	−13.2	<.001	−2.37	.018	1.51	4.11	<.001	1.11	n.s.	"			201
OP: site06	13.25	−7.82	<.001	3.54	2.00	.045	3.59	.001	0.43	−1.19	n.s.	−1.60	n.s.	"			26
STR: site07	37.54	−4.71	<.001	0.16	−4.25	<.001	−1.90	.057	4.09	2.97	.003	2.37	.018	"			71
OP: site08	29.82	−10.3	<.001	0.68	−3.36	.001	5.42	<.001	1.31	2.10	.035	−0.16	n.s.	"			136
OP: site09	44.78	−3.36	.001	0.70	−2.92	.004	5.42	<.001	1.03	0.21	n.s.	−2.11	.035	"			107
OP: site10	36.11	−5.77	<.001	0.61	−1.41	n.s.	1.57	n.s.	1.25	0.59	n.s.	−0.18	n.s.	"			78
OP: site11	57.01	−0.05	n.s.	0.45	−7.13	<.001	1.85	.064	1.09	0.69	.491	−1.60	n.s.	"			115
LTR: site12	74.13	2.92	.004	0.22	−6.12	<.001	−1.99	.046	1.59	1.65	.099	0.54	n.s.	"			57

Table 23.3
Pair-Wise Comparisons of Parameter Estimates for LOC Groups

Site	Baseline					Tx Effect					Relapse Effect				
	e^{B_0}	vs STR		vs OP		e^{B_1}	vs STR		vs OP		e^{B_2}	vs STR		vs OP	
		t	p	t	p		t	p	t	p		t	p	t	p
LTR	62.51	−1.18	n.s.	8.05	<.001	0.21	−3.37	.001	−7.85	<.001	1.65	0.93	n.s.	2.42	.016
STR	65.84			11.2	<.001	0.31			−6.98	<.001	1.45			2.36	.018
IO/IOP	42.45					0.56					1.16				

Figure 23.1
LTR, STR, OP/IOP Trends Adjusted to 0 Days in a Controlled Environment

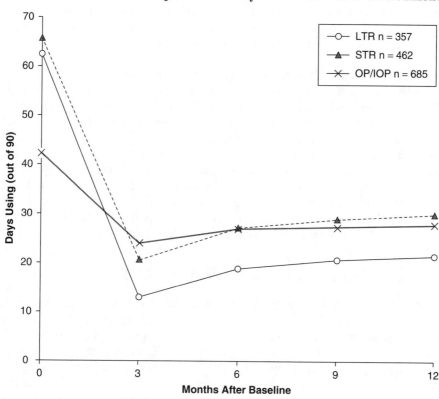

from zero; and other tests compare coefficient estimates for each LOC "vs. all" others, or for each site "vs. all" others. Table 23.3 reports *t*-tests comparing each LOC group's estimate with each other LOC group.

Figure 23.1 describes the AOD use trend (adjusted to zero days in a controlled environment) for LTR, STR, and OP/IOP groups.

Baseline Status. With respect to baseline status, AOD use was greater among LTR and STR sites than among OP/IOP sites; however, substantial variation in site averages was present within the LOC groups. Baseline AOD use ranges were: LTR (58.4 to 88.0); STR (37.5 to 79.8); and OP/IOP (13.2 to 57.0).

Treatment Effects. Beneficial treatment effects were present in all LOC groups; however, one OP site (site 6) showed a significant counter-trend effect—specifically, an increase in adjusted AOD use from baseline to three months (changing from 13.2 days to 46.9 days). Overall, LTR sites showed the best average reduction (as a percent of baseline), significantly exceeding the rate for STR and OP/IOP. The rate of reduction in use was also significantly greater, on average, for STR sites versus OP/IOP. Despite a relatively high rate of use at baseline, LTR sites averaged the lowest adjusted AOD use at three months (13.1 days), versus STR (20.7 days) and OP/IOP (23.9 days).

Each of the three LTR sites had a treatment effect significantly exceeding the average effect in the full study population. All of the OP sites had relatively weak treatment effects (versus all other sites), reaching statistical significance in three of five sites.

STR sites also tended to show relatively strong treatment effects relative to all other sites, reaching statistical significance in two of four sites. A comparison of treatment coefficient variance estimates from two-level models with no predictors, LOC predictors (2 df × 3), and site predictors (11 df × 3) indicated that approximately 62.4 percent of site variance in B_1 coefficients is accounted for by LOC.

Relapse Effects. As described above, only 0.9 percent of person variance in B_2 coefficients was explained by site. This small effect was primarily due to a marginally significant test comparing OP/IOP sites versus LTR sites, $t(1501)=2.42$, $p=.016$, and comparing OP/IOP sites versus STR sites, $t(1501)=2.36$, $p = .018$. As a percentage of adjusted three-month AOD use, in OP/IOP, STR, and LTR conditions, AOD use at twelve months increased by 16 percent, 45 percent, and 65 percent, respectively.

Although the relapse effect was relatively greater in the LTR condition, given the relatively strong treatment effect for LTR, at twelve months, adjusted AOD use was still lowest in LTR (21.6 days), as compared with OP/IOP (27.8 days) and STR (30.0 days) sites. Relative to adjusted baseline AOD use estimates, at the end of twelve months, AOD use declined by 65 percent at LTR sites, 54 percent at STR sites, and 35 percent at OP/IOP sites.

Example 3—Predicting Risk Using the CANS

This example predicts risky behavior among children receiving case management services. Using ordinal CANS risks scores from a statewide sample of children receiving varied levels of wraparound services for a diverse array of problems, it predicts a simple ordinal outcome (a four-point maximum risk rating) using a trajectory model with a polytomous logistic link function. In this case, child and caregiver needs and strengths were used to predict the four levels of risk, based on ten risk categories repeatedly assessed with the CANS. The model yields probability estimates for each of the four ordinal categories as a function of time and each child/caregiver profile on five CANS scales. The number and timing of repeated assessments were quite variable from case to case.

Sample Used. The present analyses include data from 11,236 CANS assessments of 2,823 children or adolescents treated within New Jersey's Partnership for Children program. The CANS was used to monitor caregiver and child needs and strengths while the sample received intensive wraparound services and/or less intensive case management services in a diverse array of settings. The number of repeated assessments ranged from two to fourteen (mean = 3.98), covering a range from one month to 1.6 years (mean = 0.68 years).

Instruments. CANS items, and risk items in particular, are generally structured such that ratings of 0 to 3 have particular action implications. The instrument specifies the following general rule for 0 to 3 ratings:

0 = No evidence or no reason to believe that the rated item requires any action.

1 = A need for watchful waiting, monitoring or possibly preventive action.

2 = A need for action. Some strategy is needed to address the problem/need.

3 = A need for immediate or intensive action. This level indicates an immediate safety concern or a priority for intervention.

The ten risk items assess:

1. Suicide risk
2. Self-mutilation
3. Other self-harm
4. Danger to others
5. Sexual aggression
6. Runaway risk
7. Delinquency
8. Poor judgment
9. Fire setting
10. Social behavior

A maximum rating of 0 to 3 (MAXRISK) was generated for the set of risk items, indicating the worst level of risk attained across the ten items. Given the general rule in the key above, the maximum score implies a minimum level of action indicated by the risk assessment (in at least one risk domain).

CANS domain scores at baseline were obtained by averaging similar 0 to 3 ratings in five domains: caregiver needs, caregiver strengths, child needs, child strengths, and child life domain functioning. For strength ratings, high scores indicate that a strength within a given domain is absent or not identified, or exists at such minimal capacity that considerable effort is required to allow the strength to effectively contribute to a strengths-based treatment plan. Thus, for all CANS scales, higher scores represent worse mental health status (i.e., greater needs, limited/absent strengths, and poorer functioning).

Analysis Strategy: Polytomous Logistic Link Function, Random Slope, and Intercept. A hierarchical nonlinear model was used to describe the relationship between CANS scale predictors at baseline and individual differences in MAXRISK across time.[7] Because the dependent variable was an ordinal four-category variable, the level 1 model predicted logit (natural log of the odds associated with "below threshold" scores). For each person, the log-odds was modeled as a linear function of time (measured in years after baseline), with five CANS predictors of random intercept and slope variation.

Level 1 (Repeated Measures Level):

$$\text{logit}(MAXRISK < 1, 2, \text{ or } 3) = \beta_{0p} + \beta_{0adj} + \beta_{1p} YEARS_{pt} + \varepsilon_{pt}$$

Level 2 (Person Level):

$$Intercept = \beta_{0p} = \pi_{00} + \sum_{i=1}^{j} \pi_{0i} PRED_{ip} + r_{0p}$$

$$Slope = \beta_{1p} = \pi_{10} + \sum_{i=1}^{j} \pi_{1i} PRED_{ip} + r_{1p}$$

---

[7]HLM2L software (version 5.0) was used to conduct these analyses.

Table 23.4
Odds Ratios Associated With Predictors of Intercept and Slope Variation From First-Order and Fifth-Order Models

	First-Order Model		Fifth-Order Model	
	OR	p	OR	p
For "Starting Level" slope, B_0				
CG Needs	0.36	<.001	1.12	.399
CG Strengths	0.42	<.001	0.97	.751
CH Needs	0.03	<.001	0.53	<.001
CH Strengths	0.002	<.001	0.007	<.001
CH Functioning	0.019	<.001	0.29	<.001
For "Rate of Change" slope, B_1				
CG Needs	1.59	.030	0.54	.025
CG Strengths	1.85	<.001	1.30	.103
CH Needs	13.53	<.001	1.61	.056
CH Strengths	141.77	<.001	71.64	<.001
CH Functioning	14.34	<.001	1.44	.174

In addition to intercept (B_{0p}) and slope (B_{1p}) terms, the level 1 model includes two fixed adjustments to the intercept (B_{0adj}) that alter the function so that it estimates either the log-odds that MAXRISK will be 0 or 1 (below threshold of 2), or the log-odds that MAXRISK will 0, 1, or 2 (below threshold of 3). Without these adjustments to the intercept, the function estimates log-odds that MAXRISK will be 0. So, with the threshold adjustments, the adjusted intercept $(B_{0p} + B_{0adj})$ refers to the log-odds that MAXRISK will be below threshold at baseline, and the slope (B_{1p}) refers to the rate of change in log-odds of below threshold scores per year. Regardless of whether the function estimates log-odds that MAXRISK will be less than a score of 1, 2, or 3, the fixed effects of $j = 5$ predictors of intercept (π_{0i}) and slope (π_{1i}) variation are held constant.[8]

The five CANS scales at baseline noted above (caregiver needs, caregiver strengths, child needs, child strengths, and child life domain functioning) served as predictors of intercept and slope variation in a standard regression procedure. The effect of each predictor was estimated alone (first-order models) and with all other predictors included (fifth-order models, controlling for all other predictors). The models yielded estimates of probabilities of each of four events across time for a child with any specified profile on the five predictors at baseline. Exponents of model coefficients yielded odds ratios associated with one-point changes in any predictor.

Table 23.4 reports odds ratios for predictors in both first- and fifth-order models, with inferential tests (*p*-values) from tests of all model coefficients. Table 23.5 reports

---

[8]This "equal odds" assumption defines the method as "polytomous." The odds ratios generated for each predictor are an average of three odds ratios for three possible "above threshold" events.

details on fixed and random effects for model coefficients for the fifth-order model, with associated inferential tests.

The first-order models indicate that problematic scores at baseline on all five measures tend generally to be associated with substantially worse MAXRISK scores at baseline and an improved (positive) "rate of change" in the odds of below threshold MAXRISK scores. The latter improvement is likely a "regression to the mean" effect, since the identification of strengths at baseline is highly correlated with lower MAXRISK scores, and the failure to identify strengths at baseline is highly correlated with higher MAXRISK scores. For example, with respect to baseline risk, a one-point increase (worsening) in child strengths is associated with a substantial reduction (OR=.002) in odds of below-threshold (healthier) baseline MAXRISK. On average, odds of attaining a below-threshold risk score increase by 1.44 times over the course of one year (OR for one year = 1.44, evaluated at average on all predictors). A one-point increase in child strengths increases the effect of one year on the odds of below-threshold risk by 142 times (OR = 141.77).[9] Controlling for other CANS predictors, this effect of child strengths on the odds ratio associated with one year is still substantial (OR = 71.6). The only predictor that retained a substantial unique effect on MAXRISK probabilities, controlling for other predictors, was the child strengths average.

Table 23.5 provides detailed estimates of model coefficients and random effects. As may be expected, probability estimates are substantially affected by choice of dependent variable threshold. The random effect estimates indicate that substantial reliable variation in MAXRISK remains unexplained by the current model.

The equation depicted in Table 23.5 may be used to generate MAXRISK probability estimates across time for any case. To more clearly see the implications of child strengths scores at baseline, this equation was evaluated at the average level on all other predictors, but at the twenty-fifth percentile below (CH Strengths = 0.20) versus the seventy-fifth percentile above (CH Strengths = 0.70) the mean at baseline. The probability estimates are depicted in Table 23.6.

Table 23.6 illustrates the substantial association between the identification of strengths at baseline and a child's immediate risk level at baseline. Eighty-two percent of children with limited or unidentified strengths (75th percentile) at baseline have scores of at least 2 on at least one of ten risk items at baseline, suggesting a need for risk-based intervention. On the other hand, only 15.4 percent of children with substantial identified strengths at baseline (25th percentile) show the same need for risk-based intervention at baseline. As one examines the trend in probabilities across time, there is a tendency for children without substantial strengths identification to show improvement while children with identified strengths at baseline show some worsening in maximum risk scores (regression to the mean).

---

[9]Reported ORs for all predictors are associated with substantial changes on both the time metric (one year) and each predictor (ones point corresponds to two or three standard deviations on each predictor). For example, the OR of 142 above is associated with a one-point change. If the OR were converted to the effect of a 1/10 of a point change in child strengths, this OR could be expressed as 1.64 (1.64 to the 10th power = 142). If the OR was converted to correspond to a one-standard-deviation (0.34) change in the child strengths score, this OR could be expressed as OR = 5.39. Significance levels are unaffected by these transformations, but direct interpretation of the meaning of each OR depends on the definition of a "one-point change" on the predictor.

Table 23.5
Fixed and Random Effects for Fifth-Order Models, Predicting Random Intercept and Slope Variance in Log-Odds (MAXRISK > Threshold) From Five CANS Scales at Baseline

Final estimation of fixed effects:

Fixed Effect	Coefficient	Standard Error	t	df	p
For "Starting Level" slope, B_0					
INTRCPT1, π_{00}	−0.103108	0.107038	−0.96	2817	.336
CG Needs, π_{01}	0.113448	0.134531	0.84	2817	.399
CG Strengths, π_{02}	−0.025259	0.079707	−0.32	2817	.751
CH Needs, π_{03}	−0.629500	0.126738	−4.97	2817	<.001
CH Strengths, π_{04}	−5.014558	0.206078	−24.33	2817	<.001
CH Functioning, π_{05}	−1.232158	0.129244	-9.53	2817	<.001
For "Rate of Change" slope, B_1					
INTRCPT2, π_{10}	−2.391230	0.201635	−11.86	2817	<.001
CG Needs, π_{11}	−0.620645	0.276367	−2.25	2817	.025
CG Strengths, π_{12}	0.263851	0.161946	1.63	2817	.103
CH Needs, π_{13}	0.478385	0.251195	1.90	2817	.056
CH Strengths, π_{14}	4.266024	0.359982	11.85	2817	<.001
CH Functioning, π_{15}	0.362081	0.266509	1.36	2817	.174
Threshold adjustment, B_{0adj}					
Below 2	4.065114	0.066018	61.58	11222	<.001
Below 3	7.181844	0.090087	79.72	11222	<.001

Final estimation of variance components:

Random Effect	Standard Deviation	Variance Component	df	χ^2	p
For "Starting Level" Slope:					
level 2, r_{0p}	1.20600	1.45444	2817	3741.17901	0.000
For "Rate of Change" Slope:					
level 2, r_{1p}	2.02775	4.11175	2823	3756.07269	0.000

CONCLUSIONS

Implicit in the notion of a trajectory is the belief that not all variation around a smooth, regular pattern is meaningful. All trajectory models include a level 1 error term, representing unexplained variation that is unavailable for analysis, since it deviates from the trajectory form under consideration. If one is willing to focus on an underlying regular pattern within each case, trajectory models provide versatile tools for describing change across time.

Trajectory models are particularly useful when the time periods assessed have no naturally occurring fixed range, and when repeated and variable numbers of

Table 23.6
Probability (MAXRISK = 0, 1, 2, or 3) Versus Years After Baseline Assessment

		Years After Baseline Assesment						
	MAXRISK	0	0.25	0.5	0.75	1	1.25	1.5
Identified	0	8.8%	7.1 %	5.7%	4.6%	3.7%	3.0%	2.4%
Strengths	1	75.7%	74.2%	71.8%	68.6%	64.8%	60.3%	55.4%
(ChST = .2)	2	14.6%	17.7%	21.2%	25.1%	29.5%	34.1 %	39.0%
	3	0.8%	1.0%	1.3%	1.6%	2.0%	2.6%	3.2%
	MAXRISK							
Limited/	0	0.4%	0.6%	0.8%	1.2%	1.8%	2.6%	3.9%
Unidentified	1	17.7%	24.0%	31.6%	40.2%	49.3%	58.0%	65.6%
Strengths	2	64.9%	63.2%	58.9%	52.5%	44.8%	36.5%	28.6%
(ChST = .8)	3	17.0%	12.2%	8.6%	6.0%	4.2%	2.9%	2.0%

assessments are obtained, whether by fault or by design. In health services research, there is often a clear intention to describe change as a monotonic function of treatment services (e.g., mental health outcomes as a function of psychotherapy sessions). In such a case, an appropriate and conventional monotonic math model can be applied. However, even when a monotonic model is not appropriate, trajectory models may be modified to accommodate diverse patterns of change across time. The combined step and log-linear trajectory function used to model AOD use illustrates one of an undefined variety of such models capable of capturing non-monotonic trends.

Trajectory models are also amenable to applications with dependent variables entailing any set of scaling properties. Dependent variables with nominal or ordinal scaling may be related to linear analyses of slope and intercept variation through link functions, generating person-specific parameter estimates from nonlinear model forms. We have described only two such cases (polytomous logistic link functions, Poisson link function), but there are many more.

Like most regression models, person-specific estimates of trajectories may be generated by profiling each case on predictors relevant to change, and including these predictors in the statistical model. Unlike some regression approaches, the trajectory method makes efficient use of available data (no cases are deleted due to missing data) and places more weight on cases with more reliable estimates of change parameters (unlike approaches relying on imputation, which often do the opposite).

If one is willing to focus on an underlying regular pattern within each case, trajectory models provide a powerful and effective method for describing change across time. Previous research has demonstrated the importance of using outcome trajectories to better understand the course of change experienced by adults in individual psychotherapy (Howard et al., 1986), inpatient psychiatric treatment (Lyons et al., 1997a; Lyons et al., 1997b), partial hospitalization programs (Lyons et al., 1996), and children and adolescents in residential treatment (Lyons et al., 2001; Hussey & Guo, 2002).

Other change analysis methodologies for comparing outcomes only allow researchers to demonstrate that there was a change in functioning from pre- to post-test. A simple finding of change in functioning is limited, however, because it does not allow for a more complete examination of the differences in outcome across individuals or treatment programs. Trajectory models allow researchers not only to examine individual level change over time, but to compare outcomes of treatment programs and facilities based on individual level and organizational level characteristics.

References

Bryk, A. S. & Raudenbush, S. W. (1992). *Hierarchical linear models.* Newbury Park, CA: Sage.

Dasinger, L. K., Shane, P. A. & Martinovich, Z. (2004). Assessing the effectiveness of community-based substance abuse treatment for adolescents. *Journal of Psychoactive Drugs*, 36, 27–33.

Howard, K. I., Kopta, S. M., Krause, M. S. & Orlinsky, D. E. (1986). The dose-effect relationship in psychotherapy. *American Psychologist, 41*, 159–164.

Hussey, D. L. & Guo, S. (2002). Profile characteristics and behavioral change trajectories of young residential children. *Journal of Child and Family Studies, 11*, 401–410.

Lyons, J. S., Howard, K. I., O'Mahoney, M. T. & Lish, J. D. (1997a). *The measurement and management of clinical outcomes in mental health.* New York: Wiley.

Lyons, J. S., O'Mahoney, M. T., Miller, S. I., Neme, J., Kabat, J. & Miller, F. (1997b). Predicting readmission to the psychiatric hospital in a managed care environment: Implications for quality indicators. *American Journal of Psychiatry, 154*, 337–340.

Lyons, J. S., Terry, P., Martinovich, Z., Peterson, J. & Bouska, B. (2001). Outcome trajectories for adolescents in residential treatment: A statewide evaluation. *Journal of Child and Family Studies, 10*, 333–345.

Lyons, J. S., Thompson, B. J., Finkel, S. I., Christopher, N. J., Shasha, M. & McGivern, M. (1996). Psychiatric partial hospitalization for older adults: A retrospective study of case-mix and outcome. *Continuum, 3*, 125–132.

Polaris Behavioral Health Status Scale (2000). Fairless Hills, PA: Polaris Health Directions, Inc.

Raudenbush, S. W., Bryk, A. S., Cheong, Y. F. & Congdon, R. T. (2004). *HLM 6: Hierarchical linear and nonlinear modeling.* Lincolnwood, IL: Scientific Software International.

Chapter 24

Creating Decision Support and Eligibility Models Using Clinical Assessments

by John S. Lyons, Ph.D.

INTRODUCTION

Along with quality improvement activities and outcomes monitoring, the third primary application of communimetric tools within the Total Clinical Outcomes Management (TCOM) framework is the development of decision models that support placing service recipients in the appropriate program or level of care. Decision models are approaches that support clinical decisions regarding referral to specific treatments, programs, intensity of services, or levels of care. The theory behind these models is that it is possible, and in fact desirable, to develop a clear description of clinical profiles or levels of need that indicate such referrals. This chapter provides an overview of the principles used to develop effective and efficient decision models.

PRINCIPLES OF DECISION MODEL DESIGN

Focus on Current Needs and Strengths

The first principle of decision model design is: focus on the individual's current needs and strengths, not on his service receipt history. This means that an understanding of the needs and strengths of the individuals being served will guide the management of the service system. This key principle is the foundation on which decision models are created, so that an individual's primary service recipient experience is not a central consideration. This is an important, but somewhat controversial, perspective. For example, a history of psychiatric hospitalization is often used as an eligibility criteria for some intensive community programs, for both children and adults. However, it has been demonstrated that racial disparities influence the decision to admit to the hospital (Pavkov et al., 1989). So, using a history of hospitalization in a decision model serves to institutionalize these disparities in all future decisions made regarding the affected individual.

The Child and Adolescent Level of Care Utilization System (CALOCUS), a popular decision model for children, uses compliance to prior services as an indicator of level of need. In fact, approximately one-third of the total score on the CALOCUS is related to youth and parent compliance. However, sometimes compliance is a reflection of the quality and competence of prior service providers rather than the commitment of the youth or their parents. Increasing the intensity of services or level of care based on a family's prior experience with low quality services runs a distinct risk of punishing poor families who live in service-impoverished areas. So the first principle of the development of decision models is to keep the assessment about the individual's needs and strengths and *not* about his or her prior service experience.

The design of specific assessment strategies for decision models, therefore, should be driven by consideration of the information required to inform good decision-making. In other words, an application of a communimetric tool for a mobile crisis program must consider the key information needed to determine whether an individual might require psychiatric hospitalization.

A distinct advantage in the design of communimetric tools is that their required use of action trumps (e.g., evidence/no need for action, watchful waiting/prevention, action, or immediate/intensive action) makes them adapt easily to decision models. Decision models with these tools generally involve patterns of 2 (action) and 3 (immediate/intensive action) rather than summed scores with cut-offs. This strategy makes it possible to describe clinically individuals for whom a particular program, service, or level of care is intended; for example, treatment foster care is intended for children with an actionable behavioral health need and either a functional disability or an actionable risk behavior. Using profiles in this way is generally palpable to more people than using cut-offs (such as a score above 120 indicating residential treatment).

Identify Those Most Likely to Benefit

The second principle of design is that the clinical indicators used in the model should identify those most likely to benefit from the program or level of care to which they are referred or recommended. Ultimately, any decision model should increase the likelihood of identifying individuals who are more likely to obtain positive outcomes from services. The Philadelphia treatment foster care (TFC) decision model discussed by Hirsch, Elfman, and Oberleithner in Chapter 6 is an excellent example of using data on program outcomes to validate the design of a decision model. In this application, the TFC model was validated on the population of children currently at this level of care by comparing outcomes for children who fit the criteria versus those who did not.

Unfortunately, we do not currently have good outcome data for all services, program types, or levels of care. When it is not yet possible to predict expected outcomes, then clinical strategies based on experience or other research can be used to assist in the initial decision of decision models. For example, we know that youth with higher needs and significant risk behaviors appear to benefit more from episodes of residential treatment than do youth with lower levels of needs (Lyons & McCollough, 2006). So, using these data to design decision models for residential treatment is an acceptable initial strategy. However, these models should be followed over time and adjusted based on data on outcomes from the treatment.

Keep It Simple and Relevant

The third principle is to keep decision-making simple and relevant. The implementation of decision models varies around the country with different applications in different settings. However, the common thread is that decisions must be made in an efficient manner by individuals who do not always have access to an exhaustive amount of information. Team decision-making appears to be generally superior to decisions by individuals because usually more information comes to light in a group of individuals who all know the service recipient, compared to any single individual (including the recipient).

For accessibility of the assessment information to inform decision-making across diverse groups, you need an easy-to-understand, universal language assessment approach. This requires that the ability to describe an individual's needs and strengths should be a characteristic embraced by the entire system. Diagnosis may be a specialty assessment that only certain professionals can apply; however, description must be accessible to everyone. Requiring decision models based on assessment strategies that are only permitted to small groups of professionals places much too much power on these individuals, thereby risking notable distortions in the functioning of service systems. For example, if only a psychiatrist can decide whether or not a child is placed in residential treatment, then, without oversight, this decision model can result in an over- or under-use of this valuable and expensive resource too dependent on practice pattern variations.

Make Models Local and Flexible

The fourth principle is that decision models should reflect local systems and be flexible within those systems. Every local system, whether state, county, or municipality, has unique service options and availability. Some systems have more developed intensive community services than others. Rural areas sometime suffer to provide home-based services due to transportation challenges. Further, different systems call similar services by different names. These complexities challenge our ability to make uniform decision models that might apply universally. For these reasons, we believe strongly that decision models must be local. Localizing models has the further advantage of building system partner buy-in and respecting the current status of a particular system. Overwhelming a system with forced transformation caused by applying a universal model that does not fit local capacity will result in a failure of that implementation.

Related to this, it is important to respect the fact that systems change. New services become available. We learn over time to better understand which individuals benefit from which service. Therefore, initial decision models should not be presented as the final model. The idea, of course, is to use these models to support movement towards a more fair and effective service system. While the decision models are meant to hold the system more accountable to the needs and strengths of the individuals served, it is also true that the system must hold the decision model to a similar level of accountability. Elsewhere we have called this concept *matrix accountability*. Everyone is accountable to everyone else simultaneously in a complex system, and designing reciprocal accountability mechanisms is important. For decision models, this means that the development of the model is never ended and always subject to adjustments based on circumstances or experience.

Field Reliability Is Critical

The fifth principle is that field reliability is critical. Inter-rater reliability is the primary concern with communimetric tools, and it requires that everyone use the same language. Consistency in the use of language translates into reliability when numbers are assigned to the communications. The reliability question concerns whether different people completing the same assessment get comparable findings. Decisions about program referral, service referral, or level of care, which carry great import, can become controversial in a limited resource environment, making the reliability of the assessment information on which these decisions are made critical.

Achieving high reliability requires following a set of straightforward principles and procedures, as follows:

- Everyone using the assessments should be trained for reliability. No one who is not trained or has not demonstrated reliability should be allowed to use the assessment.

- Assessments used for decision support should be shared with relevant partners so that everyone is aware of the information input into the decision. This open procedure allows anyone to provide corrective information who believes that an assessment is incorrect.

- Reliability should be monitored in the field. Two methods are available. Recertification, at least annually, should be used to ensure that training is not forgotten and to remind those who use the assessments of the importance of reliabilities. Audits should be instituted on randomly selected cases over regular intervals. Audits involve taking information from complementary sources of information covering the same time frame as the assessment and completing the assessment independently using these data. Audit reliability is the reliability between the original assessment and the one completed on parallel information.

By adopting uniform training and reliability certification and monitoring reliability in the field through audits and recertification, it is possible to create a reliable assessment tool for use with decision models. But the single most important means to ensure ongoing reliability is to ensure that the assessments remain open and widely accessed and used. Involving all partners in the assessment process and communicating findings openly across these partners helps build trust, a fundamental aspect of the ongoing utility of any decision model approach.

METHODS OF DECISION MODELING

There are two essential methods used in decision models: decision support and eligibility. The basic distinction between these two approaches is the degree to which the assessment data and decision model determine the actual decision about program referral or level of care. In the decision support model, the assessment and recommendation from the model are only one possible input into a variety of factors that might influence the actual decision. The decision is left up to an individual or a team—the recommendation of the decision model is not final. In the eligibility approach, the recommendation coming out of the decision model is the actual decision. Partners involved in the planning for a specific individual can appeal the decision; however, the planning starts by accepting the result of the application of the decision model to existing assessment information.

Decision Support Approach

A decision support approach is the easiest and most widely used method in using decision models. As described above, decision support considers assessment results and recommended referrals as one form of input into the decision-making process. In some applications, this input actually can come after the decision is already made through a quality improvement approach (see Leon's discussion in Chapter 9).

The Illinois Department of Children and Family Services (IDCFS) has implemented a decision support application of the CANS for all decisions regarding placement of a child at a level above regular or kinship foster care. The IDCFS established child and youth investment teams (CAYIT) that use a team decision-making approach to decide whether a child should be placed in specialized foster care, a group home, residential treatment, a transitional living program, or independent living. CAYIT are organized across the state, with each team comprised of a CANS reviewer, a facilitator, and an implementation manager. The CANS reviewer obtains information about the child before the meeting and completes the IDCFS version of the CANS based on this information. The reviewer presents his findings to the CAYIT, and the team members make adjustments based on updated or otherwise unavailable information that becomes available when all partners (including the youth, when appropriate) meet together. The facilitator ensures that everyone involved is invited to the meeting and that everyone gets an equal voice in the process. Once the team decides whether a program referral is indicated, it will develop an action plan. The implementation manager then assists the youth and case worker in putting the recommendations arising from the plan into action.

Table 24.1 presents the decision model used by the CAYIT. The model has six referral levels, including services provided in regular/kinship foster care. It is noteworthy that three different decision models were generated, for different age groups. The IDCFS's thinking behind the different thresholds was that it should be difficult to place a child age twelve years or younger into a group home; and for youth age fifteen and older with attachment problems, a group home may be an equal or better option than specialized foster care.

Review of CAYIT decisions over the first ten months of implementation suggested that CANS recommendations were followed about 60 percent of the time, and that decisions were within one level of the CANS recommendation more than 80 percent of the time. The main discontinuity between the CANS recommendation and the CAYIT decision involved group homes and transitional living programs (TLP). Early experience was that few youth who had need profiles consistent with TLP referral on the CANS actually were placed in TLPs. Review of these data revealed a significant lack of options for these referrals. The IDCFS used these data to support the investment in an additional 200 beds for TLPs.

The IDCFS is now building profiles of each CAYIT team to monitor their decision-making relative to the other teams. As more data accrues, it will be possible to inform judgments of the quality of CAYIT decision-making based on outcomes from the resultant placements. In other words, tracking outcomes for children placed in group homes and residential treatment centers will inform the decision-model, but also will give the IDCFS and the CAYITs feedback on the impact of their different decisions across children and program types.

Eligibility Approach

The eligibility model is used to make the actual decision regarding program referral or level of care, based on assessment results. We noted earlier Philadelphia's use of the eligibility model with its TFC referrals, as described in Chapter 6. Several unique characteristics of this implementation are worth noting. First, Philadelphia's Department of Human Services (DHS) uses an independent assessor to complete the CANS. This removes any conflict of interest. Foster care providers who might benefit financially from a referral do not complete the assessment, and DHS staff who would save money by not referring a child are removed from the assessment process. This helps ensure the accuracy of the assessment by eliminating any motivation for over-rating or underrating needs. While not always feasible due to the expense of creating a "CANS Unit," this strategy is very useful when there is a lack of trust between funding sources and providers regarding the accuracy of assessments.

Second, the use of an independent assessment unit reduces the training demands and makes maintaining reliability throughout the implementation a smaller task than the statewide assessment implementation as described in New Jersey. Assessors in the Philadelphia CANS unit are recertified quarterly, which helps ensure continuing reliability. As the DHS expanded the use of the CANS from only treatment foster care eligibility to group homes and institutions, they had a new decision model designed for these levels of care and expanded the CANS unit to serve the additional assessment needs for a higher volume of referrals.

The key reason for using an eligibility model is that you have a clear idea of who is likely to benefit from a particular program referral or level of care. In situations in which this knowledge is available, not using it to guide the decision might even be considered unethical. However, in most cases, we do not currently have good information on differential outcomes for youth with different needs and strengths profiles. In the absence of this information, decision support models are probably more ethical in that they allow "clinical brilliance" to influence decisions more easily than do eligibility models.

SUMMARY

As described in this chapter and a number of other chapters throughout this book, decision models are a valuable aspect of the TCOM approach. When the focus is on the current needs and strengths of the individual served, the application of either decision support or eligibility approaches is consistent with the full implementation of TCOM. In their simplest form, communimetric tools naturally translate into individual-level service planning. This can be seen as a low-level decision support implementation. The inherent design features of tools like the CANS and the Adult Needs and Strengths Assessment (ANSA), with their action levels, translate easily into decision support applications. The keys to successful implementation include achieving and maintaining reliability and identifying who benefits from what program or level of care.

Table 24.1
CANS Comprehensive Decision Support Model for the Illinois Department of Children and Family Services

---

REFERRAL 1. REGULAR/KINSHIP FOSTER CARE WITH SERVICES

Criterion 1.1. Child is age 5 or younger and receives a 2 on at least one of the following:
Communication
Failure to Thrive
Regulatory Problems
Pica
Substance Exposure

Criterion 1.2. At least one 2 or 3 on any of the Behavioral/Emotional needs items:
Psychosis
Attention Deficit/Impulse
Depression
Anxiety
Oppositional Behavior
Antisocial Behavior
Attachment
Adjustment to Trauma
Substance Use
Anger Control
Affect Dysregulation
Eating Disturbance
Behavioral Regression
Somatization

To be suggested for foster care with services referral, a child must meet Criteria 1.1 OR 1.2.

REFERRAL 2. SPECIALIZED FOSTER CARE

Criterion 2.1. A rating of 2 or 3 on Medical/Physical or Somatization.

Criterion 2.2. At least one 2 or 3 on one of the following:
Psychosis
Attention Deficit/Impulse
Depression
Anxiety
Oppositional Behavior
Antisocial Behavior
Anger Control
Attachment

(Continued)

Table 24.1 (Continued)

Adjustment to Trauma
Substance Use
Anger Control
Affect Dysregulation
Eating Disturbance
Behavioral Regression

Criterion 2.3. A rating of 3 on at least one of the following:
Motor
Sensory
Intellectual
Communication
Failure to Thrive
Regulatory Problems
Substance Exposure
Developmental
Self Care

Criterion 2.4. A rating of 3 on at least one of the following:
School Behavior
Social Behavior
Sexually Reactive Behavior

Criterion 2.5. A rating of 2 or 3 on at least one of the following:
Suicide Risk
Self-Mutilation
Other Self Harm
Danger to Others
Runaway
Sexual Aggression
Fire Setting
Delinquency

A child is suggested for Specialized Foster, if he/she meets EITHER
　　a. Criteria 2.1 for referral to Medically Complex, OR
　　b. Criteria 2.2 and (EITHER 2.3 OR 2.4 OR 2.5) for Mental Health.

Note: Unless a youth is 15 years old or older and Attachment is rated as a 2 or 3, then consider Group Home (see Group Home criteria below).

Table 24.1 (Continued)

REFERRAL 3. GROUP HOME/TREATMENT GROUP HOME

For this level, three different threshold models should be used, depending on the age of the child.

For Children less than 12 years old:

Criterion 3a.1. At least one or more 3 or two or more 2 among the following needs:
   Psychosis
   Attention Deficit/Impulse
   Depression
   Anxiety
   Oppositional Behavior
   Antisocial Behavior
   Attachment
   Adjustment to Trauma
   Substance Use
   Anger Control
   Affect Dysregulation
   Eating Disturbance
   Behavioral Regression

Criterion 3a.2. A rating of at least 2 on Developmental.

Criterion 3a.3. One 3 among the following risk behaviors:
   Suicide Risk
   Self-Mutilation
   Other Self Harm
   Danger to Others
   Sexual Aggression
   Fire Setting
   Delinquency

Criterion 3a.4. Two or more 2 among the following risk behaviors:
   Suicide Risk
   Self-Mutilation
   Other Self Harm
   Danger to Others
   Runaway
   Sexual Aggression
   Fire Setting
   Delinquency

(Continued)

Table 24.1 (Continued)

A child who is less than age 12 to be suggested for Group Home, if he/she meets (EITHER Criterion 3a.1 OR Criterion 3a.2) *AND* (Criterion 3a.3 OR Criterion 3a.4):

- If Criterion 3a.2 is met consider a specialty program.
- If Sexual Aggression is rated a 2 or 3 consider a specialty program.
- If Physical/Medical is rated a 2 or 3 consider a specialty program.
- If Delinquency is rated a 2 or 3 consider a specialty program.

For youth ages 12 through 14 years:

Criterion 3b.1. At least one or more 3 or two or more 2 among the following needs:
Psychosis
Attention Deficit/Impulse
Depression
Anxiety
Oppositional Behavior
Antisocial Behavior
Attachment
Adjustment to Trauma
Substance Use
Anger Control
Affect Dysregulation
Eating Disturbance
Behavioral Regression
Somatization

Criterion 3b.2. A rating of 2 or 3 on Developmental.

Criterion 3b.3. One 3 among the following risk behaviors:
Danger to Self
Self-Mutilation
Other Self Harm
Danger to Others
Sexual Aggression
Fire Setting
Delinquency
Sexually Reactive Behavior

Criterion 3b.4. Two or more 2 among the following risk behaviors:
Danger to Self
Self-Mutilation
Other Self Harm
Danger to Others

Table 24.1 (Continued)

Runaway
Sexual Aggression
Fire Setting
Delinquency
Sexually Reactive Behavior

Criterion 3b.5. A rating of 3 on at least two or more of the following:
School Attendance
Judgment
Social Behavior

A youth 12 to 14 years would be suggested for Group Home if he/she met (EITHER Criterion 3b.1 OR Criterion 3b.2) *AND* (EITHER Criterion 3b.3 OR Criterion 3b.4):

- If Criterion 3b.2 is met consider a specialty program.
- If Sexual Aggression is rated a 2 or 3 consider a specialty program.
- If Physical/Medical is rated a 2 or 3 consider a specialty program.
- If Delinquency is rated a 2 or 3 consider a specialty program.

Youth 15 years and older:

Criterion 3c.1. Attachment is rated as a 2 or 3.

Criterion 3c.2. Meets criteria for Specialized Foster Care.

Criterion 3c.3. Female ward who is pregnant (rated a 2 or 3 on Parenting Role).

A youth 15 years or older would be suggested for Group Home is he/she met criteria set for youth 12 to 14 years OR
met (both Criterion 3c.1 AND Criterion 3c.2) OR
met Criterion 3c.3:

- If Criterion 3c.2 is met consider a specialty program.
- If Sexual Aggression is rated a 2 or 3 consider a specialty program.
- If Physical/Medical is rated a 2 or 3 consider a specialty program.
- If Delinquency is rated a 2 or 3 consider a specialty program.
- If Criterion 3c.3 is met consider a specialty program.

REFERRAL 4. RESIDENTIAL TREATMENT CENTER

Criterion 4.1. At least two or more 3 among the following needs:
Psychosis
Attention Deficit/Impulse
Depression
Anxiety
Oppositional Behavior

(Continued)

Table 24.1 (Continued)

               Antisocial Behavior
               Attachment
               Adjustment to Trauma
               Substance Use
               Anger Control
               Affect Dysregulation
               Eating Disturbance
               Behavioral Regression
               Somatization

Criterion 4.2. Three or more 2 among the following needs:
               Psychosis
               Attention Deficit/Impulse
               Depression
               Anxiety
               Oppositional Behavior
               Antisocial Behavior
               Attachment
               Adjustment to Trauma
               Substance Use
               Anger Control
               Affect Dysregulation
               Eating Disturbance
               Behavioral Regression
               Somatization

Criterion 4.3. A rating of 2 or 3 on Developmental.

Criterion 4.4. At least one 3 among the following risk behaviors:
               Suicide Risk
               Self-Mutilation
               Other Self Harm
               Danger to Others
               Sexual Aggression
               Fire Setting
               Delinquency

Criterion 4.5. Three or more 2 among the following risk behaviors:
               Suicide Risk
               Self-Mutilation
               Other Self Harm

Table 24.1 (Continued)

Danger to Others
Runaway
Sexual Aggression
Fire Setting
Delinquency
Judgment
Social Behavior
Sexually Reactive Behavior

**To be suggested for RTC, a child should meet
(EITHER Criteria 4.1 OR 4.2 OR 4.3)** *AND*
(Criteria 4.4 OR 4.5):

- If Criterion 4.3 is met consider a specialty program.
- If Sexual Aggression is rated a 2 or 3 consider a specialty program.
- If Physical/Medical is rated a 2 or 3 consider a specialty program.
- If Delinquency is rated a 2 or 3 consider a specialty program.

REFERRAL 5. TRANSITIONAL LIVING

Criterion 5.1. Youth is 17 to 19 years old.

Criterion 5.2. Youth is 19 to 21 years old.

Criterion 5.3. A rating of 2 or 3 on Independent Living Skills.

Criterion 5.4. A rating of 2 or 3 on any of the following:
Intimate Relations
Parenting Role
Victimization
Medication Compliance

Criterion 5.5. A rating of 1 or higher on Educational Attainment and has not graduated from high school.

Criterion 5.6. Does not meet criteria for Group Home or Residential Treatment.

Criterion 5.7. Youth is NOT currently living in a stable foster home.

A youth would be suggested for:

(Continued)

Table 24.1 (Continued)

Level 1   Transitional Living if he/she meets Criterion 5.1 and 5.3 and 5.6 and 5.7.
Level 2   Transitional Living if he/she meets
          Criterion 5.1 and (Criterion 5.3 *AND* Criterion 5.4) and Criterion 5.6 and 5.7.
Level 3   Transitional Living if he/she meets Criterion 5.2 *AND*
          (Criterion 5.3 AND Criterion 5.5) and Criterion 5.6 and 5.7.

REFERRAL 6. INDEPENDENT LIVING

Criterion 6.1. Youth is 19 years or older.

Criterion 6.2. A rating of 0 or 1 on Independent Living Skills.

Criterion 6.3. Youth does not meet criteria for Group Home or Residential Treatment.

Criterion 6.4. Youth is NOT living in a stable foster home.

A youth is suggested for Independent Living if he/she meets Criterion 6.1 *AND* Criterion 6.2 AND Criterion 6.3 AND Criterion 6.4.

References

Lyons, J. S. & McCollough, J. R. (2006). Monitoring and managing outcomes in residential treatment: Practice-base evidence in search of evidence-based practice. *Journal of the American Academy of Child & Adolescent Psychiatry*, *45*, 257–251.

Pavkov, T., Lewis, D. & Lyons, J. S. (1989). Psychiatric diagnosis and racial bias: An empirical investigation. *Professional Psychology: Research and Practice*, *20*, 364–368.

Chapter 25

Reflections and Future Directions

by John S. Lyons, Ph.D. and Dana A. Weiner, Ph.D.

PRESENT AND FUTURE NEEDS

Two things are obvious to anyone who has read the preceding chapters. First, the full implementation of Total Clinical Outcomes Management (TCOM) has not been realized anywhere. Second, significant progress towards the goal of full implementation has been made at the individual, program, and system levels. The emerging question is: what things need to happen if we are to realize the full vision of making behavioral health service systems work on the shared vision of serving individuals in need? We can identify at least the following:

- Development of clear linkages between identified strengths and needs and empirically supported treatment approaches, evidence-based practices, and provider networks.

- Use of technology to support the rapid collection, management, and reporting of assessment data so that it can be used in real time case management, supervision, and program management.

- Development of communities of individuals, agencies, and systems committed to the full implementation of the approach.

ASSESSMENT AND TREATMENT LINKAGES

Currently there are a number of projects that attempt to refine our understanding of the relationship between assessed needs and strengths and specific treatment approaches. Much of this work is originating at sites that began by using decision modeling approaches for level of care or program referral. Using the results of assessment processes to become more specific with regards to the treatments recommended is a natural outgrowth of that work.

Initially, the work must be informed by clinical judgments. For example, evidence-based practices for trauma should be indicated by adjustment to trauma symptoms or symptoms of posttraumatic stress disorder (PTSD). Similarly, treatment for oppositional deviant disorder should be indicated by the presence of relevant behavioral problems. Over time, these models can be empirically validated or evolved to maximize outcomes in the field based on matching criteria. Currently, in Illinois's Department of Child and Family Services, we are piloting three evidence-based practices for treatment trauma in children. The question becomes whether these treatments, developed in clinical trial research, can be applied in the real world of a complex child welfare environment and result in positive outcomes for the children served.

Making decisions about indicated services based on individual needs is a good place to start, but overly simplistic. Ultimately, this one-for-one match between an identified need and an empirically supported treatment is likely to be insufficient. Often people have multiple and complex needs. As we have seen from research documenting the reduced effectiveness of treatments with coexisting mental illness and substance-related disorders, it is not likely accurate to think that an individual with multiple needs would benefit from specific, but separate, treatments for each of those needs. In other words, a depressed individual, with alcohol abuse problems and symptoms of PTSD, might not benefit from the simultaneous application of different, empirically supported treatments for these three needs. At some point the design of empirically supported treatment approaches must account for the actual complexity of presentation in the field. TCOM can support the creation of profiles of needs that might require integrated treatment approaches rather than the applications of separated treatments.

USE OF TECHNOLOGY

The last two decades have seen an explosion in technology. At the dawn of the Information Age, the potential for technological applications to support the management of behavioral health services seems limitless. However, anyone who has been working in the field over these decades has likely experienced the over-promise of technological solutions to very human problems. We also have come to believe that behavioral health care attracts individuals who are cautious about the use of technology or perhaps even unable or unwilling to consider technological solutions, further complicating the implementation of technology in support of case and system management. That said, there is a renewed opportunity to manage services and systems in a way that maintains our humanity but takes advantages of technological efficiencies never before available.

Perhaps the most useful tool that is now widely available is the Internet. Web-based technology makes it possible to provide database support with easy access to any location with a high-speed connection. Given the economy of scale available through Internet applications, the cost of these systems is very low compared to stand-alone computer systems of the past. While public sector services have been slow to get online, most providers and agencies now have high-speed Internet access or the ability to obtain it easily. While both confidentiality (e.g., Health Insurance Portability and Accountability Act, or HIPPA) and work force management (e.g., no shopping or visiting pornography sites) represent legitimate concerns, security applications exist that allow for the effective and secure management of web-based systems.

As discussed in Chapter 22, the future of these applications will allow the real time matching of a specific individual's profile of needs with available providers in geographic proximity who have the capacity to provide effective treatment. This same technology allows systems to clearly define unmet need not only by type of need, but by the location/geography of individuals having a profile of needs. Once fully developed and available, such technology will be a core element of a systems-level TCOM approach.

COMMUNITIES OF INDIVIDUALS, AGENCIES, AND SYSTEMS

Of course, any long term success of TCOM requires communities that endorse TCOM principles and become committed to its full implementation. Creating such communities is no small task. One strategy we have begun to work on to support their development is to establish learning collaboratives. Three such groups exist. The first, a government-level collaborative, uses a monthly phone call and a web-based "meeting place" model. In this group are representatives from a number of states that are implementing communimetric tools and engaging in at least some aspects of the TCOM approach.

A second learning collaborative, an organization of private sector agencies, has just begun to try to establish consistent communication. This collaborative's objective is to support the use of communimetric tools and TCOM strategies in programs and agencies. Currently about fifty programs and agencies have indicated interest in participating in this collaborative.

A third learning collaborative has begun to take shape. This group is a collection of academics researchers and program evaluation consultants who are interested in sharing methodological and statistical experiences and data in their pursuit of behavioral health services research informed through the use of communimetric tools. About ten university-based researchers have begun to correspond in this collaborative.

A second strategy we have begun to develop is something that was originally titled the SuperUser program when it was originally initiated in New Jersey. The idea is to identify individuals in the field who are involved in and experienced with training and quality improvement activities. Once identified, these individuals are provided additional training and meeting experiences to support their ability to implement communimetric tools and support the implementation of the principles of TCOM in their home agencies. Thus the SuperUser model is an adult learning strategy to support the development of a workforce with the knowledge and skills to implement TCOM in the field. In addition to the small SuperUser program initiated in New Jersey, we are launching larger programs in Illinois and Indiana with the goal of about 250 individuals participating in each state.

The issues discussed above may confound our ability to fully realize the explicit vision of the TCOM approach, but additional considerations abound as well. Financing support from the information infrastructure needed to access information, and the training and technical assistance needed to create a workforce with the requisite skills, are two other areas of need, among others.

A PARADIGM SHIFT

The last decade has seen a considerable shift in the degree to which measuring and monitoring outcomes has become accepted in the behavioral health system. As a field, we appear poised to move to the next level in which outcomes are actually used to manage services and systems. We believe the implementation of TCOM represents a natural and valuable next step in this process. Further, we believe that a full implementation of TCOM is nothing short of a paradigm shift in how the business of behavioral health care is managed. We look forward to continuing to work to create an environment that supports this fundamental change in practice.

Table of Acronyms

ABC	Activity-based costing
ABCTC	Arthur Brisbane Child Treatment Center
ACLU	American Civil Liberties Union
ACS	Administration of children's services
ACT	Assertive community treatment
AHCPR	Agency for Health Care and Policy Research
ANCOVA	Analysis of covariance
ANOVA	Analysis of variance
ANSA	Adult Needs and Strengths Assessment
AOD	Alcohol or other drugs
APPA	American Probation and Parole Association
ARC	Attachment, Self-Regulation, and Competency (treatment framework)
ARCH	ACT Resources for the Chronically Homeless Program
ArcIMS	Arc Internet Map Server
ASEBA	Achenbach System of Empirically Based Assessment
ASI	Addiction Severity Index
ATM	Adolescent treatment models
AYI	Alaska Youth Initiative
BASIS-32	Behavior and Symptom Identification Scale
BHOS	Behavioral Health Overlay Services
BHS	Beck Hopelessness Scale; Behavioral health system
BHS-CBH	Behavioral Health Services-Community Behavioral Health
BHS T-score	Beck Hopelessness Scale total score
BOCES	Board of Cooperative Educational Services
BPI	Best Practices Institute
C/L	Consultation/Liaison (psychiatry)
CAFAS	Child and Adolescent Functioning Assessment Scale
CAIRS	Child and adolescent information reporting system
CALOCUS	Child and Adolescent Level of Care Utilization System
CANS	Child and Adolescent Needs and Strengths
CANS-CW	Child and Adolescent Needs and Strengths —Child Welfare
CANS-DD	Child and Adolescent Needs and Strengths —Developmental Disabilities
CANS-EC	Child and Adolescent Needs and Strengths—Early Childhood
CANS-JJ	Child and Adolescent Needs and Strengths —Juvenile Justice
CANS-MH	Child and Adolescent Needs and Strengths —Mental Health
CANS-SD	Child and Adolescent Needs and Strengths—Sexual Development
CAPE	Contract administration and program evaluation
CAPI	Childhood Acuity of Psychiatric Illness Scale
CARTS	Case assessment resource teams
CASII	Child and Adolescent Service Intensity Instrument
CASSP	Child and Adolescent Service System Principles
CAT	Crisis Assessment Tool
CAYIT	Child and Youth Investment Teams (IDCFS program)

CBCL	Child Behavior Checklist
CBH	Community behavioral health
CBT	Cognitive behavioral therapy
CCF	Community Connections for Families; Council on Children and Families
CCIS	Children's crisis intervention services
CCJCC	Cook County Juvenile Court Clinic
CD	Compact disk
CDHS	Chicago Department of Human Services
CEO	Chief executive officer
CGAS	Children's global assessment scale
CHAMPUS	Civilian Health and Medical Program of the Uniformed Services
CHEO	Children's Hospital of Eastern Ontario
CHINS	Children in need of services
CIACC	County Inter-Agency Coordinating Councils for Children
C-Info	Oneida County, N.Y. database version of CANS information system
CIP	Community inpatient program
CLMHD	Conference of Local Mental Hygiene Directors
CMHS	Center for Mental Health Services (part of SAMHSA)
CMO	Case management organization
COMPRI	Care complexity prediction instrument
COO	Chief operating officer
CQI	Continuous quality improvement
CRCY	Community residences for children and youth
CSA	Contracted systems administrator
CSAT	Center for Substance Abuse Treatment
CSE	Committee on Special Education
CSPI	Childhood Severity of Psychiatric Illness (tool)
CtC	Communities that care
DASA	Division of Alcoholism and Substance Abuse (Illinois)
DCBHS	Division of Child Behavioral Health Services
DCFS	Department of Children and Family Services (Illinois, Los Angeles)
DCS	Department of Children's Services (Indiana)
DHHS	Department of Health and Human Services
DHS	Department of Human Services
DHS/BHS	Philadelphia's child welfare and behavioral health systems
DMHS	Division of Mental Mealth Services (New Jersey)
DPCA	Department of Probation and Correctional Alternatives
DPCP	Division of Prevention and Community Partnerships
DRG	Diagnosis-related group
DSS	Department of Social Services
DYFS	Department of Youth and Family Services (New Jersey); Division of Youth and Family Services
EBP	Evidence-based practice
EBPD	Evidence-based practice dissemination
EPSDT	Early and periodic screening, diagnostic, and treatment instruments
ERASOR	Estimate of Risk of Adolescent Sexual Offense Recidivism (instrument)
ERIC	Education Resource Information Center

ESRI	Environmental Systems Research Institute
ETR	Expected treatment response
FAST	Family assessment services team; Family assessment support tool
FBT	Family-based treatment
FCM	Family case manager
FFA	Foster Family Agency
FFT	Functional family therapy
FFTA	Foster Family Treatment Association
FSN	Family support network
FSO	Family support organization
FY	Fiscal year
GIS	Geographic information system (ESRI computer software)
HADS	Hospital anxiety and depression scale
HAPI-C	Hoosier Assurance Plan Instrument: Children and Adolescents
Hba_{1c}	Glycosylated hemoglobin (fraction of hemaglobin to which glucose has nonenzymatically attached in the blood stream)
HBCI	Home-based crisis intervention
HIPAA	Health Insurance Portability and Accountability Act of 1996, P. L. No. 104-191
HRSA	Health Resources and Services Administration
HUD	Housing and Urban Development
ICC	Intraclass correlation coefficient
ICM	Intensive case management
ICS	Intensive community services
ICU	Intensive care unit
IDCFS	Illinois Department of Child and Families Services
IDHS	Illinois Department of Human Services
IDOC	Iowa Department of Corrections
IEP	Individualized education plans
IIC	Intensive in-community (services providers)
ILP	Independent living program
IMDS	Information management and decision support
IOM	Institutes of Medicine (U.S.)
IPA-T	Interpersonal therapy for adolescents
ISP	Individualized service plan; Iowa State Penitentiary
ISPD	IDCFS Statewide Provider Database
IST	Instructional support team
IT	Information technology
JJC	Juvenile Justice Commission (New Jersey)
JRI	Justice Resource Institute (Brookline, Mass.)
J-SOAP-II	Juvenile Sex Offender Assessment Protocol II
LCP	Life-course persistent
LOC	Level of care
LOS	Length of stay
LTR	Long-term residential
MAYSI-2	Massachusetts Youth Screening Instrument-2
MCC	MacLaren Children's Center (Los Angeles)
MCH	Maternal and child health (programs)
MDR	Monthly administrative data report

MECCA	Marshfield Enhanced Charting and Code Acquisition
MHJJ	Mental health juvenile justice
MHPSU	Mental Health Patient Service Unit
MHST	Mental Health Screening Tool
MIS	Management information system
MISA	Mental Illness/Substance Abuse Institute (Illinois)
MRO	Medicaid rehabilitation option
MRSS	Mobile response and stabilization services
MS	Multiple sclerosis
MST	Multi-systemic treatment; Multi-systemic therapy
NCHS	National Center for Health Statistics
NCS-R	National Co-Morbidity Survey Replication Study
NCTSN	National Child Trauma Stress Network
NECTAC	National Early Childhood Technical Assistance Center
NIC	National Institute of Corrections
NIMH	National Institutes of Mental Health
NS	Not significant
OASAS	Office of Alcoholism and Substance Abuse Services
OCFS	Office of Children and Family Services
OCS	Office of Children's Services
OJJDP	Office of Juvenile Justice and Delinquency Prevention
OMH	Office of Mental Health
OP/IOP	Outpatient/intensive outpatient
P3	Permanency planning process
PA	Provider agency
PAC	Parent assessment of care; Placement advisory committee
PCE	Proportion of time in a controlled environment
PHMS	Philadelphia Health Management Corporation
PMHCC	Philadelphia Mental Health Care Corporation
PMT	Project management team
POE	Points of engagement
Polaris CD	Polaris-Chemical Dependency (outcomes)
PTSD	Posttraumatic stress disorder
QA	Quality assurance
QI	Quality indicators
QMHC	Qualified mental health professional
RBS	Residentially based services
RCTS	Residential continuum of treatment services
RFP	Request for proposal
RFQ	Request for qualifications
ROH	Royal Ottawa Hospital
ROMS	Recovery Outcome Management System
RPESCY	Regional Psychiatric Emergency Service for Children and Youth
RPRT	Regional placement review team
RTC	Residential treatment center
RTF	Residential treatment facility
RTOS	Residential Treatment Outcomes Study (Illinois)
RUM	Resource utilization management
SAMHSA	Substance Abuse and Mental Health Services Administration, United States Department of Health and Human Services

SASS	Screening assessment and supportive services
SAVRY	Structured assessment of violence risk in youth
SCM	Supportive case management
SDM	Structured decision-making
SDQ	Strengths and Difficulties Questionnaire
SEBD	Serious emotional or behavioral disorders
SED	State Education Department
SIL	Supervised independent living
SNA	Strength and needs assessment
SOC	System of care
SOCPR	System of Care Practice Review
SOIP	State-operated inpatient unit
SPANS	Service Process Adherence to Needs and Strengths
SPFY	School partnership for youth
SPI	Severity of psychiatric illness
SPMI	Severe and persistent mental illness
SPOA	Single point of access
SPOA/A	Single point of access and accountability
SQL server	Structured query language server (to interact with a database)
STR	Short-term residential
SU	Substance use
SUVA	Swiss National Accident Insurance Fund (Schweizerische Unfallversicherungsanstalt)
TCOM	Total Clinical Outcomes Management
TDM	Team decision-making
TFC	Treatment foster care
TFI	Treatment Fidelity Index
THINK	Tampa Hillsborough Integrated Network for Kids
TLP	Transitional living program
TRAAY	Treatment recommendations for use of antipsychotics with aggressive youth
TRF	Teachers Report Form
T-score	Total score; Test score (in psychometrics)
TSCYC	Trauma Symptom Checklist for Young Children
TST	Trauma systems therapy
t-test	Statistical text
TX	Treatment
UBHC	University Behavioral Health Care
UCR	Uniform case record
UM	Utilization management
VA	Veterans Affairs
WFI	Wraparound Fidelity Index
WHO	World Health Organization
WOF	Wraparound Observation Form
YAC	Youth assessment of care
YCM	Youth case management
YMCA	Young Men's Christian Association
YSR	Youth self-report

Index

[References are to pages.]